pauline frommer's

IRELAND

spend less see more

1st Edition

RETIRÉ DE LA COLLECTION UNIVERSELLE
Bibliothèque et Archives nationales du Québec

by Dr. Keith Bain & Emily Hourican

or: Pauline Frommer

WILEY

Wiley Publishing, Inc.

Published by:

Wiley Publishing, Inc.

111 River St.
Hoboken, NJ 07030-5774

Copyright © 2009 Wiley Publishing, Inc., Hoboken, New Jersey. All rights reserved.
No part of this publication may be reproduced, stored in a retrieval system or trans-
mitted in any form or by any means, electronic, mechanical, photocopying, recording, scanning or otherwise, except as permitted under Sections 107 or 108 of the
1976 United States Copyright Act, without either the prior written permission of
the Publisher, or authorization through payment of the appropriate per-copy fee to
the Copyright Clearance Center, 222 Rosewood Drive, Danvers, MA 01923,
978/750-8400, fax 978/646-8600. Requests to the Publisher for permission should
be addressed to the Permissions Department, John Wiley & Sons, Inc., 111 River
Street, Hoboken, NJ 07030, 201/748-6011, fax 201/748-6008, or online at
http://www.wiley.com/go/permissions.

Wiley and the Wiley Publishing logo are trademarks or registered trademarks of
John Wiley & Sons, Inc. and/or its affiliates. Frommer's is a trademark or registered
trademark of Arthur Frommer. Used under license. All other trademarks are the
property of their respective owners. Wiley Publishing, Inc. is not associated with any
product or vendor mentioned in this book.

ISBN 978-0-470-12172-6

Editor: Melinda Quintero
Production Editor: Eric T. Schroeder
Cartographer: Roberta Stockwell
Photo Editor: Richard Fox
Interior Design: Lissa Auciello-Brogan
Production by Wiley Indianapolis Composition Services
Front and back cover photo © Alberto Paredes/Alamy Images
Cover photo of Pauline Frommer by Janette Beckmann

For information on our other products and services or to obtain technical support,
please contact our Customer Care Department within the U.S. at 877/762-2974,
outside the U.S. at 317/572-3993 or fax 317/572-4002.

Wiley also publishes its books in a variety of electronic formats. Some content that
appears in print may not be available in electronic formats.

Manufactured in the United States of America

5 4 3 2 1

Contents

List of Maps

About the Authors

Keith Bain has moved around his home country, South Africa, all his life—so the travel bug is in his blood. Nevertheless, he managed to sit still long enough to get a doctoral degree in drama, and for a few years even amused himself writing and performing for the stage. He's also served his time lecturing future filmmakers, actors, and dramatists, but has now quit academia to more rigorously explore the world. Besides developing a fondness for Guinness in Ireland, his assignments for Frommer's have  sent him to India, Italy, Romania, Slovenia, Botswana's Okavango Delta, and even out onto the streets of Johannesburg. He's most recently completed work on the first edition of *Frommer's Kenya & Tanzania*, and has been covering Cape Town—where he's now comfortably settled—for the latest edition of *Frommer's South Africa*.

Emily Hourican lives in Dublin and is a prolific freelance writer.

An Invitation to the Reader

In researching this book, we discovered many wonderful places—hotels, restaurants, shops, and more. We're sure you'll find others. Please tell us about them, so we can share the information with your fellow travelers in upcoming editions. If you were disappointed with a recommendation, we'd love to know that, too. Please write to:

Pauline Frommer's Ireland, 1st Edition
Wiley Publishing, Inc. • 111 River St. • Hoboken, NJ 07030-5774

An Additional Note

Please be advised that travel information is subject to change at any time—and this is especially true of prices. We therefore suggest that you write or call ahead for confirmation when making your travel plans. The authors, editors, and publisher cannot be held responsible for the experiences of readers while traveling. Your safety is important to us, however, so we encourage you to stay alert and be aware of your surroundings. Keep a close eye on cameras, purses, and wallets, all favorite targets of thieves and pickpockets.

Star Ratings, Icons & Abbreviations

Every restaurant, hotel and attraction is rated with stars ★, indicating our opinion of that facility's desirability; this relates not to price, but to the value you receive for the price you pay. The stars mean:

No stars: Good
    ★ Very good
  ★★ Great
★★★ Outstanding! A must!

Accommodations within each neighborhood are listed in ascending order of cost, starting with the cheapest and increasing to the occasional "splurge." Each hotel review is preceded by one, two, three or four dollar signs, indicating the price range per double room. Restaurants work on a similar system, with dollar signs indicating the price range per three-course meal.

Accommodations		**Dining**	
$	Up to $100/night	$	Meals for $7 or less
$$	$101–$135	$$	$8–$12
$$$	$136–$175	$$$	$12–$17
$$$$	Over $176 per night	$$$$	$18 and up

In addition, we've included a kids icon 🧒 to denote attractions, restaurants, and lodgings that are particularly child friendly.

Frommers.com

Now that you have this guidebook to help you plan a great trip, visit our website at **www.frommers.com** for additional travel information on more than 4,000 destinations. We update features regularly to give you instant access to the most current trip-planning information available. At Frommers.com, you'll find scoops on the best airfares, lodging rates, and car rental bargains. You can even book your travel online through our reliable travel booking partners. Other popular features include:

- Online updates of our most popular guidebooks
- Vacation sweepstakes and contest giveaways
- Newsletters highlighting the hottest travel trends
- Podcasts, interactive maps, and up-to-the-minute events listings
- Opinionated blog entries by Arthur Frommer himself
- Online travel message boards with featured travel discussions

I started traveling with my guidebook-writing parents, Arthur Frommer and Hope Arthur, when I was just four months old. To avoid lugging around a crib, they would simply swaddle me and stick me in an open drawer for the night. For half of my childhood, my home was a succession of hotels and B&Bs throughout Europe, as we dashed around every year to update Europe on $5 a Day (and then $10 a day, and then $20 . . .).

We always traveled on a budget, staying at the Mom-and-Pop joints Dad featured in the guide, getting around by public transportation, eating where the locals ate. And that's still the way I travel today, because I learned—from the master—that these types of vacations not only save money, but offer a richer, deeper experience of the culture. You spend time in local neighborhoods, meeting and talking with the people who live there. For me, making friends and having meaningful exchanges is always the highlight of my journeys— and the main reason I decided to become a travel writer and editor as well.

I've conceived these books as budget guides for a new generation. They have all the outspoken commentary and detailed pricing information of the Frommer's guides, but they take bargain hunting into the 21st century, with more information on using the Internet and air/hotel packages to save money. Most important, we stress "alternative accommodations"—apartment rentals, private B&Bs, religious retreat houses, and more—not simply to save you money, but to give you a more authentic experience in the places you visit.

A highlight of each chapter is the section called "The Other" side of the destinations, the one visitors rarely see. These sections will actively immerse you in the life that residents enjoy. The result, I hope, is a valuable new addition to the world of guidebooks. Please let us know how we've done! E-mail me at editor@frommers.com.

Happy traveling!

Pauline Frommer

Pauline Frommer

1 The Best of Ireland

by Keith Bain

IN MANY WAYS, IRELAND CLINGS—IN THE POPULAR IMAGINATION ESPE-cially—to the idea of itself as a small, mostly rural, and eternally countrified realm still tuned in to a way of life long forgotten. Vast uninterrupted swaths of green rolling hills; shaggy sheep forever grazing along cliffs that tumble down to a raging ocean; luminous shamrocks emblazoned on everything from airplanes to guesthouse signboards; and tributes to the national pastime—Guinness drinking—posted on any available surface. These are some of the endearing images that permeate the popular conception of Ireland.

And yes, some of the stereotypes hold true. It's true about the Irish being tremendously gregarious. They're largely Catholic, too, with large chunks of their country given over to agriculture. But don't be fooled into thinking that village charm and bucolic meadow scenes are all there is to the country. As the late great Irish author John McGahern wrote, Ireland "is a peculiar society in the sense that it was a 19th century society up to about 1970 and then it almost bypassed the 20th century." It's been Ireland's great economic boom—its "Celtic Tiger" phase, a phrase first coined in 1994 to describe a suddenly vibrant Irish economy—that has perhaps brought some of the most obvious changes throughout the island. With foreign capital pouring in, much of the landscape has been recently transformed as holiday homes, cluster developments, and—on the positive side—decent roads were built. Large-scale hotels are replacing family-run B&Bs, BMWs have taken over from tractors, and rather than hearing Yeats recited in a pub, you're likely to hear familiar rhetoric on mortgage repayments.

The other great change, of course, has been arrival of peace. The IRA's announcement (also in 1994) that it intended a "cessation of military activity," fundamentally altered the prospects and culture of the Emerald Isle. Yes, lingering resentments still exist, particularly in Northern Ireland, but after centuries of conflict—between warring tribes, with invading Vikings and Brits, and between Protestants and Catholics—hope has gained the upper hand over hatred. And this change, along with economic progress, has fundamentally reshaped life here.

Learning about this history of conflict—which you'll see in Ireland's ruined monasteries, ancient fortresses, and bullet-pocked walls and hear about in pubs in every town big and small—is part of the experience of visiting a land that constantly reveals itself to be a far more complex, complicated, and intriguing destination than you might have imagined.

But you also visit, well, to hang out with the Irish and discover the joys of *craic*—pronounced "crack" and denoting nothing more complicated than good old-fashioned fun. After only a short time here, I think you'll find, as I have, that you wish you'd been born Irish, too.

A QUICK LOOK AT ALL IRELAND

The island of Ireland consists of four ancient provinces—Ulster, Leinster, Munster, and Connacht. Today these are largely used to denote the competitive sports terrain, and express historical allegiances. Modern Ireland is divided into 33 counties—six of them in Northern Ireland, and the rest in the independent Republic of Ireland, sometimes referred to by the Northern Irish as the "South" despite the anomalous fact that the Republic's northernmost point, in County Donegal—is actually farther north than any point in Northern Ireland. Now that's Ireland for you . . .

DUBLIN

Established by the Vikings and now the country's financial powerhouse where everything from hamburgers to houses are pricier than anywhere else in Europe, except maybe Stockholm or Moscow, Dublin is a mad, busy place where around 40% of the nation's 4.1

> ❝ *When anyone asks me about the Irish chracter, I say look at the trees. Maimed, stark and misshapen, but ferociously tenacious.* ❞
>
> —Edna O'Brien, author

million people live within commuting distance. People say that success has changed everything about the city, and there are those who bemoan the ebb of traditional culture. But there's good reason for Dublin's reputation as a fun little capital—there's plenty here to see and do, with a brilliant social scene, cultural activities and festivals galore, and an urban center brimming with history.

DUBLIN'S NEIGHBORS

Easily overlooked because of their proximity to the feisty capital, the counties around Dublin have an intriguing history as the last line of English defense against the savage Irish hordes who dwelt farther west—beyond the Pale. Today, Dublin's neighbors are an excellent place to discover picturesque towns and villages, spectacular gardens (especially in County Wicklow), and intriguing ancient Celtic archaeological sites (notably Newgrange in County Meath).

THE SOUTHEAST

Ireland's southeast—Counties Kilkenny, Wexford, Waterford, South Tipperary, and Carlow—enjoys the best of both worlds: a dazzling coastline powered by more sunlight than anywhere else in the country, and a sublime countryside with tranquil waterways coursing through pristine, unruffled villages. Wexford and Waterford were both ancient Viking strongholds, and Kilkenny was once the headquarters of the powerful Ormonde clan, making this an important region in the riveting history of fierce sieges and mighty battles.

THE SOUTHWEST

With five ruggedly beautiful peninsulas stretching out into the Atlantic, the southwest is the most popular region in Ireland (for all the good and bad that implies). Still, there's a fantastic social scene in Cork City, remote boho enclaves around the West of Cork, and some of the most gob-smackingly gorgeous scenery as you drive all along the coast.

COUNTY CLARE

County Clare is known for its traditional music sessions, the dramatic Cliffs of Moher, and the boulder-strewn otherwordly surface of the Burren, perhaps the most engrossing landscape in Ireland.

GALWAY CITY & COUNTY

One of Ireland's most cosmopolitan and culturally-active cities, Galway is as vibrant and glittering as you could hope, with a line-up of carnival-style festivals celebrating everything from oysters to movie-making. But don't just stick to the city; County Galway also impresses with the brooding landscape of the Connemara Peninsula, forever immortalized in the film *The Quiet Man*.

ALONG THE SHANNON

Seldom-explored, and often only seen by tourists as they hightail it from one coast of the country to the other, this is a great part of the country to escape the masses, become friendly with the locals, and—while seeing some of Ireland's hidden treasures—bedding down in some of the country's loveliest family-run guesthouses.

COUNTIES MAYO, SLIGO & DONEGAL

Sligo is Yeats country and it delivers a landscape that's as rugged and heart-stirring as the poetry which the land inspired. It's also known for its surfing and for the chance to take a bath in seaweed and to hike through hills dotted with Neolithic cairns. Donegal includes the country's most northerly point, Malin Head, and all along the county's sublime coastline are feisty villages packed with personality (some also surfing meccas). Mayo, meanwhile, is very much an extension of Connemara, Galway's rugged, rural hinterland. Here's where you'll discover abandoned islands where communities once thrived, while on the mainland, towns, and villages are exuberant and picturesque enough to be attractions in their own right.

NORTHERN IRELAND

Home to 1.7 million people, Northern Ireland was for so long relegated to "no go" status because of the ongoing political trouble between militant Republicans and Loyalists. The tension has now calmed to a near-indiscernible simmer and many might wonder what all the fuss was about. You can learn about that turbulent, tragic recent history on various fascinating walking tours and often simply by strolling through once-cursed neighborhoods. But your biggest impression of the North will be its friendly, open welcome, its geographic beauty, and fabulously unfettered rural hinterland.

Belfast

Northern Ireland's capital is celebrating a social and cultural Renaissance. Considering its size—under 500,000 people live in the greater Belfast area—the energy in this once strife-torn city is fantastic. Nightlife is booming, shops are doing a wild trade, and there's a burgeoning restaurant scene. There's so much going on, in fact, you might be forgiven for forgetting to stop and stare at all the marvelous architecture bestowed upon Belfast during its glory days as one of the most powerful port cities on earth.

Derry & the Western Counties

Derry is the North's second city—once a world leader in the textile industry, it became a major center for violence during the Troubles, and is now an intriguing place to gain insight into the centuries-old conflict that has defined the history of this island. Among the highlights of the North's seldom-visited western counties are the lush, boggy Sperrin Mountains, and the tranquil lakelands of tiny Fermanagh.

Counties Antrim & Down

Northern Ireland's two eastern counties are also its coastal gems. Antrim's Causeway coast is a geological phenomenon so astonishing it is mythically said to have been fashioned by a love-crazed giant, while Down's brooding Mountains of Mourne have inspired popular songs and fantasy literature. There are further myths, too—like fairy folk who make their home in the beautiful Glens of Antrim, and the legendary St. Patrick, who arrived by way of Strangford Lough, and bestowed on Ireland her greatest cultural icons.

ENCOUNTER NATURE'S MARVELS

EXPLORE THE SOUTHWEST'S ICONIC PENINSULAS   Dramatic cliffs and furious sea spray defines much of the glorious coastline that hugs each of the five peninsulas of southwest Ireland. You could devote your entire vacation to either the **Dingle** (p. 185) or **Iveragh** (p. 174) peninsulas, both of which are famous for their superb coastal drives and melancholic villages. Or lose yourself in a dreamy, undiscovered wilderness on **Sheep's Head** (p. 226), **Beara** (p. 230), or **Mizen Head** (p. 224), each captivating for their idyllic mix of jagged cliffs, serene coves, shaggy grass-covered hills, and a blissful sense of remoteness.

WITNESS DROP-DEAD CLIFFS   Join the millions of enthralled visitors who annually arrive to gape at the reality-defying **Cliffs of Moher** (p. 236)—it's arguably the finest spot in the country to witness the land being ravaged by the sea (although there are other, even higher cliffs off the northern coast of County Mayo if you'd like to do a comparison, p. 309). At their highest (and most popular) point, Moher's ancient precipices—said to be 300-million years old—rise some 214m (702 ft.) above the water, creating some of the most iconic imagery in Ireland. And as if Clare weren't blessed enough, just south of Moher, there's the spectacle of more precarious edge-of-the-world vistas and ocean-plunging seacliffs around the peninsular tip at **Loop Head** (p. 237). The careening cliffs and craggy caves are all there, but the crowds are wonderfully non-existent.

> " Geographically, Ireland is a medium-sized rural island that is slowly but steadily being consumed by sheep. "
>
> —Dave Barry, comedian

DRIFT ACROSS A LUNAR LANDSCAPE   In the west of Ireland, County Clare is known primarily for its dramatic oceanfront cliffs and spectacular line-up of traditional music. But almost half the county is given over to one of Ireland's

Walkabouts & Bike Trips

Pack your hiking boots because—when it's not raining—Ireland is best seen on foot. Marked trails are found throughout the country, but particularly worthwhile are the **Wicklow Way** (p. 92), the **Burren Way** (p. 251), and parts of the **Ulster Way** (p. 406) that take you along the Causeway Coast and through the Glens of Antrim. Excellent day walks are possible along the **Slieve Bloom Way** (p. 105) straddling the hills of Laois and Offaly, the **Southwest** (p. 183), and the **Slieve League cliffs** (p. 350) in Donegal. The **Mourne Mountains** (p. 430)—said to have inspired C. S. Lewis's *Chronicles of Narnia*—are another fabulous hiking destination in Northern Ireland, while in the **Sperrins** (p. 446) you may well run into a number of mystifying stone circles.

Many of the most popular driving routes in Ireland are suitable for cyclists—but top of the heap for bikers are the **Kerry Way** (p. 174) or the stunning **Connemara Loop** (p. 283).

most mesmerizing landscapes—simply called the Burren. Its magnificent boulder-strewn topography looks like nothing else on earth and has the eerie ability to make you lose your sense of perspective—tiny rocks mysteriously become huge hills as you wander though this captivating otherworldly space. As you hike, bike or drive through the population-deprived rockscape, you'll encounter exotic plants, ancient ringforts, and prehistoric tombs that add immeasurably to the surreal experience. See chapter 6.

FOLLOW IN THE FOOTSTEPS OF GIANTS   Along the northernmost coast of Northern Ireland, thousands of basalt pillars in geometrical shapes form a wondrous stonework tapestry terrace that disappears into the sea. It's called the **Giant's Causeway,** and legend dictates that a lovesick giant built it in order to find his way to his would-be lover across the ocean. Ireland boasts some pretty captivating geological marvels, but the splendid precision of these colossal stepping stones borders on the miraculous, and will surely have you, too, believing the Irish myths. See p. 410.

VENTURE THROUGH FAIRYTALE PARKS   A setting worthy of a starring movie role, there seems to be no end to the loveliness of **Killarney National Park** (p. 180)—its legendary beauty not only won over Queen Victoria, but has seduced visitors and awed potential conquerors through the ages. You can row across the shimmering mirror-surface of its lakes; discover enchanted islands plump with ancient monastic ruins; explore cultivated gardens; hike through forests and climb mountains; walk or cycle through the awesome Gap of Dunloe; or simply head for higher ground and take it all in from above. Farther north, in the wilds of Donegal, **Glenveagh National Park** (p. 355) is Ireland's biggest single attraction—literally. It's a massive (6,475 hectare/16,000 acre) protected landscape incorporating mountains, bogland, lakes, and forests, not to mention a recently introduced population of golden eagles.

GO ISLAND-HOPPING   Ireland may be an island, but it's also the mainland for a number of tiny offshore enclaves worth visiting for the pure adventure of the often-bumpy sea journey and thrill of discovering the magical impact of centuries of relative isolation. Life unfolds at a languid, timeless pace on several of these islands that have indeed been tamed and managed to remain inhabited—excursions to the **Sherkin** and **Cape Clear islands** (p. 222), **Aran Islands** (p. 277), **Tory Island** (p. 356) or **Clare Island** (p. 321) will reveal a way of life that you might no longer have thought possible. Meanwhile, the **Skelligs** (p. 179), **Great Blasket Island** (p. 191), and **Innishmurray Island** (p. 340) are hauntingly uninhabited rocks that have either been abandoned by a once-hardy human population, or were never fit for habitation in the first place. One delightful oddity is the fascinating **Garinish Island** (p. 229), established as an immense pleasure garden in the early-Twentieth Century, and still going strong.

OGLE MAN-MADE WONDERS

MYSTICAL STONE CIRCLES   Ireland's ancient ruins represent some of the oldest evidence of human creativity and ingenuity, and draw on a diversity of cultural traditions and influences. Among the world's most intriguing Neolithic sites, **Newgrange** (p. 113) and its lesser-known cousin, **Knowth** (p. 113), are older than the Giza pyramids and Stonehenge, and both continue to baffle scientists because of their perplexing astronomical alignments. These are among the most important ancient monuments on earth, set amidst mystical landscapes that many believe to have profound spiritual significance. Whatever purpose these immense passage tombs might once have served, it's impossible not to admire their creators for their engineering ingenuity and sheer determination.

PRE-HISTORIC MINIMALISM   The **Poulnabrone Portal Dolmen** (p. 248) in County Clare, may look like nothing more than an avant garde stone table, but to see it standing there—in a patch of grass amidst the bewitching landscape of the Burren—thousands of years after it was erected as part of an ancient tomb, is an experience nothing short of mystical and sublime.

BASTIONS OF EARLY CHRISTIANITY   Near the bellybutton of Ireland are two of the world's great ecclesiastical sites—the early Christian ruins at **Clonmacnoise** (p. 296) overlooking the River Shannon, and the hilltop **Rock of Cashel** (p. 162), where St. Patrick supposedly converted Celtic kings to the new faith. While much of their original splendor has dwindled with time, there's no denying the visual impact of the human endeavor—magnificent High Crosses, elegant architecture, and intricate sculptural effects—that made these holy sites such tremendous beacons of Christian scholarship at a time when the rest of Europe was slogging through a medieval wilderness.

FORTIFIED DEFENSIVE STRUCTURES   The main attraction in one of Ireland's tidiest little towns, **Trim Castle** (or King John's Castle, p. 115) is one of the best places to discover why medieval castles look the way they do—and why, for example, their inhabitants filled their moats with raw sewage! Although partially in ruins, the castle was dazzling enough to feature in *Braveheart*, not to mention playing a starring role in a surfeit of battles and sieges over the centuries. With its back to the ocean and a hazardous cliff-edge location, the ruins of **Dunluce Castle** (p. 413) in County Antrim remain tantalizingly evocative; the dramatic setting is enough to make your heart skip a beat. And then you're reminded that people once lived here . . .

SHOWSTOPPER REAL ESTATE   If there's any defining quality to more recent Irish architecture, it's probably the dissimilarity of styles and wide range of influences. Grand mansions stand like monuments to the high life near humble whitewashed thatched cottages; planned Georgian towns created to make life more civilized vie with severe forts designed to keep invaders at bay. But one thing Ireland's rich seldom skimped on was their propensity for spending mountains of cash on mansions, castles, and show-off holiday homes. Considered Ireland's most beautiful building, Wicklow's **Russborough House** (p. 94) is hailed for its impeccable Palladian symmetry, packed with one-of-a-kind furniture, and set within lush designer gardens on the edge of Blessington Lake. It's worth stopping in the Midlands to check out the humungous, superbly grotesque facade of **Tullynally Castle** (p. 298), surely the most enormous faux-Gothic enterprise in the country, and—in stark contrast with Russborough—lacking any semblance of symmetry whatsoever. A tour through **Kilkenny Castle** (p. 140) reveals some of the country's best public and private living spaces, once inhabited by one of the most powerful families in pre-independent Ireland. In a similar spirit of aristocratic excess, **Muckross House** (p. 184) just outside Killarney looks much as it did when it was extensively renovated for a visit by Queen Victoria—there's so much to see here, you'll need to take the tour twice to take even half of it in.

QUIRKY DESIGNER PROPERTIES   Don't for one instant think that the architects to the rich and famous didn't have loads of fun putting together some of the country's most intriguing (and perplexing) monuments. Dublin's **Casino Marino** (p. 61) is a stunning agglomeration of architectural tricks starting with one in which you think you're visiting a miniature classical temple. Even more tricksy is the beautifully inventive **Swiss Cottage** (p. 164), built purely as an ornamental conceit by aristocrats who got a kick out of pretending to be commoners as a form of entertainment for their guests. Fortunately, their architect managed to foist fistfuls of masterful design—inspired by nature—into the mix, so the end result is one of Ireland's most superb (and beguilingly simple) freestanding buildings. And if bizarre excess is a measure of fashion consciousness, then don't skip the schizophrenically-designed **Castle Ward** (p. 424) where two distinct aesthetic sensibilities are appeased in a single building on an aristocratic estate in bucolic County Down.

PAY TRIBUTE TO THE ARTS

WITNESS INCREDIBLE MANUSCRIPTS   More museum-gallery than library, the **Chester Beatty Library** (p. 52) is one of Dublin's most riveting indoor attractions where one man's love of books spawned perhaps the most significant collection of tomes on earth. Among the hand-written manuscripts and beautifully type-set volumes are some of the earliest Biblical texts, as well as an impeccable selection of elaborately crafted Oriental documents, wall-hangings, canvases, and even authentic samurai armor.

BROWSE THE ULTIMATE LIBRARY   Some of Ireland's brightest talents attended Dublin's landmark university, **Trinity College** (p. 54), and these days tourists queue up to get a peek at some of the world's most eye-poppingly beautiful, medieval illuminated manuscripts—including the austerely guarded Book of Kells, kept in a dimly lit vault-like modern chamber. While the manuscripts are worth fighting the crowds for, the best part of the tour continues into the utterly fantastic Long Room, surely the most beautiful medieval library you'll ever likely lay eyes on.

STUDY ICONIC IRISH IMAGES   George Bernard Shaw called Dublin's **National Museum of Modern Art** (p. 58) one of his universities. A sumptuous repository of great Irish art, this is the ultimate place to become familiar with the iconic Irish masters, including Jack B. Yeats (brother of the great poet, William Butler), Paul Henry, Séan Keating, and William Orpen, all of whom manage to capture the agony and ecstasy of Ireland in mesmerizing, often haunting, canvases.

UNDERSTAND VIKING HERITAGE   Although most people go to Waterford to see crystal being crafted, it's **Museum of Treasures** (p. 153) is one of the very best places in the world to admire Viking artifacts—the city is Ireland's oldest, and a considerable portion of the nation's Viking heritage has been unearthed here.

ENCOUNTER IRELAND'S LITERARY HERITAGE   Ireland has a fiercely proud literary tradition, and you'll encounter myriad sites associated with this articulate country's poets, playwrights, authors, and musicians. You'll traverse landscapes that have inspired great poetry and prose, and gone on to appear in silver screen epics as breathtaking backdrops. Dublin is popping with tributes to Ireland's greatest wordsmiths; besides statues and museums dedicated to brilliant men—Wilde, Shaw, Yeats, Joyce, Beckett—there are **literary walks** and **city tours** that focus on their life and times (p. 57). And, on the other side of the country, many of Ireland's greatest writers and artists, including George Bernard Shaw and W.B. Yeats, spent long creative periods at the estate house at County Galway's **Coole Park** (p. 284), once the residence of Lady Augusta Gregory, and an essential visit for anyone who takes their love of literature to a higher level.

LEARN WITH A MASTER CRAFTSMAN   You could haul out the photos and tell your friends about the wonders you've seen—or you could take home evidence that you've embraced a new art form and acquired a useful skill during your travels through artsy West Cork where some of the nation's finest craftsmen and women hold classes (p. 232). You can **learn to make a chair** using natural wood which you'll collect from the forest floor in Rossnagoose; or you can take up **pottery** under an expert, nurturing teacher in fabled Kinsale; or develop a flair for raku under one of Ireland's most respected **ceramicists**.

SPECIAL PLACES FOR A NIP OR A PINT

MOST ENTICING TRADITIONAL PUBS   Ireland's traditional pubs have long served as vanguards of social intercourse, unique places where locals in even the tiniest villages can meet up, exchange the latest news or gossip, enjoy a glass or two of the black stuff—yes, Guinness really is the drink of choice—and perhaps even stock up on groceries. Steadily, the old-style watering holes are disappearing and being replaced by look-alike super-pubs and late bars that lack both the character and the characters that have always made ordering a pint in this country something of an event. While we hate to play favorites, there are two true pubs—one in each of the capitals—that you absolutely daren't miss. In the south of Dublin, near the city's largest cemetery, Kavanagh's **Gravediggers** (p. 78) is anything but morbid—in fact, it's one of the merriest places in the city for a pint, and it draws a discerning following that includes, well, savvy gravediggers. In Belfast, the **Duke of York** (p. 388) is particularly memorable, its walls packed with memorabilia and its floors always brimming with a lovely, uproarious crowd.

IRELAND'S PARTY CAPITALS   We could tell you to head straight to Dublin for the non-stop social scene that spills out of Temple Bar and seems to wend its way down every imaginable sidestreet. We could encourage you to make a beeline for Belfast where the pub scene pulsates with an unmistakable energy any night of the week. We could insist that you sample the rich musical cadences of Cork's unshakeable late night music scene. Or we could remind you that tiny **Kilkenny** (p. 131) not only has a stout named after it, but more pubs and bars than you could possibly know what to do with! But what we won't do is suggest you try all four fabulous cities so you can decide for yourself and let us know where you think the richest party pickings preside.

ANCIENT & NOTEWORTHY   In Athlone—smack dab in the very center of Ireland—**Seán's Pub** (p. 296) is thought to be the world's oldest pub, and already holds the Guinness record as the oldest pub in Ireland. Pre-dating the town itself, Seán's fills to capacity every night with a crowd as mixed and vibrant as you'd hope to see in any big city watering hole, only here you'll have sawdust underfoot and the very authentic sense that the entire pub slopes to one side.

MOST SWOON-WORTHY DECOR   Belfast probably has the edge on Dublin for its broad selection of noteworthy historic pubs, many of them in mint vintage condition, and with a sociability score to match. More than just a place to put away a pint, the heritage-listed **Crown Liquor Saloon** (p. 377) is an especially beautiful High Victorian drinking hole with original gas lighting, opulently decorated private snugs, colorful mosaic tilework, and ornate detailing that tremendously distracting. Thank goodness that the clientele is equally entrancing.

TOP SPOTS FOR TRADITIONAL MUSIC   Some of the best traditional music can be heard in County Clare. Although the little village of Doolin has become a regular stop on the well-trodden tourist circuit, you can still hear wonderful *seisiúns* here; our favorite is **McDermott's Pub** (p. 241), where some of the nation's hottest artists have played to crowds intoxicated not by booze, but by the

Find Out Why the Irish Have the Gift of Gab

Not everyone in Ireland has kissed the **Blarney Stone** (p. 213), but you'll quickly notice that the Irish gift of the gab is virtually genetic. Storytelling is traditionally a major part of Irish culture, but is sadly a dying art form; fortunately, events focused on preserving this great tradition still happen regularly at festivals around the country—look out for professional storytellers like **Eddie Lenihan** (p. 250) from County Clare, or **Liz Weir** (p. 404) who resides in Antrim. In Wexford, you can visit **Ár mBréacha** (p. 128), a traditional Irish "rambling house," where folks gather to share tales, tea, and fun. Poetry is also wildly popular—don't be surprised if someone suddenly stands up after a few pints at the pub and starts reciting with fiery gusto. They may be witty limericks or heartfelt, woeful ballads, or perhaps something with a political edge; check out how the oul fla's do it at the **Sky & the Ground** (p. 130), a wonderfully rowdy pub in Wexford Town. For poetry that's a little more organized, there are open mic events in **Cork** (p. 209), pub poetry nights in **Limerick** (p. 256), and during Belfast's **Cathedral Quarter Festival** (p. 453), there's a poetry slam in which locals get to sound off while the audience judges the competition—if you're brave enough, you can compete for the prize.

toe-tapping beat. Further south, in the seaside town of **Dingle** (p. 185), there's trad playing virtually every night of the year and always ample opportunities to catch class acts of world repute. In Cork City you can hear music from just about every imaginable genre—but for a fiery session of inspirational trad, you need to stop off at **Sin É** (p. 212), reputedly the city's only remaining authentic pub. And, if you venture up to Northern Ireland, don't miss **Peadar O'Donnell's** (p. 445) in Derry—it's a legendary spot for excellent traditional music and the finest *craic*.

2 The Fair City of Dublin

Arguably the most vibrant, go-getter capital in Europe

by Keith Bain & Emily Hourican

GULLIVER'S TRAVELS AUTHOR JONATHAN SWIFT CALLED DUBLIN THE largest open-air asylum in Europe, and several centuries later, there are still times when it seems like a horde of lunatics has escaped and been set loose on this effervescent city. Dublin has a vitality—an unmistakable, un-put-downable exuberance—that's quite unlike anything anywhere else on earth. Perhaps it's the ridiculous youthfulness of its populace. Celtic Tiger cubs—students, young professionals, and newly arrived immigrants from foreign lands—account for vast swaths of its strutting, bitching, slagging, misbehaving population that floods the streets on any given day.

And, on top of this cult of "new and fresh" is a millennia's worth of residual energy left by a mishmash of powerful personalities who've helped shape this mad, mad society—artists, politicians, musicians, freedom fighters, and perhaps most famously, writers. You'll see evidence of their influence in the city's historic homes, museums, and galleries, which may not be the world's biggest, but are excellent, top-drawer affairs that showcase the great variety and depth of Irish culture. And, of course, Dublin's pubs and bars (now just 850 of them, compared with an all-time high of 4,000) have long been incubators for some of the country's greatest literary exponents. Writers like Brendan Behan, in fact, were as famed for their virulent drinking as for their way with words. Little wonder, perhaps, that the city's busiest attractions include a high-tech museum dedicated to Guinness, that most famous of Irish brews, and one concerned solely with the production of whiskey.

Dublin presents a worrying side, too. You'll see signs of the social fabric coming apart at the seams—it's a dirtier, tawdrier city than you'll see anywhere else in Ireland. Thanks to the recent economic downturn there are more signs of poverty and misery here, as well.

Take it as all part of Dublin's hearty stew of experiences. Somehow, along with the great musicians and up-and-coming buskers, the boozers, and the misfits, multitudes of tourists manage to find space within this compact jigsaw puzzle that is one of the world's great cities. Enjoy!

DON'T LEAVE DUBLIN WITHOUT . . .

WALKING THE WALK   Sign up for one of the many brilliant walking tours on offer, an ideal way to get the insider's scoop on this fascinating city. See p. 56.

HAVING AT LEAST ONE LILLIPUT MOMENT   At Casino Marino (p. 61) you'll be surprised (and perplexed) by how the architecture plays tricks on you, convincing you that you're entering a tiny temple, when in fact it's a size-able stately home. Meanwhile, at St. Patrick's Cathedral you can walk Ireland's longest nave (p. 53). At Trinity College, you simply must visit the fantastical "Long Room," a medieval library with an astonishing collection of bookshelves arranged to appear to be part of some kind of ancient optical illusion (p. 54).

GETTING TO GRIPS WITH AN ANCIENT GAME   Hurling may sound like an activity practiced late at night after one too many drinks, but in Ireland it refers to one of the world's most ancient sports—also considered one of the fastest ball games on earth. Croke Park, Dublin's much-loved stadium, is the spiritual home to the traditional Irish games of Gaelic football and hurling. It's the most exciting place in the country to witness either of the two sports. Even if you can't make it to a live game, catch one on the telly at just about any local pub, and visit the stadium's museum where you can learn everything there is to know about the games, and even go behind the scenes on a stadium tour. See p. 68.

TOSSING COINS IN A HAT   Dublin's pedestrian zones—particularly Grafton Street—brim with street performers. Many of them are astonishingly good, and considering how many big name musicians Dublin has bred, there's a good chance your small donation could inspire a future star. See p. 48.

HAVING A QUIET PINT IN ONE OF THE CITY'S CLASSIC BARS   Get ready to shamelessly eavesdrop in the selection of Oul Fla's (Old Man's) pubs that still cut the grade for our choice of Dublin originals. See p. 77.

A BRIEF HISTORY OF DUBLIN

The history of Dublin, like that of the whole country, is that of various waves of settlers. The first inhabitants of the area came in around 8000 B.C., though very little is known of them. The Gaels, who arrived around the first century, are thought to have come up with the name Dubhlinn (the black pool), referring to a part of the now submerged River Poddle, while the modern Irish version, Baile Atha Cliath, meaning Ford of the Hurdles, is reckoned to have been the name of an ancient Celtic settlement. However, nothing structural went up until the Vikings made Dublin their base from which to plunder surrounding regions in the 9th century. The city grew rich on the spoils of pillage, and the first perma-nent dwellings were constructed close to what is now Temple Bar. Once the English arrived, invited over by the deposed King of Leinster, they naturally took Dublin as their seat of power, and so it became the heart of the Pale, the region most firmly under their rule for the next 1,000 years.

During the medieval years, Dublin was as filthy, squalid, and overcrowded as any large town, crammed with many poor and starving people—who were said, in 1295, to have eaten the criminals from the gallows, such was their plight. Barely 100 years later, the Black Death swept across the city, killing about a third of the then 35,000 inhabitants.

The battle between Catholicism and Protestantism in England and across the rest of Ireland meant that by the time Cromwell arrived in the mid 1600s, Dublin was a predominantly Protestant city. Its Catholic inhabitants had either been dispatched by starvation and disease, or banished. Those who remained were summarily dealt with by Cromwell, who stabled his horses in St. Patrick's Cathedral.

The British restoration of the monarchy brought better times to Dublin, and much of the fine building work that characterizes parts of the city was begun under the deputyship of the Duke of Ormond. Squares, parks, broad streets, and neo-classical grandeur were the architectural hallmarks of this era. The late 1700s were the city's Golden Age, when it was second only to London for music, theater, and writing. Composer George Frederick Handel lived on Abbey Street at the time; playwrights Richard Sheridan, Oliver Goldsmith, and William Congreve were also in situ, as was Edmund Burke, philosopher and writer, and Jonathan Swift. However, beyond the city's boundaries the country was deeply troubled, and gradually disaffected Catholics began migrating into Dublin, completely changing the tone of the city and adding a new note of violence to its streets. Rival gangs would regularly come to blows and mete out bloody justice on each other.

Years of rebellion and uprising led to the Act of Union in 1801, which saw all political power removed from Dublin to London. The city effectively became a ghost town, as the ruling class up and left, taking their money with them. This too aided the rebels' cause, as did the devastating potato famine of the mid-1800s, with the ferment coming to full fruition with the Easter Rising of 1916, an event that can still be traced in the physical structure of the city: the bullet holes in the columns of the General Post Office; Kilmainham Gaol, where the rebellion leaders were imprisoned and then executed; the Shelbourne Hotel, where British soldiers took up position and fired into St. Stephen's Green; Bolands Mill, where Eamon De Valera was quartered.

During the long, bloody war of independence, Dublin was a violent and unsafe place, with British troops and IRA men fighting it out in the streets, indifferent to who got caught in the crossfire. The Civil War that greeted the arrival of something like independence was little better, as pro- and anti-Treaty sides attacked each other under cover of many of the city's finest buildings, frequently destroying them in the process.

It wasn't until the 1930s that Dublin began to be rebuilt and re-imagined, with new shops, theaters, cafes, and public buildings. However, the many waves of emigration throughout the 20th century meant that Dublin was a relatively empty city. Most of its inhabitants lived in relative poverty, and the city's grime—and filth of the River Liffey—were as much part of its identity as O'Connell Street or Trinity College. It wasn't until the Celtic Tiger years began that it really became the bustling, busy, crowded, thoroughly modern city you see today.

LAY OF THE LAND

Dublin is a city of many waters. Bounded by the **Irish Sea** right along one side, it is further bisected by the **River Liffey,** which flows through the city center, dividing it into north and south sides. Traditional rivalry between the two sides of the river date back generations, with the Northside being dismissed by those on the South as impoverished and lacking culture. In truth, plenty of pockets of deprivation dot the Southside, and just as many highly desirable and expensive neighborhoods can be found on the Northside.

The city is further criss-crossed by the **Grand** and **Royal** canals, which connect Dublin with the **River Shannon** in the west and are navigable by barge. Facing the coast line are the **Dublin Mountains,** which can be seen from spots around the city and provide fine views on good days.

Today, tourism tends to center on the areas immediately around **Temple Bar** and **Grafton Street** on the Southside of the River Liffey, and around **O'Connell Street** to the north. The hub of accommodations, restaurants, and attractions are situated within a fairly small radius around the center, although there are plenty of opportunities to escape the crowds and explore nearby suburbs, as well as small towns and villages elsewhere in County Dublin. The coastline is the main focus of the housing market, with all the most desirable suburbs.

GETTING THERE

BY AIR

If you are arriving from outside Ireland, chances are it'll be by air. **Dublin Airport** (☎ 01/874-1111; www.dublinairport.com) is the main point of arrival into Ireland, and the country's most chaotic air terminal. It is still entirely inadequate for the amount of traffic that goes through it these days. Please don't feel compelled to fly in to Dublin as you can often find cheaper flights to other airports around the country (or in Belfast), and then easily catch a bus or train to the capital. That said, there is certainly no shortage of flights into Dublin, and finding inexpensive flights (especially from London and any number of other European cities) is a cinch. Despite financial problems in 2008, Ireland's national carrier **Aer Lingus** (13 St. Stephens Green, Dublin 2; ☎ 01/705-3333; www.aerlingus.com) was offering heavily discounted tickets for flights booked directly through its website. Note that on its short haul flights (including all flights from London Heathrow and Gatwick), Aer Lingus operates as a no-frills airline, meaning you'll pay for checked luggage and all in-flight catering. A similar policy applies to **Ryanair** (Dublin Airport; ☎ 01/844-4400; www.ryanair.com), Ireland's homegrown budget airline (and international success story), which connects Dublin with London, as well as numerous other European cities. You'll probably find little price difference between Aer Lingus and Ryanair on flights from European hubs, but service on Aer Lingus is superior. Also, Aer Lingus has frequent services from North America.

Getting to the City from the Airport

Dublin Airport is 11.25km (7 miles) north of the city. The most affordable way to get from the airport into the city is by public bus. You pay €1.90 for a ticket valid for 90 minutes, and catch one of the regular buses that takes around 30 to 40 minutes to get to town (stopping frequently along the way). The more time efficient but less economic option is to hop on the **Aircoach** (☎ 01/844-7118; www.aircoach.ie; €7 one-way, €12 round-trip), which provides regular city transfers; it's an unmistakable, large, blue private coach operating directly opposite the arrivals hall and runs into town and out to the south suburbs every 10 minutes between 6:30am and 8pm. Service outside these hours is slightly less frequent. Regular stops are at all the main city junctions—O'Connell Street, Trinity College, Merrion Square—and drivers are decent about pulling in elsewhere on the route to let you hop off. The end point for the main route is Stillorgan, via Donnybrook; a secondary route takes in the city center and then Leopardstown. You can also buy the **Dublin Pass** at the Aircoach office (see "Dublin VIP? Maybe Not . . . ," p. 17). A taxi costs at least €20 to €25 into the center (20 min.), and will almost certainly involve a long wait at the taxi rank (still, if there are more than two of you, a taxi is a more attractive option than Aircoach).

BY CAR

Getting in and out of Dublin by car is a schlep—all the main roads, such as the M1 to the north, the M11 to the south, the M4 and M7 to the west, are heavily congested morning and evening, and fairly nightmarish on bank holidays, too. *Note:* If you're planning on renting a car to tour Ireland, you should consider picking it up at the end of your Dublin stay; driving here will be bothersome, as will finding parking, which you'll inevitably pay dearly for, too.

BY BUS OR TRAIN

If you arrive from elsewhere in Ireland, you will most likely end your journey at **Busaras** (the Main Bus Station) if you come by coach, and **Heuston** or **Connolly Stations** if you come by train. **Busaras** (Store St., Dublin 1; ☎ 01/836-6111; www. buseireann.ie) is right beside O'Connell Street with easy connection to all city buses and the DART.

Heuston Station (Victoria Quay, south bank of the Liffey; ☎ 01/677-1871 or 01/703-4434) is the largest Dublin train station, recently upgraded, and serves Kildare, Galway, Westport, Ballina, Tralee, Cork, Limerick, Ennis, and Waterford. **Connolly Station** (Amiens St.; ☎ 01/836-3333 or 01/703-4434) serves Belfast, Rosslare, Wexford, and Sligo. Many rail routes are in the process of being upgraded, which means occasional delays and frequently old, grotty InterCity trains. Bikes can be carried on most mainline routes, but ask where to store them as it varies with the type of train.

BY SEA

If you arrive in Dublin by ferry from England, you will be coming into **Dublin port** (www.dublinport.ie; ☎ 01/872-2777), which is about 3km (2 miles) from the city center and served by the number 53A bus, or into the seaside suburb of **Dún Laoghaire** (www.stenaline.ie; ☎ 01/204-7777), which is on the DART line (20 min. from the city) and is well served by buses.

GETTING AROUND

Forget about driving in Dublin; that'll be a waste of time, money, and emotional well-being

Dublin VIP? Maybe Not . . .

Longing to jump the queue at the zoo or be first in line for your free pint of Guinness? The **Dublin Pass** (www.dublinpass.ie) promises all that. It's one of those sightseeing cards that bundles entry to many of the city's top attractions with a "free" airport transfer, presumably making the whole lot substantially cheaper. You can bypass the ticket queue at 28 visitor attractions and get in without paying another dime with this card—and this includes some popular and expensive places (both cathedrals, Dublin Castle, Kilmainham Gaol, and, of course, the Guinness Storehouse) as well as some less-discovered gems (like the Casino at Marino).

So why are we warning you against getting the card? Several reasons:

- **Many of Dublin's best experiences are free anyway,** including six covered by this card (at these you get a discount on a pricey purchase in the attached cafe or shop).
- **The card doesn't cover Trinity College** or the city's terrific walking tours, but does steer visitors to sights that aren't worth their time.
- **Users aren't given sufficient time to see all the sites on the card** (and thus make their money back). The moment you use your card to catch the bus in from the airport, the "countdown" begins. Unless you plan your stay in Dublin with mechanical precision—and what fun is that?—it's unlikely you'll get to all you want to with the card (and you'll feel a lot of needless pressure trying to do so).
- **Jumping the line to get in sounds good on paper,** but at many of the sites you have to wait for a guided tour anyway, so no time is actually saved.
- **Oh, and by the way, when we last checked,** some of the sights were displaying "No Dublin Pass Queue-jumping" signs. Farewell, VIP fantasy . . .

If you still want to weigh up your options, visit the website. A 1-day pass starts at €31; variations include a 6-day pass (€89). You can purchase your pass online and collect it at the airport, at Dún Laoghaire ferry terminal, or a number of city center locations, upon arrival. Stopwatch not included.

Buses criss-cross the city in every direction and although they can be very slow at rush hour, they are an otherwise efficient way to travel. **Dublin Bus** (59 O'Connell St.; ☎ 01/873-4222; www.dublinbus.ie; office hours Mon 8:30am–5:30pm, Tues–Fri 9am–5:30pm, Sat 9am–2pm, Sun 9:30am–2pm) tirelessly provides information on bus routes. Be warned that drivers can't give change—it's exact fare only, so carry coins (if you really must pay with a note, they'll issue you a refund voucher). Single trips cost €1 to €1.90 (€.70–€.90 children 15 years old and younger). Buses run 7am to midnight.

With a name that means "speed" in Irish, the **LUAS** (☎ 01-800/300604; www. luas.ie) is a brand new light rail system running across the city and connecting many of the top attractions as well as the major shopping districts. The red line runs from Connolly train station to Tallaght in the southwest, and the green line runs from St. Stephen's Green to Sandyford in the south suburbs. Single fares start at €1.40 and you need to buy tickets before boarding. Ticket machines are located at every stop.

The **DART** (Dublin Area Rapid Transit; www.irishrail.ie) is Dublin's suburban railway and runs parallel with the coast from north to south. Services are frequent. At peak hours trains arrive every 5 minutes or so, but off-peak frequency can drop to one every 25 minutes. The most central stations are Pearse Street, Connelly Station, and Tara Street.

As a last resort, call for a **taxi.** Taxis are expensive in Dublin, but plentiful, except for late at night when large unruly queues form in the city center. They are no more uncertain/smelly/unreliable or prone to rip-offs than any other major city, but if you do have a complaint, call the **Irish Taxi Federation** (☎ 01/ 836-4166). Fares start at €3.40 for the first kilometer or 4 minutes, and then each additional sixth of a kilometer or 15 seconds is charged at €.15 between 8am and 10pm; don't expect to pay less than €6 to €10 for a short journey. You'll also pay €.50 extra for animals and any luggage that needs to be stowed in the trunk, although they will usually take a child's buggy without the extra charge. There are plenty of cab companies and stands throughout the city and in front of all major hotels, but a couple of good ones are listed in "The ABCs of Dublin," at the end of this chapter.

ACCOMMODATIONS, BOTH STANDARD & NOT
VACATION RENTALS

For its size, Dublin has a surprisingly large number of vacation rentals. Since these have the twin benefits of allowing visitors to live like locals while often saving a good deal of money (not only on accommodations but on meals, as these can be cooked), we'll discuss the rental option in full before moving on.

The biggest of the rental agencies, and one that operates a bit differently from the rest, is **stayDublin.com** (☎ 800/789-8734 toll-free U.S. and Canada, or 01/677-6600) which is part of a chain of rental organizations also operating in Liverpool, Manchester, Marbella, Amsterdam, and Paris. As in those cities, stayDublin.com doesn't simply act as a middle-man between apartment owners and the public. Instead it leases and furnishes apartments, so what you get is in some ways more akin to a hotel in ambience than your typical vacation rental. Furnishings are always quite stylish and sleek—leather couches, brushed metal lamps, duvets—and there won't be any pictures of Aunt Fiona taped to the fridge, as no one has ever lived in these apartments for more than a month or two tops.

With most of their 230-plus properties slap bang in the center of town, stayDublin.com has an enviable portfolio. In addition to inspections by their staff, they employ "mystery shoppers" to comment on their product, so you can be sure that maintenance standards are a priority. And their rates often beat hotel pricing, staring at just €69 a night for a one-bedroom apartment, €89 for a two-bedroom, and €139 for a three-bedroom. All apartments have sleeper sofas making them

What's Your Number?

You'll notice that whenever "Dublin" is used in an address, it is followed by a number. This is the postal code for a particular part of the city. If you'd like to start operating like a local from the get-go, keep in mind that all the even numbers refer to neighborhoods and suburbs south of the River Liffey, while odd numbers refer to areas on the Northside. For the "city center" general, look for Dublin 1 and Dublin 2. Don't assume the numbers have a logical pattern, although you can generally assume that the lower numbers are relatively near the center.

eminently shareable. **Millennium Apartments** (25 Upper Abbey St., Dublin 1; 23-hr. reception desk) is their most recently refurbished property; they also own **Augustine Apartments** (p. 22), but there's no competition between the website of that particular apartment house and stayDublin.com's website: You'll get the same rate no matter which site you surf.

With 15 years experience, **Your Home from Home** (The Moorings, Fitzwilliam Quay, Dublin 4; ☎ 01/678-1100) has a solid reputation and a fine spread of properties in a range of price brackets. This is the site to search if you'd prefer to be away from the center, as they've staked a claim in some hot properties out in the 'burbs (which, in Dublin, usually means walking distance to the center!). Unlike stayDublin.com with their hotel-like reception desks, here an employee personally meets you and ushers you into the apartment. You'll also have round-the-clock access to someone who can assist with any problems that may crop up, and they'll provide a back-up property should yours fall foul to any mishap. Also take note that while they have regularly advertised rates (like those given below), this agency runs specials throughout the year, with some one-bedroom apartments from €70 per night.

Your Home from Home has two sets of apartments in fairly central suburbs that we particularly like. First up, **Baggot Rath Apartments** ✪ in the trendy south Dublin haven of Ballsbridge have been designed to accommodate corporate clients, so they're clean and contemporary, with a Scandinavian look (lots of blond woods, shiny floors, bold colors for the couches and curtains). Rates for the one-bedroom units used to start at €80 a night. **Sunburry Gardens** ✪✪ in the leafy suburb of Rathmines is a large, red-brick Georgian house converted into one- and two-bedroom apartments. Here, there's a rather intriguing marriage of contemporary style (particularly in the sleeping quarters, where beds are plush and firm and graced by luscious linens) and some period charm (lovely ornamental plasterwork on the ceilings, large Georgian windows and fireplaces). Some of the furnishings, too, pre-date the modern minimalist look evident in so many other properties. One-bedrooms start at €110 per night, or €710 for the week, while two-bedroom units are from €150 (or €800 by the week).

Kenneth and Susan Allen's **My Dublin Home** (☎ 800/687-2764 toll-free U.S. or 01/493-6080) only takes weeklong rentals, but for those who can stay that length of time, its rates beat the rest (starting at just €350 a week). Like Your Home from Home, its focus is on suburban areas—specifically in the prime real estate of Ballsbridge and Donnybrook, known for their Georgian terraces. As for

Where to Stay in Dublin

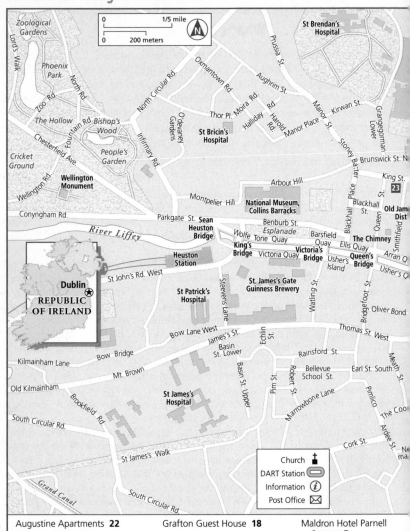

Augustine Apartments **22**	Grafton Guest House **18**	Maldron Hotel Parnell Square **5**
Baggot Court Townhouse **12**	Harding Hotel **20**	
Baggot Rath Apartments **11**	Harrington Hall **15**	Maldron Hotel Smithfield **23**
Charles Stewart B&B **4**	Harvey's Guest House **1**	Mercer Court **16**
Clifden House **3**	Kilronan House **14**	Millennium Apartments **8**
Dergvale Hotel **2**	Kinlay House **19**	Townhouse **6**
Four Courts Hostel **21**	Latchfords Self Catering Apartments **13**	Trinity Capital Hotel **9**
Globetrotters Tourist Hostel **6**	Litton Lane Hostel **7**	Trinity College **10**
Grafton Capital Hotel **17**		

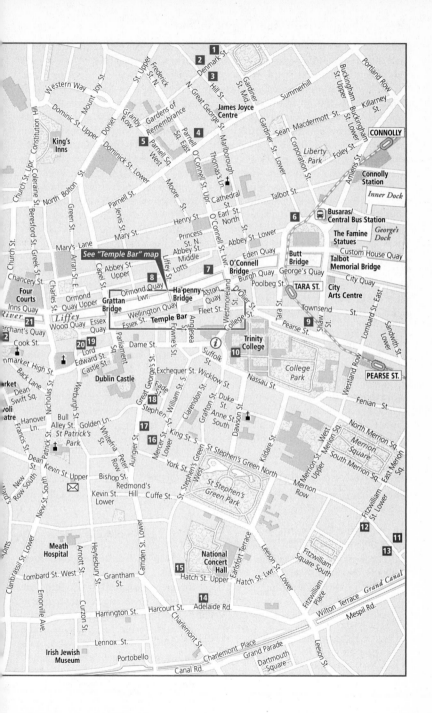

decor, the Allen's properties—which include houses as well as apartments—don't have the same contemporary design, but some might prefer that. These homes feel homey, with an eclectic assortment of furnishings, always nicely maintained but with a bit more character. So a living room might boast a kitschy hand-painted screen in front of the fireplace, a blindingly tangerine-colored couch, or bookshelves filled with well-loved paperbacks. Their portfolio stretches from apartments in fashionable Ballsbridge (studio from €440 per week; one-bedroom apartment from €470), to an apartment in the south Dublin suburb of Rath-farnham (one-bedroom €395 per week), to a two-bedroom town house in Palmerstown, which is farther from the city, but comes in at €350 per week.

If you're okay with being outside the city entirely (but obviously within easy striking distance, thanks to good bus and train services), consider **Monkstown Properties** ✦ (☎ 087/270-7678 or 01/280-7797; www.self-cater.com) self-cater-ing apartments in the towns of Donnybrook, Monkstown, and Dún Laighaire. Prices tend to be lower than what you'd pay for a much smaller apartment in the city, though decor generally looks a little thrown-together. On offer are seven dif-ferent apartments priced from €480 to €595 per week, depending on size (they're all either for two or three people) and location. Nightly rates, starting at €80, are also doable. Everything is included, except for your electricity, which is metered, and telephone calls. Best of all, the prices don't change season to season.

Lastly, there's always **Craigslist** (www.dublin.craigslist.org)—and while the listings for short-term accommodation aren't as comprehensive as that of, say, New York, it's still possible to root out a short-term bargain or two; we have friends who recently stayed in a charming one-bedroom apartment just off O'Connell Street for €50 a night. That's even cheaper than most hostels—and distinctly more luxurious. Just bear in mind that you're not dealing with an agency, but pretty much on the good will of the private advertiser—ask lots of questions before agreeing on a deal. Key question: Is there anyone I can call if something goes wrong? If you can't get a good answer on that one, we recommend you move on.

Recommended Rental Apartment Complexes

When looking at the offerings of the agencies, keep an eye out for the following properties (or contact them directly):

◆ **Augustine Apartments** ✦✦ (42–76 Saint Augustine St., Dublin 8; ☎ 01/677-6600, reception ☎ 01/645-8150; www.augustineapartments.com): The needs of budget-conscious travelers have been carefully considered here. Offering bright, airy one- and two-bedroom apartments (from €79 per night in winter) with big open-plan living areas, balconies overlooking the city, and the added bonus of a rollaway sofa bed, these apartments represent everything that's right about city rentals. Compared with hotels, rooms here are wonderfully spacious, particularly if you're opting for a two-bedroom unit (from €99 per night). Since they're new, they're also clean and mod-ern—soft white linens, plenty of dark wood, straight no-nonsense edges, and the odd painting to pretty things up. Included in the rate is parking, heat-ing, linen and towels, and Internet access, so there are no unpleasant sur-prises. Round-the-clock help at the reception desk is available. Just a

10-minute walk from St. Stephen's Green, this is a great base from which to explore the city.

- **Latchfords Self Catering Apartments** ✸ (99–100 Lower Baggot St., Dublin 2; ☎ 01/676-0784; www.latchfords.ie): Set in two converted Georgian buildings on Lower Baggot Street, in the heart of the affluent "Golden Mile" (a stretch of upmarket restaurants and hotels, running from St. Stephen's Green to the canal), these apartments have the advantage of location, location, location. Nightly rates, therefore, may be a bit rich for budget travelers' blood; however, if you can book by the week, prices drop to a reasonable €715 for a studio. Parking will set you back €7 a night (subject to availability; bear in mind parking is at least €2.50 an hour in this part of Dublin, so you'll be grateful for any savings). As you'd expect from this part of the city the rooms are grandly spacious, with high ceilings and massive windows—it's also surprisingly quiet around here at night, a bonus.

- **Tibradden Farm Cottages** ✸✸✸ (☎ 01/493-2559; www.dublincottages. com): Chris and Valerie Keogh's award-winning cottages are in Rathfarnham (Dublin 16), some 13km (8 miles) from Dublin center. You'll need a car to get to these large two-, three-, and four-bedroom whitewashed cottages, but when you set eyes on the location—out in the Dublin Mountains—you'll know the effort was worth it. The three lovely vacation homes have all modern amenities (full kitchen, with dishwasher, laundry facilities, fresh linens, towels, TVs, the works) but their architecture harks to an earlier era—wood beam ceilings, slate and timber floors, and peat-burning Stanley stoves in cozy Inglenook fireplaces. The largest house—Fern Cottage—sleeps up to nine people in four bedrooms, while the Loft has two bedrooms and sleeps up to six (two on a sofa bed). Decor isn't luxurious, but with good-quality pine furniture, an excellent kitchen, plenty of light, and some simple decorative touches. These are very special places to stay, in an unbeatable location. And prices are good, too. The smallest unit costs €450 to €680 per week, while the three-bedroom unit starts at €600.

HOTELS, B&BS & GUESTHOUSES
Dublin 2

CITY CENTER SOUTHSIDE

€€   Within walking distance to, well, everything you'll want to visit (not to mention stellar restaurants and shops), **Grafton Guest House** ✸✸ (26–27 South Great George's St.; ☎ 01/679-2041; www.graftonguesthouse.com; AE, MC, V) is an unassuming, peaceable retreat—the kind of place we really wish there were more of. Bedrooms are bright and contemporary—deep red carpets set off white or wallpapered walls, and the superbly comfy beds are swathed in comforting white linens. Although bedrooms are compact, there's a sense of considerable effort to make these budget accommodations feel as special as they can possibly be (down to the rainfall showers in some of the bathrooms). Everything you might need—wardrobe, desk, bedside tables, and light fittings that have been individually chosen rather than bought in bulk—and all the regular amenities (flatscreen TV, kettle, bedside lamps) are here, too. Some of the units on the top floor have skylight windows, so you can't look out unless you stand on the bed or a table—the benefit is tremendous peace and quiet. A double room here will run €95 to €110, while triples are €120 to €135.

€€–€€€   At the quieter end on Temple Bar—without the concentration of pubs—and practically across the road from Dublin Castle, **Harding Hotel** (Fishamble St., Christchurch; ☎ 01/679-6500; www.hardinghotel.ie; AE, MC, V) is a solid, reliable hotel that may lack a bit in character but makes up for it with good year-round rates (without breakfast, doubles run €90–€125 depending on season and time of the week, but can drop to as little as €65 when booked online). Among its 52 bedrooms, a batch of 10 oversize units can be used for three or even a small family (€25 supplement for the third person); singles are a good value, too, at €65 to €70. Don't expect miracles from the decor—everything is very neat, clean, and functional, but totally ordinary, and the bathrooms (showers only) are rather dinky. Wi-Fi is free. Still, considering what you'll pay nearby, the Harding's a decent choice.

€€–€€€€   If you don't mind cramped quarters, you may appreciate the pleasant atmosphere and clean rooms at **Eliza Lodge** ✯ (23–24 Wellington Quay, corner of Eustace St., Temple Bar; ☎ 01/671-8044; www.elizalodge.com; AE, MC, V), a wee guesthouse carved out of a sliver of riverside real estate. Let's reiterate: Bedrooms are very small but the riverside location, try-hard staff, and reasonable rates may be reason enough to stay. In summer, singles go for just €80 a night, doubles €100 (down to just €60 in winter and at the last minute online). In most rooms, large beds fill the space almost entirely, but you could reserve one of the larger "penthouse suites," which have private balconies and sometimes start at €115 (although these can soar to €250). Even if you're not that lucky, most rooms—simple, with natural woods and quality orthopedic mattresses—boast large windows with panoramic views (stand at one and you may feel a bit less cramped!).

€€–€€€€   Nearby, and this time offering a degree of luxury at rates that lately (thanks to the economic downturn) have been surprisingly affordable, is the **Paramount Hotel** ✯✯ (Parliament St. and Essex Gate, Temple Bar; ☎ 01/417-9900; www.paramounthotel.ie; AE, MC, V), one of the slickest operations in Temple Bar. Though nightly rates can soar to €350, the sales manager recently assured us that the average price for a room was really around €100, and over December and January that drops to €75. Converted from five adjoining apartment blocks, designers opted to retain the original Deco ambience; the decor reflects a distinct 1930's love affair with burgundy, heavy wood, and pale, natural shades. Arranged inside a rather labyrinthine space, bedrooms are carpeted and elegantly furnished with leather headboards, armchairs, proper desks, and exceptional beds. They do, however, come in all sizes, so ask for one of the corner units if space is important to you. Downstairs, the Gaudi-esque Turk's Head is a warren of mosaic-tiled pillars, colorful alcoves, and four different bars servicing a nightclub with hot DJs and late-night dancing.

€€–€€€€   The O'Dwyer brothers are a couple of novel fellows; having built up their business on the back of a successful series of superpubs (the Capital Bars empire), the duo set their sights on the hotel business, just in time to see visitor numbers to the city hit the roof. One of their most popular ventures, the **Grafton Capital Hotel** ✯ (Lower Stephen's St.; ☎ 01/648-1100; www.graftoncapital-hotel.com; AE, MC, V), is skillfully tacked on to the side of their trendy late bar, Break for the Border. It's a fairly low-key central hideaway that's big on comfort—the king-size beds here are as snug as you're going to get, at any price point. The hotel should also be commended for its commitment to the environment; it recently joined a government scheme aimed at reducing its carbon footprint. This also means, however, the rooms don't have A/C, and given the hotel's proximity to the nightclub, opening the windows isn't a great option either (not that we've ever really felt the need for air-conditioning here in Dublin). Doubles start at €89 room only but can fluctuate between €99 and €169; check online for special offers, such as "3 nights for the price of 2."

€€–€€€€   Also part of the O'Dwyers' portfolio is the **Trinity Capital Hotel** ✯✯✯ (Pearse St.; ☎ 01/648-1000; www.trinitycapitalhotel.com; AE, MC, V), just opposite Trinity College. Again, massive beds are key, along with whirlpool baths and spectacularly inventive decor, the kind that wouldn't be out of place in a New Orleans burlesque house (vivid colors, luxurious fabrics, furniture straight out of *Alice in Wonderland,* and all kinds of weird and wonderful statuary that adorns the public areas). All guests at this hotel (and the Grafton Capital, for that matter) get free priority entrance to any of the bars in the Capital Bars portfolio (www.capitalbars.com), which includes a formidable number of the city's hottest venues. Rates at Trinity Capital depend on demand—and it's an understandably popular place—but you can actually bag a room here from €99 in winter and €119 for a weeknight in summer (weekends, however, can be up to €50 higher).

ST. STEPHEN'S GREEN & BEYOND

€€   Just around the corner from the National Concert Hall, **Kilronan House** ✯✯ (70 Adelaide Rd.; ☎ 01/475-5266; www.kilronanhouse.com; AE, MC, V) is a much-loved anomaly, charging as little as €89 per room B&B in an area that could command two or three times that. Built in 1834 and recently refurbished, this 12-room guesthouse has been in operation for the past 60 years, giving the staff plenty of rehearsal time in the art of the traditional Irish welcome. Bedrooms aren't enormous, but are bright and have fabulously plush beds—with thick, back-supporting mattresses—that dominate a well-supplied space with everything you could need for a comfortable stay (including great big wardrobes, excellent showers, and plasma TVs). Breakfasts here are a bit of an event—you choose from a thoughtfully composed menu and are served with professionalism and good cheer in equal measure.

€€–€€€   Within easy striking distance of the city center—roughly midway between busy Grafton Street and upmarket Ballsbridge—**Baggot Court Townhouse** ✯ (92 Lower Baggot St.; ☎ 01/661-2819; www.baggotcourt.com; MC, V) was built in 1829 and is one of those real Georgian houses; its first resident, Timothy O'Brien, became Lord Mayor of Dublin in 1844. It's located directly across the street from where Francis Bacon was born and is today a friendly, professional little lodge sporting a variety of accommodations. It goes without saying that the higher up your room, the more stairs you'll need to negotiate (and this is

Cheapies, but Goodies

If there's one thing a well-established chain hotel can do, it's offer good value—even if the experience ends up being commensurate with staying in a hotel anywhere on earth. What these branded places do is give you spotless accommodations, comfortable beds, and the attentions of a professional (if occasionally disinterested) staff. Often room rates here go up and down like the stock exchange, but you've every hope of scoring a price that's on a par with (or even cheaper than) a simple B&B.

◆ There is, happily, a growing market in reasonably stylish, modern, budget accommodation, and Travelodge is central to the genre. Dublin has four of them, of which **Travelodge Rathmines** kids (Lower Rathmines Rd., Dublin 6; ☎ 01/491-1402; www.travelodge.ie; AE, MC, V) is by far the most practical as a base from which to explore the city. The vibe here is clean, fairly cozy, and very functional, complete with king-size beds, big duvets, and cheery, spacious rooms, available in singles, doubles, twins, or triples (happily, family rooms with pull-out beds cost as much as doubles). Prices are a bit of a moveable feast, but you might snag a room here for just €49 if you book early and online (though €70 is more common). Don't bother with the continental breakfast—Rathmines is heaving with cafes, and the city center is only about 10-minutes' walk away.

◆ Log on to the website of **Bewley's Hotel Ballsbridge** ★★ kids (Merrion Rd., Ballsbridge, Dublin 4; ☎ 01/668-1111; www.bewleys hotels.com/ballsbridge; AE, MC, V) and there it is: a message stating "Every Room, Every Night €99." Now how can you pass up an offer like that? (Not low enough? Try to haggle; it sometimes works here.)

true of all our Georgian recommendations—so ask if you need to be close to the landing). Knee strain aside, Baggot Court is a good value with comfortably sized bedrooms—all with bright blue carpets, vintage wood furnishings, armchairs, and smallish double beds with quality mattresses and new duvets. A handful of rooms also come with their own tiny kitchenettes. Things aren't perfect here, though. Thanks to the conversion from a Georgian home to modern guesthouse, some of the bathrooms are spatially awkward, and we've heard some ominous groans emerging from the plumbing (this calms down at night, thankfully).

€€–€€€   Guesthouses with a glimmer of grandeur (even if it's slightly faded) are a weakness of ours, and **Harrington Hall** ★ (70 Harcourt St.; ☎ 01/475-3497; www.harringtonhall.com; AE, DC, MC, V), once the home of Timothy Charles Harrington, counselor to Charles Stewart Parnell and Dublin Lord Mayor, is one such example. The high, ornamental ceilings and Georgian fireplaces echo bygone glory days, while the sound-proofed windows in the bedrooms are a godsend once

A great big historical building is what you get, and although bed-rooms lack any of the character suggested by the striking red-brick Victorian facade and large lawn out front, they're certainly comfort-able, with plumped-up hypoallergenic duvets and splendidly springy mattresses. And the rate covers family rooms, too, which means you get a double, a single, and a pull-out bed for the same price. There are a number of other branches as well (including an airport one with good soundproofing if you have an early morning flight). One warn-ing: Don't bring a car, as parking is €8 per day.

* Formerly known as Comfort Inn, a brand new name in hotels hit Ireland toward the end of 2008: Maldron. Four Dublin hotels are in the stable, which quadruples your chances of bagging a good deal. We love the location of the **Maldron Hotel Smithfield** (Smithfield Village, Dublin 7; ☎ 01/485-0900; www.maldronhotels.com; AE, MC, V) near the Smithfield Market (ask for a room with a balcony over-looking all its hustle and bustle). Cushy beds with soft white linens stand out in rooms that cap off their inoffensiveness with plenty of neutral tan and beige; bathrooms—with gleaming tiles and large mir-rors—tend to vary in size, but mostly have tubs with excellent show-ers. "Room only" deals start as low as €79 per night (and that's for two or three people), although it's always pricier at weekends. **Maldron Hotel Parnell Square** ✶ (Parnell Square West, Dublin 1; ☎ 01/871-6800; www.maldronhotels.com; AE, MC, V) is another solid choice with prices here sometimes dropping to just €65. It's a 2-minute walk from O'Connell Street, yet out of the way of the city center hum.

Harcourt Street's nightclubs empty on a Saturday night. Try to nab a room at the front if you can; they're larger than those at the back, and are a great spot from which to take in ye olde glamor of this part of Dublin. We're also fond of room 38 (ask for it), which is especially large, with a great king-size bed and a view of the Iveagh Gardens. Rates for regular doubles start as low as €79 (without break-fast), but are most likely to cost €119 midweek (rising to as much as €209 on very busy weekends). Note that the elegant suites are often booked as family units (you won't pay extra for any children traveling with you, and they can comfort-ably sleep on the convertible sofas in the huge lounge area below the mezzanine-style main bedroom). Breakfasts are sumptuous (check if it's included, though).

Dublin 1
NORTHSIDE
Hotels and guesthouses of various levels of distinction are clustered around O'Connell Street, and an almost endless string of B&Bs, hostels, and small hotels

Picking Up a Good Deal in Dublin: Five Simple Rules

1. **Pick your days.** At smaller hotels, guesthouses, and hostels, weekdays are always cheaper. Larger business hotels tend to either have the same rate all year round, or may even lower their rates on weekends (try to bargain).
2. **Pick your seasons.** For some reason, the entire world feels it's important to descend on Dublin—and Ireland—during "summer." Let's set you straight: In 2007 and 2008, the entire population complained that there was no summer in Ireland, and that it rained perpetually between May and September. We've enjoyed beautiful weather either side of summer, and we love the fact that there are fewer people around. Lower demand means that hoteliers are more likely to drop their prices.
3. **Pick your price.** Nearly all hotels run regular website deals, and no matter what rate they advertise, will probably have a better price if you play their online system like a pro. Don't stop looking when you see the home page advertising unfathomable rates starting way above your budget. It'll be worthwhile keying in your dates and details and seeing what rates are actually offered. We can't guarantee that you'll always get what you want, but we've found that—at least with every hotel and guesthouse listed in this chapter—we've been able to score a rate lower than the one originally advertised.
4. **Pick your neighborhood.** Demand is high for such neighborhoods as Temple Bar, so establishments there have less need to run specials. You're more likely to get a deal out of the center. Remember, Dublin is a compact city, so you'll seldom be beyond walking distance of the hub.
5. **Try to bargain.** Heck, it can't hurt. When it comes to room rates . . . there are no rules.

---

line Gardiner Street, which runs parallel to O'Connell. This can be a lively neck of the woods, with local dives and restaurants vying for your attention alongside the nation's Abbey Theatre and all the shopping you'll ever need.

€–€€ Practically across the road from the Gate Theatre, the **Charles Stewart B&B** ★ (5–6 Parnell Sq. East; ☎ 01/878-0350; www.charlestewart.ie; MC, V) occupies a cluster of Georgian houses, one of which was the birthplace of Oliver St. John Gogarty, probably best know for first sharing digs with James Joyce and later becoming something of a rival to him. The way the guest rooms have been carved into the space creates a bit of a disorienting maze, but room quality is solid. The presence of proper wood furniture (not the modular cheap stuff you might expect at a place charging just €60 a night double, including a full Irish breakfast) and due regard for traveler's needs (a desk/dresser, table, bedside lamps, and well-pressurized shower) moves this property several notches above hostel status. All in all, you can easily disregard some of the dour service, and thank your lucky stars for a firm mattress at a reasonable rate. *Tip:* Rooms in the front of the house are quite sizeable, but ones farther back, away from the street, can be shoebox tiny, so be very clear to specify that you want a large room when booking.

€€   The homey atmosphere of **Clifden House** (32 Gardiner Place; ☎ 01/874-6364; www.clifdenhouse.com; MC, V), which is set in a 200-year-old Georgian building, has more to do with the friendly demeanor of host Mary Lalor than the bedroom decor—frankly, the beds are a bit hit-or-miss (some are a bit concave), while a couple of the rooms are cell-like. That said, Clifden House scores highly in terms of its location, and with double rooms starting from €60, including a full Irish breakfast. It's a perfectly fine place for a night or two.

€€–€€€   Also standing out among the slew of average (and worse) B&Bs in this area is **Harvey's Guest House** ✯ (11 Upper Gardiner St.; ☎ 01/874-8384; www. harveysguesthouse.com; MC, V), a family-operated establishment with a handful of big and bright bedrooms (and some smaller, cramped ones, too). But again, the welcome is particularly warm and heartfelt. In fact, when you walk into this guesthouse, it's as though you're visiting a long-lost Irish relative, so helpful and accommodating are the staff. What's more, unlike the rooms in many B&Bs hereabouts (most of which have rooms that look like they belong to a missing teenager), bedrooms all look like they've been designed (rather than thrown together) with guests in mind; they're very neat with solid wood furnishings, and although a little worn in places, are well looked after (with proper wardrobes and sleigh beds). Breakfast is a European buffet, with fruit and yogurt, cereals, and fluffy scrambled eggs. The big negative? Soft, slightly lumpy mattresses. Rates at Harvey's are volatile and vary with demand. A double room could cost you just €70 during the week, but as much as €140 on a busy summer night (the average seems to be €100). *Tip:* Try to haggle, especially if you're staying longer than 2 nights. There are a couple of family rooms, too, for which you'll pay around €120.

€€–€€€€   Just around the corner from Harvey's is the ever-popular **Dergvale Hotel** ✯✯ (4 Gardiner Place; ☎ 01/874-4753; www.dergvalehotel.com; AE, MC, V); like Harvey's, it's a well managed family-run property, but looks fairly unappealing from the outside (the grotty sign above the door hasn't been smartened up for years). Nevertheless, it's a pleasant, welcoming spot inside, particularly well loved by Irish travelers who know that this was once the home of GAA co-founder, Michael Cusack. Which explains why the hotel is a regular meeting place for enthusiastic Gaelic Games supporters (avoid weekends when there are matches in Croke Park as the hotel can get rowdy). The decor in many of the rooms is definitely a throwback to the 1970s—although with a pleasant, orderly edge to it (and white linens offset by chintzy bedspreads). On average, double room rates range from €70 to €125, depending on time of year, but may fetch €165 when there's a sporting event. The hotel also has its own traditional bar, which many claim serves the best pint of Guinness in the city. *One warning:* There's no elevator here, so if you have mobility issues, ask for a room on a lower floor.

€€–€€€   Owned by the same people who run Globetrotters Hostel (p. 34), the **Townhouse** ★★★ (47–48 Lower Gardiner St.; ☎ 01/878-8808; www.town houseofdublin.com; AE, MC, V) has some of the most creatively designed bedrooms in the city. Inspired by the fact that the original town houses were once home to 19th-century playwrights Dion Boucicault and Lafcadio Hearn, the rooms have been named for their offbeat-sounding literary works (like "Queen of Spades" and "Vampire"). Each guest room has an artful individuality—even where space is limited (and sometimes even a bit cramped). "Rip van Winkle," for example, is one of the rather decently proportioned rooms, and has a great four-poster bed (blessed with a wonderfully firm mattress), an antique kist (large wooden chest), two armchairs, and wonderfully dramatic color scheme underscored by shocking red walls. Despite the varying decor, all rooms are comfortable and have a full list of amenities (kettle, TV, hair dryer, safe, and Wi-Fi). Double rooms go for €115 to €130; breakfast is included.

Dublin's Suburbs

€€   In the Northside suburb of Phibsborough, **Charleville Lodge** (268–272 North Circular Rd., Phibsborough, Dublin 7; ☎ 01/838-6633; www.charlevillelodge. ie; MC, V) has it all from a location standpoint; it's no more than 15 minutes' walk to town and about the same by car to the airport. It's also served by a number of central bus routes. What's more, room rates are excellent—doubles are €69 midweek and €89 on weekends, and there are even sweeter deals to be had, such as 3 nights for the price of 2 during the winter, and 4 for the price of 3 in the summer. If that's not enough, there's a 10% discount if you pre-pay and a further 5% off if you print the map off the website and present it at check in. All good news from a value point of view, but is the place actually any good? Absolutely. Besides the large bedrooms and equally spacious bathrooms, there's a bit of a 19th-century ambience thanks to all the high ceilings and ornamental fittings. Manager Paul Stenson and his staff are attentive and friendly, and try their best to deliver, even when things get busy.

€€   **Nua Haven** ★★ (41 Priory Rd., Harold's Cross, Dublin 6W; ☎ 087/686-7062; www.nuahaven.com; MC, V) may sound like an odd name for an Irish B&B, but you won't think so once you've met owner, Bruno Breathnach. He's a practitioner of Buddhist meditation, an artist who dabbles in music and films, and he likes to keep things calm and tranquil. Which accounts for the relaxing time you'll have at what is essentially a purpose-built guesthouse with four comfortable bedrooms upstairs and a big open-plan lounge-dining-kitchen space below. It's a bit New York–loft in style, with pristine bedrooms (€100 double); they're carpeted, with white, white walls, large beds, exceptionally comfortable mattresses (possibly accounting for the all-morning breakfast policy—guests here tend to sleep in), and good, strong showers. Bruno and his partner, Michael, will share insider tips on attractions, dining, and nightlife, both gay and straight. Having grown up in a country where homosexuality was illegal until the early-1990s, these guys happily welcome anyone into their relaxing home. Buses head into the city (10 min. away) for €1.50, or it's a pleasant 25-minute walk.

€€–€€€   Ballsbridge is home to a number of fine guesthouses, but be warned: Not all adhere to the desired standards. Standing way above the many overpriced duds, however, is the excellent **Ariel House** ✪✪✪ (50–54 Lansdowne Rd., just down from Ballsbridge Court Hotel; ☎ 01/668-5512; www.ariel-house.net; AE, MC, V), a Victorian mansion just down the road from Landsdowne Stadium. Sporting high ceilings, beautiful wallpaper, chandeliers, and original stucco detailing, this is really something of a boutique hotel in the period design mold. While the 29 bedrooms in the original 150-year-old house are splendid—with thick-pile mattresses, luxurious bedding, and more Victorian features—eight top-quality smaller "standard" bedrooms in the 1960s annex at the back of the main house go for just €79 if you book online (the "superior" rooms start in the region of €130). Either way, you'll be scoring a good-value bargain, and Ariel has many of the lavish extras you might only expect of a hotel twice the price, including a damn good breakfast (have the stacked pancakes with summer berries), and sumptuous communal areas in which to spend a chatty evening, or get stuck into a sing-song around the in-house baby grand.

HOSTELS & UNIVERSITY ROOMS

Location, location, location. That's the main draw of the majority of Dublin's hostels—at least 70% of them are located within a 1km (⅔-mile) radius of each other, and are, at most, 5 minutes' walk from busy O'Connell Bridge, the main focal point joining the north and south sides of the city. In the summer, visitors also have the option of bunking in the dorm rooms temporarily vacated by the city's many university students, and these are just as well located, and sometimes much nicer than the standard hostel digs. Both types of lodging have no age limit and do not require that you be a student (see box, "For One Season Only: Student Digs at Bargain Prices," p. 32).

The Southside

€€   While the standards at **Barnacles Temple Bar House** (19 Temple Lane South, Temple Bar, Dublin 2; ☎ 01/671-6277; www.barnacles.ie; MC, V) are high, staff are lovely, and safety is paramount (a key card is required to gain access to guest areas), be warned—the noise from the street carries inside, especially on weekends. So, it's doable only if you're a partier (or don't mind wearing earplugs to bed). Cheapest digs here are the beds in 11-person rooms at €15 a night, a six-bedder is €22 each, a quad €25. Don't even consider the twin/double rooms (€70–€83 including breakfast, but with shared bathrooms)—they're tiny, with barely enough space for luggage, let alone people. You'll find similar pricing and problems (more than decent rooms, lovely staff, alas too much noise) at **Oliver St. John Gogarty** (58–59 Fleet St., Temple Bar; ☎ 01/671-1822; www.gogartys.ie; MC, V), another Temple Bar Hostel.

€–€€   On the outskirts of touristy Temple Bar, occupying a late-Victorian building that looks over Christ Church Cathedral, **Kinlay House** ✪✪ (2–12 Lord Edward St., Dublin 2; ☎ 01/679-6644; www.kinlaydublin.ie; MC, V) is a far better bet. Not only is it slightly removed from the mayhem of Temple Bar proper (yet still just moments away from plenty of boozers, eateries, and cultural opportunities), it's a better-value, and surprisingly clean and well maintained. Operating since 1985, Kinlay offers an assortment of digs, from doubles and twins (€60–€76 double; add €4–€6 if you prefer a room with a private, attached shower) to dorms big (16-, 20-, and 24-beds; €18–€24 per bunk) and small

For One Season Only: Student Digs at Bargain Prices

When the future physicians studying at the Royal College of Surgeons take their summer vacation (June 25–Sept 25), their digs at **Mercer Court** ✦ (Lower Mercer St., Dublin 2; ☎ 01/474-4120; www.mecercourt.ie; MC, V) become available to paying guests looking for affordable, central lodgings. All in all, that's 100 private guest rooms, each with small, private attached showers, in a rather excellent location (right behind St. Stephen's Green shopping center) in the heart of the city center (although it must be said that it can get noisy hereabouts). As you might expect, rooms are unexceptional—small and basic—but they're well maintained and linens are a step up from what you might expect in a typical student's room. Also, many guests delight at the cheerfulness of the staff. Single (€45) and double rooms (€70) are available, and you have the option of including breakfast in your package as well. Be sure to periodically check the website, where you might find sales and deals, such as a third night free for every 2 nights you book (Sun–Thurs only), meaning that you could end up paying just €47 per night double, or €27 single.

Since it's also one of the city's major tourist attractions, most visitors often don't realize that **Trinity College** (College Green, Dublin 2; ☎ 01/896-1177; www.tcd.ie/accommodation; MC, V) also offers an abundance of cheap summer campus accommodation. From June to September, Trinity opens up its 800 or so on-site residential rooms to visitors, and while the quality of the rooms themselves varies—you can almost tell the art students' rooms from those studying science—all dorms are within 10 minutes' walk of the heart of the city and many have an atmospheric

(€24–€33 per night, depending on season, time of the week, and whether or not you're in an en suite room). A very light breakfast (toast and coffee) is included, as is Wi-Fi and access to a neat little kitchen. We also have to applaud them for a range of clever, useful amenities including a weighing facility to check that your luggage isn't over the limit before you fly; umbrellas for purchase at the reception (pure genius!); and staff who will oversee the recharging of your phone or batteries. Showers look and feel a lot better than many others in town, thanks to frosted glass doors that make them feel fresh and contemporary. The TV lounge—besides enjoying a view of Christ Church Cathedral—is neatly stocked with books, videos, and DVDs. And, best of all, there's none of that smell that pervades some of the hostels we decided not to recommend in this book.

€–€€   Merchants Quay is another area that has undergone significant gentrification in recent years, and while there's still a drug rehab and homeless clinic only a few doors down from **Four Courts Hostel** ✦ (15–17 Merchant's Quay, Dublin 8; ☎ 01/672-5839; www.fourcourtshostel.com; MC, V), you've nothing to worry about in this safe, comfortable location (it's directly opposite Ireland's House of Justice, the Four Courts). Set in three refurbished Georgian buildings, it still quaintness of their very own. While the hotels that surround Trinity may charge upwards of €300 a night, a standard double/twin room on campus will set you back €120. Also on offer are pretty swank two-bedrooms (with lovely ceiling moldings, solid furnishings, and huge windows) for €144, though it'll be less if children are part of your party. Prices include a continental breakfast, with a "full-Irish" available for an extra €3.60. Plus, with many rooms located in one of the oldest parts of the campus, who's to say former alumni Jonathan Swift or Samuel Beckett didn't fall through your door at one point in varying states of inebriation?

Finally, there are also summer-only student accommodations 4km (2½ miles) north of city center in Glasnevin. Easily accessible from the city, and only a 10-minute taxi ride from the airport, **Dublin City University** (Ballymun Rd., Glasnevin; ☎ 01/700-5736; campus.residences@dcu.ie; AE, MC, V) offers cheap but highly functional digs. Over 1,000 rooms are available, all en suite. The Hampstead Apartments (€81 double with breakfast, €65 without) and College Park Apartments (€84 double), all come with a microwave, oven, and toaster for added convenience, while shared kitchen facilities are also available. Yes, the rooms are small, and all the vacuuming in the world won't remove the general student "ambience" from the carpets, but it's hard to find fault with such otherwise good-quality accommodation at this price. For an extra €10, you can also gain access to the campus sports facilities, including a swimming pool, fitness center, and sauna.

retains plenty of old-world glamour with high ceilings, wooden floors, and large windows, but with an aura of modernity in the form of extras like swipe-card locks on the doors. And it's considered by many (including ourselves) to be one of the finest hostels in the city. Sure the pillows can be a bit thin, and the staff's a bit overstretched, but where it counts—security, cleanliness, and maintenance—things are generally jacked. And we rather appreciate that the neat duvets were turned down for us upon arrival. Twin rooms start at €64 (or €70 if you prefer a private shower). Dorm beds (seven to a room) cost €19 (€21 Fri–Sat), while more cramped dorms are slightly cheaper, but are claustrophobic. Family rooms (with two sets of bunks) run €27 per person. Be sure to check the website for deals on longer stays.

The Northside

€–€€   It used to be easy to distinguish the more affluent Southside from the more "working class" Northside. The Celtic Tiger years changed all that, of course, but parts of the north inner city are still relatively unsafe at night, while the standard of many "hostels" up here may leave you scratching your head and wondering how to get your deposit back. That said, there are many exceptions, and the **Globetrotters Tourist Hostel** ✷✷ (47–48 Lower Gardiner St., Dublin 1; ☎ 01/873-5893; www.globetrotterdublin.com; AE, MC, V) is probably the ultimate exception, with impeccably clean dorms (all with comfy bunks and en suite showers), a smart little lounge with TV, board games, and an altogether grown-up ambience—heck, the breakfast room looks out over a Japanese garden! Guests can avail of the courtyard outside, not to mention all kinds of attractive indoor spaces in an arrangement that carefully and unobtrusively shares premises with the adjoining Townhouse guesthouse (same owners; p. 30). A bed in a dorm costs €24 to €28.

€–€€   **Litton Lane Hostel** ✷ (2–4 Litton Lane, Dublin 1; ☎ 01/872-8389; www. littonlane.hostel.com; AE, MC, V) is full of character, in no small part thanks to its history as a former studio where the likes of U2 once recorded; apparently record deals involving Van Morrison were struck here, and there are ample stories of famed, famous, and future boy bands having passed through here. Today, you get a sense of that rock 'n' roll history largely through the poppy murals and neatly framed posters—particularly in the orderly lounge, where late-night conversations expounding the virtues of vinyl draw strangers closer together. Unlike some of the hostels across the river, there's no elevator here, but then again, everything's on a bit more of a human scale. Twin and double rooms cost €75, regardless of the time of year; dorms beds cost €18 to €20 during the week and €21 to €23 weekends. In keeping with the hostel's roots, musicians can exchange their talents for a free night's stay. There's also free Wi-Fi.

DINING FOR ALL TASTES

We'd better start with a warning: Central Dublin caters extensively to late-night revelers looking to soak up excess alcohol with anything they can get down their throats. And many of the eateries there know that they can pass just about anything off as food because of this. So you can really have a stinker of a meal in Dublin if you're not careful. To help avoid that, we've listed our favorite good-value eateries. If you don't have time for a sit-down meal, pick up something nutritious from a market like **Dunnes** (South Great Georges St.; ☎ 01/611-1600; daily till 11pm; AE, MC, V); they have everything from bananas and strawberries to packaged sandwiches (€2.50–€6), and just about anything to stock the fridge if you're renting (or if you're in a hostel with a usable kitchen).

We should also tell you about **Fallon & Byrne** ✷✷✷ (11–17 Exchequer St.; ☎ 01/472-1010; www.fallonandbyrne.com; Mon–Fri 8am–10pm; Sat 9am–9pm; Sun 11am–9pm; AE, MC, V), arguably the finest food emporium in the city with everything you could possibly need to stock the pantry. The owners—Brian and Fiona Fallon and Fred Byrne—traveled to New York to scour its foodhalls for the best ideas, and came back to create Dublin's foodie paradise (it's not unlike Dean & DeLuca's). Besides selling top-quality produce, there are also ready-made dishes (to eat in or takeaway); massive chalkboards in the deli section list an astonishing variety of savories: Sandwiches run €3.90 to €6.60, salads are €13 to €15 per kilo, and you can get a meal-size cooked dish for €5.95 to €8.25. Downstairs is the **Wine Cellar** ✷✷ (Mon–Wed 11am–10pm; Thurs–Sat 11am–11pm; Sun 12:30–9pm) where you can sit at casual tables amidst thousands of tempting vintages and order light eats like olives and salads, or choose from a selection of

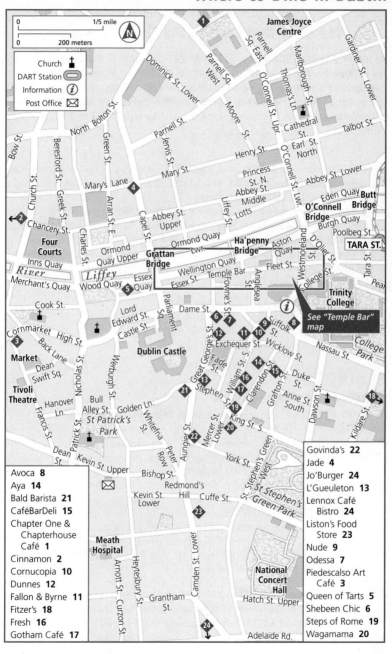

0 — **1/5 mile**
0 — **200 meters**

Church ✝
DART Station ⊖
Information ⓘ
Post Office ✉

James Joyce
Centre

Four
Courts

Grattan
Bridge

Ha'penny
Bridge

Butt
Bridge

O'Connell
Bridge

TARA ST.

River *Liffey*

Trinity
College

Dublin Castle

Market

Tivoli
Theatre

St Patrick's
Park

See "Temple Bar"
map

Meath
Hospital

National
Concert
Hall

St. Stephen's
Green Park

Avoca **8**
Aya **14**
Bald Barista **21**
CaféBarDeli **15**
Chapter One &
   Chapterhouse
   Café **1**
Cinnamon **2**
Cornucopia **10**
Dunnes **12**
Fallon & Byrne **11**
Fitzer's **18**
Fresh **16**
Gotham Café **17**

Govinda's **22**
Jade **4**
Jo'Burger **24**
L'Gueuleton **13**
Lennox Café
   Bistro **24**
Liston's Food
   Store **23**
Nude **9**
Odessa **7**
Piedescalso Art
   Café **3**
Queen of Tarts **5**
Shebeen Chic **6**
Steps of Rome **19**
Wagamama **20**

The Early Bird Catches the Three-Course Meal

If you're prepared to eat at 6:30pm during the week, it is perfectly possible to have three courses of decent fare for under €30, even at some of the city's most highly touted eateries. So if a particular restaurant catches your eye but the prices seem scary, investigate further. Chances are they will have more options than they initially let on.

platters (cheeseboards are €9, pâté plates €8), or go for a chunky Mediterranean fish stew (€8.50). On Mondays, you can purchase wine from the cellar and pay just €1 corkage to drink it right there.

A final recommended picnic stop is **Liston's Food Store** ★★★ (26 Lower Camden St.; ☎ 01/405-4779; Mon–Fri 10:30am–6:30pm; Sat 10am–6pm; MC, V), a deli selling superb Irish artisan foodstuffs and gourmet sandwiches (€4.75), plus personal-size quiches that are light, creamy, and simply melt in your mouth (try one with bacon, chives, and mushroom, €4.15). Incidentally, the espresso here was voted the city's best by the *Irish Times* in 2008.

€	Main courses under €8
€€	Main courses €8 to €14
€€€	Main courses €15 to €21
€€€€	Main courses €22 plus

SOUTHSIDE
Temple Bar & Christ Church

€–€€€   The no-booking policy at **Gruel** ★★ (68a Dame St.; ☎ 01/670-7119; daily noon–10pm; cash only) means you may have to wait for a table. But that's little hardship. The retro industrial interior is an excellent spot for people-watching (both those going about their business outside on busy Dame Street and those eating at the tables inside). Bide your time as you scan the boards for the day's offerings—there'll be something new and innovative each time you visit. The lunchtime roll, top value at €7.25, changes daily, but one classic variation is roast pork with stuffing and apple sauce. Prices on the dinner menu creep up—pan-fried salmon with baby potatoes is €13—but still knock the socks off most of the city's restaurants. Staff is a bit scarily cool and usually under too much pressure to chat, but pick a quiet time of day (there are very few . . .) and they can be pleasant and helpful with local info on places to go.

€   Laid-back **LemonJelly** 🧒 (10–11B East Essex St., Temple Bar; ☎ 01/677-6297; Mon–Thurs 8:15am–9pm; Fri 8:15am–10pm; Sat 10am–10pm; Sun 10am–9pm; cash only) specializes in preparing large, fresh crepes (€6.20–€7.80) made as you order them. While this goes on, chat with the staff and—in no time at all—not only will your food be ready, but you'll have become part of the family of local regulars who use this casual little eatery as a social club. The crepes themselves—like the people who work here—are light and delicious. The Fishamble

Elephant Wings

How's this for a complex backstory? The original **Elephant & Castle** ✹✹ (kids) (18 Temple Bar; ☎ 01/679-3121; www.elephantandcastle.ie; Mon–Fri 8am– 11:30pm; Sat–Sun 10:30am–11:30pm; AE, DC, MC, V) was a pub in London originally named *Enfanta de Castile* when it looked like the British monarch Charles I was going to marry a Spanish princess. That didn't happen, of course (he refused to convert to Catholicism), and later that same year (1625) the two countries went to war and the misguided publican realized he needed to change the name of his establishment—and quick! The newly named pub thrived until World War II when it was leveled during the Blitz (and is now a major London traffic hub). Cut to 1974, when two young entrepreneurs decided to borrow the name and the rough hewn atmosphere to create a bit of the British Isles in New York's Greenwich Village. When one of the Irish chefs who was emigrating to work there was denied a visa, the owners decided to build him his own Elephant Castle right here in Dublin. Whew!

Going strong since 1983, this Irish version of a New York take on a London pub combines its myriad influences in lovely ways. Its burger menu (€10–€14)—a tip of the hat to the Big Apple—swells with variations on the theme, such as roasted garlic-laden burgers, burgers topped with cur- ried sour cream and bacon, and Stilton cheese–laden patties. Brunch and breakfast are creative affairs that range from Mexican scrambled eggs (€10) to Irish pinhead oatmeal (€3.25). You can also order up sand- wiches, salads, and full mains, but according to everyone who comes here regularly (and that's about everyone we know!), there's one item that would be criminal to neglect: the legendary spicy chicken wings (€13). Whatever you order, you'll leave feeling full (and pretty darn happy).

Melt, for example, is stuffed with tuna and cheddar. You can also invent your own combinations (or use ours: spinach, cheese, and crispy bacon), or go weak at the knees over a sweet crepe filled with ice-cream and Nutella (which actually goes very well with the finest damn coffee in Temple Bar). And remember—don't come here for salads, or bagels or sandwiches (there are other spots that handle that better)—just stick to the crepes.

€–€€   You'll smell **Queen of Tarts** ✹✹ (Dame St.; ☎ 01/670-7499; www. queenoftarts.ie; daily 7:30am–7pm; MC, V) before you even get in from the street—warm breads, fresh-out-of-the-oven muffins, and all kinds of tarts and pastries in various stages of preparation scent the air with an aroma that's impos- sible to resist. So don't even try. Your nose isn't lying: The baked goods here (cakes especially; the warm apple crumble, or a slice of New York baked cheesecake— both €5.50) are simply exquisite. But don't stop with those. The ladies behind the counter also serve deliciously creamy savory tarts (their brie, pinenut, and spinach tart, €9.95, is spectacular), as well as generously stuffed sandwiches, served with salad for €7.95, and healthy breakfasts. You'll down your meal in a cozy (some might say cramped) space that nonetheless has its charms—vintage music plays as if from an ancient gramophone, while a relaxed clientele sits cheek by jowl with jars of cookies, plates piled with chocolate-oozing scones, and overflowing baskets. A larger but less atmospheric branch is just around the corner down Cow's Lane (☎ 01/633-4681).

€€–€€€€   For a restaurant that once seemed a little too self-consciously stylish for Dublin, **Eden** (Meeting House Sq.; ☎ 01/670-5372; Mon–Sat noon–3pm and 6–10:30pm; Sun noon–3pm; AE, MC, V) has settled very nicely, and is now one of the more consistent and established local eateries. Adventurous fish and seafood—think smoked haddock with *creme fraiche,* spring onion, and melted cheddar cheese—dominate the menu; the three-course pre-theater menu (weekdays, before 6:30pm), with four choices on each course, is great value at €25, and the weekend brunch menu has a fantastic bouillabaisse for just €9.50. Bag a table on the terrace for top people-watching, and summer Saturday night free cinema screenings by the Irish Film Institute.

Great Georges Street to Stephen's Green

€–€€   The Hare Krishna influenced **Govinda's** ✸ (4 Aungier St.; ☎ 01/475-0309; Mon–Sat noon–9pm; cash only) has a definite whiff of sanctimony about it—the proud boast here is "karma-free meals." Nevertheless, homemade, seasonal soup of the day with chunky bread is €3.35, delicious veggie samosas with a savory dip coast in at €3.80, while mains hover around the €9 mark (so who's complaining?). Specials change daily—if moussaka is on the board, grab it fast—and mostly come with steamed basmati rice and vegetables. The interior is fairly faded, but a second outlet opened recently around the corner (83 Middle Abbey St.), so they must be doing something right.

€–€€   It may pass itself off as a relaxed neighborhood cafe during the week, but come weekends the **Lennox Café Bistro** ✸✸ (Lennox St., at the top of Synge St.; ☎ 01/478-9966; daily 9:30am–5pm; MC, V) has devotees queuing up for their fix of fine, wholesome food and excellent coffee. This contemporary-looking newcomer (think pale, pale walls, with whispers of blue and dramatic chandeliers dangling) staffed by attractive young people, is just down the drag from the house where George Bernard Shaw was born—in what some refer to as Dublin's Jewish quarter. After sampling their breakfast—homemade muesli with oats, nuts, grated apple, honey, yogurt, and red berry compote (€9.50)—and such lunch specials as bagels with smoked salmon (€7.95); fish and chips with mushy peas (€15); and quesadillas (€11), it was clear they had the comfort food down. But what really impressed us was their way around salad. How about crab with pink grapefruit, avocado, and ginger (€14)? Or warm figs, walnuts, cherry tomatoes, crispy Parma ham, and shaved Parmesan (€12)? On a sunny day we can't imagine anything better than sitting under their umbrellas (there are only two, so timing is everything), with a salad and a glass of chilled Chardonnay.

€–€€   You see, smell, and hear evidence of authenticity even before you've entered the **Steps of Rome** ✸✸ (1 Chatham Court, Chatham St.; ☎ 01/670-5630;

stepsofrome@hotmail.com; Sun–Wed noon–11pm; Thurs–Sat noon–11:30pm; cash only), just a few steps away from Grafton Street and the hubbub of daily Dublin. Once inside, the aroma of baking pizza dough and freshly prepared sauces can be completely intoxicating. It's small, simple, and thoroughly unpretentious, a Dublin original that has been going strong since the Roman family who own it arrived here 13 years ago. Office workers from all around crowd in at lunch time, choosing between single ready-made pizza slices (try the ever-popular *patate*—mozzarella with potato, olive oil, and rosemary; €3.40 takeaway, €4 eat in) and filling pastas (€11–€13). From 6pm, you can also order full round pizzas; they're mostly around €12, and second to none in Dublin.

€–€€ Although it has the look of a Middle Eastern fast food joint—and in fact, basically is a Middle Eastern fast food joint—**Zaytoon** ★ 🅺 (14–15 Parliament St.; ☎ 01/677-3595; daily noon–4pm; cash only) does the best fish kabob in town; big chunks of marinated salmon on flatbread straight out of the stone oven. Stand-alone it costs an appealing €8.50; upgrade to a meal deal and you get chips and drink for €11. The atmosphere is loud and buzzy, with plenty of raucous chat from the guys grilling behind the counter. Yes, this place is popular with a post-pub crowd—it stays open until midnight—but it is authentic Persian fare with no fuss at all. We like that.

€–€ Okay, so you'd expect any place with U2 connections to be trading on its degrees of separation celebrity "cool" factor. But, the truth is, that even though Bono's brother owns one of our downtown favorites, **Nude** ★★★ 🅺 (21 Suffolk St.; ☎ 01/677-4804; www.nude.ie; Mon–Sat 7:30am–10pm; Sun 10am–8pm; AE, MC, V), there's not an ounce of name-dropping involved. In fact, thanks to the youthful ambience and healthy (often organic and vegetarian) cuisine, this wonderful fast food–style cafe generates more than enough pulling power. Choose from sandwiches and wraps (€3.50–€5.50) and healthful drinks and smoothies; we love the hot dishes here—especially the stew bowls served in large hollowed out thick crusted buns (€8.50). Order from the counter, grab a number, and choose your seat at one of the shared tables. Bring sunglasses for people-watching (and celeb-stalking) and check out the varied and vibrant clientele. Toward closing time, there are always two-for-one specials as they try to clear out the day's stock . . . since everything tomorrow must be fresh.

€–€€ Far more stylish is the Brit Isles Asian noodle chain **Wagamama,** ★ 🅺 (South King St., ☎ 01/478-2152; www.wagamama.ie; Mon–Sat noon–11pm; Sun noon–10pm; AE, DC, MC, V), set in an open basement canteen space off St. Stephen's Green. Long communal bench-and-table combos and a no-bookings policy mean turnaround is fast and you won't be encouraged to linger, which is fine, because it's also noisy. That said, the food is fresh and very tasty. It's all about the noodles here, either udon (fat), ramen (thin), or soba (buckwheat), topped with slices of meat or fish and stripes of bright colored vegetables, scattered with cheerful fresh herbs. If you prefer rice, order the cha han (€11). Kids get mini-versions of the grown-up menu, for around €6 each. Juices are good, but dessert is not worth the wait.

A Museum Meal

Tucked inside the Millennium Wing of the National Gallery under its soaring glass roof, **Fitzer's** ✹✹ (Merrion Sq.; ☎ 01/663-3500; www.fitzers.ie; restaurant Mon–Fri noon–3pm; Sat–Sun noon–4pm; AE, DC, MC, V) is a swank but affordable place to grab a lighter meal, sandwich, or pastry. It's clearly no secret—this place buzzes all afternoon as Dubliners queue up at the self-service counter, but the food is worth the time you may have to spend waiting to get it, particularly the savory, inventive soups (like broccoli and almond, or artichoke and Parma ham) for €4.50, and fresh salads. Since admission to the gallery is free, you can easily take a spin through the art (p. 56), which should prove as aesthetically toothsome as the grub here.

€€   Grafton Street isn't exactly a foodies mecca, but behind the vintage facade of Bewley's Oriental Café (a Dublin landmark and well worth a peak for the beautiful Harry Clarke stained glass windows), sits **CaféBarDeli** ✹ (kids) (78–79 Grafton St.; ☎ 01/672-7720; Mon–Tues 12:30–10pm; Wed–Sat 12:30–11pm; Sun 2–10pm; AE, MC, V), a favored haunt of everyone from large families to hip, young professionals. There are two more branches across the city—in Ranelagh and down the road on South Great Georges Street—but this is by far the one with the most interesting people-watching potential. Grab a seat, sit back, and observe the post-shopping spree troops as they assemble for their afternoon tea. If it's dining you're after, come prepared for hearty Mediterranean food, with an emphasis on antipasti, pizza, pasta, and salads. Pizza and pasta specials change daily, but the gourmet pizza—roasted red peppers, pine nuts, tomato, goat cheese, mozzarella, and pesto, for €14, is usually a good bet. They also do gluten-free pasta and spelt bread.

€–€€€   The style-savvy and dedicated people behind **Aya** (kids) (49/52 Clarendon St.; ☎ 01/677-1544; Mon–Fri 12:30–10pm; Sat 12:30–10:30pm; Sun 1–9pm; AE, MC, V) are constantly involved in maintaining and upgrading the stripped-back, rather 1970s look of this Japanese restaurant and sushi bar. Constant re-designs, re-imaginings, and re-positionings mean that the interior feels as fresh and contemporary as ever. This isn't particularly a cheap restaurant if you go a la carte, but the owner, Yoichi, is the king of the deal. At lunchtime, you can grab their Quick Menu and choose from 12 or 14 main courses—think miso-glazed pork strips with wok-fried vegetables and rice, or black tiger prawns, sea bass, and vegetables in batter with a ginger dip—for €13. The sushi bar is actually a conveyor belt, which meanders around the bar area, transporting little dishes of sushi, sashimi, and maki, interspersed with plates of vegetables, noodles, and skewers of deep fried chicken or prawn. Usually those little plates are color-coded by price, and can rack up to a hefty total, but in the afternoons (Sun–Fri 2:30–4:30pm), all dishes are just €1.50.

Great Java, No Jive

Our search for Ireland's finest espresso finally ended when New Zealander Brent "Buzz" Fendall opened his consummate cafe, the **Bald Barista** ★★★ (68 Aungier St.; ☎ 01/475-8616; www.thebaldbarista.com; Mon–Thurs 7am–8pm; Fri 7am–6pm; Sat 8am–6pm; Sun 8am–4pm; cash only) in 2008. Buzz—you'll recognize him instantly, since he named the cafe after himself—has personally layered Brazilian, Sumatran, and Ethiopian coffee beans to create a coffee blend specifically designed for the Irish palate. We're not entirely sure what that means, but we've got to agree that he's created a rich, flavorful coffee that outstrips the competition. He's so obsessed about the quality of what he serves that he'll only serve espressos that make it to the table within 15 seconds of preparation. Decorated with birds of paradise, designer chairs, and leather sofas, this small, bright, very orange shop buzzes with on-the-ball energy. There are no newspapers (only quality magazines, "Because you've come here to escape reality," says Buzz). At lunchtime, you can get a sandwich, salad,

€–€€€   It took a long time for the city to wake up to the fact that behind the alterno-crusty vibe at **Cornucopia** ★★ (19 Wicklow St.; ☎ 01/677-7583; Mon–Fri 8:30am–9pm; Sat 8:30am–8pm; Sun noon–7pm; MC, V) was some of the best veggie food the city has to offer. This is good, simple cooking; the kind of thing your mother would whip up if your mother was a conscientious objector to all things globalized and non-ecological. Hearty mains, such as the Moroccan chickpea tagine with lemon and coriander couscous (€11) make the absence of meat totally painless, while the vegetarian breakfast is a sure-fire winner—giant herb-stuffed flat cap mushroom, sesame-crusted veggie sausages, homemade baked beans, and caramelized red onion with fresh herbs (€9.25). The premises are small but to the wide selection of health-conscious diners who regularly queue for tables, this is no big deal. Desserts—brownies, cookies, crumbles, fruit tarts, puddings—almost all gluten and wheat free, are excellent.

€–€€€   The spacious top floor cafe in the Powerscourt Townhouse Centre, **fresh** (South William St.; ☎ 01/671-9669; Mon–Fri 10am–6pm; Sat 9am–6pm; www.cafe-fresh.com; MC, V) is another monument to wholesome, meat-free goodness. Miso soup, varied, tasty salads, and main courses are a lesson in how to prepare all those things you know you should be eating—like lentils, legumes, and sprouted stuff—but usually just can't face. Specials change daily, but expect something along the lines of fennel, mushroom, and potato gratin with Drumlin smoked cheese (€8.95), or perhaps a very tasty Indian-style curry with potatoes, peas, and aubergine (€12). Desserts are less successful—the lack of sugar, and often eggs, makes itself felt here.

€–€€€   The top floor cafe at the knitwear store **Avoca** ★★★ (11–13 Suffolk St.; ☎ 01/677-4215; Mon–Sat 10am–5pm; Sun 11am–5pm; AE, MC, V) is, believe it or not, a lovely place to lunch . . . if you can get a table. And that can be rough when the shoppers stop shopping and head upstairs en mass right at the stroke of noon (go a bit earlier or later to avoid the rush). Menus emphasize local, seasonal, and often organic ingredients, while staying simple and homey. Dishes change frequently, depending on the seasons, but expect something like hearty fish pie with baby leaves (€14) or organic beef burger with chunky chips on a homemade bap and tomato salsa (€16). The cakes are excellent, so is the coffee, and the homemade lemonade has real bite.

€€–€€€   Popular and pop culturist, **Gotham Café** ★ (8 South Anne St.; ☎ 01/679-5266; daily 10am–11pm or midnight; MC, V)—its walls are plastered with framed *Rolling Stone* magazine covers—wears its love affair with New York City proudly on its sleeve. Like the city from which it draws inspiration, the menu suggests wide-ranging cultural influences—there are some Asian dishes, but also plenty of Italian comfort food, and variety that runs from enormous lunchtime sandwiches (€8.95, with plates packed with potato wedges or roast baby potatoes) to duck and meat dishes (€20) that are admirably better priced than similar dishes in neighboring steak joints. Named for New York districts, the pizzas are very popular, and the regular nine-inchers cost €11 to €13 (we favor the Harlem, which is covered with sundried tomatoes and goat cheese). If you want to get in on the evening action here any time from Wednesday through Sunday, make reservations.

€–€€€€   **Shebeen Chic** ★★ (4 South Great Georges St.; ☎ 085/118-6108; daily 12:30pm–midnight; MC, V) is a bit like an antique or vintage store thrown together by a preppy designer who knows just where to draw the line between sexy and unkempt. It's bohemia meets garage sale meets grandma's garden shed— old suitcases, elaborate candelabras, hurleys, porcelain gnomes, religious icons, framed paintings, and toilet seats as wall art. The result is cool and visually exciting enough to be distracting; we reckon a good game to play here would be to sit through an entire meal without staring at the decor. But what of the food? Renowned chef Seamus O'Connell is clearly trying to revitalize traditional Irish favorites. So, among the starters you'll find seaweed salad (€5.50), lamb's kidneys (with mushroom, leek, and mustard; €7.50), and pig trotters (crubeens) with pickled cauliflower (€6.50). There's also a selection of boxty (a potato-based dish)—with such intriguing variants as "leek and blood" (€8.50). Main dishes run the gamut from Irish stew with pearl barley and mash (€15) to eel prepared with lemon, ginger, and coriander (€15), and "spudballs" with broccoli, mushrooms, and "ould" cheddar (€12). If you are afraid of dinnertime prices, stop by for lunch, when most dishes are on special (€10).

€€–€€€   For a good while after it opened, **L'Gueuleton** ★★★ 🧒 (1 Fade St.; ☎ 01/675-3708; Mon–Sat 12:30–3pm and 6–10pm; MC, V) was doing something nowhere else in this city seemed able, serving really good food at fairly low prices. This they achieved by mixing up the starter-mains-dessert format, and moving away from the classic cuts of meat so beloved of Irish diners—fillet steak, sirloin,

The Burger King Has Arrived

The burger is king in Dublin right now, particularly the gourmet, organic kind with a stylish new joint appearing shotgun-style every couple of weeks. Our current favorite (and hitting the #7 position on The Dubliner's Top 100 Restaurant list in 2008) is **Jo'Burger** ★★★ (kids) (137 Rathmines Rd.; ☎ 01/491-3731; www.joburger.ie; Mon–Wed noon–11pm; Thurs–Fri noon–midnight; Sat 11am–late; Sun 11am–9pm; MC, V), where a 7 oz. organic burger with a wide range of toppings—we're fans of the brie, pear, and ginger relish (it's delish)—is €10. It's a fun and spunky spot, with bopping music (spun by a different resident DJ nightly Wed–Sat, while Mon–Tues is open mic night, when you can sing for your supper if you dare!), servers who'll sit down beside you while taking your order, menus tacked inside old British comic book albums (remember Beano, Dandy, and Desperate Dan?), and bright Pop Art murals. Burgers all have whacky-sounding names, but there's method here—they're all named after South African townships (and Jo'burg, of course, is a nickname for Johannesburg). Even the sides are special—sweet potato chips are a healthy alternative to your standard french fries, so be sure to try them (although one portion between two is more than ample).

But, if you're looking to dine right in the city center, **Odessa** ★★ (14 Dame Court; ☎ 01/670-7634; Mon–Fri noon–3pm; Sat–Sun 11:30am–4:30pm; daily 6–11:30pm; MC, V) still does a sure-fire organic burger, best enjoyed with red onion compote, smoked bacon, and tomato relish,

pork loin, chicken breast—and delving into the world of cheaper cuts, like pork belly or pig trotters. Now everyone is doing it, but this seductive, atmospheric, intimate little French bistro is still the most assured; blackboards showing daily specials, shiny wooden surfaces, stuffed animal heads, and dusty old wine bottles all add a degree of charm. At lunchtime it's possible to make a hearty meal of French onion soup with Gruyere croute for just €7.90, or try the pan-fried haddock with marinated tomato and watercress for €15. Although too cramped really for strollers, the relaxed, noisy atmosphere makes it good for kids—you won't be made to feel you're spoiling anyone else's meal. And the staff is very good about bringing your child's order out fast. The only downside is that you can't book and queues are often long.

The Liberties

€–€€€   Time your day carefully, and you could easily stop in at **Piedescalso Art Café** ★★★ (78 Thomas St.; no phone; baldindenny@hotmail.com; Mon–Sat 9:30 or 10am–10pm; MC, V) on your walk back from the Guinness Storehouse. And what a change in atmosphere that'll be, because this place is all heart and 100% bopping with Dubliners. The name means "barefoot," and—truly—if you

A Literary Lunch

If you're planning one special meal in Dublin, let it be **Chapter One** ★★★ (Writers Museum basement, 18–19 Parnell Sq.; ☎ 01/873-2266; www.chapteronerestaurant.com; Tues–Fri 12:30–2pm; Tues–Sat 6–11pm; AE, MC, V), a Michelin-starred restaurant loved by critics and regular foodies alike. The food is Modern French with an Irish twist—think Ballotine of organic cured salmon with mustard dressing and spring salad, followed by slow-cooked shoulder of spring lamb with cevenne onion puree, spring veg, and mint jus. The fierce loyalty of Chapter One's regular clientele means you won't get a table on a Saturday night—it's booked out months in advance—but try your hand for a lunch or early evening slot, when you'll also get a better value meal. While the normal dinner menu offers three courses for a mind-blowing €63, you can enjoy the same food (and the same quality) if you arrive for the "Pre-Theatre Menu" (served Mon–Sat 6–7pm) for €38, which is basically the price of any single main dish on their a la carte menu—gulp!

Still shuddering at those prices? Don't despair. The same kitchen also does the food for the **Chapterhouse Café** ★★ (☎ 01/872-2077; Mon–Sat 10am–5pm; Sun 11am–5pm; cash only) upstairs in the **Writers Museum;** here's a real chance to sample chef Ross Lewis's finest at a fraction of the cost. Wooden trays, woven breadbaskets, and blackboards showing the daily specials give this place a quality rustic feel, and food is equally simple. Soup of the day with homemade bread is €3.65, while the daily specials—perhaps meatloaf, or spaghetti with a fragrant tomato sauce—are

come in here shoeless or even topless, we doubt anyone would mind. The narrow, cluttered space is packed with tiny tables and chatting regulars; the walls are hung with eclectic artwork; the menu comes in a file stashed with poems and stories (mostly by the owner, Denny Baldin, who wants you to think he's actually a writer pretending to be a restaurateur). Then you notice the finer details—a rose on each table, staff rewarding customers with sincere smiles, and great-tasting, good-value food. While there are soups and hot sandwiches (€5.20–€5.90), we favor the line-up of pastas (€9–€14)—the selection rotates every 3 days and always includes a vegetarian option. At lunch you can get a plate of pasta and glass of wine for €13. But save some room: The tiramisu may well be the best in Dublin.

NORTHSIDE

A bit of a desert as far as food is concerned, the Northside, however, does have a few places we can recommend.

€–€€   In a lively, compact, wood-paneled space that feels every bit the neighborhood gathering spot that it is, **Cinnamon** ★★ (Coke Lane, Smithfield; ☎ 01/872-6567; cinnamoncafe@gmail.com; Mon–Fri 6:30am–6pm; Sat 9am–3pm; cash only)—offers low-key, uncomplicated comfort grub that's been upgraded and redesigned. So, while pies are a specialty here, you can expect the chef to have come up with some interesting, alternative flavors—like chicken chardonnay (€6.25) or venison in red wine (€7.15). Sided by creamy mash and a choice of peas or beans, they cost €11 and will really fill you up. This is a great breakfast spot, too, and they serve a huge bowl of steaming porridge (€3) topped with mixed berries or rhubarb.

€–€€   Not far from the Smithfield Market, **Jade** ★★ (27 Little Mary St.; ☎ 01/887-4468; daily noon–midnight; MC, V) seems on the surface like a most unassuming Chinese eatery. Although it's small and tucked out of the limelight (more or less midway between O'Connell St. and the Old Jameson Distillery), it has drawn the attention of—among other publications—the *New York Times*. What caught their notice? Jade's superb, authentic food that focuses on the tastes of China's northeastern provinces. Ask for the Chinese menu (it has English translations) to get the dishes with a full range of spice, such as the slightly fiery, slightly sweet Yu-Xiang pork (€7.90) or the unctuously tasty Jing Chong duck. At lunch most of what's available is under €8, and at dinner there's a broader choice for a couple of extra euros. After you dine, head upstairs to belt out a few tunes at the raucous karaoke parlor.

WHY YOU'RE HERE: TOP SIGHTS & ATTRACTIONS

When thinking about their home town, Dubliners themselves divide the city into Northside and Southside and will refer to themselves and each other as Northsiders and Southsiders, respectively. (The Southside is considered more affluent, though looked down upon as somewhat foolish and not truly Dublinese.) However these subtle native discernments have no geographical effect on the location of attractions in this vibrant but unkempt city. Ex-tenements sit cheek by jowl with grandiose buildings and the famous roll call of world class literary and artistic geniuses who have lived and flourished (and continue to do so) provide attractions all of their own. We've divided the city's top attractions into manageable, bite-size pockets, and organized them according to area.

Note: If you happen to be in Dublin (or Ireland for that matter) during **Heritage Week** (www.heritageireland.ie), the last week in August every year, most of the attractions mentioned here are free.

TEMPLE BAR, COLLEGE GREEN & GRAFTON STREET

College Green acts a bit like a fulcrum connecting different parts of central Dublin. Standing here, you have Trinity College on one side, and the hedonistic

Open & Shut Case

Generally, where Dublin attractions are open on Bank Holidays, they will operate according to a Sunday schedule.

Exploring Dublin

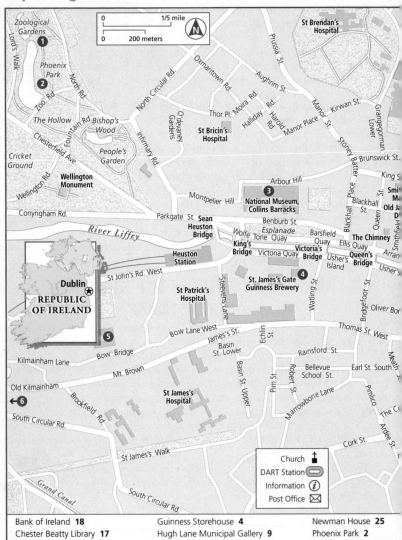

Bank of Ireland **18**	Guinness Storehouse **4**	Newman House **25**
Chester Beatty Library **17**	Hugh Lane Municipal Gallery **9**	Phoenix Park **2**
Christ Church Cathedral **14**	Irish Museum of Modern Art **5**	Science Gallery **20**
Dublin Castle **15**	Iveagh Gardens **26**	Shelbourne Hotel **23**
Dublin City Hall **16**	Kilmainham Gaol **6**	St. Audoen's Church **7**
Dublin Writers Museum **8**	Marsh's Library **27**	St. Mary's Abbey **11**
Dublin Zoo **1**	Museum of Decorative Arts	St. Patrick's Cathedral **2**
Dublinia & Viking World **13**	and History **3**	St. Stephen's Green **24**
Four Courts **12**	National Gallery of Ireland **21**	Trinity College **19**
General Post Office **10**	National Museum of Ireland **22**	

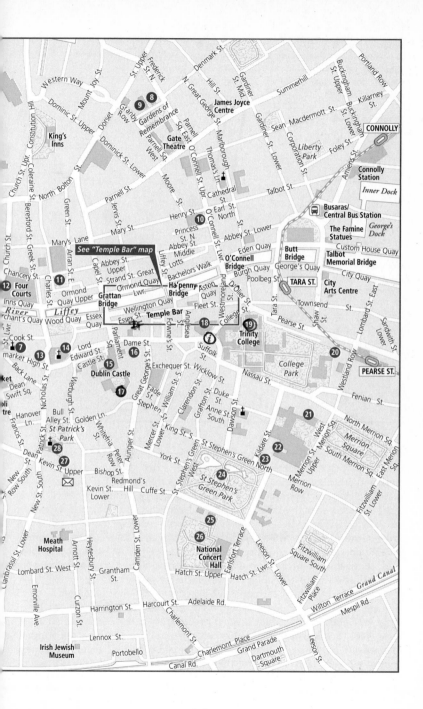

Temple Bar

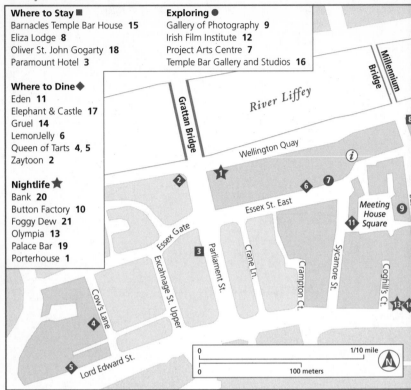

den that is Temple Bar, on the other. Head west along College Green and the street soon transforms into **Dame Street,** with a rich selection of pubs, restaurants, and other entertainments, while at Trinity's front gates, College Green itself curves north onto **Westmoreland Street,** leading in turn to O'Connell Bridge which stretches over the Liffey to Dublin's Northside. Also radiating away from the gates of Trinity is Ireland's trendiest, glitziest, and most expensive shopping strip—**Grafton Street** ★★★, a throbbing pedestrian sector always brimming with shoppers, tourists, and street performers. It's easy to be baffled by the powerful, contrasting choices that present themselves, and no matter which way you go, you'll find a piece of Dublin that will intrigue you.

Nevertheless, while at the corner of Dame and Westmoreland streets, take a moment to survey the unmistakable **Bank of Ireland** ★★ (2 College Green; ☎ 01/677-6801; www.visitdublin.com; free admission; Mon, Tues, and Fri 10am–4pm, Wed 10:30am–4pm, Thurs 10am–5pm)—look for the six fat Corinthian columns along the front facade—originally created to house Ireland's Parliament. Built in the early 18th century to a design by Edward Lovett Pearse, this was the first parliamentary building to house both chambers of the legislature—the

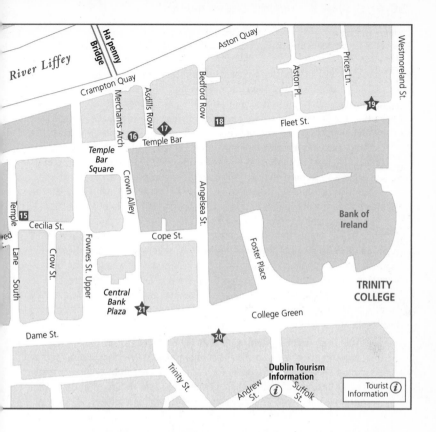

House of Lords and the House of Commons—under one roof. Although that sounds very democratic, you'll notice that while the bank's main doors face College Green, a separate entrance on Westmoreland Street, just around the corner, had to be specially built for the aristocrats who sat in the House of Lords when they complained about using the same entrance as the commoners. Parliament House didn't get to serve its purpose for very long: In 1799, the Act of Union was debated here and passed (although only after a second vote and much bribery) and Irish representatives relocated to London.

The founder of the Bank of Ireland, George LeTouche, who happened to be a former parliamentarian, paid £40,000 for what had become a superfluous building. The former House of Commons was divvied up into various banking halls, while the chamber used by the House of Lords remained pretty much as it is today. Public visits—accompanied by a "lecture" on the building—are on Tuesdays (at 10:30, 11:30am, and 1:45pm); you'll sit around a large table in the former House of Lords and hear a detailed history of the building and its part in Irish political history—it's pretty action packed actually. Don't miss the original tapestries that hang here—they triumphantly depict the Siege of Derry and the

What's Up with Temple Bar?

First-time visitors to the city will undoubtedly be drawn to **Temple Bar** (☎ 01/677-2255; www.templebar.ie), a hub of activity wedged between Dame Street and the Liffey and stretching from Westmoreland Street to Parliament Street. It's either your idea of heaven, or a real-life depiction of the worst sort of Hieronymus Bosch nightmare—either way, it's a swirling, heaving mass of humanity that comes to life at night (weekends especially), and really has to be seen to be believed. There are more pubs per square mile here than in any part of the country; a couple of years back, a noted American songstress in town described her shock at the area's "overflowing pubs, drunks, urine stains, and pools of vomit."

But a concerted effort by the local city council and local traders has since made Temple Bar an altogether more hospitable district. The fact is, in addition to some of the grungier aspects of Temple Bar, it's where many of the city's important cultural institutions are based, and you can browse art, listen to music (with or without merit), explore some great little shops, and easily get caught up in the general enthusiasm of the area. By day, there really is a bit of a neighborhood feel here, and off the cobbled streets are some cultural centers you should visit:

- **The Irish Film Institute** ✪✪✪ (6 Eustace St.; ☎ 01/679-3477; www.irishfilm.ie) occupies a former Quaker meeting house, and is more than a mere hangout for arty and intellectual types—it really is a bastion of art-house cinema. It's also where the Irish Film Archives are held, and you can spend hours here looking at difficult-to-find Irish movies (it costs about €6 for a good session, and you get to chat to the knowledgeable archivists while you're at it).
- **The Gallery of Photography** (Meeting House Sq.; ☎ 01/671-4654; www.galleryofphotography.ie; free admission; Tues–Sat 11am–6pm; Sun 1–6pm) hosts changing exhibits and has a superb specialist bookstore on the ground level.
- **Project Arts Centre** ✪✪ (39 Essex St. East; ☎ 01/881-9613 or 01/881-9614; www.project.ie) deals in contemporary art in its myriad forms through exhibitions, film screenings, dance performances, theater, and music.
- **Temple Bar Gallery and Studios** (5–9 Temple Bar; ☎ 01/671-0073; www.templebargallery.com; free admission; Tues–Sat 11am–6pm; Thurs 11am–7pm) showcases work by leading Irish artists as well as work from abroad; resident artists also keep studios here, so it's a fine place to talk to practitioners about their work.

The Tart with the Cart

One of Dublin's favorite photographic hotspots is the marvelously ugly statue of **Molly Malone,** an imaginary figure concocted of assorted emblematic figures who might have occupied these streets once upon a time. Whether she's a street vendor or a prostitute, the buxom "tart with the cart" who peddles her wares at the bottom of Grafton Street is crass, cheesy, and seriously lacking in aesthetic value. These days, Dubliners are pretty affectionate toward the statue, but it wasn't always so. Some years ago, a fiery young art student (incidentally, the daughter of poet Paul Durkin) expressed her disgust by tipping a bucket of indelible fluorescent green paint over it. It took a good year for the paint to wear off, but now Molly is once again posing with tourists.

Battle of the Boyne, both signaling that this was always a parliament for the Protestant minority.

DUBLIN CASTLE & AROUND

At the western end of Dame Street, you come face to face with **Dublin City Hall** ✪✪ (Dame St.; ☎ 01/672-2204; www.dublincity.ie; Mon–Sat 10am–5:15pm; Sun 2–5pm), a minor attraction on the scale of things, but rather beautiful (and where you can occasionally catch an organized protest). Through the main Dame Street portico, you will find yourself in a large, domed atrium designed by Thomas Cooley with mosaic floor and sweeping staircases, originally as the Royal Exchange. Around the central space are frescoes by James Ward, showing scenes from the history of Dublin, such as the battle of Clontarf. In the basement is the **Story of the Capital** ✪✪ (€4), an excellent exhibition detailing various aspects of the city's history, with an emphasis on matters of local government. That might sound a little dull, but in truth, it's packed with enlightening vignettes—newsreels from the 1918 Rebellion, medieval artifacts, and even the original roll signed by famed personalities who've been granted freedom of the city.

Behind City Hall is **Dublin Castle** ✪✪✪ (Dame St.; ☎ 01/677-7129 or 01/645-8813; www.dublincastle.ie; €4.50; Mon–Fri 10am–4:45pm; Sat–Sun 2–4:45pm), the "heart" of the city, and the site of a 10th-century Viking fortress. In fact, Dublin derives its name from the "black pool"—or Dubh Linn—that occupied what is now the handsome Castle Garden. A hot seat of power down through the ages, it is centrally located—physically, historically, and culturally—and has played many roles in the life of the country. It has functioned as a military fortress, prison, treasury, courts of law, and the seat of English administration in Ireland for 700 years. Originally completed for King John in 1230 (to replace an earlier Norman fort), the Castle was largely destroyed by fire in 1684, and consequently rebuilt to a Georgian aesthetic. The British government in Ireland was headquartered here until independence in 1922, and the Castle is now used for important State receptions and Presidential inaugurations. On the flipside, as the setting for the country's interminable tribunals, investigating serious official misbehavior, it is also synonymous with corruption in Irish life. Out in the courtyard, above the

Dublin's Other Castle

On 101 hectares (250 acres) out in the suburban town of Malahide, **Malahide Castle** ✪ 🎈 (Malahide, Co. Dublin; ☎ 01/846-2184; www.malahidecastle.com; €7.50; Mon–Sat 10am–5pm; Sun 11am–5pm; closed for tours 12:45–2pm) is the historic home of the de Talbot family and is an intriguing jumble of architectural styles; Norman and Gothic features sit happily alongside elegant period furniture, and everywhere you look a different era seems to be represented. But the reasons children adore this place has nothing to do with turrets and furniture. Its **Fry Model Railway,** a re-creation in miniature of Heuston and Cork stations with handmade model trains from as far back as the 1920s, is highly popular among trainspotters and children, while the **Doll's Museum** should make girly-girls weak at the knees. Outside is an excellent adventure playground. Malahide Castle also has the lovely **Talbot Botanic Gardens;** the Walled Garden (guided tours only, Wed 2pm) is where Milo, last of the de Talbots, established a fine collection of rare plants from Australia and New Zealand. Summer is obviously the best time to visit the gardens, but even in winter, thanks to careful and imaginative planting, there is something to see here.

main entrance, you'll see a representation of Justice—Dubliners have long liked to joke that it's fitting that in this version, she has her back to the people.

Visits to the Castle are by guided tour only, and take in the various State Apartments where English royalty have slept, all kinds of aristocrats have plotted, cavorted, and dined, and Stanley Kubrick filmed his 18th-century period masterpiece *Barry Lyndon.* The tour also takes in the Undercroft, where you get to see parts of the city's medieval foundations, much of them under water. Occasionally Dublin Castle is closed at very short notice for government business but there is no way of predicting when.

Even if the Castle is closed, don't miss the **Chester Beatty Library** ✪✪✪ 🎈 (Dublin Castle; ☎ 01/407-0750; www.cbl.ie; free admission; Mon–Fri 10am–5pm; Sat 11am–5pm; Sun 1–5pm), on its grounds, which can be visited separately. An absolute jewel of a gallery, it contains one of the world's more important collections of Eastern and Western books and manuscripts. Donated to the state by a philanthropic Canadian mining-millionaire, Sir Alfred Chester Beatty, who made Dublin his home in 1953, the collection is rivaled only by the Gulbenkian in Lisbon. Beatty employed experts throughout the world, for 60 years, to identify, not just good but superlative examples of objects and written works from ancient Jewish, Buddhist, Islamic, Christian, and other traditions. The illuminated medieval manuscripts are as stunning, if not more, than the Book of Kells. The museum shop is a treasure in itself, and a far superior choice to the heritage shop at Dublin Castle.

TWO CATHEDRALS & A DESCENT INTO "HELL"

From the Chester Beatty, it's a short walk to 800-year-old **St. Patrick's Cathedral** ★★ (3 St. Patrick's Close; ☎ 01/475-4817; www.stpatrickscathedral.ie; €5.50; Mar–Oct daily 9am–5:30pm; Nov–Feb Mon–Fri 9am–5:30pm; Sat 9am–5pm; Sun 9am–3pm; no tours during Sunday service), at 91m (300 ft.) the longest medieval church in Ireland and considered to have the most impressive nave of any church in the country; the Normans originally built it in 1191 on an island between two branches of the River Poddle, near to where St. Patrick is believed to have performed baptisms many centuries before. Author and satirist Jonathan Swift is famously linked to the church, having served as its dean from 1713 to 1745; his grave (and death mask) are found here, and some of the most touching details within the church are tributes to his memory.

Just a few steps down from St. Patrick's is **Marsh's Library** ★★ (St Patrick's Close; ☎ 01/454-3511; €1.50; Mon and Wed–Fri 10am–12:45pm and 2–5pm; Sat 10:30am–12:45pm), the oldest public library in Ireland, and a fascinating (and largely undiscovered) slice of 18th-century heritage. Inside are wire cages, where visitors were locked in with particularly precious books. Incidentally, it is believed that the ghost of Bishop Narcissus Marsh, who established the library in 1701, haunts it to this day. Apparently his spirit is restlessly searching for a letter of remorse written by his young niece who secretly eloped. She hid the note in one of Marsh's books, but he never did find it . . .

North of St. Patrick's Cathedral, a few minutes' walk along Patrick Street, will bring you into an area now known for the towering church which was for hundreds of years the political and ecclesiastical center of Dublin—**Christ Church Cathedral.** However, before reaching the cathedral, turn left into High Street to see sections of the original **medieval walls** and boundaries of the city, not to mention the 12th-century **St. Audoen's Church** ★★ (Cornmarket, High St.; ☎ 01/677-0088; free admission; May–Oct daily 9:30am–5:30pm), the city's only remaining medieval parish church still in use. At the back of the church is a small exhibition on medieval Dublin, and some curious memorials and tombs (staff here

---

Hell's Wandering Spirit

Wall-to-wall with whorehouses and drug dens, the district that stretches between Christ Church to St. Audoen's Church was once known as "Hell"—it was here that Darkey Kelly, a notorious 18th-century Madame, kept a brothel known as the Maiden Tower (which is where Darkey Kelly's pub now stands). When Darkey fell pregnant with the child of the Sheriff of Dublin, Simon Luttrell, she demanded financial compensation, but he disavowed his child, accusing the Madame of witchcraft and of murdering the baby. Kelly was sentenced to death and burnt alive while the crowds jeered her for her crimes. Since then, it's said that her ghost wanders the streets of "Hell" toward the bottom of the infamous 40 steps at the gate to St. Audoen's Church—it was here that, traditionally, unwanted babies were abandoned by their mothers.

enjoy talking about the site, so make an effort to chat with them). Be sure to go around the far side of the church and follow the 40 steps down to the only surviving city gate, **St. Audoen's Gate,** built in 1275.

Overarching this historic hub, quite literally, is **Christ Church Cathedral** ✪✪✪ (Christchurch Place, Cornmarket St. and High St.; ☎ 01/677-8099; www.cccdub.ie; €6; daily July–Aug 10am–6pm; Sept–May 9:45am–5pm or 6pm; closed for services). It was first founded on this spot in 1038 by the Norse King of Dublin, Sitric Silkenbeard (nothing remains of that building). The current structure straddling the street was built by a famous Norman general Strongbow, whose marriage to Aoife is depicted in a gargantuan painting that dominates the wall of the ballroom of the National Gallery. Huge, intriguing, but slightly gloomy, Christ Church is Dublin's oldest building. With a thousand years of history, architectural restorations, and players to go through, a guide is recommended. If you do plumb for DIY, allow yourself a good few hours to explore all it has to offer, including the crypt, the chapel housing the reputed relics of St. Laurence, modern sculptural monuments, and the "Treasures of Christ Church" exhibition, containing spectacular examples of gold and silver wares.

Across St. Michael's Hill, which connects the cathedral by a covered bridge, is Synod Hall, now transformed into **Dublinia** and the **Viking World** 🧒 (St. Michael's Hill, Christchurch; ☎ 01/679-4611; www.dublinia.ie; €6.25; combined Dublinia/Christ Church ticket less 20%; Apr–Sept daily 10am–5pm; Oct–Mar Mon–Sat 11am–4pm and Sun 10am–4pm), one of those annoying museums that re-creates lifeless scenes from bygone times using simulated sound effects and voice recordings (some of which drown one another out). The topic here is ancient Dublin life. Unless you're with kids, skip it; and if you see a school group coming, definitely avoid it.

LEARNED DUBLIN: TRINITY COLLEGE

Trinity College ✪✪✪ is Ireland's oldest university. A little world within a world, it has plenty to explore. Founded by Elizabeth I it was meant to reform "the barbarism of this rude people," because so many Protestant Anglo-Irish were traveling abroad and becoming "infected with Popery and other ill qualities," which in turn made them "evil subjects." Past pupils include Bram Stoker, Jonathan Swift, J.M. Synge, Samuel Beckett, and Oscar Wilde; also Edmund Burke—philosopher, statesman, and a man who saw nothing contradictory in asserting Ireland's right to independence while insisting it remain part of the British Empire—and Oliver Goldsmith, poet and general wit, who's statue stands guard over the main College Green entrance.

Catholics were welcome within Trinity's walls as long as they changed their religion, and by the time this decree was lifted, in the late 18th century, the boot was on the other foot. Until 1970, the Catholic Hierarchy banned all Catholics from attending unless granted a special dispensation from the archbishop; one not lightly given.

The **Rubrics** are now the oldest surviving building on campus, c. 1700. There are four entrances but the main one is the one to use. It leads in under the entrance arch to Front Square and faces the extremely pretty **Campanile,** designed by Lanyon, which rises 30m (100 ft.), framing beautiful ancient maple trees (tradition decrees any freshman walking under this will not finish their degree). Guided tours (€5, or €10 if combined with Library entrance) are available during the summer months, every 40 minutes or so, depending on numbers; inquire at the Porter's office inside the arch. Trinity is also perfect for gentle strolling, with notable sculptures scattered on the lawns—Henry Moore, Alexander Calder, and Arnaldo Pomodoro are all represented. There is also the often baffling avant garde art in the **Douglas Hyde Gallery,** while

> **"** *Dublin University contains the cream of Ireland: Rich and thick.* **"**
>
> —Samuel Beckett

the **Weingreen Museum of Biblical Antiquities** (by appointment only; ☎ 01/677-2941) contains intriguing objects from ancient Egypt, Palestine, Greece, Rome, and Mesopotamia. The Venetian Gothic Museum's exterior is the most decorated in the city, and two giant Irish deer's skeletons greet you in the hallway. If you like rocks, head up the polychrome marble staircase to the geographical museum.

Vying with St. Patrick's for the most majestic interior award is **Trinity College Old Library** ✮✮✮ (College Green; www.tcd.ie; ☎ 01/608-2320; €9; Mon–Sat 9:30am–5pm; May–Sept Sun 9:30am–4:30pm; Oct–Apr noon–4:40pm). If we had a 4th star to deploy here, we'd use it. Designed by Thomas Burgh, this is quite simply one of the most beautiful rooms in Europe and the largest single chamber library in the world. Known as "The Long Room," its barrel vaulted ceiling and two levels of bookcases are breathtaking. Over 5,000 manuscripts and two million books dating from 1601 are housed here, while down the center of the room are 10 large glass cases devoted to texts on Robert Emmet, Trinity's most famous expulsee. Kicked out during a purge of United Irishmen in 1798, Emmet's brief, dramatic life and extraordinarily moving and eloquent speech from the dock before his execution have inspired countless newspaper columns, contemporary accounts, biographies, plays, and conspiracy theories, many of which are to be read up on here.

To get to the Library you must enter through the Colonnades exhibition, where Trinity's principal pride and joy—the 7th century **Book of Durrow,** 8th century **Book of Dimma,** and 9th century **Book of Kells** are on display. Trinity's most famous artifact, the Book of Kells, suffers slightly from Mona Lisa syndrome—so endlessly reproduced that it is slightly underwhelming in the flesh. The remarkable craftwork and intricate design are impressive, but not show stopping. The book, designed around the 9th century, is an illuminated copy of the Gospels in Latin, lovingly created by early Christian monks and at any one time four pages are on display—two illustrated and two text—inside a bullet-proof glass case. The Book of Durrow is an even earlier illuminated manuscript of the Gospels created in about A.D. 675. It disappeared in the 16th century, for an entire century, during which time it was used as a kind of lucky charm by a farmer—he used to pour water on it to cure his cattle. At peak tourist season (which is now most of the year), both the Library and Books can be annoyingly overrun, so if you really want to view them in peace arrive before 9:30am and be first through the door. And if you want your very own Book of Kells pages, the shop sells first rate reproductions.

Top Walking Tours (Plus One Bus Tour)

So much history is etched into the very cobblestones of Dublin that taking a good tour is as rewarding as any of the individual attractions you might visit. Here are our favorites; along with these, foodies should consider Dublin's brilliant new **Fabulous Food Trails** (p. 66):

* **Musical Pub Crawl** ✪✪✪ (commences from upstairs Oliver St. John Gogarty's, corner Fleet St. and Anglesea St., Temple Bar; ☎ 01/475-3313; www.discoverdublin.ie; €12; Apr–Oct daily 7:30pm; Nov–Mar Thurs–Sat 7:30pm): Dublin's legendary pub crawl is far more enlightening than its name suggests. You'll hop to a couple of low-key pubs (well off the beaten trail), where you'll gather in upstairs lounges, complete with a private bar, for private trad sessions with accomplished local musicians. Along with hearing them play, they talk about the music, their instruments, and about how the tunes and techniques vary from county to county. All in all the experience is far more valuable than the cost of a ticket.

* **Dublin's Rock 'n' Roll Bus Tour** ✪✪ (commences Westmoreland St.; ☎ 01/620-3929; www.dublinrocktour.ie; €15; daily 12:30, 2:30, 4:30, and 6:30pm): This 75-minute tour is more of a traditional sightseeing jaunt, as it swings by key locations in Dublin rock history, sometimes racing past the first venue where so-and-so performed or idling in the vicinity of the U2 studios (dependent on whether or not they're in, of course). A video is played to fill in the parts of the story you won't see in the streets. Participants stay on the bus, so if you like to get out and touch or photograph places, this is not the tour for you. However, the owners of the bus have personal links with the music industry and feed in tasty, up-to-date tidbits that keep the tour fresh and topical.

* **1916 Rebellion Walking Tour** ✪✪✪ (☎ 086/858-3847; www.1916 rising.com; €12; Mon–Sat 11:30am; Sun 1pm): Lorcan Collins may just be the most entertaining and witty Dubliner you'll ever meet. Wry, intelligent, and engaging, he co-authored a book on the 1916 Rebellion, and shares his knowledge of that time in this compelling 2-hour walk, unspooling the tale of how the Rebellion set off events

DUBLIN'S MUSEUM QUARTER

Just around the corner from Trinity is the **National Gallery of Ireland** ✪✪✪ (Corner of Merrion Sq. West and Clare St.; ☎ 01/661-5133; www.nationalgallery.ie; free admission; Mon–Sat 9:30am–5:30pm; Thurs 9:30am–8:30pm; Sun noon–5:30pm), which George Bernard Shaw loved so much (he called it one of his universities) that he bequeathed much of his estate to ensure its continued success. Though it houses important 14th- to 20th-century that led to independence. Kicking off at the historic International Bar (p. 79), you'll pass a number of famous city attractions (Lorcan gives you his candid opinion of their worth) as you soldier forth; part of the joy of this tour is that you get to see another Dublin—one which isn't highlighted much, and gets a blast of energy from your eloquent guide. Don't panic if Lorcan isn't leading the tour; he works with Conor Kostick (who co-authored the book) and Shane MacThomais, both excellent guides in their own right.

◆ **Dublin Literary Pub Crawl** ✯✯✯ (commences from upstairs at The Duke, 9 Duke St.; ☎ 01/670-5602; www.dublinpubcrawl.com; €12; Apr–Oct daily 7:30pm; Nov–Mar Thurs–Sun 7:30pm): The pub crawl that inspired imitators in cities around the world, after 2 decades, this remains one of the most entertaining (and informative) nights out you can have in Dublin. Sage actor-tour guides Colm and Brendan perform scenes from plays and novels by some of Dublin's best-loved writers, filling the words with gusto and good humor, and all the while injecting plenty of anecdotal information. Such as, did you know that Beckett co-authored the steamy, hideous musical *Oh! Calcutta*? Or that a first edition copy of *Ulysses* will set you back €35,000? There are rewards for paying attention, by the way. A literature-related quiz runs through the evening.

◆ **Dublin Footsteps Walking Tours** ✯✯✯ (☎ 087/779-1979; €12; Mon, Fri, and Sat 10:30am, and Wed 2:30pm): A one-man show led by Rob McElroy, a young, devoted follower of Irish history and Celtic mythology; these tours usually commence from outside Bewley's Café on Grafton Street. McElroy churns out intimate tales about the authors, playwrights, and poets who've lived, died, and gotten drunk in Dublin. This is a great opportunity to hear the bohemian angle, revealed by someone who not only loves the great writers, but is himself a poet. McElroy will tell you which writers drank, and where, and he's a good one for shooting down the establishment. Call ahead to book and confirm details.

art from all over Europe (most notably Caravaggio's *The Taking of Christ*), your time will be best spent in the galleries devoted to the iconic Irish masters from the haunting, simple landscapes of Paul Henry to Limerick-born Séan Keating's colorful modernism. The museum's pinnacle is the Yeats Room, which explores the multi-generational genius of the Yeats family including attempts at fine art by the poet William Butler and the unequivocal masterpieces of his brother Jack B.—it's extraordinary to follow the evolution of his style, culminating with *Grief*, which he painted in 1951 at the age of 80, 6 years before his death. We also have a soft spot for the National Portrait Collection, where evocative images of James Joyce, W. B. Yeats, and Bono share wall space with Irish politicians, artists, and other heroes, revealing (especially when you listen to the audio-guide commentary) genuine insights into the Irish psyche.

Practically around the corner (okay, it's a big corner) from the Gallery is the **National Museum of Ireland** ✪✪ (Kildare St.; ☎ 01/677-7444; www.museum.ie; free admission; Tues–Sat 10am–5pm; Sun 2–5pm), another mammoth collection, impossible to tackle in one visit. But, without a doubt, the most intriguing section is one devoted to a series of bog-preserved human bodies, believed to have been victims of ritual execution or perhaps sacrifice. The detail you can see on leather-like skin and sections through the corpses themselves is astounding, and—so long as you're not squeamish—worth devoting some time. The second most worthwhile collection here are the Viking artifacts found in various corners of the city, although ultimately the scope is not as wide as the collection in Waterford's Treasures Museum (p. 153; if you're planning on also visiting Waterford you can skip this exhibit). Ultimately, the museum's haul is so extensive that only part of it can be exhibited here. A whole other section devoted principally to history (as opposed to the archaeology collection housed here) and the decorative arts is on display across the Liffey at Collins Barracks (p. 61).

PINTS & PUNISHMENT: THE LIBERTIES & DUBLIN WEST

We're sorry to say, but Dublin's most popular (and busiest) attraction is a sorry letdown. Despite fabulous views over the city from the top (where, yes, you exchange your expensive ticket for a "free" pint of porter), we think that the **Guinness Storehouse** (St. James's Gate; ☎ 01/408-4800; www.guinness-storehouse.com; €13.50; daily Sept–June 9:30am–5pm; July–Aug 9:30am–8pm; Bus 51B, 78A, 123) is simply an elaborate bore. An interactive celebration of Ireland's most famous brand—housed in an impressive six-storey building designed around a pint-shaped glass atrium—the Storehouse never offers a chance to witness stout being brewed (now, that would be something intriguing). Instead, you spend at least an hour cooped up in an endless succession of digital exhibitions and displays. We think you can skip it.

Farther west, however, is the site of one of Dublin's most authentic and intriguing attractions. Every famous Irish felon for 200 years, until 1924 when it was closed, was held at **Kilmainham Gaol** ✪✪✪ (Inchicore Rd.; ☎ 01/453-5984; www.heritageireland.ie; Heritage Card or €5.30; guided tour only, daily May–Sept 9:30am–5pm; Oct–Apr 9:30am–4:30pm; Bus 51B, 78A, 79), now an evocative museum space. The cold, bare, concrete speaks volumes about the terrible times visited upon the men and women who were interred here. We've seen visitors teary-eyed at the end of the tour, so strong is the emotional connection with events that have shaped the Republic of Ireland (and it doesn't hurt that the guides who take you around are crack storytellers). Robert Emmet, Padraig Pearse, Joseph Plunkett, Eamon De Valera (who was the last prisoner ever released from here, and the first leader of independent Ireland)—it's a who's who of Irish history. Once the prison was ordered closed, it was left untouched and thus is today exactly as it always has been. A bleakly informative display gives an overview of the truly appalling conditions in operation here, and there's a multimedia display

When Vikings Were Stand-ups

Okay, so they're awfully gimmicky, but the **Viking Splash Tours** (kids) (Depart from 65 Patrick's St. and St. Stephen's Green North; ☎ 01/707-6000; www.vikingsplash.ie; €20; daily) can be a great deal of fun, too, and they're the only tours of the city that give tourists the chance to try to (intentionally) frighten the natives. Prepare to wear a plastic Viking helmet and roar "WHAAAAY!" at startled Celts (pedestrians). They're also the only bus tour of Dublin that covers the city's Viking roots and its evolving Docklands' future. Once you're done with the land bit, these World War II amphibian trucks—vehicles known as "duks"—trundle into the Grand Canal basin and paddle around the revamped, regenerated Docklands area, where you get within meters of U2's recording studios and hear about Colin Farrell's penthouse. The tour commentary resembles a comedian's routine and is given either by the driver or by a designated guide (the latter is preferable, so ask before you book).

on hanging (including a chance to log your vote in the debate over capital punishment), but the real appeal is the connection with the past.

From the gaol, a long pathway through cultivated gardens leads to the **Irish Museum of Modern Art** ✯ (IMMA, Royal Hospital, Kilmainham; ☎ 01/612-9900; www.imma.ie; free admission; Tues and Thurs–Sat 10am–5:30pm; Wed 10:30am–5:30pm; Sun noon–5:30pm), occupying the extensively restored Royal Hospital. Alas, the museum interiors are stark and clinical (perhaps appropriate for a disused hospital), and the exhibits—including the permanent collection—tend to be laid out in a similarly sterile manner, leaving us as cold as the brilliant-white walls and floors against which the artworks are displayed. Overly intellectual, the museum ends up being a bit disengaging, lacking in visceral pull. There are a few solitary gems, of course, and it'd be worth coming here to check out the Chapel, the most beautiful room in the building, with an unparalleled Baroque Caroline floral ceiling; it can be visited only on hourly scheduled tours.

ACROSS THE LIFFEY: EXPLORING THE NORTHSIDE

Historically, the most significant building in this area is the **General Post Office** ✯✯✯ (GPO, O'Connell St.; ☎ 01/705-1000; Mon–Sat 8am–8pm), which still functions in its original capacity. It was outside the GPO that the 1916 Rebellion got underway when, on Easter Monday, the commander-in-chief of the rebel Irish forces, Padraig Pearse, read the Proclamation of the Irish Republic, declaring independence after over 750 years of British rule. In a surprise move, key locations around the city were occupied by rebel insurgents and for a brief 1-week period, there was war on the streets of Dublin. During the short-lived uprising, the GPO and many surrounding buildings were heavily bombarded by British artillery and reduced to smoldering ruin; you can still see bullet wounds in the walls and columns out front. Once the British had quashed the uprising, and hundreds of combatants and civilians lay dead, the leaders of the Rebellion were jailed and executed at Kilmainham (p. 58). Effectively, these men became martyrs, swinging the tide of opinion so heavily against the British that the Rebellion ultimately sparked the final transition to independence. If you go into the vast main lobby of the GPO, you'll see 10 paintings that give a snapshot look at different stages of the Rebellion, including the fighting that took place in this very building (now entirely restored).

Back outside, if there's one thing on this road you can't miss, it's the **Spire,** a massive, soaring, needle-shaped modern artwork that rises to an intimidating 120m (394 ft.); it was erected in 2002 and 2003 in celebration of the renewal of O'Connell Street. It also occupies the spot where there formerly stood a statue of Horatio Nelson, for many a symbol of British Imperialism. Nelson's stone column was blown up by the IRA in 1966. Locals have given the Spire countless unflattering nicknames—from the "Phallus by the Palace" to "Stiffy by the Liffey!" Clearly nothing—not even a tall spike—is sacred.

DUBLIN'S LITERARY HEROES

North of O'Connell Street—beyond the Gate Theatre and facing the Garden of Remembrance—is **Parnell Square** and the **Dublin Writers Museum** ✯ (18 Parnell Sq. North; ☎ 01/872-2077; www.writersmuseum.com; €7.25; Mon–Sat 10am–5pm; Sun 11am–5pm; June–Aug 11am–6pm). It's strictly for enthusiasts, who will enjoy the reams of information it offers on Ireland's writing fraternity. It's not a big museum, but if you get into it, you can wile away an hour expanding your perspective on the last 300 years of Irish literary history. Most intriguing, perhaps, is the "revelation" that Bram Stoker pretty much cloned his Dracula tale from Joseph Sheridan Le Fanu's earlier Gothic novel, *Carmilla.*

Right next door to the Writers Museum, and guaranteed to give you a rush (if fine art is your thing), is the **Hugh Lane Municipal Gallery** ✯✯ (Charlemont House, Parnell Sq. North; ☎ 01/222-5550; www.hughlane.ie; free admission; Tues–Thurs 10am–6pm; Fri–Sat 10am–5pm; Sun 11am–5pm). Its holding of Continental, Irish, and British art from the 19th and 20th centuries is extensive.

Joyce in the Suburbs

A jaunt to Sandycove, easily doable from central Dublin, is richly rewarded with walks along the piers and a visit to the **Joyce Museum** ✯✯ (Joyce Tower, Sandycove; ☎ 01/280-9265; €7.25; Apr–Oct Mon–Sat 10am–1pm and 2–5pm; Sun 2–6pm; Nov–Mar by arrangement only). The home it inhabits is the setting for the opening chapter of *Ulysses* in which Joyce mocks his one-time friend and later rival, Oliver St. John Gogarty, calling him "Stately plump Buck Mulligan." Devised by Sylvia Beech in 1962, the interior has been restored to match Joyce's description. Exhibits are basically a collection of memorabilia: walking stick, cigar case, guitar, death mask, and many letters. Also on display is a beautifully illustrated edition of *Ulysses* with line drawings by Matisse.

Renoir, Manet, Monet, and Corot all jostle for your attention; a Bossi fireplace is on the first floor; the Francis Bacon Studio and artworks are a hackle-raising slaughterhouse of modern art. In the wintertime stop by for free classical music recitals on Sunday afternoon from high caliber international performers.

For insights into ancient Dublin, **St. Mary's Abbey** (Meetinghouse Lane, off Capel St.; ☎ 01/833-1618; free admission; mid-June to mid-Sept Wed and Fri 10am–5pm; last admission 30 min. before closing) is the spot. One of Dublin's best-kept secrets, it was founded in 1139 and was once the wealthiest and most important (in terms of the role it played in affairs for state) Cistercian Abbey in Ireland. It was in the Chapter House here that "Silken" Thomas Fitzgerald started his unsuccessful rebellion and it is in this context that the Abbey gets a pretty write up in the "Wandering Rocks" chapter of James Joyce's *Ulysses*. King Henry VII dissolved the Abbey, along with many others, and now only two rooms remain—that same Chapter House and the Slype. They contain a fascinating exhibition put together by the Office of Public Works along with the Dublin Archaeological Society and the History of Art Department of Trinity College, Dublin. It is self guiding, but off season tours can be arranged (☎ 086/606-2729). If you happen to be in Dublin on June 16th—Bloomsday—Joycean events are held here. To get here, from O'Connell Street follow Luas Line down Abbey Street Upper, cross Capel Street to street called Mary's Abbey, then turn right into Meetinghouse Lane.

More recent history is surveyed at Collins Barracks, which now houses the extensive collections of the **Museum of Decorative Arts and History** (Benburb St.; ☎ 01/677-7444 or 01/648-6453; www.museum.ie; free admission; Tues–Sat 10am–5pm; Sun 2–5pm), a branch of the National Museum. While the National Museum is a definitive archeological experience, Collins Barracks is rather special-ist and eclectic. The exceptional talent on display here is Eileen Gray, Irish furni-ture designer extraordinaire, many of whose pieces are modern design classics.

ALICE IN WONDERLAND GOES NORTH

The Hugh Lane Gallery (p. 60) was originally built as the city residence for the extravagant and fun-loving James Caulfield, 1st Earl of Charlemont, who also commissioned the **Casino at Marino** ✪✪✪ (Cherrymount Crescent, off the Malahide Rd., Marino; ☎ 01/833-1618; www.heritage.ie; Heritage Card or €2.90; Mar and Nov Sat–Sun noon–4pm; Apr Sat–Sun noon–5pm; May and Oct daily 10am–5pm; June–Sept daily 10am–6pm; last tour 45 min. before closing; Bus 20B, 27, 27B, 42, 42A, 42B from Lower Abbey St., and 123 Imp Bus from O'Connell St., Dart to Clontarf Road Station), perhaps our favorite piece of Dublin architecture. We love it because—as when Alice enters Wonderland or Gulliver discovers Lilliput—nothing here is as it seems, and everything you think you know about size and proportion goes down the tubes. As you approach it, the Casino looks a bit like a small classical temple; step inside and you discover that it's cunningly divided into 16 gorgeously decorated little chambers. You'll also dis-cover that the urns on the roof are actually chimneys, the pillars are hollow drains, doors are hidden, and corners painted in. Built as a playhouse in which the Earl entertained friends at his country residence, this is one of Europe's finest 18th-century neo-classical buildings (and nearly ruined the Duke financially). Visitors are taken around in small groups (16 people maximum) by knowledgeable guides;

Dublin's Visit-Worthy Parks

The city's most central, and most formal, park is **St. Stephen's Green** ★★★ (Dublin 2), an elegant city center of tree-lined lawns, a wide, duck-filled pond, a pretty pagoda, children's playground, and plenty of space to ramble around. While today there are frequent outdoor summer exhibitions and regular lunchtime music programs, until the 17th century this was a site for regular public hangings and other grisly punishments. Sir Arthur Guinness—yes, a member of the brewing clan—oversaw a new design in 1880, when it took on the handsome, ornamental layout it retains today. Look out for the statue of one of Dublin's largely unsung 19th-century figures, James Clarence Mangan, whom Oscar Wilde called the greatest Celtic poet. He led a most unorthodox life, apparently at one stage even sharing a bed in a poorhouse with a leper; he died from complications resulting from alcohol and opium use. The park has plenty more recognizable statues, too—Henry Moore's rather functional rendition of James Joyce, and a bust of Countess Marciewicz, the major female figure involved in the 1916 Rebellion. Probably its finest statue is George Moore's expressionist image of W.B. Yeats.

Around Stephen's Green, as locals call it, are two famous addresses, the **Shelbourne Hotel** ★ (27 St. Stephen's Green; ☎ 01/676-6471) where the constitution of the Irish Free State was drafted in 1921; and on the opposite side of the Square, **Newman House** ★ (85–86 St. Stephen's Green; ☎ 01/716-7422; www.visitdublin.com), which was designed by the great architect Richard Castle and is considered one of the highlights of Georgian Dublin. It housed the first Catholic university in Ireland and was attended by James Joyce from 1899 to 1902. Limited guided visits to the house are available in summer (€5; June–Aug Tues–Fri at noon, 2, 3, and 4pm), but you can freely wander through the magnificent **Iveagh Gardens** ★★★ (Clonmel St.; ☎ 01/475-7816) at the back of the house by taking one of the entrances off Harcourt Street. Dotted with classical statuary fountains, a maze, and a rustic grotto, the Iveagh was laid out in 1863 and is a lovely spot for a picnic.

Set over 12 hectares (30 acres) once belonging to a pair of eccentric sisters, the Overends, **Airfield Trust** ★★ kids (Upper Kilmacud Rd., Dundrum; ☎ 01/298-4301; €5) has a cute working farm, with goats, geese, sheep, cows, donkeys, and miniature horses as well as lovely old walled gardens

you'll be provided with special slippers to protect the delicate parquetry floors, some of which include wood from trees that are now extinct. The tour takes about an hour. Be sure to take in the terrific view of Dublin Bay from the garden.

Also of fairy-tale quality are the **National Botanic Gardens** ★★ (Glasnevin; ☎ 01/837-7596; www.botanicgardens.ie; free admission; €2 guided tours by prior arrangement; free guided tours Sun 12:30–2:30pm; daily summer 9am–6pm;

and a vintage car museum filled with gorgeous Rolls Royces. A swell spot for families; there's also a cafe on site.

Heading north, across the Liffey, the largest enclosed public park in any capital city in Europe is the **Phoenix Park** 🧒 (Dublin 8; ☎ 01/677-0095; free admission), originally formed as a royal hunting park in the 1660s after it was confiscated from a priory. Opened to the public in 1747, it's still grazed today by large herds of fallow deer; most of them are relatively bold, and it's possible to sneak quite close up before they bother fleeing. The Phoenix Monument sits in the center though it's thought the park gets it name from the spring underneath it. The building adjoining the Phoenix Park Visitor Centre is Ashtown Castle, a medieval tower house built sometime prior to the 17th century. If you have children, they'd probably love you to bring them to the **Dublin Zoo** 🌟 🧒 (Phoenix Park; ☎ 01/677-1425; www.dublinzoo.ie; €14.50; Apr–Sept Mon–Sat 9:30am–6:30pm and Sun 10:30am–6:30pm; hours slightly reduced rest of the year). Founded in 1830, it's the world's third-oldest public zoo and a recent far-reaching renovation has greatly enhanced the facilities, with an African plains section that looks and feels very much like a trip halfway around the world. The highlight, though, is watching the gorillas in their glass enclosure just beyond the Arctic section.

Out of town, **Bull Island** 🌟 is a UNESCO Biosphere nature and wildlife reserve reached by a spindly bridge, well signposted off the main Clontarf Road. The island is just 200 years old and was formed by the gathering of sand when the Great South Wall was built in the 1700s. Sandbanks gradually became locked together by sea grass and other hardy plants, and its dunes and mudflats are now home to many types of bird and plant life. A swimming beach runs the length of the island. Opposite Bull Island Bridge is **St. Anne's Park** (☎ 01/833-1181; daily dawn–dusk), once part of the Guinness estate, bought by old Sir Benjamin in 1832. The Clontarf Road approach is most unremarkable; in fact, it looks like scrubland, but behind that are 109 hectares (270 acres) of straight, formal walkways with a duck pond, tennis courts, numerous playing fields, and cute little old stables. Don't miss the flowers! Within the park are a miniature rose garden, with bower and fountain, and a large rose garden with hundreds of bushes, with every variety of rose; during high summer the scent is intoxicating.

winter 9am–4:30pm), which boast 15,000 plant species and cultivars from a variety of habitats from all around the world. Famous for its exquisitely restored and planted greenhouses, the gardens have lately made a name for themselves as a center for conservation. They are home to over 300 endangered plant species from around the world, including six species already extinct in the wild. Covering 19.5 hectares (48 acres), the Gardens were officially founded in 1795, but are actually older, since the demesne originally belonged to the poet Thomas Ticknell (1686–1740).

Nearby **Glasnevin Cemetery** (Prospect Rd.; ☎ 01/830-1133; www.glasnevin-cemetery.ie; Mon–Fri 9:30am–1pm and 2–4:30pm; Sat 9:30am–noon) is filled with memorials to some of Ireland's greatest heroes. Many of the country's best and brightest from the political, theatrical, entertainment, and literary worlds are buried here, including Daniel O'Connell, Michael Collins, Eamon De Valera, Brendan Behan, and Maud Gonne, and—since many of the important gravesites are fairly nondescript—guided tours are given Wednesdays and Fridays at 2:30pm. Once you've paid homage to some of Ireland's greats, head over to **Gravediggers,** one of our favorite pubs in the city, and just a short walk from the main cemetery entrance (p. 78).

THE OTHER DUBLIN

Sneak into Trinity College Chapel, to the right on Trinity's Main Square as you stand facing the main entrance, around 5pm on a Thursday during term time and you will catch the church choir at Evensong. Their voices soar and the sounds echo around the elegant nave. Look around—you won't see another tourist in sight.

Well, that's one way of seeing—and hearing—a side of Dublin that most tourists will never know about. But how about some opportunities to really get involved? Here we discuss a wide range of activities that'll enable you to spend time alongside ordinary Dubliners or to learn from extraordinary locals who'll reward your time and effort with memories that mere sightseeing can never replicate.

DUBLIN AT WORK: THE COURTS

Dublin's **Four Courts** (15–24 Phoenix St., Inns Quay, Smithfield; ☎ 01/872-5555; www.courts.ie) have been at the center of Irish law for 200 years; this emblematic complex was commissioned when, in 1775, it was decided to bring the country's legal system under one roof and thereby end the nomadic Irish court system that had been in place for centuries. And anyone who's interested is allowed to go inside this majestic edifice and witness the Irish legal system in action by attending a trial. Simply find your way to the Reception and Information desk and ask to see the Courts Diary which lists current proceedings. All but those with "In Camera" notices on the door are open to the public.

The scene inside is fascinating, a bizarre juxtaposition of stenographers working on modern computers in the foreground, and judges and lawyers sporting ancient-looking hairpieces (yes, the funny wigs with the curlicues) and flowing robes calmly arguing and discussing the case. If you're very lucky, one of the state's popular corruption cases will be in session, or—better still—you may have the opportunity to listen in on a Supreme Court hearing. Here, you'll see the finest judges in the land making precedent-setting decisions, and you'll come away with insight into just how the cogs of this country's legal system turn—or, as one repeat offender who recently accused the Irish defense minister of assaulting him in a pub suggested, how the courts conspire against the common man. No prizes for guessing how his case went!

Some of the country's great legal cases have been heard here, and iconic figures from Ireland's turbulent past, including Daniel O'Connell, have had their words echo through its chambers. While most visitors to Dublin see the Courts, and perhaps take time to admire the iconic dome atop the central Round Hall, few are aware that the buildings are bustling with activity every day of the week.

WATCHING A TV TAPING

Believe it or not, Ireland's most popular television program—*The Late Late Show*—is also the longest running chat show in the world; it was originally conceived as a short filler program for the summer of 1962, but now it's an Irish institution that frequently generates quite a stir thanks to some of the cutting-edge and controversial issues that are debated and hot celebs (everyone from Mother Theresa to Elton John to Colin Farrell have stopped by) that appear. If you want to take the pulse of Ireland, watch this show.

And watching a live taping, with all the backstage maneuverings, the working up of the crowd, and the tech wizardry, is certainly the most fascinating way to take that pulse. The live 2-hour show tapes each Friday from September to May. It's not easy to snag a seat, but it is possible . . . and it's as simple as submitting an online application (www.rte.ie/tv/latelate), which will put you into huge pool of potential audience members. You could also opt for a last-minute ticket, which is possibly the most favorable option if you're here for a short while. It doesn't mean you'll get onto the show, but if you do, you'll be contacted up to a mere 3 hours before the show. You'll obviously need to give a local phone number (we always provide a mobile number rather than the guesthouse or hotel contact and are still waiting to be summoned . . .) and then be on standby to receive instructions. If they do call, then good for you . . . if not . . . well, most Dubliners haven't made it onto the show yet, so you'll be sharing the experience with them.

DUBLIN AT SCHOOL: CLASSES, LECTURES & WORKSHOPS OF ALL SORTS

Dublin's spiffy all-new **Science Gallery** (Pearse St., Trinity College; ☎ 01/896-4091; www.sciencegallery.com) is a far more exciting and fun place to hang than its name suggests. In a big, contemporary space bathed in light through massive glass walls, this Trinity college initiative puts on some of the best interactive-yet-educational events in town. A schedule of changing exhibitions runs through most of the year (there are brief breaks between different projects) and aims to bring the supposedly divergent worlds of art and science together. Call the Gallery or check their website for events during your stay. And the exhibits aren't at all like museum installations. Instead, they're designed a bit like a futuristic laboratory where visitors like us can take part in experiments (nothing harmful, of course), sit in on lectures and debates, build robots, or even watch a high tech fashion show. The aim is to make science fun and to strip down the perceived barriers that technophobes might think exist between themselves and the scientists.

When we last visited, the Gallery had just launched its month-long "Pay Attention—Donate your Brain to Science" project, during which we took part in various brain power tests, memory games, and even a mind control experiment in which we used our brain's own Alpha waves to move a solid object. It was freaky! All the "experiments" were conducted by friendly, engaging Trinity students in crisp white lab coats, who loved chatting to us about what they were doing . . . and about life at the College, too. Some of the other projects at the Gallery in 2008 included: "Pills," which explored our relationship with pharmaceuticals;

"Artbots," which investigated the relationship between sophisticated technology and art, including a musical performance by robots, and in one fascinating workshop—"What's in your pocket?"—where visitors got to make their own miniature robot using simple, everyday objects.

Tip: Become a member of the Science Gallery online (it's free), entitling you to free Wi-Fi access when you're there, and discounts on the few events that have admission fees.

WRITING YOUR OWN GREAT NOVEL

If you have ever harbored the belief that you have a novel in you, Dublin is the place to begin excavating it. And if you need help doing that, the **Irish Writers Centre** (19 Parnell Sq.; ☎ 01/872-1302; www.writerscentre.ie) runs regular 1-, 2-, and 3-day workshops with top-class published writers, such as Roddy Doyle, Carlo Gebler, and Claire Hennessy. Typically you will have to actually write a couple of pages of your novel, which you then bring with you and show to the great man or woman. They will offer criticism, advice, and a (usually) much-needed kick in the butt to get you on the right path. One-day courses are pricey at around €240, but most people feel lucky to get to work with the great minds on staff here. Be warned, they book up fast—if there's one thing Dubliners are passionate about, it's writing. You will also get the chance to mingle and meet other attendees, many of whom are surprisingly well-known writers already.

LEARNING MORE ABOUT NEW (& OLD) IRISH CUISINE
A Food Walk

For food-lovers, the best way to explore the city is—without question—by signing up for one of Dublin's **Fabulous Food Trails** (☎ 01/497-1245; www.fabulous foodtrails.ie), which we think is a stunning introduction, not only to Irish cuisine, but to the city itself. Led by grub-besotted Rosin Fallon, these tours venture into hidden parts of the city; you're taken (usually with a good contingent of Dubliners who're as curious about the secret life of Dublin) to some really special culinary venues. When we joined the Friday morning "Dublin Tasting Trail," we were introduced to all kinds of people—from artisan cheesemongers, to a salt-of-the-earth publican, an old-school butcher, the city's best barista, and a secreted-away cafe that produces heavenly chocolate tarts. Between meeting food experts and neighborhood heroes, we got to taste, and taste, and taste (and drink a bit, too—little nips of whiskey). At €45 for the morning (which lasted 3 tasty hours), it's a great, fun way to see Dublin, meet its creative businessfolk, and taste the excellent fruits of their labor.

Incidentally, Fabulous Food Trails only started operating in spring 2008, and they already have a repertoire of "other" trails that focus on specific ethnic cuisines (so far, they have Thai, Indian, and Japanese trails), with demonstrations and tastings run by some of Dublin's leading restaurant chefs; there's also a chocolate trail, during which an award-winning chocolatier, Benoit Lorge, teaches participants how to make their own (it's tempting, top-class stuff, but costs €120 for 3 hr., so is definitely a special occasion splurge).

A Food Talk

It's frequently said that during the British occupation of Ireland, the colonists spent a great deal of time wondering how the Irish could be so happy despite their overwhelming poverty. One obvious answer lies in the tremendous sociability of the local people. Their fondness for getting together, sharing a song, belting out a tune, telling a story, and generally contributing to a convivial social environment, forms a sturdy context for all-round well-being. That's the theory put forward by Johnny Daly, who is a local expert on Irish history and culture, and a big fan of the common potato. In his **Evening of Food, Folk, and Fairies** (☎ 800/251-052 or 01/492-2543; www.irishfolktours.com; €44; May to early Nov Tues–Sat 7pm), you can learn about Irish culinary history while enjoying a night of storytelling packed with information, curious anecdotes, and curious Irish myths. At the same time, you get to tuck into a laid-on feast that embellishes the spoken words with tastes and smells.

The event happens upstairs at Dublin's oldest pub, the Brazen Head, which has held a license since 1198, is packed with atmospheric detail, but is definitely overflowing with tourists. The 3-hour evening with Johnny Daly includes dinner (acceptable, if not exceptional), but any booze is extra.

An Opportunity to Cook

Among the variety of cooking workshops and classes at **Cooks Academy** (2 Charlemont Terrace, Crofton Rd., Dún Laoghaire; ☎ 01/214-5002; www.cooksacademy.com) is a very hands-on workshop, indispensable for visiting foodies looking to take home some insider knowledge on cooking the Irish way. The class, which runs for 3 hours from 10am on weekdays, costs €75, and includes information on the history of Irish food, and culminates—of course—with a genuine Irish lunch. Other courses are also on offer, and perhaps aimed more at locals, meaning they're an opportunity to rub shoulders with Dubliners who love their food (asking them about their favorite dining hangouts is a good way to break the ice). Daytime workshops (€150) and evening workshops (€70) focus on more general skills.

ACTIVE DUBLIN

BEACHES

Dublin has plenty of good swimming spots, but our favorite by far is **Seapoint** (DART to Seapoint on the Southbound route). At low tide it is impossible to get water higher than your knees, frustrating if you want a swim, but making this stretch of sandy beach great for kids. When the tide comes in, it laps right over the Victorian walkway. On really sunny days, the place is packed, mainly with families with young children, and if it's a weekend there can be loud, messy gangs of young teenagers with loud music and bad litter habits. Seapoint has a blue flag, meaning water is clean, and during the summer is patrolled by lifeguards.

Farther out along the coast is the **Forty-Foot** (DART to Dún Laoghaire, then walk along the seafront, past Sandycove), a year-round bathing spot once famous for being men-only. It was named for the Fortieth Foot regiment, once quartered in what is now known as Joyce's **Martello Tower** during the 19th century, and not, as is often thought, because it is 40 ft. deep. However, deep it is, and tides

Take Me Out to the Ball Game(s)

If you thought Yankee stadium was spectacular, you ain't seen nothin' yet. **Croke Park** (St. Joseph's Ave., Drumcondra; ☎ 01/819-2300; www.croke park.ie) is the undisputed home of field sports in Ireland, truly coming alive in the summer months, with capacity crowds of 82,300 attending the latter stages of the GAA All-Ireland Football and Hurling Championships. A writer for *Sports Illustrated* recently described the attendance levels "in a nation of 3.9 million, the per capita equivalent of 5 million Americans attending an AFC wild-card game." And the overwhelming enthusiasm and passion will make you proud to be Irish . . . even if you're not. Tickets are generally nationally distributed through clubs, but limited tickets are available through **Ticketmaster** (☎ 0818/719300; www.ticketmaster.ie), with some tickets also available through the **GAA telephone ticket line** (☎ 01/865-8657). Until 2010, Croke Park is also to play host to Irish rugby and soccer internationals; check www.fai.ie (soccer) and www.irfu.ie (rugby) for details.

Even if there's nothing scheduled, "Croker," as it's locally known, is well worth a visit all year round, housing as it does the fine **GAA Museum** ★★ (Jones Rd.; ☎ 01/819-2323; http://museum.gaa.ie; museum only €5.50; museum and stadium tour €10.50; Mon–Sat 9:30am–5pm; Sun noon–5pm; July–Aug 9:30am–6pm), which is an immense celebration of anything and everything related to the Gaelic games. Besides videos of important matches and blow-by-blow accounts of some thrilling finals, you can also learn about the rules, and the staff is incredibly knowledgeable and enthusiastic. Feel free to ask away, and don't miss the chance to test your own hurling and Gaelic football skills in an interactive games area, without the cuts and bruises (unless you're that way inclined). For real enthusiasts, you can take an optional behind-the-scenes tour of the stadium itself. You'll also hear about the tragedy known as Bloody Sunday that happened here on November 21, 1920, when British soldiers entered the stadium 15 minutes into a game and killed 13 people. And if, for any reason, you're not impressed by what you see here, just remember that all GAA teams are amateurs who play purely for their love of the game and commitment to their teams and their fans.

make little difference to water levels here. Sunny weekends are overly busy, with gangs of adrenalin-seeking kids jumping off the rocks into the water.

The **Vico bathing spot** (DART to Dalkey, walk along Vico Rd. for 10 min.) is where many of the gentlemen swimmers from the Forty-Foot seem to have migrated, and it is still unashamedly nudist. This is a rocky spot and access to the water can be difficult on windy days. However, it is friendly and social for regulars and blow-ins alike, and with views across Dalkey Bay and the odd large yacht drifting by, can feel very like La Med on a good day.

GOING TO THE DOGS & HORSES

Horse racing is regarded as a predominantly rural pastime in Ireland (see Kildare, p. 97), but few racecourses boast the facilities and accessibility of **Leopardstown Racecourse** (Dublin 18, easily accessible from M50 motorway at junction 13, or a 5 min. walk from the Luas Green Line Sandyford DART stop; ☎ 01/289-0500; www.leopardstown.com), set at the foot of the Dublin mountains, around 9km (6 miles) from the city center. Based on the U.K.'s prestigious Sandown racecourse, and having little to do with big cats (the name, Leopardstown, has it's roots in a "leper" hospital that once stood in the area, aka "lepers-town"), the track hosts around 25 races a year; the Hennessy Cognac Gold Cup, held in February, is probably the most notable, followed closely by the Irish Champion Stakes in September. It may lack the extrovert exuberance of racecourses like Ballybrit during the Galway Races (p. 273) or the hardened professionalism of the Curragh (p. 105), but Leopardstown is a fine diversion for an afternoon, evening, and, on weekends, all night long—the course boasts its own nightclub, **Club 92** (☎ 01/ 289-5686; €10; Thurs–Sun 11pm–2:30am); be warned, though, the crowd is more teenage filly than mature thoroughbred.

Racing of the canine variety is found all week long at two of the city's premier greyhound tracks, with **Harold's Cross Greyhound Stadium** (Harold's Cross, Dublin 6W; no phone; www.igb.ie; €10; Bus: 16, 16A, or 49) taking care of Mondays, Tuesdays, and Fridays, while **Shelbourne Park** (South Lotts Rd., Ringsend, Dublin 4; no phone; www.igb.ie; €10; Bus: 2 or 3) covers Wednesdays, Thursdays, and Saturdays. Each night carries between 10 and 12 races, every 15 minutes or so. Any tips? Our money's on the hare.

GOLF

It's not that long ago that a young Padraig Harrington was cutting up the bunkers at his local **Stackstown Golf Course** (Kellystown Rd.; ☎ 01/494-1993; www. stackstowngolfclub.ie), located in the south Dublin suburb of Rathfarnham, and while "Pad Rag" has since gone on to bigger and better things—a Major or two never hurt anyone—Dublin still retains an allure to golfers few other counties can boast. There's no shortage of challenges for players of all skill levels and wallet sizes—green fees run just €30 (weekdays) and €40 (weekends), and you pay just €20 before 10am Monday through Wednesday.

Also on the south side of the city, the **Dublin City Golf Club** (Ballinascorney, Tallaght; ☎ 01/451-6430; www.dublincitygolf.net)—don't be fooled, you don't tee off from O'Connell Street—is one of the county's most challenging parkland courses, set in the scenic valley of Glen na Smol, just beyond the town of Tallaght. Green fees starts at €25 midweek and €30 to €35 weekends.

Down the road, in Clondalkin, you'll find even sweeter green fees (from €21 weekdays) at the equally challenging **Grange Castle Golf Club** (off Nangor Rd. in Clondalkin, opposite Grange Castle Business Park; ☎ 01/464-1043; http:// grangecastle.ie), one of the few courses in the country to boast greens of United States Golfing Association standard. The course recently underwent a bit of a refurb to take further advantage of the seven lakes and myriad streams that crisscross through here, so it's probably a good idea to take along a spare ball or two.

Northside has its fair share of memorable courses as well, the pride of which has to be **Portmarnock Hotel Golf Links** (Portmarnock; ☎ 01/846-0611;

By Sail or By Rail, Even Beyond the Pale . . .

Sometimes getting there is half the adventure, particularly if you do it by historic train or inflatable boat. This is especially true if you decide to take a day trip from Dublin City with the **Irish Railway Preservation Society** (www.rpsi-online.org; from €10; Apr–Oct and Christmas), which operates four old steam trains that make regular journeys as far afield as Belfast, Mullingar, and Wexford. Shorter excursions run to scenic Greystones, generally leaving from Pearse Street station. The trains are beautifully preserved and look like a picture book illustration brought to life.

For a spin around Dublin bay, including a visit to Skerries Island, Ireland's Eye, the Liffey basin, Rockabill Lighthouse, and more, by inflatable boat, try **Sea Safari** (☎ 01/855-7600; www.seasafari.ie; €30). Expect to see seals, cormorants, kittiwakes, and maybe even a dolphin or two along the way. Departing Malahide Marina or Dublin City Moorings, opposite the IFSC (International Financial Services Centre), each trip lasts an hour and is always entertaining.

www.portmarnock.com), around 18km (11 miles) north of the capital. Originally the private golf course of the Jameson family—only those fond of a drop could come up with a location this challenging!—and designed by Bernhard Langer, it's a championship links course that takes full advantage of the Dublin coastline, with close to 100 bunkers, wild grasses and gorse, and invigorating sea breezes providing ample challenge for even the most experienced golfer. Until recently, the course banned women from playing golf—now the wheel has come full circle, and the course is home to the Irish Ladies Open. Such liberation comes at a price, however; green fees, at €165, are some of the highest in the county.

Far easier on the wallet, if not as breathtakingly picturesque, is **Clontarf Golf Club** (Donnycarney House, Malahide Rd.; ☎ 01/833-1892; www.clontarfgolfclub.ie), the nearest golf club to Dublin City, and an oasis of sorts in the northern suburban belt. It's a short course, with plenty of challenging narrow fairways and pine trees looming along both sides; the so-called "Quarry hole," the 12th, is the main talking point here, and the tricky approach to the green has ruined many a fine scorecard. Green fees range from €33 midweek and €65 on weekends (Nov–Mar), but are pricier during the rest of the year. There's a special midweek rate of €33 if you hit the grass before 9:30am.

WALKING

Walking in Dublin is generally the kind of pastime for those who miss the last bus home, but for true trekking enthusiasts, a number of interesting walks loop around **Howth Head.** Looking out over Dublin Bay from the south side of the city, it's difficult to miss **Howth** (DART, or Bus 31, 31A to Lower Abbey St.), a sullen mass of rock jutting out to sea across the bay. Choose from myriad paths: The lower cliff loop and tramline loop can be completed in about 1½ hours and are suitable for everyone; more experienced types should check out the 3-hour

"Bog of Frogs" loop, which incorporates stunning views of Dublin Bay to the south and the Mourne Mountains stretching away to the north. Experienced walkers should also note that the **Wicklow Way** (p. 84; www.wicklowway.com), which stretches 132km (82 miles) from north to south Wicklow, begins in the Dublin suburb of Rathfarnham, at Marlay Park, which is well served by the no. 16 bus from O'Connell Street.

ATTENTION, SHOPPERS!

Look-alike high street fashion boutiques aside, as long you're prepared to do a bit of legwork to find the best of Dublin's shops, rest assured there are gems.

The area around **Castle Market** and the **Powerscourt Townhouse Centre** in particular have a cheery, eclectic selection of shops, from boutiques to beauty emporiums and interiors stores, all good fun to wander into and around. Tax-free shopping for non-E.U. visitors has clear appeal. Obviously, those stores trading with an eye to the tourism market—and that means anywhere they're selling iconic Irish products, namely linen, crystal, china, wool—will offer the option, and anywhere that displays the "Tax Free" logo is worth a peek—check out some of the stores along and near Nassau Street.

CLOTHING

If you love labels, **Brown Thomas** (Grafton St.; ☎ 01/605-6666; www.brownthomas. com; AE, MC, V), the country's glitziest department store, is where to shop. Windows are always gorgeous and worth a peek, particularly at Christmastime. And although they sure know how to mark up, they also have the most dramatic sales in town. So, if it's January or July, pop in.

Savvy ladies looking for a Big Day dress should head directly for **Costume** ✪✪✪ (10 Castle Market; ☎ 01/679-4188; MC, V), surely Dublin's most delightful boutique, thrilling enough with its inventory to make even pure browsing enjoyable. Alongside top class international designers, Costume stocks local success story (and daughter of the owner) Leigh Tucker's label Leighlee, as well as fabulous sashes by Helen James, another local girl, and their own brand of coats. The best bargains here though are the very smart leather gloves, in a range of jewel-like colors. Think shocking pink and turquoise for about €40 a pop.

Close by, **Jenny Vanders** ✪✪ (50 Drury St.; ☎ 01/677-0406; MC, V), is a vintage boutique with plenty of pedigree. Here you'll find gorgeous, unique pieces from the Victorian era through to the 1970s, in excellent condition and, almost best of all, stylish umbrellas from a time when elegance and functionality weren't mutually exclusive.

Marie Murphy honed her aesthetic back in the days when U2 were gigging in any dive that would have them, and was even pals with legendary rocker Phil

---

Shop till You Drop, or at Least until . . .

Unless otherwise stated, shops are open roughly 9am to 6:30pm, with late opening on Thursday until 9pm. Larger stores open on Sunday, usually 10am to 4pm.

Lynott of Thin Lizzy. Her retro and vintage outlet, **A Store is Born** (34 Clarendon St.; ☎ 01/285-7627; Sat only 10am–6pm; cash only) stocks everything from second-hand cashmere (in the region of €50) and retro silk scarves for as little as €10, to elegant evening dresses, all without so much as a hint of moth ball. Marie herself is glamorous, smart, sassy, and, crucially, will tell you exactly what looks good on you and what stinks.

If tweeds really are your thing, **Kevin and Howlin** (31 Nassau St.; ☎ 01/677-0257; www.kevinandhowlin.com) do a very fine selection. From old-man-of-the-islands caps to smart, well-cut lady's jackets, and cozy travel rugs, all in unique, handwoven tweed.

Local designer gear is best bought at the indoor fashion market, the **Loft** (Top Floor, Powerscourt Townhouse Centre; www.powerscourtcentre.com; Sat–Sun noon–6pm; most stalls cash only). This New York–style market is the place to go to pick up the Lainey Keoghs and Louise Kennedys of tomorrow: It has a proven track record in up-and-coming talent, showcasing them before they hit the big time and get snapped up by boutiques who add their own hefty markups. Clothes, shoes, bags, accessories, and art all jostle for space, and there is even some international talent. Oh, and a DJ or two to keep the energy up.

ARTS, CRAFTS & SOUVENIRS THAT SCREAM "IRELAND"

For many visitors **Avoca** ✮✮ (11–13 Suffolk St.; ☎ 01/677-4215; www.avoca.ie) defines one-stop shopping. It's an attractive jumble of super-soft wool and cashmere rugs, clothes, picnic hampers, cookbooks, kitchen utensils, pretty Wellington boots (if you can imagine such a thing), garden furniture, cute toys with a charming yester-year feel, bags, sparkly jewelry, and so much more. Best of all, there is something for all budgets. Alongside stripped pine dressers for €800 are snugly cashmere throws for €60 and even pretty, sparkly photo frames for €10. The only drawback to this place is that space is very tight, and it's always pumping with customers—so it's not a place you want to bring kids.

Competitor House of Ireland (37–38 Nassau St.; ☎ 01/671-1111; www.houseofireland.com) may look a bit self-consciously tweedy from the outside, but their luxurious selection of wool, cashmere, and silk-mix clothes and rugs is really good. Alongside some rather tortured-looking silver and crystalware you will also find sleek, modern pieces by John Rocha for Waterford Crystal, and contemporary-looking Belleek china.

If you have a yen for Irish linen and if you don't mind doing a bit of stitching yourself, buying lengths of excellent quality fabric and turning it into a luxurious double sheet, or a pocket handkerchief, is not just good value, but satisfying, too. **Murphy Sheehy** (14 Castle Market; ☎ 01/677-0316; www.murphysheehy.com; cash only) sells proper Irish linens, exactly as they've always been made, and all that's missing is a hem. Averaging €15 a meter, and given that you need about 5m for a double sheet, you're looking at about €75 for the fabric; which knocks the socks off every other price we've been able to find.

MUSIC & BOOKS

Dublin's literary pedigree ensures plenty of bookstores, though it's surprising there aren't more independent bookshops. Yes, the big names have a big presence— **Hodges Figgis** ✮✮ (56–58 Dawson St.; ☎ 01/677-4754) and **Waterstones** ✮✮

To Market, to Market!

Temple Bar, especially on the weekend, is a market mecca thanks to its food market in **Meeting House Square** (Sat 10am–4:30pm), the **book market** around the corner (Temple Bar Square, Sat–Sun 11am–6pm) and the **design market** (Cow's Lane; Sat 10am–5pm). The food market is our favorite hangout, its eye-catching stalls packed with organic vegetables, artisanal breads and cakes, olives, cheese, chocolate, and even soap. Some of these guys come all the way from Cork to help Dubliners stock their pantries.

The world of organic and sustainable food is big news in Dublin these days, and regular farmer's markets are to be found in almost every borough. For a chance to chat to traders and discover the scene, try the most relaxed and pleasant of these, **Supernatural** (St. Andrews Resource Centre, Pearse St.; Sat 9am–4pm), which has housed a whole foods market for over 30 years now. Originally set up by anti-war and nuclear arms protesters, the market has changed with the times and is now a reasonably sophisticated and moderate enterprise. The center is a Victorian building, which adds a touch of class—as does the wide range of eco-friendly, sustainable but luxurious cosmetics on offer. Bread, veg, fruit, meat, and basic household items are all to be found here, along with a stall doing excellent coffee. Best of all, the traders are a fascinating, learned bunch, willing to chat about every aspect of what they do.

(7 Dawson St.; ☎ 01/679-1260; www.waterstones.com) sit opposite each other and have the new book market pretty well carved up between themselves (several branches of **Easons** are scattered throughout the center, too; often this is where you'll find a couple of bargains, so browse here, by all means).

But for second-hand books at outrageously good prices, we'll steer you to the **Winding Stair Bookshop** ✪✪✪ (40 Ormond Quay; ☎ 01/872-6576; Tues–Sun noon–5pm). A 1970s kind of cool place, with battered old typewriters and squashy old sofas, its books are chosen with a sure touch by manager Regan Hutchins, who mixes up vintage paperbacks, hardback classics, and cult new titles. There's even a smattering of well-chosen children's books.

Finally, as the name suggests, the **Secret Bookstore** ✪✪ (15A Wicklow St.; ☎ 01/679-7272) is brilliantly undercover, inexplicably hiding in one of the busiest parts of town. You could browse the excellent selection of new and used books and Irish literature selection for hours. Part of the secret is that one part of the bookstore is actually **Freebird Records** ✪, a fine place to paw through CDs and vinyl in hopes of finding that one U2 album missing from your collection.

Speaking of music, **Claddagh Records** ✪✪✪ (2 Cecilia St., Temple Bar; ☎ 01/677-0262; www.claddaghrecords.com) is far and away the best place in the city to start a collection of authentic Irish music. The choice ranges from trad to contemporary, and staff will usually find just about anything for you.

NIGHTLIFE

The transition from day to night in Dublin is seamless: By day the city is a heaving mass of humanity, and at night things simply do not slow down. It's only the loci of action that steadily shift as the evening progresses. Pop into a pub for a late afternoon pint, and you may find your self caught up in conversation, or listening to an impromptu music session, without ever having cause to relocate until bedtime. Or you could spend the entire evening drifting from one busy little spot to the next, experiencing a mix of entertainment genres that spans the gamut from sweaty dancefloors to transvestite cabaret. For a city this size, Dublin packs a wallop, and, besides its reputation for drinking holes, also does an excellent trade in cultural activities—there are theaters aplenty here, with something to tempt every taste. Traversing Dublin's streets by night can be both exhilarating and terrifying in equal measure—depending on your state of mind and/or inebriation.

Be sure to take a look at the map "Temple Bar," on p. 48.

WHERE TO CATCH A SHOW: TOP DUBLIN THEATRES

With its connection to great dramatists—Shaw, Beckett, Synge—you can imagine Dublin to be heaving with performances spaces . . . and you wouldn't be wrong. Here are a few that you must know about.

The **Gate Theatre** ✸✸✸ (1 Cavendish Row, Parnell Sq.; ☎ 01/874-4045 or 01/874-6042; www.gate-theatre.ie) is by far the most elegant stage in Dublin. Under its proscenium arch unfold polished plays from the 20th-century canon of American, Irish, and British greats. Director Michael Colgan mixes international stars (Sam Shepard, Frances McDormand, and Ralph Fiennes have all appeared recently) with local greats to pull in the crowds. The bill of fare is typically intellectual and occasionally hard edged, but seldom innovative, experimental or frown inducing. The Gate celebrated its 80th anniversary in 2008 and Godot, Pinter, and Ibsen were all in attendance. Previews, Monday shows, and matinees are €25, Tuesday to Thursday performances are €32, and Friday and Saturday shows are €34.

The **Abbey** ✸✸ (26 Lower Abbey St.; ☎ 01/878-7222; www.abbeytheatre.ie), Ireland's National Theatre, is no looker (cast as it is in an ugly behemoth concrete block on the Northside), but it was founded back in 1904 by Yeats and Lady Gregory (in another, Southside, venue that's now boarded up), and holds a special place in the hearts of Dubliners. It tends to stick to the tried and tested, which includes fine examples from the Irish canon—Sheridan, Synge, O'Casey—with a few British and American favorites (Shakespeare, especially). Evening shows (7:30pm) range €20 to €35, but matinees (Sat 2pm) and previews cost just €18 to €22. The Abbey's underground (or rather, downstairs) progeny is the **Peacock** ✸✸ (same contact details) and is Dublin's most versatile, intimate space—a moveable stage so the show can be in the round or it can point at the audience like an arrow. The Abbey spawned the Peacock to show new drama, but the offspring has now overtaken the parent—at least in having a more focused identity. Plays at the Peacock tend to be intense, new, and experimental, and if established, then overhauled with a dash of "radicalism"; head here if you prefer your theater to be cutting edge.

Andrew's Lane Theatre ✸ (Andrews Ln.; ☎ 01/679-5720; €15–€23), just off Trinity Street, has two theaters. Upstairs is very small and anything goes—it's

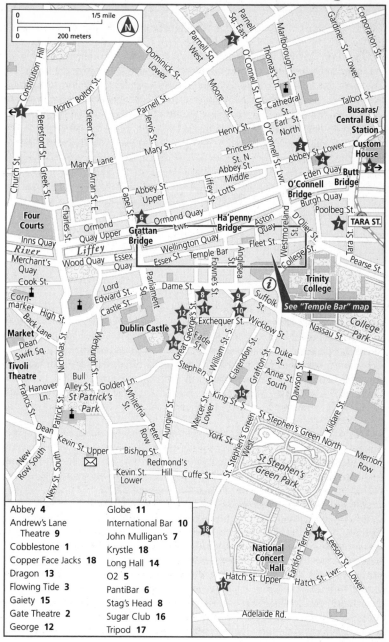

Abbey **4**
Andrew's Lane Theatre **9**
Cobblestone **1**
Copper Face Jacks **18**
Dragon **13**
Flowing Tide **3**
Gaiety **15**
Gate Theatre **2**
George **12**
Globe **11**
International Bar **10**
John Mulligan's **7**
Krystle **18**
Long Hall **14**
O2 **5**
PantiBar **6**
Stag's Head **8**
Sugar Club **16**
Tripod **17**

Dublin Nightlife 101

A few words of advice before you set out to conquer Dublin's social scene:

1. **Avoid the bars on Dawson Street.** Unless you're looking for the lowest common denominator theme-bar and Dublin's Neanderthal doorman experience. As most savvy Dubliners will tell you, this is not the Irish capital's most cosmopolitan corner. The exception to the rule is Dawson Lounge (the tiniest pub in Dublin), which is really quite twee and a bit of a delight.

2. **Dress the part (perhaps).** Many Dublin nightspots have a strict entrance policy, sometimes with rules about age (if you look under 30, bring your ID), and dress sense. If you fear being turned away (oh, the shame!), wear smart casual clothes and avoid jeans, football shirts, and sneakers. Of course, these are also the types of places that charge sometimes steep admissions for unspectacular surrounds, dull commercial music, and tired bar service. Rule #2 is really: Avoid bars and clubs with dress codes!

3. **Avoid Temple Bar after dark.** The only people who go there are (a) tourists, and (b) locals looking to pick up tourists. This is particularly true of the touristy, terrible bar that takes the name **Temple Bar** (47–48 Temple Bar). The exception to the rule would be one or two pubs (see below) on the fringes of the area. While in Temple Bar, be aware that you're probably going to cough up more than the citywide average for a pint, and that—particularly on weekends—the area quickly transforms into a drunken pick-up joint. After dark watch where you walk so you don't inadvertently step in the evidence that some long-suffering party animal couldn't hold his (or her) drink.

You have been warned . . . now set forth and conquer.

---

where fledgling companies can have a go (a good thing for them, a doubtful pleasure for the audience). The downstairs theater is larger and hosts visiting companies. Atmosphere is vaguely bohemian and fare is quirky but popular. Management seems to favor American plays that are well known but not yet canonized, such as *One Flew Over the Cuckoo's Nest* and *Proof.*

The **Project Arts Centre** ★ (39 East Essex St.; ☎ 01/881-9613; www.project.ie; €14–€20) has ambitions to be the most avant-garde theater in Dublin and has two great spaces—including one of the few "black box" theaters in Dublin—but it takes itself perhaps a bit too seriously. Having hosted brilliant productions by local heroes Rough Magic, it's also been known to stage exhaustingly earnest productions by the black polo neck brigade, which can be testing for audiences after lighter entertainment.

The **Gaiety** (South King St.; ☎ 01/677-1717; www.gaietytheatre.ie; €17–€20), opposite St. Stephen's Mall near the top of Grafton Street, is your best bet if you've missed any of the big headline musicals on the West End or Broadway. On weekends the space transforms into a club style salsa party venue.

The **Olympia** ★★ (72 Dame St.; ☎ 01/679-3323; reservations ☎ 081/871-9330; €30–€35) is Dublin's oldest theater and you get a sense of its history from the way it seems carved into the side street, its facade appearing to cry out to passersby on busy Dame Street, and Dublin Castle, just across the way. During the Dublin Theatre Festival, you can catch some authentic, top-notch theater here, but the focus is usually on commercial musicals, including tribute shows that, for some, don't qualify as theater at all.

DOWNING A PINT IN DUBLIN
Temple Bar Watering Holes

To savor "real Dublin" in this part of town, head for watering holes at the outer fringes of Temple Bar. Facing onto Central Bank Square, the **Foggy Dew** ✖ (1 Fownes St.; ☎ 01/677-9328; www.thefoggydew.ie) is a solid choice; both the kind of rustic olde-worlde pub that you're likely to find at the end of a lane in rural Ireland and a lively nightspot with a well-mannered obsession for rock music. You find neither blaring chart music nor a cheery fiddler in the corner indulging in a bit of old "tiddly-aye." Instead, as you enter you'll note walls covered in rock 'n' roll memorabilia—gold discs, album covers, posters, photos, and even a couple of electric guitars signed by Keith Richards and David Bowie. And then, of course, there's the young contingent of rock 'n' roll wannabes, their guitars tucked behind their chairs. Don't be put off by the trying-to-be-scary teens moping around outside; Central Bank Square is a popular meeting point for the local Goth fraternity—they're harmless, even if slightly vampiric.

Another top spot—this time at the other end of Temple Bar—is the **Porterhouse** ✖ (16–18 Parliament St.; ☎ 01/679-8847; www.theporterhouse.ie), a micro-brewery pub opened in 1996 and now something of a Dublin institution—on the back of the success of this place, the owners have since opened another three bars around Dublin and one in London, all bearing the Porterhouse name. Unlike so many other franchises, this is one that's in no danger of losing its luster. The main attractions here are the home-produced beers and ales that the business has become famous for; if you're planning on spending the whole evening there, be sure to tackle the "Brain Blásta" at some point, a fulsome, 7% ABV ale that will undoubtedly put hairs on your chest . . . even the women.

Distinctly free of tourists, **Palace Bar** ✖✖✖ (21 Fleet St.; ☎ 01/671-7388 or 01/677-9290) is located at the Westmoreland Street end of Temple Bar, and one of the few pubs in the area where the real music that fills the air is that of fine conversation. Get ready to eavesdrop shamelessly—many true Dubliners have their

Closing Time

Locals laws generally dictate pub and bar closing times. Most operate Monday to Wednesday 10:30am to 11pm, and stay open a little longer Thursday through Saturday (closing time will be 12:30am). Times are reduced on Sundays (12:30–11pm). When the publican starts announcing final rounds, you'd better move your butt, 'cause he generally means business—we've even seen one pub-owner kicking the musicians out while they were still playing. Late bars and nightclubs operate according to different licenses and obviously can go on until much later.

best conversations here, before the city's nightlife gets into full swing. Alternatively, the upstairs lounge features solid trad music sessions 4 nights a week (Wed–Thurs and Sat–Sun) kicking off around 9pm.

While waiting for the clubs to open, don't pass up the chance to hang with a hip crowd at the **Globe** ✪✪✪ (11 South Great George's St.; ☎ 01/671-1220; www.globe.ie), a cool all-day hangout that has drawn all kinds of comparisons (notably with places in Paris and New York's East Village), but is really a quintessential modern Dublin haven. Before nightfall, you can comfortably enjoy the morning paper—or a game of chess—and then freefall into a night of uninhibited grown-up fun.

Around the corner, directly across the road from the Bank of Ireland, is the **Bank** ✪ (College Green; ☎ 01/677-0677; www.bankoncollegegreen.com), a bar and restaurant carved out of the Victorian edifice of what was once the Belfast Bank building. Head up to the mezzanine to admire the imported mahogany woodwork, mosaic tile flooring, stained glass windows, and chandeliers dangling from the high ceilings. It feels a bit like the set of a period film, but not yet sufficiently aged (it only opened in 2003); the ATM and scrolling stock exchange prices on an electronic banner also give the game away a bit. Better clues to this building's former life are downstairs, where the original Chatwood bank vaults mark the entrance to the toilets.

The Northside

When we head across to the Abbey Theatre, there's always one indispensable stop before the curtain goes up: the **Flowing Tide** ✪✪✪ (Lower Abbey St.; ☎ 01/874-0842). An oasis of calm, restrained imbibing, its careful atmosphere is retained by the welcome absence of televisions and other such distraction—the focus is impressively on the art of conversation.

Staying Northside, but quite a distance west, in Smithfield, **Cobblestone** ✪✪✪ (77 North King St.; ☎ 01/872-1799; www.myspace.com/thecobblestone) conjures up some of the finest traditional Irish music in town—always streets ahead of the tourist-pleasing stuff you'll hear in Temple Bar. There's a lively mix of punters here, too, as workers from Smithfield's Market stop by on their way home from work (and sometime stay put all night)—a truly democratic social mélange.

It should be against the law to leave Dublin without sampling the porter at the redoubtable **Kavanagh's Gravediggers** ✪✪✪ (1 Prospect Sq., Glasnevin; no phone). It's right beside Glasnevin Cemetery and has long been the traditional hangout of, well, gravediggers. When we asked directions of the veteran flower seller outside the cemetery, she beamed with delight and pointed us down the road, saying "Just turn in at the hole in the wall . . . Best pints in Dublin!" Established in 1833 and covered from top to bottom in wood, this is an authentic "Oul Fla's pub"—precisely the sort of place that will make your time in Dublin memorable.

Beyond Temple Bar: Southside's Best Traditional Pubs

When it comes to Dublin pubs, "old-fashioned" isn't a criticism but an enviable label; successfully retaining the authentic flavor and atmosphere of an earlier era—preferably one that matches the period when a place was established or perhaps when a place was the preferred hangout of some famed author or drunkard—is ideal. One such seemingly unchanged tippling spot is much-loved **John Mulligan's** ✯✯✯ (8 Poolbeg St.; ☎ 01/677-5582; www.mulligans.ie), frequented by all kinds of notable personages and one of the few really authentic pubs in the city center; it's mentioned in "Counterparts" in Joyce's *Dubliners,* and apart from a few things like TV sets, the layout, and atmosphere—dark and a little brooding—isn't much different from the way so many pubs once were. Of course, everyone knows this, and that makes it popular and, consequently, very crowded at night. For a more relaxed drink, arrive before 6pm.

The **Stag's Head** ✯✯✯ (Dame Court; ☎ 01/679-3701) is pretty much a must-see Dublin watering hole; despite its fame it never feels like a tourist trap. You'll know you've arrived when you catch sight of the massive stuffed and mounted stag in question eyeing you from above the bar. The place is beautifully paneled in wood and mirrors, while vintage light fittings adorn the ceiling. Visit late in the afternoon to drink some of the finest Guinness in the country and soak up delicious conversation. Live traditional music starts up from time to time.

Occupying a listed building and every bit the grand historical monument you might expect that to signify, the **Long Hall** ✯✯✯ (51 South Great George's St.; ☎ 01/475-1590) is frequently referred to as Dublin's finest pub. We're not naming an all-out favorite, but there's something hypnotic about the mix of twinkling Victorian chandelier, polished antique mahogany, plasterwork ceilings, and glistening mirrors here (you may recognize it from a Thin Lizzy music video).

With its beautiful hand-carved oak counter, the **International Bar** ✯✯ (23 Wicklow St.; ☎ 01/677-9250; www.international-bar.com) has been in the O'Donaghue family for six generations. It first opened in the 1700s, and since being done up in 1847 doesn't appear to have changed very much at all—although they no longer have a whiskey-bottling unit in the basement. The slim ground-level bar boasts stained glass windows, mosaic tile flooring, moulded ceilings, and carved wooden figures by a master craftsman—they certainly don't make them like this anymore. For 2 decades, the bar has been home to the **International Comedy Club** (http://theinternationalcomedyclub.com; €10; Thurs–Sat 9:15pm) which has a formidable reputation for its mix of top-name professionals and fresh young talent. Trad music sessions happen Sundays 1 to 4pm.

NIGHTCLUBS & LIVE MUSIC VENUES

Once the pubs shut down, the place where Dubliners choose to let their hair down as the evening progresses becomes a fair reflection of their aspirations for the evening. Singles descend upon the hedonistic mosh pit that is **Copper Face Jacks** (29 Harcourt St.; ☎ 01/475-8777; www.jackson-court.ie; €8–€10) every Friday and Saturday evening—and right through the week, to be fair—hoping to nuzzle up with a stranger. It tends to get a lot of off-duty policemen and nurses.

Stepping into the **Krystle** ✯ (21–25 Harcourt St.; ☎ 01/478-4066; www.krystlenightclub.com; €10, or €25 VIP) you'd be forgiven for thinking you had been transported to Pacha in Ibiza or Les Caves du Roi in St. Tropez; the venue oozes sophistication, yet doesn't price itself out of its target market—a range of cocktails start at €11, and bottle service is available for less than you'll pay in neighboring clubs. It's frequented by both local and international glitterati—Colin Farrell once proclaimed that the VIP area reminded him of those in Miami clubs. Dress to impress!

Just down the road, heading a little away from the city center (but still within easy walking—or stumbling—distance), the three-venue **tripod** ✪✪✪ (Old Harcourt Station, Harcourt St.; ☎ 01/476-3374; www.tripod.ie) is a multi-purpose entertainment music and dance venue that opened in September 2008; it's an extension of **POD** ✪✪✪, an underground (literally) dance venue that's been a beacon of sorts for techno and house fanatics since it first opened its doors some 15 years ago. While POD ("Place of Dance") fuses raw and futuristic design, the new venue is more industrial chic. The former Harcourt Street train station forms the venue's shell, and the slick, high-tech, contemporary interior trades in both live and electronic music gigs and is Dublin's largest dance venue. Wednesday and Thursday are student nights (€8; starts 10:30pm); Friday is **515** ✪✪, with dirty electro in one room, and old school and disco in another (€8 before midnight, €10 after; doors open 11pm); and on Saturday it's an over-21's night with eclectic, mostly retro, tunes (€12; doors open 11pm). The **live music venue** ✪✪ here is brilliantly laid out so you can see the act from anywhere in the room. And we love that the line-up is so varied—Nouvelle Vague, Grandmaster Flash, Stereolab, the Dandy Warhols, and even the Human League were on the bill at the end of 2008.

Under the same ownership as POD and tripod is the **Button Factory** ✪✪✪ (Curved St.; ☎ 01/670-9202; www.buttonfactory.ie), a swish venue that caters to all imaginable tastes, from punk to progressive rock, and all points in between. There's no set formula to this place—the bill, admission times, and prices vary nightly—but, when it comes to live venues, this is one of Dublin's best.

More consistent, and with an extra degree of sassiness, the **Sugar Club** ✪✪✪ (8 Lower Leeson St.; ☎ 01/678-7188; www.thesugarclub.com) is a wood-paneled venue in the premises of the former Irish Film Theatre that epitomizes cool; whether it's the regular burlesque performances or hard-to-find '60s records on continuous playback, the place has an unmistakable swagger that rarely misses the mark. Velvet banquettes and tables replaced the old tiered cinema seating providing a great line of sight down toward the stage. Live acts are the focus, with performances followed on weekends by late-night parties. Fridays it's **Strictly Handbag** ✪✪✪ (from 11pm; €10, two-for-one before midnight)—the longest-running regular nightclub in Dublin ('80s, electro, and Indie tunes), while Saturdays are all about soul, salsa, ska, and Latin beats (from 11pm; €15).

Dublin's newest concert area, the **02** (Northwall Quay; ☎ 01/676-6170; www.the02.ie)—in the same neighborhood as U2's upcoming recording studios—is guaranteed to become the city's top music entertainment venue, as its state-of-the-art facilities have had all the biggest names (Coldplay, Kings of Leon) in music lining up to sign gig contracts.

GAY DUBLIN

Loud, proud, and certainly worth seeking out, Dublin's gay scene is memorable, even if it's so extensively merged with the mainstream as to be—at times—almost imperceptible. We've heard it said that there are more gay people per capita in Dublin than San Francisco. While some have gone so far as to say that a "GBF" (gay best friend) is a popular Dublin accessory, it's worth remembering that homophobia can still rear its ugly head in rougher boozers and neighborhoods; name-calling and even physical assault is not unheard of. The time you want to be in Dublin more than any other (except that it's in also when the city is at its busiest) is for the annual **Dublin LGBTQ Pride Festival** (www.dublinpride.org), which celebrates its 26th anniversary in 2009.

If you're looking to meet people other than in a club or bar, stop by Dublin's gay community center, **Outhouse** (105 Capel St.; ☎ 01/873-4932; www.outhouse. ie), where there's a cafe, free Internet access, a library, and you can pick up lots of information on the local scene. Another healthy way to meet people is to join the gay and lesbian walking group, **Out and About Hiking** (www.gay-hiking.org) on one of their weekly rambles. They set off at 10am every Sunday; pick-up is from outside the National Concert Hall in Earlsfort Terrace and there are different routes every week, usually in neighboring County Wicklow, and cover on average 10 to 16km (6–10 miles). A €2 fee covers costs, but you need to bring water and food for the outing.

As for gay clubs, the king is the **George** ★★ (South Great George's St.; ☎ 01/ 478-2983; www.capitalbars.com). You can get away with just about anything here, and just about everyone is welcome (troublemakers will be turned away by butch bouncers, though). Shirley Temple Bar, who's a hot TV celeb, hosts Sunday-night bingo, and we've caught some fairly acceptable karaoke on Saturdays, just before the dance floor turns into a throbbing mass of bouncing bodies. Bar staff is spectacularly friendly (and so very easy on the eye), and in our experience, you'll come away with heaps of new friends. There's a cover charge on weekends later in the evening, so arrive early.

Just a few steps up the road, and owned by the same brothers, the **Dragon** ★★★ (South Great George's St.; ☎ 01/478-1590; www.capitalbars.com) has a combustible reputation for being a pounding house club with great aesthetics. Above the dance floor, witness a bulging Hercules getting to grips with a giant snake, while there's enough comfortable lounge space around the bar to escape the sweaty mélange for a while. Arrive early and you can avoid the cover charge (usually around €10).

PantiBar ★★★ (7–8 Capel St.; ☎ 01/989-7777; www.pantibar.com) offers arguably the most innovative club line-up in town—it's the brainchild of a fabulous Dolly Parton–worshipping transvestite who is something of a Dublin celeb. Monday kicks off with "Make and Do-Do with Panti," when you take part in a craft-making workshop (from making puppets to redesigning T-shirts) down in the PantiBar Homo Activity Centre, a gay movie night on Wednesdays ("Movies in Her Living Room"), and DJs on weekends.

The ABCs of Dublin

Area Code The area code for Dublin is **01**.

Banks & Foreign Exchange Banks generally operate weekdays 9am to 4pm and until 5pm on Thursday; some banks do open on Saturday mornings. ATMs are ubiquitous and practically all of them can deal with MasterCard and Visa credit cards. You can change money at the Dublin Tourism Centre on Suffolk Street.

Embassies **Australia** (7th Floor, Fitzwilton House, Wilton Terrace; ☎ 01/664-5300); **Canada** (65 St. Stephen's Green; ☎ 01/417-4100); **United Kingdom** (29 Merrion Rd.; ☎ 01/205-3700); **U.S.A.** (42 Elgin Rd.; ☎ 01/668-8777).

Emergencies Dial ☎ **999** or **112** for any emergency, including police, ambulance, fire services, and marine and coastal emergencies.

Hospital **Mater Misericordiae** is on Eccles Street (☎ 01/803-2000) and has an emergency department, as does **St. James's** on James Street (☎ 01/410-3000).

Opening Hours **Stores** Are generally open Monday to Saturday 9:30am to 6pm and until 8pm on Thursdays; those that open on Sunday do so between noon and 6pm. **Pubs** are open from Monday to Thursday 10:30am to 11:30pm, Friday and Saturday 10:30am to 12:30am, and Sun noon to 11pm. **Bars** and **clubs** have much later opening hours, although these tend to vary wildly and change from night to night.

Police Call ☎ **999** in case of any emergency. Tourists who are victims of crime also have access to the **Irish Tourist Assistance Service** (Block 1, Garda Headquarters, Harcourt St.; ☎ 01/478-5295; www.itas.ie).

Post Office The **GPO** (General Post Office; O'Connell St.; ☎ 01/705-1000) is also one of the city's architectural highlights and an important historical landmark. Visit even if you don't need to post anything. It's open Monday to Saturday 8am to 8pm; parcel service ends at 7pm. Another branch is opposite the Tourist Office on Suffolk Street.

Restrooms A few pay-per-use high-tech toilet cubicles are scattered around the center; shopping malls all have free restroom facilities. Most pubs aren't too fussed about passersby using their facilities—just don't be too conspicuous about single-mindedly barging in off the street.

Taxis Reliable taxi companies include **Metro Cabs** (☎ 1-800/444700 or 01/668-3333); **Satellite Taxis** (☎ 01/836-5555 Northside; 01/454-3333 Southside); **NRC Taxis** (☎ 01/677-2222); **Pony Cabs** (☎ 01/661-2233); and **City Cabs** (☎ 01/668-3333 or 01/872-2222).

Tourist Offices Dublin Tourism has its **headquarters** in a converted former church (St. Andrew's) on Suffolk Street not far from Temple Bar (☎ 01/605-7700; www.visitdublin.com; Jun–Aug Mon–Sat 9am–8:30pm; Sept–May Mon–Sat 9am–5:30pm); you can get information on just about anything here; book accommodations, tours, and shows; change currency; and browse assorted souvenirs. Branches are also in the **Dublin Airport** in the Arrivals Hall (Mon–Sat 8am–10pm); on **Baggot Street Bridge** (Mon–Fri 9:30am–noon and 12:15–5pm); on **O'Connell Street** (Mon–Sat 9am–5pm); and at **Dún Laoghaire Ferry Port.**

3

Meet Dublin's Neighbors

The intriguing counties surrounding the capital

by Keith Bain & Emily Hourican

THE PALE. ONCE A STRONGHOLD OF ENGLISH COLONIAL POWER; IN essence, these counties directly surrounding Dublin were for long an imaginary boundary dividing British crown and Irish native. It was here—not too far from the protective aura of English sensibility—that formidable mansions and palatial estates were established, so as to ensconce and nurture the mannered aristocracy, keeping loyal English subjects close to the "center of the civilized world." And so it was for hundreds of years, when fortified towns and castles represented the perimeter of colonial manners and civility. And it was here, too, that historic battles were fought and, during the Battle of the Boyne especially, Ireland's long-suffering political fate was decided.

Today, reasons for visiting the Pale have little to do with war and social division and more to do with coming face to face with a history that spans thousands of years, starting with great Neolithic tombs and mysterious stone formations. Or with enjoying the multitudinous horse farms and racetracks of Kildare. South of Dublin, County Wicklow has spawned many fine gardened estates, and names like Powerscourt and Russborough are synonymous with monumental Palladian mansions. Those who prefer the outdoors in its wilder, untempered form are drawn to hike the Wicklow Way or cycle some of its arduous but sumptuous routes.

Yes, these counties are close enough to the capital to mean that they're packed with commuter towns. But spend a little time here, and you'll discover that there's so much to see and do you might consider skipping Dublin altogether.

DON'T LEAVE DUBLIN'S NEIGHBORS WITHOUT . . .

COMMUNING WITH ANCIENT CELTIC CIVILIZATION Passage tombs, and ancient spiritual sites litter Ireland's northeast. Make your own pilgrimage to Newgrange (apparently the oldest building on earth, p. 113) or the Hill of Tara (the ancient seat of Ireland's Celtic kings, p. 114) in County Meath—both are said to embody mystical powers.

GOING GREEN IN THE GARDENS OF WICKLOW Among some of the finest gardened estates on the planet—Powerscourt and Huntington are right here in County Wicklow (p. 84), famously known as "the Garden of Ireland." Even if you don't get to any of these cultivated plots, there are endless stretches of pristine, beautiful greenery, to enjoy while hiking the world famed Wicklow Way (p. 95).

DISCOVERING THE SECRETS OF NEW IRISH CUISINE   At historic Castle Leslie and Catherine Fulvio's Ballyknocken Cookery School (p. 96) are exciting learning opportunities for foodies.

COUNTY WICKLOW

Wicklow is nicknamed "the Garden of Ireland" because of its captivating scenery; few counties in Ireland have such a range of landscapes in such a compact area. More literally, it also has a number of fine gardens, some of which are attached to aristocratic estates open to visitors. Stretching from just beyond Enniskerry right down to Rathdrum, the Wicklow Mountains dominate the landscape, and the county has earned an international reputation as a hillwalkers' paradise, with the massive, 132km (82-mile) Wicklow Way (p. 95) king of the many trails. Head east, only a few miles, and you come across the Irish Sea, with golden sand stretching away from soaring clifftops and hidden coves. The best way to take it all in, incidentally, is simply to take the train—the main Dublin-to-Arklow line runs parallel with the sea for most of the journey, and once you get beyond Dalkey, the view alone is worth the fare.

A BRIEF HISTORY OF COUNTY WICKLOW

Like its neighbors, Wicklow's hills hide a history that stretches back before the time of Christ. Pre-Christian tombs and monuments pockmark the landscape, particularly along known walking routes. The most famous of these is probably the **Mottee Stone,** a huge granite boulder standing isolated atop a hillside just beyond the pretty village of Avoca—legend has it that renowned Irish hero Fionn MacCumhaill, in a fit of rage—or perhaps just bravado—hurled the stone here from the nearby Lugnaquilla mountain, Wicklow's highest point. We now know that its presence here is probably more to do with glacial flow than throwing ability, but stones like these were looked upon for centuries as reminders of Ireland's heroic past. During the 19th century, one over-zealous priest even blew several of them up, believing they were pagan.

County Wicklow also gets called "the last county," as it was the last of the current Irish counties to be established. The land on which it sits was best known for centuries as O'Byrne County, named for a fierce local family who kept Wicklow free from invasion until the start of the 17th century. Henry VIII tried to forge an agreement with the family in 1542, even going so far as to agree to terms with the leader of the clan, Thadeus O'Byrne. But the rest of the family had other ideas; they replaced Thadeus as leader, and held out until 1603, when Wicklow was finally designated a county.

The mountainous landscape also proved difficult for British forces in the wake of the 1798 rebellion, with large pockets of Irish resistance holding out in the mountains. Refusing to be bested, the British army built the Military Road, from Rathfarnham in south Dublin to Aghavannagh in south Wicklow, crossing the mountains and providing them with direct access to what had been a native troublespot for centuries. Following independence, parts of the Military Road developed into the **Wicklow Way,** much of which follows the route the soldiers would have taken, through some of the most majestic countryside on the east coast.

Castleblayney
Carlingford Lough Kilkeel
N2
N1
Greenore
Dundalk
CAVAN
Carrickmacross
LOUTH
Dundalk Bay
Bailieborough
Kingscourt
Ardee
Dunleer
Virginia
Collon
Clogher Head
Clogher Head
MEATH
Baltray
Loughcrew
Kells
Slane
Drogheda
Crossakiel
Newgrange
Donore
N1
Delvin
N51
Navan
Duleek
Balbriggan
Athboy
N2
Skerries
Kinnegad
Trim
N3
Garristown
Rush
Summerhill
Swords
Malahide
Enfield
Kilcock
DUBLIN
Howth
Irish Sea
N4
Maynooth
Lucan
DUBLIN
Leixlip
Leixlip
Dun Laoghaire
Prosperous
Dalkey
River Liffey
Naas
Bray
Edenderry
Enniskerry
Greystones
Newbridge
Blessington
WICKLOW MOUNTAINS NAT'L PARK
Newtownmountkennedy
Monasterevan
N7
Kildare
Emo
Roundwood
←**Portalaoise**
KILDARE
Laragh
Rathnew
Wicklow
Ardscull
Wicklow Head
Stradbally
Athy
Rathdrum
Glenealy
LAOIS
N81
WICKLOW
Brittas Bay
Avoca
Aughrim
Woodenbridge
Carlow
Tinahely
Arklow
Tullow
Shillelagh
N11
Castlecomer
N9
N80
Carnew
CARLOW
Bunclody
Gorey
Kilkenny
WEXFORD
0   5 mi
0   5 km

area of detail
Dublin
REPUBLIC OF IRELAND

In recent years, Wicklow's landscape has been in hot demand for international movies—Mel Gibson's *Braveheart* and John Boorman's *Excalibur* both feature the countryside quite spectacularly—and Bray's Ardmore Studios, established in 1958, are still involved in the creation of many well-known productions.

LAY OF THE LAND

Wicklow is one of Ireland's most mountainous counties, but it's hardly the Alps—the highest peak, Lugnaquilla, is 925m (3,034 ft.) high, and many of the hills and mountains that dot the landscape can be scaled in a half day or so. The river Liffey, which flows right through Dublin City, starts in Wicklow, while the area known as Glendalough is home to many spectacular lakes and rivers—Lough Dan and Lough Tay in particular—which formed during the last ice age. The east coast of Wicklow also has many beautiful beaches, such as Brittas Bay and Silver Strand.

GETTING THERE & GETTING AROUND

In the past decade or so, due to its location immediately south of Dublin, parts of North Wicklow have been gobbled up by the capital's outward sprawl, and so traffic in the county can be bad during rush hours. The main road through Wicklow, the **M11/N11,** begins just before Shankill on Dublin's Southside, and continues along the eastern side of the county, towards Wexford. The **M50** motorway, which circles Dublin, joins up with the N11 just before Bray, providing access to the airport, but be warned—this can be a very busy route. Further inland, due to the mountains, the roads can be scarily twisty and tight, but they're also some of the country's most picturesque roadways. The **R759** (from Enniskerry to Ballymore Eustace), which crosses part of the Wicklow mountains known as the Sally Gap, winds through stunning scenery; but again a warning: Driving this road can become dangerous during and immediately after a heavy storm.

Bus Eireann (www.buseireann.ie) operate a number of bus routes to Wicklow (from Dublin €7.20 one-way, €12 round-trip), some of which go on an hourly basis, meaning that you could potentially do without a rental car, particularly if you're hoping to get to Bray, Newtownmountkennedy, Newcastle, Ashford, Rathnew, and Wicklow (very frequent service to these towns). Check the website for fare specials. Another popular bus provider, and one which stops at many of the B&Bs in the rural heart of the county, is the privately owned **Saint Kevin's Bus** (www.glendaloughbus.com), which runs twice daily (11:30am and 6pm) from St. Stephen's Green to Bray, Kilmacanougue, Roundwood, Annamoe, and Laragh, finishing in Glendalough (€13 one-way, €20 round-trip). The same bus runs twice daily from Glendalough service to Bray only as well. The route, incidentally, follows that of the 6th century Saint Kevin, who took a self-imposed exile in Glendalough and founded the monastic site there.

But as we said in the intro, the train is the best way to really enjoy the sights—if you're going toward the sea, that is. **Irish Rail** (www.irishrail.ie) serves only the coastal towns in Wicklow. **DART** services run from Dublin to Bray (€2.50 one-way, €4.30 same-day return) and Greystones from approximately 6am to 11:20pm Monday to Sunday—as often as every 6 minutes at peak times, mornings and early evenings, but with long waits at quieter times. Intercity/Arrow trains run from Dublin Connolly to Wexford/Rosslare (€21 one-way, €26 round-trip) four times daily, stopping at Bray, Greystones, Wicklow, Rathdrum, Arklow.

MT Cabs (1 Quinnsboro Rd., Bray; ☎ 01/286-3633) is a reliable taxi service that operates out of Bray and serves most of the major hotels in Wicklow directly—indeed, in many hotels you'll find a direct dial telephone to its switchboard. In the heart of Wicklow, meanwhile, **Red's Taxis** (Avoca, Arklow; ☎ 0402/35000) operate out of Avoca, with capacity for up to eight persons per taxi, while the **Philip Davis Taxi Service** (☎ 087/614-1297) operates a hackney taxi service in Roundwood, Laragh, and Glendalough.

WHERE TO STAY & DINE
North Wicklow

€   As of summer 2007, Enniskerry became home to Ireland's first Ritz-Carlton Hotel, with its own signature Gordon Ramsay restaurant, and prices that don't so much astound as baffle. Feel free to pop in for a quick look, although Ramsay himself rarely makes an appearance. You'll enjoy it all the more knowing that you're being well looked after just a short drive away, for a tenth of the cost. Double rooms at the **Knockree Youth Hostel** ★ (7km/4 miles from Enniskerry, along Glencree Rd.; ☎ 01/276-7981; www.knockreehostel.com; cash only) don't rise above €60 all year round and for real bargain hunters, there are a number of six-bed dorm rooms with beds costing €16 a night. A new-build—expect lots of glass and steel tacked onto the old farmhouse—Knockree is way more up-market than standard youth hostels, being spacious, modern, and comfortable—and all rooms have private bathrooms. There's even a truly state-of-the-art communal kitchen if you fancy giving Gordon a run for his money.

€   Although not technically a suburb of Dublin, Bray certainly feels that way, and even has its own rail link to the city center—incidentally, a spectacular cliff-top journey, well worth taking. Although we wouldn't recommend you stay here—there are too many other more idyllic spots in Wicklow—Bray has a couple of decent cafes. Our favorite, **Molloy's** (Quinsboro Rd., about 500m/1,640 ft. from DART station, Bray; ☎ 01/286-2196; daily 7am–6pm; cash only) enjoys massive local support, no surprise when you check out its great selection of pastries, danishes, strudel, and meringues—a slice of cake will cost you just under €1. Lunch specials for €8 are also a top buy, many of them cafe-staples such as fish of the day, lasagna, shepherd's pie, and vegetable quiche. For a quick lunch, pick up one of their chicken or ham salad sandwiches for just €4.50. Yes, this little, open plan cafe is a tad old-fashioned, and the menu is hardly pioneering stuff, but its longevity alone is proof of the affection it inspires.

€€   It's not the easiest place to find, set a couple of kilometers from the main road, but once you make your way to **Wicklow Way Lodge** ★★ (follow Lough Dan signs from Roundwood, take left at Y junction marked Laragh/Glendalough; ☎ 01/281-8489; www.wicklowwaylodge.com; MC, V), you'll appreciate its seclusion, and the fact that it has been designed over three levels to maximize the backdrop of the mountains and woodlands. Try to nab a room with a balcony for some of the most beautiful views in the county. If you can tear yourself away from the

Cottage Stays in Ireland's Garden

Scattered throughout "the Garden of Ireland" are fine deals on holiday rentals that put you right in the heart of some of the loveliest hiking, biking, and outdoor-sightseeing locations in the land. Here are but a few:

- **Glendale Holiday Homes** ★ (☎ 0404/45410; www.glendale-glendalough.com): Comprised of a handful of three-bedroom cottages with log-fires, open-plan living/dining areas, and a full complement of modern day amenities. Weekly rates—for up to six people—run €340 to €460 most of the year (but shoot up to €700 July–Aug). B&B type stays are also available, and your hosts, Christy and Valerie Merrigan, are on hand to lend a hand, give advice, and point you in the direction of the nearest pub; they'll also organize babysitting. Best of all, you're a mere 1.5km (1 mile) from Glendalough—bring your hiking boots.

- **Minmore Mews** ★★ (☎ 053/942-9147; www.minmoremews.com): John Hayden rents four graciously restored stone cottages on his farmstead in Shillelagh. Each one has a different configuration, with living areas and bedrooms carved from the hulls of the various farm buildings. Interiors are woodsy with solid and comfy (if not particularly stylish) furnishing, though the two-person Coach House has a rather neat, contemporary-looking en suite bedroom. The Barn and the Loft sleep up to four people. Two hectares (4½ acres) of inviting gardens surround the cottages, and there's a small play area for children and game room (with billiard table) for all ages. You're within easy driving distance of the beach, neighboring golf courses (John can provide the clubs), and some primo hiking trails. Weekly rates go from €200 to €270 most of the year, and €250 to €420 in summer (June–Sept).

- **Tynte House** ★★★ (☎ 045/401561; www.tyntehouse.com): With access to all facilities (including a tennis court, children's play area, and gardens) offered to guests staying in their beautiful B&B in Dunlavin, John and Caroline Lawler's self-catering cottages have the best of both worlds. You can pop in for dinner (€25 per person) when you're too lazy to cook, or stay put when you're wanting privacy. There's also a bit of choice here, between eight different-size mews cottages in the courtyard of the main house. They sleep up to nine people, and weekly rentals start at €245 to €430 for a two-bedroom mews (sleeps five), while a four-bedroom unit is €320 to €550; heating is charged extra. The Lawlers are consummate hosts, and because they're busy with the on-site B&B, there's always help at hand should problems arise. They've also done a good job of making the cottages look respectable. Timber floors, smart pine furniture, and open fireplaces sit side-by-side with modern amenities—including a full self-contained kitchen. Incidentally, B&B at Tynte House is scenery, host Marilyn Kinlan lays on a fantastic breakfast, with delicious home-made breads and the kind of porridge that takes you back to your childhood. Power showers and underfloor heating in all the rooms seal the deal for me. Rates range from €90 to €100 a night, double. Bear in mind that you'll need a car—it's a tricky place to reach, though worth the trek.

€€   In the center of Enniskerry village, Josie Corcoran's **Ferndale House** (Main Sq., Enniskerry; ☎ 01/286-3518; www.ferndalehouse.com; cash only) is a charming 190-year old Victorian house with roses rambling around the front and an acre of garden at the back. It isn't madly grand—think well-to-do local doctor rather than lord of the manor—and there is a faint fussiness to the very traditional interiors, but the beds are big old brass ones, the thread count on bed linen is high, and the back garden is a riot of color and scent. The Corcorans charge €90 double year-round, which is the going rate for B&Bs in the area, though few can match the quality on offer here.

€€   Directly opposite Ferndale House is **Poppies** ✮✮✮ (The Square, Enniskerry; ☎ 01/282-8869; www.poppies.ie; daily 8:30am–6pm; MC, V), not so much a restaurant as an institution. Good, wholesome country cooking is the order of the day here, with the majority of dishes (each €6.50) made in-house; as well as the likes of quiches and cottage pie, there's Poppies chicken—creamy chicken with celery, onion, almonds, and cornflakes, a local favorite and one you'll be bound to write home about (not to mention to the rhubarb crumble, €5.25). The low ceilings and hunched together tables might be off-putting in a different setting, but here they only add to the homey feel.

€€€   Down the road, pretty little Greystones has, like Bray, recently seen massive housing growth—the DART rail system was extended out here in 2001, increasing traffic through the once sleepy village. Not that Pat Keown, owner of the **Hungry Monk** ✮ (Church Rd., Greystones; ☎ 01/287-5759; www.thehungry monk.ie; Restaurant: Wed–Sat 6:30–11pm; Sun 12:30–8pm; Wine Bar Bistro: Mon–Sat 5–11pm; Sun 4–9pm; AE, MC, V) notices that much—he's been drawing crowds from all over Dublin for over 20 years now. The Hungry Monk is actually two restaurants, with a bistro downstairs, where mains range from €12 to €21, and a formal restaurant upstairs, with mains around the €20 to €25 mark. Ask Pat about his seafood specials, which change daily, depending on how the local fishermen fared that morning.

€€€   Opposite the Hungry Monk, **Backstage @ Bels** (Church Rd., Greystones; ☎ 01/201-6990; www.bels.ie; Tues–Sat noon–4pm and 6–10pm; Sun noon–8pm; MC, V) has recently been given a new lease of life by husband and wife team Tara and Jeff Norman. Tara breezes around the front of house; Jeff pours his heart out in the kitchen. The backstage theme, if you're wondering, is a nod to the new local theater next door, and is reflected in the menu, which is divided up like the acts of a play: Act One is starter, Act Two main course, and so on. Gimmicky, but kind of cute, too. Daily lunch specials start at €10, and the pre-theater menu is a great value; three "Acts" for €23 between 5 and 7pm Thursday and Friday, and all night Tuesday and Wednesday. Be sure to try the smoked salmon platter from local supplier Terry Butterly (€11)—you'll struggle to find anything that comes even close elsewhere.

In & Around Wicklow Town

The Irish Landmark Trust (p. 99) has one of its quirkiest properties right here in Wicklow: the **Wicklow Head Lighthouse** ★★★ (Dunbur Head, Co. Wicklow; Reservations: The Irish Landmark Trust, 25 Eustace St., Temple Bar, Dublin 2; ☎ 01/670-4733; www.irishlandmark.com). First built in 1781, it was never much use as a lighthouse. Fog rendered its 20-candle lantern ineffective, so it was decommissioned. In the mid-1800s, a lighting strike burnt out the interior. When the Trust undertook to rebuild in 1996, everything from floors to windows had to be installed. Six octagonal rooms were built on six levels, and the resulting spaces were fitted out by Kilkenny-based *tromp l'oeil* artist Orla Kelly. She used simple furniture, pale blue painted pine wood, mosaic tile bathrooms, and a faintly nautical theme (sea charts and maps decorate the lounge, while a telescope, a model ship, and water-tight ship's windows remind you of being at sea) to create an elegant-yet-timeless atmosphere—so no bland modernism here. A generously stocked bookcase, cushy armchairs, and plenty of fine extras (spruce linens, good mattresses) complete the picture, while arched windows provide enchanting views of the countryside and coastline, and meter-thick walls stave off the elements.

All in all, there are two double bedrooms and one bathroom, and—perhaps to the horror of some—a kitchen at the very top. Alas, there is no elevator in this lighthouse, so those 109 winding steps need to be climbed to reach the galley. This may not be the cheapest rental in the country, but it's not outrageous either: A week here in low season costs between €1,134 (for four people) and €1,260. This might sound hefty but works out to €41 to €45 per person per night, which is generally what you'll pay in a very ordinary B&B. We can't imagine a better spot for quiet, calm contemplation.

€–€€   Although it's a large enough town, Wicklow Town is hardly a foodie paradise—every second eatery seems to be either a "chipper" or generic Chinese—but if you're close by, the **Bakery** (Church St., Wicklow Town; ☎ 0404/66770; Tues–Sat 5–9:30pm; Sun noon–9:30pm; cash only) is worth wandering into. Don't bother with the menu; just check out the daily blackboard specials. The last time we were there, the special was baked sea bream on mango and coriander salsa with lemongrass sauce (€15), and a veggie option of wild nettle and onion tart for €9.95. Clearly, someone in the kitchen is trying hard, because, although ambitious, both were quite good.

€€   Geographically, Annamoe marks the start of the Wicklow Gap, a solitary path through some of the most lovely landscape in Ireland. Judy and Jim Doyle's **Bracken B&B** (just outside Laragh, 3km/2 miles from Glendalough; ☎ 0404/45300; http://brackenlodge.com; cash only) is about the last house on the route, and a popular base for walkers. It is also one of few guesthouses in the area on any kind of public transport—the twice daily St. Kevin's bus from Trinity College to Glendalough stops right at the gate—so there's no need to rent a car. Rates start at €66 double, including breakfast, but it's the dinners you'll really cherish—Jim is an avid cook, hunter, and fly-fisherman, and his meals are hearty fare, spiced up with organic herbs from the guesthouse garden. Good sustenance for the mountain climb ahead, and at €25 for four courses, not bad value either.

€€ With possibly the best location of any guesthouse in the country, **Derrymore House** ✹✹ (Lake Rd., Glendalough; ☎ 0404/45493; http://home page.eircom.net/~derrymore; cash only), situated 2km (1 mile) from Laragh village overlooks the lower lake in the heart of the Glendalough valley and is just 2-minutes' walk from the 6th-century monastic settlement that gives the area its name. You could forgive Pat and Penny Kelleher for resting on their laurels—a steady stream of tourist business is almost guaranteed—but you love them all the more because they don't. In fact, the Kellehers are part of the local attraction—don't be surprised to see the family pick up flute, fiddle, and tin whistle, with Pat on the banjo or mandolin, and launch into an impromptu trad session in the evenings. A novel pricing structure means a double room will set you back €80 per night, €76 per night for 2 nights, or €72 for 3 nights. Last time we were there, we asked Pat whether he had ever won any awards. "I got a bronze medal for the breast stroke in 1962," he responded. "Does that count?"

€€€ Catherine Fulvio took over **Ballyknocken House** ✹✹ (Ashford; ☎ 0404/44627; www.ballyknocken.com; closed Dec and Jan; MC, V) in 1999, after three generations of ownership by the Byrne family, and while it took a while to settle, she's now truly found her groove. Yes, the rooms are wonderfully luxurious and elegant, with free-standing Victorian baths and lovingly polished old furniture, but Catherine and her cooking are the real draw here. She gives practical, down-to-earth cooking classes (p. 96). Built in the 1850s, rates at this seven room guesthouse start at €130 double (€118 if you plan on sticking around for a week), including a full Irish breakfast, and while that is clearly a bit on the pricey side, it's worth it for the chance to hang out with the incredibly dynamic Catherine and enjoy her spectacular breakfasts. To get there, turn right after Texaco petrol station in Ashford, follow road for around 5km (3 miles).

€€€€ The only certified organic restaurant in Ireland, the **Strawberry Tree** ✹✹ (in the Brooklodge Hotel, signposted from Aughrim village in Macreddin; ☎ 0402/36444; www.brooklodge.com; daily 7–9:30pm; AE, MC, V), is a charming spot that deserves all its many awards. Chef Evan Doyle selects the best organic ingredients the region has to offer—and trust me, there are plenty—and blends them with care and precision to create one of the most innovative menus in the country. Think chicken with sun-dried tomato and lentil stew; couscous and shitake mushroom salad, or the trout with mange tout. Most mains are around €20.

Near Shillelagh, South Wicklow

€€ **Stoops Guesthouse** (3km/2 miles east of Shillelagh; ☎ 053/942-6530; http://stoopsguesthouse.ie; MC, V), just outside the village, is just the kind of rural hideaway Wicklow is famous for—a winding, wooded driveway leads to a cozy, revamped farmhouse, with airy bedrooms, modern artwork, and flatscreen TVs on the walls, and a large communal area for visitors to while away the evening swapping stories. A double room will set you back €85, although discounts for children and senior citizens are available if you ask.

WHY YOU'RE HERE: TOP SIGHTS & ATTRACTIONS

The legacy of Saint Kevin's self-imposed hermitage to the Wicklow Mountains in the 6th century is still with us in the form of the magnificent monastic remains at Glendalough, and the **Glendalough Visitor Centre** ✪✪ (follow R756 from Laragh, 5km/3 miles along on left hand side; ☎ 0404/45425; www.wicklow.com/glendalough; €2.90; Mar–Oct 9:30am–6pm; Oct–Mar 9:30am–5pm) is probably the most-visited tourist attraction in the county—it's simply breathtaking. Set in a glaciated valley between two lakes, features include a magnificent round tower, ruined churches, and countless stone crosses, all intricately carved, while further up the hillside, a stone fort stands guard over the valley. Stand at the foot of the round tower (an iconic image), gaze upward, and contemplate one of the jewels of Irish ecclesiastical history.

Spanning some 20,000 sq. hectares (122,222 sq. acres), with a landscape that features everything from blanket bogs to mountain peaks, the **Wicklow Mountains National Park** ✪✪✪ (Upper Lake, Glendalough, 2km/1 mile from Glendalough Visitor Centre; ☎ 0404/45425 or 0404/45338; www.wicklownational park.ie) is arguably Ireland's finest national park. The Wicklow Way bisects the park from North to South, with countless walking trails leading off it. While much of the terrain can be heavy going, even for experienced walkers, there are also trails for novices who want to savor all the park has to offer, without getting too up-close and dirty. Must-see features along the route include the **Lugnaquilla** and **Liffey Head Bog complexes, Glendalough Wood Nature Reserve,** and **Lugnaquilla Mountain** (Wicklow's highest peak)—also keep an eye out for one of the park's most treasured residents, the peregrine falcon. Access to the park is free for all, but we recommend getting hold of an official **Wicklow Way Map Guide** (€5.50)—available from the National Park Information Office, near Glendalough's Upper Lake—which breaks the walking trail into individual sections.

Wicklow's Treasured Gardens & Estates

Wicklow may be the "garden county" in its wild, undisturbed state, but to get some sense of the pleasures to be had from a perfectly cultivated garden, you've really got to take a gander at one or two of the county's famous estates. Chief among these—and among the finest gardens in Europe—are **Powerscourt Gardens** ✪✪✪ (Enniskerry; ☎ 01/204-6000; www.powerscourt.ie; €8; daily Mar–Oct 9:30am–5:30pm; Nov–Feb 9:30am–dusk), which occupy a pristine estate in Enniskerry at the foot of Sugar Loaf Mountain. Here, the great Palladian architect Richard Castle was hired by the first viscount of Powerscourt to build what, in 1740—after 9 years of construction and a great deal of financial investment—was one of Ireland's most sumptuous homes. Powerscourt's renown was legendary, and even attracted a visit from King George IV in 1821.

Alas, the house itself no longer looks the way it did back then—a vicious fire gutted it in 1974, and while the exterior remains arresting, there's little inside (aside, perhaps, from the ballroom) that truly captures the original grandeur of the residence. Small worry, though, since it's really the gardens that you should make every effort to see. They're an amalgam of plans and designs by various owners and landscapists over the years, including the architect Daniel Robertson, who was clearly influenced by the Italian Renaissance villas. Robertson apparently supervised his workers from a wheelbarrow while polishing off a bottle of sherry

Getting Around the Park

Wicklow Mountains National Park holds several guided walks throughout the year (☎ 0404/45425; http://wicklownationalpark.ie for details on upcoming walks), all of which are free, but are on a first come, first served basis. If you do plan on going it alone, the Park is well mapped out, with color coded walks of varying difficulties.

First timers to the area may want to try out the **Miners' Road** (purple) and **Green Road** (green) walks to get accustomed. Both take less than an hour and will undoubtedly get you in the mood for the more ambitious **Derrybawn Woodland Trail** (orange) or **Spinc and Glenealo Valley** (white) walks, both of which involve high climbs but reward you with stunning views over the valley.

If you're short of time, or don't fancy a muddy trek, there are countless bus tours serving Wicklow, most of which depart from Dublin city center, with pick-up stops on the way south. **Day Tours Unplugged** (☎ 01/834-0941; http://daytoursunplugged.ie; €28) operate daily tours around Glendalough, which depart from Gardiner Street in the city center at 8:50am, returning at 5pm, and take in a pub lunch (not included in price) along the way. Cheaper again, if only slightly, is the Day Tour of Wicklow operated by **Coach Tours of Ireland** (☎ 044/934-8479; http://coachtours ofireland.com; €24), which leaves Suffolk Street at 9am, returning at 5pm, via Glendalough, and Avoca in the south of the county, home of a flourishing crafts industry. For €25, the Wicklow Mountains tour by **Gray Line Tours** (☎ 01/605-7705; www.irishcitytours.com; tickets €30, €25 on Tues–Thurs; departs O'Connell St. at 9:45am) takes in most of Wicklow's sights, and features a 2-hour stop at Glendalough.

And of course, you could always simply drive the routes these busses take in your rental car.

---

each working day. Despite his debilitating gout, Robertson laid out magnificent terraces adorned with a collection of statuary, ironwork, and decorative features that elevate them to the realm of fantasy. When you visit, don't miss the enchanting walled gardens, which are the oldest features on the estate grounds, and check out the "Pet's Cemetery," a real marker of eccentricity, where formal headstones mark the graves of domestic animals that belonged to the estate's latter-day owners—the Wingfield and Slazenger families. Between them, they managed to create Ireland's largest private pet burial ground. There are more conventional parts of the gardens to explore, too, including the Japanese garden, established in 1908 with Japanese maples, azaleas, and Chinese fortune palms.

If you're looking for a good picnicking spot, head for **Powerscourt Waterfall** (€5; daily Nov–Feb 10:30am–4pm; Mar–Apr and Sept–Oct 10:30am–5:30pm; May–Aug 9:30am–7pm), which, at 121m (398 ft.), is Ireland's highest waterfall, fed by the Dargle River.

Not far from Enniskerry, right near the border with County Kildare, Wicklow's other great estate overlooks vast Blessington Lake. Unlike Powerscourt, **Russborough House** ✿✿✿ (Blessington; ☎ 045/865239; www.russborough.ie; €10; May–Sept daily 10:30am–5pm; Oct–Apr Sun 10:30am–5pm) has been perfectly preserved. Unusually harmonious features—its perfect Palladian symmetry, its handsome silver-gray granite, and its massive facade (at 200m/700 ft. it's the longest of any dwelling in the country)—have led many to name it the most beautiful house in Ireland. The eye candy continues inside with the Lafranchini plasterwork, hand-carved mahogany staircases, and Italian marble and Kilkenny limestone polished to a high sheen. Among its treasures are a 16th-century Lotto rug from Anatolia in Turkey, a scagliola console table top from Vallombrosa (dated 1750), a gilt bronze microscope by Gozzi of Parma (1772), and a fine collection of French clocks. This is another of Richard Castle's architectural creations—considered his finest—commissioned by Joseph Leeson, the first Earl of Milltown, in 1741. Hourly, 45-minute long guided tours of the house take in its "greatest hits" rooms and offer an insightful commentary on the architecture and furnishings. From the upstairs bedrooms, you get a great view over the lake, and after exploring the house, you can try getting lost in the adjacent **Beech Hedge Maze** 🧒 (€3).

If you want the glories of Wicklow nature without the overt meddling of architects and landscape artists, **Kilmacurragh Arboretum** (5km/3 miles off N11, south of Rathnew, turn right at the Beehive pub; ☎ 0404/48844; www.botanicgardens.ie; free admission; daily Nov–Feb 9am–4pm; Feb–Nov 9am–6pm) is an alternative, a living museum of plant species from around the world, planted during the 19th century by the Moore family, curators of the National Botanic Gardens in Dublin at the time. Unlike the Dublin gardens, however, the soil and climactic conditions of Kilmacurragh are well suited to many species found nowhere else in the country, including rare rhododendrons and conifers. Guided tours of the arboretum are available between noon and 3pm daily and are free of charge.

ACTIVE WICKLOW

Wicklow is walking country, so don't forget your hiking boots. Walkers of all ages and experience will find a walk that suits them along the **Wicklow Way,** which stretches 132km (82 miles) from north to south Wicklow (divided into seven sections; see **www.wicklowway.com** for information on routes). The route begins in the Dublin suburb of Rathfarnham, at Marlay Park (served by the no. 16 bus from Dublin City center); if you'd prefer to tackle the route from the bottom up, head for the Carlow village of Clonegal (the main Dublin to Waterford bus route will drop you at Kildavin, 3km/2 miles from Clonegal).

Other walks of note in the area include **Saint Kevin's Walk,** which follows the 6th-century monk's progress through the valleys of Glendalough, and the **Bray to Greystones Cliff Walk** (both Bray and Greystones are served by regular DART trains), an 8km (5-mile) route over Bray Head, with spectacular views of Dublin Bay—on a clear day you can make out Wales in the distance. And, of course, there are rewarding treks within Wicklow Mountains National Park (p. 92).

Wicklow is, of course, a fine golfing county, with some of Ireland's most renowned courses. Chief among these is **Druid's Glen** (Woodstock House,

The Wicklow Way

Even though the Wicklow Mountains rise to just 924m (3,000 ft.) at their highest point, their barren, desolate expanse and jagged hillside plunges make the whole experience feel far more wild than anything this close to the capital should be. There are miles and miles of remote trails to follow, some hard, some leisurely, past lakes, forests, fast-flowing streams, and steep-sided valleys. Many days' walking can be done here—in fact, you can begin in Dublin and walk all the way to County Carlow.

The Wicklow Way **website** (www.wicklowway.com) is packed with details of walks, trail descriptions, advice, and recommendations for conservation measures, and it lists companies that will help you arrange advance transportation for your baggage if you intend to get serious and hike the stages. But equally, you could just drive to Roundwood, Glendalough, Laragh, or Enniskerry, park, and wander.

signposted from Newtownmountkennedy; ☎ 01/287-3600; www.druidsglen.ie), known as the "Augusta of Europe," which has played host to countless international events, such as the biannual Seve Trophy. With green fees starting around the €175 mark (€110 if booked in advance), it's one to save for a very, very, *very* special occasion.

Much better value, and arguably with better views, is **Bray Golf Club** (Greystones Rd., take turn from N11 for Bray/Greystones; ☎ 01/276-3200; http://braygolfclub.com), which has Killiney Bay on one side and the Wicklow Mountains looming large on the other; green fees range from €25 for a 7:30 to 9:30am slot, Monday, Thursday, and Friday, to €70 for a peak time slot on a Saturday. Midweek offers are also available; four play for the price of three between 7:30 and 9:30am.

Other reasonable options include **Greystones Golf Club** (Whitshed Rd., Greystones; ☎ 01/287-4136; www.greystonesgc.com), which dates back to 1895, and charges €55 on Mondays, Tuesdays, and Fridays and €60 on Sundays (closed Wed, Thurs, and Sat; Mon and Fri €40 before 9:30am), and **Coollattin Golf Club** (follow N11 through Aughrim, Coolboy and on to Coollattin; ☎ 055/29125; www.coollattingolfclub.com; €35 Mon–Fri; €45 Sat and Sun), set among the redwood, oak, and beech woodland of the south of the county.

Wicklow is well known for its excellent cycling terrain; this was where future Tour de France winner Stephen Roche trained when he was an amateur. It's also home to Ireland's biggest cycling event, the **Wicklow 200** (Baltinglass; ☎ 059/648-1350; www.wicklow200.ie), which takes place on the Sunday after the June Bank Holiday Weekend, and celebrates its 27th anniversary in 2009. If you're not up for a competitive ride through the county, but want to rent a bike, there are several choice options, including **Hillcrest Hire** (Main St., Blessington; ☎ 045/865066) and the **Bray Cycle Centre** (The Boulevard Centre, Bray; ☎ 01/286-3357). At the latter, owner and expert cyclist Brian Murphy will make

---

Beach Bunnies

Wicklow has a good selection of lovely beaches on the stretch off the R750 towards Arklow. First up, about 5km (3 miles) from Arklow town, is the aptly named **Silver Strand,** a sheltered cove of fine, soft sand that is protected enough to be a good spot for small children. The enormous curve of **Brittas Bay**—3km (2 miles) long, with its endless grassy dunes—is another 10 minutes or so down the same road. Although well worth a visit for its bracing, wind-blown expanses on an indifferent day, Brittas can be horribly crowded on sunny weekends with Dubliners escaping the city. Large family parties and scuffling groups of teenagers can make it a fairly fraught experience. Go to walk, not to swim.

---

suggestions about routes and advise on what sort of bike you should take (so we'd give it a slight edge over Hillcrest, though both charge €10 per day).

For a spot of angling, head for **Annamoe Trout Fisheries** (Annamoe; ☎ 0404/45470; www.annamoetroutfishery.com). The 2-hectare (4-acre) brown and rainbow trout lake provides year-round fly-fishing; a day ticket for catch-and-release fishing costs €24. Rod hire and bait cost €5, and you must pay €3 for each fish caught that you wish to keep.

THE OTHER WICKLOW

"Modern Irish cuisine" is a term that foodies across the land have been bandying around for several years now. Most people have a fair idea what it means: locally sourced ingredients (preferably organic) in simple, traditional Irish dishes, which can be a bit confusing, since far too many people the world over still associate Ireland with potatoes, potatoes, potatoes. Banish such misgivings with a few lessons from one of Ireland's most renowned proponents of country-style cooking. At **Ballyknocken Cookery School** (☎ 0404/44627; www.thecookeryschool.ie; year-round courses, primarily weekends), culinary whiz Catherine Fulvio will teach you what this cuisine is all about. What you get here, Catherine suggests, is "a tranquil, friendly experience in the country—but in a modern kitchen." It's that simple.

Classes take place in a renovated milking parlor (now sporting gleaming, state-of-the-art kitchenware) on the grounds of Ballyknocken House (p. 91), where Catherine also runs a fabulous countryside B&B (her mother started the first farmhouse B&B in Ireland in 1969). She's become established enough to have appeared on cooking programs around the world and is the food writer for *Irish Garden* magazine. Classes range from hands-on bread-making to special-edition sessions focused on preparing only food that is pink (think salmon and strawberry salad). Classes are typically in the morning (9:30am–1:30pm) or afternoon (2:30–6:30pm) and cost €110 per person; this includes either lunch or a light supper. Also in the mix are wine masterclasses, and a few children's classes (€55).

If conservation is your thing, the voluntary **Bray Coastcare Group** (www.volunteerwicklow.ie) is always looking for help picking up litter and maintaining the coastline. This can involve cutting back undergrowth and clearing rock fall as well as clearing the debris of a thousand day-trippers. The group—a dedicated gang of local enthusiasts—go out on the second Saturday of the month and take immense pride in their good work. As a welcome by-product, most are also chatty and wonderfully opinionated on local doings and happenings.

ATTENTION, SHOPPERS!

There is a great tradition of the local "everything" shop in Ireland, where clothes, jigsaws, industrial torches, loo paper, and bits of string are all sold together, often along with bottles of whiskey and the odd packet of crisps, and not even the proprietor knows the extent of what's available. One place successfully working this tradition is **Fishers of Newtownmountkennedy** ✪ (The Old Schoolhouse, Newtownmountkennedy; ☎ 0281/9404; www.fishers.ie), where casual and formal clothes for men and women sit alongside fishing gear, gadgets, golf clubs, china, and pretty silver jewelry by the owners' daughter. The Fishers folk are friendly, helpful, and chatty, with time to spare for everyone. A dedicated gang of locals as well as considerable passing trade from tourists signals the many things these guys do right.

Also in Wicklow is **Avoca** ✪✪ (The Mill at Avoca Village, Wicklow; ☎ 0402/ 35105; www.avoca.ie). The heart of the empire, it's located in a white-washed working 18th-century mill, where much of the cloth for their own-brand scarves, rugs, and throws is made. The large, light-filled store has the usual great Avoca selection of clothes, jewelry, homewares, interiors, cookbooks, and food. The Pratt family, originators of the Avoca concept, have done as much as anyone to make small-town, local Irish goods and food popular. Incidentally, Avoca is the town where the fictional *Ballykissangel* BBC series was shot, and thus played its part in launching Colin Farrell to fame.

NIGHTLIFE

County Wicklow is teeming with atmospheric pubs, especially around the east coast, and Wicklow Town's oldest pub, the **Bridge Tavern** (Bridge St., Wicklow Town; ☎ 0404/67718) is also one of the most fun, with live music sessions every night, all year round. **The Coach House** (Main St., Roundwood; ☎ 01/281-8157; www.thecoachhouse.com) also has regular energetic trad sessions and ballad singing in the evenings, but with enough nooks and crannies that you can avoid the mayhem and enjoy a quiet pint if you wish. Slightly quieter, but equally popular due to its proximity to the N11, is **Ashford House** (off N11, Ashford; ☎ 0404/ 40481), a major stop off point for tourists exploring the south of the county, and a pub with a strong local following among the people of Ashford.

KILDARE

Since 1790, when the first Turf Club was founded at what is now the Curragh horse racing circuit, Kildare has been all about the horsey set. And it's not difficult to see why; from the tip of the Wicklow mountains in the east, to the raised Bog of Allen on the west, lies some of the most fertile, grassy land in the country, the undulating hills of the Curragh, with springy turf just perfect for racing. According to legend, around the time that St. Brigid came to Kildare to found a monastery, she asked the High King of Leinster for the land on which to build it. The unimpressed king, laughing, granted her "as much land as her cloak would cover." St. Brigid placed her cloak on the ground to cover the entire Curragh plain. Today, a millennium or two later, her legacy lives on (she is one of the country's favorite saints)—although the king himself is conspicuously forgotten.

A BRIEF HISTORY OF KILDARE

While there's evidence of at least one or two settlements in modern day County Kildare stretching back to the time of Christ, it wasn't until the 5th and 6th centuries that the monastery that gives it its name was founded. Cill Dara, meaning "Church of the Oak," was founded by St. Brigid in A.D. 524. Since then, Kildare has made its mark on Irish history; the country's first college was founded in Maynooth in 1518, and is still in use today (it's also an excellent place to stay; see p. 99), while the first shots of the 1798 rebellion, an uprising against British rule, were fired in the county.

Kildare has been a pioneering conduit to Irish industry over the years, with the county at the center of Ireland's inland waterway system. Constructed during the 1830s and 1840s, canal systems run through the county and link the capital with Waterford, Limerick, and Athlone (the Royal Canal, in the north of the county, runs along the border with Meath). Toward the end of the 20th century, Kildare played an important role in the development of the "Celtic Tiger" economy, as multinational firms Intel and Hewlett-Packard established operations there in the early 1990s, as well as pharmaceutical giant Wyeth.

LAY OF THE LAND

Kildare's location directly west of Dublin means that it acts as a hub of sorts for most of the major westward routes out of the city. The **N4/M4** (Dublin to Sligo) runs along the north of the county, passing the towns of Maynooth, Cellbridge, and Leixlip, three towns very much in Dublin's commuter belt. The **N7/M7** runs through the middle of the county, connecting Dublin with three of Kildare's most prominent towns—Naas, Newbridge, and Kildare Town—while the **N9/M9,** which starts in Newbridge, links the county with Waterford in the south of the country. Athy, in the south of the country, is served by the N78, again from Newbridge.

GETTING THERE & GETTING AROUND

Kildare's proximity to Dublin means transport networks are plentiful, with **Intercity/Arrow** rail services (www.irishrail.ie) between Dublin and Kildare operating twice every hour, direct, Monday to Friday. Hourly services also run to Cellbridge, Sallins, Naas, and Newbridge on the same route (Dublin to Portlaoise, €20).

Because of their commuter town status, Maynooth and Cellbridge are served by **Dublin Bus**—route 67 runs three times hourly Monday to Saturday and twice hourly on Sundays in both directions (€6.80). It takes approximately 80 minutes to get from Pearse St. (Dublin) to Maynooth. **Bus Éireann** (www.buseireann.ie) also operate a number of routes to Kildare (€9.30 one-way, €12 round-trip).

M7 Taxis (☎ 045/875270), based in Naas, are a good option for travel within the county, while **Top Mark Cabs** (Main St., Leixlip; ☎ 01/624-7500), based in Leixlip are well situated for access to the capital, close to the M50 and access to Dublin airport. Meanwhile, **Xpert Digi Taxis** (☎ 01/628-1777;

King of the Castle(town)

The town of Celbridge's main claim to fame is as the site of Castletown House, one of the country's great 18th-century Palladian mansions. Gracing the entrance to the Castletown Estate, at the end of the tree-lined avenue leading to the House, are excellent rental opportunities—two of the three gate lodges that were also built in the 1700s, and have been elegantly restored by the **Irish Landmark Trust** (Reservations: 25 Eustace St., Temple Bar, Dublin 2; ☎ 01/670-4733; www.irishlandmark.com). The properties, the **Gate House** ✹✹✹ and the **Round House** ✹✹✹, feature period furniture, attractive pastel color schemes, and modern conveniences (dishwasher, washing machine, microwave, radio—but no TV), while bedrooms have stripped pine floors, rugs, lots of dark wood, and just enough antique detailing to suggest the influence of a proper designer. Soothing white linens and quality mattresses emphasize comfort. The smaller of the two, the Gate House (€581–€686 per week), sleeps three people in two bedrooms. Sleeping six people in three bedrooms, The Round House (€847–€1,106 per week) is a bit more architecturally quirky (as the name suggests), with unusually shaped rooms, but loads of space. Wake up here and you may just have to pinch yourself to check that you haven't traveled back in time. No need to fear—indoor plumbing has long been installed!

http://xperttaxis.com) recently opened an office in West Dublin covering the Leixlip and Celbridge areas—unlike many other firms, the company also allows booking of taxis over the Internet (subject to availability).

WHERE TO STAY & DINE
Maynooth

As home to the oldest college campus in Ireland, the north Kildare settlement of Maynooth has all the telltale signs of a university town—plenty of low-cost sandwich and bagel joints, and pubs. It's also where you can find campus accommodation, surprisingly available most of the year.

€–€€ **Maynooth Campus** ✹✹✹ (Kilcock Rd., Maynooth town; ☎ 01/708-6402; http://maynoothcampus.com; AE, MC, V) has seven options for accommodations, most available year round (except for short periods around Christmas and Easter), with the most basic room rates starting at just €47 for two people sharing, or €58 for two single rooms. These rooms, originally designed for use by seminarians attending the college, are as spartan as you would expect and do not have private bathrooms. However, a limited number of more comfortable rooms with private facilities are available in the south campus (rates starting at €72 double), and there are even a couple of darn luxurious suites in grand old Georgian buildings. A sense of history hits as you walk through the college gates to the cloisters lined with portraits of distinguished clergy—such subtle, clever faces. The south campus, where the seminary is located, is all Neo-Gothic buildings dating from the mid-1800s, while Pugin Hall, where guests take breakfast (toast, croissants, jam for €7.40 extra) is a dead ringer for the dining hall Hogwarts in the Harry Potter movies. Be aware that many of the students are studying for the priesthood, so respect and quiet is expected.

€–€€€   Catering perhaps less to students (unless they're looking for a romantic night out) is **Avenue Café** ✸✸ (Main St., Maynooth; ☎ 01/628-5003; Mon–Sat noon–10pm; MC, V), a pleasant surprise among all the fast food joints in town. It's a smooth, contemporary-looking place, an oasis of calm and good service. Although the menu offers plenty to scratch your head over—from paninis and wraps (€6.50–€7.50), to salads (try goat cheese and baby spinach with beetroot and orange salsa; €8.50), and burgers (made with pure Irish beef; €12–€15)—best usually are the chalked-up specials. Particularly when these include the classic beef and Guinness pie served with french fries (€15). There are a few pricier main dishes over €15, but you'll have no need to even glance at them—the cheaper dishes are just as good.

Kildare Town

While it is practically choking with history and heritage, up until very recently Kildare Town was better known for its traffic—a famous bottleneck on the way from Dublin to the southwest. Now that the N7 bypasses the town, it's generally quieter than other towns in the county, but still has a good range of cafes. We don't recommend staying in Kildare town—there are better lodgings values elsewhere—but it's a sure bet if you're looking for a good meal.

€   **Cafe Lutetia** (Main St., Naas; ☎ 045/520905; daily 8:30am–11pm; cash only) serves a range of no-nonsense breakfast, lunch, and dinner items. We'll give it an honorable mention for its veggie selection, particularly its Mediterranean Melt—peppers, courgette, aubergine, feta cheese, and pesto for €7.50. A whopping Irish breakfast (eggs, beans, sautéed mushrooms, hash browns, grilled tomato, and toast) goes for just for just €6.

€€-€€€   If you can ignore the off-putting name, the chef's special at the usually busy and buzzing **Ristorante Colosseus** (Main St.; ☎ 045/520570; daily 5–10pm; MC, V), is a good deal—three courses for €25. Risotto is the house specialty, either with mushrooms, shallots, and chicken or mixed seafood, shallots, and fresh tomatoes (both €20). The restaurant has a decent antipasti selection as well, ranging from a well-priced Mediterranean salad (€8.50) to the house special Antipasto Colosseus—king prawns, grilled tomatoes, and aubergines, topped with parmesan cheese.

Newbridge

To tap into the growing Irish obsession with local, seasonal produce, pop by **Newbridge Farmers Market** (beside the Courtyard Shopping Centre; Sat 9am–2pm). Excellent organic produce from all over the country is on offer, as well as a range of delicious jams, chutneys, and juices.

Kildare's Silky Smooth One-Stop Pub

Named after the Irish rebel—"Silken Thomas" FitzGerald—who stood up to Henry VIII in 1534, the **Silken Thomas** ★ (The Square, Kildare; ☎ 045/522232; www.silkenthomas.com; MC, V; daily 8am–11pm) is an all-encompassing type of place, with enough *va-va-voom* and edible sustenance to do justice to the memory of the upstart rebel. It truly is a one-stop shop: There's a full-blown restaurant, **Chapter 16,** a bar-style dining venue, **Flanagan's Lounge,** two pubs—**Squires** and **Lil Flanagan's** (aka **Lil's**)— and even a nightclub, **Tigerlily** (☎ 045/521389; Fri–Sun 11pm–late; cover €8–€12; VIP tickets €15–€20).

Even if you find the whole entertainment complex idea a bit forced and "diddly-aye," it's certainly a worthy stop for a meal. Chapter 16 mixes European, Mexican, and Asian styles for solid house specials such as the Chapter 16 Caesar salad (€13, €17 with Cajun chicken), Silken smoky chicken on a bed of penne pasta (€15), or the shareable Chapter 16 Grill Platter—sausage, bacon, eggs, mushrooms, grilled tomato, lamb cutlet, or minute steak, and Clonakilty pudding (€19). It's basic, but acceptable fare—and you're guaranteed not to go hungry.

Lil's is all about steaks and burgers—including a variety of gourmet burgers, such as a whopper of a chili burger laden with Mexican spicy beef (€12), and the Lord Edward, topped with blue cheese and sun-dried tomatoes (it's our favorite; €12). What the room lacks in authenticity, it makes up for in enthusiasm, and the location alongside a 13th-century Norman castle, is intriguing.

And, if all the wining, dining, and hip-swinging have been a bit too much (and it's all-too-easy to fall victim to the good vibes here), you can simply swing on round the back for a comfortable night's sleep at the Silken's own built-in B&B, the **Lord Edward Guest House** (☎ 045/522389), which occupies a "reinvented" 18th-century building (though, it must be said that little that is original remains). It offers 18 well-priced, relatively comfortable rooms (€55–€65 double; €45 single); after a punishing night on the dance floor (if that's your thing), you can look forward to tucking yourself up in a clean, cozy, fuss-free room with crisp white linens and a decent mattress. Rooms are equipped with all the usual amenities, but breakfast, although available, is not included in the rate.

€€–€€€   Slap bang in the center of the county, and just down the road from Newbridge, the **Hanged Man's Pub and Restaurant** (follow R418 out of Newbridge, or R416 out of Kildare; ☎ 045/431515; www.hangedmans.ie; daily 5–11pm; Sun noon–10pm; MC, V) is a great place to spend an evening, with a stone fireplace and lit candles providing a snug respite, particularly if high winds are raging outside. The early bird menu (Mon–Thurs 5–6.30pm) offers two courses for €25. Owner Patrick Keane is particularly proud of his steaks, and rightly so.

€€€   Pascal Moreau's **L'Olivier** (Limerick Lane; ☎ 045/436893; Tues–Sun 1:30–10pm; MC, V), unrelated to the San Francisco restaurant of the same name, is just off Newbridge's main thoroughfare, and in the words of the man himself, offers "real French food, that French people eat; not some kind of snobbish, so-called 'cuisine'." You have to admire his honesty. The menu is indeed packed with a wide selection of lesser-known, traditional French dishes such as the *salade landaise* (€7.95), veal saltimbocca (€23), or beef *bernaise* (€25). Italian dishes are similarly well priced, with pizzas and pasta dishes generally around €9.50 to €11. Lunch is just €9, while an early bird menu (Tues–Fri to 7:30pm) offers three courses for €15.

Athy

Located right where the Grand Canal meets the River Barrow, Athy—often over-looked by visitors—has been a busy market town for centuries, and all that history shows; it's everywhere, including in the choice of guesthouses.

€–€€   **Moate Lodge** ★★ (Off Dublin Rd., 6km/4 miles from Athy; ☎ 059/862-6137; www.moatelodge.com; MC, V) is a solid, comforting 18th-century Georgian farmhouse full of original features. Bedrooms are done up in a charm-ing jumble of mismatched but good old furniture, family portraits, old books, and pretty fabrics. Moate is a working farm, so expect to catch glimpses of cows going about their business, or hear the cluck of hens in passing; but that only adds to the drowsy serenity. Rates start at just €65 for a double room, with a €10 reduc-tion for guests staying 3 nights or more. Breakfast is included, but it's dinner (€25, book before noon) that really showcases host Mary Pelin's cooking ability—I'm a particular fan of her desserts; excellent, hearty pies and crumbles made with fruit from the garden. Husband Raymond is an expert on both World War II and Munster's rugby team—and historical discussions on both can last long into the night. There is a good rental opportunity here also; four pretty converted cottages grouped around a restored 18th-century cobbled courtyard. They look very olde worlde, but the magic wand of modernity has transformed the interiors, with spa-cious, functional kitchens and bathrooms. All cottages sleep four, in one double and one twin room, and one of them is purposely wheelchair friendly. High

---

Home on the Range

The pace of life in Ireland today is too darn fast sometimes. Thank heavens for firms like **Kilvahan Horse-Drawn Caravans** (Tullibards Stud, 5km/3 miles from Coolrain in neighboring Laois; ☎ 057/873-5178; www.horsedrawn caravans.com), which offer visitors the chance to step outside the everyday bustle and take in the countryside the way it used to be enjoyed—via horse and cart. Such serenity has a price tag, of course, with caravan rentals start-ing at €600 per week. Each caravan sleeps four people. For more info on how these caravans operate, see p. 316.

season rates are €300 per week, though this can be haggled down "a fair bit" off peak, and the location is perfect for day trips to Kilkenny and Wicklow as well as Kildare. The only snag: They tend to get snapped up pretty fast.

€–€€ In Athy, things don't really get more "local" and relaxed than at **Bradbury's Bakery** 🧒 (Main St.; ☎ 059/863-1845; www.bradburys.ie; Mon–Sat 8am–6pm; Sun 9am–5pm; MC, V), which has been going (quite strong, we'd say) for at least 80 years. It's not, as advertised, a restaurant, but rather a cafeteria-style hang-out. Things are pretty straight down the line here. For big eaters, the lunch plate of the day usually satisfies (€7.90–€9.95; served from noon daily). Otherwise, go for a filled panini (€4.95) or baguette (€4.20)—you can choose whatever ingredients your heart desires and your sandwich will be stuffed full to overflowing (no one leaves this place hungry—ever!). If it's a fine day, sit in the small outdoor garden.

€€ Also in Athy, **Ballindrum Farm** ✖ (turn left at Ardscull from Athy; ☎ 059/862-6294; www.ballindrumfarm.com; MC, V) is another shining example of the burgeoning agri-tourism industry in Ireland; as a working dairy and tillage farm that has won a host of national awards—guests are encouraged to reconnect with nature by watching a milking, or touring the farmyard, though 5am wakeup calls are mercifully optional. Though newer and less grand than Moate Lodge (p. 102), there is a warm and generous welcome at Vincent and Mary Gorman's five-bedroom guesthouse, with rates starting at €70 double, and 1-week's accommodation on offer for €420. The rooms are cozy and very peaceful. From the second you sit down to homemade scones and jam upon arrival, to the time you leave, the Gorman family will treat you like long-lost friends in this picture postcard setting. There's also a wheelchair-friendly cottage for rent.

€€€ The recently opened **Carlton Abbey Hotel** (Monasterevin Rd.; ☎ 059/863-0100; www.carltonabbeyhotel.com; MC, V) is in the town center. Located in a former Sisters of Mercy Convent, the design of the hotel has stayed faithful to many of the old features—the hotel bar is located in what was once the convent chapel—even though the general air is far more modern than monastic. A new pool, leisure center, and spa are good for chilling out. Rooms and bathrooms are big and appealingly uncluttered, and prices are all over the map. Off season an Internet special may bag you one for €59 a night if you're very lucky, though you're more likely to pay between €90 and €140.

WHY YOU'RE HERE: TOP SIGHTS & ATTRACTIONS

Kildare's horsey heritage is well represented at the **Irish National Stud** (Tully Estate, off R415 near Kildare Town; ☎ 045/521617; www.irish-national-stud.ie; €10.50; Feb–Dec daily 9:30am–6pm), which also, and conveniently, includes another popular attraction, the **Japanese Gardens,** within its 405-hectare (1,000 acre) estate. This working stud farm is a hugely popular draw—some of Ireland's most famous thoroughbreds, such as Tulyar and Royal Charger, started their careers here—and a visit includes the opportunity to meet the next generation of mares and foals along the Tully Walk. Two years ago, the Stud opened the National Horse Museum, a state-of-the-art facility charting Ireland's contribution to the "sport of kings." The **Japanese Gardens,** accessed through the Stud, were designed at the start of the 20th century by Lord Wavertree to symbolize the "Life of Man." A monument to the bonds forged between Eastern and Western cultures, these gardens are among the finest of their kind in Europe. To mark the start of the 21st century, the Irish National Stud created a **commemorative garden to St. Fiachra,** Patron Saint of Gardeners, which references the ruggedness of the Irish landscape along themes of rock and water. Best of all, admission charge gives access to all four of the attractions, meaning you can make a long afternoon of it.

The horsey set have always liked the finer things in life, so it's unsurprising that Kildare fairly bristles with magnificent country houses. Some, like **Carton House** (5 min. from N4 "Leixlip West" exit; ☎ 01/505-2000; www.cartonhouse.com) have been converted into hotels; others, like that at **Castletown Estate** ★ (take the Celbridge West/Leixlip West exit off the M4, then first left, then right at the Castletown gate; ☎ 01/628-8252; www.castletown.ie; €4.50; Easter–Sept Mon–Fri 10am–6pm; Sat–Sun 1–6pm; Oct Mon–Fri 10am–5pm; Sun 1–5pm; Nov Sun 1–5pm) are a fantastic relic of the gentrification of rural Ireland during the 17th and 18th centuries. Castletown was built in 1722 for the then speaker of the Irish House of Commons, William Connolly, with several noted architects of the time employed, such as Alessandro Galilei, Sir William Chambers, and Sir Edward Lovett Pearce.

Few explorers knew the Polar regions like Sir Ernest Shackleton, and the Kilkea-born adventurer and national hero is recognized at **Athy Heritage Centre** ★ (Town Hall, Emily Sq., Athy; ☎ 059/863-3075; www.athyheritagecentremuseum.ie; €3; Mon–Fri 10am–5pm), where a permanent exhibit commemorates his daring Antarctic expeditions of the early 20th century. The exhibit features an original sledge and harness from his Antarctic expeditions, a 5-m (15-ft.) model of his ship, *Endurance,* unique Shackleton family photographs, and an audiovisual presentation showing footage of the expeditions. The Centre also houses a World War I exhibit and a nostalgic look back at the Gordon Bennett car races, which ran through the county, but really, Shackleton's story is why you're here.

In nearby Laois County

As Queen's County, Laois was probably the most settled of all Irish counties during the plantation years, and while the English and Scottish settlers have long since gone home, the legacy of the former British aristocracy lives on in country estates like **Emo Court** ★★ (7km/4 miles from Portarlington train station, off N7; ☎ 057/862-6573; €2.90; Easter–Oct 10am–6pm). A magnificent example of the neo-classical style of architecture, the house at Emo Court was designed for the Earls of Portarlington by James Gandon, who is better known as the architect of the Customs House and Kings Inns in Dublin. Dating from 1790, the house is fronted by formal lawns, a lake, and a woodland that contains many Giant Sequoias, one of few places in Ireland the species is found. The gardens are divided into two areas: the Clucker, featuring a bright array of azaleas, rhododendrons, and other shrubs; and the Grapery, an arboretum with many twisty, winding pathways. A gem of the past, still standing proud today.

Similarly impressive gardens are found at **Heywood Gardens** ★ (7km/4⅓ miles southeast of Abbeyleix, off R432; ☎ 057/873-3563; free admission; daily

8:30am–7pm) in the south of the county, which were completed in 1912 and designed by the renowned architect Edwin Luytens, better known for designing the Cenotaph in London and the official residence of the British viceroy in New Delhi. Circular terraces in the sunken garden descend to a central pool, flanked by inquisitive statues of turtles gazing at the grand fountain, while kingfishers and moorhens keep guard over the manmade lake at the center of the property.

Finally, for nature lovers, Laois's most prominent feature is the steeply rising **Slieve Bloom Mountains,** which cover an area of 1,553 sq. km (600 sq. miles) and cast a formidable impression over the region, despite rising no more than 610m (2,001 ft.) at their peak. Views, nonetheless, are not to be sneered at, and the terrain is a rich mixture of vast bogland (it's the country's largest blanket bog), forest, and glens formed by water dripping steadily down from the bogs. The **Slieve Bloom Way** covers a circular route of around 32km (20 miles) and is rightly the most famous walk in the county (and the perfect way to explore the mountain scenery here). You can obtain the *Slieve Bloom Way Walking Guide* from the **Portlaoise tourist office** (County Hall, Portlaoise) for €5; and you can also navigate to **www.slievebloom.ie** for exacting details on all possible routes.

Getting There: For a headache free vacation, rent a car. Apart from that, **Bus Éireann**'s (www.buseireann.ie) no. 124 bus (Dublin to Mountmellick, €9.90 one-way, €14 round-trip) runs through Ballybrittas, Portlaoise, and Mountmellick, but this only operates once daily in both directions at 6:40am from Mountmellick and at 5:30pm from Dublin. **Irish Rail** (www.irishrail.ie) operates an Intercity route from Dublin Heuston to Portarlington (€17) and Portlaoise (€20) every 2 hours, but it's difficult to get from those areas to the sights you'll want to see (though you could take a taxi; try **Carroll's Xpress Taxis** ☎ 057/866-5000 or **Ace Taxis** ☎ 057/868-0080).

ACTIVE KILDARE

If you're lucky, your time in Kildare will correspond with a race at either Curragh or Punchestown. Whatever your level of knowledge about the racing business— does anyone really know how to read a form?—a day at the races is not to be missed. The **Curragh** ✪✪ (take junction 12 off M7, between Newbridge and Kildare Town; ☎ 045/441205; www.curragh.ie) is universally known as the home of flat racing in Ireland; the area has been used for equine activities for centuries, and even the word "Curragh" means "place of the running horse." From March

Extra Savings

Ireland's national tourist board, Fáilte Ireland, have released a free pocket-size guide to Ireland's East Coast that includes eight pages of two-for-one and discount vouchers for most of the attractions featured in this guidebook, as well as myriad other attractions in Louth, Meath, Wicklow, Kildare, Laois, Offaly, Westmeath, and Longford. Visit **www.eastcoastmidlands.ie** for details of how to get hold of it.

to October every year, the calendar is packed with classic race meetings including the 1000 and 2000 Guineas, the Irish Oaks, the Irish St. Leger, and of course, the Irish Derby, which takes place at the end of June or start of July. The 5-day Punchestown Festival, at **Punchestown Racecourse** ✪✪ (take R140 off N7, near Naas; ☎ 045/897704; www.punchestown.ie), at the end of April, is one of the unmissable events on the racing calendar, full of glamor and action. Events take place right through the winter, while during the summer, the racecourse is often used to host music events.

If you fancy getting closer to the game, Kildare is also home to several equestrian centers, with **Abbeyfield Equestrian and Outdoor Activity Centre** (4km/2½ miles from Barberstown Castle, Richardstown, near Clane; ☎ 045/868188; www.abbeyfieldfarm.com) chief among these—set over 81 hectares (200 acres) of Kildare countryside, over 40 horses are available for riders of all levels of experience. You'll pay €40 per hour to ride.

As the home of the 2006 Ryder Cup, Kildare's **K Club** (Straffan; ☎ 01/601-7200; www.kclub.ie) golf course attracts would-be Tiger Woods from all over the world—don't expect the experience to be a cheap one, however, with green fees on the Arnold Palmer–designed course ranging from €105 to €225. Far better value is **Kilkea Castle** (take a right turn in Castledermot for Athy, continue 3km/2 miles to Kilkea village; ☎ 059/914-5555; www.kilkeacastlegolfresort.ie) golf club, featuring views of the 12th-century castle grounds, the River Griese and two large lakes. Green fees are €40 Monday to Thursday and €50 Friday to Sunday. Cheaper still is **Newbridge Golf Club** (Barretstown, 2km/1 mile from Newbridge town; ☎ 045/486110; www.newbridgegolfclub.com), a challenging course set around the brooding Hill of Allen. Green fees start at €25 midweek and €30 at weekends. Lastly, those interested in the history of the area should check out the **South Kildare Heritage Trail,** (see www.kildare.ie/SouthKildare HeritageTrail for route), a winding route through some of the county's most notable heritage sites.

THE OTHER KILDARE

Kildare has a strong following among artists, drawn to paint its ever-changing scenery. Many head straight for **Kilkea Lodge Farm** ✪ (Kilkea; ☎ 059/914-5112; www.kilkealodgefarm.com) and the regular art classes offered by watercolor guru Charles Evans, who has a devoted following. Evans teaches everyone from beginners to semi-pros, encouraging them along the next step of their artistic journey. However, even in Evans's absence, you'll find plenty of talented, dedicated teachers here who share your passion for painting and are eager to pass on their knowledge. Kilkea Lodge Farm is a pretty little farmhouse—quirky, even slightly eccentric bedroom furnishings, with knitted patchwork quilts, and brightly colored wall hangings—at a fairly reasonable price. B&B rates start at €45 per person per night, and hostess Marion Greene is a most charming landlady—her family has lived in the house since 1740, and she is quietly opinionated on everything worth seeing or doing in the area. In general this is a restful spot—you'll be more likely to be woken by the bark of a fox at night than rowdy fellow guests—but Marion has, on occasion, hosted a series of music appreciation weekends . . . where everybody is expected to sing.

Ireland's great cultural associations often obscure the fact that the country also has a rich natural heritage, including its own unique wildlife. Some bright sparks at the **Kildare Heritage Office** have been working to make people more aware of the county's biodiversity. For the last 2 years, they've been running a series of **workshops** dealing with different aspects of Irish Wildlife. Workshops take place primarily in the summer (late-May through Oct) and have in the past covered such topics as "Identifying Wild Plants," "Bats," "How to Read a Map," and "The National Bird Atlas." Each session is presented by a different expert, many of whom work for national agencies such as BirdWatch Ireland, Bat Conservation Ireland, or the Ancient Tree Forum. While the session may start with a brief introductory talk, they quickly move outdoors where there's plenty of hands-on learning (you'll need waterproof footwear) that might include taking part in a survey of plants or animals, for example, as well as a good deal of interaction with the tutors. To find out about this year's program of events, contact **Bridget Loughlin** (Kildare Co. Council; ☎ 045/980791; heritageofficer@kildarecoco.ie), or visit www.kildare.ie, Workshops are free, and happen on Saturday mornings (usually 10am–1pm); venues vary.

An associated organization, the **Irish Peatland Conservation Council** (IPCC; Bog of Allen Nature Centre, Lullymore, Rathangan, Co. Kildare; ☎ 045/860133; www.ipcc.ie) was established in 1982 to campaign for the conservation of a representative sample of living intact Irish bogs and peatlands. The IPCC holds a rather more extensive program of workshops, seminars, and all kinds of events (including hosting celebrations on International Bog Day in July) throughout the year, focusing on different aspects of wildlife and bogland conservation. They, too, welcome anyone who wishes to attend, and most of what's on offer is free or involves a small fee to offset costs. Again, these are not regular happenings, so you need to check their website for upcoming activities, and then confirm that you'll be attending by calling or sending an e-mail.

The IPCC also has a busy contingent of **volunteers** and plenty of opportunities at the Bog of Allen Nature Centre to learn through doing. Volunteers are heartily welcomed and have the chance to get some first hand experience in peatland conservation. Hands-on volunteer work includes helping at the garden centers, where you'll be taught to weed and mulch plant beds, help with planting, construction of pathways, survey bird and other wildlife, and even water carnivorous plants. Or you could possibly end up assisting a conservationist on surface topography studies of drains, identifying where dams need to be inserted, and then helping to insert the dams and remove invasive plant species. Full training is always given. To volunteer, contact Catherine O'Connell (info@ipcc.ie).

ATTENTION, SHOPPERS!

As economic reality bites, the world of outlet shopping is becoming increasingly attractive in Ireland. Probably the best designer outlet in the country is **Kildare Village** ★★ (Nurney Rd., Co. Kildare, just off exit 13 of the M7; www.kildare village.com), where labels like Karen Millen, LK Bennett, Bally, Thomas Pink, Molton Brown cosmetics, homewares by Armani Casa, Le Creuset pots, and Kenneth Turner home fragrances come at a ferocious discount. Kildare Village is laid out just like a regular shopping center, only everything is at a knock-down price, sometimes as low as 70%.

Naas is a decent little shopping hot-spot, with **Kalu Emporium** (23 North Main St., Naas; ☎ 045/896222) topping the charts in terms of designer gear. However, unless it's sale time, or you want to browse the fabulous Lainey Keogh dresses for fun, there probably isn't much point. Far more accessible is **Prouts** (18 North Main St., Naas; ☎ 045/89732), one of those traditional, anything goes country shops. A family-run business for generations now, it has wool and linen as well as children's clothes, womenswear, and a very good selection of jewelry.

NIGHTLIFE

The county is well served by pubs and **Thomas Fletcher's** ★ (Main St., Naas, beside Superquinn; ☎ 045/897328) is one of the county's hidden gems; an atmospheric place that hasn't changed much since it first opened in the 1800s. It's like walking into a museum—sturdy rustic furniture, stained glass panels, and a beautiful long mahogany bar. **Coffey's** (Main St., Newbridge; ☎ 045/431316) in Newbridge is another find, a pub on two floors with a wisecracking staff and a younger crowd on the weekend; it's the social hub of Newbridge town. And the **Bridgewater Inn** (Kildare; ☎ 045/880682; www.bridgewater.ie), on the banks of the Grand Canal in Sallins, has one of the prettiest settings of any pub in the country, and is easily reachable (1km/less than 1 mile from the M7 motorway). It's a new build, and so lacks some of the atmosphere of other pubs, but is well worth a pit stop on the motorway.

Lastly, **Time Nightclub** (Devoy Quarter, Naas; ☎ 045/881222; www.time venue.com) is where Kildare's bright young things come to party, and while the venue is certainly spectacular, with nine bars spread out over four floors, be warned that it can get very crowded.

MEATH

County Meath seems to have a starring role in every era of Irish history, from the 5,000-year-old monuments at **Newgrange** and **Knowth,** through to the monastic heritage that produced the Book of Kells and on to the Battle of the Boyne in the 17th century. Known as the Royal County—the High Kings of Ireland used to sit at Tara in the center of the county—Meath is a vibrant, busy place. Meath has just 12km (7 miles) of coastline, but the resorts of Laytown and Bettystown are popular with families—particularly those with small children—during the summer. Meath also has the only surviving Gaeltacht areas in the province of Leinster, Ráth Cairn, and Báile Ghib.

A BRIEF HISTORY OF COUNTY MEATH

Where do we start? The 5,000-year-old monuments in Newgrange, Knowth, and Dowth (p. 113) represent the beginnings of a rich and varied local history, and are linked inexorably with the feudal history of the whole country. The High Kings of Ireland ruled from the Hill of Tara, also the site of one of the key druidic religious centers in the country. During the 5th century, legend has it that St. Patrick was summoned to appear before the king after he dared light a flame on the neighboring Hill of Slane before the druids lit their ceremonial fire at Tara. His meeting served a crucial purpose in Irish history; it was Patrick who managed to convert the king, and thus the whole of Ireland, to Christianity. Recently, Tara has been the subject of controversy, as conservationists and authorities have clashed over the proposed routing of a major motorway close to the fabled site.

The Boyne river, which flows through, forms the backdrop for most of the county's history; from **King John's Castle** (p. 115) at Trim, dating from the 13th century, the ruins of the 12th century **Bective Abbey**, and on down to the UNESCO World Heritage Site at **Newgrange** (p. 113). Much of the Battle of the Boyne, fought in 1690 between Jacobite (Catholic) and Williamite (Protestant) forces seeking to gain control of the British crown, took place along the river, while the Irish rebellion of 1798 also shaped Meath history, with monuments to Irish rebels seen at Summerhill, Dunshaughlin, and Curraha.

More recently, Meath has become known for its farmland, with two major meat processing plants at Clonee and Navan, and a flourishing potato industry— the county produces more potatoes than any other. Navan was also the center of the Irish furniture industry until very recently, when rising prices drove manufacturers overseas. The largest zinc producing mine in Europe, Tara Mines, is located close to Navan, although that's not something you're likely to want to see.

LAY OF THE LAND

Just like Wicklow, the south serves as part of Dublin's commuter belt and so is often very clogged up at commuter rush times. Meath is served by four major roads out of Dublin. The **N3** (Dublin to Cavan) is the main road through the county, going through the towns of Dunshaughlin, Navan, and Kells. Controversial plans are underway to turn this road into a motorway in certain areas. The **M4** motorway passes through Meath at its southernmost tip, serving the town of Enfield, while the **M1** (Dublin to Belfast) again only passes through a small part of the county, near Laytown and Bettystown on the east coast. The **N2** (Dublin to Monaghan) road passes through the county as well, bypassing Ashbourne and passing through Slane.

GETTING THERE & GETTING AROUND

As part of Meath falls into Dublin's commuter belt, the county is well serviced by buses, with **Bus Éireann** operating regular routes to the four corners of the county. Buses are a better option than rail in this neck of Ireland as only the coastal towns of Laytown (€5.40 one-way, €9 round-trip) and Bettystown get frequent commuter service (while the busses go to literally every town in the county, often on an hourly basis). Enfield is on the main Dublin to Sligo route out of Dublin's Connolly Station, and while a train link to Drogheda is in place in Navan, at the moment it is only reserved for traffic coming from the Tara Mines site.

Grab A Cab (☎ 046/903-0400) operate a large fleet of taxis out of Navan, as do **Town Radio Taxis** (24 Flower Hill; ☎ 046/907-8999), which recently updated its fleet.

WHERE TO STAY & DINE

Near Newgrange

€–€€   There are more than a handful of accommodation options lining the road that leads to the **Newgrange Visitor Centre**—it's a busy spot where many tourists stand in queues for hours each day, or find themselves being turned away because the daily quota for shuttle buses to the country's most popular Celtic heritage site has been reached. A good idea is to spend the night at **Newgrange Lodge** ✪✪ (follow signs from Donore; ☎ 041/988-2478; www.newgrangelodge.com; MC, V), where staff will book your place on the first tour of the following morning. After breakfast, you can simply walk the 200m (656 ft.) to the Visitor Centre and jump the queue. And the Lodge caters to a wide variety of travelers offering dorms as well as private rooms, all with private bathrooms. Formerly an old farmhouse, the 27-room guesthouse has been almost totally remodeled, although atmospheric use is made of the old brick walls. Communal areas have a vaguely Casbah-feel to them, with long, low leather sofas and heaps of velvet cushions; bedrooms are a mixed bag, but all extremely pleasant, impeccably clean, and come with private bathrooms and beds that position you on the luxurious side of "good-value." The staff is incredibly helpful and you can get access to the communal kitchen if you'd like to prepare a simple meal. But in truth, we love the fact that you're allowed to bring your own drinks—and the terrace is a lovely place from which to enjoy the sunset with a glass of wine. Rates for a double room go from €60 to €70, family rooms from €90 to €110 depending on the time of year. If you're really stretched, three dormitories have rates starting at €18 a night (for a bed in a 10-bedded unit, with bathroom attached). A simple continental breakfast is included in the tariff.

€–€€€€   The estate village of Slane is just 10km (6 miles) from Newgrange, and is where famous Slane Castle has hosted some killer concerts over the years. It's also where you'll find our favorite Meath dining establishment: the **Old Post Office** ✿✿✿ (Main St.; ☎ 041/982-4090; www.theoldpostoffice.ie; Mon–Sat 9am–4:30pm; Sun 10am–6pm; Tues–Sat 6:30–9:30pm; MC, V). Owned by a Turkish-Irish couple, Levent and Olivia Güneyer, this bright, modern little bistro attracts all kinds of people—to its credit, it's usually busier outside the tourist season, showing how loved it is by locals. We're mad about their warm Roquefort salad (€9.50), which makes a wonderful accompaniment (shared, if you like) to a bowl of fresh spaghetti with a putanesca sauce (€14) or the vegetarian gnocchi Parisienne (in Mornay sauce, gratinee, with Gruyere cheese; €14). Seafood is top-notch, too, sourced from a fishmonger at nearby Clare Head. If you time your visit well—coming here after a morning tour of Newgrange and Nowth—you'll be able to avail of the excellent-value menu at lunchtime (all mains €5.95–€12). And, after hours of feasting and chatting to amiable Levent, you can happily stroll outside to partake of the *craic* at either of the two good pubs across the road.

You could also spend the night in one of the rooms right upstairs from the restaurant. The **Old Post Office B&B** ✿ has chic little doubles at €80 per night (and triples for €100). Although compact, each of the five rooms has a fresh, contemporary look, done out in earthy tones, with firm mattresses, good little showers, an armchair to lounge in, and plenty of wardrobe space. The great bonus here—which you'll find in very few B&Bs anywhere—is that you can happily order room service, choosing from anything on the bistro menu (including breakfast, served in the downstairs restaurant when it opens in the morning).

Kells

Although Kells itself is hardly a hot tip for a holiday, it is a convenient spot to base yourself if you have a couple of days visiting planned in Meath.

€   The cheapest place for a base is **Kells Holiday Hostel** (Carrick St.; ☎ 046/ 924-9995; www.kellshostel.com; AE, MC, V), which is perfectly clean and functional if nothing to write home about. A room with private bathroom costs €20 to €24 per person here, though a third consecutive night will cost you half that. Dorm beds come in at just €18 (by contrast, when we stayed at the beautifully located but rather disheveled hostel in nearby Trim, we paid €25 for a dorm bed). Located just beside the main Kells bus stop—35 buses run daily between Kells and Dublin—it's also a great stop off point on the way to Newgrange, 30km (20 miles) away.

€   **Smiley Bites** (Newmarket St.; ☎ 046/929-3060; daily 7am–9pm; cash only) isn't a looker, with plastic chairs and retro (in a bad way) upholstery, but it does some fairly interesting, reasonably priced local and Indian cuisine. All mains are €9.50 (except for the special Biriyani—chicken, lamb, or prawns cooked with a mix of spices, coriander, and an omelette, €11), and for breakfast you can bag a full-Irish for €7.50.

€€€   There's little difference between the menu at the **Ground Floor** kids (Bective Sq.; ☎ 046/924-9688; daily 5:30–10:30pm; MC, V) and its sister restaurants in Navan (The Loft) and Cavan (The Side Door), but the buzzy atmosphere of this family-friendly restaurant makes it a great place to spend a lazy afternoon listening in on local gossip. Head chef Carl Rennicks and manager Patrick Stapleton oversee a simple but effective menu: lightly fried brie (€8), and crab and buffalo mozzarella (€8.50) to start; teriyaki beef (€21) and roast vegetable calzonette (€17) to follow. Keep an eye out for the daily specials.

Navan

Although it lacks charm, Navan is big and busy enough to have a couple of decent dining and lodgings options.

€€   Tops among the places to pillow your head is Hilda Vance's spacious, stand-alone guesthouse just off the Dublin Road. The **Yellow House** (Springfield Glen, off Dublin Rd.; ☎ 046/907-3338; www.theyellowhouse.ie; MC, V) is a large, modern property, within 2 minutes' walk of the main bus route to Dublin, and the regular 109a bus to the airport. Hilda managed the Durhamstown Castle equestrian center outside Navan for 18 years before opening this guesthouse in 1996, and is a mine of information about local horse riding activities—she'll even drop you off if she has time. Rates are €40 per person, including a wide-ranging, mostly organic breakfast.

€–€€€   If you have children in tow, the **Loft** kids (26 Trimgate St.; ☎ 046/907-1755; daily 5:30–10pm; MC, V), sister spot to the Ground Floor in Kells (see above), is a good place for eats (it's loud enough that no one will be bothered by a crying baby and with a broad enough menu to service even picky eaters). Bright daubs by Northern Ireland artist Terry Bradly light up the walls, daily specials are jotted on the blackboards, and staff is buzzed up and friendly. Mains range from about €16 to €25, with the daily pasta special around €18. Otherwise, try the **Russell** (Ludlow St.; ☎ 046/903-1607; Tues–Thurs and Sat 6–10pm; Fri and Sun 5–9pm; MC, V), a reasonably stylish restaurant with cute waiters and airy, ambient house music wafting from the speakers. The menu sticks pretty close to the old tried and trusted bistro formula—steak, burgers, grills, but the set menu

(Tues–Fri 6–7:30pm and Sat 6–7pm) will get you two courses for €25 and three for €30. Our tip? Start with the crispy potato skins or deep-fried Camembert, follow with chicken teriyaki or the Russell gourmet burger, finish with a decent slice of Bailey's cheesecake, and you will be perfectly happy.

In & Around Trim

A short drive from Trim will bring you to a cluster of large holiday bungalows, well-hidden from the main road. On a sprawling 14-hectare (35-acre) property, **Beechwood Lodge Holiday Homes** ✩✩✩ (kids) (Readstown, Trim; ☎ 046/943-6926 or 046/943-8743; www.beechwood-lodge.com; MC, V), offers some of the best rental accommodation in the county. Covered with trees, lush gardens, tennis courts, a children's play area, and even its own archaeological "henge" site (basically, "like Stonehenge, but without the stones!"), this is an ideal vacation stop, professionally managed and lovingly tended by the family owners. Accommodations in the three free-standing, self-catering bungalows are light-filled, superbly spacious, and come with such niceties as underfloor heating and great big open-plan living areas. Each has three sizeable bedrooms sleeping six or even seven people who share two bathrooms. These cost €495 to €750 per week (shorter stays are possible Sept–June). There are smaller units, too, with various accommodation combinations on two levels, and rates from €395 to €495; these sleep up to five people and are slightly less lavish, but still very comfortable. They can also be taken on a B&B basis (€80 double).

€–€€   For once, you'll find rather good dining located right at the heart of this town's main attraction. The **Ramparts Coffee Shop** (kids) (Castle St., Trim; ☎ 046/943-7227; Mon–Sat 9:30am–5:30pm; cash only) serves up fresh and tasty simple meals that go down perfectly after you've explored the castle and are still trying to fathom how our forebears ever lived in such appalling conditions. It's located in the same space that provides local tourist information (just around the corner from the entrance to the castle), so it's not exactly brimming with atmosphere, but there's good value to be had. The daily fare ranges from fruit scones (€1.80) to bagels with smoked salmon (€4.95) to lasagna served with a side portion of salad (€8.50). However, we rather enjoy the sardines served with brown bread (€6) that's sometimes available—it might sound a little left of center, but it's a tasty treat, and quite filling.

€€   At the mansion-like period home turned guesthouse **Highfield House** ✩✩✩ (Maudlins Rd., Trim; ☎ 046/943-6386; www.highfieldguesthouse.com; MC, V), owners Geraldine and Eddie Duignan have gone all out to evoke a real sense of grandeur. Decor is a mix of classic antiques, chunkily framed portraits, brocaded drapes, and all-round richly decorated public spaces. The house was built around 1806 and spent 84 years as a maternity hospital, which probably explains the rather generous proportions. Bedrooms are a mixed bag, but the Duigans have made every effort to give each of them that special something (expect wood frame beds, lithographs on the walls, and tiny bathrooms). Ask for a room with a window facing the Boyne and the abbey; these get the best light and, of course, the best view. Geraldine told us that they allow guests to bring takeaway meals into the dining room (she'll even provide cutlery and crockery), and she's more than happy for you to enjoy a bottle of wine or even a few beers in the sitting room. To our minds, such generosity is already a sensible reason to stay here. Another reason is the incredible value—doubles here cost €84 to €88.

€€   If fishing is your thing, you will find far more than just reasonable accommodation at Marc O'Regan's **Crannmor Guesthouse** ★ (Dunderry Rd., just outside Trim on R161; ☎ 046/943-1635; www.crannmor.com; MC, V). Marc is one of the country's leading authorities on pike fishing, and operates a busy angling business out of the large, attractive, ivy-clad house, set in 2 hectares (5 acres) of mature gardens. There are just four rooms, with rates of €80 double (with breakfast), which is good for the area, especially when you consider the size and rather careful design of the rooms—they're elegant, stripped of clutter, with matching furniture. Big beds and thick mattresses, too. The house itself is 180 years old, so it's one of those solid pieces of architecture with plenty of space and character—and Marc himself is something of a character. If you do plan on hitting the water, give plenty of notice, as the cost is negotiable.

€€   Don't be alarmed by the Mock Tudor facade of **Tigh Catháin** (take roundabout to Kilcock, 2nd roundabout to Longwood, just outside Trim; ☎ 046/943-1996; www.tighcathaintrim.com; cash only)! This is a wonderfully comfortable guest house, run by the ever-chatty Marie Keane, whose taste clearly runs to the old-fashioned. Expect Chesterfield sofas, antique wooden cabinets, small chandeliers, as well as fine linen in the bedrooms and an equally old-fashioned sense of hospitality. Marie runs a tight ship here, making all the breakfasts herself (and there are a number of different choices on the menu, such as homemade muesli or fruit compote), and providing those welcome little extras, like hand cream and face-wipes in the bathrooms. Rates are €75 per room per night, all rooms are en suite, and free Internet access is included.

WHY YOU'RE HERE: TOP SIGHTS & ATTRACTIONS

Alongside the Book of Kells, the Blarney Stone, and the Cliffs of Moher, the passage tombs at **Newgrange** and **Knowth** ★★★ rank as one of Ireland's true iconic sights. And of these, they're certainly the most mysterious. No records exist as to how they were built (we know that some of the 16-ton stones came from as far away as County Wicklow, but nobody knows how they were transported here) or who the tombs were meant to hold. The advanced engineering that went into them is also a question mark: How did our Neolithic ancestors manage to build this massive structure (the mound at Newgrange is 11m/36 ft. tall and 78m/256 ft. in diameter) in such a way that it would remain watertight and intact for some 5,000 years? Remember: These UNESCO World Heritage sites predate the pyramids of Giza and Stonehenge in the U.K. by several hundred (perhaps thousand) years—that's pretty darn ancient. Questions exist as well about the swirling patterns that mark the door to the tomb and the many kerbstones that surround it; similarly patterned stones have been found in such far flung places as Sicily and the Isle of Wight. A final mysterious feat of architecture is the play of light that only occurs here during the winter solstice. The rest of the year, the inside of the tomb is pitch black but at that time, for 17 minutes, a ray of light enters the tomb at dawn and snakes its way through the passage and up the back wall. It's a mystical sight and one that's so coveted, places to watch it are booked up years in advance (enter the lottery for tickets at **www.knowth.eu/newgrange-solstice-lottery.htm** if you want to chance it). Happily, for a few days either side of that, the experience can just be as mesmerizing. ***Note:*** It will mean getting up at 4am, or earlier.

Access is only through the **Bru Na Boinne Visitor Centre** (2km/1 mile west of Donore along river Boyne; ☎ 041/988-0300; www.knowth.com; daily 9:30am–6pm); a shuttle bus runs from the center to both sites, and tailor-made packages are available for those who want either the full experience, which includes a comprehensive exhibition, Newgrange, and Knowth (€10.30), or either one of the monuments, individually (€5.80).

Similarly inspirational, though often omitted by guidebooks, are the **Loughcrew Cairns** ✪✪✪ (Corstown, near Oldcastle; ☎ 049/854-1240; www.loughcrew.com; free admission; June–Aug daily 10am–6pm), also known as the Hills of the Witch, a group of Neolithic passage tombs almost as old as those at Newgrange and Knowth. The tombs are located on three different hills, and Cairn T, the largest of these is also the most notable; just like at Newgrange, the tomb lines up with the morning sunlight, this time on the Vernal and Autumnal equinoxes, while the inner chamber of the tomb is decorated with beautiful examples of neolithic art. Bear in mind, while these cairns are of general access to the public, it's not simply a case of walking up to them—the key for Cairn T is held at **Loughcrew Garden Visitor Centre** (☎ 049/854-1060) some 3km (nearly 2 miles) from the Cairns, and a passport or driving license and deposit of €50 are required.

Head south from Loughcrew along the N3 motorway and you'll sooner or later pass through the Tara-Skryne valley, home of the third of the county's great Neolithic monuments, the **Hill of Tara** (signposted, 12km/7½ miles from Navan along N3; ☎ 046/902-5903; €2.10; May–Sept daily 10am–6pm). Archeologists are still arguing as to the significance of this pretty hill. It was thought that, until the 6th century A.D., this was the seat of the High Kings of Ireland, but recent excavations seem to suggest the ruins found here aren't of the scale that would have supported the king's largest court. Instead, they now think that the site was used ritually every few years, for large gatherings at which laws were enacted, disputes settled, and much ancient liquor drunk. On the hill are an ancient passage grave, a large standing stone where, legend has it, the kings were crowned (Irish myths tell of the stone screaming at the touch of a new king), two ring forts, and a ceremonial avenue (long thought to be the remains of a banqueting hall) approaching the main sites. Beyond Tara's historical importance, pagans believed it was the home of the goddess Maeve. Watch the well-done film at the visitor's center for more background on the site.

The significance of such sites is reflected by the number of bus tours that service the region from the capital. Bus Éireann's **Newgrange and Boyne Valley Tour** (☎ 01/836-6111; departs Busaras 10am, returns 5:45pm daily; €36, 10% discount available by booking online at www.buseireann.ie) takes in Newgrange, the Boyne Valley visitor center, the Hill of Tara, and Mellifont Abbey (Louth), over an 8-hour period, with the admission charges to Newgrange and the Bru na Boinne Visitor Centre included. **Mary Gibbons Tours** operates daily tours to Newgrange (with the promise of no queuing), the Hill of Tara, and the village of

Neat & Tidy Trim

There is a touch of smugness to Trim, a town that clearly revels in its heritage status. But it's hard *not* to forgive local pride in a burg that has so many wonderful medieval ruins and relics, handsome Tudor-style houses, as well as its own tumbledown castle. (Sad that little remains of its once great cathedral, founded in 1206, which had been the largest Gothic church in Ireland and is alas, no more.) **Trim Castle** ✪✪✪ (Co. Mouth, Trim; ☎ 046/943-8619; www.heritageireland.com; Heritage Card or €3.70; Easter–Sept daily 10am–6pm; Oct daily 10am–5:30pm; Nov–Easter Sat; Sun 10am–5pm), remains a draw, its luster burnished by Mel Gibson, of all people, who featured it in his film *Braveheart*. Of course, the castle's fame stretches much further back as it was frequently the site of battles between the British and the Irish.

The castle (aka King John's Castle) is the largest remaining Anglo-Norman castle in Europe, and is unique throughout the continent as it was built in the shape of a Greek cross. It's been magnificently preserved rather than refurbished (as has happened to so many other castles in Ireland), and retains many of its original scars. A visit here is indispensable for anyone wanting to know more about how these castles once functioned. In fact, the very entertaining tour includes vivid accounts of daily life in this castle and the ins and outs of siege warfare. There's a cheaper entrance fee if you only want to see the castle grounds, but here's a case when spending that €2 will definitely be worth it, as the interior is much more interesting than the grounds.

Some advice: Arrive early and sign up for the first (least crowded) tour of the day. And afterward, if tidy Trim starts to grate, you can always head out of town to take a peek at Laracor Vicarage, the little church where Dean Jonathan Swift spent so many happy years in the early 1700s; to get there, take the Summerhill Road (R160).

Slane (☎ 086/355-1355; www.newgrangetours.com; €35, includes all entry fees; departs Mespil Hotel, Donnybrook at 9:30am, returns 4:15pm). Cheapest of all, however, is the **Newgrange Shuttlebus** (☎ 1800/424252; €18 return), which runs twice daily from Suffolk Street (departs 8:45am and 11:45am) to Newgrange (departs 1 and 4pm), and includes access to Newgrange only.

THE OTHER MEATH
Getting Down with Modern-Day Druids

The UNESCO world heritage site of Newgrange, draws visitors the world over, many of whom are interested in Celtic mysticism. And lately, those enthusiasts are mixing visits to these passage tombs with courses at the **Irish Centre for**

Shamanic Studies (Dunderry Park, Navan; ☎ 046/907-4455; www.shamanism ireland.com). Established by Martin Duffy (an accredited Jungian psychotherapist and former health care professional), the center promotes both traditional and contemporary Shamanism through courses and workshops.

So just what is "Shamanism" in this context? That's a bit hard to explain. According to Duffy it's "an ancient spiritual system dating back over 50,000 years" that's traceable as the root of all forms of healing and spirituality, whether they be Celtic, European, American, or Aboriginal. And a shaman is an individual who is able to use different techniques (drumming, dancing, even dreaming) to change their state of consciousness and travel outside time and ordinary human understanding. Pretty esoteric, we know. Duffy's parents were traditional folk healers, and his own research and practice—which have taken him as far as the Amazon and Mongolia—is heavily influenced by the ancient Druid traditions.

The Centre occupies a 200-year-old restored Georgian residence on a 10-hectare (25-acre) estate (with parkland, lush woods, and its own lake) and operates workshops throughout the year. All first timers to the center take "The Shaman's Journey," a 3-day introductory course in which, among other awareness-shifting activities, you get to experience the journey with the drum, the Celtic fire ceremony, and trance dancing. The course is residential and the €295 tuition fee includes accommodation (shared doubles, triples, and quads) and food (strictly vegetarian). Workshops are held in March, August, and November.

Not forgetting children, the center also offers special 1-day youth workshops (for children age 8–18) twice-yearly (€100; 10am–7pm), and has special events around the sacred Celtic sites during the solstices.

Gaelic Football 101

On a slightly more mundane level, while driving through Meath during the summer months, you can't help but notice green and yellow flags tied to lampposts, houses, trees, or anything capable of supporting them. The colors in question are the county colors of **Meath's GAA** team, one of the most successful Gaelic football sides in the country, with seven national championships and 20 Leinster championships under their belt. Besides an excellent track record, the reason Gaelic Football is held in such high esteem here is because the game might actually have originated here—in fact, the first recorded game reportedly took place in the village of Slane in 1712. Meath play their home games at **Páirc Tailteann** (Navan; ☎ 046/902-2780; www.meath.gaa.ie), and with fixtures running throughout the summer, it's a great way to feel the depths of true local passion. Even if you're not able to attend a game, you can experience the passion that's felt for the sport by popping into the **Village Inn** (Main St., Slane; ☎ 041/24230), a wonderful pub in Slane (right across the road from The Old Post Office Bistro) and the local hangout for every GAA enthusiast in the village. Watching here is a bit like attending a college class in Gaelic Football—perfect if you want to hear a very personal version of the history, the rules, and the reasons why GAA outstrips soccer and rugby. A word of warning, however: Don't arrive too late, as the pre-Guinness conversation will be far more edifying!

Food from the, um, Fairies

And if you can't stick any more sports' talk, head instead for Ratoath, where you'll find one of the country's best cooking schools, the **Fairyhouse Food and Wine School** (Fairyhouse Rd., Ratoath; ☎ 01/689-6476; www.fairyhousecookery school.com), which offers 1-day courses from €120, covering everything from choosing the right ingredients to pairing wine with your dish. Given the recent trend toward "healthy eating," there's also a popular 1-day course (€75) on urban gardening—focusing on how even the contents of your window box can be used in cooking. A range of evening courses (€60) are interestingly tailored to men only.

Getting Crafty in Neighboring Louth

An unexpected boom in the craft trade around County Louth has meant not just increased retail opportunities and the chance to take home unique, handmade items, but also a chance to see some of the country's most talented artists at work, and to explore their vision. **Craftmark** (Sarah Mallon, Quayside Business Park, Mill St., Dundalk; ☎ 042/939-6944; www.craftmark.ie) is an organization dedicated to preserving and furthering the work of artists North and South of the border. To that end, it organizes free studio visits with the surprisingly large number of artists in the area. If you have ever wondered about the creation of the classic pendulum clock, or wanted to watch wood carvers or potters at work, this is how to go about satisfying that curiosity. Craftmark represents over 20 local artists, working in everything from silver to leather, all of whom are happy to chat about what they do. This is a chance to learn about applied art in a totally unique way, and maybe commission a piece or two.

ACTIVE MEATH

The shores of the Boyne Valley are heaven for angling enthusiasts—Meath poet Francis Ledwidge once paid tribute to these waters "where the jewelled trout are leaping/And the heron flings his spear"—and the **Rathbeggan Lakes** (just beyond Black Bull on the N3; ☎ 01/824-0197; www.rathbegganlakes.com; a full day's fishing starts at €30, with an extra €5 charge for every fish you want to take home) near Dunshaughlin is one of the best spots in the country for game angling. Consisting of five lakes, including two mature fly-fishing lakes, over 3 hectares (8 acres), the area is well stocked with carp, tench, bream, and rudd, not to mention a plentiful supply of rainbow trout, while equipment is available to hire from the on-site offices. True, fishing like this is a bit of a cheat—the lakes are regularly restocked—but there's little chance of going away empty handed, which makes the experience more satisfying, don't you think? For anglers who prefer a real challenge, the River Boyne and its tributaries have extensive stocks of wild brown trout, but bear in mind that the majority of angling in the Boyne is controlled by different angling associations, with many parts maintained by private fishery owners. For more information, and to apply for a fishing permit, visit the website of the **Eastern Regional Fisheries Board,** at www.fishingireland.net.

Like Kildare, Meath's lush green pastures lend themselves well to horse racing, and **Fairyhouse Racecourse** (Ratoath, ☎ 01/825-6167; www.fairyhouserace course.ie) is the home of one of the highlights of the racing calendar, the Irish Grand National, traditionally run on Easter Monday every year. Unlike many other racetracks around the country, the 1 mile, 6 furlong circuit has races all year round; information is available from the course website, www.fairyhouserace course.ie.

NIGHTLIFE

The **Solstice Arts Centre** ✶ (Railway St., Navan; ☎ 046/909-2300; www.solstice artscentre.com), in Navan, is the center of Meath's artistic scene, with ongoing art and photography exhibitions by local and national artists in three galleries, and a 320-seater theater that draws groups and performers from across Ireland. The center, in its own words, highlights the "importance of living, expressive and diverse culture that enriches the lives of the people of Meath." Anytime I've been there, there's been no shortage of all three.

It wasn't that long ago that busloads of Dubliners would make the pilgrimage every weekend to towns like Dunshaughlin to while away the hours in pubs and nightclubs, and although the numbers have lessened in recent years, Meath is still a good place to throw a party. **Crean's Gardens** (no phone) and **Caffrey's** (☎ 049/854-2679) in Oldcastle are two of the county's number one music spots, featuring mainly local artists; the cover charge for both varies between €5 and €10. **The Lantern Bar** (32 Watergate St., Navan; ☎ 046/902-3535) in Navan is the home of the Backroom Sessions, a weekly live indie-rock club featuring the hottest Irish bands of the moment, again for little more than a tenner admission. **Taboo Nightclub** (Kenny Rd., Navan; ☎ 046/907-0077; www.taboo.ie; €10), is one of the county's most popular late-night venues, and while the crowd is generally fairly young, the club also boasts a more relaxed chill-out area, the Red Room (pre-booking essential), for more sophisticated clubbers.

4

The Yin & Yang of the Southeast

Party pubs, Viking towns, crystal factories & pastoral backwaters

by Keith Bain

THE SOUTHEAST IS AN AREA OF "FIRSTS." IT WAS HERE THAT THE VIKINGS established their first towns—at Wexford and Waterford—and it was here, too, that the Anglo-Normans began their takeover of the island of Ireland. Centuries before those outsider plunderers arrived, St. Patrick allegedly made a national symbol of the shamrock by using it to explain the Holy Trinity, while preaching atop the Rock of Cashel.

Though the threat of invasion by Vikings and Cromwellians has been replaced by troops of die-hard partiers who pack out Kilkenny City on weekends and armies of curious tourists keen to see how glass is produced in Waterford's famous crystal factory, there's still plenty to remind visitors of an intriguing history. Fantastic castles, ancient city walls, Viking heritage, and pubs so old they're virtual museums—it's enough to make your head spin. At least in certain parts. Because just as there are pockets of bustling activity—commerce in Waterford, nightlife and action-packed Gaelic sports in Kilkenny, and rather vibrant craft industries in country villages—there are plenty of patches of pure pastoral bliss, both along the magnificent coastline and in vast stretches of unspoiled countryside, where time may just as well have stood still.

It's that yin and yang nature of the Southeast, in fact, that's its greatest asset. Here you can join the weekend crowds in rollicking fun in its party-central cities, or just as easily idle away the days in serene backwoods villages with little more than a gently flowing river and ruined abbey for company.

DON'T LEAVE THE SOUTHEAST WITHOUT . . .

PARTYING HARD IN IRELAND'S SMALLEST "CITY" For a relatively wee place, Kilkenny packs a hefty punch, particularly as a weekend nightlife destination. Walk the two main streets, and you'll find an endless supply of places to socialize, no matter what your poison. See p. 131.

POSING WITH PICTURE-PERFECT VILLAGES The Southeast has a wealth of pretty villages where you can get in touch with your bucolic side. Lismore in north Waterford has one of the country's loveliest castles (p. 162), while St. Mullins in south Carlow basically has just the one pub, but the riverside setting is blissful (p. 135).

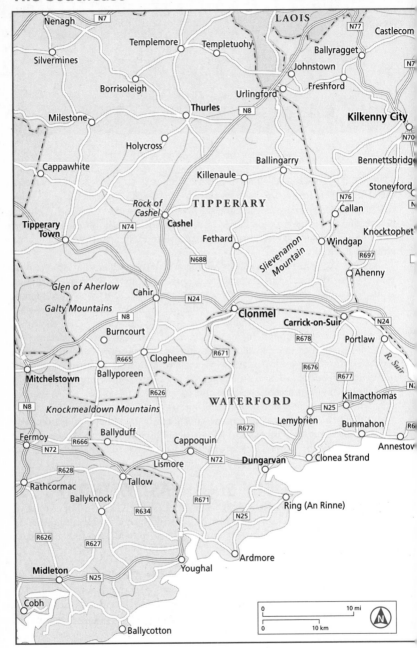

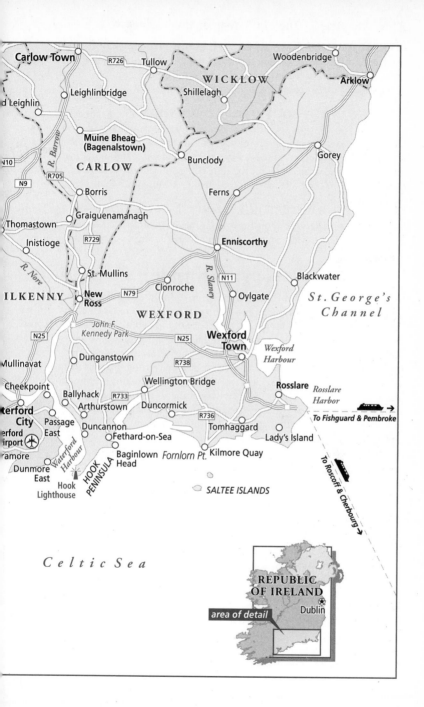

Carlow Town

R726   Tullow

d Leighlin   Leighlinbridge

WICKLOW   Woodenbridge

Shillelagh   Arklow

R. Barrow

Muine Bheag
(Bagenalstown)

CARLOW   Bunclody   Gorey

N10

N9   R705   Borris   Ferns

Thomastown   Graiguenamanagh

Inistioge   R729   Enniscorthy

R. Nore   St. Mullins   Clonroche   Blackwater

ILKENNY   New   N79   N11   St. George's
Ross   WEXFORD   R. Slaney   Oylgate   Channel

John F.
Kennedy Park   N25   Wexford
Town

N25   Mullinavat   Dunganstown   R738   Wexford
Harbour

Cheekpoint   Wellington Bridge   Rosslare   Rosslare
Harbour

erford   Ballyhack   R733   Arthurstown   Duncormick   R736   To Fishguard & Pembroke

City   Passage   Duncannon   Tomhaggard

erford   East   Fethard-on-Sea   Lady's Island   To Roscoff & Cherbourg

irport   Baginlown   Fornlorn Pt.   Kilmore Quay

ramore   Dunmore   Head

East   Hook   Waterford
Harbour   HOOK
PENINSULA   SALTEE ISLANDS

Hook
Lighthouse

Celtic Sea

REPUBLIC
OF IRELAND

area of detail   Dublin

ADMIRING THE VIEW FROM THE ROCK   The Rock of Cashel in southern Tipperary is one of the world's most famous ecclesiastical monuments and its history is the stuff of legend; it's worth getting up there, however, simply to take in the view of the surrounding countryside. See p. 162.

WALKING IN THE FOOTSTEPS OF THE VIKINGS   In the narrow streets of Wexford you'll still get a sense of the heady days when it was a walled Viking town. Not too far away, Waterford is the oldest city in Ireland where some of the most exciting Viking archaeological remains have been unearthed. Although a major Viking museum is in the works here, for the time being you can check some of these fascinating exhibits at the brilliant Waterford Treasures Museum. See p. 147.

TOURING THE WATERFORD COAST   The scenic coastline along County Waterford is dotted with beautiful coves, some of them backed by plunging cliffs and gorgeous beaches; it's worth spending a day driving or cycling through here. See p. 147.

WEXFORD TOWN

Wexford Town isn't an obvious tourist destination, but I think that's what makes it such an enjoyable, if offbeat, place to visit. And it has some elements that will appeal to outsiders: its Viking roots are visible in the way it's put together. Wander the narrow muddle of streets at night, and it's easy to imagine yourself 1,000 years back in a place inhabited by fierce seafaring warriors. Step inside its pubs, though, and that image is quickly replaced by one of a welcoming, hospitable people.

Wexford is the Anglicized form of Waesfjord, the Viking's "mudflat harbor," one of their most important trade centers in the south of Ireland. With much of its harbor activity now given over to mussel dredging and pleasure cruises, 20th-century Wexford turned its attention to cultural pursuits. The Wexford Festival Opera is one of Ireland's most anticipated events. Based here, you can easily explore the entire Wexford coastline, starting with languid Kilmore Quay, a nearby village of thatched fishermen's cottages, ultra-fresh seafood, and pristine beaches. Rumors are bouncing around that Wexford is hyping up to claim city status, but even that won't alter its small town appeal.

A BRIEF HISTORY

Ancient Wexford traces its history back at least to the 2nd century, which is when Ptolemy noted it on one of his maps; back then it was called Loch Garman, named, according to legend, after a man who died at the mouth of the River Slaney when an angry witch released a tidal torrent. Christianity here predates St. Patrick, and the evangelization of the local people is attributed to St. Ibar, a bishop who came from County Down and started Wexford's first monastery, on Begerin Island. Ibar legendarily banished all the rats from Wexford, prompting locals to note that today it's only two-legged rats—politicians—who roam the town. The Vikings sailed up the Slaney and invaded in the 9th century, and their Waesfjord remained a Viking town for over 3 centuries. The Normans first arrived in Ireland at Bannow Bay in County Wexford, so this was one of the first places where they moved in and kicked the Irish and the Vikings out, altering the course of Irish history forever. Walls were extended, and the Irish and Norsemen were excluded; Wexford became a stronghold of old—meaning pre-Protestant—English culture and language.

In the 1640s County Wexford strongly supported Confederate Ireland, and Cromwell consequently wreaked awful revenge here in 1649, sacking the town and massacring 2,500 men, women, and children. Little wonder then that Wexford was central in 1798 Rebellion against the English Crown; the town was a rebel stronghold and the United Irishmen infamously massacred scores of local Loyalists. In June 1798, Wexford declared itself a republic, which lasted just one week. An important harbor since the days of the Vikings, Wexford went into decline during the 20th century as the harbor became silted up making it necessary to dredge the channel for use by larger ships. By the 1960s, regular dredging was no longer feasible. The port is now used for mussel farming.

GETTING THERE & GETTING AROUND

Wexford town is close to the **Rosslare Europort,** a major point of arrival for waterborne Europeans, and commonly referred to as the Gateway to Europe because of its major ferry crossings to and from the continent. Rosslare is 16km (10 miles) from Wexford, on the R470.

The **N11** links Wexford with Dublin, via Enniscorthy; and the **N25** is the most direct (if least inspiring) route to Waterford, by way of New Ross. From Kilkenny, a series of small backroads leads to New Ross and then the N25 reaches Wexford, or you can go via Waterford.

You can catch a train from Dublin's Connolly Station to Wexford's **O'Hanranhan (North) Station** (Redmond Sq.; ☎ 053/912-2522); the journey takes under 3 hours and costs around €24 return. A far more affordable way of getting there is by **bus** (around €15), which takes the same time, but has many more departures; buses also pull in at the train station.

Wexford is a medieval town and really doesn't make much sense; too-narrow streets that feel hemmed in, emanate from just about anywhere—you'd do well to park your car in one of Wexford's parking areas, and explore on foot; this really will give you a more authentic feel for the city. There are pay-and-display lots near the riverside **Tourist Information Centre** (The Quay; ☎ 053/912-3111; Mon–Sat 9:15am–1pm and 2–5pm). If you're exploring places farther from the center, you'll need to drive.

ACCOMMODATIONS, BOTH STANDARD & NOT

Wexford's biggest draw is its annual Opera Festival; opera-lovers from around Ireland fill up hotels and restaurants each October, when you'll pay premium rates for accommodations and will need to book months in advance.

€ The new owners of Wexford's hostel have painted the walls, cleaned up the old mess, and are making an earnest, honest attempt to bring **Kirwan House** (3 Mary St.; ☎ 053/912-1208; www.wexfordhostel.com; cash only) into the 21st century. Digs range from six- to eight-bedded en suite units (with wooden bunks, €20) to smaller rooms suitable for couples (€50 double), families or even solo travelers (€30 single). There's a decent kitchen and an outdoor courtyard area (with promises to make good and tidy here, too), and the central location is a great bonus.

A Country Retreat en Route to the Southeast

Just south of the Wexford-Wicklow county border, **Woodlands Country House** ✿✿✿ (Killineirin, Gorey; ☎ 0402/37125; www.woodlandscountry house.com; Apr–Sept; MC, V) is the ideal B&B address. This wonderfully maintained family home dates back to 1836; in a former incarnation it belonged to wealthy landowners who ran a mill where the tennis court is today. After a curse was placed on them by a local tenant woman, the farmstead mansion fell into disrepair. Nearly 40 years ago, homemakers Philomena and John O'Sullivan bought and upgraded the house and in so doing must have lifted the curse because they've been welcoming guests—trouble-free—ever since. Philomena is a meticulous hostess: the house is filled with all kinds of dainty trifles—antique furniture, hand-embroidered cushions, artisan quilts, and such cushy extras as electric blankets, decent toiletries, and bedside chocolates. The fine, sublime countryside setting doesn't hurt (woodlands and beach are within easy reach) nor do the smashing breakfasts. Besides all-round *craic*, Philomena will share the tale of the house (and its curse), and John is a great fol-lower of hurling and Gaelic football, so here's where to pad your knowl-edge on all things Irish. Doubles cost €100, while superior rooms (with

€€   On the street where Oscar Wilde's mother once lived, is one of Wexford's best-value lodgings, a B&B named for an obvious feature—the **Blue Door** ✿ kids (18 Lower George St.; ☎ 053/912-1047; www.thebluedoorwexford.com; MC, V). Blue carpets mark the near-spiral staircase that leads up to the bedrooms in this tall, narrow, 200-year-old house. Rooms are spacious and tidy, with high beds, pine furniture, and a sofa; despite the slightly lumpy mattresses, they're comfort-able and have decent attached showers. Windows are double-glazed to keep out night noise (it's bang in the center). Doubles cost €70, and family rooms are no more than €85—a real value.

€€   About 10 minutes by foot from the town center, Carol and Tim Kelly have upgraded, refurbished, and refurnished **Rosemount House** ✿✿ (Spawell Rd.; ☎ 053/912-4609; www.wexfordbedandbreakfast.ie; MC, V), transforming it into my favorite right-in-Wexford lodging. Built in 1803, the house was originally a Protestant school, which explains not only why it is so wonderfully light-filled—in those days a tax was levied on windows, but schools were obviously exempt—but also why the rooms are large enough to be called "extravagant." Judicious distribution of French antique furniture and rococo ornaments has provided a luxurious atmosphere. Of the three bedrooms, my favorite is massive unit 2 with its ornately carved high wooden bed (and firm mattress), inlaid wooden chest of drawers, chandelier, beautiful armchair, flatscreen TV, and large bathroom with tub and shower. Besides getting a lot of light, the house has loads of character and if you book room 2, you'll be overwhelmed by space. Doubles cost €80, but rise to €100 May to October, and €120 in opera season.

€€–€€€€ If you prefer hotel-style lodgings, then head across the river to the **Riverbank House Hotel** ✪ (The Bridge; ☎ 053/912-3611; www.riverbankhouse hotel.com; AE, MC, V), where there's heaps of old world charm and Victorian atmosphere, particularly in the bar and restaurant. Here, the design is borderline bohemian—dark wood furniture, flickering candles, textured wallpaper, and the pleasant scent of burnt incense. It all certainly feels intimate and warm, and a young staff provides service to match. Bedrooms aren't quite as lavish—they're neat with a faintly derivative antique look, huge beds, double-glazed windows, functional little bathrooms (half with shower only), and one fresh rose suggesting that personal touch. In quieter months (Oct–May), rates are €120 double on weekends, and €100 during the week; in summer, prices climb to €140 to €160. Breakfast is included.

Kilmore Quay

€€ Simple, affordable, and well-groomed, **Quay House** ✪ (Kilmore Quay; ☎ 053/912-9988; www.kilmorequay.net; MC, V) is everything you want in a seaside guesthouse. It's in an ideal location, within strolling distance of everything in Kilmore Quay, including the sea, just .5km (⅓ mile) away. The house, which has a faintly nautical feel, was the local post office-cum-shop back in the 1950s. The upstairs bedrooms have pitch pine floors, pine furniture, and pale pink walls; they're spacious enough, with dressing tables and tubs in the en suite bathrooms. Ask for a corner unit with a view of the Saltee Islands—you can see them from your bed in room 3. You'll pay €90 to €100.

DINING FOR ALL TASTES

€–€€ Although it's not a place of dining innovation, **la Cuisine** (80 North Main St.; ☎ 053/912-4986; Mon–Sat 9am–5:30pm; MC, V) is where many of Wexford's old timers have been gathering since 1985 to exchange gossip over a cup of tea and a plate of wholesome "homemade" food. Breakfast (try a hot bacon sandwich, €4) is served for most of the day, and there are various light meals and deli items (quiche, €8; lasagna, €8.25) which you can eat in or take away; this is a reasonable place to sample that ultimate traditional Irish dish—an unpretentious plate of bacon and cabbage, served with creamed potatoes and parsley sauce (€10).

€–€€ Locals queue for authentic Italian fare at **La Dolce Vita** ✪✪ (6–7 Trimmer's Ln.; ☎ 053/917-0806; Mon–Sat 9am–5:30pm; MC, V), a small daytime cafe tucked down a side street off North Main Street, and marked by its green, white, and red awnings. With affordable dining options (pastas are a great value, mostly around €10, and paninis stuffed with fresh deli ingredients to eat in or take away) and the heady buzz of loyal fans (yup, you'll most likely have to wait if you want a table), you may as well convince yourself to splash out on a bottle of house wine, or at least pig out on dessert.

€–€€€€ Down on the quayside, the **Potato Market** ✪ (O'Donovan's Wharf, Crescent Quay; ☎ 053/914-1131; Mon–Wed 8am–5:45pm; Thurs–Sat 9am–9:15pm;

Sun 9am–4:30pm; AE, MC, V) is expensive at night, but does simpler, cafe-style meals and quick-bite pastas, salads, burgers, and sandwiches during the day. George Leahy, the owner, runs cookery classes and demonstrations here, too. He told me that visitors are welcome to drop in for a day, and either watch or participate; for €20 to €25, you get a day's tuition, a bite to eat, and a glass of wine.

€–€€€€   A simple, relaxed coffee shop commandeers the front part of Wexford's stylish, newish yuppie-hangout, the **Yard** ✩✩ (3 Lower Georges St.; ☎ 053/914-4083; daily 8:30am–10pm; MC, V). Here you can order from an all-day sandwich bar with plain or toasted sandwiches from €3. Step into the restaurant, and prices head upstream, although you can get tasty lunchtime items for €8 to €12 (try the lip-smacking marinated pork ribs for €9).

Kilmore Quay

€–€€€€   Ask just about any Wexford foodie, and they'll tell you that the place for eat-your-heart-out seafood is **Kehoe's Pub** ✩✩ (Kilmore Quay; ☎ 053/912-9830; Mon–Thurs 11am–11:30pm; Fri–Sat 11am–12:30am; Sun 12:30–11pm; MC, V). Step inside and take a whiff: Kehoe's is saturated with a permanent scent that can only be described as "ocean-going" (the nautical decor only adds to the ambiance). Beloved by locals—you might share a toast with the parish priest or a resident fishermen—it boasts a broad menu including sandwiches (€5), lunch specials like roast lamb (€10), or even a great big sirloin steak (€22). But there's no real excuse to come all this way and not order something that was likely swimming that morning. What you get will typically depend on what's come off the boat today—the great triumph here is the "famous" trilogy of fish for €20.

WHY YOU'RE HERE: TOP SIGHTS & ATTRACTIONS

You can explore Wexford town without urgent need to see very much at all. This is a good place to simply wander, picking your way through narrow roads and chancing upon various ruins, such as those of the **old town walls,** first built by the Vikings and later expanded by the Normans. There were originally five gates, but only the fortified **West Gate,** with its square tower built of red sandstone, survives; completed in 1300, it's been wonderfully restored and the gateway leads to the area known as **Selskar,** which was where the original Gaels had their settlement. Here, the 12th-century **Selskar Abbey** (Selskar St.) was founded by a Norman knight who returned from the Third Crusade only to discover that his fiancée had become a nun; overcome by grief, he became a monk himself and appointed himself head of his own religious house. When Cromwell arrived in Wexford, he destroyed the abbey, but although he ordered that its bells be made into cannons, they now toll at a church in Liverpool.

At the heart of the compact little town, the **Bull Ring** is the unofficial town square; the name derives from the practice of bull baiting that took place here in less-civilized times for the amusement of the citizens, but was especially popular with well-to-do Normans. Notice **Furlong's butchery?** It's been there since 1621 and was responsible for supplying the bull for this activity. The bull was tied to a rope, the other end of which was speared into the ground—fierce dogs were then unleashed to attack the beast until it was dead. The bull's hide was then given to the mayor and the meat was distributed to the poor; the activity was banned in 1777. When Cromwell sacked the town, he had 2,500 citizens butchered in the Bull Ring.

In the center of the square, the **"Pikeman"** statue is a memorial to the 1798 Rebellion; the hooked part of the pike would have been used to pull mounted soldiers off their horses. The statue faces one of Wexford's oldest taverns the **Cape of Good Hope,** now simply known as the Cape (p. 130), where a prized captive of the Rebellion, Lord Kingsborough, was held for some time. Just off the Bull Ring is **Main Street**—famous for its extraordinarily narrow width in places—which runs more or less parallel to the **Slaney River;** a number of atmospheric streets and lanes connect Main Street with the redeveloped quayside area.

On Main Street, just around the corner from the Bull Ring, **St. Iberius' Church** ✸ stands on the site of St. Ibar's second monastery; the present church was built in 1760, designed by John Roberts, who was the architect of many of Waterford's most prominent buildings. Nearby, on High Street, the intimate **Theatre Royal** was expanded to accommodate the Wexford Festival Opera, which first happened in 1951.

With their spires poking out of the Wexford skyline, the town is particularly proud of its twin churches—the **Church of the Immaculate Conception** on Rowe Street, and about .5km (⅓ mile) away, the **Church of the Assumption** on Bride Street. Both were designed by Richard Pierce, a pupil of Augustin Pugin, the great master of gothic-revival. Built of Wicklow granite and local sandstone they opened in April 1858 within a week of each other; they're identical except for the ways in which they're decorated and ornamented; if you visit, take note of the mosaics, executed in pebble paving, at the front doors.

ATTRACTIONS NEAR WEXFORD TOWN

Birders should give their attention to the **Wexford Wildfowl Reserve** ✸✸ (North Slob, Wexford Harbour; ☎ 053/912-3129; free admission; daily 10am–5pm), which lies 5km (3 miles) northeast of town on the other side of the river; follow the signs from Castlebridge Road. The reserve consists of 200 hectares (500 acres) of slobs—or mudflats—that draw between 8,000 and 10,000 endangered Greenland Whitefronted geese for the winter. Also to be seen are numerous wader species, ducks, three varieties of swan (Whooper, Mute, and Bewick's), and birds of prey, including kestrels, sparrowhawks, and harriers, and—more rarely—red kite and goshawks. Beyond the slobs, 10km (6 miles) northeast of Wexford, film fundis may want to take a gawk at Curracloe Beach, where the epic opening sequence of *Saving Private Ryan* was shot. If it's a sunny day, take your bathing suit and towel—this popular beach seems to stretch on forever.

Southwest of Wexford Town the exquisite **Johnstown Castle Gardens** ✸✸✸ (6km/4 miles southwest of Wexford, off the N25; ☎ 053/914-2888; €5 per car, €2 pedestrians and cyclists, free Oct–Apr; daily 9am–5:30pm) ensconce a magnificent Victorian Gothic Revival style mansion that looks less like it was built to be the home of the Grogan-Morgan family than created to star in a movie. Although built between 1810 and 1855—long after the days of fortified castles—it's awash with turrets and battlements forming a sturdy, jaw-dropping chunk of period fantasy. The "castle" does actually incorporate an authentic, more ancient castle, and it sits at the edge of a 2-hectare (5-acre) man-made lake which also has gothic towers rising from it; from the lakeside terrace a favorite view is of the castle, reflected on the water's surface over which it hovers. Aside from the entrance hall, the castle itself is out of bounds (it's an agricultural college), so much of your time here will be spent exploring the grounds and admiring the redwoods, cypresses, firs, cedars, magnolias from China and dogwoods from Japan. Also be sure to seek out the gargoyle-festooned Devil's Gate which leads to a walled Victorian garden. *Note for birders:* Two more lakes on the property attract grebes, heron, mallards, and swans.

And I'll mention one last attraction near Wexford Town simply to warn you off: the **Irish National Heritage Park** 👶 (Ferrycarrig; ☎ 053/912-0733; www.inhp.com; €8; daily Apr–Sept 9:30am–6:30pm; Oct–Mar 9:30am–5:30pm), an open-air museum that re-creates various kinds of Irish habitation through the ages, from prehistoric dwellings to medieval castles. Frankly, this is precisely the kind of lame, dull tourist trap you want to avoid.

An Outing to Kilmore Quay

Within striking distance of Wexford City, the sleepy fishing village of **Kilmore Quay** ✫✫✫ consists of time-forgotten thatched cottages clustered along a single road. Probably the most popular activity out of Kilmore Quay is exploring the **Saltee Islands** by boat; as the islands with the highest number of birds anywhere off the Irish coast, the main thrill is seeing thousands of puffins, gannets, razor-bills, kittiwakes, guillemots, cormorants, shearwaters, and—for some variation—basking seals. The most favorable months for seeing the birds are April through July. There are a number of operators (including several that offer angling trips, too; see "Active Wexford," below); based at the Kilmore Quay Marina, is **Saltee Cruises** (☎ 087/252-9736 or 053/912-9684). Beyond the boat trip, you may want to simply drift into town and after strolling along the harbor or seeking out a beautiful stretch of coastline, wander into the famous maritime-themed **Kehoe Pub** (p. 126) where you can rub shoulders with a sample of the village's 150 or so residents.

THE OTHER WEXFORD

"Rambling Houses" are revival spaces for traditional Irish culture: storytelling, singing, and dancing constitute pre-TV-era entertainment where the community gets together to have traditional fun that harks back to the days when the entire universe could revolve around the campfire. Traditionally, these events would be run by local women who'd prepare tea and cornbread for all the revelers. If you turn up, you'd usually see a stick being passed around, and when the stick is handed to you, it's your turn to perform. It's definitely a chance to mingle with a truly local crowd. There are a couple of such houses in Wexford, but the most organized is **Ár mBréacha–The House of Storytelling** (☎ 087/650-8929), located north of Enniscorthy, in Raheen, Ballyduff, 5km (3 miles) from the village of Camolin (from where it's signposted) in the county's north. Evenings of poetry, storytelling, dancing, and music in a spontaneous, totally open and welcoming environment happen in or around a thatched white-walled cottage on the first Tuesday of every month, and every Tuesday in July and August (they usually run from 8 to 10:30pm, and attendance is free). I suggest you call ahead to confirm times and to get good directions, and prepare to discover how Celtic culture is being sustained in Ireland's smaller, tight-knit communities.

Literary types should look out for the 3-day **Wexford Book Festival** (☎ 053/912-2226; www.wexfordbook.ie) in April, featuring readings, workshops, and lectures by a wide range of Irish authors (for grown-ups and children), providing a social-yet-intellectual opportunity for getting together with locals other than hanging out with them in the pub. At most events, you get the chance to meet the author, too, and you'll be able to pick up a new book and get it signed.

One venue with a regular line-up of workshops and lectures (many especially for children) catering to all kinds of tastes, is the **Wexford Arts Centre** (p. 130).

Award-winning chef Phelim Byrne is Wexford's top professional caterer; not only does he have a newspaper column through which his recipes find their way into kitchens across the country, but he also has a culinary slot on South East Radio. And in order to get closer to "the people," he has his own **Cookery Academy** (Rosslare Rd., Wexford; ☎ 053/918-4995; www.phelimbyrne.ie) and does courses ranging from 1 day (or night) to 10-week intensive programs. Saturday courses, for example, include a mix of demonstration-style teaching and hands-on cooking, and run from 10am to 4:30pm. They cost €110 to €135, including a huge lunch and nonstop tasting of everything that's being prepared; tea, coffee, and freshly baked scones are also provided, and there are no more than 12 people in the class. Friday evening classes go from 7 to 10:30pm, when Phelim teaches you how to source and prepare six to nine dishes; the class costs about €75 and culminates in a full-blown meal. On the website you'll find the full line-up of classes, which really do cover the gamut of possibilities . . . but are really just a great way to mingle with local people and spend time in the presence of a Wexford hero.

ACTIVE WEXFORD

With its 200km (124-mile) coastline, Wexford is paradise for water-babies. Beside lazing on the beach or bobbing in the waves, the region is popular for exploration by boat and also offers some of the country's top sea fishing; at least 35 different fish types—including bass, dogfish, codling, and coalfish—have been recorded by anglers setting off from Kilmore Quay. **Angling** and **boating** from Kilmore Quay are possible with **Eamonn Hayes** (☎ 087/213-5308 or 053/912-9723; www.kilmoreangling.com), who skippers the Autumn Dream. He'll set you up with whatever equipment you need (€10 rod and reel hire), and charges €60 per person per day, or €385 to charter the whole boat. His trips round the Saltee Islands cost €20 per person, and he also does trips out to some of the wrecks off the coast. Also recommended is Leslie Bates's operation, **Mermaid Angling** (Killag, Duncormick, Co. Wexford; ☎ 087/249-2718 or 053/912-9806; www.mermaid angling.com), with much the same rates.

If fishing isn't your scene, you could try your hand at **sailing** off the Wexford coast. **Sailing Ireland** (Sallystown, Murrintown, Co. Wexford; ☎ 086/171-3800 or 053/913-9163; www.sailingireland.ie) offers courses for beginners, as well as opportunities for experienced sea hands to skipper a yacht around the Saltee Islands and as far as the Hook Peninsula. The "Introduction to Sailing" beginners course consists of six 4-hour lessons and costs €380. More advanced courses (including a 5-day "live aboard" course) are also available.

Enthusiasts who prefer to get closer to the water should head for the **Rosslare Watersport Centre** (Rosslare; ☎ 053/913-2566 or 053/913-2202) where it's possible not only to rent body boards, kayaks, and canoes, but also take introductory windsurfing and kayaking lessons.

ATTENTION, SHOPPERS!

Westgate Design (22 North Main St.; ☎ 053/912-3787) is probably *the* touchstone shopping venue for visitors to Wexford, with a mixed selection of arts, crafts, jewelry, and clothing.

You need to head out of town (along the N25) to reach the studio-outlet for **Paul Maloney Pottery** ✭ (Ballindinas, Barntown; ☎ 053/912-0188; www.paul maloneypottery.com; Mon–Sat 10am–6pm), where Paul, a master craftsman, makes hand thrown pottery with a contemporary, earthy look.

NIGHTLIFE

It's long been said, "Don't bring your secrets to Wexford because the locals will extract them from you!" This is especially true during the 18-day **Wexford Festival Opera** ✭✭✭ (☎ 053/912-2400; www.wexfordopera.com), far and away the biggest happening in town. What makes Wexford's festival special is its focus on reviving neglected or ignored operas, such as Bizet's *The Pearl Fisher,* performed here in 1971 and now among the repertoires of opera houses around the world. David Agler, the current Artistic Director, also enjoys choosing operas by living composers, so there's the chance to see something cutting-edge. In recent years, Wexford has been holding its breath for the arrival of its brand new state-of-the-art Opera House—with a 780-seat main auditorium and a second 170-seat drama theater—that opened in 2008, forever changing the town's skyline and reinvigorating the festival. The 58th annual festival begins mid-October 2009; if you can't be around then, at least check out the new opera house, where organizers are planning all sorts of innovative musical theater for the remainder of the year.

Serious plays, comedies and intimate music shows are staged at the **Wexford Arts Centre** (Cornmarket; ☎ 053/912-3764; www.wexfordartscentre.ie), housed in the 18th-century Cornmarket House, which stands on the site of the Vikings' central market.

Top marks for authentic pub atmosphere go to the **Sky & the Ground** ✭✭✭ (112 South Main St.; ☎ 053/912-4877) where the crowd is dynamic and the traditional entertainment (music and beyond) is out of this world. Arrive later in the evening (after 9pm at least) to catch riveting performances; one Monday I watched as five musicians were spontaneously joined by an ancient man who sang in a voice so pure, sad, somber, and melodious, it gave me goose flesh. When he was done—and the stunned crowd had come back down to earth—another man took the spotlight with a flourish of his eyebrows and recited a ballad that he might have remembered from his schooldays, perhaps 70 years ago. Spine-tingling stuff.

To warm up for the Sky, stop by the **Cape** ✭ (Bull Ring; ☎ 053/912-2949) where owner Eddie Mackin still has "Undertaker" emblazoned over one window. Originally called the Cape of Good Hope Bar, and dating back several centuries, this is an excellent place to share heartfelt *craic* and meet some new friends.

KILKENNY CITY & AROUND

Like moths to a flame, people have always been drawn to Kilkenny. As a monastic center, it drew religious and learned men. Then came the Vikings and the Normans, including the most powerful Norman family in Ireland, the Butlers, who established their residence here. From Holland, it drew Edmund Smithwick who started one of Ireland's most famous breweries here. Now, people flock to Kilkenny on weekends, drawn by its arty, alternative vibe and not insubstantial number of pubs.

It's a remarkably ambitious little town—that's dubbed itself "the Marble City"—yet is compact enough to explore in just a few hours. Nighttime revelers be warned, though, it's also fresh and exciting enough to hold your attention for a few days, with a heady pub and party scene that somehow caters to just about every conceivable taste—along one stretch of Parliament Street, six public houses stand side by side, each with a slightly different atmosphere. Yes, there are times when this feels like a mini-London, but with traditional music sessions filling in the gaps between bopping clubs and more serious bars. As you might imagine, Kilkenny gets inundated over weekends, especially in summer. But there are more than ample opportunities for escape, and Kilkenny is at the heart of an area rich with picturesque villages.

A BRIEF HISTORY

Medieval Kilkenny, which grew out of a monastic settlement first established in the 6th century by St. Canice, was shaped a bit like a figure eight; it comprised two parts—a monastic town and a merchant town—at the center of a wheat-growing region. When the Anglo-Norman knight, Strongbow, arrived here, he built a small fort to protect the crossing of the River Nore. Later, as the town expanded and was walled, the local population—the Irish Catholic community—was forced into the area north of the city (around St. Canice's original monastic settlement), which became known as Irishtown. By the end of the 14th century, the powerful Butler clan had taken over and moved into the stone castle which had replaced Strongbow's fort.

The 1366 Statutes of Kilkenny took their name from the Irish Parliament which resided in Kilkenny; these were designed to reduce the influence of the native Irish on the Anglo-Normans. Irish customs, culture (including games like hurling), and language were suppressed and intermarriage was banned. After the 1641 Rebellion, Kilkenny became the capital of Confederate Ireland—formed by an allegiance of Catholic landowners who had lost their lands to English settlers, and loyalist supporters of Charles I—which lasted from 1642 and 1649, until the city surrendered to Cromwell during his conquest of Ireland.

Kilkenny's core retains its medieval influence, and while the walls of the city are gone, you can still see reminders of those days when stone and mortar formed a physical barrier between the Irish and Normans. Although abandoned by the Butlers after Ireland achieved independence, Kilkenny Castle has been dutifully restored and remains the city's principal attraction. Today, Kilkenny is renowned for its craft industries; the city is the HQ of the Crafts Council of Ireland, and many potters, leatherworkers, jewelers, and other artists have established their workshop studios in villages around the county.

THE LAY OF THE LAND

Although it's officially a city, Kilkenny is tiny; in the main center are two major intersecting stretches of road, with various side-streets and laneways trailing off these. You can cover the major sights in a couple of hours, but the real fun here is venturing forth at night when the action can get combustible. Try to spend at least 1 full day getting out into the surrounding countryside—the nearby villages (some of which are in neighboring County Carlow) are disarmingly pretty, typically with a riverside location and backed by rolling, wooded hills that are ideal for walking and cycling.

GETTING THERE & GETTING AROUND

Kilkenny City lies on the **N10,** which is a short detour off the N9 which links Waterford to Carlow Town and then, further north, eventually merges with the M7/N7 to Dublin. To get here from Wexford, take the N25/N30 to New Ross and then follow the R700 through Thomastown and on to Kilkenny.

Getting here by **bus** from Dublin takes 2 hours (€11); from Cork 3 hours (€17); from Waterford 1½ hours (€10). If you want to get here by bus from Wexford, you need to go through Waterford (€15). The main bus depot is at the train station on the Dublin Road, but you should source onward tickets from the tourist office as buses also depart from Patrick Street. **Trains** running between Dublin (€16; 2 hr.) and Waterford (€8; 45 min.) pull in at **MacDonagh Station** (Dublin Rd.; ☎ 051/772-2024).

The official **Tourist Office** (Rose Inn St.; ☎ 051/775-1500) dispenses information and maps, and also sells bus tickets; theoretically they should be able to help with accommodation bookings; I've found them lacking, though. You can rent bikes from **Connick Cycles** (9 John St.; ☎ 056/776-5168).

ACCOMMODATIONS, BOTH STANDARD & NOT

Kilkenny's popularity as a getaway destination means that hoteliers push up their prices, and entrepreneurial property owners rent out dives for inflated rates. In fact, many of the rentals in the center are targeted at groups of young people who come to town for a party, so while they may have plenty of beds, they tend to feel more like dorm spaces than homes. The agencies at work in town aren't particularly helpful, either. If you would prefer to self-cater, I'd suggest a place in the country, such as the **Old Grainstore,** a wonderfully restored riverside property in St. Mullins (p. 135).

Camping on the outskirts of Kilkenny City at **Treegrove** (Danville House, New Ross Rd.; ☎ 086/830-8845 or 056/777-0302; www.treegrovecamping.com; cash only) is also an option for penny pinchers; it has both caravan and tent pitches. Campers are charged €6.50 to €7.50 each, plus €1 per tent and €2 per car; showers are free, and there's a laundry, kitchen facility, and TV room. Kilkenny's nightlife is a 25-minute walk away, or you can rent a bike and cycle along the riverside path that leads into town. Things are family-run and pretty casual; reception is in a wooden hut.

Kilkenny City

€   If you're literally counting every cent, consider the well-located, if slightly grungy **Kilkenny Tourist Hostel** (35 Parliament St.; ☎ 056/776-3541; cash

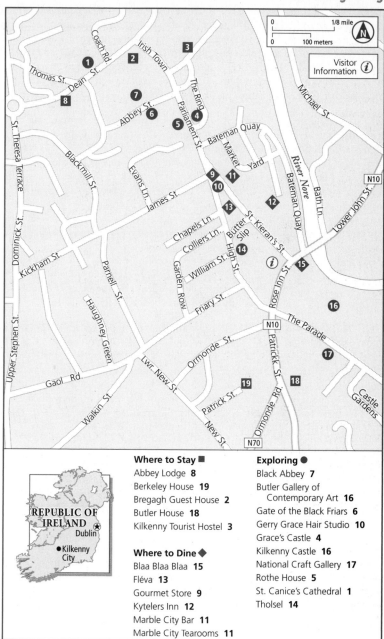

Where to Stay ■
Abbey Lodge **8**
Berkeley House **19**
Bregagh Guest House **2**
Butler House **18**
Kilkenny Tourist Hostel **3**

Where to Dine ◆
Blaa Blaa Blaa **15**
Fléva **13**
Gourmet Store **9**
Kytelers Inn **12**
Marble City Bar **11**
Marble City Tearooms **11**

Exploring ●
Black Abbey **7**
Butler Gallery of
  Contemporary Art **16**
Gate of the Black Friars **6**
Gerry Grace Hair Studio **10**
Grace's Castle **4**
Kilkenny Castle **16**
National Craft Gallery **17**
Rothe House **5**
St. Canice's Cathedral **1**
Tholsel **14**

REPUBLIC OF
IRELAND
  Dublin
● Kilkenny
  City

only), where a dorm bed is €17. You'll have access to a well-equipped (though small, and often overcrowded) kitchen, be able to use the Zen-atmosphere lounge (until 11pm, at least, when you're summarily kicked out), get free Wi-Fi (there are safes for your laptop and valuables), do your laundry (€5 per load), and even get a fairly comfortable night's sleep—although, in the dorms, a few extra pints of Guinness would go a long way to smooth the way through a haze of potentially loud snoring. Twin rooms (not en suite) cost €42.

€€   Virtually in the shadow of St. Canice's Cathedral, just around the corner from the northern end of Parliament Street, Rosanne and John Brennan's big ocher-colored **Bregagh Guest House** ✪✪ (Dean St.; ☎ 086/109-9348 or 056/772-2315; www.bregaghhouse.com; cash only) is one of the nicest B&Bs in Kilkenny. Named after the river that flows at the back of the house, it's not only a warm, cozy home-away-from-home, but has an excellent, tranquil garden and conservatory that gets plenty of sun. The fair-size bedrooms are neat, clean and carpeted, with big windows (double-glazed to keep out any noise), wall-mounted mirrors, large wardrobes, and stylish contemporary linens; only the bathrooms (with very good shower cubicles) are perhaps "smallish." Although there's no front desk, and the atmosphere is informal and absolutely family-run, the place feels ever so slightly like a small hotel—even the little breakfast room, with its leather seats, is a chic upgrade of what's usually on offer. The Brennans charge €80 to €90 per double, and have family and double-bedded single units, too.

€€   Further along Dean Street, and no longer such an easy walk to town, the Brennan's daughter, Rosie Keenan, recently opened **Abbey Lodge** ✪✪ (The Waterbarracks, Dean St.; ☎ 056/777-1866; www.abbeylodge.ie; cash only), a contemporary-style B&B in a purpose-built house. Rosie is aiming at a luxury boutique type guesthouse, so the minimalist design includes plenty of straight lines, crisp modern linens, wall-mounted plasma TVs, and modern finishes. For the best bang for your buck, you'll want a room with a view of the Black Abbey that also gets plenty of sun; unit 5 is the best double (€80–€90), and 6 is a good choice for families. My only worry is that two of Rosie's bedrooms are for five and six people, respectively (at around €35–€40 per person), meaning they may fill up with partying groups, which may impact the serenity of the place.

€–€€€   If you'd prefer to be closer to town, and want something more akin to a small hotel, then **Berkeley House** (5 Lower Patrick St.; ☎ 056/776-4848; www.berkeleyhousekilkenny.com; AE, MC, V) is probably your best option, with dull, neatly maintained rooms in a Georgian residence once occupied by George Berkeley. Bedrooms are a little boxy, with modular furnishings and all the standard amenities (including ironing facilities), but clean and tidy. Although prices go all the way up to €90 or even €130 in summer (and €150 during festivals), you can score a standard room for €60 during the week in low season (Oct–Feb). Berkeley's owner, Vincent, also has a number of self-catering houses for rent (just be sure to avoid the "Base Apartment," a rather rudimentary option).

€€–€€€€   Three presidents have stayed in the only Presidential suite in Kilkenny, and despite agreeable prices, **Butler House** ✪✪✪ (16 Patrick St.;

☎ 056/772-2828 or 056/776-5707; www.butler.ie; AE, DC, MC, V) remains, unquestionably, the loveliest address in Kilkenny. It offers what no other establishment in town can: a real sense of history. Overlooking a magnificent garden and beyond that, Kilkenny Castle, this large townhouse was first refurbished as a guesthouse by designer Jenny Trigwell in the 1960s; when the rooms were renovated in 2007, Ms. Trigwell worked with the new team to retain the same soothing retro minimalism that makes each of the 13 bedrooms feel a bit like a work of art. In fact, each huge bedroom contains great, unique artworks, perfectly complementing the elegant, comfortable furnishings; those upstairs have vast bay windows. Breakfast is served at the restaurant of the Kilkenny Design Centre; the chef comes to take your hot food order (anything goes), while you help yourself to a generous buffet. I include this luxe property because it's sometimes an affordable option: Prices often drop to €120 during the low season (Nov–Jan), though you're likely to pay up €180 at peak times (May–Oct).

Near Thomastown

€€ Another of my favorite spots in the southeast (I admit there are a few) is **Ballyduff House** ★★★ 🎒 (Thomastown; ☎ 056/775-8488; www.ballyduff house.com; cash only). It's one of those places that, by the time you've driven up the long, tree-lined driveway, you're wishing you'd booked an extra week. The "house" is attached to 750-year-old Ballyduff Castle, while the rest is a mere 300 years old. Despite its distinguished pedigree, Ballyduff feels much like a lovingly lived-in home, and Brede Thomas welcomes you with easygoing hospitality. Red-carpeted stairs lead up to big, sumptuous bedrooms, each filled with Georgian antiques, books, and framed artworks. One room is exactly as it looked for the scene where Colin Firth beds Saffron Burrows in the film *Circle of Friends,* which was shot here and launched Minnie Driver's career. If you must have a room with private bathroom, ask. The B&B rate is €100 double, and €130 for a family room. By the way, the appeal here is as much outdoor as indoor: This place is a perfect setting-out-point for long countryside walks, relaxing alongside the river, or watching the sheep nibbling the lawn (that same lawn features soccer nets and a trampoline for the wee ones).

St. Mullins

In an idyllic "nobody will find me here" setting at the edge of the Barrow River, the **Old Grainstore** ★★★ (St. Mullins; ☎ 087/258-4663 or 051/424440; www.oldgrainstorecottages.ie) is a set of three blissful little self-catering cottages around an old stable yard that lies on a bend in the river. They're handsomely decorated, imbued with a bright, fresh, crisp look and plenty of cottage-style pine, modern kitchen facilities, and a cozy, furnace-warmed sitting area; bedrooms are stylish and simple, with wood floors and contemporary linens. The two one-bedroom units cost €380 per week (May–Sept) and sleep two people in a wonderfully comfortable double bed; and for families, a two-bedroom unit sleeps four people (a double plus one twin bed; €480). Cottages are rented from Saturday to Saturday, and are €80 cheaper October to April. You can rent fishing equipment and bicycles here, and learn from the handful of locals how to take life at a gentler pace.

€€   Blessed with eye-popping views over the Barrow Valley and located at the top of one of the most picturesque villages in Ireland, **Mulvarra House** ✮✮✮ (St. Mullins; ☎ 051/424936; www.mulvarra.com; MC, V) is where you'll find your country groove. Nothing fancy, just filled with home-fashioned warmth and Noreen Ardill's easygoing welcome—"I don't think I've ever refused anybody anything," she says. But she also assists with sightseeing itineraries, does laundry, provides an Internet facility, cooks evening meals (€30 for a five-course dinner), and offers massage and spa treatments. All five of the bedrooms are upstairs, built into the pitched roof, so feel a bit like large attic rooms, and four of them have little balconies with those spectacular views. Rooms, which go for €80, all have private bathrooms (with great big showers), but no dressers or desks (though there's ample room to leave your luggage ajar). I'd reckon this is the perfect base if you're self-driving and want to explore the counties of Kilkenny, Carlow, and Wexford from a central, serene, picturesque home.

DINING FOR ALL TASTES
Kilkenny City

€   Kilkenny has two grade-A essential stops for sandwiches. Around lunch time, you'll often see hungry locals waiting for their daily fix of filled bread outside the tiny premises of **Blaa Blaa Blaa** ✮✮ (Canal Square; ☎ 056/775-2212; Mon–Fri 8:30am–4pm; cash only), right near the bridge, around the corner from the castle entrance. A husband and wife team, the Clandillons turn out "a couple of hundred sandwiches a day," and you can either throw together your own ingredients, or choose from a tasty menu: "The Blasse" is a grilled sandwich with roast peppers, goat cheese, and hummus (€4.30), and there's a breakfast-in-a-sandwich (with bacon, sausage, black pudding, and egg) for €3.80.

€   Since Blaa Blaa Blaa doesn't operate on weekends, you'll have little excuse not to head over to the **Gourmet Store** ✮✮ (56 High St.; ☎ 056/777-1727; www.thegourmetstorekilkennycity.com; daily 9am–6pm; MC, V), where each toasted panini (or bagel or sandwich; all €3.60) is more delicious than the next. I'm totally hooked on their "Sicily" (goat cheese, semi-dried tomatoes, and basil pesto) and the "Turin" (French brie, hummus, mixed peppers, and sundried tomato pesto). The shelves are packed with take-home gourmet items—pastas, homemade Irish preserves, bottled sweets (try the rhubarb chunks), cheeses, chili sauces, olives, and meats.

€–€€€   Directly opposite Keyteler's Inn (p. 137), one of the most atmospheric places for a light lunch or afternoon cup of java is the **Marble City Tearooms** ✮ (St. Kieran's St.; ☎ 056/776-1143; daily 9am–7pm; summer 9am–9:30pm; MC, V). A wee outdoor area is ideal for dry, warmer days, but step inside and you'll enjoy overhearing the constant buzz of customers engaged in daily gossip. Besides an extensive menu of teas (all fair trade, and some organic) and cakes, are some good-value light meals, like salmon fillet (€9.50), chicken burger (€8.50), and a variety of sandwiches and stuffed bagels. Upstairs, in the **Marble City Bar** (66 High St.; daily 9am–10pm), there's more focus on pints and pub grub served in a chic, contemporary setting.

Kyteler's Revenge

Deep in the heart of the city, **Kytelers Inn** (St. Kieran St.; ☎ 056/772-1064; www.kytelersinn.ie; food served all day until 9pm; AE, MC, V) was established in 1324 and is the progeny of one of Kilkenny's most famous legends—that of the Kilkenny witch, Dame Alice le Kyteler, the original owner of the Inn.

Born in 1280, Alice was a beautiful and buxom Belgian lass, and she collected husbands and enemies—both partially because she came from a family of moneylenders and bankers. It didn't help that each of her husbands died mysteriously and all were presumed to have been poisoned. Little wonder, then, that her stepchildren began rumors that she was involved in witchcraft. These were taken to heart by the new local bishop, a Frenchman, who had her accused and found guilty. But wily Alice had friends in high places, and in a legal coup, they had the bishop imprisoned for 17 days, instead. Although Alice was arrested and thrown into the castle dungeons, her friends helped her escape from Kilkenny. Meanwhile, her maid, Petronilla, and son, William, had also been implicated as witches, and were left to bear the brunt of the consequences. Petronilla was tortured for a week before being burned at the stake, and William bought a pardon by agreeing to put a new lead roof on the bishop's church. However, in an ironic twist, the leaden roof proved too heavy and eventually collapsed 50 years after the witch trials.

Although Alice was never officially heard of again, her, um, spirit lives on at Kyteler's Inn, particularly in its dungeon-esque (yet mysteriously modern-looking) downstairs tavern, where moody red lighting, stone walls, and vaulted arches conjure up a bygone era. A wonderfully authentic pub on the ground level displays historic memorabilia, has neat tables for meals, and a decent-enough menu (although I'd say the place does tend to trade a bit on reputation). Still, you can get a good ol' Irish stew (€12) and other such bar grub (mostly around €13). But be warned: The early bird specials here (like smoked salmon and a glass of Guinness for €15) are not really good deals at all, since the beer comes in a teensy glass.

€€–€€€€   If all goes according to plan, when you leave **Fléva** ★★★ 🧒 (84 High St.; ☎ 056/777-0021; www.fleva.ie; Tues–Sun 12:30–2:30pm and 6–9:15pm; Fri–Sat 6–10:30pm; AE, MC, V) you'll feel right as rain, your day brightened and your mood lightened, all after a dining experience accompanied by cheerful service, organic ingredients, interesting menu choices, and mood-enhancing decor—"It's feng shui . . . what I call acupuncture for buildings," says owner Kayrin Connery. Through a tiny doorway on High Street and up the stairs, you'll see what she means: Brightly colored walls, eye-catching artworks, quirky chandeliers, spunky Latino music, and elegantly laid out tables. Fléva prepares world cuisine-inspired updates of classic Irish dishes, so there are some interesting twists. Like couscous with almond crusted aubergine (€9.50), or salmon, cod, and monkfish fishcakes (€13). If you want something that really explodes with flavor, start with the scrumptious ginger spiced pork wontons (€9.50). Lunch is more affordable than dinner; otherwise, come early (6–7:15pm) and enjoy a two-course meal for €22. There's a special slow food menu just for kids, culminating with either Tipperary ice cream or traditional bread and butter pudding, and costs €12.

Inistioge

€€–€€€€   Blessed with perfectly glorious views of lolling hills and the Nore River valley stretching out down below, **Bassetts at Woodstock** ✪✪✪ (Woodstock Gardens; ☎ 056/775-8820; www.bassetts.ie; weekend reservations recommended; Wed–Sat noon–4pm and 7:30pm–late; Sun 1–5pm; MC, V) is one of my favorite dining discoveries, right at the entrance to Woodstock Gardens (p. 142). It's a small place that, thanks to a menu that's a little different and a setting that can't be beat, has quickly found its way into the hearts of foodies and nature-lovers alike. At lunch (certainly the best time to come for views), the standout is a crispy bacon and egg sandwich (served with chips, €14) made with pigs reared in the adjacent field. Beef is also raised right here, and the fish comes straight from the local market (best on Thurs). On warm, sunny days, you can sit on the outdoor deck overlooking the valley; inside, the decor is simple and modern with the light, breezy ambience of a cool cafe-bistro.

WHY YOU'RE HERE: TOP SIGHTS & ATTRACTIONS

With a good guide, you'll come away knowing more about Kilkenny than most people who live here. One such gem is **Liam Bolger** (ask for him by name), who takes visitors around the city on behalf of **Pat Tynan's Walking Tours of Medieval Kilkenny** ✪✪✪ (☎ 087/265-1745 or 056/776-3955; www.tynantours.com; €6), and is one of the most talented guides I've had in Ireland. Tours run from mid-March through October, and start at 10:30am, 12:15, 3, and 4:30pm Monday to Saturday, and at 11:15am and 12:30pm on Sunday. Tours start out from the **Tourist Office** on Rose Inn Street (☎ 056/775-1500), which, incidentally, is housed in the 16th-century **Shee Alms House,** built by a charitable aristocrat as a shelter for the poor. It also served as an underground Catholic church from 1800 to 1829.

Exploring Medieval Kilkenny

With its medieval layout still very much in evidence (particularly when it comes to traffic), Kilkenny is a marvelously compact, dynamic place to explore. Starting at the massive, unwieldy intersection where the Parade meets Patrick Street, make your way slowly north along the **High Street** (first laid out in 1203, but enlarged in the 1800s), and venture off down its atmospheric side-street laneways—or "slips"—that connect with **St. Kieran's Street,** and you'll soon unearth the "flavor" of the city. **Butter Slip,** for example was once where butter was sold, prompting a little ditty that goes like this:

If you ever go to Kilkenny, look for a hole in the wall.
There you will get 24 eggs for a penny, and butter for nothing at all!

Down on St. Kieran's Street are many wonderful bars and pubs, the most famous of which is **Keyteler's Inn** ✴✴, started by a woman purported to be a witch (p. 137). Notice how many of the windows of Keyteler's are bricked up? That's because of a medieval tax on windows—a mean-fisted scheme that coined the phrase "daylight robbery."

Along High Street, the stand-out monument is the **Tholsel** ✴, an Anglo-Saxon term for "house of taxes," and which still serves as the City Hall, albeit one which was rebuilt after a fire in 1985. If you study the surviving walls, however, you can still make out carved symbols of Norman power—look for images of archers at the ready on the top of tower walls. Medieval Kilkenny was surrounded by 6m (20-ft.) walls, completed in 1400 and built to keep the native Irish out. When it was built in the 1700s, the Tholsel was where criminals were tried and imprisoned—and, in some cases, executed. Naughty, lawbreaking youngsters were placed in a whirligig (a type of iron cage) that was suspended from the portico archway, so that passing citizens could spin them as a kind of public humiliation. The Tholsel, you will notice, appears to be built of marble. In fact, as you explore this part of town, notice how an abundance of polished black stone is used everywhere, on sidewalks and buildings; actually, it's this imitation marble that earned Kilkenny the moniker "Marble City," although the stone in question is actually limestone. The marbled effect is created by fossil shells.

Incidentally, on the other side of the road, the house that is now **Gerry Grace Hair Studio** (44 High St.) was once the home of James Hoburn, the man who designed the White House and much of Washington D.C., and also owned the American capital's first brothel. Walt Disney's grandfather also lived on this road, at number 21.

As you continue north along High Street it soon merges with St. Kieran's Street to become **Parliament Street.** Notice the **sculpted bust?** It's a limestone depiction of Kilkenny's first priest, Cainneach, erected here in 1999. Interestingly, the sculptor chose to give the priest Egyptian features, symbolizing an ancient connection with the people of North Africa. Gene pool testing has revealed that the ancient Irish in fact came from Egypt some 7,000 years ago.

Considered the most beautiful piece of architecture in Kilkenny, **Rothe House** (Parliament St.; ☎ 056/772-2893; www.rothehouse.com; €5; Nov–Mar Mon–Sat 10:30am–4:30pm; Apr–Oct Mon–Sat 10:30am–5pm; Sun 3–5pm) was built in 1594 for a wealthy, high-class drapery merchant, John Rothe. Today, it consists of three interconnected houses, the 2nd and 3rd houses added for Rothe's offspring. The family's life of privilege ended abruptly in 1650 when Cromwell arrived in town with 30,000 troops and presented Rothe an ultimatum; rather than renounce Catholicism, the family moved to France. One of the Rothes became a lady-in-waiting to Marie Antoinette, and was actually beheaded alongside her. Rothe House is now the headquarters of the Kilkenny Archaeological Society which hosts an exhibition of ancient and medieval relics; at the back a medieval garden has been redeveloped.

Opposite Rothe House is **Grace's Castle,** which is the county courthouse (closed for renovation since Mar 2008); the neo-classical facade dates from the 1780s, and conceals dank, gloomy cells. Although the cells were designed to take four inmates each, at one stage in the early-1800s, there were as many as 200 prisoners stuffed in here like sardines. Nearly 1,000 young girls were marched from these prisons to Cork, where they were put on ships destined for Australia.

The Cathedral & the Black Abbey

Built between 1202 and 1285, the Anglican **St. Canice's Cathedral** ✹ (The Close; ☎ 056/776-4971; www.stcanicescathedral.ie; €4; Apr–May and Sept Mon–Sat 10am–1pm and 2–5pm; June–Aug Mon–Sat 9am–6pm; Oct–Mar Mon–Sat 10am–1pm and 2–4pm; Sun from 2pm all year) lies north of Parliament Street, beyond the original confines of the medieval Anglo-Norman market town, where St. Canice first built his original wooden church. Most visitors head straight for the door and proceed inside to uncover the history of this place, but I like to wander through the grounds—with loads of gravestones—first. Once inside the church, you need to take care not to trip over the grave slabs that form part of the undulating floor. If pieced together cleverly, the many stone artifacts collected here help tell part of the city's history; there's even a model of Kilkenny as it looked in 1642. Just outside, you can climb to the top of the 30.5m (102-ft.) round tower (€3, or €6 for a combo ticket), which predates the church itself. Built in the 9th century by the king of Ossory, the tower is a remnant of St. Canice's original monastic settlement from where **360-degree views** ✹ of Kilkenny are the reward for a stiff climb up a narrow staircase.

South of the Cathedral, hidden amidst Kilkenny's ancient backstreets, **Black Abbey** ✹✹ (Abbey St.; ☎ 056/772-1279; free admission; Apr–Sept Mon–Sat 7:30am–7pm; Sun 9am–7pm; Oct–Mar 7:30am–5:30pm) is a spectacular work of medieval architecture that's survived more than its fair share of nicks and bruises; to reach it from Parliament Street, walk down the narrow lane (Abbey St.) across the road from the Watergate Theatre. En route, you'll pass through the **Gate of the Black Friars**—or Black Freren Gate—which is the only survivor among the original seven city gateways. The iron gate alongside the archway was made by a Kilkenny family named Wilkinson, now globally famous for producing Wilkinson Sword razor blades. A triumphant example of defensive ecclesiastical architecture, Black Abbey is one of the oldest surviving Catholic churches in Ireland. Extensively damaged by Cromwell, who also ousted its religious community, it remained roofless and windowless until the Dominicans were able to return in the 19th century. Only one precious statue survived Cromwell, a lovely effigy of Christ, sculpted in 1264, and plastered over by the locals so that it would not be found. The other highlight: a magnificent stained glass Rosary Window that has over 10,000 pieces of glass; when it was re-leaded, it took 14 men 6 months and cost £75,000.

Kilkenny Castle

Looking at it from across the River Nore, **Kilkenny Castle** ✹✹✹ (The Parade; ☎ 056/770-4100; www.heritageireland.ie; Heritage Card or €5.30; daily Oct–May 10:30am–5pm; June–Aug 9:30am–7pm; Sept 10am–6pm) dominates the city. Its walled grounds—where children play, jugglers juggle, the healthy jog, and town councilors strut—seem to stretch out into eternity (never mind the 20 hectares/50 acres today, the ruling landowners once controlled land spanning several counties and much of Munster), and the whopping big castle itself seems entirely out of proportion, given the marginal size of the city. Which makes a visit essential; you've just got to get an eyeful of what's lurking behind those grey

Gothic-Victorian walls. A guided tour takes you through various stately rooms and hallways, now restored, including a William Morris-designed bedroom, with an en suite loo specially installed for a visit by King Edward VII.

Home to the mighty Butler clan until 1935, the site where the castle stands is where Strongbow (otherwise known as Richard, Earl of Pembroke) established a fortress in 1172. When Strongbow's son-in-law took over the kingdom of Leinster, he built the first complete castle here, some of which still survives. In the 14th century, the government met here and passed the infamous Statutes of Kilkenny which effectively banned Irish culture. James Butler, who headed up a long line that would become the earls of Ormonde, bought the castle in 1391. One of his descendants, another James, remodeled the castle in the guise of a very big French chateau in 1660, following a grueling cannonball attack by Cromwell a decade before. The second great remodeling happened in the 1820s, when all the early-Victorian fixings were added, transforming the place into the fairytale monument you see today. Although the Butlers were always a family of fence-sitters when it came to the "war" between Catholics and Protestants, and indeed the Irish and English, they maintained close allegiances with the crown, and the castle did host King George V. And when the Irish Free State was created, they left the castle and its contents were auctioned off. In the late-1960s, it was sold to the local community for a paltry fee, and the process of restoring what had fallen into considerable disrepair was begun.

Of all its lavish rooms, the most thrilling is the Long Gallery, an enormous salon shaped like an upside down Viking longboat with a magnificent painted Norwegian pine ceiling. Created to house a collection of 200 spectacular paintings—including portraits of William of Orange and Queen Mary, who both stayed here—the space is a marvel of design, with hammer beam trusses and a Carrera Italian marble fireplace. While you're waiting for your guided tour to begin (and I suggest you turn up early to book your place), pop down to the **Butler Gallery of Contemporary Art** ✪✪✪ (free admission), which occupies a section of the original servants' rooms in the basement of one wing of the castle.

Across the road from the castle, another essential stop is the **National Craft Gallery** ✪✪✪ (Castle Yard; ☎ 056/776-1804; www.ccoi.ie; free admission; Mon–Sat 10am–6pm; Apr–Dec Sun 11am–6pm), established by the Crafts Council of Ireland in 2000 as a showcase for Irish and international arts and crafts. Occupying the former palace stables, which were built in 1776 by Walter Butler, the line up of exhibitions includes the work of inventive, cutting-edge artists working in such diverse areas as sculpting, basketmaking, jewelry design, and ceramics. You'll see eye-catching designs by crafters, functional as well as avant garde and offbeat works, and will often come away with new ideas about something you may have long taken for granted; the excellent **Kilkenny Design Centre** (p. 145) is also here.

A Roadtrip: Unspoiled Towns & Villages near Kilkenny

Kilkenny is ideally situated close to quite a number of truly delectable villages—for some this roadtrip should be the best part of a visit to Kilkenny.

Take the R700 south to **Bennettsbridge,** a tiny community straddling the Nore and linked in the middle by a handsome 18th-century stone bridge; the village is home to two important pottery studios—Nicholas Mosse and Stoneware Jackson (see "Attention, Shoppers!" on p. 145).

Another 9km (5½ miles) south lies **Thomastown,** once known as Grennan, which was at the heart of the ancient kingdom of Ossory. Thomas Fitz Anthony Walsh, the Norman lord who built his castle here, gave the town its modern name and also built the defensive walls of which only a few ruins still remain. Along the Nore you can still see a number of defunct mills that were the driving force in the town's principal industry until the 1960s. The town's famous Mount Juliet Conrad hotel and golf course draws the well-to-do, while one of the country's finest Cistercian abbeys lies 2km (1 mile) south of Thomastown on the N9. You can't miss the defensive tower added on to **Jerpoint Abbey** ✯✯ (☎ 056/772-4623; www.heritageireland.ie; Heritage Card or €2.90; daily Mar–May and mid-Sept to Oct 10am–5pm; June to mid-Sept 10am–6pm; Nov–Feb 10am–4pm) in the 15th century. This remarkable example of Romanesque ecclesiastical architecture was first founded as a Benedictine abbey, however, most of what we see today was built shortly after the site was taken over by 12th-century Cistercians. The ruins are in good enough shape to give a fairly good idea of how the abbey would have functioned (I find the structure evokes the past quite vividly). Another great surprise is that you can clearly make out some of the details in the stonework carvings: Norman knights who wear armor, and holy men who dress in robes and carry staffs. Not far from the abbey, you can watch glassblowing at **Jerpoint Glass Studio** ✯✯ (Stoneyford; ☎ 056/772-4350; www.jerpointglass.com; Mon–Thurs 10am–4:30pm; Fri 10am–2pm; shop open Mon–Sat 10am–6pm; Sun noon–5pm), a wonderfully non-commercial alternative to Waterford Crystal (p. 153). And it's free. Movie buffs will be interested to know that a piece of Jerpoint glassware is featured in *Harry Potter and the Order of the Phoenix,* when a toast to the young wizard is raised with a set of specially commissioned trumpet wineglasses.

Head south from Thomastown following the River Nore, to **Inistioge** ✯✯✯, another adorable village (sorry, there's no other word for it) with its sumptuous **Woodstock Gardens & Arboretum** ✯ (☎ 087/858-0502; www.woodstock.ie; car €4, pedestrians free admission; daily May–Sept 9am–8pm; Oct–Apr 10am–4:30pm), first laid out in Victorian times with many exotic trees and shrubs that were considered rare or unknown at the time (Japanese cedar, Golden Monterey cypress, Chilean myrtle to name a few). Ongoing restoration is constantly improving the gardens and walks, providing impressive views over Inistioge and the Nore River valley below.

To get to **Graiguenamanagh** ✯✯, you can head east from Thomastown, or you can take an extremely quiet country backroad signposted just over Inistioge's 10-arch bridge. Although difficult on the tongue, this old-worldly village (it's pronounced graige-nah-manna; say it 5 times and you'll get it) is very easy on the eye, pressed into a gentle fold between the Barrow River and Brandon Hill. The village's centerpiece is the massive **Duiske Abbey;** established in 1204 by Norman monks from Stanley Abbey in Wiltshire, this was once Ireland's biggest Cistercian abbey with hundreds of lay priests supporting a community that included a school, hospital, hostelry, and farm. Although the present structure bears the obvious marks of its restoration during the 1970s, the soaring whitewashed walls do a good job of showing off two sets of particularly lovely tall stained-glass windows. The village is a popular destination for the boating and fishing crowds, and the quayside guesthouse, **Waterside** ✯✯ (☎ 059/972-4246; www.watersideguesthouse.com; AE, MC, V; €84–€105 double with breakfast) does an excellent four-course Sunday lunch for under €25.

A little farther out, across the border in the south of County Carlow, **St. Mullins** ✿✿✿ may just be one of the loveliest spots in the southwest; perched on a tranquil stretch along the River Barrow, nestled between the Blackstairs Mountains and Brandon Hill, the highlight of this tiny village is a collection of church ruins—dating as far back as 1000 A.D.—gathered amidst a mass of gravestones. Beyond a few houses, there's little more than the local pub, Blanchfields, which doubles as the local post office. The ecclesiastical ruins at St. Mullins may not be as extensive as at Jerpoint, but there's a wonderful mystique around the site, not least because of the devastation which took place in 1323, when the church here was burned along with local men, women, and children. St. Moling, after whom the village is named, was a 7th-century prince, poet, and cleric who is said to have hand-dug a mile-long water channel here in order to power his mill. St. Moling died in 697, and is believed to be buried on the church grounds along with men who died in the 1798 Rebellion, and several ancient kings of Leinster. Outside the ruins of the medieval abbey, stands a wonderfully carved 9th-century high cross engraved with depictions of the crucifixion and a swirling Celtic pattern. The holy well of St. Moling, nearby, is meant to have the power to cure, among other things, the plague.

Incidentally, the **Barrow Way,** a towpath that runs alongside the Barrow River that was originally used to pull boats or barges along the water, is an excellent walking route; from St. Mullins, you can use it to reach Graiguenamanagh in 40 minutes (6km/4 miles), or—if you've got real time on your hands—walk all the way to Lowtown, some 113km (70 miles) north. You'll pass myriad tiny villages along the way, not to mention old bridges, castles, and ruined ecclesiastical monuments that are far away from the beaten tourist track.

THE OTHER KILKENNY

You'll get a sense of the hustle and bustle of daily life (and meet local producers) at Kilkenny **farmers' market** held each Thursday morning on Mayor's Walk. It's not a huge market, with about 20 stalls selling all kinds of foodstuffs and fresh produce, but you can buy coffee, get take-out food, and spend time chatting with the people who work and shop here. Don't miss the **Truffle Fairy** (☎ 087/286-2634; www.trufflefairy.com) where you can buy mouthwatering chunks of

---

Alternative Dental Hygiene

Buried at St. Mullins on the monastery grounds is Daniel Kavanagh, a friar descended from the kings of Leinster, the MacMurrough Kavanaghs. He apparently had the power to heal, and it's believed that even in death he can cure a toothache. Admittedly, I haven't tried this out yet, but here's how the locals say it works. Grab a bit of soil from outside the churchyard and exchange it for a bit of clay from Daniel's grave. Then, say a quick prayer and pop the clay into your mouth and head down the hill to St. Moling's well, where you should use the water to wash out your mouth.

Catch the Cats in Action

Kilkenny's sports scene is legendary, and the county's favorite team is nicknamed the "Kilkenny Cats," considered one of the "Big Three" in the world of hurling, far and away the dominant sport in the county. The Cats have won the All-Ireland hurling championship 30 times, their last victory in 2007, which makes them the reigning champions as I write this (watch the press for details).

The team takes its name from an old expression "fighting like Kilkenny cats," which was used to describe the ongoing brawls that happened at the gate which once separated the walled Norman part of town from Irish Town. That expression, or so the story goes, came from a cruel sport practiced in the city by Cromwell's men. Apparently they would amuse themselves by tying the tails of two cats together and hang them from a wire, an inhumane act which would induce a feline fight to the death.

Thankfully, the sports scene in Kilkenny is very different today. Kilkenny's GAA grounds are at **Nowlan Park** (☎ 056/772-1236). Just remember that you'll be supporting the lads wearing black and amber vertical stripes. Fans will be only too happy to explain what's going on, so use this as an opportunity to make new friends. Matches typically happen on Sunday afternoons, and as the build-up to the finals of the All-Ireland Championships goes into full swing, you'll be assured of catching a thrilling game (especially in June and July). Find out what fixtures are planned at the GAA's (Gaelic Athletic Association) website, www.gaa.ie, or simply ask almost anyone in town.

homemade fudge (try chai espresso and lime chili-flavored fudge, which has a slight edge to it). For information about the market, call **Mary Merritts** (☎ 086/815-6182).

As mentioned, the **National Craft Gallery** (p. 141) is a hub of top-quality Irish craftsmanship. Part of the program includes occasional workshops, seminars, and even demonstrations to coincide with current exhibitions. Among the events put together for crafts enthusiasts in 2008, there was a 1-day basketmaking conference; a seminar in which artists, architects, and designers spoke about how we will live in the future; and a "Breaking Out" seminar focused on emerging artists and crafters. To find out if anything is happening when you're in town, go online (**www.ccoi.ie**) and search the "Exhibitions Programme"; special events (and seminar booking details) are mentioned here.

ACTIVE KILKENNY

Mount Juliet Estate (☎ 056/777-3064; www.mountjuliet.ie) near Thomastown is considered one of the country's premiere golfing facilities. Designed by Jack Nicklaus, and voted Ireland's Best Parkland Golf Course in 2008 by *Backspin Golf*

Magazine, the course draws many of the world's top-rated pros; major international events are hosted here. For just €12, enthusiasts can sample the 18 hole putting course which is the venue for Ireland's annual National Putting Championship. Terrain includes mini-bunkers and rock-bordered lakes, making the experience fun and exciting, yet a heck of a lot more affordable than the main course (green fees €90–€190). It's popular, so book ahead.

For **canoe** trips on the River Barrow, contact **Go with the Flow River Adventures** (☎ 087/252-9700; www.gowiththeflow.ie). Charlie Horan's team of instructors lead adventure outings that combine gentle stretches, weirs, rapids, and waterfalls; there's plenty of white water action. Wetsuits and buoyancy aids are provided, as are clear instructions; most canoeing sessions happen on weekends, last around 4 hours, and cost €49 per person. Canoeists meet up near the little village of Borris (around 20 min. from Kilkenny). Guided river treks are also available, as are instruction courses.

Graiguenamanagh has been associated with eel **fishing** for 800 years; the monks of Duiske monastery were in control of this lucrative little industry for much of that time. The Barrow which passes right through Graigue also gets some trout and salmon (Mar–Sept), and the river is considered one of the best in the country for coarse fishing; there's an annual shad run in May. To find out about where best to buy a fishing license and pick up supplies, call **Carlow Coarse Angling Supplies** (☎ 059/913-7664). There's also lake fishing in Thomastown at **Mount Juliet** (☎ 056/777-3000), and at **Wallslough Village** (☎ 056/772-3838) in Bennettsbridge.

As mentioned, this part of the southeast offers plentiful opportunities for **walking.** Graiguenamanagh is a great starting point for hikes up Brandon Hill (515m/1,689 ft.), exploring the Blackstairs Mountains, and reaching the top of Mount Leinster (795m/2,608 ft.). If you prefer taking things at a gentler pace, then set off along the Barrow Way (p. 143), which you can also tackle from other starting points. You'll find trail maps on site.

The gentle country roads of the Barrow, Nore, and Suir river valleys make for ideal cycling terrain. **Celtic Cycling** (22 Ballybricken, Waterford; ☎ 051/850228) puts together hassle-free cycling holidays in this region, with 7- or 14-day itineraries in addition to tailor-made options. Accommodations range from quality B&Bs to heritage properties, and the organizers make all luggage arrangements for you; you can even combine your biking holiday with pre-arranged golfing sessions. A 7-day cycling tour costs €725 per person sharing.

ATTENTION, SHOPPERS!

Kilkenny is known for its remarkable variety of artists and craftspeople, many of whom have set up studios or workshops in quiet (and stereotypically picturesque) villages within easy striking distance of Kilkenny City. Start by visiting the **Kilkenny Design Centre** ★★★ (Castle Yard; ☎ 056/772-2118) located in the castle's restored stable yard. You can watch gold and silversmiths at work, browse art exhibitions, craft, and design, and pick out some gifts of exemplary quality. There's more eye-catching high-end jewelry and crafts at **Red Aesthetic** ★★★ (2 Rose Inn St., Kilkenny City; ☎ 056/776-5526; www.redaesthetic.com).

Ten kilometers (6 miles) out of Kilkenny, on the way to Bennettsbridge, it's worth stopping at the **Bridge Pottery** (Coalsfarm, Burnchurch; ☎ 056/772-9156;

www.bridgepottery.com) to peruse award-winning ceramics created by Mark Campden and Mary O'Gorman. Farther along the R700, in Bennettsbridge, **Nicholas Mosse Pottery** (Big Mill; ☎ 056/772-7105; www.nicholasmosse.com; Mon–Sat 10am–6pm; Sun 1:30–5pm) is now a booming business, albeit one where you can stop in at the studio to watch how the signature spongeware pottery is made. Mosse has become a huge name in Irish pottery (and quite pricey, I feel), but **Stoneware Jackson Pottery** ✹ (☎ 056/772-7175; www.stonewarejackson.com; Mon–Sat 10am–6pm) just outside Bennettsbridge, is a bit more low key, and therefore even more enticing. I just love the big, chunky floral designs produced on useful homeware items in bold, imaginative colors. Michael and Mary's pottery also goes by the name Michael Jackson Ceramics, but is not to be confused with the iconic pop star.

In Thomastown, lovers of quirk must check out **Clay Creations** (Low St.; ☎ 056/772-4977; Tues–Sat 10am–1pm and 2–5pm), the studio-gallery of ceramic artist, Brid Lyons. She creates delightful sculptural pieces with a comic, eye-catching edge—lovable dogs with egg-shaped heads, and red-lipped long-necked ladies—and also hosts the work of other artists. While in Thomastown, you'd do well to spend awhile at **Earthworks Ceramics Studio and Gallery** (Grennan Watermill; ☎ 086/166-3691) where a number of crafters operate and sell their work; there's usually someone on hand who will let you watch them in action. The best work here is produced by **Karen Morgan** (www.karenmorgan ceramics.com), who uses wheel-potted fine white porcelain to create serving vessels that "bridge the gap between art and functionality." Jewelry-lovers should make a point of getting to Sue Bowden's Thomastown studio workshop, **All That Glitters** (Ladywell Corner; ☎ 056/772-4081; www.allthatglitters.ie; Mon–Sat 9:30am–1pm and 2–5:30pm). Sue uses fossils, semi-precious stones, crystals, and local stone—such as Kilkenny "marble"—to make really lovely, totally unique pieces, many of which will look wonderful around your neck. You can also commission a design which Sue will make for you while explore Thomastown. If you can't get out this way, visit her store on Ormonde Street in Kilkenny.

Booklovers shouldn't miss Graiguenamanagh's well-stocked **Antiquarian Bookmarket** ✹ (Main St.; ☎ 086/406-1049) which is just across the road from the town's centerpiece abbey. Shop hours are limited (Fri–Sun 1–4pm, although usually extended in summer), but if you can get here you're sure to pick up an armload of bargains. It can look a bit chaotic, but there are boxes filled with cut-price second-hand books and CDs; there some interesting titles (including many by Irish authors) and collector editions sought out by a consortium of different book dealers with divergent interests.

NIGHTLIFE

The mixed line-up of drama, comedy, and dance at **Watergate Theatre** (Parliament St.; ☎ 056/776-1674; www.watergatekilkenny.com) battles to compete with the more lucrative liquid entertainment scene; as with many of the theaters in smaller Irish towns the program often comprises touring productions, so I wouldn't lose too much sleep over missing a show here in favor of a good old pub crawl. What does draw in the crowds is the **Smithwick's Cat Laughs Comedy Festival** ✹✹✹ (www.smithwickscatlaughs.ie), showcasing top stand-up acts and impressive enough that some critics have gone so far as to call it the best comedy festival in the world. If you plan to be here in early-June, organize accommodations well in advance and get tickets to the best shows pronto.

Kilkenny has all kinds of places where you can wet your whistle, all concentrated along John and Parliament streets. I can recommend many of them, but there's one place I love for its authenticity: **Tynan's** ✪✪✪ (John's Bridge; ☎ 056/772-1291), which has been buzzing for over 3 centuries—you can still see the cubbyhole drawers from the days when this place doubled as a grocery store. It's also one place where *craic* takes precedent; when I last sat at the bar I swear I could've penned an award-winning script by just transcribing the comically acid dialogue being flung around. Sure, Kilkenny banter may not be suitable for sensitive listeners (definitely not for children), but the ribald is always softened by lilting voices, and I can't imagine a more relaxed spot to kick off the evening.

Tynan's is music-free, but you can catch cracking-good live music at **Andrew Ryan's** ✪✪✪ (Friary St.; no phone) on one of the roads off High Street. Practically every taste is catered for, but Thursdays are set aside for traditional sets, and on weekends they mix it up with a variety of bands, mostly playing rock 'n' roll.

More live entertainment—ranging from trad sessions to theatrical events—can be had at **Cleere's** ✪✪ (28 Parliament St.; ☎ 056/776-2573), the popularity of which seems to know no end.

Right next door, the **Pump House** (26 Parliament St.; ☎ 056/776-3924) puts on a formidable variety of music acts; genres run the gamut from commercial and rock (usually only on weekends when big city crowds descend), to toe-tappingly traditional.

With its variegated spaces (upstairs it's a pub, downstairs anything goes—including dancing), no trip to Kilkenny is complete without a round of drinks at legendary **Kyteler's Inn** ✪✪ (p. 137). More contemporary tastes will be satisfied at the **Marble City Bar** ✪✪ (66 High St.; ☎ 056/776-1143), where the look is sleek, polished, and cheerful.

Finally, the ultra-stylish **Carrigan's Liquor Bar** ✪✪ (2 High St.; ☎ 056/770-3979) is often heralded as the shining light among Kilkenny's more polished drinking venues. Classy design works well with traditional music each Monday, and there's a gay night twice a month (Fri).

Incidentally, as the night wears on, often the best way to figure out directions to the latest hip and happening late night venue, is to simply follow the foot traffic. On weekends it can seem as though the whole world is out on the prowl.

WATERFORD CITY & THE COAST

As with all Viking settlements, Waterford was built up along a stretch of river, the Suir, which empties into Waterford Harbour just east of here. Your first encounter of the city will probably have you panicking as you tussle with vexing traffic and one-way street systems through a fairly unattractive industrial cityscape. You need to ply all the way to the riverside Quay—the historic heart of the city—to discover the place those early Vikings made their home. While handcrafted cut glass is perhaps the city's most obvious attraction these days (though no longer made in Ireland), it's worth coming to grips with its history in other, less commercial, ways. The city has two cathedrals built by a master of Georgian design, its history museum is filled with archaeological treasures, and a visit to Reginald's Tower—the first Irish building made with mortar (albeit a grisly mix of blood, hair, and mud)—reveals some fascinating quirks of architectural evolution. By night, Waterford's messy industrial look is replaced by twinkling lights on the river surface, and pubs that fill up with eager, enthusiastic crowds—you find it's a jollier place than you might imagine (glassware being so formal). And, in the morning, you can make for the beaches, where surfers and nature-lovers congregate in the summer, or drive the entire Waterford coastline, admiring spectacular cliffs from Dunmore East all the way to Ardmore, near the Cork border.

A BRIEF HISTORY

Ireland's oldest city was founded by Vikings in 914 A.D., 74 years before they settled Dublin. Waterford is also older than Oslo, Stockholm, Copenhagen, and Reykjavik. The Vikings began developing towns when they started trading in addition to their regular activity of plundering monasteries for their wealth, livestock, and ready supply of slaves (i.e. the monks). In the mid-12th century, the King of Leinster, Diarmait MacMurrough, tried to capture Waterford from the Ostmen (descendents of a united Viking and Irish community) and failed. He returned in 1170 with the Anglo-Norman knight, Strongbow, to whom he had promised the hand of his daughter in marriage. The Normans took Waterford and in 1171 it was declared a royal city; this really marked the start of the fall of Ireland to English rule, symbolized by the marriage between Strongbow and Aoife, MacMurrough's daughter. The Normans spent the entire Middle Ages (until about 1530) expanding, fortifying and walling the original triangle-shaped Viking city, and by incorporating agricultural lands, they made it virtually self-sufficient—only wine, iron, and luxury goods needed to be imported.

When Henry VIII suppressed the Catholic church, Waterford remained a strongly Catholic city; early-17th-century Waterford was known as Parva Roma—"Little Rome"—thanks to the many scholars and churchmen who had assembled there. Even after the Protestant Reformation, Waterford tried to assert its Catholic identity and took part in the Confederation of Kilkenny, which was an independent Catholic government that lasted from 1642 until 1649 when Charles I was executed and Cromwell set about squashing the perceived Irish threat. He failed to make Waterford capitulate (famously the only Irish city that he besieged and did not conquer), but 8 months later, Cromwell's son-in-law, Henry Ireton, took the city after a major siege and he expelled the Catholic merchant class, replacing it with Parliamentary supporters.

Waterford saw something of a Georgian rebirth during the 18th century, largely under the stewardship of local architect John Roberts who designed, among many other buildings, both the Catholic and the Protestant cathedrals. With its river providing such excellent harbor access, Waterford's industrial prosperity continued, thanks largely to a boom in 19th-century shipbuilding and the exportation of its world-class crystal glass between 1783 and 1851 (Waterford Crystal was only revived again in 1946). With World War II and a general downturn in the economy, Waterford petered out until the upswing of the Celtic Tiger in the 1990s.

GETTING THERE & GETTING AROUND

Waterford lies directly south of Kilkenny on the **N10/N9.** The city lies on the **N25** that links Cork with Wexford, however, if you're coming from Wexford, I'd strongly urge you to travel along the coastal roads between Kilmore Quay and Ballyhack, taking time to explore Hook Peninsula along the way. At Ballyhack, take the **car ferry** (☎ 051/382480; www.passageferry.com; €8 one-way; €11 return) across Waterford Harbour, touching down in the prim, proper little village of Passage East, just a short drive from Waterford. Similarly, if you're coming from Cork, rather avoid the N25 and stick to the coast-hugging roads, for a far more scenic—at times spectacular—drive through seaside villages like Ardmore, Ring, Dungarvan (back on the N25), Stradbally, Annestown, Tramore, and Dunmore East, from where you head north along the R684 to reach Waterford.

Potentially useful if you prefer arriving at very quiet airports, **Aer Arann** (www.aerarann.ie) has daily flights from London Luton to **Waterford Airport** (☎ 051/875589; www.flywaterford.com; from £27 one-way), 10km (6 miles) south of Waterford City; a cab into the city shouldn't cost more than €20. **Trains** from Dublin (via Kildare, Kilkenny, and Thomastown) pull into **Waterford's Plunkett Station** (☎ 051/873401) four times a day (€16–€32). Waterford is connected to Wexford by 2 trains arriving from Rosslare each day. From Limerick, there is 1 daily connection via Cahir. **Buses** present a more frequent and affordable way of getting here as well as exploring the region. Around 10 buses a day arrive at **Waterford Bus Station** (☎ 051/879000) from Dublin (€11), and there are even more from Cork, and a handful each day from Limerick, Wexford, and Kilkenny.

Given its size, Waterford's traffic is intolerable, but fortunately—with the exception of the Waterford Crystal Factory (for which there is a bus service, so ask at the tourist office)—all its attractions and points of historical interest are located within a relatively compact area around the quayside area along the Suir's south bank, and this is relatively manageable on foot.

ACCOMMODATIONS, BOTH STANDARD & NOT

Waterford City's best accommodations deals are in its highly competitive hotels, some of them offering attractive packages, particularly if you play your cards—or rather the Internet—like a pro. You can also score great deals on self-catering properties out in the country; **Woodstown Holiday Homes** (☎ 051/382611; www.woodstownhh.com), for example, is a cluster of very pretty mews-style two- and three-bedroom cottages on a parkland estate where Jackie Kennedy stayed in 1967. It's 5 minutes from the coast and not too far from Waterford City, either. Rates start at €350 per week for a unit that sleeps four people in low season, while two nights cost €200 to €300. In Dunmore East, one of Waterford's loveliest coastal villages, **Dunmore Holiday Villas** (☎ 051/383699; www.waterford-dunmore.com) offers comfortable lodgings in freestanding houses that sleep six people for between €360 and €775 per week.

€ You'll share bathrooms at **Mayor's Walk House** (12 Mayor's Walk; ☎ 051/855427; www.mayorswalk.com; cash only), but you'll save enough euros to grab an extra couple of pints. Owner Jane Hovenden keeps a clean house and her four simple rooms are probably the cheapest in town (€50 double).

€–€€   When the local **Travelodge** (N25 Cork Rd.; ☎051/358885; www. travelodge.co.uk; AE, DC, MC, V) puts out its saver rates, you'll pay just €40 for a double or a family room (Travelodge allows parents with kids to pay the same for a converted quad—with pull-out trundle sofa—as others pay for a double). And this is a company that's always throwing sales, so sign up for their e-mails if you want to be alerted. At other times of the year, you'll pay between €50 and €69. You'll get a rather pre-fab looking room, but comfortable, clean, well-maintained and located just opposite the Waterford Crystal Factory.

€–€€   Just a touch pricier than Mayor's Walk, but several leaps up the style ladder, is John and Margaret Fogarty's **Avondale House** ✭ (2 Parnell St.; ☎ 051/ 852267; www.staywithus.net; MC, V). An excellent budget choice, with rooms that are modest, yet smart, and come with modern necessities like TVs. Doubles start at €60, and you can bag a triple for €70, but note that breakfast is not served.

€€   Even though it's outside the city, **Diamond Hill Country House** ✭✭ (Slieverue; ☎ 051/832855; www.stayatdiamondhill.com; MC, V) is a good option if you have your own transport. Accommodations are reasonably priced (€70–€90, depending on season) and the setting, amidst ⅔ hectare (1½ acres) of pretty gardens, doesn't hurt. Bedrooms are quiet, pleasantly refurbished, and have wonderful big beds to go with all the usual amenities.

€€–€€€   For a central and convenient location and a warm Waterford welcome, nothing beats the **Granville Hotel** ✭✭ (65 The Quay; ☎ 051/305555; www.granville-hotel.ie; AE, MC, V) which has a special place in the city's history and is one of Ireland's oldest hotels. Charles Stewart Parnell ("the uncrowned king of Ireland") made many speeches from a window on the first floor, and Daniel "the Liberator" O'Connell was a regular visitor. Today, the Cusack family, who've owned it since 1979, regularly think up excellent money-saving deals to help your budget go a little further. Comfortable, well-proportioned, unfussy bedrooms retain hints of Old World charm, but are thoroughly up to date, with modern amenities and the sheen that comes from regular refurbishment. Downstairs, a crowd always packs in the very schmoozy, sociable bar. Normal rates run from €98 (Nov–Apr) to €110 (May–Oct), but you'll get the best value from a mid-season special, where 2 nights plus one dinner for two people cost €178 the last time investigated.

DINING FOR ALL TASTES

Besides the choices below, affordable meals are usually available all-day in many of Waterford's pubs. There's also a very pleasant, popular cafe—the **Granary** (Mon–Sat 8am–5pm)—attached to the Museum of Treasures (p. 153).

€–€€   It's a cinch to find a decent, affordable meal in Waterford, particularly if you're prepared to pull up your sleeves and hang with the locals at some of their favorite low-key eateries. Case in point: **Café Lucia** ✭ 🧒 (2 Orundel Ln.; ☎ 051/ 852553; Mon–Thurs and Sat 9:30am–5pm; Fri 9:30am–7pm; MC, V) where residents go for their caffeine fix, served—along with breakfast, wholesome lunches, and in-between light meals—in restful, laidback, unpretentious surrounds. Hearty soup of the day makes a meal here, sided by delicious homemade bread

(€4.25), and I'm also a fan of the warm, crispy bacon, pear, blue cheese, and walnut salad (€11) as a healthful lunch. Otherwise, there are mountainous classic club sandwiches (€9); tasty Thai fishcakes, made with lemongrass and ginger, and served with salad and potato wedges (€11); roast chicken, bacon, and mushroom lasagna (€11); and different daily specials all the time (€8.50–€11). A children's menu has nothing over €6.

€–€€ Not as exotic as its name, but certainly comfortable (and in a real way, comforting, too) **Sumatra** ✪✪ (53 John St.; ☎ 051/876404; Mon–Wed 9am–7pm; Thurs 9am–9pm; Fri–Sat 9am–11pm; Sun 11am–7pm; MC, V) is an all-day cafe with restaurant aspirations. Set along a strip of junky fast-food joints, it boasts an artful look, piles of magazines and newspapers to peruse, and good, wholesome food. Options include paninis, wraps, and toasted sandwiches (€7.25–€9), burgers (€10–€11), pastas (€10–€11), and daily specials, too. The "blue plate" when I last stopped by was a steak and bacon pie (€11)—the beef cooked in red wine gravy and then blended with bacon, thyme, and mushrooms and baked inside a delicate puff pastry. Truly delish.

€€–€€€ Simple as it may seem, **Kashmir Tandoori** ✪ (18 High St.; ☎ 051/853630; Sun–Thurs 4:30–11pm; Fri–Sat 4:30–11:30pm; MC, V) is the best Indian eatery in the southeast, and benefits from a corkage-free BYO policy, so you can pick up an affordable bottle of vino from the Wine Vault next door and head on over for a most satisfactory, affordable meal. Ultra-polite waiters and relaxing music set just the right mood, despite the bright lighting and plain decor. All the main contenders—from "very hot" vindaloos to milder tandooris (with yogurt, ginger, a touch of lemon, and Himalyan herbs)—are here; they're decently priced—from €9.50 to €14 for their main dishes—and all come with either rice or (since this is Ireland) chips. My suggestion is that you arrive for the 5 to 7pm early dining special; for €16 you get a starter plus main course, with rice or nan bread, and tea or coffee. Curry dishes are served in copper bowls on candle burners, which adds a dash of atmosphere.

€€–€€€€ Right next door to Sumatra, the place for a bit of a splurge is colorful, vibrant **Bodéga!** ✪✪✪ (kids) (54 John St.; ☎ 051/844177; www.bodega waterford.com; Mon–Fri noon–10pm; Sat 5–10:30pm; AE, MC, V), widely considered the hip, fun, happening place to dine. As per the norm, it's much cheaper to do lunch here (served until 5pm), when you can get steamed Wexford mussels with shallots, garlic, and white wine, or duck leg confit, for €15. Tantalizing starter-size dishes (€6.50–€9.50), and up-market burgers (€14) and sandwiches (€9.50) are also an affordable choice. Bodéga! has been reviewed and praised by just about every guidebook in the business, so you might think it would develop a big head, but it still attracts its loyal, local following, with families packing it out at lunchtime (so have no qualms about bringing the kids along).

WHY YOU'RE HERE: TOP SIGHTS & ATTRACTIONS

The best way to quickly get a grasp of the city is to take one of Jack Burtchaell's informative and quick-paced **Walking Tours of Historic Waterford** ✪✪ (from Waterford Treasures Museum; ☎ 051/873711; €7; mid-Mar to mid-Oct daily 11:45am and 1:45pm). Jack—or one of his guides—takes you through over 1,000 years of history, using the monuments in the oldest part of town to explain what went down, when, and why. He brings to light unusual anecdotal facts that give Waterford a far cooler sheen than it probably deserves. But what the hell—it's a fun and entertaining way to spend an hour.

One of the monuments you shouldn't (and can't) miss as you're trawling Waterford's quayside stretch is **Reginald's Tower** ✪✪ (The Quay; ☎ 051/304220; Heritage Card or €2.10; daily Easter–May and Oct 10am–5pm; June–Sept 10am–6pm; Nov–Easter Wed–Sun 10am–5pm), one of six original defensive medieval towers around the city. Considered the oldest urban civic building in Ireland, the round tower is a 12th-century upgrade of an original wooden Viking tower, and is supposedly the first building in Ireland built with mortar; this consisted of silt, animal blood, and mud, and if you look closely at the walls, you can still see strands of hair (animal and human) that were also in the concoction. It may not look like a heck of a monument, but to have withstood all that it has and still be in such fantastic shape is remarkable. Built in the early-13th century, and much enhanced in the 15th century, it has served various functions—a mint (the oldest in Ireland), an arsenal, a prison, a family home (until 1950!), and a city museum. The guided tour will help you understand the architectural styles that evolved in response to changing military technologies. You'll also hear how mediaeval long drop lavatories were used to keep fleas and lice out of clothing. Yuck? My thoughts exactly.

Standing inconspicuously in one corner of John Roberts Square, the **Holy Trinity Cathedral** ✪ (Barronstrand St.; ☎ 051/875166; free admission; daily 8:30am–5:30pm) is the oldest Roman Catholic cathedral in Ireland, commissioned in 1793 during a time when penal laws against Catholic worship still meant that its churches were required to be discreet, almost unnoticeable. At one time, there was a wall in front of the sedate, simple facade, ensuring that it did not face a main street. Venture inside, and you'll discover an altogether more riotous assemblage of color and decoration—its powder blue Corinthian columns are rather striking against the cream walls and stained glass windows, and some of the oldest Waterford crystal chandeliers hang inside this church. In more recent years, several millions have been spent preventing the cathedral from sinking into the soft ground below.

Protestant Christ Church Cathedral ✪✪ (Henrietta St.; ☎ 051/858958; www.christchurchwaterford.com; free admission; Mar–Oct Mon–Fri 10am–6pm; Sat 10am–4pm; guided tours €5, daily 11:30am and 3:30pm) is the only Neoclassical Georgian church in Ireland. Christian worship has been taking place on this site for 900 years; when the Anglo-Normans took over the city, they knocked down the original Viking church (yes, even those "marauding pagans" had been converted) and built their own Gothic church. But in the 18th century, the city fathers were feeling that the church was dark and unpleasant and they tricked the bishop into thinking that it was falling apart (they apparently had choirboys drop stones from the rafters) so he agreed to let it be demolished in 1773, making way for the current edifice. Inside, you can still view part of the original Norman church foundations, and there are some intriguing artifacts such as the late-15th-century sarcophagus-tomb of 11-time Waterford mayor, James Rice—a spooky, gruesome, gory skeletal carving straight out of a ghoulish horror film, with worms and frogs crawling over the hollow-eyed, dismembered figure; the tomb is meant

Waterford's Great Builder

John Roberts is Waterford's stand-out Georgia architect, and designed both the Catholic and Protestant cathedrals. Born to a working-class Protestant family in 1714, he eloped as a teenager with a wealthy French Huguenot girl and fled to London with her. There, Roberts put himself through college, legitimized his marriage at age 22, and returned to Waterford where he bought the 16th-century house that still stands adjacent the Christ Church Cathedral. During his career, he built at least 25 town houses as well as a number of Waterford's public buildings—including the City Hall—not to mention his work in other centers. He also produced 22 children. Busy Roberts died at the age of 82 of chill-fuelled pneumonia contracted while putting the finishing touches on the country's oldest Catholic Cathedral. Waterford hosts a weekend-long festival celebrating the work of John Roberts each April; events include lectures, exhibitions, and architectural tours, and you can check the program at www.johnrobertsweekend.ie.

to be a warning to the living of the fate that awaits them in death. While there's much to explore within the lofty, naturally lit interior, it always strikes me as exceedingly odd—and almost a transgression—to find a gift shop inside a house of worship; well, here it's worse, since they have set up a little cafe!

Brilliantly curated by Eamonn McEnealey, an expert on Viking and mediaeval history, **Waterford Museum of Treasures** ✪✪✪ (The Granary, Merchant's Quay; ☎ 051/304500; www.waterfordtreasures.com; €7; Apr–Sept Mon–Sat 9:30am–6pm; Sun 11am–5pm; Oct–Mar Mon–Sat 10am–5pm; Sun 11am–5pm) is one of the best museums in Ireland, tying its phenomenal collection of cherished artifacts into an enlightening narrative. As you gradually move through the ages, you'll see fascinating pieces from the excavation of original Viking settlements, including a 12th-century dog collar, and personal grooming devices that say a great deal about the hygiene habits of those Norse people so often stereotyped as unkempt savages (actually, much of what we think we know about the Vikings comes to us from Arab writers who probably described them as dirty since their own hygiene practices were so advanced—proof, yet again, that history is relative). A highlight of the collection is the Great Charter Roll of 1372 which features the earliest-rendered medieval image of any English king, namely Edward III. Part of the exhibition is also given over to the history of glass production in Waterford, so is a good primer for the city's other "must see" attraction.

Remember Stomp!, that wild, rollicking perfectly choreographed stage show in which industrial boot-wearing workers pounded out riveting beats with their feet and dustbin lids? Well, during the best parts of the **Waterford Crystal Factory Tour** ✪✪ (Kilbarry; ☎ 051/332500; www.waterfordvisitorcentre.com; €10; Nov–Feb Mon–Fri 9am–3:15pm; Mar–Oct daily 8:30am–4pm), that's what I was reminded of. Never mind that this is where the original Times Square Millennium

A Splendid Side Trip, by Hook or by Crooke

Planning his siege of Waterford in 1719, General Oliver Cromwell is reported to have said that he would take the town "by Hook or by Crooke." He likely unwittingly invented that catch phrase, though in truth he was simply plotting his geographic staging points. Crooke was a small town on the Suir estuary and Hook referred to the Hook Peninsula.

Nearly 300 years later, the so-called "Ring of Hook" is still a marvelous staging point for a "touristic invasion" of Waterford (or at least a fun side trip). Beyond its eye-popping natural beauty—secluded cove beaches alternate with wave-slammed rocky headlands—it's a history-rich peninsula with many rewarding sights.

I highly recommend snaking your way from Fethard-on-Sea to Churchtown, and beyond until you come to the medieval **Hook Lighthouse** ★★ (☎ 051/397055; www.thehook-wexford.com; €6; daily 9:30am–5pm; May and Sept 9:30am–5:30pm; June–Aug 9:30am–6pm), said to be the oldest functioning lighthouse on earth (but that's a yarn I'm sure is spun elsewhere, too). Built by the Earl of Pembroke in the 13th century, it's an almost intact four-storey tower that bears some resemblance to the lighthouse at Pharos in Alexandria. Also on the peninsula, stop to explore **Duncannon Fort,** described during the reign of Charles II as the second most important fort in the British Empire; views from its bastions are splendid. And outside the town of Wellington Bridge are the haunting ruins of Clonmines, a 13th-century Norman walled village.

Near the head of Waterford Harbour, the tiny village of **Ballyhack** enjoys an enviable position along the slope of a steep green hill. Here, the square squat tower house of **Ballyhack Castle** ★ (☎ 051/389468; free admission;

ball was produced, or that these craftsmen produce a lot of kitschy ornaments, glass trophies, and twee crystal "art." The real thrill is in watching what looks like an industrial theater piece, as the men in question smelt, blow, and shape the glassware—only without the synchronized choreography or pace-keeping soundtrack. What you witness is the organized chaos as red-hot blobs of molten glass are pulled, folded, stretched, and cut, and furnace doors are opened and closed in some kind of elaborate, organic rhythm. This minor spectacle is set to an incessant chorus of mechanical hums, hisses, blasts, and whirs. And backing it all up is a supporting act of heavy machinery, severe-looking equipment, intense hot-burning flames, and assorted twirling bits. It's not the least bit glamorous, and the show has shrunk since the company laid off the majority of its Irish workers in late 2008 and moved production to eastern Europe. But it's still a worthwhile place to visit (and perhaps enough visitors expressing their displeasure with the outsourcing of Waterford may return some jobs to this factory).

The 1-hour tour commences from the maelstrom of the factory's mall-like **Visitor Centre** (daily Nov–Feb 9am–5pm; Mar–Oct 8:30am–6pm), which mid-June to mid-Sept daily 10am–6pm) comes as a sudden shock amidst the dainty neighboring residences. Built around 1450 by the Knights Hospitallers of St. John, the castle still seems to keep watch over the **car ferry** (€8 one-way, €12 return; 5 min.) that runs from Ballyhack to Passage East.

If you decide to lodge in the area—highly recommended—choose **Glendine Country House** ✪✪✪ 🅺🅸🅳🅂 (Arthurstown, around the corner from Ballyhack; ☎ 051/389500 or 051/389258; www.glendinehouse.com; MC, V). Built in the early 1800s as the dower house to Dunbrody Estate (now an expensive hotel, spa, and cooking school), it's an enchanting destination in its own right, and one of my favorite B&Bs. A farmhouse set on grounds grazed by deer, cattle, and quizzical-looking Jacob sheep, it's also a great place for kids (wide open fields, a trampoline and playground, books for younger readers, and plenty of fresh air). The spacious bedrooms have elegant furniture and views of Waterford Harbour; breakfast is an all-organic feast. Ann Crosbie is a tireless hostess, and although she jokes that "nothing much happens here," she'll give you plenty of ideas about what's worth exploring, and which of the nearby beaches to visit. The B&B rate is €100 double or €130 for the big suite, but attached to the main house are Glendine's two self-catering cottages, each with two bedrooms (one with a king-size bed, and one with three singles; both have attached bathrooms) and a full kitchen, for which you'll pay between €250 and €550 (most expensive during July and Aug) per week. Glendine is perfectly situated for day trips to Waterford City, Wexford Town, and many coastal spots.

receives 350,000 tourists per year; from here, you're jostled onto a shuttle bus for the short trip to the factory. It's not quite as exhilarating as everyone suggests, but you'll probably kick yourself if you pass this way without seeing it for yourself.

Waterford's Coast

Waterford's beaches are popular summer holiday destinations, particularly loved by surfers who—along with numerous youngsters—flock to the tacky seaside resort of **Tramore** (see "Active Waterford," p. 156). There are far lovelier spots along Waterford's coast, though. **Dunmore East** ✪ is a pretty fishing village set around a cove, backed by black craggy cliffs that drop off into the glistening waters. A small cluster of whitewashed thatch cottages sits at the edge of a miniature natural harbor, which gives on to a picturesque bay. West of here, I suggest you whiz straight through the Ferris wheel-and-candy floss beach resort of Tramore, and perhaps slow down in the more remote, totally serene village of **Annestown.** Roughly 2km (1¼ miles) beyond Annestown, at Kilmurran, you'll see my favorite **beach** ✪✪✪ along this coast—a pebbly crescent-shaped cove against ragged, rocky cliffs that stagger down to the ice-blue water (you will know it when it pops into view). In fact, this stretch of shoreline, from Annestown to Bunmahon, 6km (3¾ miles), is the most rewarding, studded with lovely inlets, perfectly formed coves, pebble beaches, and steep rockfaces stretching like fingers into the blue, blue ocean. After Bunmahon, the road veers inland, now affording vivid views of the Knockmealdown Mountains. Some 9km (5½ miles) before Dungarvan you'll be back alongside the sea. Just after this busy little fishing town at the edge of Dungarvan Bay, you can turn off the N25 to check out the Gaeltacht community of **An Rinne** (which translates as "Ring," but there are no English signs in this Irish language outpost). Further west, close to the Waterford-Cork border, is pretty little **Ardmore** ★ with a long narrow beach, and—at the top of the village—a graveyard centered on a roofless church and a round tower that looks set to star in a film version of Rumpelstiltskin.

THE OTHER WATERFORD

In its day, Waterford was considered the country's wine capital, and was the port of entry for most imported liquor into Ireland; in fact, wealth literally poured into Waterford thanks to a Royal Charter which meant that the city paid only half the usual taxes on wine. No stranger to the pleasures of wine, Waterford has its fair share of wine aficionados and, of course, people who love to learn about, talk about, and—of course—drink wine. Monthly wine events are held in the 13th-century cellar at the **Wine Vault** (High St.; ☎ 051/853444; www.waterford winevault.com), a most auspicious meeting place, and boutique-style wine store. These evenings usually revolve around an international winemaker brought in to promote a new label featured in the shop. In attendance are Waterford's most dedicated wine enthusiasts who come to indulge in wine-focused *craic*.

If you're interested in learning a rare skill, consider a **glassblowing workshop** with a former Waterford Crystal craftsman. John Cuddihy is a second generation master Waterford glassblower, and after years working on important designs and training new glassworkers, began presenting courses to the public in late 2007. John teaches classes on how to work with molten glass using demonstrations; students then practice the techniques until they have a reasonable handle on them. Things start relatively slowly, as you first have to learn how to gather the molten glass on the end of the "punty" (the long, hollow metal rod which is used to turn, work, heat, and ultimately blow into the molten glass); you then learn techniques for shaping, and later how to add color to the glass. Of course, glassblowing takes years to master, so you shouldn't expect to come away ready to restock your entire bar with self-made glassware. Courses last 5 days (Mon–Fri 9am–4pm) and cost €875. Sessions are held at the Waterford Crystal Factory, where you work in the well-stocked, spacious training area incorporating its impressive furnace, large glory hole, and gas-fired kiln. To find out when the next course will be held, contact **Crystal Studio Ireland** (www.crystalstudioireland.com).

ACTIVE WATERFORD

Surfing lessons in Tramore are a great way to meet aquatically athletic residents, as well as visitors from other parts of Ireland; in summer this resort town gets crazy. Family-run **Oceanic Manoeuvres** (The Red Cottage, Tramore; ☎ 051/390944; www.oceanicmanoeuvres.ie) offers a variety of programs, from 1-day courses (two sessions of 2 hr. each) for those of you who haven't ever picked up a board, to advanced modular courses that can run over either four weeks or be packed into 2 days and include such need-to-know surfing skills as surfing etiquette and wave forecasting. This outfit claims a 98% success rate—even with ultra-first timers—but, even if you don't manage to stay on that board, you'll have spent some quality time with some talented resident surfers whose enthusiasm will leave you inspired enough to keep on trying.

NIGHTLIFE

For concerts (€15), theater (€15), and also film screenings (€8), usually of the offbeat and arthouse variety, head to the **Garter Lane Art Centre** ★★ (22A O'Connell St.; ☎ 051/855038; www.garterlane.ie), which is the town's cultural heart. For more populist events, check the program of the **Forum** (The Glen; ☎ 051/871111; www.forumwaterford.com), which stages all sorts of entertainment, from music concerts and bodybuilding competitions to international DJ parties, and Goth, fetish, and industrial-alternative bashes.

With its neo-baroque styling—chunky chandeliers, blackamoor figurines, huge framed mirrors, mosaic tiles, plenty of faux-leather—and contemporary funk-rock soundtrack, **KazBar** ★★ (57 John St.; ☎ 051/843730) has a seductive atmosphere and a mixed crowd. It's an all-day place with live bands and quality DJs on weekends, when the party goes till 2am. Across the road, wood-paneled **Geoff's** (8 John St.; ☎ 051/874787) gets packed with a loyal crowd, many of whom arrive soon after their university lectures have ended.

Occupying a Tudor-style house that sticks out on the pedestrian quarter just off John Roberts Square, **T&H Doolans** ★ (George St.; ☎ 051/841504) has over 300 years behind it. It maintains a reputation for its live music scene, but I've found that you can just as easily turn up to find yourself bombarded by super-touristy, kitschy, folksy, faux-Irish honky-tonk ear-strain.

Drinking Beneath the Bridge

Dating back to 1705, **Jack Meades** ★★★ (Halfway House, Cheekpoint Rd.; ☎ 051/850950; MC, V), billed as "Ireland's only fly-over pub" because it's right beneath an old stone bridge—is pretty much in the middle of nowhere. You'll need your own set of wheels to get there but it's worth it. This is one of the coziest, most atmospheric spots in the southeast. Set in a pretty little cottage, the original pub is a dark, low-ceilinged space packed with a curious assortment of memorabilia, antiques, and photos; there's even a piece of the Berlin Wall. When I sat down for a pint, even the locals were discussing how awfully quiet it was, while a couple of beaming tourists had their cameras on automatic. Outside is a new bar in a large beer garden, a children's playground (with ducks), and access to walking paths that take you past some ruined buildings; food is served daily from 12:30 to 9pm. The "pub under the bridge" is on the R683, some 6.5km (4 miles) from the city.

CASHEL, CAHIR & LISMORE

The Rock of Cashel in southern Tipperary is one of the most important and famous monuments in Ireland. It was at Cashel (or "stone fort") that the kings of Munster were crowned during the glory days of Celtic history even before St. Patrick turned up and turned things on their head. Upon the famous Rock, popular mythology tells us, the saint used a shamrock to explain the concept of the Holy Trinity, and he then converted the king to the new religion of Rome. While Cashel of the Kings is a beacon for tourists, much of the outlying terrain is little explored and retains a pastoral ambience. Farming is the main activity here, not tourism, and between castle and church ruins you should make a point of getting out into the country. Better still, head for the exquisite Knockmealdown Mountains with fine views all the way as you cross into County Waterford, chancing upon unassuming villages en route to picture-perfect Lismore.

GETTING THERE & GETTING AROUND

From Dublin, Cashel is a 2-hour road journey, on the **N8;** from Cork, it's 1 hour, also on the N8. Cashel lies on the **N24,** more or less midway between Limerick and Waterford, so the road journey from either city is 1 hour.

The Rock of Cashel is one of Ireland's biggest tourist attractions and draws numerous day-trippers, the majority of them on tour buses; there are also **Éireann buses** from Dublin and other major towns and cities, including Waterford and Cork; most buses stop in Cahir en route to Cashel. Buses to Lismore are similarly priced, but service is less frequent. Cahir is connected to Dublin, Limerick and Waterford by **train;** tickets are up to three times the cost of a bus ride, and can take longer. The 15-minute bus trip from Cashel to Cahir costs €4.10 (€5.50 return). Lismore is best visited by **car** as part of a journey from Cahir, through the Knockmealdown Mountains along the "Vee" Road that goes through Clogheen.

Cashel's **Heritage Centre** (Main St.; ☎ 062/62511; Mar–June daily 9:30am–5:30pm; July–Aug daily 9:30am–8pm; Feb and Sept Mon–Fri 9:30am–5:30pm) in the center of town doubles as a friendly tourist information office where you can also book B&Bs. If you'd like to investigate the area by **bike,** pop into **McInerney's Bicycle Hire** (☎ 062/61225) on Main Street.

Right in the center of town, the **Lismore Heritage Centre** (The Courthouse Building, Lismore; ☎ 058/54975; www.discoverlismore.com; Mon–Fri 9:30am–5:30pm; Sat 10am–5:30pm; May–Oct Sun noon–5:30pm) dispenses information and sells an informative walking-tour guidebook (€3).

WHERE TO STAY & DINE

In & Around Cashel

€–€€   Modest and modestly priced, **Bruden Fidelma Bed & Breakfast** (5 John St., Cashel; ☎ 062/62330; www.sisterfidelmabandb.com; MC, V) offers simple, clean rooms (€60 with shared bath, €70 with private, €105 family room) in an early-19th-century Georgian townhouse. The look is unglamorous, yes, but things are generally comfortable, with rooms named for the characters in Peter Traymane's mystery novels about the eponymous Sister Fidelma, a 7th-century female crime-solver. The lounge—with its old-fashioned wood-and-leather sofas—has a wood-burning fire in winter, and free Internet. *One note:* Rates include breakfast; however, if you prefer to go without you can usually negotiate a €10 per person discount (ask).

The B&B owners also run a hostel right next door (**Cashel Holiday Hostel;** same details), with bunk beds in rooms sleeping anywhere from 2 to 10 people for €16 to €22 per person. Single rooms cost €25. I'll be frank: It's a bit run down, with grubby carpets, broken shower doors, and a credit card machine that may not work. Still it has some nice extras like a laundry, help-yourself kitchen, wood-tabled dining area, and a big common room with books, games, old leather sofas, a fireplace, and TV.

€€ Just down the road from Bruden Fidelma, at Michael and Laura Ryan's **Ashmore House** (John St.; ☎ 062/61286; www.ashmorehouse.ie; MC, V), you'll find comfortable lodgings in an even earlier Georgian house packed with antiques and memorabilia—plates, wall-hangings, glassware—collected over the years by this couple who've been running their B&B for almost 20 years. Bedrooms are a mixed bag, varying in size and shape (some are a bit of a tight squeeze), but they're all fairly simple with pine furniture and new, firm mattresses; room 6 is probably the best double in terms of size. The Ryan's have included some useful touches, like an indoor smoking zone, free Wi-Fi (and a PC), and there's off-street parking. Rates are reasonable: Two people in a double room pay €70 to €80, or you can have a larger family room for €90.

€€ A tree-lined avenue off a road running through fields of frolicking horses and grazing cows leads to **Derrynaflan** ✦✦✦ (Ballinure; ☎ 052/56406; www. derrynaflanhouse.com; AE, MC, V), a 300-year-old farmhouse where Shelia O'Sullivan and her family offer B&B accommodation and great hospitality (€80 double, €50 single). Bedrooms are supplied with original antiques, wardrobes, wooden floors, and rugs, and high metal frame beds that Sheila's says are "as old as the hills," but have brand new mattresses. Instead of TVs, most rooms have gorgeous views across the farm; ask for the room with the best view—it's the unit to the right of the tea service in the passageway (rooms aren't numbered). Breakfast—a superb farmhouse spread with homemade yogurt, bread, preserves, and cheese—is served at a communal table. Darrynaflan is open April to November; to get there, take the R691 to Dualla (9km/5½ miles), and from there it's another 3km (2 miles). *Note:* The entrance is concealed, so drive carefully, particularly upon departure.

€€–€€€ It may not be set in a former church like its more famous next-door cousin, Chez Hans, but **Café Hans** ✦✦ (Moor Ln.; ☎ 062/63660; Tues–Sat noon–5:30pm; cash only) offers excellent daytime dining in a fairly up-market, modern setting. Even though some items from the lavish Chez Hans menu have found their way over here, and it is pricier than your average cafe, a meal here won't bankrupt your budget. Especially if you go for a meal-size salad (like Bluebell Falls organic goat cheese, roasted aubergines, red peppers, and organic leaves, €12; or smoked salmon with baby new potatoes, €13), or try one of their open sandwiches (served with homemade French fries)—the "ham and cheese," for example, is made with Coleeney cheese and honey-roasted pork loin, and finished off with a red pepper and tomato chutney (€12). And, after lunch, head up to the Rock to watch the sun set—better than dessert.

In & Around Cahir

€€   Named after William Tinsley, the man who remodeled Cahir in the 19th century, **Tinsley House** ★ (The Square; ☎ 086/842-6345 or 052/41947; www.tinsleyhouse.com; cash only) is a cute little place, a former antique shop actually, right on the town square (so it's ideal if you're using public transport). Its four bedrooms (€70 for two people and €45 for singles) are all well-proportioned and homey in ambiance (think floral wallpapers and curtains, homemade quilts on the beds); one of the "suites" is ideal for families with two bedrooms plus tub and shower. I'm awarding the star, however, for its history-buff owner Liam, who delights in discussing the town and its environs and can give you the inside scoop on the best local walks and fishing spots. If you want to hire him for the day, he offers more formal local tours (€20 for a small group).

€€   You arrive at **Kilmaneen Farmhouse** ★★ (Newcastle, Clonmel; ☎ 052/ 36231; www.kilmaneen.com; MC, V) already relaxed into a spirit of country living just from the drive in; for kilometers in every direction are wide expanses of green pastures and grazing cows, and above you, the most painterly cloud formations. It's pretty, with accommodations—in a smart country style—to match. Room 3 is the largest and most attractive, with a massive wardrobe, TV, and dresser; the other two are a bit smaller and less grand; all cost €90 double (with discounts of stays of 3 nights or more), and that includes a fine farmhouse breakfast. Some excellent walks start and end here (walking sticks are provided, and Kevin O'Donnell is a fount of knowledge on the surrounding Knockmealdowns), and you're just a short drive from Cahir. Besides the excellent B&B, there's the option of renting a self-catering cottage—either as a one-bedroom unit (with a sofa bed suitable for a child) or as a two-bedroom unit that sleeps six altogether. Either way, what you get is very quaint, large, and excellent value—full kitchen, washing machine, dishwasher, lounge-cum-dining room with fireplace and TV, plenty of packing space, and a private entrance. Weekly rates run €275 to €425 (one-bedroom) or €325 to €525 (two-bedroom).

€–€€   Directly opposite Cahir's castle is **River House** (1 Castle St.; ☎ 052/ 41951; Mon–Wed 9am–5pm; Thurs–Sat 9am–9pm; Sun 9am–7pm; MC, V), a modish restaurant-cum-"cafe-bar." Since taking on new management, things have been getting progressively better and more interesting here; you can sit through the day sipping smoothies and cappuccinos, availing of free Wi-Fi, and selecting from a deli-style selection of salads, sandwiches, and quiches (mostly under €10). Or, if you're busting a more serious hunger, there's beef and Guinness casserole (€11) and similarly hearty, traditional meals.

€–€€€   For pub grub, my top pick is the **Galtee Inn** (The Square; ☎ 052/ 41247; daily 9:30am–10pm; MC, V), which serves up fantastic *craic* and delicious pints. The menu rotates daily, so there's a potential surprise in store, based on what's available (everything is sourced locally). Double-decker rye sandwiches, grilled wraps, and stuffed pita bread are good if you're after something light (at lunchtime), and at night there's a range of usual suspects: roast beef, pasta, lamb cutlet, chicken curry (all €11), and steak, of course (€20).

Spiritual Accommodations in a Tranquil Setting

The Cistercian—or Trappist—**Mount Melleray Abbey** ★★★ enjoys a sublime setting in the Knockmealdown Mountains. It's possible to visit the abbey (there's an exhibition on its history, and you can wander the lovely grounds and explore its church), but you can also come here to stay on "quiet, personal retreats." Part of the abbey's mission "is to render assistance to those who come to the monastery looking for deeper prayer," and this is fulfilled by the provision of shelter. Meaning you can arrange to stay for a while, but—and this, the abbey's officials asked me to reiterate—this is not simply a cheap accommodation option for backpackers. This is a place for silent, peaceful contemplation (and simple digs, naturally), where you'll be among silent monks and an environment of calm spirituality. Advance reservation is necessary (e-mail guestmaster@ mountmellerayabbey.org, or call ☎ 0581/54404) and although there's no set fee, a reasonable donation is expected; for details, visit www.mount mellerayabbey.org.

Lismore

€€   With ponies in the adjoining field and a fine front lawn and immaculate garden of its own, **Pine Tree House** ★ (Ballyanchor; ☎ 058/53282; pinetree house@oceanfree.net; MC V), is one of Lismore's loveliest B&Bs, where you stay with a family who'll help you get to know their little community. The B&B is about a 10-minute walk from the village; when you enter Lismore, turn right and continue straight; it's directly across from the GAA grounds, just beyond the Blackwater Community School. You'll feel like you're out in the country. The three rooms (€80 a night, double) are simple and cottage-like, with the pine furniture evoking a pleasant farmhouse vibe.

€€   At the upper end of this price bracket, but offering luxury for a relatively bargain price, **Lismore House Hotel** ★ (Main St.; ☎ 058/72966; www.lismore househotel.com; MC, V) is smart and very central, and has double rooms for €120.

€–€€   The **Summerhouse** ★★ (Main St.; ☎ 058/54148; www.thesummer house.ie; Tues–Sat 10am–5:30pm; Sun noon–5pm; AE, MC, V) is a lovely cafe that serves light meals—sandwiches (€4.50), paninis (€8.50), soups (€4), and more substantial fare—in a relaxed environment that really is quite "summery"— Mövenpick ice-cream is a perennial, year round. Half the house is actually a store, selling organic wines, homemade jams, attractive homeware items, and soaps.

€–€€   On the other side of Main Street, the top pub in these parts is **Eamonn's Place** ★★ (Main St.; ☎ 058/54025; lunch served from 12:30pm; cash only), a crisp, wood-paneled space with its smart little benches and snug leather armchairs. The food is enticing, too. Particularly if you're after a hearty, warming,

Get Out of Town: Lismore

If you have the time, I encourage you to try this day trip, modeled upon one undertaken by Victorian novelist William Makepeace Thackeray. Here's what the author of *Vanity Fair* had to say about this jaunt: "The beautiful Blackwater River suddenly opened up before us, and driving along it for three miles through some of the most beautiful rich country ever seen, we came to Lismore. Nothing can be certainly more magnificent than this drive." Interested? Here's how to do it.

From Cahir, head south along the R668 on a course for, and through, the **Knockmealdown Mountains** ✯✯✯, which have the unusual appearance of rounded summits divided by deep gaps, which form natural mountain passes. The most famous of these is the **Vee Gap,** where motorists stop for wraparound views of the mountains and plains of Tipperary. Beyond the Vee, you can continue on the R668 directly to Lismore, or head along the R669 towards **Cappoquin,** and look out for signs to **Mount Melleray Abbey** ✯✯; founded by Cistercians in 1832, after 64 Irish and English monks were forced to leave France, this was the first post-Reformation monastery in Ireland, and the monks chose a majestic site, affording breathtaking views. Their monastery isn't too shabby, either. (See "Spiritual Accommodations in a Tranquil Setting," p. 161.)

Attractive little **Lismore** ✯✯✯ (37km/23 miles south of Cahir) was founded by St. Carthage in 636 A.D., and grew to become the greatest monastic school of the 8th century; both St. Malachy and King Alfred the Great were students here. Vikings repeatedly burnt Lismore, but it rose from the ashes, and after the Norman settlement the local population was known to speak both Irish and French; in fact, if you listen to the

---

traditional meal—Eamonn serves two daily lunch specials, such as burgers or liver and bacon casserole, for €8.50 each, and does lighter meals like salads, sandwiches (around €3.50), and paninis (€7.25)

WHY YOU'RE HERE: TOP SIGHTS & ATTRACTIONS
Cashel & the Rock

Cashel, in southern Tipperary, might today seem reliant on tourism, but it is in fact a market center for many neighboring villages, and its importance stretches back to the 4th century, when it first became the seat of the kings of Munster, making it one of the most prominent centers in Celtic history. Catching sight of the fabled **Rock of Cashel** ✯✯✯ (Cashel; ☎ 062/61437; www.heritageireland.ie; Heritage Card or €5.30; daily mid-Mar to mid-June and mid-Sept to mid-Oct 9am–5:30pm; mid-June to mid-Sept 9am–7pm; mid-Oct to mid-Mar 9am–4:30pm) as you approach the town is a bit of a mind-blast. It's one of Europe's top medieval sites—a glorious triumph of architecture perched high upon a limestone hill. The history of the Rock goes back to the time when St. Patrick legendarily converted

Lismore accent today, there is still a discernible trace of that early Norman influence.

Today, the mere sight of **Lismore Castle** ✦✦✦ screams romance; it's probably the most fabulously set castle in the country, perched atop a steep ravine on the outskirts of the village. This is where the scientist, Robert Boyle (yes, he of Boyles Law, also known as the "Father of Modern Chemistry") was born. Before that, the castle was owned by Sir Walter Raleigh who had masses of land throughout the southeast and was responsible for large-scale deforestation here. Entire forests were cut down to fuel his ironworks and build ships for the Elizabethan fleet. To his credit, though, he also brought potatoes and cherry trees to Ireland. The castle remains the Irish residence of the Duke and Duchess of Devonshire, meaning that only the **Castle Gardens** ✦✦ (€7; late-Apr to late-Sept daily 11am–4:45pm) are open to the public.

In Lismore Village, you could do worse than to simply roam the tidy collection of streets to visit the two handsome church buildings, or hang out in the pubs that dot the main street. As you pass the castle and enter town, you'll see the **Lismore Experience** (Lismore Heritage Centre, Main St.; ☎ 058/54975; www.discoverlismore.com; Mon–Fri 9:30am–5:30pm; May–Oct Sat 10am–5:30pm; Sun noon–5:30pm) directly ahead of you—this is part tourist information center (useful for booking accommodation and finding out about walks in the area), and part historical introduction to the village. The latter bit is a half-hour film presentation (€5), but you can also ask for a guided tour of Lismore, which costs the same as the virtual experience.

the local king, Aenghus, to Christianity, and it was here that Brian Ború was crowned King of Ireland in the 11th century. In fact, this limestone bastion was occupied by the kings of Munster for centuries before what we see on it today was even considered possible; the base on which St. Patrick's Cross now stands is thought to have been the coronation stone for these kings. The Rock was presented to the church as a gift in 1101, and the first monks to settle here were Cistercian or White monks who came from France. Prominent features here include a 15th-century castle, 13th-century Gothic cathedral, and the 12th-century round tower, a High Cross, and the exemplary Cormac's Chapel. The latter is the finest Hiberno-Romanesque chapel in existence, its twin towers and rounded doorways revealing the influence of foreign design on Irish architecture at the time when it was built.

If you're lusting for more ecclesiastical architecture, ask one of the guides to point you towards **Hore Abbey** ✦, the last Cistercian monastery built in Ireland, in the field across the road directly below the Rock. At the base of the Rock, the **Brú Ború Centre** (☎ 062/61122; www.comhaltas.com) is known for its evening entertainments (see "Nightlife," p. 165), but I've found the less well-know **Sounds of History** ✪✪ exhibition (€5; Mon–Fri 9am–8pm and Sat in summer) quite engaging—particularly if you've an interest in cultural anthropology, especially relating to the development of music. It's a well thought-out interactive exhibit that includes early Irish instruments (including a Bronze Age *crothal,* a bell that looks like a hand-grenade, and fantastic bronze horns that produce a sound akin to that made on a didgeridoo, which is believed to have been played at ancient ceremonies). Vintage film clips reveal how a strong music and dance tradition survived the hard times of the wars and the Troubles. The center also has a shop that stocks books, crafts, and assorted souvenirs.

Cahir's Castle & the Fairytale Cottage

The main reason to visit Cahir (pronounced care) is to explore its centerpiece **Cahir Castle** ✪✪ (Castle St.; ☎ 052/41011; www.heritageireland.ie; Heritage Card or €2.90; daily mid-Mar to mid-June and mid-Sept to mid-Oct 9:30am–5:30pm; mid-June to mid-Sept 9:30am–7pm; mid-Oct to mid-Mar 9:30am–4:30pm), built on a rocky island outcrop on the River Suir; the effect is brilliant—the magnificently preserved castle appears to emerge right out of the rock itself. Poking around the bastions, crenellated towers, dank cells, and unprotected stairways that you have to turn sideways to negotiate, this feels like the "real deal" of castles, perfect for imagining sieges, battles, and military intrigues. But, as the main exhibition in one of the rooms reveals, the castle was only ever taken once by force; that was in 1599, when the Earl of Essex (supposedly Queen Elizabeth's lover) besieged the Anglo-Norman Butler clan who had built most of what remains of the castle today.

After exploring the castle, and the Georgian town center nearby, prepare yourself for the best part of Cahir—this time entirely attributable to Richard Butler, the Earl of Glengall, who commissioned one of the strangest, and loveliest, houses in Ireland: **Swiss Cottage** ✪✪✪ (Kilcommon, Cahir; ☎ 052/41144; www.heritage ireland.ie; Heritage Card or €2.90; mid-Mar to mid-Apr Tues–Sun 10am–1pm and 2–6pm; mid-Apr to mid-Oct daily 10am–6pm; mid-Oct to mid-Nov Tues–Sun 10am–1pm and 2–4:30pm). A so-called "cottage *orné,*" it was designed by the famous Regency architect John Nash and looks a bit like a gigantic two-storey mushroom with undulating thatched roof and log-colonnaded wraparound patio (hence the "ornamental cottage" moniker). Its quirky design comes as welcome relief from the grey stone walls of all the castles and church ruins hereabouts. So, what's it all about? When it was built in 1810, it was fashionable for the wealthy to play at being commoners. So, the ornamental chalet was a rich society approximation—a fantasy imitation, if you will—of the type of dwelling inhabited by the poor. Needless to say, any hint at poverty is wholesale illusion, for the interior is lovingly designed and decorated to the highest standards. What's interesting, however, is that the entire house is filled with intentional imperfections—no two windows, doorways or floor levels are the same, which is a symbolic reference to the triumph of nature (because this is a simulation of a pastoral home) over civilization. As you're taken through the house, you'll also see numerous visual motifs that represent nature in its myriad forms—whether in an etched mirror frame or chairs carved to resemble wood bark. Who'd ever imagine being a privileged aristocrat involved so many conceits?

NIGHTLIFE

Adjacent the Rock of Cashel, at the **BrúBorú Centre,** you can catch a live song and dance act. Called "BrúBorú," it features 33 performers who present traditional music, haunting voices, and folk dance routines that may feel a little hammy (you know, the over-rehearsed showgirlsy variety), but has nevertheless entertained multitudes of fans around the world—from Frank Sinatra to the Sultan of Oman. A summer-only production, it plays Tuesday to Saturday at 9pm; tickets are €20. Some pay €50 for the pre-show dinner, commencing at 7pm (but I don't recommend it). Call ☎ 062/61122 to book.

For a convivial drink in a traditional pub that still bears a resemblance to its earlier incarnation as a grocery store-cum-pub, visit **Mikey Ryan's** ✭✭ (76 Main St., Cashel; ☎ 062/61431), where locals gather to exchange the latest bits of gossip and huddle in front of the TV for the next big game . . . whatever it might be.

5 The Famed Southwest

Splendid scenery, real Irish culture &
yes, the Ring of Kerry

by Keith Bain

WITH SOME OF THE SHOWIEST COASTLINE ON EARTH, IRELAND'S SOUTH-
west is probably its most visited region, and its famous Ring of Kerry—a 175km
(110-mile) coastal road route around the largest of the southwest's five rugged,
sea-battered peninsulas—is easily the most popular journey undertaken by visitors
to Ireland. That's bad news as well as good. With traffic jams of tour busses, and
souvenir shops overrunning some of the small towns along the Ring, many feel
that this is an area that's being loved to death.

Still, there are scores of less-saturated areas to visit in the Southwest and you'll
find that each peninsula has its own quixotic appeal. At the edges of each, crag-
torn cliffs plummet into the pounding sea to produce intensely visual drama, go
inland and you're never far from an idyllic, colorful village, a castle ruin, or a set of
magnificent lakes, mountains, and woodlands such as you'll find in the Killarney
National Park—its fairy tale terrain so magical, it made a tourist out of Queen
Victoria. The Queen, who stayed at Killarney's magnificent Muckross House
(p. 184), was so enchanted by the grandeur of the parklands that she had ferns, ivy,
and even leaves sent back home to remind her of her stay. Today, the National Park
and Kerry's backbone mountain range—Macgillycuddy's Reeks—remain a compelling draw, relatively unscathed by the tourist bug that's grabbed Killarney itself.
Not far from Killarney, the Dingle Peninsula has long been a popular silver screen
backdrop, but it's also remarkable for its archaeological finds, phenomenal surfing,
and hiking routes that follow in the footsteps of saints and pagans.

Nature aside, the southwest is also a brilliant cultural destination. Lurking in
the shadows here, amidst the tranquility and good cheer, are tales of fierce sieges,
swarthy pirates, and the gloom of devastation during the Great Famine.
"Rebellious" Cork City sees itself a rival to Dublin, and when it comes to nightlife
and music, it stands out for the sheer quantity and variety of what it delivers. And
scattered throughout West Cork artists and craftspeople find inspiration in the
solitude of its remote villages and prepossessing seascapes.

DON'T LEAVE THE SOUTHWEST WITHOUT . . .

TAPPING INTO THE BEST MUSIC SCENE   One thing's for sure, if you get
to Cork City, you're going to find music. Just about everywhere. From brilliant
trad sessions, to experimental rock, to innovative avant garde, classical, or fusion,
you'll definitely find your groove in this buzzing little city. See p. 195.

GOING NATIVE WITH THE ISLANDERS The waters off the coast of West Cork and Kerry are studded with remote islands, some inhabited, some not. Try to get to at least one of them, by boat or—in the case of Dursey Island—by cable car. It may just be the ride of your life. See p. 230.

LOSING YOURSELF IN THE SLEEPY WILDERNESS OF A TIME-FOR-GOTTEN PENINSULA Kerry's Iveragh Peninsula is where *everyone* goes, and its beauty is astounding—but to get off the beaten track, submit to the wilder, untamed gorgeousness of smaller, more-rugged peninsulas, like Beara or Sheep's Head. See p. 230 and 226, respectively.

MEETING AN ARTIST West Cork is a haven for artists and craftspeople; many people escape here to focus their creative energies, and as you travel the region, you'll soon discover why. Take time out from ogling the coastline to browse a gallery, join a workshop, or attend a class where you can learn a skill that will forever remind you of the rhapsodic beauty of this place. See p. 232.

LAY OF THE LAND

Cork is also the main city in County Cork (254km/158 miles from Dublin), and also the biggest hub in terms of transport—there's an international airport here—so you might start out there. You can also explore the region starting in Kerry's northernmost peninsula of Dingle, and then travel the region in reverse. As with any part of Ireland, the best way to get around these two counties—if you really want to see the best it has to offer—is by car. For up-to-date travel information specific to this region, log on to **www.corkkerry.ie**.

KENMARE

Ireland's first planned town, Kenmare was established in 1670 by Sir William Petty who planted the region with Protestants from England and Wales. A century later, one of Petty's progeny rebuilt the town and christened it; he then went on to become the British Prime Minister. With gracious Georgian houses and colorful limestone shop facades—their hand-painted wooden signs preserving an Old World atmosphere—Kenmare remains an appealing little town. It also has more than its fair share of excellent restaurants and—for such refined town—the after-dark scene can build up considerable momentum. However, Kenmare's principal benefit is its prime position as a base for forays around both the Ring of Kerry and Beara's less-traveled coastline. Smaller and more attractive than Killarney (although without the benefit of Killarney's National Park on its doorstep), Kenmare is also used by watersport enthusiasts, who dive and boat in the wide Kenmare River. As far as sights go, the only thing to see in town is a Bronze Age stone circle; the largest of its kind in the Southwest, the circle is centered on a dolmen burial monument.

LAY OF THE LAND

Kenmare's action happens on and around a triangle of streets: **Henry, Main,** and **Shelburne,** with the town's square located in the broad area stretching out from the intersection of Henry and Main.

Counties Cork & Kerry

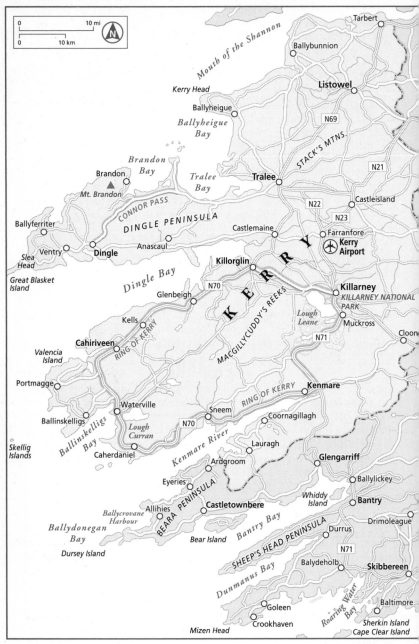

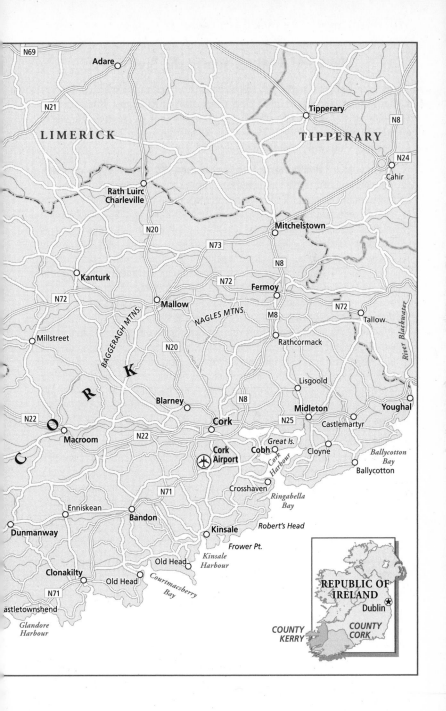

Vacation Rentals across the Southwest

Because Ireland's southwest has so much to offer, many travelers set-up-house here, and spend their time simply taking day trips. This approach yields up to 2 weeks of satisfying sightseeing (not to mention the pleasure of living like a local). To find the rental that's right for you, I recommend the following three companies:

Kenmare-based **Dream Ireland Holiday Homes** (☎ 064/41170; www.dream ireland.com) offers a broad inventory of houses, cottages, and apartments throughout the region (and across Ireland). Currently, they have access to 35 different sets of properties in Cork, and 99 in Kerry, many of which are in holiday home developments, which means that the houses or cottages are often in clusters—like small holiday villages—where you're not exactly living among locals, but rather spending time with other vacationers, often from Dublin. A selection of freestanding cottages (sometimes in wonderfully isolated spots with sublime views, like **Reen Cottage,** p. 225), apartments, and homes right in the villages are also available. Decor at these homes will run the gamut from minimalist contemporary, to homey, and old-fashioned. A minimum 2-night stay is always required, but you'll always get the better deal if you stay for a week. For example, when I looked at the prices of the two-bedroom cottages in the popular Barley Cove development on the Mizen Head Peninsula, they were €482 for a week in September 2009, but €302 for 2 nights during the same period. Their best out-of-season deal along the coast of County Cork is €280 for a six-person cottage in Castletownbere.

West Coast Holidays (☎ 061/335799; www.westcoastholidays.ie) represents pockets of holiday villages concentrated around certain towns—like West Cork's Clonakilty (a hotspot popular with Irish vacationers, no doubt because of it's proximity to Inchydoney Beach). It doesn't necessarily have the far-reaching access to properties in unique locations that Dream

You can learn about Kenmare's history as a modern town at the **Heritage Centre** (The Square; ☎ 064/41233), which also has tourist information and a Heritage Trail map.

GETTING THERE & GETTING AROUND

From Cork, you can drive directly to Kenmare along the **R569;** from Killarney, follow the **N71.** However, if you've been following the West Cork coastal route, you'll probably arrive from Glengarriff, 21km (13 miles) south. Getting around is a breeze if you're on foot and a bit pointless if you're in a car—it really is that small.

Bus Éireann operates services between Cork and Kenmare (via Glengarriff and Skibbereen) from June through September; the trip takes 4 hours and costs around €14. The 1-hour bus trip from Killarney costs around €8.

Ireland does, but proximity to a town does have its perks, and there's more chance of having access to a support staff when things go wrong (you know—plumbing leaks, malfunctioning central heating). And while you may blanch at the architectural detailing of many of its properties (yeah, they're built as quick, urgent investments), some are neutral enough to be, well, fine. Among the rentals I've found through this agency have been one- or two-bedroom apartments in Youghal (either way it's €249–€499 per week); three-bedroom houses in Clonakilty (€379–€699 per week); and four-bedroom cottages in Caherdaniel on the Iveragh Peninsula (average price €499 per week). And remember, the top price is only ever charged in July and August.

Finally, the advantage of choosing an agency like **Rent an Irish Cottage** (☎ 061/411109; www.rentacottage.ie) is that you'll be more likely to find a historic property, such as one of their courtyard cottages at **Ardnagashel Estate,** 3km (2 miles) from Ballylickey (West Cork), for which you could pay as little as €175 for a week. Don't be deceived by their cutesy name, however—their "cottages" are often modern developments, too, and also include townhouses. Such as the colorful row of three-bedroom houses—called **Fairfield Close**—in Dingle Town; a house here for the week costs between €320 and €575 for most of the year. Don't expect miracles from the decor, which tends to be on the satisfactory side of garage sale mix 'n' match; you'll have everything that you need and want, but it won't necessarily hang together very fetchingly. But that's a minor quibble: In just about every rental here, you'll have a homey space to call your own for a spell, and the pleasure of feeling more resident than passer-by will make up for any lapses in the designer's taste.

One tiny, but nevertheless annoying, concern about most of these agencies: You are more than likely going to pay extra for towels. And you always need to check if electricity and heating oil is included or not.

ACCOMMODATIONS, BOTH STANDARD & NOT

€ Centrally located and clean, **Kenmare Lodge Hostel** ✦ (Main St.; ☎ 064/40662; kenmarehostel@eircom.net; MC, V) does just about fall into its self-proclaimed "luxury budget" category. Choose from eight-bedded dorms (€15–€17 per person), en suite doubles (€50), and family rooms sleeping four (€80). Bedrooms are well-maintained, with TVs and wardrobes in the private rooms; linen and towels are provided, and there's a properly equipped kitchen and laundry facility. There's even a courtyard at the back.

€€ The real benefit of a night at **Virginia's Guesthouse** ✦✦✦ (Henry St.; ☎ 064/41021; www.virginias-kenmare.com; MC, V)—besides the good rates—lies in the hands-on attention of husband-and-wife owners Noreen and Neil, who take good care of their guests, especially when it comes to Noreen's breakfasts. Her pear slices smothered with melted Cashel blue cheese, served with crispy bacon and homemade tomato and apple chutney in particular, are scrumptious. The guesthouse is well located in the heart of Kenmare, right above Mulcahy's (one of the best restaurants in a town that's known for it's dining); and bedrooms are compact, cozy, and freshly painted, featuring solid wood furniture, comfy beds, and such individual, if twee, touches as teddy bears. Rates are fair: Typically a room will cost €70, going up to €90 or €100 in summer.

€€   Many guests at Mary and Noel O'Brien's **Hawthorn House** ✸✸ (Shelburne St.; ☎ 064/42035; www.hawthornhousekenmare.com; MC, V) come back time and again. "We come back for Mary," I've heard some of them joke, but when you witness the cheerful repartee she enjoys with visitors, you'll understand why this place is so popular. "Great rooms and fantastic breakfasts," is why one regularly returning golfer prefers to stay here; and I can add primo location. Here's another: Double rooms start at €80, and are €100 in peak season.

€€€–€€€€   Although it's pricier than my other Kenmare favorites, **Shelburne Lodge** ✸✸✸ (Shelburne St.; ☎ 064/41013; www.shelburnelodge.com; closed Dec–Feb; MC, V) really outshines everyone else when it comes to style and historic ambience. The oldest house in town, it was built in the mid-18th century for Lord Shelburne, who rebuilt Kenmare and became British Prime Minister. Set in sumptuous grounds, with magnolia-filled gardens and trees covered in ghost-like moss, the house offers splendidly individual accommodations (pale, bone-finish antique furniture, big mirrors; and great bathrooms with tub-shower combos. And the smaller "queen"-size rooms are not too big of a splurge at €100 to €140 double, (larger "king" units cost €160). An eclectic art collection fills the house—from textile wall-hangings to religious icons and contemporary canvases—while an open-fire warms the sitting room, filled with more antiques and piles of coffee table tomes. Breakfast is another elegant affair where you're spoilt for choice.

DINING FOR ALL TASTES

€–€€   Deli, bakery, and cafe all in one, **Jam** (6 Henry St.; ☎ 064/41591; Mon–Sat 8am–5pm; summer 8am–6pm; MC, V) is now a small County Kerry franchise, good for light lunches (daily specials around €8) and made-to-order sandwiches (€3.50) stuffed with fresh, local ingredients.

€–€€   However, I find you get even better take-home meals from **Truffle Pig Fine Foods** ✸✸ (The Square on Market St.; ☎ 064/42953; Mon–Sat 9:30am–6pm; cash only), where you can sniff around for exciting, good-value ready-to-serve meals—just add heat. Among a wide selection, there's Kerry beef slow-cooked in Guinness (€6); braised lamb shanks (€7.25); Greek-style aromatic chicken with wine, olives, and cinnamon (€6); vegetarian moussaka with aubergines, lentils, and potato (€6); and Spanish-style pork (€6). Most of these portions will serve two people, or one very hungry soul. You can also buy cheeses, pates, pastas, olives, and various homemade breads and preserves here, making this an ideal stop if you're stocking up for a week in a vacation home.

€–€€€   For bar food a couple of notches above the average, the **Purple Heather** ✿✿ (Henry St.; ☎ 064/41016; daily 11:45am–5pm; MC, V) opened in 1964, when it was called "the model for a new kind of eating place—a seamless blend of pub and cafe." While the model has now been adopted widely across Ireland, this remains a haven of good food, elegant boho style, and a friendly, civilized atmosphere. The menu is also far more intriguing than you could hope to find in a traditional pub: chicken liver pâté (€9.80); seafood soup (€8.20); organic salads (€5.80); a very popular Purple Heather omelet (€9); and cheeses served with homemade bread and apple chutney (€9.80). It's simple, excellent fare that has earned a loyal following over the years.

€€–€€€   My other favorite easy-dining restaurant hereabouts is unpretentious and always packed to bursting—even when tourists aren't around, which says a great deal. As the name suggests, **Prego** ✿✿ 🄺🄸🄳🅂 (18 Henry St.; ☎ 064/42350; daily 9am–9:30pm; MC, V) is Italian, and the interior—candles flickering on the hand-painted wooden tables—certainly evokes a warm Mediterranean ambience, greatly enhanced by the awesome buzz of lively families, intimate couples, and a music soundtrack by Afro Celtic Sound System (recorded, but still magical). There's a formidable pizza selection (€11–€14) and great variety of pastas (€13–€14), and although I'm assured that the chef, owner, and staff are all 100% Irish, the food is as richly toothsome as anything you'd find in Bologna.

ATTENTION, SHOPPERS!

Nest (2 Shelbourne St.; ☎ 064/41802 or 085/753-4278) is one of Kenmare's loveliest little shops, selling a mix of quality children's items (toys and clothing—look for knitwear by Julie Dillon), knickknacks for the home, and assorted oddities that make fine gifts for anyone preparing to, well, "nest."

Kenmare Bookshop (Shelbourne St.; ☎ 064/41578) carries an outstanding selection of books on anything and everything Irish, from history to hurling, as well as books specifically on Kenmare, Kerry, and Cork.

On the other side of town, just past the Heritage Centre and across the road from the Kenmare Art Gallery, don't neglect **Noel & Holland's Second Hand Books** (Bridge St.; ☎ 064/42464) with a selection that includes rare and vintage books. Even the window display can be intrepid—one of the best I've seen is *Fanny Hill's Cook Book* (with its naughty cover depicting a buxom redhead preparing fish in the buff) displayed ironically alongside the very serious *Hunger—An Unnatural History.* Pure genius.

NIGHTLIFE

Kenmare's nightlife revolves around dining out, followed by pounding the sidewalks in search of a pub with live music; no hardship this, since an abundance of pubs and bars line both Henry and Main streets. There's DJ-driven commercial stuff, too, with more than one disco yielding some of the most atrocious dance moves I've seen in these parts; look for the bars with doormen checking IDs at the entrances. One such venue is the **Square Pint** (Main St.; ☎ 064/42357), where there's usually dance-floor action (and a €5 cover) on weekends, but things can get downright dull if the regulars don't show up. **McCarthy's** (☎ 064/41516) on Main Street is the best place for traditional music, although it sometimes has what I would deem "commercialized" traditional, meaning you'll hear the type of heartfelt guitar-accompanied crooning you can hear just about anywhere. Another favorite for regular traditional music is **Crowley's** (Henry St.; ☎ 064/41472), which can get pretty rowdy.

If you want to escape the outsiders and get an eye-opening look at life on the inside track, step inside **Roughty Bar** (17 Main St.; no phone) which, as some locals put it to me, is frequented by "part-time workers and professional drinkers." Here, beneath stuffed animal trophies, you'll find the local lads playing cards in ancient upholstered benches, and others nursing their last, final, "perhaps one more," pint while staring at TV sports. Sometimes you'll spot someone's wife suddenly appear, threateningly, in the doorway; and just as quickly, she'll disappear . . . with husband in tow. She'll probably be the only woman you see here, unless an unwitting tourist accidentally wonders in. Some might find Roughty a little threadbare, but this is the "real thing" which the superpubs simply cannot replicate.

THE IVERAGH PENINSULA & RING OF KERRY

Millions (yes, millions) of gawking people come to the Iveragh Peninsula to do "The Ring of Kerry"—really a cheesy marketing moniker for a circular road route that misses some of the best the Iveragh has to offer (mainly because their buses stick to the wider roads). To really experience this place, you need to venture off the main route whenever possible, and spend a night or two so you can appreciate the coast's magical beauty at both sunset and sunrise, unhindered by crowds. That's when you'll be able to appreciate the scenery that drew all the folks here in the first place: rocky cliffs battered by relentless waves, wild islands piercing the ocean surface, lush hills terraced all the way down to sandy coves. That's what makes the coast of the Iveragh Peninsula memorable (not the kitsch-filled souvenir stands). The hinterland, meanwhile, beckons with verdant forests, shimmering lakes, and Ireland's highest mountain (Carrantuohill, 1,038m/3,405 ft.). Take time to walk a little or cycle, notably the Kerry Way, for an opportunity to commune with the region in a most profound way.

"DOING" THE RING OF KERRY

The Ring of Kerry is a 176km (109-mile) road trip, much of it along the Iveragh's often-spectacular coast. In truth, the best part is along its most westerly reaches, more or less from Castle Cove to Valentia Island, with myriad points affording gobsmacking views. Whether of plunging cliffs, sharp-rising islands, or the heady bombardment of waves against rock—it's a cold heart that isn't moved.

From Kenmare, the N70 leads to **Sneem** (27km/17 miles), the first village of any note and completely touristy (€3 espresso? I think not): Press on, better things lie ahead. Next up, you may want to stop for a dip or a beach walk at wild and lovely **White Strand,** just before you reach **Castlecove** (14km/8⅔ miles from Sneem), where the roadside bar may tempt you to stop. Instead, look for the turn-off to **Staigue Fort** ✦, an interesting diversion, 4km (2½ miles) off the main road, this incredible stone ring fort was built around 2 millennia ago and now belongs to a local farmer (€1 honesty box). Back on the Ring, it's 6km (3¾ miles) to **Caherdaniel,** the place where Daniel O'Connell (see box, "Iveragh: Land of the Liberator") was born and where you can visit his nearby home, **Derrynane House** ✦ (☎ 066/947-5113; Heritage Card or €2.90; closed Nov–Mar), or simply explore the adjacent sandy beach.

Iveragh: Land of the Liberator

More than just a pretty stretch of peninsula, the Iveragh holds a special place in the hearts of Irish people as the home of **Daniel O'Connell,** the man who brought religious freedom to Ireland. Known as "the Liberator," O'Connell was born in Cahersiveen to a family of smugglers and was sent to study in France. Solid education opened his eyes to the need to challenge the English government on the oppressive penal laws which had been introduced to limit the rights of Catholics. As a barrister and parliamentarian, he became a great advocate for the cause and his political activism, with fierce popular support, finally won civil liberties and rights for Irish Catholics in 1829. Incidentally, O'Connell also campaigned for the abolition of slavery, and was a supporter of women's rights. O'Connell's home was at Derrynane—with a perfectly formed smugglers' cove—just below his namesake village of Caherdaniel; today his house is a museum celebrating his life (p. 174).

Just beyond Caherdaniel, you come upon the precariously positioned **Scarriff Inn** (p. 178) affording breathtaking clifftop views—the Scarriff and Deenish islands as a backdrop to treacherous Scarriff Bay. Another viewing spot lies just beyond, at the head of the **Coomakista Pass;** at the bottom of the Pass, you reach the mellow seaside town of **Waterville** which has long been a holiday destination—Charlie Chaplin was a fan.

Beyond Waterville, most people continue along the N70 to Cahersiveen: Don't! Look for the R567 turn-off to **Ballinskelligs** (marked only as Baile an Sceilge on some signs), and take in the less-explored **Ring of Skellig,** or R566. For a real treat, ask for directions (there are no signs of any kind) to **Cill Rialaig,** a "famine village" situated high on the Bolus headland. A group of stone houses—left deserted after famine decimated the population—have been handsomely restored with slate or straw roofs and brightly painted doors and window-frames to create an artist retreat. Beyond here, the road meanders even higher above the cliff-face, with awesome dropaway views; it eventually culminates in a threatening "No Entry" sign at the entrance to a farmer's property, so consider rather doing this last bit on foot (there's no turning point beyond Cill Rialaig without trespassing). Head back towards Ballinskelligs village and continue on the R566 to Portmagee.

For much of this route, you'll be overlooking **St. Finan's Bay,** with the Skelligs and Puffin Island bobbing in the water—have your binoculars ready for the view (on a good day you'll see as far as the islands) from the Skelligs View Telescope.

At the summit of the gorgeous **Coomanspic Mountain pass,** there's another great viewing point (just park and roam), but be warned that at the signposted cafe, **Blasket View House** (☎ 066/948-0985), a little further along, you'll be charged €3.50 to park your car, get a pair of binoculars, and walk 10 minutes for one of the finest views on the peninsular cliffs: From up here, you not only can see the Blasket Islands off the tip of the Dingle Peninsula, but you can also get a very good look at the Skelligs.

This Way or That: Which Way Round the Ring?

Squadrons of tour buses tackle the Ring of Kerry each summer, commencing from Killarney; they are required to all travel counter-clockwise in order to prevent massive pile-ups around sharp, narrow corners along the way. "Doing the Ring of Kerry" (p. 174) describes the route if you're starting in Kenmare which takes you around the edge of the peninsula in a clockwise direction. The benefit of starting from Kenmare is that you avoid the potential risk of having buses intimidate you from behind; and when you're trying to enjoy a leisurely drive for the sake of taking in the views, there's nothing worse than being tailgated by an impatient and overbearing bus driver with a schedule to keep.

However if you prefer to start from Killarney, wait until after 10am (after the tour busses have left and then take your time, and you should avoid most of the crowds. Although you can probably drive the Ring in as few as 3 or 4 hours, ideally you should spend the entire day. There's another argument which favors following the buses, because then you avoid the chance of meeting them head on if you do start out in Kenmare.

One drawback of starting out from Kenmare is that you miss the spectacular stretch of scenery between Moll's Gap and Killarney at the end of the journey, so be sure to factor this in later, if you do start from Kenmare. In short, there's no sure fire method.

You are now just outside **Portmagee,** an ideal spot for a bite to eat, or even to spend the night (see "Where to Stay & Dine," below), this is also where you'll find several boat launches that go to the **Skellig Islands** ✿✿✿, perhaps one of the most exhilarating trips you can take in Ireland; one operator is **Joe Roddy & Sons** (☎ 087/120-9924; www.skelligstrips.com) who's been launching from Portmagee Pier for 40 years. A bridge at Portmagee links the mainland with Valentia Island which you can zip across in a few minutes, or explore at leisure for a taste of remote wilderness. As you cross the bridge onto the island, there's a virtual tour of the Skellig islands at the **Skellig Experience** (☎ 066/947-6306; www.skellig experience.com; €5; daily Apr–June and Sept 9:30am–5pm; July–Aug 9:30am–7pm), which is strictly for anyone who's not done the real thing (in fact, the film presentation may just be rubbing your nose in what you've missed out on; see "Your Skellig Island Adventure," on p. 179). Valentia, incidentally, is where scientists have identified tetrapod footprints that are 360-million years old; there's also evidence that Neolithic man lived here some 5,000 years ago.

At the other end of Valentia, from hauntingly situated **Knightstown,** you can catch the ferry (€5 one-way, €8 return) back to the mainland at **Cahersiveen,** where Daniel O'Connell was born in 1775. There are two tributes to this political legend—the **O'Connell Memorial Church** (1888), and a display at the **Cahersiveen Heritage Centre**—although there's little need to stop for either of them. The 27km (16¾ mile) stretch to **Glenbeigh** affords views across Dingle Bay to the Dingle Peninsula—particularly as the road begins to climb after the village of **Kells.** With an excellent beach nearby, Glenbeigh is also visited for the **Kerry**

Bog Village Museum (www.kerrybogvillage.ie), but the experience is a bit hollow for my tastes. Rather, follow signs to idyllic, mountain-encircled **Caragh Lake** (a chance to see some of the Iveragh's majestic hinterland) before picking your way back to the N70 for the final leg, passing through **Killorglin**—home of the annual pagan-style Puck Fair in August—which is just 22km (13⅔ miles) short of Killarney.

Of course, if you can do all this by bike, it'll be all the more blissful; my co-author, Emily, says that the stretch between Killorglin and Derrynane is her favorite cycle route in the country.

TAKING A BREAK ON THE RING OF KERRY: WHERE TO STAY & DINE

Naturally, there are plenty of places to stay throughout the peninsula; highlighted below are a few that I think are ideal for touring the best of the Iveragh's coast— **Derrynane** is practically midway along the ring and the setting is miraculous, while **Portmagee** is great for the Ring of Skelligs and, indeed, for trips to the Skellig Islands.

Ballinskelligs

€–€€€   Part of the Ballinskelligs Inn, **Cable O'Leary's** (☎ 066/947-9104; www. ballinskelligsinn.com; daily 6–10pm; MC, V) is one of the Iveragh's most popular venues for live music. The bar-cum-restaurant also serves simple meals, including sandwiches for around €6.

In & Around Caherdaniel

€   Caherdaniel has its own homey hostel, the **Traveller's Rest** (Caherdaniel; ☎ 066/947-5175; www.myderrynane.com/hostel.htm; cash only), with dorms (€16) and private rooms (€19 per person) in a converted house. The atmosphere is decidedly unlike that experienced in city hostels—this is particularly warm, cozy, and personal.

€–€€€€   Also in Caherdaniel is **Freddy's Bar** ☆ (☎ 066/947-5400; summer daily 8:30am–late; call ahead in winter), where Freddy—a relative of the great Daniel O'Connell—has been pulling pints for over 41 years; his family built this bar (which is attached to Freddy's grocery store where you can pick up supplies for a picnic) in 1832. As one of the locals told me "This is a real drinking man's pub." (Don't worry; lots of women tipple here, too.) Across the road at the **Blind Piper** (☎ 066/947-5126; food served Mon–Fri noon–3pm and 6–8pm; Sat–Sun 12:30–8pm; MC, V) there's live music many nights, too.

€€   About 1km (⅔ mile) from Caherdaniel village, are immaculate, comfortable lodgings to be had at **Derrynane Bay House** ☆ 🎈 (Caherdaniel; ☎ 066/947-5404; www.ringofkerry.net; closed Nov to mid-Mar; MC, V). Although it's a small B&B, it offers six biggish bedrooms, each individually decorated and neatly maintained, with thick duvets on the beds. Views from the dining room (dinner costs €25) and lounge take in Derrynane Bay. Doubles cost €76 to €80; family-size rooms are also available.

€€ First, I must warn you that Katie O'Carroll's precariously positioned **Scarriff Inn** ✪✪ (Caherdaniel; ☎ 066/947-5132; www.caherdaniel.net; closed Nov to mid-Mar; MC, V) is a popular lunch stop on the summer tour bus route. And there's good reason: The views from here are awesome, and Katie prepares satisfying food (her cooking was praised by Andrew Lloyd Webber when he came to Iveragh 10 years ago). So, definitely check out the Irish stew (€13) even if you can't overnight (such a shame). The trick is to arrive here after 2pm once the buses have departed and normality has been restored. And you really do want to be here—although the bedrooms (just five of them at €80–€90 a pop) are pretty compact and simple—they offer the priceless reward of unimpeded views over Derrynane Bay below. And, spend some time chatting with Katie—she'll share many insider insights about the region.

€€–€€€€ Proclaiming itself Ireland's only beach bar, **O'Carroll's Cove Beach Bar and Restaurant** (Caherdaniel; ☎ 066/947-5151; food served June–Aug daily noon–9pm; MC, V) is as much a spot for a bit of island-style fun as it is for solid pub grub, with a focus on seafood. Your location will tell you exactly how fresh everything is.

€€€ Way down below, practically on the water, **Iskeroon** ✪✪✪ (Iskeroon, Caherdaniel; ☎ 066/947-5119; www.iskeroon.com; closed Oct–Apr; MC, V) is a haven for anyone who wants to get well away from it all. Situated right on Derrynane Harbor (which the Washington Post called "arrestingly beautiful"), Iskeroon is an ultra-luxurious B&B with such plush amenities as iPod docking stations, a private jetty, and huge, suite-size rooms. Problem is, you pay dearly; rooms are €160 per room per night, and there's a 2-night minimum. Iskeroon's equally chichi self-catering "apartment" is the solution: Big enough for two—full kitchen included, with lovely color-saturated decor (tastefully done), and very soft, inviting linens—it's much more affordable at just €500 to €550 per week for two people.

Portmagee

Margaret MacCarthy is one of Port Magee's dear souls, and I like her all the more after checking out the large **vacation house** ✪✪ (New Road, Port Magee; ☎ 066/947-7193; cash only) she rents out on the road leading into town. With four big bedrooms (three en suite) and plenty of space to relax—inside and out—this is a great bargain for €500 per week (or €700 July–Aug).

€€ Right next door, but this time catering to modernists who prefer a slightly luxe B&B experience, is **Portmagee Heights** ✪✪ (New Rd.; ☎ 087/272-2503 or 066/947-7251; www.portmageeheights.com; MC, V). A contemporary house with packed Valentia slate walls, attractive wood finishes, and a green ethos (alternative energy is used here), this is a really smart, spacious, option; unimpeded views across the water take in Valentia Island. Bedrooms have wooden floors, fine linens, powerful showers, and either an armchair or sofa. Surprisingly, luxury like this comes at a budget price—€70 double, and €80 for a "superior" room.

€€–€€€ Down at the harbor, Gerard Kennedy offers stylish, hotel-standard lodgings at the **Moorings** ✪✪ (Portmagee; ☎ 087/239-0010 or 066/947-7108;

Your Skellig Island Adventure

Prepare for a bumpy ride on wild waters as you set sail for the **Skellig Islands** ✮✮✮, 10km (6 miles) off the Iveragh coast. Rising sharply out of the water, untamed Skellig Michael (Great Skellig) is where adorable, clown-faced puffins congregate during their breeding season—from April until August. An otherworldly monastic settlement, constructed here (heavens alone knows how) some 1,300 years ago, is also a kick to explore. Guides on the island will explain the unusual architecture and layout of the monastic community—reached via hundreds of steep steps—and how the innovative monks (who finally left in the 12th century) traded seal steaks, feathers, and birds' eggs for luxuries from passing ships.

Your boat will also pass close to the off-limits gannet colony on Little Skellig; around 33,000 birds dock here from the west coast of Africa.

This is perhaps the most adventure you can pack into a single day around these parts, so you'll want to be prepared; get your timing right, dress warmly, and prepare for the wet. If conditions are bad, boats don't sail, so check ahead: You can contact **Sean Feehan—Skellig Cruise** (☎ 086/417-6612 or 066/947-9182; www.skelligsboats.com)—who sets off from Ballinskelligs Pier at 11am each day, for a heads-up on the situation. From Ballinskelligs, it takes around 45 minutes to reach Skellig Michael and you get to spend 1½ to 2½ hours on the island before heading back, taking in Little Skellig and the Washerwoman's Rock along the way; if you've got luck on your side, you may spot dolphins, minke whales, and basking sharks. Settle on devoting the better part of a half-day to this

www.moorings.ie; AE, MC, V), where the lobby features pictures of Gerard hanging out with Irish celebrities and politicians. Standard bedrooms (from €90) are neat-as-a-pin and comfortable—but if you want a view and upscale luxury, you'll need to upgrade to one of their blissful "Seaview" rooms (mini-suites, really, from €120). Downstairs, the action happens in the Bridge Bar—with its strong nautical theme and upbeat crowd—it also serves some of the Iveragh's best seafood. Regular music sessions include Gerard himself singing on Tuesday nights and set dancing that erupts quite spontaneously.

Sneem

€–€€€€   The **Blue Bull** (South Sq.; ☎ 064/45382; food served daily noon–9pm; AE, MC, V) is another pub that has long been pulling in the summer crowds; don't think twice about sharing a main course here, they're huge.

Waterville

€–€€€€   The **Lobster Bar** (☎ 066/947-4629; daily noon–9:30pm; MC, V) is a vast pine-furnished venue that's long been trusted for its laid-back, unpretentious meals. Affordable lunchtime favorites include homemade fisherman's soup (€5.75) and the prawn fishcakes, served with chips and salad (€10); a variety of sandwiches go for between €3.50 and €12.

ATTENTION, SHOPPERS!

To my mind, there's only one shop you need to bother with on the Iveragh, and that's Portmagee's handsome white and blue store, **Cois Cuain** ✪✪ (The Moorings; ☎ 066/947-7108) which carries an assortment of quality items: tableware by Philip Kenny if you want something substantial; marine-themed ornaments if you're after an affordable gift; and great homemade deli items—preserves, breads, and artisan cheeses—if you want to nibble.

KILLARNEY & THE NATIONAL PARK

When Queen Victoria visited Killarney in 1861, she set off a tourism craze which flourishes to this day. Initially developed around a fledgling linen industry and known for the quality of its woodwork, Killarney now seems to exist almost exclusively for the whims and fantasies of holidaymakers. Yes, the hype can be daunting, but its allure lies in its position at the foot of Ireland's highest mountain range—the Macgillycuddy's Reeks—and proximity to its namesake National Park, a natural preserve of magnificent woodland punctuated with fairy-tale lakes. Surprisingly, given its obvious attractiveness for nature lovers, Killarney is actually a huge party destination, with much of the after dark goings on unfortunately inauthentic and increasingly "citified." I'd suggest you use this primarily as a base and spend most of your time getting out and about in the Park.

GETTING THERE & GETTING AROUND

The nearest airport is **Kerry International** (18km/11 miles), although there is more access via **Cork International Airport** (85km/52¾ miles) and **Shannon International Airport** (128km/79⅓ miles). Frequent **trains** and **buses** connect Dublin, Cork, Limerick, Galway, and other urban hubs. North from Kenmare, Killarney town lies on the **N71.**

Killarney itself is small and, for what it's worth, entirely manageable on foot; it's not too much effort to walk to Ross Island, either. The other main center of activity, **Muckross House,** is 6½km (4 miles) from town along the **N71** (Kenmare Road); this is the principal access point for the Park.

ACCOMMODATIONS, BOTH STANDARD & NOT

Since much of your downtime in Killarney should be spent recuperating from long days out in the Park or exploring the nearby peninsulas, being self-sufficient—with a place all of you own—is ideal. For chic vacation rentals in Killarney's center, try **Park Place Apartments** ✪✪ (www.parkplacekillarney.com), a purpose-built facility with 73 one- and two-bedroom apartments and 15 two-bedroom townhouses; they're all kitted out to contemporary standards (large flatscreen TVs with satellite, laundry facilities, free Wi-Fi) and some have balconies and Jacuzzi baths. The two-bedroom units have an extra fold-out bed so they sleep five people comfortably, and management can also organize babysitting. They're not bad value, either—from €250 per week for a one-bedroom unit, and €307 for a two-bedroom place; the most you'll pay is €595 or €707 during the busy month of July. Because they have such a large inventory of flats, they're able to undercut other holiday rentals, and also offer shorter stay options—so you needn't check-in for an entire week.

If the units at Park Place don't appeal, consider using one of the rental agencies discussed on p. 187.

€   Killarney's best-known hostel is **Neptunes** (www.neptuneshostel.com), but I prefer the more intimate **Sugan** ✪ (Lewis Rd.; ☎ 064/663-3104; cash only), just next door to the Fairview, and a mere 100m (328 ft.) from the bus station. Although it's small, and all bathrooms are shared, it's clean, well-managed, and caters less to rowdy party-hungry youths than to responsible, budget-conscious backpackers. Private double rooms (with basin, desk, and heater) cost €40, while dorms (with either wood- or metal-frame bunk beds) sleep four (€16) or eight (€15) people. A small kitchen is available as is bike rental.

€–€€   As you might imagine, Killarney is overrun with B&Bs; the majority offer good, reliable comfort, and a warm welcome. That's particularly true at **Chelmsford House** ✪ (Muckross View, Countess Grove; ☎ 064/663-6402; www. chelmsfordhouse.com; MC, V). With views across Killarney's lakes and mountains, owner Louise Griffin's house is immaculate and run with a personal touch (it's her family home, after all). I particularly like the size of the bedrooms (which have wooden floors, good little private showers, and white, modular, functional furnishings), and one of them has a small, balcony. Rates start at €60 for two people, and go up to €90 in summer. Best of all, despite being out of the center, you're just a five-minute walk away via a set of steps.

€€   If Louise is full, try **Northwood House** ✪ (5 Muckross View, Countess Grove; ☎ 064/663-7181; www.northwoodhouse.com; MC, V) just down the road; the owner, Josephine Lawlor, offers much of the same comfort (doubles here cost €64–€80 depending on season) in slightly smaller rooms but in a much-newer house. And, like Chelmsford House, there's a pleasing absence of twee, frilly effects; bedrooms are orderly and smart. Josephine also has a small stash of vacation rentals. Her self-catering townhouse has three bedrooms and sleeps six to eight people (€600–€900 per week), while her two-bedroom apartment sleeps four to six and costs €450 to €650 per week.

€€–€€€   I don't think there's a more delightfully simple, straightforward place in the heart of Killarney than the **Copper Kettle** ✪ (Lewis Rd.; ☎ 064/663-4164; www.copperkettlekillarney.com; AE, MC, V); it's a top pick for a well-priced, comfortable stay. The house has a warm, homey ambience, with compressed granite floors, textured wallpaper, floral fabrics, and plenty of pine. Doubles start at €70 (and superior rooms go up to €120 in July), but you should check the internet for discounted rates from €65.

€€€   Bubbly Kathleen O'Regan-Sheppard is so enthusiastic about Kerry that you'll remember her larger-than-life smile and knowledge of the region long after you've left the comfort of **Kathleen's Country House** ✪✪ (Madam's Height, Tralee Rd.; ☎ 064/663-2810; www.kathleens.net; MC, V). Just a mile outside Killarney, set on a huge landscaped garden, Kathleen's house has a large assortment of cottagey bedrooms done up to hotel standard (pine furniture, original artwork in each, and all with tubs and high-power showers); some are less spacious than others (so ask for a "big" room), but all have countryside views from windows that open completely. Kathleen charges €130 to €140 per night in peak season; triples are €180.

€€–€€€   Carol Foley, the energetic force behind **Foley's Townhouse** ✪✪✪ (23 High St.; ☎ 064/663-1217; www.foleystownhouse.com; AE, MC, V) still remembers playing in the streets in front of what has become one of Kerry's most exceptional lodgings. Carol's mother started this guesthouse as a tiny restaurant in 1949—back then there were fires and hot water bottles in the bedrooms, now there are Jacuzzi tubs. Yet, the hands-on, family-run approach prevails. "Make it your home . . . if you want anything, just ask" is what Carol tells guests. What she doesn't tell them is that she still decorates the rooms herself (€110–€150, Wi-Fi included)—not a fan of modern minimalism, they're sumptuous, spacious, and tasteful, with excellent mattresses, antique-style furnishings and silks brought back from India. Downstairs, **Carol's Restaurant** ✪✪✪ is Killarney's best—the medallions of monkfish are blissfully good, perfectly prepared with chanterelles, leeks, ginger, and port jus (€29), while the seafood platter is a veritable feast (actually a mountain of food, suitable for two people; €30).

€€–€€€€   James O'Neill grew up in the house that has become one of Killarney's best guesthouses, the **Fairview** ✪✪ (College St.; ☎ 064/663-4164; www.fairviewkillarney.com; AE, MC, V). Upmarket and stylish, it is nevertheless one of the better-value places to stay, and although it's pretty much like a hotel, there is a sense of hands-on, personal attention from your host. All the rooms are personally designed and decorated by James's wife, Shelley, who has a keen eye for detail as well as a love of contemporary luxuries, so you'll feel quite pampered. James, meanwhile, arranges tours and itineraries, and fusses over guests as though they really were in his own home. There's also a smart in-house restaurant, the **Fifth Season,** where elegant breakfasts are served. While official standard room rates are €105 to €184, if you book online, you get a 25% discount, meaning you pay €79 to €138, depending on season.

DINING FOR ALL TASTES

€   If all those morning fry-ups and late night pints are getting to your waistline (or your immune system), pop into **Shyne Pancake & Smoothie House** (1 Old Market Lane, Killarney; ☎ 064/663-2686; www.shyne.ie; summer daily 8:45am–10pm; winter Mon–Sat 10am–6pm; Sun noon–6pm; cash only) for freshly squeezed healthy juices, which you can enhance with the addition of immune boosters; or choose from a menu of organic teas and Fairtrade coffees; dairy-free ("skinny") smoothies are available for the ultra-health conscious (€3.50–€4.80). Since mid-2008, the real draw here has been the tantalizing menu of sweet and savory pancakes. Rather than spending heavily on a full-blown restaurant meal elsewhere, stop here to order a filling crêpe stuffed with bacon, cheese, and sunblushed tomatoes (€6.90); and at the end of a day of outdoor adventures, you can reward your kids (or yourself) with a dessert pancake decadently smothered with melted Mars bar, or Nutella (€4.90).

€–€€   At **Cathleen's Country Kitchen** (17 New St.; ☎ 064/663-3778; June–
Aug Mon–Fri 9am–8pm; Sat 9am–6pm; Sept–June Mon–Sat 9am–6pm; cash only)
you can either join the locals for affordable, homecooked meals, or grab a takeaway. All meals are under €10, and include lasagna, shepherd's pie, and traditional bacon with cabbage. Sandwiches and sweets are also served.

€€–€€€   Probably the best-value restaurant in town, stone-walled **Stonechat** ✫
(Fleming's Ln.; ☎ 064/663-4295; Mon 6:30–10pm; Tues–Sat 12:30–3pm and 6:30–
10pm; MC, V) is an unpretentious cafe-style eatery tucked into one of Killarney's
little side-streets. The kitchen uses locally sourced organic ingredients to prepare
hearty soups, goulash, meat dishes, and lots of veggie-fare. You'd do well to fill up
at lunch, when dishes cost between €7 and €11, since dinner mains start at
around €14 and go up to €20.

WHY YOU'RE HERE: EXPLORING KILLARNEY NATIONAL PARK

Within the **National Park** is a network of surfaced tracks and nature trails ideal
for walking and cycling. **Boats** are strategically positioned to take visitors out to
see the islands on Killarney's beautiful lakes; you can choose from a seat in a large
waterbus—such as the **Lily of Killarney** (☎ 064/663-1068; €8) which is stationed at Ross Castle—or, for €10, hire a small rowboat and propel your family
across the water. Just beyond the Park, the Gap of Dunloe is only doable on foot,
by bicycle, or on a jaunting horse-drawn cart—the latter being a big tradition
hereabouts, and a pricey, kitschy one at that. "Jaunting cars"—driven by "jar-
veys"—are stationed at key points throughout the area; their rates vary tremendously and go up when demand goes up.

Maps of the Park can be obtained from the info center at Muckross House and
from the **Discover Ireland** (☎ 064/663-1633) tourist center on Beech Road in
town; across the road, you can rent a bike from **O'Sullian's Cycles** (☎ 064/662-
2389; €15 per day). Equipment for the outdoors, camping, and hiking, is available from the **Outdoor Shop** (18 New St.; ☎ 064/662-6927).

The Castle on the Lake & the Gap of Dunloe

A castle at the edge of a silver mirror-surface lake. Throw in several dozen islands.
Cue the swans. Add veiled mist for atmosphere. Voila! If this tranquil scene
sounds a bit too much like a shot from Excalibur, wait until you see the real thing.
Ross Castle ✫✫ (Knockreer Estate, off Muckross Rd.; ☎ 064/663-5851; Heritage
Card or €5.30; daily June–Aug 9am–6:30pm; mid-Mar to May and Sept to mid-Oct
9:30am–5:30pm; mid-Oct to mid-Nov 9:30am–4:30pm) was probably built in the
15th century by an Irish chieftain who chose an inspired position on the edge of
Lough Leane. While the defensive nature of the tower and its fortified walls
(notice the many embrasures and musket loops) indicate that he was mostly concerned with defending his family, he also created a most idyllic scene—one that
inspired Tennyson's poem *The Splendour Falls on Castle Walls.*

Tours of the castle (about 40 min.) are extremely popular, meaning you should
arrive early to avoid the crowds. The castle was used as an English army barracks
until 1825, but restoration has rendered it much as it might have looked during
the 150-year medieval tenure of the O'Donoghues, who built it and used it for

domestic and civil purposes. If you're spending enough time in Ireland to see other, less-frequented castles elsewhere, you can happily skip the interior of this one—although restoration has been so sensitive that medieval building techniques were used in the process, it's been scrubbed to the extent that is does tend to feel a bit "showy," even inauthentic, at times. But, if this is your one medieval tower house experience, it's worth battling the masses.

Ross Castle is the setting-off point for several different boat trips, and one of the most rewarding goes to **Innisfallen Island** ✪✪ which shelter the ruins of an abbey established by St. Finian in the early-7th century, possibly as a leper colony. Now kept at Dublin's Trinity College, the Annals of Innisfallen—a manuscript containing the history of the world until the 5th century as well as an account of early Christian Ireland—were compiled by monks living here.

Also accessible by boat from Ross Castle is one of Mother Nature's great triumphs-by-misadventure, the **Gap of Dunloe** ✪✪✪ 🅺, which was gouged out of the Macgillycuddy's Reeks by glacial movement at the end of the last Ice Age. That was some 12,000 years ago, and the intervening millennia have layered this 6.5km (4-mile) gulch between the Reeks and the Purple Mountains with gigantic boulders, lakes, streams, and sheep-grazed fields (it really is stunning). The Gap is mostly off-limits to cars, which makes the hike (or bike ride) through it memorable for the right reasons. Because of the circuitous nature of the hike through the Gap (2½ hr.), it's best undertaken with the logistical support offered either by the tourism office (p. 186), or by a company like **Gap of Dunloe Tours** (7 High St.; ☎ 064/663-0200; www.gapofdunloetours.com). They'll arrange the 11km (7-mile) transfer to the foot of the Gap at Kate Kearney's Cottage. You then do the Gap and at the other end, a boat will transport you from Lord Brandon's Cottage (a seasonal cafe; ☎ 064/663-4730) at the edge of Upper Lake back to Ross Castle, from where there's another transfer into town (total tour price around €30). The route can also be done in reverse, which—if you're going by bike—also becomes a more affordable option (€15). Cyclists can first catch a boat from Ross Castle, and then, after cycling through the Gap, continue back to town by road, thus eliminating the need for the shuttle bus.

Muckross Estate

There's much to see on and around vast Muckross Estate, where—some 3km (2 miles) south of Killarney—stately **Muckross House** ✪✪✪ (Muckross Rd.; ☎ 064/ 667-0144; www.muckross-house.ie; Heritage Card or €6.50; daily Nov to mid-Mar 9am–5:30pm; mid-Mar to June and Sept–Oct 9am–6pm; July–Aug 9am–7pm; last entry 1 hr. before closing) doubles as headquarters for the National Park. Overlooking Muckross Lake and surrounded by magnificent gardens, this Neo-Elizabethan mansion—built in 1843 at a cost of £30,000—is a stand-out for its opulent Victorian interiors, filled with such a rich assortment of fine furnishings, artworks, and historic decoration that I cannot help but feel that the 50- to 60-minute guided tour is unsympathetically rushed; in fact, one guide I spoke to said it would take an entire day to walk visitors through adequately. Fascinatingly, the owners—hungry for better titles and a grant of more land—spent six years preparing the house for Queen Victoria's much-anticipated visit to Muckross. As queens do, she arrived with an entourage of 80 people, and stayed just 2 nights; unfortunately for her hosts, Prince Albert died soon after the visit, and Victoria went into mourning, and forgot to repay her host's generosity with the titles they'd

Getting a Good View

The three favored vantage positions for spectacular views over Killarney's lakes and the Park are:

- **Agadhoe,** the traditional starting point for the Ring of Kerry, reached by taking the Aghadoe Junction off the N22; however, instead of proceeding directly on to the Ring, it's wise to get out of your car at Agadhoe and gaze across the whole of Killarney below and, stretched out behind the town, the Park, its lakes, and the Macgillycuddys.
- Famous for offering the view most preferred by Queen Victoria's ladies-in-waiting, **Ladies' View** lies 16km (10 miles) from Killarney along the N71.
- Excellent views can be had all along the way between Ladies' View and **Moll's Gap** as you follow the N71.

wanted. Muckross's owners weren't able to recoup the loss incurred to make the house more comfortable for Victoria, so their children eventually mortgaged it.

Once you've seen the house, take the very pleasant 2km (1⅓-mile) walk through the gardens and along the lake toward the foot of Torc Mountain, where signs point you in the direction of **Torc Waterfall** ✸✸, which is particularly engrossing after heavy rains. A walk in the opposite direction will take you to well-preserved **Muckross Friary** ✸ (free admission; mid-June to early-Sept daily 10am–5pm), the evocative, if damp and ominously dark, ruins of a Franciscan friary first built in the 15th century.

ATTENTION, SHOPPERS!

Actually, the heading here should read "Warning, Shoppers!" since I'm inclined to suggest that you skip shopping in this touristy town. Prices for quality goods are high, and the conversation during my last poke around the souvenir shops in Killarney went like this:

"It's not all bad—the wall-mounted Celtic cross brass ashtray is beyond expectation!"

"Yes, but look at that little sculpture of a leprechaun spinning wool directly from the back of his bewildered little sheep 'friend.' Gosh."

Meaning: Beware the kitsch.

DINGLE & THE DINGLE PENINSULA

Wild, rugged, and very popular, Dingle is northernmost of Cork and Kerry's five westward-pointing peninsulas. Like Iveragh and Beara, it has an abundance of dropaway rock faces standing their ground against the ocean's furious attack. Again, the spectacle of waves battering headland is a great attraction here, while the immediacy of Mount Brandon and the range from whence it soars—forming the backbone of Dingle's northern ridge—adds great drama. While most people touring the gorgeous Slea Head tend to concentrate on the great oceanside views, it's worth stopping to also check out a handful of over 2,000 archaeological sites that dot the peninsula. And for hikers and purveyors of high-altitude views, the path that leads to the summit of Mount Brandon is the same one used for centuries by religious pilgrims. For more solitude, you can head over Ireland's highest motorable mountain passage, Connor Pass, and witness the broad expanse of Brandon Bay, a world-class location for wave-riders. Dingle is a crowd-puller, but it's not that difficult to get far away from the masses and have great vistas all to yourself. Much of Dingle is a Gaeltacht (Irish language) area, meaning that Irish-only road signs are in full force here—much to the disgruntlement of many locals counting on tourist trade. It is fun, however, to hear Irish being spoken in public, a sure sign that you aren't entirely surrounded by visitors like yourself.

GETTING THERE & GETTING AROUND

Dingle Town (*Daingean Uí Chúis* in Irish—abbreviated to *An Daingean* on signposts) is the main settlement and just about the only town of any significant size. It's the most convenient (and touristy) base from which to explore the peninsula's highlights. *An Daingean* lies at the end of the **N86,** 18km (11 miles) from Annascaul—the peninsula's first worthwhile stop—which is 49km (30 miles) from Killarney; many time-pressed visitors use Killarney as a base for speedy day trips around Dingle—it's that small, and that easy. West of *An Daingean* is the **Slea Head** circuit, a more or less circular, clockwise route of 40km (25 miles), with many stop-for-a-photo moments along the way.

From *An Daingean,* the **R560** north becomes the Connor Pass, a scenic mountain road that cuts through to Brandon Bay on the peninsula's northern coast. Here, tiny villages like Cloghane and Brandon are calming respite after touristy *An Daingean,* while farther east lie the popular surfing beach at Castlegregory.

Dingle is your best bet for **bicycle rental,** and for picking up hiking maps at **Dingle Tourist Information Office** (The Quay; ☎ 066/915-1188).

DINGLE TOWN

Dingle Town was granted its charter by King James in 1607, and became the second largest port on Ireland's west coast, thanks to trade links with France and Spain. Today, its small town affability works well with its wonderful position, perched at the edge of Dingle Bay, and it draws a regular summer pilgrimage of tourists; many come to spot and even swim with the resident dolphin, Fungi, which must rank as one of the silliest tourist-hyped attractions in Ireland (a fixture in the harbor since 1983). Kitsch references to Fungi notwithstanding, you'll find myriad boat trips and swimming excursions offered by the dolphin hustlers down at the pier; the deal usually comes with a money back guarantee—no Fungi, no charge (of around €18). Be warned that the town packs out with visitors in summer, many of them inspired to discover Dingle's legendary music scene; you can catch live music sessions just about every night of the year here, and there'll be at least a dozen traditional music sessions happening on any summer's night. To have a crack at the accompanying *craic* (good time), simply stroll the streets and keep an ear open as you pass the myriad pubs—or turn directly to the round-up of nightlife venues on p. 194. Connoisseurs of an "authentic" Irish music scene, be warned: Dingle's status as a music mecca means that it's also popular with visiting artists, so on a busy night you're just as likely to find yourself listening to a foreign band (perhaps even from your home country) as local lads.

Accommodations, Both Standard & Not

If you're looking for a **vacation rental,** Dingle Town is a mere 20-minute walk from one of the newest and best-looking developments in Kerry: **Ballintaggart Holiday Homes** ✪✪ (www.holidayrental.ie). Twelve large three-bedroom houses on the grounds of a 300-year-old hunting lodge have been built in stone to echo the character of the original house. All modern amenities, including broadband and an up-to-date open-plan kitchen, have been included, and rental here starts at €490 per week (though it will vary by date). Towels and linens are included, but you're charged €5 to €8 per day for electricity and heating.

€   About 1km (⅔ miles) out of town, there are neat, clean, spruced-up digs at **Rainbow Hostel** 🄺 (Dingle; ☎ 066/915-1044; www.rainbowhosteldingle.com; cash only), a converted family home with private rooms (€20 per person), dorms (€16), and camping sites (€8 per person, with access to the hostel's indoor facilities). Among the private rooms is a very large family room with dormer windows, wooden floors, plenty of packing space, and duvets on the comfy beds. Other pluses: a laundry, a good-size kitchen for guest use, free Wi-Fi, parking; and on-site bike rental (€10 per day). Linens are provided, and towels can be rented (€2). There's no curfew or lockout.

€   Just about everyone in Dingle Town has a room or house to rent (if you turn up without a reservation, go to the tourist office), but the cheapest private rooms are those above the **Goat Street Café** (Goat St., Dingle; ☎ 086/826-4118 or 066/915-2770; MC, V); they cost €40 throughout the year. There are two very basic, clean rooms, and they share a bathroom; one is dinky, but the so-called "Red Room" is larger and even has a bit of a view. Breakfast is not included, but the cafe downstairs starts serving at 10am.

€–€€   **Dillon's B&B** (Conor Pass Rd.; ☎ 066/915-1724; cash only) is wonderfully clean, and bedrooms (most of which are en suite) are bright and light-filled. You'll be far removed from the tourist maelstrom in town: Ask for a room overlooking the adjacent fields, and you can watch grazing sheep and catch a partial glimpse of distant Dingle Bay. The owner will even knock a few euros off the price (€60–€70 double) if you ask to forgo breakfast.

€€   Back nearer the town center, however, there's also good value-for-money at Stella Doyle's seasonal two-bedroom B&B, in a grape-colored house simply called **Number Fifty Five** ✪✪ (55 John St., Dingle; ☎ 066/915-2378; www.stelladoyle.com; cash only). Stella is a convivial host; once just about the best-known restaurateur in town, she treats guests like time-honored friends, and (unlike many B&B-owners) doesn't discriminate against solo travelers. When I visited her in mid-2008, she'd just unpacked two brand-new mattresses for her guest rooms (€75 double), but the real treat here is the spectacularly bright, art-filled open plan lounge, kitchen, and dining area upstairs, with great views of a cow-grazed field stretched out in front of the Connor Pass. Needless to say, Stella prepares splendid breakfasts.

€€–€€€   Views, views, and—crikey—more views. Cast your eyes across the spectacle of Dingle Bay—and, like me, you'll be captivated by the scene below.

John O'Farrell—who tirelessly ensures that his guests are happy and well-informed—provides abundant charm at his aesthetically exciting **Pax House** ★★★ (Upper John St., Dingle; ☎ 066/915-1518; www.pax-house.com; MC, V). The easy style here proves that luxury needn't be stuffy or overblown; bold, colorful paintings add a sense of drama and pizzazz. And, because you're about 1km (½ mile) from town, you needn't put up with the tourist hordes when they descend. Rates are better March to May and October (€100–€120), while from June to September, rooms start at €120, and those with the best views cost €160. Such a pity John closes in low season.

€€–€€€€   Just down the road, closer to town, John and Mary Curran run a tight ship at **Greenmount House** ★★★ (Upper John St., Dingle; ☎ 066/915-1414; www.greenmounthouse.ie; MC, V) where they've established a reputation for their luxurious accommodations and award-winning breakfasts (Julia Roberts is a fan). As at Pax House, views from up here are marvelous, and there's plenty of space to unwind—two lounges, plenty of books, and even a hot tub out back. The day starts with one of Mary's formidable breakfasts and ends with the comfort afforded by luxurious linens and an excellent bed. You can either stay in one of the original, more classically styled bedrooms, or opt for one of the massive new wood-floored units which are light-filled and have a slick contemporary design. Rooms are well-endowed—wardrobes, sofas, and bathrooms with showers and tubs. Rates vary according to season and the size of room you take: In low season you can bag a room for as little as €80 to €110, while in July and August, you'll spend between €110 and €170. My only complaint is that all the many extras that are offered (internet, for example), are price tagged.

Dining for All Tastes

€   For a miniature, indulgent splurge, cough up €3.50 for a scoop of deliciously creamy, award-winning ice-cream at **Murphy's Ice Cream** ★★★ (Strand St.; ☎ 066/915-2644; www.murphysicecream.ie; summer 11am–10pm; winter 11am–6:30pm; cash only), the now-famous handiwork of Séan and Kieran Murphy. If "brown bread and Guinness" is available, it's a must . . . and goes very well with a scoop of Skelligs truffle.

€–€€   Cool lounge music sets a mellow vibe at the **Goat Street Café** ★ (Goat St.; ☎ 066/915-2770; Wed–Mon 10am–5pm; Fri–Sun 6–9:30pm; MC, V), a calm, friendly little place owned by a French-Irish couple who emphasize fresh ingredients—and put them to good use. Ideal for such karma-conscious dishes as Mediterranean bean, tomato, and herb stew (€11), or a warm beetroot and goat cheese salad with glazed walnuts (€11). Breakfast is also available (€6–€8), as are sandwiches and daily specials.

€€   The **Garden Café** ★ (Green St., Dingle; ☎ 087/781-5126; sheilamegan@eircom.net; Mon and Wed–Thurs 10:30am–5:30pm; Fri–Sat 10:30am–6pm; Sun noon–4pm, summer 10:30am–8pm; cash only) focuses on healthful, wholesome dishes that can be enjoyed over a long afternoon, preferably with a relaxing bottle of vino (all bottles €18). Try the warm brie, pear, and walnut bruschetta (€8),

Seisiúns: The Lowdown

So, you've been tapping your toes to a group of musicians who seem to have met up accidentally, whipped out their (sometimes unlikely looking) instruments and started jamming. This impromptu performance is called a session, and it's a phenomenon to behold. The musicians always seem to know what to play, and they always seem to know when it's time for the song to come to an end. Since there's no sheet music and no sign of a conductor, it's as though they're psychically linked.

But there's no voodoo here. According to the folks at the **Dingle Music School** (see "The Other Dingle," p. 192), improvisation is only part of the performance. These trad musicians have acquired an intimate knowledge of a fairly wide range of tunes. Each time a group (often, strangers) plays together, they are dipping into a pool of shared knowledge.

And there is some underlying structure to the proceedings. Traditional tunes generally have two parts and the players know to play each part twice through to the very end, and then the entire tune is played from the start again; typically, this tune cycle will be played two to four times, when a member of the group (often whoever started the tune the first time round) uses a gesture—a nod, a wink, or a glance—to signal a change, and then moves full tilt into the next tune. It may even be in a different key. So even if the entire set looks convincingly pre-arranged and rehearsed, the level of spontaneity is such that not even the musicians know exactly what tune is next up.

which is served with salad, or choose from the specials chalked up on the board—all are under €10 (you might find, for example, lamb and rosemary sausage and sweet potato hot pot). Platters of artisan cheeses with salami and fruit (€12) can be shared between two.

€–€€€ Pubs serving ho-hum meals are dime a dozen in Dingle (and I've had some dodgy meals here), but one decently priced spot that doesn't skimp on quality (all fish comes straight off local boats, and beef and poultry are from Dingle farms) is **Danno's** (Pier Head, Strand St.; ☎ 066/915-1855; Tues–Sun 12:30–2:30pm and 6–9pm; MC, V) where most meals cost around €13—including a big portion of freshly steamed Dingle Bay mussels.

€€–€€€ Orla and Fernando serve authentic Italian fare at **Novecento** ✪ (John St., Dingle; ☎ 066/915-2584; daily 6–11pm; MC, V), where the best deals are to be had before 7pm, when an early-diner's menu is offered. You won't find better pizza on the peninsula, and you can save a few euros by ordering yours from the attached takeaway shop.

WHY YOU'RE HERE: SLEA HEAD DRIVE, CONNOR PASS & MT. BRANDON

Although you're likely to encounter the odd road-hogging bus—particularly in summer's silly season—you won't forgive yourself for missing this magical circular route out of Dingle, known as the **Slea Head Drive** ✪✪✪. The route passes from the village of **Ventry** (Ceann Trá), along the eponymous view-intensive cliffs at **Slea Head,** through **Dunquin** (Dún Chaoin), and then back to Dingle Town via **Ballyferriter** (Baile an Fheirtéaigh). (Take note of the Irish names of these places, as signposting conforms strictly to Gaeltacht regulations.)

Apart from stopping often to gasp at the drop-dead vistas, you can also get out and inspect archaeological sites along the way. In the Fahan area on the imposing hillside along the Slea Head Drive, there is evidence of over 400 **beehive huts** ✪— or Clocháns—ancient drystone structures corbelled with such astonishing skill (similar to what was used at Newgrange) that several survive intact. In fact, this style of structure was used as recently as the early 20th century; those along Slea Head were probably built in the 12th century when native Irish people were forced into this part of the peninsula by invading Normans. You'll see a couple of signposted "beehive" sites, where farmers usually charge around €2 for you to get close to these stone huts, impressive for being rainproof despite their total absence of mortar.

Beyond Fahan, the most dramatic part of the journey is the stretch along the **Slea Head** ✪✪✪, from which eagle views of Great Blasket Island, and—across Dingle Bay—the northern coast of the Iveragh Peninsula and even as far as the Skelligs off the Iveragh's most westerly point. You'll also see magnificent **Coomeenole Strand,** where David Lean shot parts of *Ryan's Daughter*. At Dún Chaoin, if weather or season has prevented you from taking a ferry to the Blasket Islands (see "Become a Blasket-case," p. 191) it's worth stopping at the **Blascaod Centre** ✪ (Dún Chaoin; ☎ 066/915-6444; Heritage Card or €3.70; daily Easter–June and Sept–Oct 10am–6pm; July–Aug 10am–7pm) which presents a richly textured celebration of the history and culture of the Blasket Islanders, starting with a short, dramatic film with scenes of life on the Great Blasket (which was evacuated entirely in 1953), and coverage of the island's literary tradition. North of the Blascaod Centre, spend time admiring the views from Clogher Head, and if you divert from the R559 at Baile an Fheirtéaigh (Ballyferriter), you can explore Sybil Head for views over Smerwick Harbour.

Near Ballyferriter, a Gaeltacht community (parts of which featured in *Far and Away*), is **Gallarus Oratory** ✪ (☎ 066/915-5333; €3; daily Mar–Oct 9am–9pm; Nov–Feb 10am–5pm) an extraordinary 1,300-year-old stone building constructed by early Christians using dry rubble masonry. Although attacks by Vikings and Normans decimated the settlements around the oratory, its pitched roof, formed by the gradual rise of the side walls—no cement, no mortar—keeps rainwater out to this day. You can view the structure from the road, but paying for a ticket means you can get inside the rudimentary, tiny space; it's a sublime, but brief, encounter with ancient architecture, but likely to disappoint anyone expecting riveting entertainment from their €3 (the short film on Dingle's ancient built heritage doesn't quite make the experience any more fulfilling).

Nearly 2km (about a mile) from Gallarus, the 12th-century **Kilmalkedar Church** ✪ is another worthy stop. The church is a fine example of Irish-Romanesque

Become a Blasket-case

From Slea Head, the mere sight of the Blaskets—and the surf-battered headland that reaches out toward them—is intoxicating; it's probably the most memorable scene on any of the five peninsulas of Ireland's southwest. A vast ragtag sweep of near-vertical plunging cliffs steps into the breakers and juts out towards the wild uninhabited rock islands.

Rugged, unspoiled **Great Blasket Island** ☆☆☆ lies 4.75km (3 miles) off the coast, and was inhabited by hardy seafaring islanders until 1953. Although there is evidence of Iron Age and early Christian habitation, modern life there might have begun around 1290 when Great Blasket was leased to the Ferriter family by the Earl of Desmond for an annual rent of two hawks. In 1756 there were five or six families living there, but the population rose quite dramatically in the 19th century due to the eviction of native Irish on the mainland; the island became a refuge. By the time it was abandoned, there were just 20 people left, and without a school or church, community life was no longer possible.

If you plan properly, you can get out to Great Blasket on one of the most memorable (and perhaps cold and bumpy) outings you'll have in Ireland. Ferries to the island depart from **Dún Chaoin Pier**, in Dunquin—once the mainland harbor for Blasket islanders who fished from canvas-covered canoes called *naomhóg*—giving you the chance to explore the dramatic desolation of a place that feels totally cut off from the world. Often, in fact, weather did cut the islanders off from the rest of civilization, and as you'll discover, they existed with none of the comforts or advances of the modern world (locals lived by fishing and turf cutting). It's a haunting, deeply memorable experience to wander the island for a couple of hours imbibing the sense of isolation these people must have experienced and the unimaginable hardships they endured. Island life became the subject of some great books—such as *The Island Man, Peig,* and *Twenty Years A-Growing*—and these works are all that remain of this community along with the ruins of their simple homes, some of which have now been refurbished (there's a cafe, and a hostel sometimes operates here).

You'd be well advised to phone ahead to check if the ferry is sailing, since weather and surf conditions impact the schedule. **Blasket Island Ferries** (☎ 066/915-1344 or 066/915-6422; www.blasketisland.com; €30 round-trip; May–Sept).

architecture, with decorative carved animal heads, round-topped doorways and windows, high-pitched gables, and geometric designs on some of the columns. Fragments of the original barrel-vaulted roof are visible, too. The graveyard includes an Ogham stone (recognizable by the hole at the top), and there are other carved stonework pieces—one of which is believed to be a type of sundial—that pre-date Christ. Saint's Road, which runs from the church to the summit of Mt. Brandon, is a popular hiking route (below) and still used by pilgrims celebrating St. Brendan's feast day on June 29th each year.

Exploring Mt. Brandon & the Connor Pass

Rising 938m (3,127 ft.), Mount Brandon looms over the Dingle landscape. The summit was an important pagan pilgrimage destination, and worship there was later Christianized and dedicated to St. Brandon who may or may not have discovered America in the 6th century, after setting sail from Brandon Bay.

To really experience Mt. Brandon take up the pilgrim's challenge by hiking the **Pilgrim's Route** from Kilmalkedar Church to the summit, passing ancient forts and Christian ruins along the way. Set aside the better part of a day to reach the summit and get back, taking plenty of water (and perhaps a picnic) for the hike.

You can also get a good look at Mt. Brandon by checking out the view as you drive from Dingle Town over the magnificent **Connor Pass** (457m/1,499 ft.) and down to the tiny enclaves of Cloghane and Brandon. As you head down the Pass with Brandon Bay spread out before you, Mt. Brandon looms on your left. Along the way are a number of excellent stopping points, where you'll want to whip out your camera. These stops can also be used for short but often thrilling hikes into the surrounding mountainside.

Cloghane and Brandon each have two pleasant pubs where you can hear the murmur of local life (the two villages have a combined population of around 100, although I've heard it said that "a funeral in Cloghane is like a wedding anywhere else in the world"), and Cloghane is a fine place to set off on any number of walks into the mountains (the tourist office only opens in summer, so you might want to stock up on maps and information in Dingle Town). But the highlight of a trip here lies at the very end of the narrow, sheep-trundled road, culminating at **Brandon Point** ✰✰✰, a cliff edge spot (with a car park) where it feels that you have the entire ocean at your feet. From here you can sit on the grassy outcrop and watch for hours as marine birds—including crow-like choughs—glide on the updraft. It's an exceptionally windy place, so come prepared for the cold, and mind your footing as you explore the cliff's edge.

If you're willing to brave it, you can head farther up the mountain on foot, to reach the summit of Mt. Brandon—the route isn't always clear and it can get wet and steep, but the higher you go, the more rewarding the view. Avoid tackling this in inclement or misty weather.

THE OTHER DINGLE

Much of Dingle is a Gaeltacht area, meaning that Irish is actively promoted as the main (and, to the distress of many citizens, the only official) language. This means that it's possible to walk into a pub and hear locals conversing in Irish—Dick Mack's is a good place to start (p. 194).

If you'd prefer a more academic approach to local culture, contact **An Díseart Institute of Education and Celtic Culture** (Green St., beside St. Mary's Church, Dingle Town; ☎ 066/915-2476; www.diseart.ie; Mon–Sat 9am–5pm). This small local organization promotes research, runs courses, and hosts cultural events that aim to keep the Celtic spirit alive. They do a range of activities—from putting on exhibitions to archaeological tours—but you'll need to speak to someone in person to find out what's on the agenda, since (by their own admission) they can be rather disorganized.

South for the Summer

En route to Dingle, an essential stop is the **South Pole Inn** ★★ (☎ 066/915-7388; MC, V), a famous little pub in a blue house in the colorful town of Annascaul. Although reasonable bar food is served here from noon until 8pm (sandwiches €4–€7, burgers €4.20–€10 and more), the chief attraction is the pub's association with Tom Crean, the legendary Antarctic explorer who is famed for his epic bravery demonstrated on expeditions undertaken with the likes of Robert Scott and Sir Ernest Shackleton. After retiring to his hometown and marrying in 1920, Crean established the pub to make up for the fact that he never quite made it to the South Pole. The place remains a tastefully executed shrine to Crean, memorialized in black and white photos, drawings, newspaper clippings, and copies of his biography for sale. Besides live music on Saturday night, Wednesday evenings are dedicated Irish nights—this is a great spot to listen to (or try your hand at) a bit of conversational Irish. And—of course—there's always great *craic*.

A fun way to learn Irish—although usually geared towards groups—is with **Gaeilge Beo** (☎ 087/246-0507, 066/915-5300, or 066/915-5429; www.gaeilge beo.com) a small organization that puts together "Irish culture" packages. Various activities—Irish dancing, hill walking, music lessons, an introduction to Irish place names, quizzes, even pottery classes and sporting events—are combined (over a weekend, usually) to help participants learn a wee bit of Irish through immersion in traditional culture. While some programs are 100% Irish, with no English spoken, Gaeilge Beo offers a bilingual format so even if you've never spoken a word of Irish in your life, there's no need to sweat the language issue. Courses are fun and informal; there are no tests at the end. The organizers have their own lodge, so accommodations are usually included in the package (from self-catered to fully catered). The cost of a weekend program starts at around €60 to €75 per person (with self-catering accommodation).

Irish music is another part of Celtic culture that is nurtured here. If, after listening to a couple of sessions, you find you've caught the bug, why not try your hand at playing one of the traditional instruments yourself? At the **Dingle Music School** (Dykegate Lane, Dingle Town; ☎ 086/319-1438; www.dinglemusicschool.com), visitors are encouraged to drop by for an introduction to the *bodhrán* (the Irish handheld circular drum played with a stick and pronounced "bough-ron") and the tin whistle, and—if you give them some warning—they'll even fix you up with a tutor for more specialized instruments, like the uillean pipes (*uillean* is Irish for "elbow," and these are the traditional pipes of Ireland). John Ryan, who runs the school, says that most people are surprised at how much they can learn even with just a short lesson. The school is open daily and offers beginner *bodhrán* workshops in the summer—usually Wednesdays for an hour from noon, and Saturdays from 11am (€15 per hour, *bodhrán* provided). Tin whistle workshops happen on Mondays from 11am to 1pm (€30 per session). Private one-on-one lessons cost €35 per hour.

ACTIVE DINGLE

For a more hands-on, active immersion in one of Dingle's favorite subcultures, head for Castlegregory. This laid-back village provides access to some of the best surf spots in the country—the **Maharees Peninsula**—with great stretches of sandy beaches around Brandon Bay, Scraggane Bay, and Sandy Bay; in fact, legendary Brandon is considered some of the best windsurfing territory in the world (it recently hosted the World Cup), with ideal down-the-line wave sailing conditions.

The relative absence of tourists makes this an ideal place to stop if you'd like to catch some waves—the kitesurfing is wicked, too. For all your equipment and wetsuit needs, go to **Jamie Knox Watersport** (☎ 066/713-9411; www.jamieknox. com). If you've never tried any of these watersports before, or if you'd like to master the waves with a pro instructor, Jamie Knox—who is an ex-world circuit professional—also offers a range of lessons in wave-riding. All equipment—including wetsuits, boots, and boards—is provided, and courses are available for all levels. A 2-hour taster windsurfing lesson costs €40, while a 2-day (8-hr.) intro course would be €175. Surfing courses are similarly priced. Kitesurfing is more expensive (€340 for 12 hr. over 2 days), but instruction is on a 2-to-1 or even 1-to-1 basis.

If you'd prefer to rent your board and wetsuit (€20 per day for both) back in Dingle Town, go to **Finn McCool's** (Green St.; ☎ 066/915-0833). Dingle's marina is also where you can investigate opportunities to dive the harbor—it's not just tame, slippery mammals you get to see, but shipwrecks, too.

For those who prefer to stay dry, read about hiking to the summit of Mt. Brandon on p. 192, or consider a gentler—but no less scenic—route along the Dingle Way.

ATTENTION, SHOPPERS!

Many artists and artisans have made Dingle their home; it's peaceful, the environment is inspiring, and there are just enough passing tourists whipping around the Slea Head to and from Dingle to sustain a lucrative income. **Louis Malcahy** (Clogher, Ballyferriter; ☎ 066/915-6229; www.louismalcahy.com) is one such potter who has hit the big time, and just about everyone ventures into his little empire where you can now watch his team of potters hard at work in the workshop (daily winter 9am–5:30pm, summer 9am–7pm) attached to the rather large outlet. Personally, I'd rather go for the work of a small time, less-commercial, artist like **Sinéad Lough** ★★ (Baile na nÁth, near Gallarus; ☎ 066/915-5787; www.sineadloughceramics.com) who makes beautiful handthrown ceramic pots and bowls using white earthenware which is then tastefully—often subtly—decorated with colored glazes and slips. Her pots are contemporary, yet have a timeless quality; each is unique. Sinéad's workshop is open March through December, Tues–Sat 10am–5pm.

Bibliophiles should made a effort to visit Dingle Town's original bookstore-cum-cafe, **An Café Liteartha** ★★ (Bothar An Dadhgaide; ☎ 066/915-2204); it carries a wide selection of old, new, and offbeat titles and obscure local imprints (like a book that deals with a single rugby match between Kerry and Offaly).

NIGHTLIFE IN DINGLE TOWN

Across the road from St. Mary's Church, **Dick Mack's** ★★★ (Green St.; ☎ 066/ 915-1960) is legendary; with wooden benches and shoe racks from the days when this doubled as a boot store, you'll run into all kinds of spirited, and spirits-induced, merrymaking. The local rogues who hang here really know how to make visitors feel part of the crowd, so expect to be drawn into conversation or regaled by Irish song, often supervised by the storytelling owner, Oliver. The downside? Tourists have "discovered" this place, too—as have a couple of celebrities.

As I've said, much has been made of Dingle's legendary music scene, so don't leave town without witnessing something authentic. Opposite the tourist office, **John Benny's** ★★★ (Strand St.; ☎ 066/915-1215) is a good place to catch not only some lively, real-deal trad, but on Mondays, local dancers hit the floor with their flashiest set dancing routines. In summer live music is lined up every night except Thursday and Sunday, and even then, you never know what might happen. See if you can catch a session with the Dingle White Females, featuring songstress Éilís Kennedy, of whom *Roots Music Magazine* wrote, "Her voice is a thing of gentle sublime beauty, the like for which mothers would be sold and kings ransoms exchanged." Incidentally, John Benny's also serves food.

If you're at a loose end on a Sunday, head early to the nearby **Marina Inn** (Strand St.; ☎ 066/915-1660), where the session starts at 6pm and you're welcome to bring your own instrument. It's not unusual to catch a virtual orchestra spontaneously erupt—imagine five fiddlers, two guitarists, a squeezebox player, and another guy playing both harmonica and concertina. In summer, sessions happen nightly; stick to the booze, though, as the food here is a bit iffy.

A family business since the early-19th-century, and for many years also run as a grocer's and a bakery, **MacCarthy's Pub** ★★ (Goat St.; ☎ 066/915-1205) has a mini-theater in the back and not only hosts local and international music talents (even Nigel Kennedy has organized a gig here), but puts on poetry and drama performances.

Renowned for its nightly traditional music sessions is **An Droichead Beag** ★★ ("The Small Bridge," Lower Main St.; ☎ 066/915-1723; www.thesmallbridge.com), where the crowd is pretty mixed thanks to the variety of entertainments on offer—there's sport on the large screen TVs, pool tables, legendary music, and weekend disco upstairs, too. Each weeknight sees a different bunch of talented local musicians, and guest artists from farther afield appear too. *One warning:* Mind your head on the ceiling beams.

More intimate, and just as likely to reward your presence with an evening of traditional tunes, is **O'Flaherty's** ★★ (Bridge St.; ☎ 066/915-1983). Bear in mind that trad sessions typically only get going later in the evening (around 9:30pm), although anything's possible on a convivial afternoon.

CORK CITY

Of all Ireland's smaller cities (beyond Dublin, they're all small), Cork has certainly found its groove. Give anyone in Cork half a chance to talk and they'll effervesce about Cork itself. And their enthusiasm is both contagious and—in many respects—an accurate measure of a place that has come a long way since it was known as the "Great Marsh of Munster."

By day, a palpable buzz hums along its pedestrian thoroughfares, in its bustling market, and at the tables of its sociable cafes; by night, a rhythm rises from the constant chatter in its many late bars, and endless supply of cutting-edge music pouring out of abundant venues. A lot of what makes Cork a worthy city destination are the discoveries you'll make down lanes and narrow alleys—listen for the music and laughter and you'll find Cork's soul. Because when it comes to sights and attractions, there are few on the ground, and even fewer worth detouring for— most visitors make beelines for nearby Blarney Castle (lovely, yes), Cobh (pro- nounced cove, but rather go to Kinsale), and Midleton's Jameson Distillery (free whiskey, expensive tour), but Cork itself is a top place just to hang out. This may be an island, but its vibrant cultural and music scene means it's certainly not cut off; in fact, if personality, pizzazz, and pure wit, are the measure, Cork isn't that small after all.

A BRIEF HISTORY OF CORK

Cork was once an archipelago of islands in a muddy marshland. Legend tells that it was first settled in the 6th century when St. Finbarre (did he even exist?) estab- lished a monastery on the south bank of the River Lee—where St. Fin Barre's Cathedral is today.

Its location made it an easy target for Vikings (who settled here and became known as the Ostmen or Eastmen) and then the Normans who took over in 1177. In 1185, Prince John—Lord of Ireland—gave Cork its city charter; its new Norman rulers transformed Cork into a great walled port city. Linked to fertile agricultural lands, it was a major exporter of wool, grain, and beef, while ships brought in wine, textiles, and spices.

But politics, poor sanitation, and the Black Plague brought economic decline from the mid-14th century, later exacerbated by the struggle between Catholics and Protestants; the capital of the "Rebel County" fell to Williamite forces after a tremendous siege in 1690, when the city walls were largely destroyed.

Nevertheless, by 1800, Cork was the most important transatlantic port in Europe; there are accounts of up to 400 ships departing from here in a single day. Cork had the largest units for brewing, distilling, and gun powder manufacture in Ireland, as well as the largest sailcloth factory in Europe. Cork's harbor played a major part in sheltering vessels during the American War of Independence and later during the Napoleonic Wars. Accounts tell of a harbor where you could hear such a wide range of languages that it was impossible to tell where in the world you were. Meanwhile, Cork emerged as Ireland's slaughterhouse, exporting masses of salted beef and pork, and its butter market was the word's largest in the 19th century.

This was also when the Lee was finally dammed in order to leave a single island—the hub, heart, and central business district of Cork City—between two channels of the river. So, as you move around the city, be aware that when you cross any of its numerous bridges, you are actually moving on and off a great man- made island. And Cork, as you will notice looking at its skyline, continues to evolve. In preparation for its 2005 tenure as European City of Culture, its main streets were completely redesigned, bringing a fresh look and plenty of public scrutiny at the start of the new millennium.

LAY OF THE LAND

Technically a manmade island, Cork City centers on the area between the North and South channels of the River Lee; here you'll find the principal shopping and dining areas, as well as the hub of Cork's near-fabled nightlife. One-way roads dominate here, and several pedestrian-priority roads are in the dense area strad- dling Grand Parade, Oliver Plunkett Street, and the bow-shaped St. Patrick

Put a Cork in It!

Cork is a place of intriguing banter, much of it unfathomable to anyone who doesn't have some insight into the specialized vocabulary of the locals. While some of the lingo traces its roots to Hiberno-English—which is the absorption of Irish and Irishisms into English—much of it is pure Cork. You'll definitely hear the phrases "That's grand!" frequently, and the same goes for "So it is . . . "; and sometimes the marriage of the two as "That's grand, so it is, so it is!" which indicates either extreme approval or may mean "Thanks for paying your bill." You'll also commonly hear strange turns of phrase like "I'm just after my tea" and "I do be doing." Here are some howlers:

- "Chats" is Cork slang for "breasts," but has also been used as a slang term for small inferior potatoes.
- "Langer" is generally accepted to be a term of abuse meaning either "an eejit" (Irish slang for "idiot") or "a penis," while referring to someone as "langered," means that they are drunk.

Corkonians are also renowned for their wit, although often it's completely unwitting, and it takes a carefully attuned listener to point out the punchline. There's even a website, **Overheard in Cork** (www.overheardincork.com), dedicated to earwitness accounts of the wonderful comments the locals make.

Street—this is truly the hub of city life, known as **City Centre South.** West of this central hub is **Washington Village;** also with its fair share of attractions and entertainment options, it straddles the south channel of the Lee, and includes St. Fin Barre's Cathedral, where Cork was first settled.

The north and south banks of the city are connected to the island by numerous bridges, and the roads skirting either bank of the Lee's two channels are referred to as quays, honoring their originals as genuine harborside docking points for merchant ships. On the north bank is the historic **Shandon** area, where Cork's famous Butter Exchange and beef market once brought fame and economic glory to the city; east of Shandon, is **City Centre North,** where—particularly along MacCurtain Street—a number of fine hotels, excellent pubs, and a faintly bohemian scene have helped shape a very lively off-island neighborhood. West of Shandon is the former **City Gaol** (now a museum), while the tiny village of **Blarney,** known for a certain kissing stone (p. 213), is just a few miles out of town. **University College Cork** lies on the South Bank towards the end of Lancaster Quay; here, too, is a lively scene greatly enhanced by the vibrant student population. Also on the South Bank, but nearer the central business district, are **St. Fin Barre's Cathedral** and **City Hall.**

On Grand Parade, **Tourist House** (☎ 021/425-5100; June–Aug Mon–Fri 9am–7pm; Sat 9am–5pm; Sun 10am–5pm; Sept–May Mon–Sat 9:15am–5:15pm) is good for dishing out flyers and reading matter, but not very eloquent when it comes to useful advice; you can, however, book accommodations—including rentals—here (for a small fee). Walking tours also commence here.

GETTING THERE

You can fly directly to **Cork Airport** (☎ 021/431-3131; www.corkairport.com), which is 6km (4 miles) south of the city. Several budget airlines, including Ryanair, fly here, as does Aer Lingus. Buses from the airport run regularly into the city (€4), stopping at the bus terminal on Parnell Place; a taxi will run you in for around €20. **Trains** pull in at **Kent Station** (Lower Glanmire Rd; ☎ 021/450-6766; www.irishrail.ie), but you'll save money if you take a **bus** (Bus Éireann)—the 4½-hour journey from Dublin costs around €10; train fare is about six times this, but only takes 3 hours. The popular Cork-Killarney route takes 2 hours, and costs €14. All intercity buses arrive at **Parnell Place** (☎ 021/450-8188).

GETTING AROUND

Even if you have your own car, you'll want to leave it at your digs and **walk** wherever possible; one-way traffic, and a few wafer thin roads on the north bank, makes driving frustrating. Parking is a hassle, with a pre-paid scratch-and-display disc required almost everywhere (parking is free Sun). Pick up **bus** time tables from Tourist House (see above) or from the terminal on Parnell Place; services run until 11:15pm. **Cork Taxi Co-op** (☎ 021/427-2222; www.corktaxi.ie) has been operating since 1971, so you know who to call when you've made a late night of it.

ACCOMMODATIONS, BOTH STANDARD & NOT

Rental Apartments

Some of the most convenient self-catering options in Cork City are the eight two-bedroom units offered by Dominic Carney at **Westview Apartments** ✰✰ (16 Washington St. West; ☎ 086/356-4246 or 021/494-4910; www.westview.ie; AE, MC, V), an eye-catching piece of riverside architecture in Washington Village. Of these, the best five have balconies overlooking the River Lee; the others look over Washington Street. Although the layout varies a bit, decor is pretty standard—it's contemporary, minimalist, and functional and all the amenities of modern life are accounted for. Towels are provided (unlike many rentals), and babysitting can be arranged, too. Reception is at the downstairs wine bar, **Café de la Paix** (p. 202), so there's someone on hand to deal with issues any time of day, and most of the evening. The weekly cost varies somewhat; starting at €495, but soaring to €980 in July and August. One night costs from €110 (and up to €170).

DeansHall (Crosses Green; ☎ 021/431-2623; www.deanshall.com) is a more budget-geared option, as it's student housing during the winter months, but open to all from mid-July to mid-August. These three- and five-bedroom apartments sit directly across the road from St. Fin Barre's Cathedral, in the most ancient part of Cork, close to the city center as well as the university (church spires loom above). There's a full kitchen and lounge, and each flat has one double bedroom (with private bathroom) plus either two or four single rooms. They're not lavish, but have a simple, modern look of, well, student housing. A communal laundry room in each block completes the amenities. A week in a three-bedroom unit that sleeps four, costs €750 (€155 1 night), while the larger units (which sleep six) go for €800 (or €215 1 night); there's a 2-night minimum. Electricity is included, but bath towels are not. To book, go to the website and click on "Crosses Green Holiday Apartments."

Hotels, B&Bs & Guesthouses

Accommodations are spread out all over town; a string of easily spotted B&Bs sits along Western Road, so head there if you've neglected to book one of the choices below. In addition to these recommendations, Cork also has two B&Bs exclusively for gay guests; read about them in "Gay Cork," p. 210.

€–€€   Though its closer to the airport than the City Center, the **Travelodge Cork Airport** (kids) (Black Ash, Kinsale Rd. Roundabout, Frankfield Rd.; ☎ 021/431-0722; www.travelodge.co.uk; AE, DC, MC, V) must be mentioned as its such a good find for families. At all Travelodges, "family rooms," sleeping up to four, are the same price as doubles (in this case an average of €79, though periodic specials can drop that rate to €59) a serious savings for folks traveling with kids. Digs include one cushy, duvet-topped queen-sized bed and a "trundle-couch"—a long, bed-like sofa, with another mattress that pops out from the bottom. And don't worry: The British Isle's chain has no relation to the somewhat grubby American chain. Here the decor is Ikea-style cheery, the mattresses high quality, and the upkeep solid.

€€   Overlooking the city, above semi-boho MacCurtain Street, is the fair-priced **Auburn House** ★ (kids) (3 Garfield Terrace, Wellington Rd.; ☎ 021/450-8555; www.auburnguesthouse.com; MC, V), a great little B&B operated by Olive and Kieran Barry-Murphy. Skinny red-carpeted stairs lead up, up, and up to clean, comfortable bedrooms, the finest of which have front and back views. While not on the island, the location is surrounded by a number of cool pubs and good restaurants. Kieran makes breakfast and Olive dishes out advice on where to catch live gigs. Their annex across the road has three more rooms; I'd go for one of these—nos. 12 and 13 are big and light-filled, and there are no stairs to negotiate (they're a good bet if you're traveling with kids). Prices? Doubles with en suite facilities are €74 to €84; or you can shave off a few euros by sharing facilities (€68–€74 double). Free parking is available at the church just around the corner.

€€   Diagonally across town, right near the University, on the south bank, is Tony and Avril Lyon's **Fernroyd House** ★★ (kids) (4 O'Donovan Rossa Rd.; ☎ 021/427-1460; www.fernroydhouse.com; AE, MC, V). Actually, there are two houses, both located on a quiet cul de sac. The original house is immaculate and homey, with comfortable bedrooms (€85 double, great showers, and a garden at the back. A short walk away is their new "overspill house," also with its own garden, and a kitchen area. If you're traveling with a larger family, you should definitely ask to be put up here—bedrooms are larger and done out in a more contemporary aesthetic, and you're likely to have the place to yourself (it's usually reserved for small groups). Everyone has breakfast at the main house, though, and there's free Wi-Fi, off-street parking, and a very warm welcome for all guests.

€€   Nearby, but this time on busy Western Road, a distinctive B&B amidst a slew of similar establishments is smart, ever-so-slightly upmarket **Garnish House** ★ (Western Rd., Cork; ☎ 021/427-5111; www.garnish.ie; MC, V), where the hands-on owners like to make guests feel pampered. Upon arrival, you'll be served tea with fresh-from-the-oven scones, and possibly even homemade tart. Then, up to your sizeable bedroom (€80–€110)—elegant but comfy, with firm mattresses,

Cork City

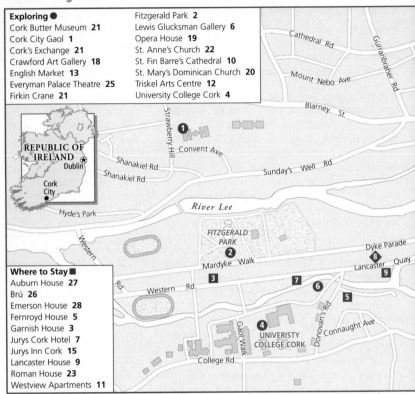

Exploring ●
Cork Butter Museum **21**
Cork City Gaol **1**
Cork's Exchange **21**
Crawford Art Gallery **18**
English Market **13**
Everyman Palace Theatre **25**
Firkin Crane **21**

Fitzgerald Park **2**
Lewis Glucksman Gallery **6**
Opera House **19**
St. Anne's Church **22**
St. Fin Barre's Cathedral **10**
St. Mary's Dominican Church **20**
Triskel Arts Centre **12**
University College Cork **4**

REPUBLIC OF IRELAND
Dublin ✪
Cork City

Where to Stay ■
Auburn House **27**
Brú **26**
Emerson House **28**
Fernroyd House **5**
Garnish House **3**
Jurys Cork Hotel **7**
Jurys Inn Cork **15**
Lancaster House **9**
Roman House **23**
Westview Apartments **11**

quality linens, big wardrobes, and pristine en suite bathrooms. The stand-out here is the extensive breakfast menu; when I was here, Mrs. Lucey had 30 different items to choose from.

€€–€€€   Part of an ever-expanding Dublin-based budget hotel chain, **Jurys Inn Cork** ✪ 🅺 (Anderson's Quay, Cork; ☎ 021/494-3000 or 01/607-5000; www.jurysinns.com; AE, MC, V) offers a good deal at the edge of the river, down near the port end of the island. Rates work on a "rate of the day" policy, which means you can never really pinpoint precisely what you'll pay until you jump on the internet and key in your dates; but you can score a room-only rate of between €89 and €139, and rooms—which are a bit plusher than those at the Travelodge, and very comfortable—are suitable for up to three adults (or two adults and two children), since they come with a pull-out couch.

€€–€€€   A good location and decent price make **Lancaster Lodge** ✪ (Lancaster Quay, Western Rd.; ☎ 021/425-1125; www.lancasterlodge.com; AE, D, MC, V) worth a mention, even if facilities are on the lean side. Designers went to the effort of smartening up all the bedrooms with that contemporary (if bland) look

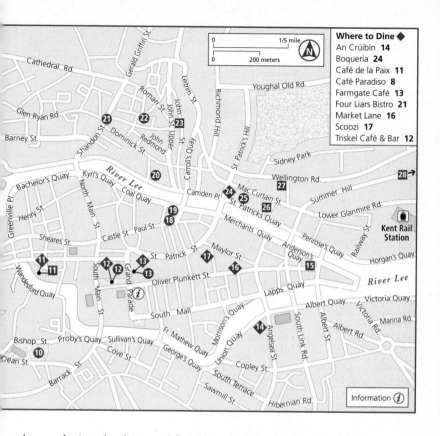

Where to Dine ◆

An Crúibín **14**
Boqueria **24**
Café de la Paix **11**
Café Paradiso **8**
Farmgate Café **13**
Four Liars Bistro **21**
Market Lane **16**
Scoozi **17**
Triskel Café & Bar **12**

that emphasizes cleanliness and feels like something bordering on luxury—wood furniture, brushed metal fittings, good bathrooms (with tub/shower combo), decent amenities (including a flatscreen TV), and modish color schemes (like purple and olive green). As long as you can secure a room with a view of the river rather than the parking lot, you'll be very satisfied (a double goes for €89–€125; up to €130 on summer weekends). The public spaces leave me a little cold—they're stiff and alienating, even if "comfortable"; the breakfast room is especially institutional, designed to make you eat and run.

€€–€€€€   Nearby, and not to be confused with Jurys Inn (see above), **Jurys Cork Hotel** ★★ (Western Rd.; ☎ 021/425-2700; www.jurysdoyle.com/cork; AE, D, MC, V) is one of those gleaming, modern (and some would say ugly) edifices situated at the edge of the Lee's south bank. It's also upmarket, complete with leisure center, spa, and bedrooms done out in the chichi look of "today." So, if you prefer a big, stylish hotel with the usual urban luxuries, heaps of amenities, and a lobby packed with guests, then it's worth keeping this option in mind. When I spoke to Joseph Downing, one of the managers, he assured me that their rate of the day policy means that savvy bargain hunters can bag a standard room for as little as €109, and since the normal rate is €269, it's an exceptional deal. The trick? Well, don't bother with the website (which starts with "specials" from around €129). Rather, keep your fingers crossed and telephone the hotel to ask if there are any last minute deals.

A Hostel Option

€   Unlikely sounding **Brú** (57 MacCurtain St.; ☎ 021/450-1074; www.bruhostel. com; MC, V) is a modern backpackers' hostel above a popular bar. This might sound like a bad idea if you value sleep over a good night out (the bar is open until 4am), but the facilities (kitchen, TV/DVD lounge, towel hire, laundry facility—and the onsite bar, of course) and atmosphere are quite conducive to having a fun time (even for those who enjoy sleep; good design means the place is relatively quiet). Not only that, but management is on the ball when it comes to keeping things clean. Located on active MacCurtain Street, it's quite central and walkable from the bus and train stations. Beds cost between €21 (four-bed dorm) and €18 (six-bed). Private rooms can sleep three (a bunk system with a double below and single above) and cost €50 Sunday to Thursday or €60 on the weekend. Most rooms have private bathrooms. To strengthen the deal, Brú offers free internet and breakfast, and will store luggage free of charge.

DINING FOR ALL TASTES

€–€€   In the funky Triskel Art Centre in Washington Village, **Triskel Café & Bar** ✿ (Tobin St.; ☎ 086/604-6004; Tues–Sat 9:30am–6pm; Fri 9:30am–midnight; cash only) combines healthy dining with gentle entertainments. Live music sets the scene on Friday nights—usually jazz or blues—and Triskel is also the setting for the occasional book launch. Breakfast is available all morning, and thoughtfully prepared soups and sandwiches cost €5 at lunchtime, when you can also hook up one of the day's specials—lamb tagine (€13), perhaps, or the latest pasta (€12). Like the atmosphere here (with cut flowers on the tables, and an artful chandelier above), everything that comes out of the tiny kitchen is fresh. *Be warned:* The lunch menu frequently sells out by 4pm.

€–€€   It's the riverside balcony that I most appreciate at **Café de la Paix** ✿ (16 Washington St.; ☎ 021/427-9556; www.cafedelapaix.ie; Mon–Thurs 8am–11:30pm; Fri 8am–12:30am; Sat 10am–12:30am; Sun noon–11am; AE, MC, V), a pleasant wine bar-style cafe with light meals and *tapas*. Breakfast (€5–€9) is served all morning. In the afternoon, choose from soup of the day with brown health bread (€4), salads, paninis, triple-decker sandwiches, or baked ciabatta (stuffed with slow-roasted vegetables topped with a basil, tomato, and mozzarella; €9). Happily, the evening menu doesn't go up all that much price-wise, either.

€–€€€€   Right next door to the Butter Museum, is Brendan Murphy's **Four Liars Bistro** ✿ (kids) (Butter Exchange, Shandon; ☎ 021/439-4040; www.fourliars bistro.com; Mon–Sat 5:30–10pm; Sun noon–10pm; AE, MC, V) where the atmosphere is casual (paper napkins stuffed into water glasses), family-friendly, and upbeat. Brendan is something of a celebrity, having cooked for, among others, the Queen of England, George Bush, Liz Taylor, and Elton John. But that was in another life, and since 1992, he's been using the culinary skills he's picked up

Meal with an Eagle's View

Cork dining institution **Farmgate Café** ✦✦ (English Market; ☎ 021/427-8134; Mon–Sat 8:30am–5pm; MC, V) is prime people-watching territory. Set in the gallery above the English Market, it offers peerless views of the action-packed market scene below. Turn right at the top of the stairs for the popular deli-style eatery (to the left is a pricier restaurant); you may need to scramble for a place to sit, and then someone needs to join the queue (with a tray) to place an order. Plenty of traditional fare is on offer—tripe and onions (€10); Irish lamb stew (€14); lamb's liver and bacon (€14)—and, watching the butcher's stalls below, you'll know exactly where the ingredients come from. Lighter meals, and vegetarian dishes are also available.

around the world to keep his local, loyal diners satisfied, without emptying their wallets. Clever foodies take advantage of special early dinner deals (Mon–Sat 5:30–7:15pm, Sun 5–8pm), and even better deals on a so-called "tourist menu," when all starters cost around €4 to €5, and mains (reminiscent of pub food) will run you €7.50 to €10. I last went for just a starter of deep fried brie and cranberry sauce—served with sliced strawberries and a small mountain of greens and coleslaw—and didn't need another morsel.

€€–€€€   One of the new kids on the dining block **Market Lane** ✦✦ 🧒 (5–6 Oliver Plunkett St.; ☎ 021/427-4710; www.marketlane.ie; reservations only for parties of 6 or more; Mon–Thurs noon–10pm; Fri–Sat noon–10:30pm; Sun 1–9pm; MC, V) sources the freshest possible ingredients—either from local producers or from the English Market. There's genuine, robust cooking here, with an eye on attentive service, even when it gets busy (which it does). Lunchtime options are cheapest: interesting salads (like deep-fried sesame goat cheese with baby leaves, semi-sundried tomatoes, and pine nuts—€8.50) and deli-fresh sandwiches (€6.80; try white sourdough filled with Cooleeney cheese, arugala, and sundried tomato pesto). More filling items (€11–€17) include fish stew, or vegetarian lasagna (both €14). Half-liters of house wine go for around €12. A special children's menu is available for €6, with healthier choices than the usual line-up of burgers and hot dogs.

€€–€€€   If you want to eat where locals eat, don't overlook **Scoozi** ✦ 🧒 (3–6 Winthrop Ave.; ☎ 021/427-5077; www.scoozis.ie; Mon–Sat 9am–11pm; Sun noon–10pm; MC, V), where it's as much about hanging out as it is about getting a reasonably priced meal. Which means you may have to wait for a table (they don't take reservations); it'll be worth it, not only for the great-tasting food, but the relaxed, "feel at home" atmosphere. Ignore the starters—you'll be overwhelmed by the portion sizes of the unpretentious mains: Burgers, salads, pastas, steak, chicken, and pizzas pack out the menu. This is my top pick for an interesting

Small Plates, Big Tastes

In Cork, *tapas* may be the new black. And here they come in all varieties. At **An Crúibín** ✪✪✪ (Union Quay; ☎ 021/450-5819; Mon–Sat 10am–5:30pm; cash only)—"The Pig's Foot"—the emphasis is definitely, well, porky. As well as charcuterie, the menu often includes traditional pigs' trotters, pigs' cheek, and even pigs' tails. It's a popular lineup and the place is small so it can get cramped (suits, sailors, students—they all come here, adding to the ambiance). A big draw are owners Paul and Frank, who work the bar and charm, amuse, and delight as they dispense drinks. *Tapas* are chalked up on the board, and range from as little as €4 for a small nibble of something tasty and rich, to around €6.50 or €8.

Another big venue for small plates **Boqueria** ✪✪ (6 Bridge St.; ☎ 021/455-9049; www.boqueria.ie; food served Mon–Sat 9:30am–11pm; Sun 5:30–10pm; winter brunch from noon; MC, V), offers authentic Iberian *tapas* and a few creative Irish additions—shaved garlic-marinated Serrano ham on baguette, with goat cheese (€8.50), perhaps, or an Irish *tapas* variant like chickpeas with black pudding, garlic, and parsley (€7). Remember, though, that not all these morsels are equally diminutive, so ask about size before you order.

pizza (all made, by the way, from a recipe brought back from Chicago in 1978): My choice, always, is the Aztec—an unusual pizza, firstly because it's grilled, and secondly because, instead of the usual tomato base, it comes smothered in pesto, topped with strips of marinated chicken, red onion, black olives, parmesan, and mozzarella (at €15, it's the priciest pizza, just €1.50 more than their Margherita). I like that you have a choice of either a 7-inch pizza, which comes with salad and/or French fries, or a 10-inch on its own—either way you can easily share between two people. Scoozi is an ideal family restaurant; there's even a coloring competition for kids.

€€–€€€€   Dennis Cotter is a legend among vegetarians, and his contribution to dining has made a loyal following of omnivores too. His **Café Paradiso** ✪✪✪ 🄺🄸🄳🅂 (16 Lancaster Quay; ☎ 021/427-7939; www.cafeparadiso.ie; reservations recommended; Tues–Sun noon–3pm and 6:30pm–late; last orders at 10:30pm; AE, MC, V) is among the coolest restaurants in Cork, with a lively open kitchen, spunky staff, and a devoted clientele. Part of the allure is his imaginative use of sheep's cheese along with vegetables and fruit. Flavors—even where they're subtle—are exciting and original (which is no doubt why Dennis already has a number of cookbook titles to his credit). With separate lunch and dinner menus, if you're watching your budget, arrive in the afternoon, when mains all cost around €10 to €12. When I last lunched here—amidst relaxed families whose children had been given drawing materials (lunchtime only)—I tucked into a bowl of exquisite fresh tagliolini with sea spinach, cherry tomatoes, shallots, pinenuts, chilies, and Knockalara sheep's cheese (€12).

WHY YOU'RE HERE: TOP SIGHTS & ATTRACTIONS

Cork is one of those cities that's perfect for getting lost in—if at all possible—particularly if you're deep in the thick of it, exploring narrow alleyways and side-streets where you get a sense of how haphazardly (or organically, if you prefer) the city has evolved. It was, after all, once a marsh, and much of it was under the River Lee; many of the roads were once water channels where, instead of cars, ships sailed. For a compelling introduction to the city, condensed into a detailed narrative, try **Cork Historical Walking Tours** ★ (☎ 085/100-7300; www.walk cork.ie; €10; Apr–Sept); the most extensive is the Grand Tour, covering as much history as can be managed in 2 hours. While light on the architectural history of the city, you will hear what happened, where, when, and why. As so much of what was no longer exists now, you don't always see the history so much as hear about it. Still, I was fascinated by some of the meatier anecdotes and many intimate details about how the city is put together.

Sightseeing on the "Island" of Cork

Odors both strange and familiar ravish the senses as you enter Cork's famed **English Market** ★★★ (entrances on Princes St. and Grand Parade; Mon–Sat 9am–5:30pm), so-named because back in the day it was reserved for loyal English traders—no Irish or Catholic merchants allowed; after the Battle of the Boyne, in fact, it was necessary to swear allegiance to the English king in order to get a stall here. With its roots traceable to the rule of James I in 1610, the indoor space you enter today was first opened in 1788, but was destroyed by fire in 1980. This is a hub of city sociability, and where you can find clues to its weirder culinary tastes: A favorite Cork dish is tripe and drisheen (a white sausage made by stuffing slaughterhouse offcuts into an esophagus), while pig's feet and hot-buttered eggs are still sold here. The market has easy access to **St. Patrick's Street,** Cork's main shopping stretch, lined with interesting side streets (more shops and bars). Both St. Patrick's Street and Grand Parade were redesigned by Spanish architect Beth Gali when Cork became the European Capital of Culture in 2005.

Right up against the hulking **Opera House,** the **Crawford Art Gallery** ★★ (Emmett Place; ☎ 021/490-7855; www.crawfordartgallery.ie; free admission; Mon–Sat 10am–5pm) occupies the former Custom's House; it's worth roughly ½ an hour of your time to walk past some great Irish artworks. On the first floor, excerpts from the gallery's permanent collection give a good overview of the major influences in contemporary and modern Irish art; look out for works by Sean Keating (1889–1977), who captures the melancholy of Irish life during troubled times; also search for paintings by Jack B. Yeats (1871–1957), and engravings by James Barry (1741–1806). The Cooper-Penrose Collection has portraits of tight-lipped aristocrats lending meaning to the term "stiff upper lip." John Butt's *A View of Cork* (c. 1755) provides an interesting comparative study for the layout of present day Cork—note the Dutch gables on some of the buildings, indicating Cork's mercantile links with Amsterdam. On the second floor is a photographic exhibition, with portraits of Samuel Beckett by John Minihan, and fantasy illustrations by Harry Clarke (1889–1931), known for his stained-glass window designs. An onsite cafe (☎ 021/427-4415; Mon–Sat 8:30am–4:30pm), offers such savory treats as goat's cheese salad (€11).

The University & the South Bank

Over on Cork's South Bank a towering trio of spires push heavenwards out of **St. Fin Barre's Cathedral** ✹✹ (Bishop St.; ☎ 021/496-3387; http://www.cathedral.cork.anglican.org; €3; Apr–Sept Mon–Sat 9:30am–5:30pm; Sun noon–5pm; Oct–Mar Mon–Sat 10am–12:45pm and 2–5pm), famously built where the saint established the monastery that eventually became Cork itself. Despite the site's ancient roots, this Gothic church dates from the 1870s; its sculpted facade is embellished with winged symbolic representations of the evangelists (Matthew as angel, Mark as lion, Luke as Ox, John as Eagle). It's worth paying to go inside, if only to see the beautiful stained glass rose window above the main entrance (best viewed from the Chancel); designed by William Burges (the architect responsible for the church itself), it depicts the story of Creation. Also take a look at the marble pillars around the base of the pulpit where the evangelists feature again—this time with the creature to which they're symbolically linked.

Heading farther west, you'll pass evidence of student life as you approach the precinct of **University College Cork** ✹✹, founded in the 1840s, and wedged between College Road and the south channel of the Lee. Established by Queen Victoria when she became the first reigning British monarch to visit Cork in 1845 (she came again in 1901), the campus once featured her statue. It was, however, buried by a Republican chancellor, and when it was finally dug up for the university's centenary celebrations there was such protest that it was decided to send the statue to Victoria—in Australia. It's a pretty campus with mature gardens and a well-integrated mix of historic and contemporary architecture. Of particular note is a collection of Ogham stones on which the 2,000-year-old Ogham alphabet is recorded. With beautiful mosaic covering its entire floor, the **Honan Chapel** exemplifies Hiberno-Romanesque architecture, the restrained exterior wonderfully offset by stained-glass windows, including 11 by the Irish artist Harry Clarke. Commemorated in one of the stained glass windows in the Aula Maxima (1849), is the work of George Boole, who was the university's first mathematics professor and known to schoolchildren everywhere as the inventor of Boolean algebra, from which computers have evolved. And on top of all this history, there's the ultra-modern **Lewis Glucksman Gallery** ✹✹ (☎ 021/490-1844; www.glucksman.org; free admission; Tues–Sat 10am–5pm; Thurs 10am–8pm; Sun noon–5pm), a worthy exhibition space where curators put on top-rate contemporary shows (I caught a clever Warhol-Hirst retrospective here). A visitors center—**Experience UCC** (☎ 021/490-1876; www.ucc.ie; Mon–Fri 10am–5pm)—runs campus tours (€4; May–Oct Mon, Wed, Fri–Sat 3pm).

Shandon & the North Bank

It's well-worth getting off the "island" to discover the historic Shandon area on the north bank, which rises up relatively sharply from the River Lee. Here, the narrow, still-cobbled side-streets betray its haphazard development. It was the site of Cork's original Shandon Castle, and it has traditionally been the area which connects the harbor with the "Golden Vale"—a vast agricultural region, which is perhaps the best grass-growing land in Europe. Shandon was also the center of Cork's major trade markets, dealing in beef and butter; at a time when Cork was known as the "Slaughterhouse of Ireland," there are records of 100,000 cattle being killed here in a single year. Animal blood no longer runs through the streets, but reminders of Cork's boomtime export industry still linger. Pope's Quay, for example, is where ships docked to pick up beef and butter exported around the world; you can still see the Cork Button Co., where the bones of slaughtered cattle were used to make buttons.

Facing the river, a regal neo-classical portico marks the entrance to **St. Mary's Dominican Church,** one of the first Catholic churches built in Ireland after the repeal of oppressive laws against Catholic worship; of particular note inside is a 12th-century alabaster sculpture of the Virgin which originated in France and which many believe has miraculous properties. Most visitors to the Shandon are on a mission to climb up the 120-ft. tower at **St. Anne's Church** ✸✸ 🧒 (Church St., Shandon; ☎ 021/450-5906; www.shandonbells.org; €6 tower climb, church free admission; May–Oct Mon–Sat 9:30am–4:30pm; Nov–Apr Mon–Sat 10am–3:30pm); at the top, you get rewarding views of the city, but I suspect that the bigger thrill comes from the stop on the first floor where—if you've paid to climb the tower—you get to ring the famous Shandon Bells (really, anytime you like for as long as you wish; kids love it). St. Anne's itself is quite small and according to one Shandon expert, the church is "a bit of dog's dinner," referring to the awkward, unplanned staging of its construction, which began in the 1720s and went on in widely spaced phases. A consequence: Two sides of the clock tower are limestone, while the other two are sandstone. Also, the clocks don't all tell the same time (apparently some of the gilded wooden numbers on the clock face are thicker than others and slow some of the hands down), giving it the nickname, "four-faced liar." Atop the clock tower is one of the city's favorite symbols, a weathervane in the form of golden salmon.

From the late-18th century, the Shandon became renowned for its Butter Exchange, which was at the heart of a major international export industry. During its heyday, at least 50 butter merchants churned away in Shandon, and many of the laneways hereabouts are named after them. Farmers came from as far as Kerry, traveling the old Butter Road to **Cork's Exchange** where the world's first quality control systems were developed to enforce product consistency—in reality, the powers that controlled the butter market were turning Cork butter into a brand name. Designed like an umbrella, the large circular **Firkin Crane** (Shandon; ☎ 021/450-7487; www.firkincrane.com) was built in 1855 as an annex to the Exchange. Firkin is the Danish word for "quarter barrel" and corresponded to 56 pounds of butter. The casks—or firkins—were weighed on a balance known as "the Crane," which comprised the centerpiece of the circular building. Since 1992, the Firkin Crane has been the home of Cork City Ballet. Both buildings were designed by John Benson, and the facade of the Exchange is one of the most enchanting in Cork.

Part of what was once the world's largest butter market, is now the **Cork Butter Museum** (O'Connell Sq.; ☎ 021/430-0600; www.corkbutter.museum; €3.50; daily Mar–Oct 10am–5pm; July–Aug 10am–6pm), where you can discover everything there is to know about Cork's role in Ireland's most important food export. It's a fraction more interesting than it sounds (so yes, it's skippable).

To complete the Shandon story: In 1924 the Butter Exchange closed; changes in technology, combined with Danish innovations in packaging, and the development of Dutch butterine (an amalgam of butter and margarine) all contributed to its demise. Today, though, Ireland's butter export trade continues, and all Irish dairy sold abroad is branded "Kerrygold."

Also on the north bank, but this time some distance west of Shandon, amid the terrace townhouses of Sunday's Well, is **Cork City Gaol** ✹ (Sunday's Well; ☎ 021/430-5022; www.corkcitygaol.com; €7; daily Mar–Oct 9:30am–5pm; Nov–Feb 10am–4pm), designed by Sir Thomas Deane, who was also responsible for the University and the Imperial Hotel. Today, it's probably the most popular attraction in the city. Visitors are given a pre-recorded audio guide with a very serious spoken tour of the prison's pre-Victorian wings, with a number of horrifying anecdotes thrown in for good measure. The focus is mid-19th-century prison life, and you venture into various cells to "discover" individual prisoners, learning grisly details of their ghastly incarceration. (Part of the severity of the punishment stemmed from the belief that criminal evil was contagious and that seclusion was an effective remedy; prisoners were expected to conduct themselves like Trappist monks.) What I find most stirring are the remnants of real people who were interred here: graffiti left by political prisoners from 1919 to 1921, in the buildup to Irish independence.

If you head back to the city on foot, stop off in **Fitzgerald Park** ✹✹, a lovely green belt stretched along the southern bank of the Lee's north channel.

THE OTHER CORK
Comedy, Drama & Poetry

Corkonians are known for their wicked (and occasionally ribald) sense of humor. If you want to learn how to roll with the punches, try to catch a performance by **Snatch,** Munster's only comedy improvisation troupe, comprising performers from across Ireland, and as far as Argentina. Now in their seventh year, their brand of comedy is offbeat and highly physical, and comes at you like a bullet. They're such a huge hit that they've started offering **improv comedy workshops,** interactive classes open to everybody (teens and grown-ups, actors and non-actors, locals, and visitors). Using games and exercises they teach the basic techniques of improvisation, all the while "playing" with new friends from Cork. If you're keen to join a workshop—held from September to May at **Triskel Arts Centre** (Tobin St.; ☎ 021/427-2022)—contact Marcus at ☎ 021/477-2190, 086/317-3543 or marcusbale@gmail.com. Each session costs just €10.

Serious theater is taken quite, well, seriously, at the **Everyman Palace Theatre** ✹✹ (15 MacCurtain St.; ☎ 021/450-1673; www.everymanpalace), with a focus largely on good, solid dramas. Weekly guided tours delve into the history of the theater and offer a tantalizing behind-the-scenes peek at on the current production (€5; Fri 2:30pm). And, in the spirit of reinventing itself and keeping with the times, the Everyman also hosts midnight parties on weekends: On Fridays, DJ Maike Darcy spins soul, funk, jazz, groove, and disco tracks; but the big, alternative "in" event on Saturdays is "MvM" (Movies versus Music), a fresh club-style party with danceable club tracks in the bar and cult movies screening in an intimate cinema padded with schmoozy, lounging space. Tickets cost €10.

Storytelling and original poetry are the stuff that attracts regulars to **Ó bhéal,** a weekly open-mic (Mon 8:30pm) in the Hay Loft, the upstairs venue at the **Long Valley** (Winthrop St.; ☎ 021/427-2144). Besides giving equal voice to local spoken word artists and poets who prefer to write, the event also includes a regular line-up of special guests who come to read their words, perform their poems, and sometimes present workshops in creative writing (these usually happen early evenings, prior to the Mon event). It's a democratic, open forum, where all genres are accepted. There's also room here for discussion and debate, and it's stimulating fun to interact with the regulars who come here to listen, learn, and sometimes express heartfelt opinions. Nights at Ó bhéal have drawn some venerable poets, songwriters, and storytellers—most of them are native Irish who've wracked up plenty experience in their fields (like veteran Irish poets Desmond O'Grady, John Liddy, and Matthew Sweeney). If you're keen to attend (and you can even sign up to perform yourself), contact Paul (info@obheal.ie) for details; or visit www.obheal.ie, where you can also find out about one-off creative writing classes (an ongoing workshop is every Tues), performance poetry workshops, and information on the special guests at upcoming events.

Learning in the Kitchen

Serious foodies should investigate cooking classes offered by the distinguished **Ballymaloe Cookery School** (☎ 021/464-6785; www.cookingisfun.ie) in Shanagarry, 37km (23 miles) from Cork. Now a national celebrity, Darina Allen began teaching in 1983 in order to supplement her husband's farm income; the school, along with organic gardens, an acclaimed guesthouse, and self-catering cottages, is set on a 40-hectare (100-acre) farm where many of her ingredients are grown. Her enterprise—run out of the farm's former apple sorting rooms—has become the last word in cooking training in the country. The program—a mix of longer courses (often attended by people looking to start restaurants or B&Bs) and 1-day sessions, and demonstrations, too—draws people from all over Ireland. You're taught useful skills—such as fish-filleting—and you can sign up for such specialist courses as home butchery, tea appreciation, and keeping chickens in the garden (not as pets, of course). The downside may be price: A ½-day course is €105, and a full day costs €175 to €250; 5-day courses are €835. Weekday afternoon (1:45–5pm) demonstrations cost €70, including tastings of whatever is prepared. Accommodation can be provided in on-site self-catering cottages; for short courses, the rate is €56 per night for a twin room.

ATTENTION, SHOPPERS!

In the center of the city, **Carey's Lane** and **French Church Street** are good places to start browsing through Cork's best-looking stores; there's also much to see along **Oliver Plunkett,** starting with Cork's top independent bookstore, **Ruiséal Liam Teo** (49/50 Oliver Plunkett St.; ☎ 021/427-0981; ruisealbooks@eircom. net), which has a huge selection of anything on Ireland; go upstairs to find mountains of bargains. Maps sold here are actually cheaper than you'll find at Tourist House. My other favorite bookstore is **Vibes and Scribes** (3 Bridge St.; ☎ 021/ 450-5370; www.vibesandscribes.com) on the north bank; it also carries a great selection of Irish-interest books, and has a bargain table, too. For books with a social conscience, head to **Barracka Books & CAZ Worker's Co-op** (61 Barrack St.;

Gay Cork

Cork's gay scene is small and fairly low-key, although if you're looking for it, there's much to uncover within a rather tightly knit network; everyone comes out to party for a week in June during the annual **Pride** festivities. For the lowdown on what's happening visit **www.gaycork.com**. You can get involved with local activities through the **Cork Gay Community Development Company,** a very busy organization that has different groups, including one that arranges hill-walking outings; find out more at **www.gayprojectcork.com**. Ladies can contact **L.Inc (Lesbians in Cork; www.link.ie),** which is a woman-centered resource center.

Or, you can stay at a B&B that's exclusively for gay guests—if you're looking for an instant introduction to the scene, here are 2 tidy choices:

Roman House ★ (3 St. John's Terrace, Upper John St.; ☎ 021/450-3606; www.interglobal.ie/romanhouse; cash only) is the budget option, run by an artist whose work is displayed around the house. Bedrooms are all individually designed, done out in bright colors and assorted furnishing— they're relatively up-tempo, although the smaller rooms are a fraction too compact. Room 2 is the one to aim for if you want to spread out a little. Doubles start at €75; singles are €55. A fraction pricier, but with a whole lot more style, and an emphasis on a romantic experience, is **Emerson House** ★★ (2 Clarence Terrace, Summerhill North; ☎ 086/834-0891; www.emersonhousecork.com; MC, V), not far from MacCurtain Road. Cyril, the owner, has individually styled each room, ensuring that they're smart

no phone), which offers a motley collection of second-hand books—most of them Irish interest, with a particular bend towards Irish "issues." The store, not surprisingly, has an activist bent, too—walls advertise political rallies and social gatherings.

Guys looking to overcome their fear of wearing vertical stripe shirts with striped pants should stop in at **Tony** (37 Marlboro St.; ☎ 021/427-7794). Nearby, a remarkable new ladies fashion label, **Kozae** (www.kozae.com) has its store in the 1792 Cork Library building on the corner of Pembroke Street and South Mall. While everything here is top-class exclusive, when I last visited, there was a 60% sale on—so it's worth investigating. Two more stops for fashionable ladies are opposite the Crawford Gallery: **Cocoon** (6 Emmett Place; ☎ 021/427-3393) stocks eye-catching shoes, while **Samui** (12 Drawbridge St.; ☎ 021/427-8080) is a magical little fashion boutique with garments that dare to be different. Look for knitwear by Lainey Keogh, and dresses by Roisin Linnane. You might also like to browse the shops at **Merchant's Quay,** an upmarket mall.

Opposite the Opera House, you'll find the local branch of **Kilkenny** ★★ (Emmett Place; ☎ 021/422-6703; closed Sun)—Ireland's top design outlet—carrying a range of crafts, including jewelry, ceramics, fashion, and homeware.

The favored haunt of Cork's DJ tribe, **Plugd Records** (Washington St.; ☎ 021/427-6300) stocks second-hand and new albums on vinyl and CD.

and neat as a pin—they also all have plush king-size beds (except for one twin) and a slightly "antique" finish. Free Wi-Fi and parking are provided. Doubles start at €80, including breakfast.

Next, you'll need to find a good place to let your hair down.

On the North Bank, within easy reach of both Roman House and Emerson, is **Flux!** ✭ (56 MacCurtain St.; ☎ 021/455-7900), a contemporary-looking bar with plenty of entertainment, including loads of raunchy events. And a pretty raunchy, raucous clientele, too. It's open till late on weekends, while Sundays feature bingo alongside a cabaret drag act. Across town, on the South Bank, **Instinct** ✭✭ (Sullivan's Quay; www.instinctbarcork.com; no phone; Mon–Wed 6–11:30pm, Thurs and Sun till 1:30am, Fri–Sat till 2am) is widely considered the best place to get your groove on; although it's a bar, the atmosphere is clubby, with theme and foam parties. Cover is €5, or up to €10 for big events.

Finally, if you still haven't managed to find the scene—or if you simply want to sit and unwind after a night on the town—the **Cork Gay Project** (8 South Main St.; ☎ 021/427-8470; www.gayprojectcork.com) is a drop-in center with a cafe-bar called the **Other Place** (serving paninis, salads, and smoothies); it occasionally transforms into a LGBT **disco** (www.theotherplaceclub.com) on weekends.

NIGHTLIFE

For news on most cool events in Cork this month, pick up a local edition of *Whaz On?* (www.whazon.com); it's free and fits in your pocket.

Cultural Pursuits

An exacting line-up of theater, music, and comedy events at **Triskel Arts Centre** ✭✭✭ (Tobin St., off Grand Parade; ☎ 021/427-2022; www.triskelart.com), draws audiences from across the county. Live music (lots of classical, jazz, world music, Irish music, and instrument specialists) stands out among a packed program of exhibitions, film festivals, dance, theater, and book launches. Tickets range from €12 to €35, but most shows go for €18.

Many have ridiculed its hideous external appearance (I won't comment), but inside the **Cork Opera House** ✭✭ (Emmett Place; ☎ 021/427-0022; www.corkoperahouse.ie) is a strong program in both the main auditorium and at the Half Moon Theatre, around the back. Opera, dramas, stand-up comedy, live music, and the Cork Film Festival are hosted here. A few prestigious names I saw billed here in 2008 were Mark Black, Kinky Friedman, and Preston Reed. Tickets range from €15 to €35.

Occupying the Butter Exchange's former rotunda, the **Firkin Crane** (Shandon; ☎ 021/450-7487; www.firkincrane.com) is a focal point for dance in Ireland.

Drinking Spots & Live Music Venues

Just about every second person you meet in Cork seems to be trying to break into the music scene—great if you're looking for entertainment. Follow your ears and keep your eyes peeled as the scene changes night to night; the places I'm recommending however are the most consistently entertaining (I think).

The packed program, and by that I mean entertainment every night, at the **Crane Lane Theatre** ★★★ (1 Phoenix St.; ☎ 021/427-8487), a stellar venue for live music, includes serious jazz, live electronica, psychedelic rock, electro-clash, and various contemporary sub-genres including cabaret, and even DJ events. It's billed as a "late bar," so you'll usually find action here well into the wee hours, with free midnight gigs most nights, too. The venue is tucked away on a laneway between Oliver Plunkett and South Mall; turn down Pembroke Street to find Phoenix Street. Tickets to big-name or international events run €15 to €25 and can be bought in advance at **Plugd Records** (Washington St.).

About 3½ strides from Crane Lane is **Counihans** ★★ (☎ 021/427-7850; www.counihans.com; no cover), where live music features every Sunday, starting with a classical string quartet at noon; but the crowds really pack in for the stirring sounds of Arundó, an expert band blending traditional Irish sounds (using banjo, guitar, fiddle, *bodhrán,* and spoons) and Latin rhythms.

The name simply means "That's it," and whatever it is, that's what you'll get at **Sin É** ★★★ (8 Coburg St.; ☎ 021/450-2266), probably the best place in Cork for live traditional music, and known as the only surviving "real" public house in the city ("the rest are all bars," says the owner). You'll find trad sessions on Friday and Sunday at 6:30pm and Tuesday at 9:30pm; when I was last here an impromptu group—harp, banjo, *uilleann* pipes, *bodhrán,* a fiddle, and a set of spoons—held a mesmerizing concert of what I must call "Celtic soul music."

If you can squeeze your way into the **Hi-B** ★★★ (Oliver Plunkett St.; no phone), behind the door at the top of some unlikely looking steps, be prepared for one of the strangest pubbing experiences of your life. The eccentric owner, Brian O'Donnell, has strict rules and standards which you're expected to maintain: Refrain from using your mobile phone and never ask for cocktails—if you perform these or any other annoying acts, you too may join the list of culprits who've been summarily thrown out for disrupting the atmosphere. If you leave here *without* a bevy of new friends, you may need to check your B.O.

Closer to the University, **Tom Barry** ★★★ (Barrack St.; ☎ 021/431-8489) is a neighborhood bar that services a spunky student crowd—students of life, that is, age 18 to 80. With *Irish Times* crossword puzzles, fresh flowers, and red-tinged candles on the tables, and great wine specials chalked up on the board, this place oozes charm and energy in equal measure. Up and coming bands are often to be seen at **Cyprus Avenue** ★★ (Caroline St.; ☎ 021/427-6165; www.cyprusavenue.ie), where the line-up includes some alternative, and frequently off-beat, sounds that may just prove life-altering. Tickets can be bought online, or at Plugd.

Just for Clubbers

High-energy house music, with the likes of major international DJs like Lisa Lashes and Mauro Picotto, is the terrain of **Savoy** ★★ (Patrick's St.; no phone;

www.savoycork.com), Cork's top superclub. Big name record-spinners tend to perform Fridays, but gigs are scheduled any time of the week, too, so do investigate. Cover charge is typically around €15, though big name acts can cost up to €50. A snazzy, stylish bar-restaurant through the week, **Scotts** (Caroline St.; ☎ 021/422-2779; www.scotts.ie) opens its nightclub on weekends, hosting some of Cork's best DJs who, in turn, draw a sexy crowd. Expect to pay a €6 cover charge, though it's only €4 if you get there before 11:30pm.

GET OUT OF TOWN: SIDE-TRIPS FROM CORK

Kissing the Blarney Stone

"Odds bodikins, more Blarney talk!" is supposedly the phrase uttered by Queen Elizabeth I in response to yet another missive from Dermot McCarthy, the ruler of **Blarney Castle** ★★ (Blarney; ☎ 021/438-5252; www.blarneycastle.ie; €10; May–Sept and Oct–Apr Mon–Sat 9am–6:30pm; June–Aug 9am–7pm; summer Sun 9:30am–5:30pm; winter 9:30am–sundown), who had been using small talk and feeble excuses to delay the terms of his surrender to the crown. "Blarney" has come to mean, put simply, "convincing smooth talk," and kissing the famous Blarney Stone at the top of the castle is believed to magically bestow upon the kisser the gift of eloquence which so frustrated Elizabeth. There's so much hype around that famous kissing stone, in fact, that the experience can be a bit of a letdown—especially if you arrive with the crowds in summer. Still, it's worth the 10km (6 mile) excursion to the tiny, one-square village of Blarney where the Desmonds, an Irish royal family, first built a castle, and were paid £20 a year to leave Cork in peace. Looking at it today, it's little wonder Dermot was so keen to hang on to his castle. It is a lively piece of work; built in 1446 on the site of two former castles, it's surrounded by verdant grounds, with a gently flowing stream, and rock caves for foundations. To partake of this silly farce (and it's almost unheard of to come to Ireland and not kiss the stone), you climb to the top of the castle—enjoying excellent views on the way up—and then lie on your back with your head hanging over the battlements . . . and in seconds it's all over (although there's a photographer to record the moment, and you buy your souvenir downstairs for a whopping €10). Buses run all day, every day, from Cork's main bus station to Blarney (15 min.); a round-trip ticket will cost around €5.

East Cork's Youghal

"Yawl" is the unlikely pronunciation for one of the more undeniably quaint seaside towns east of Cork City, just short of the Waterford border. And, despite never making it onto the tourist trail (to my mind, that's reason enough to visit), Youghal was once a major medieval port town, with an important place in Irish history. In 1585, Sir Walter Raleigh was given over 98,800 hectares (40,000 acres) of land confiscated from the rebellious Desmond—this included both Youghal and Lismore. Raleigh lived here, at Myrtle Grove adjacent St. Mary's Collegiate Church, and he was mayor of Youghal in 1588 and 1589. One story tells how a servant threw water over Raleigh when he spotted him smoking tobacco; more famously, Raleigh is attributed with planting the first potatoes in Ireland here. He was less successful at planting English immigrants, however, and in 1602, ended his involvement in the Plantation of Munster and sold his estate to Richard Boyle, the future Earl of Cork, for £1,500. Boyle imported large numbers of settlers from

Bristol. In more recent times, John Huston shot *Moby Dick* here—the Market Square stood in for the Massachusetts town of New Bedford; the **Moby Dick Lounge Bar** (Market Sq.; ☎ 024/92756) celebrates that brief fling with fame.

Youghal's size makes it a great place to explore—you can see all of it in just a few hours and then spend time relaxing at the water's edge or investigating the pub and restaurant scene. Better still, take one of Sheila Loughnane's **guided walking tours** ✯✯✯ (☎ 024/92502 or 024/20170; €6; summer daily 11am, or by arrangement). Sheila—a "drama queen," really—not only leads you through the town's extraordinary history, but entertains and surprises you (for 1 to 1½ hours) with natural flair. If you don't manage a tour, make your way to the **Tourist Information Office** (Market House, Market Sq.; ☎ 024/20170) to grab a map of the town, and try to see at least those sights highlighted on it; the tourist office also doubles as the town's history museum.

WHERE TO STAY & DINE

€€   If Youghal wins you over and you decide to spend the night, there's only one place to consider staying in the town itself—Phyllis Foley's **Roseville Bed & Breakfast** ✯✯ (New Catherine St., Youghal; ☎ 024/92571; www.rosevillebb.com; MC, V). It's right in the heart of town (two minutes from the bus stop), behind chunky maroon-colored walls. On offer, is simple, homey comfort—impeccably clean bedrooms (€66–€72 double, €50 single), coordinated in soothing blues and creams, with back-supporting beds, and showers in the smallish bathrooms. Phyllis loves to cook, and she'll put together just about anything you want at breakfast, including hot porridge, or a full Irish breakfast—she prepares her own jams and preserves.

€€–€€€   Some 10km (6 miles) west of Youghal, Margaret Browne runs one of the finest affordable lodgings in Ireland, **Ballymakeigh House** ✯✯✯ (Killeagh; ☎ 024/95184; www.ballymakeighhouse.com; MC, V). Having received much praise from just about every imaginable local critic, the B&B seems to grow with each new season, and the food is reason alone to break the journey to Cork (a six-course dinner costs €40). It doesn't hurt that you get to stay in a 400-year-old house with six neatly attired bedrooms (with electric blankets, heated towel rails, Egyptian cotton linens), and public areas dressed with antiques and individually sourced artworks. Doubles cost €120 to €130.

KINSALE & WEST CORK

"West Cork attracts eccentric genius," says Irish food critic John McKenna. "The weird and wonderful wash up here." I'm inclined to agree. West Cork—a magical stretch of coastline that erupts into three magnificent, rugged peninsulas—sustains people who go to find time for themselves, often for their art, creativity or personal rebirth away from the modern world. That's particularly true outside the holiday season when it fills up with boating enthusiasts, beach-lovers, and divers who come to swim with dolphins and explore colossal wrecks. Although some areas are hugely popular vacation destinations—particularly Kinsale, with it's appealing harborside location—there's no doubt that the people of West Cork understand the value of being away from it all, and there's a sense here of near self-imposed isolation.

So what does one do here? Well, you'll learn about one of the most decisive battles in Irish history, and visit the mighty Charles Fort where garrisoned soldiers

Sampling the Water of Life

According to legend, Christian missionaries learned the secret of distillation from Arab perfumers in the Middle East. These monks then brought a prototype of the alcohol pot still with them back to Ireland, and the idea later also found its way to Scotland. When and how whiskey was first invented is unclear, but the name derives from the Irish *uisce beatha* (pronounced "ishka-baha")—or "water of life."

And you can sample some of the best of this magical beverage in the small town of **Midleton,** roughly midway between Cork City and Youghal, which is one of the spiritual homes of the world's biggest-selling Irish whiskey, Jameson. Buildings that started out as a woolen mill in the 1790s and later became barracks for English troops during the Napoleonic threat, became a distillery in 1825. In 1975, a state-of-the-art distilling complex was built, so visitors today are given a tour of the **Old Distillery** (Distillery Walk; ☎ 021/461-3594; www.jamesonwhiskey.com; €12.50; daily 10am–5pm, reduced hours Nov–Mar), which takes in each and every step of the process in what now seems a bit like a ghostly museum—it's a bit sad to see ingenious Old World technology standing functionless and replaced by the modern distillery somewhere hidden round the back (totally out of bounds to visitors like you and me, it has a capacity of 50 million bottles of alcohol per year). The tour's proudest moment is showing off the largest pot still in the world, built in 1825 with a capacity of 31,648 gallons (143,873 liters). Although you don't get to see the whiskey-making process, your guide does a decent job of explaining how everything fitted together; the tour culminates in a tot of the liquid in question; two visitors per group get to do a whiskey tasting, comparing notes on different variants, which in my books is the best part of the visit (so volunteer your services rapidly when the time comes).

had their tongues bored with hot pokers if they dared commit blasphemy. Dotted along the coast are magnificent coves and tiny islands where marauding pirates once had their headquarters—today, the only signs of such violence are in the waves constantly ravishing the rocky shores. Head to the signal station at the end of the Mizen Head and you'll feel yourself virtually engulfed by the furious tumult. To share the solitude and sense of remoteness that draws many of the blow-ins, hikers and cyclists should head for the Sheep's Head and Beara peninsulas, where lack of population accounts for an even deeper sense of mystery. For anyone who values idyllic calm, and a way of life that's at ease with a more natural, effortless rhythm, West Cork is indeed a special place.

LAY OF THE LAND

West Cork stretches from the natural harbor at Kinsale to the far-westerly Beara Peninsula, which County Cork shares with neighboring Kerry. You could probably spend a day whizzing through the most prominent coastal towns, but I implore you to slow down and savor the ambiance. As you wend your way along the R600 toward Clonakilty, the first town of any size after **Kinsale,** think about detouring along even more rural roads that skirt the coastline, and definitely stop at **Timoleague** to explore its ruined abbey. From **Clonakilty**—known for its black pudding and nightlife—follow the N71 to **Skibbereen,** large enough to be considered the capital of West Cork. From Skibbereen, strike out to the harbor villages of **Castletownshend** and **Baltimore;** the latter is also my first choice for an overnight stop, and is the launch for ferries to the peaceful little islands of **Sherkin** and **Cape Clear.** West of Skibbereen is **Ballydehob,** where you should leave the N71 and explore the mountain-backed terrain of the **Mizen Head Peninsula.** Either do a circuit of the peninsula, visiting the signal station on its outermost tip, or spend the night. The adjacent peninsula is **Sheep's Head,** easily the least explored part of West Cork, and a wonderful place to disappear for a while. The towns of **Bantry** and **Glengarriff** lie between Sheep's Head and the rugged **Beara Peninsula,** a fat finger of land that some argue is a more attractive road trip than the Ring of Kerry.

KINSALE

Were it not for the outcome of certain strategic events at Kinsale just over 400 years ago, much of the English-speaking world may well today have been speaking Spanish. Such is the significance of the knife-edge gambit staged here during the Battle of Kinsale in 1601. Irish troops and their Spanish allies had managed to sandwich British forces between them and victory looked assured. But poor communications followed by an ill-organized attack led to the Irish being thwarted in what was, at that point, their last ditch efforts to reclaim their country. The Spanish scurried back home, having negotiated terms with the English. And the rest, as they say, is history; the battle's outcome led to the famous Flight of the Earls, forever ending the possibility of an Irish aristocracy.

Kinsale, of course, has more to offer than just that bit of history. Hailed as Ireland's oldest town, it also used to be considered one of its most attractive (unfortunately, ongoing sewer maintenance and a boarded up waterfront hotel construction site have transformed it into a temporary eyesore. Hopefully it will look better when you visit). Spread around the mouth of the River Bandon it spills into the inlet of Kinsale Harbour. Maritime activities are abundant in summer, while Kinsale's narrow, warren-like streets are lined with handsome Georgian terrace houses, concealing ruins and monuments that date back to the middle ages. Long a center for the importation of wine, it's fitting that Kinsale has emerged as a major culinary destination, attracting visitors not only for its salubrious location, but also for its many top-rated restaurants. Just south of Cork City, Kinsale is an obvious gateway to the tranquil towns and villages farther west, although it does have a bustling commercial side and it fills to bursting during hectic summer seasons. To see Kinsale at its best, come in spring and pray for good weather.

Getting There & Getting Around

Kinsale is easily visited as a day trip from Cork which is just 27km (17 miles) north; it's a 30-minute drive along the **R600,** clearly signposted all the way, and

bus no. 249 plies the route regularly (less frequently Sun). The town itself is easily explored on **foot,** but if you want to see what really makes this neck of the woods worthwhile—the forts, peninsula heads, and dramatic seaside spots, you should rent a bike. Pick up a free map at the **tourist office** (Emmet Place; ☎ 021/477-2234) on the waterfront.

Accommodations, Both Standard & Not

Slap-bang in the center of Kinsale's busy little town—convenient for everything eating- and drinking-wise—and yet totally private, **Boland's Townhouse** ✫✫✫ (Emmett Place; ☎ 021/477-7584; www.bolandkinsale.com) is one of those near-perfect rental deals that will soon have you feeling like you're part of the very fabric of local life. This apartment has two big en suite bedrooms; a wonderful kitchen; and great lounge-cum-dining room with red leather sofas, a gas fire, and satellite TV. There's even a patio (ideal for outdoor dining), and just about every amenity has been thought of (including a mobile phone). Weekly rates start at €450 (Nov–Mar) and €550 (Oct, Apr–May), but are heftier during the busy summer season (€860). Gas and electricity are not included.

If Boland's isn't available, try the **Sheehy Brothers** (Market St.; ☎ 021/477-2338; www.sheehybrothers.com), a small, local agency and property management firm that represents 18 Kinsale properties. Of these, five have sea views (including Boland's, above), 11 are within walking distance of the village, and two are out of town. Their most affordable options are two-bedroom ground-floor apartments in a small development not far from the center (these cost €350 per week in winter and €500 in June and Sept); they're a tad boxy, and not particularly elegant, but nevertheless make a convenient base for families (there's a double and a twin) and offer more privacy than is afforded by the B&Bs. If you want to find out about shorter rental periods—only workable outside summer—write to the agency.

€–€€   Although there are a few cheaper spots in Kinsale (notably, its hostels, which are, quite frankly, uninspiring), you'd be hard-pressed to find anything as decent as the **Kinsale Arms** (55 Main St.; ☎ 021/477-2233; www.kinsalearms. com; MC, V) in the heart of town. Formerly a pub, this smart little yellow building with daffodils growing from its window boxes, has a hodge-podge selection of neat, functional, freshly painted bedrooms on three floors. Accommodations aren't chic, and the compact size of some counts against them, but they're clean and bright; try to bag room 1, which is more spacious and has a large bathroom with a tub. Mylie Murphy, the owner, is really pulling up his sleeves on this makeover: Artworks are waiting to go up and he's creating a barbeque area in the back courtyard. Price is certainly king here: €60 to €80 gets you a double, and singles are €40 to €45.

€–€€   On the outskirts of town, **Kilcaw House** ✫ (Pewter Hole Cross; ☎ 021/477-4155; www.kilcawhouse.com; AE, MC, V) is a lovingly tended home, whose hosts diligently tend to even the fussiest guests, and always find time to give advice on what to see and do. Their B&B is neat as a pin, with light spilling into bedrooms through large windows looking out over the surrounding landscape of rolling hills and farmland. Wooden floors (real ones that creak), pine furniture, floral fabrics, fun color schemes, and decent showers, all come together in bedrooms that are homespun yet have a professional finish. Double rates are €56 to €110, varying greatly by season.

€€   Way across on the other side of town, just seven minutes on foot from the center of Kinsale, the Hosfords have transformed an immaculate home into a fine B&B. With stone walls and a matching low stone wall around a neat garden, **Woodlands House** ★✪ (Cappagh; ☎ 021/477-2633; www.woodlandskinsale.com; MC, V) offers a hint of luxury at a bargain price. Bedrooms are well-proportioned, wallpapered, and fitted with antique-style furniture and king-size beds; they have good showers, firm mattresses, and piles of magazines. I prefer room 3 for its great view, and larger-than-average bathroom. Guests have access to free Wi-Fi. A double room costs €80 to €100; a triple is €130; singles are €50 to €80—all depending on time of year.

Dining for All Tastes

Supposedly Ireland's "culinary capital" (a moniker I think is now way past its sell-by date), Kinsale is known for its sheer quantity of restaurants (many of them pricey); you certainly don't need to go hungry here.

€–€€   If you're looking to pack a picnic (a good idea hereabouts, since there are so many idyllic lunching spots), you must stop in at Guillaume Lequin's **Mange Tout** ★✪ (Pearse St.; ☎ 021/470-6899; www.mangetout.ie; Tues–Sat 9:30am–6pm; MC, V). One of the best things to hit Kinsale, this clever deli provides fresh, ready-to-go meals made to your specifications and within your budget. Whether it's pizza, pasta or quiche, give Guillaume how much you wish to pay, enough time, and he'll work something out—the question he usually asks if you order pizza: "Is there anything you don't want on it?" You can also pick up hot take-away soup (€3.15), cured meats, pâtés, croissants, olives, relishes, sauces, and a range of cheeses. Daily sandwich specials and fresh salads (from €3.50, depending on size and ingredients) are also reason to visit.

€€–€€€   It's a pub, it's a restaurant, and it's a local haunt. **Jim Edwards** ✪ (Market Quay; ☎ 021/477-2541; www.jimedwardskinsale.com; food served daily 12:30–10pm; AE, MC, V) is also always packed, which accounts for the wholeheartedly authentic atmosphere in this maritime-themed spot, carefully managed by an energetic and well-dressed staff. In the bar, you can push your budget farther, choosing from a selection of comfort food on the laminated clam-shell menu: Lasagna (€13), steak, chicken curry (€13), and grilled salmon in dill and lemon butter (€17) are favorites, but there are chalked up specials, too. It's worth bearing in mind that all mains come with huge portions of vegetables and a choice of potatoes, so you may want to order one starter (like the excellent grilled crab claws in garlic butter, €14) and one main dish between two people, and then share the sides.

€€–€€€€   Out at Summercove, just below Charles Fort, the **Bulman** ★✪ (☎ 021/477-2131; www.thebulman.com; food served Mon–Sat 12:30–3pm; Tues–Sat 6–9:30pm; Sun 1–4pm; AE, MC, V) is an institution: There's been drinking on this site since the early 1600s, and it's not unusual to see dozens of hedonists gathered at the edge of the parking area out front, beer or wine glass in hand, watching the sun set across Kinsale Harbour. Unless you're prepared to splurge, you'll need to stick to the bar menu's hearty starters—seafood chowder (€7), chili and lemongrass mussels (€7.50), salmon cakes with arugula salad and lime aioli (€8)—which will give you an idea of the adventurous mains on offer (like the sea bass, baked whole and served with warm potato, chorizo, and spinach salad, for €20). If you do decide to venture upstairs, the most reasonable dinner option is the two-course set menu for €23. But, quite frankly, even if you don't care to eat here, it's worth stopping in for a pint just to soak up the atmosphere. There's music most nights, usually unplugged, and turf fires burn in winter.

€€–€€€€ Another institution is Kinsale's famous **Fishy Fishy Café** ★★★ (Crowley's Quay; ☎ 021/477-4453; www.fishyfishy.ie; Sat–Mon noon–4:30pm; Tues–Fri noon–8pm; cash only). In a turquoise-walled, white-shuttered house down by the harbor, it's an extension of Martin and Marie Shanahan's fish shop and cafe (Tues–Sat noon–3pm) on Guardwell Street up near St. Multose Church. The daily specials are based on the catch of the day, brought in straight off the boats of local fishermen. Perennial favorites include wok-fried clams (€18, or €11 for a taster portion); a platter of oak-smoked salmon (€16, or €10); big open sandwiches with prawn and smoked salmon (€15); and a dozen oysters for €10. The mood and look of the place is thoroughly low-key. Of all Kinsale's famous restaurants, this is the one worth queuing for.

Why You're Here: Exploring Kinsale

The most entertaining hour you can spend in Kinsale is in the company of Don Herlihy, the fellow who leads the **Historic Stroll in Old Kinsale** ★★★ (☎ 087/250-0731 or 021/477-2873; €7; Apr–Sept daily 11:15am). His topnotch tour presents reams of historic detail but in a neatly packaged, witty bundle. (Don likes to compare the shock of the English when the Spanish armada landed at Kinsale, to the Cuban missile crisis.) He reveals how Kinsale grew from a 14th-century walled town into an important supplier of provisions for the wine-carrying Vintage Fleet that docked here during the 17th century. Definitely a highlight.

Without Don's help, it's pretty difficult to imagine that upscale Kinsale was once a garrison town and, in 1601, was the site of a battle that changed the course of Irish history. But there are markers of the town's turbulent history. Kinsale's biggest attraction (literally)—situated beyond the little enclave of Summercove—is **Charles Fort** ★★ (☎ 021/477-2263; www.heritageireland.ie; Heritage Card or €3.70; daily mid-Mar to Oct 10am–6pm; Nov to mid-Mar 10am–5pm), a magnificently preserved 17th-century star-shaped fortress (the size of a small town) perched on the edge of Kinsale's natural harbor. Climb up to its bastions for wonderful views of the estuary. The shape is a Dutch influence on English fortress design which took hold in the late-16th century when medieval castles were found to be useless against the increasingly heavy cannon fire of the day.

Charles Fort was the largest engineering project in 17th-century Ireland, yet took just three years to build—from commission to completion. Looking at it now, with it's lovely cobblestone courtyards and pathways and beautiful views, it's difficult to imagine that this was the scene of some grizzly military action—most significantly the Siege of 1690, when the people of Kinsale refused to swear allegiance to William of Orange—and often grueling conditions for the soldiers who

Kinsale's Annual Art Jig

Tiny Kinsale swells in summer, but is particularly lively during the annual **Kinsale Arts Week** (☎ 021/470-0010; www.kinsaleartsweek.com), attracting around 15,000 people each July. Top-of-their-class musicians grab the limelight (in 2008, these included Elkie Brooks, the Brodsky Quartet, Ska Cubano, and El Guayabero), and can be costly (up to €40); but there's also free street theater; workshops for children; literary events at the town's bookstores; art installations; walking tours and more.

lived here until 1922. Exhibitions cover the history of the fortress, and dig deeper into its design, but to get the most of a visit, join one of the guided tours (no extra charge; first tour 10:30am, last tour 3:30pm; duration 1 hour).

Across the estuary, opposite Charles Fort, **James Fort** is in less spectacular condition—it is an older construction, designed by Paul Ive, and built between 1602 and 1607—but unlike Charles, is free to visit, and the views are just as magnificent.

Kinsale's patron saint is St. Multose, and the Anglican **St. Multose Church** ✸✸ has supposedly been in continuous use since it was established by the Normans in 1190 on the site of an earlier 6th-century church. Study the stonework exterior carefully before venturing into the embrace of its soothing pink and white interior—there are still signs of medieval masonry. A much later construction is **Desmond Castle** (Cork St.; ☎ 021/477-4855; Heritage Card or €2.90; Apr 15–Oct daily 10am–6pm), a three-storey urban tower house built around 1500 by Maurice Bacach Fitzgerald, Earl of Desmond. It has served many functions, and became the arsenal for Don Juan Aguilla during the Spanish occupation which lasted 100 days prior to the Battle of Kinsale in 1601. From the 17th century, it became a prison notorious for its grim conditions; the crews of many American vessels were imprisoned here during the War of Independence.

Desmond castle also served as the town's customs house, at the center of Kinsale's once-flourishing wine trade; Kinsale was designated a "wine port" as early as the 15th century, supplying provisions to the 160-vessel Vintage Fleet which plied the route to Bordeaux. Ambitiously named, the **International Wine Museum** occupies part of the castle, but is little more than a lame exhibition detailing Ireland's links with a global wine industry. Frankly, you can flit through the castle in a few minutes, and easily skip the wine exhibition.

Finally, for the freshest air and finest views of Kinsale, the Fort and the harbor, let your legs carry you along the **Charles Fort Walk** ✸✸✸, a two-or-so hour route that starts alongside the Fort and wends its way along the edge of the natural harbor as far as the tip of the peninsula; your efforts will be well-rewarded and the walk is suitable for just about anyone.

SKIBBEREEN, BALTIMORE & THE ISLANDS

Skibbereen really only took off after Baltimore was raided by Algerian pirates in 1631—many Baltimoreans were killed and many more captured to become slaves in north Africa. A mass exodus of survivors into Skibbereen transformed the small

Underwater Adventures

With its coastline bang in the path of the Gulf Stream, Baltimore is ideally situated for diving. It's clear, unpolluted waters are brimming with marine life, intriguing undersea topography, and an unprecedented number of wrecks, including the massive supercarrier, Kowloon Bridge, and a German U-boat. It's one of Ireland's most potent diving locations, where aquatic enthusiasts get a chance to swim with seals and dolphins, and sight sunfish, leatherback turtles, and basking sharks.

The **Baltimore Diving Centre** (Harbour Dr., Baltimore; ☎ 028/20300; www.baltimorediving.com) offers a wide range of courses, starting with a 3-hour snorkeling session for €30, and 3-hour introductory scuba lessons for €65. But, if you seriously want to change your life, here's the place to get that Open Water Diving certificate; a 5-day course costs in the region of €475, and while diving isn't the cheapest hobby, you'll quickly discover that these waters are filled with enough curiosities to make this perhaps the most rewarding part of your trip.

The other reliable outfit in Baltimore, **Aquaventures** (The Stone House; ☎ 087/796-1456 or 028/20522; www.aquaventures.ie), offers guided diving and snorkeling packages and training courses catering to the very keen as well as the "just curious." Divers can be housed in Aquaventures' own B&B, the **Stone House** (☎ 028/20511; www.aquaventures.ie; MC, V), with double rooms for €71 to €80. The four rooms have private bathrooms (two have tubs as well as showers), and all have balconies with views over Baltimore harbor). Rianne Smith, who runs the B&B, also arranges self-catering rentals in Baltimore (€450–€750 per week for a house with two double bedrooms and usually several additional single beds); she can also

trade post into a town that flourished until the early-1800s, thanks to a textiles industry, agricultural trade, beer and porter brewing, and whiskey distillation.

Its size relative to other, smaller, towns in the region makes colorful Skibbereen the "capital" of southwest Cork, although the absence of coastline to my mind detracts from its usefulness for getting a proper sense of what the region is really all about. Still, the town exists as a spiritual hub, if only thanks to the terrible legacy of the Great Famine when so many people died here only to be buried in pit—or monster—graves at Abbeystrewery Graveyard, just outside town. Between eight and ten thousand famine victims are believed to have been buried here, but a proper census was never possible since so many were buried at night—those left behind were ashamed of their loss. A devastating exhibition on the Famine is on display at the **Skibbereen Heritage Centre** (Old Gasworks Building, Upper Bridge St.; ☎ 028/40900; www.skibbheritage.com; €6; Mar–May and Sept–Nov Tues–Sat 10am–6pm; June–Aug daily 10am–6pm), where the horrors of the worst period in local history are critically investigated. You can also buy a "Skibbereen Trail" leaflet (€1.75) which plots out an historic town walk.

Just 8km (5 miles) southeast of Skibbereen lies the alluring village of **Castletownshend** ✹✹, which draws the well-heeled, but is nevertheless a handsome place to visit; usually deserted, it fills up on weekends and in peak summer months. An even bigger attraction than the handsome hilltop church, **St. Barrahane's,** is the justifiably famous pub and restaurant, **Mary Ann's** ✹✹ (Main St.; ☎ 028/36146). It's a worthy stop even if not for a full (sometimes pricey) meal; the atmosphere is first-rate, and there's an art gallery upstairs.

The mellow fishing village of **Baltimore** ✹✹ is a good base for diving, sailing, and ferry trips to the remote and population-deprived islands of **Sherkin** ✹✹✹ and **Cape Clear** ✹✹. The latter is a Gaeltacht (Irish-speaking) area, meaning that Irish customs and traditions are practiced here—albeit by a mere 150 or so residents. The best way to experience this (although it's also the busiest time on the island), is during the annual **Cape Clear International Storytelling Festival** (www.capeclearstorytelling.com), held in September. Sherkin, the smaller of the two islands (population 120), can be circumnavigated on foot in a few hours—often you'll encounter nothing but sheep, cows, gorgeous beaches, and natural harbors. Close to the pier where you'll alight from the ferry is a ruined 15th-century Franciscan abbey, and just north are the remains of a castle built by the O'Driscolls, a notorious pirate clan that was headquartered on Sherkin.

Getting There & Getting Around

Skibbereen lies on the **N71A;** a handful of **buses** arrive from Cork (via Clonakilty) each day, and there is one bus from Killarney. Baltimore is 13km (8 miles) southwest of Skib along the **R595;** buses ply the route weekdays throughout the year, and Saturdays in summer. From Baltimore, **ferries to the islands** depart from the main pier: Departures to Cape Clear Island (**Cailín Óir;** ☎ 086/346-5110 or 028/39159; www.cailinoir.com; €14 round-trip) are less frequent than those for Sherkin Island (☎ 087/911-7377 or 028/20125; €10 round-trip; 8 daily departures in summer), a mere 10 minutes away.

Where to Stay & Dine

SKIBBEREEN

€€   Although Skibbereen doesn't have any watery views, it does offer a bigger variety of pubs, restaurants, and nightlife than Baltimore, so stay here if you want to be near the action. Another reason to stay is to spend a night at Mona Best's sumptuous Victorian-era **Bridge House** ✹✹✹ (Bridge St.; ☎ 028/21273; cash only). Overflowing with flowers, every room is dressed up as though you've entered a scene from Moulin Rouge. Yes, the three bedrooms are unique, with drapery, antique hairbrushes, pink-faced dolls in one, and a red boudoir-theme in the next. Only one room is en suite, while the other two share a big bathroom with a tub and a fireplace. Mona—or "Lady Mona" as she's known in Skib—says she runs her B&B as a hobby: "It's about having interesting people over—it's not about money!" For sheer pizzazz, memorable decor, and the warmest hospitality, this is a firm favorite, and as if that isn't enough, Mona tells me that her breakfasts are always photographed before being eaten—"They're so beautiful!" Doubles go for €75.

€–€€€ There may be more refined eateries in town, but I love the country kitchen feel of Angela Hurley's restaurant at **Annie May's** ✦ (11 Bridge St.; ☎ 028/22930; daily 8:30am–9pm or later; may close 3–5pm; cash only), while the *craic* in the attached old-fashioned bar is always authentic. The restaurant serves a range of old lunchtime favorites—the Irish stew here is among the best I've had (€10); and there's shepherd's pie (€9); sandwiches (from €3.50); and soup served with a crispy baguette (€3.50). Angela has a few compact, functional guest rooms, with tiny en suite showers, upstairs; a workable alternative should you find Bridge House full. You'll pay €70 to €80 for two people.

€–€€€€ If you favor culinary razzle dazzle over home-sourced recipes, **Over the Moon** ✦✦✦ (46 Bridge St.; ☎ 028/22100; www.overthemoonskibbereen.com; Mon–Sat noon–3pm and 6–10pm; Sun 5:30–8:30pm; AE, MC, V) might as well be the poster restaurant for Skib. Jennifer and François Conradie make good use of their proximity to great fresh fish, locally reared beef, duck, and lamb, not to mention an endless supply of cheeses. Lunch time prices are less fierce, and there's no beating the mussels here; plucked this morning from Roaring Water Bay, they're cooked with white wine, chorizo, garlic, and shallots (€10). Then there's warm confit duck salad with semi-sundried tomatoes, green beans, and Gabriel cheese (€8)—a good hint of the kind of tasteful experimentation the kitchen gets up to.

BALTIMORE

€€ On the mainland, a short way out of Baltimore back towards Skibbereen and up one heck of a steep driveway, Marguerite O'Driscoll's **Rathmore House** ✦ (Baltimore; ☎ 028/20362; www.baltimorebb.com; MC, V) comes as a real surprise—a great value with a spectacular location staring down at Baltimore Harbour. Of the six guest rooms—adequately sized, comfy beds, wardrobes, small showers—only three face the water, so I'd insist on one of these; room 4 is the best of the doubles, or take the big family room, no. 5. Doubles cost €70 to €75; singles are €45.

€€–€€€ On a hill above Baltimore, what was long a hostel now offers some of the most peaceable accommodation around. **Rolf's Country House** ✦✦ (kids) (Baltimore Hill; ☎ 028/20289; www.rolfsholidays.eu; MC, V) has 14 neat rooms with pine floors, good little en suite showers, tip-top beds, and a full-house of in-room amenities; going for €80 to €100 double (€50–€60 single), including breakfast served in a country-style cafe with views of the islands over Baltimore's rooftops. Also available are a handful of self-catering apartments: These have two upstairs bedrooms (each with three single beds which can be turned into doubles), while down below are well-equipped kitchens with open fireplaces to warm the living area; there's also a separate laundry room. Weekly rates are between €500 and €800 (mid-summer is most expensive; June and Sept are €650). Shorter stays are possible, but work out to be more expensive. Rolf's is set in a mature garden, with lovely outdoor seating areas and two donkeys to amuse the children. The restaurant (daily 8–11am, 12:30–2:45pm and 6–9:30pm) and wine bar here are highly regarded; besides serving everything from sandwiches (€5.50–€6.50) to monkfish (€22), they double as a gallery for revolving art exhibits with a local focus.

€–€€€   Lunch at **Glebe Garden & Café** ★★ (Glebe Gardens, Baltimore; ☎ 028/
20232; www.glebegardens.com; Easter–May Sat–Sun 10am–6pm; June–Aug Wed–
Sun 10am–late; MC, V) is an opportunity for more than just a meal. You'll dine on
wholesome, healthful food in gorgeous natural surroundings—the floral, woodland, herb, and vegetable gardens are an attraction in themselves, and boast an
exhilarating view over the water. Lunch is a particular treat here as meals are light,
seasonal, and often straight from the garden (like carrot and cardamom soup, €6;
or red pepper and goat cheese quiche, €9.50). From June, evenings liven up, too,
when former London River Club chef, Gillian Hegharty, prepares the meals following the same philosophy of preparing simple, hearty meals with top ingredients—beef stews; lamb served with garden vegetables; and good vegetarian
options. Outdoor music concerts are also held here.

ON SHERKIN ISLAND

€€   The **Horseshoe Cottage** ★ 🧒 (☎ 087/797-2366, 087/996-1557 or 028/
20598; www.gannetsway.com; cash only), a simple three-bedroom place, has no
frills but a perfect setting overlooking Horseshoe Bay, and is a truly soulful place,
ideal for absolute escape. You'll receive a warm welcome from the Astons—Joe
(a fishing skipper who provides ocean adventures) and Fiona (a homeopath who
obliges with holistic massage). A shortish walk from the pier (the Aston's have an
electric buggy to collect luggage), the Jolly Roger is the nearest pub (around 10
min. away) and usually serves meals, but the Astons can prepare food for guests—
freshly caught barbequed mackerel is a favorite. In mid-2008, Joe started building a new sunroom-cum-dining area, and was planning two family-size
bedrooms, but he says that "only God knows when they'll be ready." In the meanwhile, at €80 for two, it's a good value; or, for €300, you can combine 2 nights
with a full day's sailing.

MIZEN HEAD PENINSULA

Vertical cliffs, boulder-strewn coves, and the ever-looming presence of Mount
Gabriel—that's just part of the reward for making the effort to see Ireland's "Most
Southwesterly Point" at the population-deprived tip of the Mizen Head peninsula. With its friendly harbor and string of lodgings, the main town Schull (pronounced "skull") is well-geared for watersports, and draws a large following to its
sailing regatta in August. But the main rewards here are the unfettered tranquility offered by more remote spots. Ten minutes from Schull, Goleen is one of those
"blink and you'll miss it" pitstops, but turn off the main road and you reach one
of the best-located seafood restaurants in Cork, overlooking a tidal inlet where
fishing boats bob and seabirds glide. Wend your way around a sharp crook in the
coastline, and you come to tiny Crookhaven—an empty little village most of the
year, but swollen with Irish vacationers in summer. Bucolic charms aside, though,
the top reason to venture along this coastline, is for the thrill at the "lands end"-
style Mizen Head Signal Station, where the crash of waves against the rocky cliff
below you will redefine your place in the grand scheme of things.

Getting There & Getting Around

Drive west along the **N71** from Skibbereen until you reach Ballydehob; from
there, follow signs due west towards Schull and then on to Goleen and eventually

as far as the Mizen Head Lighthouse. **Bus** services travel only as far as Goleen from Cork and West Cork.

Where to Stay & Dine

For total privacy, rent out **Reen Cottage** ✫✫✫ 🌟 (Toormore, Goleen; ☎ 086/ 273-5150 or 01/295-0113; www.reencottage.com; MC, V), a handsome-yet-modern one-storey slate-roof cut-stone cottage on the road between Schull and Goleen. Not only is it large (4 bedrooms—2 en suites, plus a bathroom downstairs), but you have huge, wild lawns out front, and sumptuous views over the nearby cove. Decor is ideal for a seaside holiday: Lots of pine furniture, lots of space, and nothing that screams any particular style or aesthetic bent—it's just a straightforward, comfortable holiday spot with picture windows, a huge dining table in the big, fully fitted kitchen (laundry facilities, too), and the type of lounge (upstairs, to take full advantage of the view) where the whole family can gather to play board games or chill out in front of the fire (games, DVD-player, and satellite TV provided). Rental starts at €600 per week, but goes up to €1,100 in peak periods; oil and electricity are extra (€50–€75 per week), towels not included.

€€   Since Goleen is so rudimentary and downright deserted, it comes as a surprise to find it has a famous seafood restaurant with five hotel-standard bedrooms upstairs. The digs at **Heron's Cove** ✫ (The Harbor, Goleen; ☎ 028/35225; www. heronscove.com; AE, DC, MC, V) are large, tidy, and comfortable, if not luxurious (doubles are €80; family-size triples cost €100); thoughtful touches (like in-room CD-players, and a voluminous library in the passage) complement the harborfront views (teeming with seabirds) from your queen-size bed. And that's without mentioning the food and wine downstairs. Presided over by chef Sue Hill, the **restaurant** ✫✫✫ (summer daily 7–9pm; reservations essential, particularly Oct–Mar) serves excellent, splurge-worthy dishes (mains start at €20) like pan-fried monkfish served with walnut mayo (€27). Unique to Sue's restaurant are sprats (a local sardine-like fish), which are smoked and served as a tasty starter (€10).

€€€   In the heart of the peninsula, on a lush farmstead, is perhaps the best B&B in Ireland, **Rock Cottage** ✫✫✫ (Barnatonicane, Schull; ☎ 028/35538; www.rockcottage.ie; MC, V). Barbara Klötzer came to this Georgian house in 1996 and in two years transformed a dilapidated space (no electricity or running water) into a home with dreamy rooms and inviting public spaces. Outside, sheep trim the fields, and a short stroll takes you into a tree-canopied landscape. From the raised lookout point, the 360° views are among the most memorable you'll experience on your trip—mountains, farmlands, and Sheep's Head Peninsula across Dunmanus Bay, are all visible. Inside, the chic country-style bedrooms have high Georgian ceilings, wooden floors, modern cane furniture, and muted tones offset by bright accents—framed artworks, big mirrors, and healthy potted plants complete the effect. Little touches—like a full range of toiletries, French press coffee, and a chocolate on your pillow—emphasize Barbara's Teutonic attention to detail; at breakfast, too, she pulls no punches, offering some sublime and exquisitely presented choices. The B&B rate is €130 per night. If you'd prefer more privacy, Barbara rents a converted stable and hay-loft building behind her house; the loft-style apartment sleeps three and is kitted out with all you could hope for—weekly rates run €350 to €620.

Why You're Here: Exploring the Mizen Head

As you wend your way toward Mizen Head on the N71, at the tip of the peninsula, you'll pass cove beaches protected by outstretched craggy fingers. Raggedy low stone walls curve, dip, and weave through fields and grassland until you finally reach **Mizen Head Signal Station** ★★★ (☎ 028/35115; www.mizenhead.ie; €6; daily June–Sept 10:30am–6pm; mid-Mar to May and Sept 10:30am–5pm; Nov to mid-Mar Sat–Sun 11am–4pm). Whatever you do, don't forget a pair of binoculars—even from the parking lot you can watch seabirds nesting in the plunging cliffs. Once you get here, grab your tickets and head straight for the signal station (the visitor center is a silly distraction). From above, the Mizen Head looks like a set of beautiful pincers, constantly ravished by the pounding, riotous ocean waves. It's a famous, totally painless "99 steps" down (coming back is another story) towards the arched bridge that feels like it's connecting the mainland to an island. Crossing the narrow bridge is a totally safe, thrilling sensory assault, high above the tumultuous waters. The signal station itself is now mechanized and what were once offices and quarters for the men who worked here, are now a bizarre series of exhibitions memorializing the manly world of lighthouse-keeping. Never mind that; as the wind gushes around your head, perhaps threatening to blow you off, you'll be full to bursting with a Wagnerian opera of crashing waves and dancing clouds. Don't forget to locate the position of tiny Fastnet Lighthouse 14.5km (9 miles) to the west.

SHEEP'S HEAD PENINSULA

Possibly my favorite of all the dreamy peninsulas in Cork and Kerry, it's hard not to feel as though you've entered a coastal wilderness on this remote sliver of land, an unhurried, unspoiled, and—as you get farther from the mainland—practically untouched place. Best of all, there's no pressure here to "do" or "see" anything. No museums, no fancy restaurants, no visitor attractions or interpretative centers: You come here to commune with nature, to find pleasure in solitude, and disappear into the spectacle of waves bashing the rugged headland cliffs.

Getting There & Getting Around

Commence your exploration of Sheep's Head by driving (or cycling) either from Durrus (on the **R591,** between the Mizen Head Peninsula and Bantry) or by traveling due west from Bantry; either way, the trip can be undertaken as a circular route.

Where to Stay & Dine

€–€€   In peaceful, tiny Kilcrohane, Ann Donegan's yellow, one-storey **Bridge View House** ★ (☎ 027/67086; www.bridgeviewhouse.com; cash only) is a good-value B&B that has the advantage of offering home-cooked meals (useful in this remote region). Ann charges a mere €60 to €68 per night.

€€   Around 14km (8⅔ miles) from Durrus, roughly midway along the peninsula, is **Reenmore Farmhouse** ★ (Ahakista, Durrus; ☎ 027/67051; www.reenmore. com; MC, V), a traditional working dairy farm at the seaside. Spacious, simple bedrooms are awash in pastels and have large beds—my favorite has views of Reenmore Bay (ask for the "green room"). You can chill on the patio, explore the farm, or wander down to the strand; an energetic walk will get you to the Bay View pub—or Eileen's in Kilcrohane—if you need sustenance and company. A double room costs €70, with a proper farmhouse breakfast.

€€ Sue and Roger Goss have it real good. They gave up the urban bliss of cool London to settle in one of the most beautiful locations anywhere in Ireland. Remote, faraway, timeless. However you want to describe the location of **Ballyroon Mountain** ✪✪✪ (3km/2 miles from Sheep's Head lighthouse; ☎ 027/67940; www.ballyroonmountain.com; cash only), words will be inadequate. On an expansive landscape terraced all the way down to the shore, Sue and Roger offer a pretty en suite cottage. That's it. This isn't a B&B, nor a guesthouse. You get a stone cottage (with stone floors, wood frame bed, chest of drawers, hanging rack, desk, mini-fridge, and stove fire) all to yourself for €80 (and €70 for each night after the first). It's cleverly outfitted with the essentials for a romantic getaway (corkscrew/bottle opener, books, DVD-player with films, CD player and CDs), and comes with the knowledge that your hosts will always be nearby should you require anything over and above the breakfasts served in their conservatory; they'll also prepare dinners (€25–€30 for three courses) with a little notice. By day you can watch whales and dolphins, or peregrines and chuffs; or hike to forests, streams, waterfalls, and bogs. At night, Roger will gladly drop by and fetch you if you want to hit the nearest pub (which is definitely not just around the corner) where there's live music in winter, and always a top crowd. When I reminisce about Ballyroon, I'm overcome with longing.

€€–€€€ In Durrus, which is more a gateway to the peninsula than on Sheep's Head itself, you can eat at one of the southwest's best: **Good Things Café** ✪✪✪ (Ahakista Rd.; ☎ 021/62896; daily 12:30–3pm and 6:30–9pm; MC, V), where (late) brunch, lunch, dinner, and food-to-go are available, and there's an excellent cooking school as well (p. 231). Carmel Somers is the creative force—and energetic spirit—behind this much-praised venture where inspiration is drawn from the recipes and styles of the great names in Irish cooking. Seasonal, organic, local, and fresh are the watchwords here, and the finest ingredients combine for memorable dishes like a lunchtime pizza with Swiss chard, Durrus cheese, and nutmeg (€14), or Piperade (eggs lightly scrambled with a mixture of Provencal vegetables, €10). And for all her culinary flair (and loads of favorable reviews), you'll still find Carmel—her hair tucked into a bandana—hard at work in her big open-plan kitchen.

BANTRY TO GLENGARRIFF

Set on opposite ends of the head of Bantry Bay, Glengarriff and Bantry get a lot of hype, and are busy holiday spots. Bantry's short list of attractions is dominated by an aristocratic Georgian mansion with elaborately laid-out gardens and an enviable view across Bantry Bay. After leisurely strolling through the grounds, you can explore the house's decadent salons—filled with rare collections from around the world. Just 14km (8⅔ miles) away, Glengarriff is known for its subtropical microclimate which sustains a lush botany; these conditions have best been exploited on **Garinish Island** where exotic fantasy gardens were established in the early-20th century. Glengarriff itself feels touristy, but is a useful striking out point for one-with-nature hikes and trips around the Beara Peninsula.

Getting There & Getting Around

It's good to know that the **N71** which stretches from Cork to Killarney also passes through Bantry and Glengarriff, linking these towns and connecting them with other important centers in West Cork. **Bus Éireann** runs daily services from Cork to Bantry (as many as 12 departures per day Mon–Sat; €14; 2 hr.), and there are a limited number of buses connecting both towns with Killarney and Kenmare in the summer (June–Sept).

Where to Stay & Dine

Glengarriff is the traditional "gateway" to the Beara Peninsula, but its abundance of souvenir shops and shabby layout undermine its appeal. Bantry, too, feels more built-up than it needs to be, and doesn't compete with other spots along the coast.

€   You'll escape all the touristic hustle and bustle if you forsake the seafront altogether, and head inland, along peaceful back roads to one of my favorite West Cork escapes: **Hagal Healing Farm** ✪✪ (Coomleigh West, Bantry; ☎ 027/66179; www.hagalholistichealth.com; MC, V). A haven for tranquility-seekers, it's also a down-to-earth place for massage courses, organic cooking classes, and treatments in all kinds of natural and holistic therapies (see "The Other West Cork," p. 231). If you take part in one of those, the cost of accommodations will be factored in with the price of the course. You can also take a room on a purely B&B basis for €70 double; €50 to €60 single. Rooms are simple, but with pleasing touches, like slippers, hot water bottles, and access to a kitchen, relaxation room, and sauna. A large self-catering wooden sod-roof cottage with three bedrooms more suitable for families (kids can make more noise down here) is also available; it sleeps six or seven people and costs €100 to €125 per night (2-night minimum, linen and towels are extra). If you really want to rough it (but still have access to facilities enjoyed by other guests), camping sites are available. Two people camping pay €15.

IN & AROUND BANTRY

Actually, unless you rent a self-catering unit at **Bantry House's Gatelodge** ✪ (☎ 027/50047; www.bantryhouse.com), I wouldn't stay in Bantry at all. Here, for between €450 and €750 per week, you get an attractive two-bedroom unit on the massive Bantry estate, with access to its house and gardens.

€   Alternatively, head a few miles north to Ballylickey, which is more serene. A raised position, with an unimpeded view across the entire Bantry Bay gives **Aran Lodge B&B** (Ballylickey; ☎ 086/063-1361 or 027/50378; www.aran-lodge.com; MC, V) a bit of an edge over nearby, similar guest lodgings. The professionalism of owners Deidre and Joe O'Connell is also a plus; they provide quality bedrooms and substantial breakfasts for €70 (ask for one of the two rooms overlooking the Bay). On offer, too: A self-catering chalet with two double bedrooms for those who prefer more independence and privacy; it's €400 per week in peak season.

IN GLENGARRIFF

€€   Donal Deasy's great grandmother started **Casey's Hotel** ✪ (Glengarriff Village; ☎ 027/63010; www.caseyshotelglengarriff.ie; MC, V) back in 1884, and it's still going strong. Ask for one of the refurbished bedrooms (€80–€94 double), as these are fresher and altogether more comfortable, with shiny bedcovers, decent carpets and sparkling new (small) bathrooms (some with tubs). As you enter the lobby, you're usually hit by the aroma of fish being prepared for locals who frequent the bar—a worthy diversion for meals priced between €10 and €21, with specials for about €13.

Why You're Here: Top Sights & Attractions

Bantry House and Garden ✸✸ (☎ 027/50047; www.bantryhouse.com; €10; Mar–Oct daily 10am–6pm) enjoys a prime position overlooking Bantry Bay. From up here, you get the impression that the lords of the manor—the Whites—must have felt like they owned the whole world. Splendid as the natural vista is, try to tear yourself away to check out the lavish interior. Obsessed with collecting rare and luxurious things, Richard White (the Earl of Bantry) filled his home with one-of-a-kind furniture, artworks, and downright unusual objects. There are Gobelin tapestries that once belonged to King Louis Phillip and another which Louis XV hung at Versailles. One of the standout exhibits is right near the entrance—a Russian household shrine with icons dating to the 15th and 16th centuries. Upstairs bedrooms provide a window into the private (and less flamboyant) lives of the aristocracy; on the walls up the stairway, read a few of the startlingly sycophantic letters from the people of Bantry expressing their allegiance to the White family; and on the landing, glass cases display a variety of stuffed birds, cleverly juxtaposed with Edward Traviés "life" drawings of dead birds. It's a pity, though that the collection doesn't come with a decent guide, making it hard to gauge the worth of each item.

Glengarriff is famed for its forests and meadows; there's good reason to jump off here and set out on foot to discover waterfalls, bogs, and **Sugarloaf Mountain,** one of the low peaks of the Caha Mountain Range.

If you prefer your greenery more organized—perhaps with a dose of fantasy— then climb on a **ferry** bound for **Garinish Island** ✸✸✸ kids (☎ 027/63040; Heritage Card or €3.70; Mon–Sat mid-Mar to Oct 10am–4pm; Apr–June and Sept 10am–6:30pm; July–Aug 9:30am–6:30pm; reduced hours on Sun), 1.5km (1 mile) from Glengarriff. En route, you'll catch glimpses of seals balancing on rocky islets in the harbor, and end up on a little manmade garden paradise known colloquially as Ilnacullin. It's a place for contemplation—Shaw apparently found inspiration for his *Saint Joan* here—and I've often thought it would be the ideal venue for a full-moon party; a huge fantastical garden built for no other reason than sensory pleasure. Yet, despite being an oasis today, it started out as no more than a barren rock; a businessman named Annan Bryce purchased the island in 1900 and, with the help of architect and landscaper, Harold Peto, converted it into a horticultural paradise using large-scale gardening and escapist architecture. Plants from around the world have matured here, and there are enchanting built sections, too, like the Italianate garden's *casita*, and a miniature temple. Although you can explore it all pretty quickly, don't come here in a rush; the pleasure comes with the peace and solitude among the trees and shrubs (and with discovering remarkable, exotic species here, too). So, consider packing a lunch (there's also a cafe on the island) and take your time. **Blue Pool Ferry** (☎ 027/63333; www.bluepoolferry.com) provides the cheapest ride (€10; departs every ½ hr.)

THE BEARA PENINSULA

Just so you know, friends of mine who've lived in the southwest all their lives, are quick to suggest (in whispered tones, of course) that they prefer the Beara Peninsula to the famous Ring of Kerry. "It's shorter," they say, "and we think it's prettier. Besides, you hardly see a bus." Indeed, the Beara Peninsula does feel undiscovered and is free of the type of tourist traffic that can clog the main roads of the much-hyped Iveragh Peninsula (aka the Ring of Kerry, p. 174). For the benefit of unchoked roads alone it's worth coming, while the staggering views of plunging, dropaway cliffs, particularly along the northern coastline, make this—to my mind at least—a must-see.

Beara was once an important copper mining region, and the legacy of those that worked the mines is now captured in an unremarkable **mine museum** in the pretty artist retreat village of **Allihies,** towards the peninsula's west. At land's end, a cable car can take visitors to near-deserted **Dursey Island,** one of those quirky, remote spots where almost nothing happens, except some ardent bird-watching.

Getting There & Getting Around

You can do the **Ring of Beara** as a day trip—at around 140km (87 miles), it's an easy route and the interminable beauty takes the sting out of driving. You can also break the journey up, particularly useful if you're doing this as a hiking or cycling tour (the **Beara Way;** 200km/124 miles), by choosing to overnight here, preferably at the peninsula's far reaches.

From Glengarriff, follow the **R572** all the way to the very end of the peninsula where you could hop aboard the cable car (infrequent, odd hours) to Dursey Island, then double back for about 8km (5 miles) and follow the R575 towards **Allihies** and **Eyeries.** At Eyeries, depart from the main road (now the R571) and instead take the rural coastal-hugging road to **Ardgroom** (it'll take you much longer, but the views are magnificent). At Ardgroom, rejoin the R571 and continue to **Lauragh;** again, leave the main route and take the R573 to **Tuosist;** from there, the R571 follows the coast to Kenmare. Of course, you can do all this in reverse—which many say offers even finer viewing possibilities.

Where to Stay & Dine

Castletownbere is the biggest town on the peninsula, with a large natural harbor supporting a lucrative fishing industry; there's lodging and dining aplenty here, but I think the Beara's charms lie in more remote, restful spots further west.

€€　In a brightly painted yellow and lilac house on Allihies' main road, **Sea View B&B** ✹ (Beara; ☎ 027/73004; www.seaviewallihies.com; MC, V) has 10 large, well-lit, wood-floor en suite bedrooms (some with tubs), each painted in a different, bright color. Request one with a bit of a sea-view—although these look over the road, there's not an awful lot of noise around here. The hostess, Mary O'Sullivan, runs a tight ship and charges €74 double.

€–€€€　Even if you're just passing through, stop at **O'Neill's Bar** ✹ (Allihies Village; ☎ 027/73008; bar daily noon–9pm; restaurant daily 6–10pm; MC, V) for one of their famous crab sandwiches (€6; chew carefully, as bits of shell do get in with the shredded crabmeat). Or try something heartier and more adventurous, like chicken breast stuffed with black pudding (€16). Upstairs, the restaurant serves pricier dishes in a smart setting.

Attention, Shoppers!

If you are going to shop anywhere this far west in Cork, then it must be at **Adrigole Arts** ✪✪✪ (Adrigole Village; ☎ 027/60234; www.adrigolearts.com) which sells high-end, top-quality products by leading (and emerging) Irish artists and craftspeople. Look out in particular for Jill Bradly's large oil canvases of West Cork scenes; John Hurley's awesome seascapes; Marika O'Sullivan's jewelry which combines silver with lively, vivid colors; unique textured scarves and table runners from Kerry Woolen Mills; handmade Tedagh Candles; ceramics by Mairi Stone or the famous Jim Turner; porcelain and earthenware by Sara Roberts; and more oil paintings of the West Coast by Michael F. Downes. The shop is in a house on the R572 just outside tiny Adrigole; don't blink.

THE OTHER WEST CORK

West Cork is a haven for people who have chosen to embrace an alternative, creative or "less-commercial" way of life. That's doable here thanks to the inspiration offered by the landscape and of course, the low population density. Many of these people have discovered that they are teachers, too, and offer classes, workshops, and courses designed for people who aren't in a rush.

Reconnect with Yourself & Meet Like-minded Souls

Hagal Healing Farm (see "Where to Stay & Dine," p. 228) is a very special place, way off the beaten track, where Ireland's in-the-know go to meditate, contemplate, detox, recuperate, and—yeah, man—chill out, too. The lovechild of Janny and Fred Wieler, it was founded nearly 30 years ago and over the years has evolved into a holistic retreat set amidst 2 hectares (5 acres) of mature gardens—much of it wild and untamable.

Many different kinds of courses and workshops are hosted here: Reiki, massage, yoga, and there's even been a shaman workshop. But the one that got me excited is Fred's totally unique cooking course which not only imparts recipes, but also explores issues involving the energy of food. You learn how to confidently pick herbs and leaves from the garden, and how best to use them to add flavor and character to vegetarian dishes. These 2-day weekend courses cost €210 and include all meals, and accommodation on the Saturday night (you can also extend your stay over the Fri and Sun).

Time spent at Hagal is a sure-fire way to meet Irish people also looking to reinvent themselves. Yes, there are wind chimes and tie-dyed cloth, but also plenty of meaningful discussions around what it all means.

Connect with the Kitchen

Her cooking has been called the best in West Cork and she inevitably contends with the heavyweight in the all-Ireland division. Carmel Somers, the owner-chef at **Good Things Café** (☎ 027/61426; www.thegoodthingscafe.com), teaches some of the most successful and raved-about cooking classes in the country ("It started as an experiment," she recalls, "but demand has been so good . . ."). She uses the same kitchen in which she prepares food for her restaurant (see "Where to Stay &

Dine," on p. 226). The big menu of class options ranges from demonstration sessions (around €120 for a day), 1- and 2-day classes (around €195 for 2 days), to week-long professional courses. Classes are small (eight students in practical classes, 15 in demos), so you don't feel like a number in a crowd. While there's a lot of learning going on, there's also plenty of tasting, and tea and coffee (and wine, when appropriate) are provided; some classes inevitably lead to get-togethers, parties, and late-night dining sessions. Her method emphasizes the importance of using fresh, quality, organic ingredients—in one class, Carmel even encourages students to rear their own pigs!

Discover the Artist's Way

Adrian Wistreich quit the London rat race for the solitude of life just outside Kinsale. Now, this publisher-turned-potter runs and hosts a variety of classes and workshops at his **Kinsale Pottery & Art School** (Olcote, Balinacurra, Kinsale; ☎ 021/477-7758; www.kinsaleceramics.com). Wistreich now inspires around 300 people per year, and most of them are locals, although people come from all over to zero in on his effortless style.

You can take part in a 1-day pottery course, but you'll then miss out on the firing process and the thrill of seeing your work when it comes out the kiln. A weekend is ideal—you'll learn how to throw pots and hand build using clay; basic techniques include coiling and slabbing, and you also get to try out decorative processes like slip-painting, sgraffito, underglazing, and glazing. Such a course costs €225 (or €200 if you bring a friend) and includes lunch and all materials; all you need are some old clothes. Adrian makes the learning fun and easy; he subscribes to the notion that most people simply "don't understand their power" as creative beings, so for him, "teaching is about helping people reach their potential." I couldn't imagine a more Zen setting for a creative class—just less than 2km (about a mile) outside Kinsale, when you step outside the workshop and find yourself looking over fields dotted with grazing cows, and a gorgeous river flowing down to the harbor. If pottery isn't quite your scene, you might also want to investigate some of the many other classes that Adrian runs and arranges; these include bronze casting, mosaic, stained glass, glass fusing, jewelry-making, and drawing and painting, too.

While Adrian caters to a fairly broad spectrum of interests and sometimes has fairly large classes, some might prefer the more focused and intimate approach of the ceramics classes taught by **Jim Turner** (www.rossmorepottery.com or write to potterywithjim@gmail.com), one of Ireland's most respected ceramicists. Jim focuses especially on creating unique textured surfaces that look and feel organic, almost primordial. A virtuoso teacher, Jim conducts small workshops relatively infrequently (half a dozen per year), and these include 1-day taster classes (€95) in which you learn the traditional raku style of pottery and get an introduction to throwing. Although time restraints mean that you glaze and decorate a ready made piece, Jim does make you work quite hard, and the process is wonderfully exciting.

One of the more unique learning opportunities I've come across, are Alison Opsina's chair-making workshops in the off-the-beaten track village of Rossnagoose, near Skibbereen. Alison's designs are inspired by nature; they're rustic, totally organic furniture pieces made with "green" or unseasoned hazelwood.

In her classes, Alison teaches students to use the natural characteristics of the wood to inspire the final look of the chair—she wants to retain the energy of the original materials in the final product. It's a fascinating process, and students do return home with a solid understanding of how to work creatively and organically with wood (as well as their own chairs). A full 3-day chair-making course at Alison's **Green Wood Chairs** (☎ 028/21890; www.greenwoodchairs.com) costs €550, including all materials, and there are never more than two students per workshop. If time is a constraint, Alison offers a 1-day session in which you'll learn to make a stool or a table, for €185.

6

At the Mouth of the Shannon: County Clare

Some of Ireland's greatest hits, from the Cliffs of Moher to the Burren

by Keith Bain

I SUSPECT THAT OUR ANCIENT ANCESTORS ALONG IRELAND'S WESTERN seaboard might have imagined themselves at the edge of the earth. Here—in peaceable Clare, the county that encloses the northern shores of the River Shannon's 80km (50-mile) estuary—they likely saw the workings of a fierce and furious power, a force so great that it appears to have ripped away the land, leaving a jagged rocky outcrop to be forever hammered by the waves and pounded by Atlantic storms. Today, locals still sometimes speak of a mystical, mysterious power at work here, and there's much written about the magical aura that hangs over the region; perhaps it's the same supernatural power that carved the awesome Cliffs of Moher—enormous walls of rock that plunge into the ocean; or perhaps the wild natural forces that created the strange moonlike landscape of the Burren. Whatever it is that's deigned to make Clare look the way it does, it sure has an eye for spectacle—just ask any camera-wielding tourist.

Thanks to this natural exhibition, Clare has become a major tourist draw (other big hits among visitors include dolphin-spotting opportunities in the Shannon Estuary, world-renowned golfing links, and faux-medieval banquets in revitalized castles). But despite the hubbub, the aura here, on the whole, is far from commercialized. The county remains one of the best in Ireland for authentic traditional music, and the genuine friendly welcome visitors get here harks back to what many call "the Old Ireland." Clare also has more than its fair share of lesser-known curiosities—the exposed promontory at Loop Head, the biggest surfable wave in Ireland (for experts only), and hundreds of ring forts and Neolithic tombs that dot the landscape like surreal calling cards left by an ancient Irish race.

DON'T LEAVE THE MOUTH OF THE SHANNON WITHOUT . . .

MOONWALKING IN THE BURREN   It's known as the land of fertile rock, a landscape of weird grey that comes as a shock in a country of infinite green. The strange beauty of the rocky terrain is magical and intriguing, inviting you to

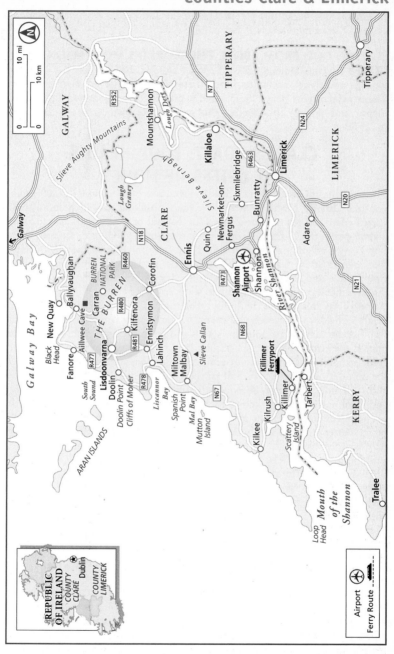

explore on foot, beckoning you to look for the unique and exotic flora that grows here, as if from the rock itself. See p. 243.

PLAYING GOD FROM ABOVE THE WORLD'S MOST MAGNIFICENT CLIFFS   Clare's famous Cliffs of Moher are the obvious draw for millions of tourists, and there's no faulting their dramatic allure (below). Further south, at Clare's westernmost point, Loop Head is practically undiscovered and has more rugged and varied cliffs, making this my favorite picnic spot in the country (p. 237).

CLARE'S COAST: LOOP HEAD & THE CLIFFS OF MOHER

The coastline of Clare shelters Ireland's biggest tourist attraction: the 300-million-year-old **Cliffs of Moher** ✪✪✪. Stretching out along 8km (5 miles) of Clare's ragged coast and rising some 214m (702 ft.) out of the Atlantic Ocean at their highest point, the Cliffs really do live up to the hype: They are a fantastical sight. The views are as impressive: On a clear day, from the edge of the cliffs, you'll see the Aran Islands, Galway Bay, as well as the Maum Turk Mountains in Connemara, and Loop Head to the south. It's unthinkable that you would pass through this way without stopping to walk along the edge.

And I say this despite the indisputable fact that the cliffs are being loved to death. Crowds, disgorged by busses on the hour, now jam large stretches of the rim. Recent additions of souvenir stands and an unnecessary visitor's center have marred the vista. The most spectacular (and highest) part of the Cliffs has been cordoned off for maximum tourist impact. But if you take the initiative (and have the time), it's still possible to find far more private spots from which to view the cliffs. All along the coast—between the surfing mecca of Lahinch to the south, and Doolin, a village well-known for its traditional music sessions, to the north—are opportunities to get out of your car and stare in amazement . . . and relative peace. Better still, you can hike the route (or part of it), stopping wherever you darn well feel like. So be sure to get off the beaten path; trust me, a little adventuring in this area will be rewarded.

As for that **Cliffs of Moher Visitor Centre** (☎ 065/708-6141; www.cliffsof moher.ie; free admission, audiovisual show €4; hours vary by month, daily winter 8:30 or 9am to 5 or 6pm, summer till 6:30 or 8:30pm), it went high-tech in 2007 with the opening of the new Visitor Experience, an interpretative exhibition and

Avoiding Parking Fees at the Cliffs of Moher

If you're loathe to part with your hard-earned cash, you could follow the many Irish folk who visit the Cliffs and refuse to use the official parking. They sneakily seek out a safe off-road spot along the side of the road within a couple of hundred meters of the center, and then walk. Just be sure not to park illegally (which means that you need to pull off the road completely).

Keeping Watch at Loop Head

As I've mentioned, Loop Head on the northern shore of the Shannon River has a wonderful land's end quality—wave-battered cliffs, dramatically swirling clouds, vast expanses of Atlantic Ocean, and hardly a sign of human habitation for kilometers around. The exception, of course, is the remote lighthouse station that marks the tip of this promontory, and has been operating here since 1670. Here, visitors have the opportunity to rent the three-bedroom **Loop Head Lightkeepers' House** ✪✪✪, which has been superbly restored, fitted out, and furnished by the Irish Landmark Trust (Reservations: 25 Eustace St., Temple Bar, Dublin 2; ☎ 01/670-4733; www.irishlandmark.com). Like all the Landmark Trust properties, accommodations have been designed to create a period atmosphere—interiors are neither modern nor old-fashioned—and decorated in a vaguely nautical theme. Shuttered windows, timber and mahogany furniture, a Victorian sofa and armchairs in front of an open fire, sturdy beds with crisp duvets, rugs on wooden floors, and an artful selection of framed pictures and prints and period lamps go toward creating an elegant, relaxed space for a peaceful stay. The kitchen has enough space for a pine table and *súgan* chairs made in nearby Kilrush. There's no TV—just a radio, a small library (with books on lighthouses and marine animals), and the drama of the ocean just outside (there's even a pair of binoculars on hand for spotting whales and dolphins). The house sleeps five people and costs €742 to €994 per week. While it's supplied with electricity and has oil heating, it isn't connected to a main water supply, so you need to bring in your own bottled water for drinking. And while you're significantly far away from the rest of the world, the nearest village, Kilbaha, is just 5km (3 miles) away and has a pub and a shop. You should definitely do your grocery shopping in either Ennis or Limerick. By the way, the lighthouse itself is now fully automated (and sadly out of bounds), so guests are no longer expected to man the watch.

audiovisual show that frankly seems a ridiculous add-on to the natural attraction you've come to see. The show is not worth the money; however, you may want to avail yourself of the free guided tours that happen daily at 11am and 2:30pm. *Note:* You don't necessarily need to visit the Cliffs when the center is open; you'll avoid the big crowds by arriving as the sun comes up, or at least before the center has opened.

Yes, the Moher Cliffs have mesmeric charm, but you definitely shouldn't miss Clare's other, less-discovered land's end experience, this time at the tip of the **Loop Head Peninsula** ✪✪✪, a horn-shaped spit of land that juts out of Clare at her most southern and westerly point, forming the upper lip of Shannon's mouth. Here, you're faced with truly precarious edge-of-the-world vistas of cliffs and craggy careening rock caves and water-battered sheer drops. While the Cliffs

Rentals Throughout Clare

Clare really is an ideal place to hole up for a while thanks, in part, to its abundance of comfy villa and condo rentals. The biggest agencies for these are both Limerick based and have a diverse spread of purpose-built houses (usually cluster-style developments) in convenient locations all around the county.

From **Rent An Irish Cottage** (☎ 061/411109; www.rentacottage.ie), for example, you could rent a modern semi-detached one-storey holiday home in a group of 12 such houses in Doolin. They're called **Doolin Court Holiday Homes** (an uninspiring name, I know) and have large open plan kitchen-cum-dining-cum-living areas and two bedrooms each. Furnishings are contemporary and you'll have most of the conveniences of home if, in some respects, modestly proportioned (TVs are small, and although the fireplace will keep you warm, don't expect a big, roaring extravaganza). Most importantly, they make a good base for exploring Clare's coast and the Burren, and you'll have Doolin's legendary music scene right on your doorstep. If you're going to stick around for a few days (on average, you'll pay around €440 for a week in a house sleeping five people), you can take advantage of nearby Doolin Pier's daily boat trips to the Aran Islands. The agency also has more traditionally styled cottages—with whitewashed walls and thatched roofs—right at the edge of the water in Ballyvaughan. It's a far larger development, called **Ballyvaughan Holiday Cottages,** with 33 cottages and up to four bedrooms, and weekly rates from €320.

An alternative Clare-wide agency is **West Coast Holidays** (www.west coastholidays.ie), which mainly deals in modern, purpose-built holiday homes, but in a number of choice locations, including Doolin, Kilkee, Lahinch, and Kilrush. Even if they're architecturally bland, they're far from off-putting, and these houses tend to be spacious and properly kitted out (decent furniture, plenty of gadgets, and good bedding). Some boast on-site extras, like tennis courts and children's play areas, or are in close

of Moher feel almost as though they've been tamed for the masses, Loop Head's tip is marked by little more than a large lighthouse complex (inaccessible) and a big parking area where you can leave your car (for free) and get out to explore the dramatic knob of land on foot. Across the water to the south you'll spot Kerry Head and Dingle Peninsula, while all along the edge you'll view an ever-changing drop-away coastline, with cliffs sculpted by Atlantic storms and tumultuous waters; cast your gaze upon the rock ledges and into the caves below, and you'll notice that they're home to seabirds and seals.

Indeed, go see the Cliffs of Moher, but know that you'll get a mighty kick and a greater sense of satisfaction out of visiting the seldom-seen Loop Head, an outing for which you must definitely pack a picnic and try to stick around for a magical sunset. Better still, you can hole up here for a few days by renting the Loop Head Lightkeepers' House (p. 237).

proximity to a reputable beach. Best deals are to be had at their Doolin properties. **Tir gan Éan,** for example, is on the grounds of a hotel (so you have access to the facilities there) slap-bang in the middle of Doolin, and offers a choice of either dormer-style or two-storey houses, each with three bedrooms and comfortably sleeping six people, with weekly rates starting at €320, or €420 to €499 in mid-season month. Slightly cheaper, but only sleeping five and located 2km (1¼ miles) from Doolin is **Doolin Holiday Village,** where the three-bedroom houses start at a mere €299 per week.

A final option: **Doolin Cottages** (Carnane, Doolin; ☎ 065/707-4187; www.doolincottages.com) is a small, family-run agency with a selection of nine cottages. Two of these are modern, semi-detached, side-by-side homes in Doolin village, while the rest are cute stone cottages on a hill with exceptional views over the surrounding landscape and, of course, the ocean. Decor is very much in the country aesthetic, with loads of wood (everywhere—floors, ceilings, furnishings, fittings) and a style that's per-haps best described as haphazard (they remind me a bit of slightly unkempt rural retreats visited on childhood holidays back in the '70s), but there's enough of everything (seating, bedding, appliances, space), and they're the types of cottages that encourage you to kick back and relax—after all, you're on holiday, and there's so much to see outside the cottage. Quality varies (as does size and number of bedrooms), but you're charged accordingly; two-bedroom units start at €250 per week (€430 in peak season), while the three-bedroom houses cost €320 to €650, depending on time of year. For romantics, there's also a quaint little one-bedroom house (€180–€330), newly renovated and fully equipped (if rather sparse), that's the perfect size for a couple—you certainly wouldn't have this amount of space (or privacy) in a hotel or guesthouse.

GETTING THERE

From Ennis to the visitor's center at the Cliffs of Moher, take the **N85** to Ennistymon; turn left onto the **N67** toward Lahinch. In Lahinch turn right onto the **R478,** passing through the village of Liscannor before reaching the Cliffs (approx. 35 min.). You'll notice a parking lot on the right side of the road, and will need to fork out €8 to park here.

If you're driving from Galway (approximately 1½ hr.), take the **N18** toward Limerick; in the village of Kilcolgan, take the **N67** for Ballyvaughan and continue to Lisdoonvarna. Turn right onto the **R478** signposted for the Cliffs of Moher, where the parking lot will be on the left.

To reach Loop Head from anywhere else in Clare, you'll need to head south to Kilrush (from Ennis, take the **N68**) and follow signs to Kilkee from there. Then head along the **R487,** passing a smattering of villages along the way. If you're setting off from Ennis, take the **N68** to Kilrush and follow signs to Kilkee from there.

WHERE TO STAY & DINE

Most people who want to stay on the coast near the Cliffs of Moher choose to bed down in **Doolin,** which is worth a visit if only for a taste of its legendary traditional music scene (there's something happening every single night in its three famous pubs). Doolin has a plethora of B&Bs, several hostels, and even a smart but bland little hotel; tourist buses make a point of stopping here, however, which can detract from the village ambience. The little harbor is a departure point for the quickest ferries to the Aran Islands (see chapter 7).

North of the Cliffs of Moher, **Lahinch** is popular with both golfers and surfers, with lodgings to satisfy both, while a little farther north is **Miltown Malbay,** a rather iffy little resort village that bursts to life during the Willie Clancy Summer School in July. Just north of here is one of the best B&Bs along this coast (see below), ideal for exploring the entire county. The area around **Spanish Point** (named for the Spanish Armada sailors who managed to make it ashore here after their ships were sunk in battle, only to be immediately executed by the British) is a final area hotspot, tops for families, thanks to a usable sandy beach.

NEAR MILTOWN MALBAY

€€   Between Loop Head and the Cliffs of Moher, Rita Meade's **Berry Lodge** ✫✫✫ (Annagh; ☎ 065/708-7022; www.berrylodge.com; MC, V) is ideal for exploring Clare's coast. Rita converted her family manse into a B&B and cookery school in 1994 and since then has offered among the loveliest, best-value lodgings in Clare. Accommodations emphasize the countryside setting (views of the surrounding farms stretch way off into the horizon, and two rooms have sea views), and although not lavish or huge, exude warmth and individual character that'll set you at rest. Rooms have wooden floors and cottage pine furniture, including wardrobes and luxurious beds; room 2 has the finest views. On arrival, you're welcomed with a tea and a baked treat just out the oven (I got a sinfully delicious chocolate torte on my last visit). Something of a culinary celebrity, Rita also prepares exquisite breakfasts—how about a cheesy mushroom waffle with bacon and mint-chive chutney cream?—and operates a seasonal restaurant; find out which nights of the week she's preparing evening meals, and plan accordingly.

Doolin

€–€€   With its attractive white and blue-shuttered exterior, **Páirc Lodge B&B** ✫ (Doolin; ☎ 065/707-4752; www.pairclodgedoolin.com; cash only), at the very end of lower Doolin, has a mildly Mediterranean feel. Here, in a modern home in the center of a neat garden, Rita Nagle offers unsuspectingly good value with up-to-date, exceptionally clean and orderly rooms going for €60 most of the year, and €65 to €70 in July and August. With plush beds (and thick, firm mattresses), attractive layout, and an innate sense of style, these guest rooms are among the very best in Doolin—and certainly the best value. The whole house, in fact, is sharply put together and wonderfully devoid of fussy frills and clutter. At breakfast, Rita pulls out all the stops with choices that go way beyond the ordinary.

€–€€€   You'll hear excellent traditional music at **McDermott's Pub** ★★★ (Doolin; ☎ 065/707-4328; food served daily noon–9:30pm; MC, V). While you're waiting for the musicians to arrive, settle in for hearty pub grub—Irish stew (€12), or a filling plate of bangers and beans (€8), guaranteed to soak up the Guinness.

€€–€€€€   Established in 1832, **Gus O'Conner's Pub** ★★ (Doolin; ☎ 065/707-4168; food served daily noon–9:30pm; MC, V) has nightly trad music sessions and hearty, filling traditional meals. Find a table and then step up to the bar where you order and pay first. The steamed garlic mussels (€13) is a mountainous affair, easily shared between everyone at the table, and the Irish beef stew (€11)—made with chunky potatoes and thick-sliced carrots—is the ideal late-lunch treat to cap off a visit to the nearby cliffs.

Quilty (Near Spanish Point)

€€   Many of the folks who start B&Bs do so because once their children are grown and moved away, they find that they have a house with too many empty bedrooms and, perhaps more importantly, they miss the sound of children giggling. You get the feeling that's the case at the **Clonmore Lodge** ★★ 🄺🄸🄳🅂 (Quilty; ☎ 065/708-7020; www.clonmorelodge.com; MC, V), a place that couldn't possibly be more welcoming . . . or family friendly. As a working farm, there are ponies for the wee ones to ride (at no extra cost), chickens to help feed and collect eggs from in the morning, and a small mini-golf course in the back. When Pauline Frommer visited with her family, Maire Daly, mistress of the house, sensing her 4-year-old was bored, invited the neighboring children over to play (now that's service!). Adults will enjoy the impromptu (and free) tour John gives most guests to a nearby ruined church and cemetery. A talented raconteur and amateur historian, he weaves compelling tales of the area along the course of the walk. As for the rooms themselves, they're knickknack laden and a tad worn, but spotlessly clean and certainly comfortable. Nothing special, but you don't come here for that, you come to the Clonmore Lodge for the privilege of joining the Daly family, at least for a short time. Rates range from €60 to €70 a night for a double including breakfast, €35 to €40 single, and €85 to €95 for a family room.

A Cool Cafe in Lahinch

€–€€€   As I've mentioned, Lahinch is something of a surfer's paradise, and those locals who aren't into golfing do try to cultivate a laid-back lifestyle. For a closer peek at this mellow surfer vibe, look no farther than **Joe's** ★★ 🄺🄸🄳🅂 (The Dell; ☎ 065/708-6113; www.joespizza.ie; daily June–Aug 9am–9pm; Feb–May and Sept–Dec 9am–5pm; MC, V), a colorful and unexpectedly classy (okay, in its own way) little cafe that serves up a great variety of dishes, starting with breakfast; sandwiches (served with chips and salad), and salads (€4.50–€7); pizzas (€7 for a "design your own" 10-incher); and going right through to hearty Moroccan lamb stew (€13) that'll warm you up after being out in the chilled Atlantic waters. Chalked-up specials (like chicken curry, €11, or carrot and parsnip soup, €4) appear daily, and there are plenty of lentil and vegetable-only dishes, too. Oh, and the washrooms are just too cool.

THE OTHER COAST OF CLARE

Clare's cliffs might draw tourists in droves, but what if you want to hang around a bit and get a deeper sense of Irish culture? I'd suggest hitting Miltown Malbay during the **Willie Clancy Summer School;** it's run by the Clare College for Traditional Studies and commemorates the town's best-known *uilleann* piper with the country's largest traditional music school (set dancing is offered, too). During the weeklong festival-style summer school, literally thousands of musicians, dancers, and singers descend on the area's classrooms and pubs to watch and listen. Lectures, workshops, and recitals fill out the program, and there's enough introductory material to make the school totally accessible to people with no prior experience or knowledge of Irish culture. So this is a chance to learn something new and meet new people, too. The summer school takes place in the first half of July; the program is posted on the **Clare College** website (www.oac.ie).

If you're passing through this part of the world, then Rita Meade is one of those fine, incredible local people you've got to meet. Particularly if cooking is one of your pleasures. Rita Meade has always been a teacher, but in 1994 she started a B&B (p. 240) and **cookery school** near the coastal resort town of Miltown Malbay. She works in a real country kitchen with an emphasis on fresh, natural, and organic ingredients, as well as Irish cooking and baking traditions. Rita's teaching is very hands on, so students get to work under her guidance rather than simply being shown what to do—she presents one or two courses each month, and each one is different from the last (because seasonal ingredients change). Rita understands that nobody wants to come to such a beautiful part of Ireland and spend the entire time in the kitchen, so her 5 hours of tuition are spread over 2 days—you can combine the course with 2 nights at her B&B (with the lunch and dinner you'll prepare in class) for €240. Non-cooking partners are welcome to join, even if they'd rather play golf. To sign up, visit **www.berrylodge.com**.

ACTIVE COAST OF CLARE

If the cooking set isn't really the crowd you want to mingle with—or if you're the outdoorsy sort, why not make Clare the place where you catch that wave and learn to surf? The bay at Lahinch opens to the Atlantic and is the "gateway" to the massive Aill na Searrach wave beneath the Cliffs of Moher, widely considered by local surfers to be the most perfect in the world, making Lahinch a surfing mecca. You can choose from several professionally run surf schools, but I think if you're going to brave these waters, you might as well team up with a top teacher. Irish surfing champ **John McCarthy** is not only a member of Ireland's national surfing team, but was one of the heroes who legendarily conquered the Aill na Searrach a few years back. He's imminently qualified, and if you're lucky enough to have him as one of your instructors at **Lahinch Surf School** (☎ 087/960-9667; www.lahinchsurfschool.com), you'll be able to ask him about his big wave experience. Classes—for kids and adults—cost €35 for a 2-hour session (of which 1½ hr. are spent in the water), with everything (wetsuits and surfboards) provided.

As I've hinted, golfing is big business in these parts, and Lahinch has a global reputation thanks to the Championship Course at the **Lahinch Golf Course** (Lahinch; ☎ 065/708-1003; www.lahinchgolf.com), renowned for both its design as well as its fantastic situation, with links stretching right along the edge of the Atlantic Ocean. Championship games have been hosted here since 1895, and you can play the Old Course for €165 (€83 students), or relax on the Castle Course for €55 (€25 students); on either course your second round is €40. Caddies cost €25 to €40 per round, per bag. When it gets busy, though, the course can be booked up months in advance, so you should definitely consider booking well ahead.

If staring at those sea cliffs has you wondering what's going on down below, consider signing up for a diving session (or lesson) through the **OceanLife Dive Centre Kilkee** (East End Pier, Kilkee; ☎ 065/905-6707; www.oceanlife.ie). The center offers a full-blown PADI open water course—with theory classes, shallow water practice, and actual dive sessions—over 5 days (Mon–Fri), or over two weekends. Cost for the course is €495, including all gear and open water dives. The undersea world hereabouts—where the Shannon spills into the Atlantic—is intriguing, although the dolphins may try to distract you from your lessons.

And, while on the subject of dolphins, from Easter through October, there are daily opportunities (weather permitting) to set off on a dolphin-spotting expedition in the mouth of the Shannon River. **Dolphinwatch** (☎ 065/905-8156; www.dolphinwatch.ie) operates a recommended 2-hour "Dolphin and Nature Tour" (€22) out of the southern Clare fishing village Carrigaholt (10km/6 miles south of Kilkee, on Loop Head peninsula), which has its own 15th-century castle. The intimate little passenger boat, Draíocht (Irish for "magic") comes complete with an underwater microphone (hydrophone) so you can listen to the dolphins as they click, whistle, and giggle beneath the surface. Officially a conservation area, this part of the Shannon is home to around 140 dolphins, and the boat (under skipper and nature-lover Geoff Magee) has a near-perfect dolphin encounter rate. To add to the experience, the boat is manned by university zoologists who mix Q&A sessions with ongoing dolphin research. Even if you're bizarrely unlucky enough not to spot a dolphin, there are plenty of seabirds—including fulmars, guillemots, and cormorants—to distract you, and the crew makes a point of talking about a variety of marine life and the coastal terrain. And, if all else fails, there's a little bar on the boat.

NIGHTLIFE

For many, a high point of a trip to Clare is listening to trad sessions in one of Doolin's famous pubs (see "Where to Stay & Dine Along Clare's Coast" under "In Doolin," above).

When you've tired of the arguably over-hyped spots in Doolin, head on down to Miltown Malbay and pop into **Hillery's Bar** ✫✫ (Main St.; ☎ 065/708-4188) in the center of the town. The pictures on the walls are snapshots of the town's early-20th-century history, and the place is known for its traditional music sessions (most nights), but the reason I love this place is to simply sit and listen to the local banter. Be warned that it's uncensored speech, often liberally laced with expletives, but it's the kind of infectious, open discussion that you'll soon want to join in, and the locals who come here will soon embrace you.

THE BURREN

Walking across the surreal rockscape of the Burren is the closest you may come in your lifetime to moonwalking (and no, I don't mean the Michael Jackson version). The region's name is derived from the Gaelic word for "great rock" or "stony place" *(boireann)* and it is, in fact, a massive plateau of limestone slabs, one of the few plateaus like it on the planet. Local legend maintains that the big rocks you see here were actually the footballs used by local giants. According to scientists, however, the massive boulders—or erratics—were once embedded in glaciers that suddenly stopped moving in this region of northern Clare, and when they melted, the rocks were deposited upon the earth here.

And while there's drama in that big picture, you need to look closer to spy the Burren's more intimate magic: Growing between the rocks are many unusual plants—Alpine, Arctic, and Mediterranean flowers coexisting—that bloom in splendid rainbow patterns, drawing aficionados on a floral pilgrimage, seeking out orchids and gentians. The limestone acts as a kind of radiator, so in the fissures—or grikes—you'll find exotics like Maidenhair fern, because the temperatures are a couple degrees higher than in the air above. Wonderful discoveries like these will make cherished memories of your time here.

The Burren is truly an otherworldly place. As one local told me: "You just have to step onto the pavement (the word for the Burren's shelves of rock) to realize the effects: peaceful, therapeutic. And spiritual, too, I'd say." As such, it's drawn people for millennia giving it Ireland's highest concentration of archaeological sites—dolmens, ring-forts, and numerous megalithic ruins remain.

LAY OF THE LAND

The Burren forms the uplands of northwest Clare and is easily accessible as a day trip from Ennis, Galway, and Limerick. Coastal Doolin (see "Clare's Coast: Loop Head & the Cliffs of Moher," above) is on the southwestern edge of the Burren, while the village of **Corofin** sits at its southeastern fringe. Corofin is just south of the **Burren National Park,** and sports a number of lakes—Lough Inchiquin, in particular, attracts anglers in droves; the village hosts an annual traditional music festival and also draws people looking to trace their Irish roots at the Genealogical Centre. Corofin also hosts an annual (international) stone throwing competition. Go figure!

More or less bang in the heart of the Burren, north of Corofin, **Carran** village (also spelt "Carron") is little more than a huddle of farmsteads, a school, and a church—it also happens to have one of the best pubs for authentic traditional food (p. 246), and a very hospitable hostel (p. 247). Overlooking a massive turlough, Carran is where Michael Cusack, the founder of the GAA (the Gaelic Athletic Association movement, which rekindled an interest in hurling and gaelic football) was born, and his home has been transformed into a totally missable visitor's center. Near Carran, the **Burren Perfumery** no longer distills scents from local flowers (as these are, mercifully, protected), but still sells candles and perfumes that are mixed on site. A short drive from Carran will bring you to the 1,000-year-old **Caherconnell Stone Fort,** which has magnificently preserved dry stone walls and was inhabited until as late as the 17th century; unfortunately, it's one of the first Burren archaeological sites to charge an entrance fee, which takes away from the allure.

On the northern edge of the Burren, sleepy-until-the-tourists-arrive **Ballyvaughan** is a popular summer retreat on the southern shores of Galway Bay; it has the advantage of affording views across the Bay toward Galway as well as fantastic vistas of the Burren hills. It's a great base for walking, and also for exploring the coastline—the road west of here affords ocean views all along the way to the village of **Fanore,** while to the east are even quieter hamlets and fascinating ecclesiastical ruins. A popular visit from Ballyvaughan is the nearby cave system of **Aillwee.**

GETTING THERE & GETTING AROUND

Public transport within the Burren is stultifying, although **buses** link the area's main towns with Ennis and Galway; contact **Bus Éireann** (☎ 065/682-4177) for timetables. Services are infrequent and slow.

If you're driving, the Burren lies along the **R480.**

An excellent source of news and information about the Burren is the website **www.burrenbeo.com**. If you want to be guided through the Burren, learning about the landscape and the flora as you go, consider contacting Shane Connolly, an experienced local guide who operates as **Burren Hill Walks** (Corkscrew Hill, Ballyvaughan; ☎ 065/707768; burrenhillwalks@eircom.net).

WHERE TO STAY & DINE

A number of great deals are available on vacation rentals in this area; you can book them through the agencies discussed in the box, "Rentals Throughout Clare" (p. 238).

In & Around Corofin

€€   Corofin is just 16km (10 miles) from Ennis, but is right at the edge of the Burren National Park. The finest B&B hereabouts is **Fergus View** ✪✪ (Kilnaboy, Corofin; ☎ 065/683-7606; www.fergusview.com; cash only), mostly because the owners, the Kellehers, resonate with the energy of the Burren and seem to have a deep understanding of its magic; they'll give you plenty of tips on how to get out and explore. In fact, the charm here is so spot-on that you easily forget that bedrooms (€76 double) are very compact and bathrooms tiny (this is a historic property, a former hostelry for teachers, and predates indoor plumbing). Nevertheless, most of the rooms have substantial views, and there's much to explore in the area, so the size of your living quarters should not be an issue. If you start feeling boxed in, head downstairs to the lovely lounge, with a wide selection of books and maps on the Burren. At breakfast, you can hear your juice being squeezed while you feast on homemade Fergus View muesli, followed by Kilnaboy goat cheese with mushrooms and bacon on toast. *One warning:* Fergus View is very popular with seasoned flower enthusiasts who return year after year (so make your reservations early). On the plus side, your fellow guests will be a wonderful additional source of information (so chat 'em up at breakfast).

€–€€€   Corofin has several homey pubs, and one that I know Burren locals like to frequent is **Anne's Kitchen at Inchiquin Inn** ✪ (Main St.; ☎ 065/683-7713; www.annecampbell.ie; Mon–Sat 9am–6pm; Sun noon–6pm; summer Tues–Sat 9am–9pm; MC, V) with breakfast until 2pm and a daily lunch carvery. Besides favorites like Irish stew (€12) and ultra-traditional bacon and cabbage (€11), there are alternatives like chicken curry from time to time; or you can have a simple "Mad Cow" sandwich made with Corofin sliced beef (€4). Also served here is the Burren's fiercest garlic bread—perfect with a bowl of homemade soup of the day. Traditional music sessions happen Friday nights (and Tues in summer).

€€–€€€   Somewhere between Corofin and Ballyvaughan, the near-unde-tectable village of Carran, overlooks the largest turlough (or "disappearing lake") in Europe—in winter it can be 81 hectares (200 acres) wide, but takes just 3 days after the rains have stopped to completely disappear. The best view of this phe-nomenon is from **Cassidy's Pub** ★★ (Carran; ☎ 065/708-9109; www.cassidys pub.com; Mon–Sat noon–9pm; Sun noon–8pm; MC, V), although that's not the main reason to seek this place out. Despite being stuck out in the middle of nowhere, Cassidy's serves some of the most memorable food in the Burren, and Friday nights feature live trad sessions. The emphasis here is on the many prod-ucts derived from local goats: kid meat (or *mionáin*), goat's milk, and cheese all feature strongly. Try the "Dolmen," a quarter-pounder of Burren *mionáin*, "embalmed" in relish and "buried" in tomato and onion under a slab of savory bun, standing on a field of salad and chips (€10). Also oddly named but worth a taste are the West Coast crab meat scones (€13), and the pizzas (try the yummy fig pizza, topped with fig jam, prosciutto, rosemary, ricotta, cheddar, and chopped scallions, €15).

Ballyvaughan

€€   Ballyvaughan is a peaceful haven along Clare's northern coast, which runs along the edge of Galway Bay. It's a popular base for Burren walkers as well as for visits to the nearby Aillwee Cave. Bang in the heart of the tiny village, the pale blue, completely unassuming house just near the local Spar (the only real shop in town) is **Teach McCoillte** ★ (Main St.; ☎ 065/708-3991; MC, V), a fine, friendly B&B. Colette, the owner, charges €70 (year-round) for each of her three smart bedrooms with wooden floors, excellent power showers, and a sense of style. Each en suite room is modern and uncluttered (much like the rest of the house), and boasts standard amenities, like TV and a kettle. This is far and away the best value in the village itself, and you'll love the back-supporting mattresses.

€€   If Teach McCoillte is full, head 1km (⅔ mile) outside Ballyvaughan village, where Philip and Mary Kyne's **Dolmen Lodge** (Tonarussa, Ballyvaughan; ☎ 065/707-7202; dolmenlodge@eircom.net; cash only) starts with a dash of kitsch (a replica dolmen burial tomb at the driveway entrance), but follows through with exceptionally clean and functional accommodations. And while the bedrooms are nothing special, there's a homey vibe thanks to the Kyne's hands-on attentions. Nearby, cottagey **Loughrask Lodge** (Loughrask, Ballyvaughan; ☎ 065/707-7151; aflanagan77@eircom.net; cash only) is an equally straightforward B&B, although all the rooms either have Burren views, or at least a view of the sea. There's also a children's play area out back, with plastic swings 'n' things. Both places charge from €70 double, and up to €80 in July and August.

€€   A bit farther out of Ballyvaughan (but still just a 2-min. drive away), **Drumcreehy House** ★★★ (Ballyvaughan; ☎ 065/707-7377; www.drumcreehy house.com; MC, V) is a beautiful house with country cottage-style rooms at an excellent rate (€80–€100 double). Bedrooms, which are large and sumptuous (antique furniture, opulent fabrics, rich ornamentation, books, plants, fresh flow-ers, and artwork), are named after Burren flowers and are coordinated in bold, contemporary colors to match their namesake bloom. Views are either toward Galway Bay or out the back toward the Burren. Public spaces are also excellent, with lots of inviting sofas, local guidebooks, and artwork to ponder; there's even an honesty bar. The breakfast spread is perhaps the most inviting you'll see in Ireland, served with aplomb to the strains of Sarah Brightman doing Lloyd-Webber showstoppers in German!

€€–€€€   Back in the village, there's loads of history at the 180-year-old **Hylands Burren Hotel** ✪ (Ballyvaughan; ☎ 065/707-7037; www.hylandsburren. com; AE, MC, V), the most affordable and hospitable standard lodgings in the Burren. With the pleasant atmosphere of a small, yet rambling old hotel, you'll find lots of quaint spaces to relax though without the intimacy of Drumcreehy (above). Bedrooms are spacious and well maintained; nine of them have Burren views. The real reward, perhaps, is that the hotel is as much a social hub as a place to lay your head, so the pub packs in locals, and many community events happen here. You'll pay €110 in winter and €140 in peak season; there are ongoing specials for stays of 2 nights or more.

€€–€€€   Although reports vary about **Monks Bar & Restaurant** ✪ (Old Pier, Ballyvaughan; ☎ 065/707-7059; www.monks.ie; MC, V), it sticks to the claim that Boris Yeltsin (!) once ate here and declared the oysters the best in Europe. Perhaps that was on a particularly good day, but I must agree with the former Russian leader by saying that the seafood here is always exquisitely fresh. Particularly the steamed mussels, plucked straight from Galway Bay (which is just across the road); the mussels are €8.85 for a starter portion—or, for €15, they come heaped up in a Pernod and garlic butter sauce, and you get enough of the little buggers to share between two. While there are vegetarian options, and one or two pricy meat dishes, seafood is definitely king here. In that vein, you can count on the chowder (€6.95), which is internationally famous (even award winning, if the menu is to be believed), and open sandwiches—with crab meat (€9.95) or smoked salmon (€9.45)—served on fresh Irish soda bread, with a salad on the side. The downside here is unprofessional service (and an absence of locals—except at night, when the bar spills its first pints)—the incessantly banging kitchen door alone was enough to drive me dilly. The oysters, by the way, are charged at celebrity prices, so don't come looking for those here . . . Galway, remember, is just across the bay!

The Burren's Best Hostel

€   In that tiny enclave of Carran, slap-bang in the center of the Burren, **Clare's Rock Hostel** ✪ (Carran; ☎ 065/708-9129; www.claresrock.com; MC, V) provides a wonderful opportunity to save more than a handful of euro. Pat Cassidy keeps a combination of immaculate and peaceful dorms (€16), private rooms (€44 double), and family rooms (€48 for three; €70 for six). There's a pleasant little sitting room, decorated with wall-mounted sports shirts, and a very good self-catering kitchen, although Cassidy's Pub (see above) is close at hand if you want someone else to do the cooking.

WHY YOU'RE HERE: TOP SIGHTS & ATTRACTIONS

While just about anywhere in the Burren is a good place to get out and explore, it would be worth your while spending a few hours picnicking on the pavement at the **Burren National Park** ✪✪✪, centered on two enormous swirling, helmet-shaped rock mounds—the Knockanes (204m/680 ft.) and Mullach Mór (188m/627 ft.)—at the edge of Loch Gealáin, a small lake next to Crag Road, which is where you park. The park is just minutes from Corofin; ask anyone for directions, or—better still—pick up a copy of Tim Robinson's *Folding Landscapes,* an exquisitely detailed map of the Burren, indispensable for walkers and anyone looking to track down the region's abundant supply of archaeological sites. If your hosts aren't able to lend you a copy, you can buy the map at the **Burren Centre** (☎ 065/708-8030; daily 10am–5pm; summer 10am–6pm) in nearby Kilfenora, a quaint village which harbors a number of magnificent carved high crosses in and around the sublime Kilfenora Cathedral. Buying a ticket (€6) for the Burren Centre itself is a waste of money (a 12 min. film and a lifeless exhibition), as are many of the "visitor centers" throughout the region—rather get out there and explore the real thing.

One other unmissable sight in the Burren is the **Poulnabrone Portal Dolmen** ✪✪✪—a prehistoric archaeological site that consists of three stones arranged like a wonky table; when you see it with your own eyes, it seems altogether impossible that it's been standing here in that awkward, lovely position for 5 millennia. At press time access to this fascinating burial site was free, but there were rumors of the imminent installation of a visitor center, which will no doubt lessen the site's immeasurable charm by changing the very landscape around it. Many of the other dolmens and wedge tombs hereabouts are more difficult to access, and I've been told by a farmer that I couldn't walk a few meters across his land to see the Poulaphuca Wedge Tomb, because "It's private!"—so do be on your toes when you go exploring.

You'll need to pay to visit the **Caherconnell Stone Fort** (near Carran; ☎ 065/708-9999; www.burrenforts.ie; €6; daily 10am–5pm, summer 10am–6pm), so that may be one you skip if you're short on time; it's been turned into a tourist attraction with the addition of a shop, cafe, and ticket desk—and visitors are given an audio guide explaining the history of the fort and the people who built it—but frankly all of these add-ons just detracts from the experience. I find the location, setting, and view of **Cahercommaun** ✪✪✪, 8.5km (5⅓ miles) to the southeast, altogether more appealing—there's no visitor center and no extortionate admission charge either. What was a busy community in the 9th and 10th centuries are now some of the most atmospheric ancient archaeological ruins in Ireland. You need to walk 1km (⅔ mile) from the road, but when you come upon the three-tier ringfort on the edge of a ravine, you'll have found the ideal picnic spot; loll in the deep grass on the cliff's edge, and try to imagine this place 1,000 years ago, when thicker, higher walls kept attacking hordes at bay.

The Burren's karstic terrain means that many caves lie beneath the surface; just outside Ballyvaughan, the best-known is the two-million-year-old **Aillwee Cave** (☎ 065/707-7036; www.aillweecave.ie; €12 cave tour only; daily 10am, last tour 5:30; July–Aug at 6:30pm), which is a bit too commercialized for my tastes, and the underground tour of frozen waterfalls and illuminated tunnels is in any case too brief (30 min.). The cave is famous for its hibernation chambers where now-extinct brown bears wore out the winter; recently introduced at the Aillwee visitor center is the **Burren Birds of Prey Centre** (www.birdofpreycentre.com; €6, or €15 combined ticket with cave tour), offering a close-up look at eagles, falcons, hawks, and owls.

A short drive from Ballyvaughan, and very close to Flaggy Shore, the **Corcomroe Abbey** ✪✪ at Bell Harbour is in spectacularly good nick. It was built

---

Of Spa Baths & Farmers' Wives

A short drive from Doolin, Corofin, or Ballyvaughan brings visitors to the therapeutic spa resort village of **Lisdoonvarna** on the Burren's southern edge; here, mineral waters containing magnesia, iodine, and iron transformed the village into a popular health resort in the early 19th century. Nowadays, Lisdoonvarna is known primarily for its annual **Matchmaking Festival** (www.matchmakerireland.com), when hordes descend to party for six consecutive weekends starting in September—purportedly with the intention of hooking up bachelor farmers with wives. Matches are arranged by Willie Daly, who is apparently the last official matchmaker in Clare. It's possibly the biggest festival of its kind in Europe, and while romantic matches are made, I think it's a bit of an excuse for some wanton hedonism. The festival includes loads of opportunities for dancing (of course), with many country music events, horseracing (not related to the eligible singles), and the crowning of Mr. Lisdoonvarna and the Queen of the Burren. So, if you're feeling lonely, and looking to find a stable mate . . .

---

by Cistercians 1,200 years ago and although mostly roofless, enjoys a wonderfully idyllic, pastoral setting that's usually completely free of other visitors. Poke around here to find effigies of bishops, and then choose a dry spot for a picnic, which you can enjoy while watching the bulls in the adjacent field meditate on their daily routine.

THE OTHER BURREN

May is undoubtedly the month to be in the Burren. It's during this time of seasonal change botanists, naturalists, and lovers of exotic flora descend as rare Arctic, Mediterranean, and Alpine plants start to bloom, covering the stone pavement in vivid, fantastic colors. And to celebrate this natural cycle, Ballyvaughan and other villages around the Burren host all kinds of activities to welcome in the new spring season. **Burren in Bloom** (☎ 065/707-7464; www.ballyvaughan ireland.com) is a monthlong smorgasbord of lectures, guided walking tours, workshops, and even a few parties. It's where you're likely to catch storytelling legend, Eddie Lenihan (see "Where Have All the Great Men Gone?" p. 250), sit in on talks by botanists and environmentalists, or join the locals at their annual family sports day (anyone for the Burren Walking Marathon?). It's not so much a festival, as a month of activities designed to remind folks (locals and visitors) that the Burren means different things to different people—and that there's actually a heck of a lot going on in this usually sleepy part of the country. Just about all the events are free, and leading up to May, fliers advertise the program just about everywhere.

With impressions of the Burren's surreal moonscape so difficult to capture in words, why not consider a short art course where you'll have the chance to describe what you see in splashes of color and shades of light and dark? The **Burren College of Art** (Newtown Castle, Ballyvaughan; ☎ 065/707-7200; www. burrencollege.ie) is a professional school offering everything from summer school

Where Have All the Great Men Gone?

Storytelling is one of the great Irish traditions. Sadly, though, a dying one. Effectively done, it's a skillful, nuanced art that holds an audience captive with lively accounts, anecdotes and legends, interweaving truth and magic in order to make a wizened point or simply entertain. Traditional Irish storytellers are known as *seanchaíthe,* and Clare is home to one of the country's few remaining *seanchaí,* Eddie Lenihan. An exuberant, bearded man who lives and breathes the tales he imparts, Lenihan made international headline news back in 1999 when he protested the removal of a whitethorn bush in the tiny Clare enclave of Latoon. The solitary plant was standing in the path of a $20-million road project, but Lenihan was of the opinion that the tree was in fact a fairy tree—a *sceach*—and as such was not to be removed. So firm were his convictions that Lenihan won out, the road was redirected and the tree saved. Protest politics aside, **Eddie Lenihan** (☎ 065/682-7191; www.eddielenihan.ie) is a famed storyteller and folklorist, with numerous volumes of collected stories (often about the fairy folk) under his belt, his own radio show, and a steady stream of requests for live appearances. If you're fortunate enough to catch Lenihan in action, it's likely to be among the most memorable experiences of your time in Ireland. He's a popular draw at the festivals celebrating storytelling, Irish folklore, or traditional culture held around the country.

Sadly, as if to remind us that the era of storytelling is truly passing, a few years after Lenihan had saved that solitary fairy tree, some malicious vandal took a chainsaw to it and lopped off its branches leaving nothing more than a stump. Talk about a fitting metaphor for the scourge of culture in decline. Make every effort to catch a storytelling session.

courses to Ph.D. programs—what's more, it's on the grounds of the 16th-century Newtown Castle, a marvelously restored four-storey round tower house. The setting, combined with the Burren location and proximity to Galway Bay and the Atlantic, certainly seems to inspire creativity. For short-term visitors, the best opportunities are May through August when the college runs several 5-day courses, each with a specific focus—like "Botanical Painting" and "Painting in the Burren Landscape" (which, incidentally, are the two most popular courses, each run twice during the season, in May and Aug). Classes are led by working artists who also happen to be great teachers, and who bring broad experience with them—for example, Susan Sex, who teaches Botanical Painting, is the artist who designed the country's Wild Flowers of Ireland postage stamp series. So you can expect top value for your money. Classes are small (12 participants maximum, so book well in advance), and some courses require you to have at least some experience (so you should at least know how to apply paint to a canvas). During the course, you'll work both in the big, bright studio (you'll have a specially allocated space) and outdoors (where you'll get to render those landscapes or unusual flowers in oil, acrylic, and watercolor). Each 5-day course costs €310 to €385 (photography courses run €540). If you forget to pack your lunch, you can grab an affordable meal from the on-site Food of the Arts Cafe. If you're not able to attend one of the art courses, the college also hosts a weekly Artists' Lecture Series during the normal semester (Sept–Apr) on Wednesdays (11am–12:30pm); local and visiting artists or scholars talk about their work in an open academic forum as part of the study program of regular students here. Admission is free and open to all, but call ahead to check the schedule.

Periodic public talks, workshops, and outings are organized by the **BurrenLIFE Project** (Old School House, Carran; ☎ 065/708-9000; www.burrenlife.com), a "farming for conservation" project with an aim toward educating people about the Burren and improving awareness about its unique heritage. There are all kinds of activities, from "summer field trips" (essentially walking lectures through the Burren itself), to pockets of Burren-related lectures held at different times through the year. These talks are given by visiting academics, many of them high-profile. Talks range in topics from a look at how the Ice Age and glacial movement impacted the landscape of County Clare, to illustrated talks on turloughs (those unusual vanishing lakes) and on the Burren's mammal wildlife. The sessions are always free and attended almost exclusively by locals, but BurrenLIFE welcomes any and all. And because they attract folks who are tuned into Burren life, they're a good place to dig up first-hand knowledge about the region. The website carries full details of all upcoming talks and events, or you can phone the BurrenLIFE to hear if there's something on while you're visiting. You can also check the "Events Calendar" pages at www.burrenbeo.com.

ACTIVE BURREN

Ideally, the best way to see and experience the Burren is on foot or by bike . . . so much of the landscape will remain unseen if you stick to the inside of your car. Many Burren highlights lie hidden in the near-microscopic details—the tiny exotic buds that pop out through the cracks in the stone in May—and in the changing sense of scale you experience as you step on and over the pavements. If you have 4 days, you can complete the entire 123km (76¼-mile) **Burren Way** ✪✪✪ walking trail, which follows a linear route commencing in Lahinch and finishing in Corofin; the first part of the route takes in some of the area discussed under "Clare's Coast: Loop Head & the Cliffs of Moher," earlier in this chapter. The trail is considered moderate to difficult, and combines a mix of rocky tracks and minor roadways; there is one steep ascent. With less time on your hands, you can still access the Burren Way at any of its six key trailheads, located at Lahinch, Doolin, Lisdoonvarna, Ballyvaughan, Carran, and Corofin. These trailheads have parking and information boards with route maps.

Bicycles can be rented for €13 per day, or €50 per week from **Burren Bike** (☎ 065/707-7061; www.burrenbike.com), located in the launderette opposite the gas station in Ballyvaughan.

ATTENTION, SHOPPERS!

Although it was once an attraction, the **Burren Perfumery** (Carran; ☎ 065/708-9102; www.burrenperfumery.com; daily May–June and Sept 9am–6pm; July–Aug 9am–7pm; Oct–Apr 10am–5pm) is a bit of a letdown these days since none of the scents that made Ireland's first perfumery famous are actually produced here. Nevertheless, there's a pleasant garden and good tea room, and you can buy hand-packaged soaps (how about fennel and mint, or cedar and lemongrass?), aromatherapy bath oils, organic herbal teas, candles, "Man of Aran" eau de cologne, and Irish parfum. There's a free slideshow with haunting music, lots of close-ups of pretty flowers, and narrated information about the Burren's botany.

While Aillwee Cave (p. 248) can be a bit too touristy for some tastes, there's nothing stopping you from visiting the food shop of the on-site **cafe** (daily 10am–6:30pm; DISC, MC, V), where you can watch smoked cheese being made, and then sample some of the unusual (and delicious) varieties, like garlic and nettle-flavored cheese, available to buy. There's also a wonderful selection of Irish jams, pâté (wild boar, guinea fowl), handmade fudge, chutneys, dried seaweed, and even that awfully sweet honey mead from Bunratty.

A famous stop for gourmet food, and specially smoked salmon, is the **Burren Smokehouse** (☎ 065/707-4432; www.burrensmokehouse.ie) in Lisdoonvarna. This is an ideal place to put together a picnic—or order smoked salmon to be sent home.

DAY TRIPS AROUND COUNTIES LIMERICK & CLARE

The rural sights and sounds are, to my mind, the big pull in Clare. But there are two urban outings, plus some famed castles, that you might want to include as an antidote to all of Clare's bucolic bliss.

LIMERICK CITY

There are two obvious temptations when thinking about Limerick City in neighboring Limerick County. The first is to draw comparisons with that other "limerick"—the five-line rhyming variety. The other is to buy in completely to the misery of circumstance so beautifully portrayed in Frank McCourt's *Angela's Ashes*. And while Limerick gets some dreadful press around the ongoing feud between two rival crime families that seem to constantly be shooting at each other (but certainly not at tourists who have never been—nor ever will be—targeted), the social horrors that once afflicted this city on the Shannon are no more a reality. What's more, with recent development around the waterfront areas, Limerick is looking decidedly perky.

Getting There & Getting Around

As a relatively large commercial center, Limerick is well connected to other principal hubs; the nearest airport is **Shannon International** (☎ 061/471444; www.shannonairport.com), which is 13km (8 miles) away. Several transatlantic carriers land here from hubs in the U.S.—New York, Philadelphia, Chicago, Atlanta, and Boston—as well as Toronto, and regular connections are available to a host of U.K. and European cities. A taxi from the airport into Limerick will cost €30; bus transfers (40 min.) cost €5. A **bus** from Dublin takes 3½ hours (around €13), while a **train** is an hour quicker but costs almost four times as much. Buses from Cork (2 hr.) and Killarney (2½ hr.) are quicker than train service. Buses arrive at **Colbert Station** (Parnell St.; ☎ 061/313333).

Limerick City has intolerable traffic, particularly at its immediate outskirts, so driving into town along the Ennis Road (from Shannon Airport or Ennis town) can involve frustrating delays. Try to limit driving as much as possible here. Parking also incurs a fee almost everywhere in and around the center; you need to purchase a scratch and display parking disc (€1), available from supermarkets.

Why You're Here: Top Sights & Attractions

You can easily conquer Limerick's top sights in half a day, although if you're driving here, you'll probably need extra time negotiating traffic (especially getting into and out of the city) and looking for parking (for which you need to pay with a pay-and-display scratch card, available from most shops). The city's most important site is **Hunt Museum** ✪✪✪ kids (Rutland St.; ☎ 061/312833; www.hunt museum.com; €7.75, free admission on Sun; Mon–Sat 10am–5pm; Sun 2–5pm), an intriguing "collection of curiosities" donated by the great English collector, John Hunt and his wife Gertrude. Beyond the regular exhibition spaces, curators have installed "curiosity cabinets," which are packed with surprises—I even found a painting by Paul Gauguin in one. Items aren't arranged chronologically, but tend to be clustered according to theme, so you'll find religious artworks in one room

Lunchtime in Limerick

Break up your explorations with a bite at one of the following fine eateries:

- **Wild Onion** ✪✪ (High St., Cornmarket; ☎ 061/440055; www.wild onioncafe.com; Tues–Fri 8am–4pm; Sat 9am–3pm; cash only) is modeled after an American diner. Known for its brilliant breakfasts, delicious cakes and cookies, spectacular coffee, and sandwiches stuffed with goodness, its light, wholesome lunch meals start at just €5.30.

- Packed to bursting during lunchtime, excellent little **Café Noir** ✪✪✪ (1–2 Roberts St.; ☎ 061/411222; Mon–Sat 8am–5:30pm and occasional summer evenings; MC, V) is a patisserie, coffee shop, and early evening wine bar that became a huge hit just moments after it opened in 2008. Diners line up and order at the counter, where you point out the ingredients you want in your design-your-own salad (€7 medium, €12 large) and sandwich (€5.70–€7.50)—with plenty of wonderful deli-fresh items to choose from. Also made fresh each morning are quiches and plenty of sinful-looking light pastries, and heartier traditional meals like steak and kidney pie (€12).

- **Sage Café** ✪✪✪ (67–68 Catherine St.; ☎ 061/409458; www.the sagecafe.com; Mon–Sat 9am–6pm; MC, V) is a deli-style eatery that's taken Limerick by storm. There's a choice of sandwiches (on brown bap or a rustic baguette) with various fillings, like home-baked ham, chicken, turkey, or steamed fish—cod, salmon, and prawn—for €6. These you can choose from behind the display counter before snagging one of the wooden tables in this bright, upbeat space. Beyond the usual, intriguing choices include goat cheese with couscous and black sesame seeds, baby leaves, green olive tapenade, and mango salsa (€9); and seared lamb's liver with leek and wild mushroom stuffing and cider jus (€12). Come early as popular dishes do run out in the course of the day.

and a fantastic collection of crucifixes next door. It feels as much like a scavenger hunt as a museum visit! In all, some 2,000 individual pieces range from a bronze horse attributed to Leonardo da Vinci to paintings by Pablo Picasso, Jack B. Yeats, Henry Moore, and Renoir. Other favorites: a 12th-century hand-warmer, the Bronze Age Ballyscullion Cauldron, the reliquary cross that belonged to Mary Queen of Scots, and a coin that's believed to have been one of the 30 pieces of silver received by Judas when he betrayed Christ. *Tip:* Because it's such an eclectic collection, I recommend calling ahead to see if you can join one of the free, illuminating guided tours. These are run by knowledgeable volunteers who aren't always on duty, so it's worth checking on tour times beforehand. Temporary exhibitions are held downstairs, and the museum hosts workshops and talks around a range of inspiring themes.

Just north of Custom House, across Mathew Bridge, is King's Island—or "English Town" as it was known when the city was segregated. Here, in Limerick's medieval warren is its flagship attraction, **King John's Castle** (Castle St.; ☎ 061/411201; €8.50; daily Apr–May 9:30am–5:30pm; June–Aug 9:30am–6pm; Sept–Mar 9:30am–5pm), which loses major points for authenticity (the modern visitor's center tacked onto the entrance just doesn't make sense) and even more points for its rather dull detailing of a history that should be *Braveheart*-thrilling. The only parts of the castle that's possibly worth the entrance fee are the views of the city from the bastions; ultimately, though, the castle is an overpriced bore. Right next door is the time-killing **Limerick Museum** (Castle Lane, Nicholas St.; ☎ 061/417826; www.limerickcity.ie; free admission; Tues–Sun 10am–1pm and 2:15–5pm), again, not worth visiting.

More worthy of your time and also on King's Island is Limerick's oldest functioning building. Predating the castle by 25 years, when you step inside **St. Mary's Cathedral** ✹✹ (Bridge St.; ☎ 061/310293; www.cathedral.limerick.anglican.org; €2; daily 9am–5pm), you feel the weight of time bearing down—the ancient arches and thick, exposed stone walls executed in brutal, solid masonry are saturated with history. It's an atmospheric space, all right, but do look out for its most treasured possession, the fantastically carved oak *misericords* ("mercy seats"), 15th-century stalls that include seats that can be raised. At a time when worshippers stood throughout lengthy church service, the lips of these clever seats enabled the occupant to rest while appearing to be standing upright. If you look at the underside of each of the *misericord* seats, you'll see that they are carved with symbolic representations of good and evil.

Beyond King's Island's narrow streets and looming walls, you'll want to get a feel for Limerick's elegant Georgian architecture. Make a beeline to Pery Square, to tour Limerick's fine **Georgian House and Garden** ✹✹ (2 Pery Sq.; ☎ 061/314130; www.georgianlimerick.com; €5; Mon–Fri 9:30am–4:30pm, weekends by appointment) across the road from the People's Park. At the time of writing, the house was undergoing extensive repair and closed to the public. Usually, there are 16 rooms showcasing the grandeur—and the furniture—of 18th-century uppercrust homelife. Juxtaposed with the marble and period detailing (greatly brought out through faithful restoration), the Coach House offers an *Angela's Ashes* exhibition, drawing attention to the film as well as the impoverished circumstances of Frank McCourt's childhood.

And if it was *Angela's Ashes* that drew you to Limerick in the first place, you might want to consider **Michael O'Donnell's Walking Tours** ✹✹ (☎ 087/635-3648 or 061/327108; www.freewebs.com/walkingtours; €10) which, in 2 hours, puts the Pulitzer Prize–winning memoir into perspective. Tours start from the **Tourist Information Office** on Arthur's Quay (☎ 061/317522) and are a good primer before setting off to explore the city's main attractions.

A Village Outing: Adare

A mere 15 minutes from Limerick City, Adare is peaches-and-cream quaint, having mustered a reputation as the "prettiest village in Ireland" (a moniker that has been flogged like a dead horse, ensuring a steady stream of tourists). They come for ancient friaries, a medieval castle, and to snap shots of a row of thatched cottages built around 1825 and now housing renowned restaurants and some very

The Other Limerick: Poetry & Prose

For an opportunity to combine your soulful intellectual side (hey, admit it, you've got one) with a totally mellow social vibe, then step up for an evening with the **White House Poets.** A weekly poetry event, held Wednesdays at the **White House Pub** (corner of Glentworth St. and O'Connell St.; ☎ 061/412377), it starts with an open mic session at 9pm. The evening—accompanied by free finger food and the polite pouring of pints—then progresses to poetry read by an established poet. For information, call **Barney** (☎ 086/865-7494) or **Dominic** (☎ 087/299-6409). By the way, if you're in town in mid-October, look out for **Cuisle,** the Limerick City International Poetry Festival, when you can catch readings and workshops presented by major poets.

When the savvy folks of Limerick look to expand their knowledge without investing in a full-blown university course, they often head to the **Hunt Museum** (p. 253) which, aside from being one of the country's finest treasure troves, puts on a good year-round program of workshops and casual classes aimed primarily at adults. The last time I was there, the focus was on fashion through the ages, and a small crowd (of nearly all-women) was listening to a lecture on different types of period costume. The discussion was happening right there, in one of the museum rooms, and original items of clothing were being modeled to demonstrate the points being made. Free lunchtime lectures happen at the museum more or less every month (usually on a Tues); while these are sometimes on obscure (although not uninteresting) subjects, they may include talks by internationally recognized artists, or fascinating left-of-center discussions about well-known authors. Admission to these events is usually free; the website carries details of upcoming activities (click on "Events").

iffy gift stores. Adare exemplifies an early-19th-century estate town, laid out according to a design by the Earl of Dunraven in 1820. Unfortunately, until a road bypass is built, the village also suffers from nonstop high-volume traffic, which does tend to spoil the illusion of gentility. Adare's present big claim to fame is as host to the Irish Open Golf Championship. If visiting by car, take the N21—it's a short drive depending on traffic (and how quickly you can escape the one-way street congestion of Limerick); buses depart for Adare every 1 to 2 hours (€4.50 one-way, €6.20 return).

SHANNON'S HISTORICAL "THEME PARK" & CASTLES

One of the most famous tourist outings in western Ireland is the much-vaunted **Bunratty Castle and Folk Park** (Bunratty, just off the N18 Limerick/Ennis Rd.; ☎ 061/361511; www.shannonheritage.com; €15; daily Nov–Mar 9:30am–5:30pm; Apr–May and Sept–Oct 9am–5:30pm; June–Aug 9am–6pm), a theme park exploring the architecture used by various communities in this part of the country;

Avoid Getting Your Fingers Dirty at Bunratty

Although Limerick's crime families don't target tourists, there's more than enough fleecing of innocent visitors going on at Bunratty. I'm talking about the themed dinners (most popular in Ireland, thanks to all the bus tour traffic) that take place in Bunratty Castle at night. Guests are promised the pomp and ceremony of a **medieval banquet** (☎ 061/360788; year-round at 5:30 and 8:45pm), complete with singing serving wenches, honey mead, and eat-with-your-fingers table rules. Throughout the night—at benches shared with strangers—cheap wine softens the blow of over-rehearsed musical routines, as the man-in-tights MC (or rather, the "butler") constantly invokes you to repeat "Sláinte is saol," a traditional toast meaning "health and long life to you" (believe me, it gets tired after a while). Along with various gimmicky entertainments, you get a subpar meal, which you must eat with your hands (as they did back in the day). At €58 per head, you'll feel like you've been caught with your trousers down. A slightly cheaper though no less cornball alternative is Bunratty's **Traditional Irish Night** (€48), held April through October (daily at 7pm), featuring Irish music, dancing, and storytelling, and a meal of Irish stew. You'll see these events advertised (and praised) everywhere, but I think there are better uses of your time and money. Consider yourself warned.

besides reconstructed houses, farmsteads, and an entire 19th-century town street, actors assuming personages from the past bring the whole thing to life and to explain the minutiae of daily life. As an exercise in experiential sociology, the park really does come off as rather cheesy, underscored by its unadulterated commercialism.

While the folk park certainly isn't going to be everyone's cup of tea (see the harsh, telling critique in Pete McCarthy's travelogue *McCarthy's Bar,* a terrific read), 15th-century **Bunratty Castle** ✦—one of almost 1,000 castles in the Shannon region—is a little more interesting, particularly if you can get in when it's not so packed with visitors (arrive very early). Touted as the most complete and authentic in Ireland (yeah, right . . . somewhat authentic it may be, but I'd be hard-pressed to figure out how you'd measure this in a country with such a rich stock of fortified buildings), the castle is the fourth one on this site, which started out as a Viking trading post in 970; this version was built by the MacNamaras in 1425, and features plenty of curious nooks and crannies filled with medieval furniture and decoration. If you train your imagination, you can conjure up a sense of what life might have been like in this motley collection of rooms and chambers. Guides in historical getup give tours of the castle (ask when you buy your ticket what time these happen—they're free), which is the only way to glean some insight into the castle's history (be warned, though, that the guides are actors, not historians, so you may want to take what they say with a pinch of salt). Failing that, don't miss the children's bedroom with its own miniature stairway, or the smaller upstairs private dining room with its painted ceiling and delicate furniture. Also, make sure you climb all the way to the top to catch views from the upper bastion. Last admissions to the park are at 5:15pm June through August, and 4:15pm the rest of the year; last entry to the castle is at 4pm throughout the year.

A far better bet if you want to explore a medieval castle (especially if you don't much care for the reconstituted village life of Bunratty's folk park) is to forgo Bunratty completely in favor of **Knappogue Castle** ★★ (R469, near Quin, Co. Clare; ☎ 061/361511; www.shannonheritage.com; €7.35; May to mid-Sept daily 9:30am–5pm). It's probably one of the most handsome tower houses in the country, and less likely to be besieged by mobs of visitors. Surrounded by magnificent gardens—including a Victorian-era walled garden centered on a representation of Bacchus, the god of wine—Knappogue was built in 1467 by Sean MacNamara. After many years of neglect and abuse, including occupation by Cromwell's soldiers in 1641, a Texas couple bought the castle in 1966 and restored its original splendor. It may not have the hype of Bunratty, but it's a more peaceable place to visit, and its rough-hewn walls fit together in a more unusual, idiosyncratic shape, making it something quite special to behold. All the furnishings at Knappogue are original to the castle, and you'll get more a sense that this served as a family home than Bunratty; among the guests who have stayed here are Charles de Gaulle, Richard Nixon, Ronald Reagan, and former Irish president, Mary Robinson.

AN AFTERNOON IN ENNIS

Straddling a crook on the River Fergus, Ennis is the only town of any significant size in County Clare. Founded in the 13th century by the descendents of Brian Boru, the first High King of Ireland, Ennis retains its medieval character, particularly evident in the narrow arched laneways—called bow-ways—that link different parts of the city (the tiny center can feel like a real rabbit warren, and that is part of the charm—one's constantly making unexpected discoveries simply by venturing down different alleyways). Nowadays, Ennis is especially known for its focus on music and traditional culture; come at the end of May and you may battle to find accommodation thanks to the **Fleadh Nua** ★★★ (www.fleadhnua.com), when the town packs out with music and dance enthusiasts from all over the country.

Buses from Shannon Airport as well as Dublin, Cork, Limerick, Galway, and other parts of the country pull in to the **bus station** (Station Rd.; ☎ 065/682-4177), adjacent the **train station** (☎ 065/684-0444). Trains connect Ennis with Dublin (5–7 departures per day; approximately €45), via Limerick (approximately €9). It's a 10-minute walk to the center—just follow Station Road until you reach O'Connell Street. If you turn right and continue until O'Connell Square, you'll find the **tourist office** (☎ 065/682-8615) down Arthur's Row.

Taking one of Jane O'Brien's **Ennis Walking Tours** ★★★ (St. Brendans, Lifford Rd; ☎ 087/648-3714; www.enniswalkingtours.com; €8; May–Oct Mon and Wed–Sat 11am) is unquestionably the best possible introduction to the town, its history, and some of its bizarre legends. Jane puts on a highly informative tour, peppering the official history with anecdotal tales that transform sleepy Ennis into a truly intriguing destination. She points out, for example, exactly where women

Boycott, the Rich B#$tard

On Ennis's pedestrian-friendly Parnell Street, Charles Stuart Parnell—the uncrowned king of Ireland—once made rousing speeches encouraging people to campaign for land ownership. It was here, in fact, that the term "boycott" was coined when he spoke out against a particularly hated man, Captain James Boycott.

were plunged into the Fergus River strapped to a Ducking Chair designed specifically to punish them for nagging or scolding. And she tells how a 70-year-old woman managed to marry a man of 20, and was thereafter tried as a witch for using a magic blue bottle to see the future. I won't give away the entire tour; suffice it to say, it's fascinating.

Alas, the **Riches of Clare Museum** (Arthur's Row; ☎ 065/682-3382; free admission; Oct–May Tues–Sat 9:30am–5pm; June–Sept Mon–Sat 9:30am–5pm; Sun 9:30am–1pm) is not nearly as absorbing, so the only real historical attraction worth visiting (besides some of the ancient-looking pubs) is **Ennis Friary** ★★ (Abbey St.; ☎ 065/682-9100; Heritage Card or €1.80; daily Easter–Sept 10am–6pm; Oct 10am–5pm), founded under the patronage of the O'Briens of Thomond in the 13th century. Although in a state of atmospheric ruin, most of the walls are still standing, as is the tower—their lofty dimensions suggesting the importance of the structure. Within are some great treasures of Irish medieval art, including five panels depicting scenes from the Passion of Christ carved around the MacMahon Tomb, dating back to 1470. Use the building plan provided when you buy your ticket to find the small carved *Ecce Homo* relief depicting an emaciated Christ with his ribs poking through his chest and his hands bound; surrounding him are allusions to his imminent crucifixion.

Without making too much fuss, I'd like to draw your attention to the fact that Ennis is considered the "boutique capital" of Ireland. No matter which direction you face, you'll probably be eyeball to eyeball with a fashion outlet of some kind. You hardly need to look much further than **O'Connell Street. Willow** ★★ (6 O'Connell St.; ☎ 065/689-1342) stocks fine international designer wear (great for beach and summer dresses) with some highly regarded brands like Ted Baker and Almost Famous. A bustling coffee shop is in the back, ideal if you need a break from trying on the store's wide range of quirky European labels.

7 Galway City & County

The arts rich city & wild, wild west

by Emily Hourican

TIME WAS WHEN GALWAY WAS BEST KNOWN FOR ITS KNITTED JUMPERS, stoic fishermen, and the unrelenting smell of burning turf in the air. No more . . . at least in the city itself, though you can still find small pockets of traditional Ireland when you get out into the countryside, but even these are fast transforming. Galway City, in particular, is one of the most cosmopolitan in Ireland, with elements of New York's Soho or London's Camden Town. In 2008, Galway was named as the eighth "sexiest" city in the world, and I think that about fits—there are few other cities where one feels so alive (though, to be fair, the title might have something to do with Galway's famed oysters). Though Galway has few iconic sights per se, rambling its 900-year-old streets, meeting its people, and ducking into its pubs is a heady experience.

One more bit of good news: Galway also has, officially, the lowest crime rate in the country; even the seagulls out on Galway harbor seem disinterested in the contents of your lunchbox—but then again, they *are* dining on some of the best seafood in Ireland.

You'll want to give the city a day or two of your time, though it's the rugged coastline of Connemara that most first-time Galway visitors flock to; a spell-bindingly dramatic, jagged peninsula, laden with pockets of Irish speaking communities. But please, don't come here expecting to sink into a world free of cars, tourists, and Internet connections; these days, most cottages have proper roofs and tractors have replaced pony-powered ploughs.

Yes, modern life has left its stamp on one of the most magnificently rustic parts of Ireland, but the stunning landscape, stretching from Lough Corrib in the East to the Atlantic in the West, still speaks of a romantic, lonely past. Sometimes, the last word just has to go to John Wayne, who points out in *The Quiet Man,* much of which was filmed in the area, "Some things a man doesn't get over so easy." Too right.

DON'T LEAVE GALWAY WITHOUT . . .

EXPLORING THE CONNEMARA PENINSULA Either by bicycle along the 85km (53-mile) Connemara Loop, which takes in some of Ireland's most majestic landscapes, or simply by car. See p. 280.

SUCKING DOWN AN OYSTER You can't say you've been to Galway, truly, until you do. And you'll taste what all the fuss is about. See p. 269.

Aran Islands **1**
Aughnanure Castle **4**
Connemara National Park **5**
Connemara Smokehouse **7**
Coole Park **2**
Glenlo Abbey **3**
Kylemore Abbey **6**

TAP YOUR TOES TO SOME TRAD MUSIC   Both in Galway City and out in the countryside, you'll find delightful sounds to feast your ear on. See p. 263 for Galway City and p. 280 for Connemara.

A BRIEF HISTORY OF GALWAY

Galway is known as the City of the Tribes, or "Cathair na dTreabh," after the 14 "Tribes" or merchant families that recaptured and took control of the city following the Norman invasion of the 13th century. Many are still remembered in the names of streets and buildings in the old part of the city (Kirwan's Lane, Lynch's Castle). In the years that followed, the walled city became almost an independent city state, trading predominantly with England, rarely fraternizing with the local Irish.

In the 18th and 19th centuries, Galway's history echoed that of the rest of Ireland. First, the relaxing of the British government's harsh Penal Laws made life easier for the native Irish settlers. Fortunes reversed, however, when the Great Irish Famine of the 1840s decimated the county's population, with those who survived taking their chances on boats headed for the United States. The industrial revolution left its mark on the county in 1850 with the first railway lines reaching the city—the same route still in use today—while the city's first university, the "Queens University of Ireland" (now National University of Ireland, Galway), opened in 1845, in honor of Queen Victoria.

Galway's role in the political upheaval that shook Irish politics at the start of the 20th century was comparatively minor; Galway City acted as the western headquarters for the British Army, and while much of the rest of the country saw fierce fighting, the local Irish Republican Army could manage little against the British forces in the city. Galway was, however, the scene of violent fighting between Pro-Treaty (regarding the taking of an oath of allegiance to the British government in the Irish Parliament) and Anti-Treaty troops in the run up to the Irish Civil War (1922).

A city on the fringes of Ireland, Galway didn't see that much investment until the 1960s, when the first major industries began to move into the region. In turn, the university expanded exponentially, drawing artists and writers to the city, creating a bohemian vibe that still pervades. As the city grew in stature, so it came to be recognized as the "jewel of the West"; Galway's population in 1950 was around 21,000, and by the end of the century that had more than doubled to 57,000.

LAY OF THE LAND

Galway covers about 6,000 sq. km, (2,316 sq. miles) and while Galway City is itself relatively easy to reach via transport networks, reaching its rugged coastline isn't as easy—such is the winding nature of these narrow roads locals joke that if you're traveling from Dublin, by the time you reach Galway City, you're only halfway there. Simply put, the western and eastern halves of Galway are separated by **Lough Corrib,** which runs through the center of the county, joining the sea just outside Galway City. The eastern half of the county is more developed and easier to access—the towns of **Loughrea** and **Oranmore** are served by the main Dublin-Galway road, the N6, and the main Dublin-Galway bus (no. 20), while **Ballinasloe** (also on the N6) and **Athenry** are reachable by train (Athenry lies on the R347, about 20km/12 miles from the city). **Tuam** (N17), **Ballinrobe** (N84), and **Moylough** (N63) are situated along the main arterial roads out of Galway City and are easily reachable by car.

Head west, beyond the city, however, and transport takes on a more rustic feel—be prepared for potholes and occasional wildlife—with the looping N59 the easiest route to follow, taking in the towns of **Recess, Clifden,** and **Leenaun** along the way. Indeed, beyond Maam Cross is where **Connemara** truly begins, around 45km (28 miles) from Galway City, with the breathtaking **Maumturk** and **Twelve Pins** mountain ranges cutting through the landscape. The zig-zagging Connemara coastline is the result of millions of years of abuse from the Atlantic Ocean, which also played a part in creating the Killary Fjord, Ireland's only fjord.

Dominating the seascape, in the southwest of the county, are the **Aran Islands**—Inis Mor, Inis Meain, and Inis Oirr—located at the mouth of Galway Bay and covering about 47 sq. km (18 sq. miles) between them. Great hunks of rock with little naturally occurring topsoil, these islands are one of the most remote parts of the country, and also the most pastoral: Irish is the official language here, and apart from the recent influx of tourists, life hasn't changed much for generations.

GALWAY CITY
GETTING THERE & GETTING AROUND
By Plane

Galway has two airports: **Galway Airport** (Carnmore, 6km/4 miles east of the city; ☎ 091/755569; http://galwayairport.com) offers a range of flights to Dublin, Waterford, Cork, and a handful of U.K. and European destinations; **Aerfort na Minna** (Inverrin, 22km/14 miles west of the city; ☎ 091/593034; http://aerarannislands.com), which operates flights to and from the Aran Islands. Unless you're renting a car, a taxi is the most logical way to get to the city from either; it will cost about €20 from Galway Airport and between €30 and €35 from Aerfort no Minna. Unfortunately only one bus to Galway Airport leaves the city daily at 1pm; no buses serve Aerfort na Minna.

By Train

Ireland's rail network links Galway's **Ceannt Station** (Just off Eyre Sq.; ☎ 091/561444; www.irishrail.ie) with the rest of the country, with seven routes between Dublin and Galway operating daily (four on Sun). Pre-book your tickets online to ensure the best fares. A one-way ticket from Galway to Dublin costs €32 when booked at the station, or €24 when booked online.

By Bus

Bus Éireann (☎ 091/562000; www.buseireann.ie), Ireland's national bus service, departs from just outside **Ceannt Station** (just off Eyre Sq.). Rates vary, with Dublin (€15 one-way, €19 return) the most expensive. Within Galway, Bus Éireann also operates a number of commuter routes. From Eyre Square, they're a convenient, cheap way to discover Galway's environs. Fares around the city and its environs average around €1.45; a weekly ticket is a good option at €16.

    City Direct (www.citydirectgalway.com) operates a number of services from the western suburbs of the city, such as Barna, Knocknacarra, and Salthill, to Eyre Square, while **JJ Kavanagh** (☎ 081/833-3222; www.jjkavanagh.ie) services the city with buses from midland counties Carlow and Kilkenny.

By Taxi

Taxis are plentiful in Galway City center, but few and far between the further you head into Connemara. There's no standard taxi rate, so be sure to shop around if you're planning a journey outside the city. Price **City Taxis** (Prospect Hill; ☎ 091/530250), **Big O Taxis** (Upper Dominick St.; ☎ 091/585858), **Locall Taxis** (Dock St.; ☎ 091/500600), or **Eco Taxis** (Eyre St.; ☎ 091/569369) when in Galway City, **Night Owl Taxi** (☎ 0909/642954) in Ballinasloe, or **Connemara Taxi Co** (☎ 095/30000) when in Clifden.

By Bicycle & By Foot

Renting a bicycle is an ideal way to see Galway City—watch out for the cobblestones!—with myriad bicycle rental options available at competitive prices. **Europa Cycles** (Earls Island; ☎ 091/563355; http://europabicycles.net) in the city center offers bikes from €6 a day or €20 a week, and train passengers can bag themselves a further 10% discount upon presentation of a valid ticket. **West**

Ireland Cycles (Upper Dominic St.; ☎ 091/58883) is another affordable option, with touring bikes available for €12 a day or €60 for the week.

Lastly, if in doubt, **walk.** A recent census indicated that almost one in three Galwegians walk to work on a regular basis, and the boutique size of the city makes excursions on foot a pleasure.

ACCOMMODATIONS, BOTH STANDARD & NOT
Student Housing

Galway's status as a student town means a good supply of great-value accommodation, bang in the city center. And don't worry: There aren't too many grungy overtones. These student villages offer travelers reduced rates for rental apartments that are well furnished and a perfect base from which to explore the West. Most importantly, they are available during the summer months (generally the first week of June to the last week of Aug), the best (and busiest) time to visit the county. As with everything, it pays to shop around; while the rates below may seem off-putting, there's still plenty of opportunity to haggle a bargain. And don't worry about accidentally stumbling into some sort of rowdy Celtic frat party—by the time you can book into these places, most students have long since packed up and gone home.

€   One more selling point: The students have managed to bag some of the best spots in the city. Case in point: **Corrib Village** 🄺 (Conference Office, NUI Galway; ☎ 091/492264; www.nuigalway.ie; MC, V), an apartment complex right on the banks of the lovely River Corrib, beside the main National University of Ireland campus (NUI Galway). Though the rooms are rather featureless and small, the location can't be beat (there's even a playground on the premises). Private rooms with shared bath go for €66 a night double, with breakfast included, while bedrooms with private facilities jump to €78.

€   Another useful way to bypass the "weekly rates" required by most student housing is to book your stay through **Hostelbookers.com**, which offers rooms at two student villages, **Glasán Holiday Village** (Dublin Rd., opposite the Galway Mayo Institute of Technology; ☎ 091/773333; www.holidaysingalway.com; MC, V) and **Dúnaras Village** (Bishop O'Donnell Rd., close to Salthill; ☎ 091/589588; www.dunaras.com; MC, V) from as little as €56 double, 2 nights minimum. Rooms are monastically simple but have plenty of natural light, decent bathrooms, comfy beds (with proper duvets), and there is much to be said for access to a washing machine and stove.

€   Moving up in the world of interior design, the student digs at **Centrepoint Galway** ✪ (Liosban Business Park, Tuam Rd.; ☎ 091/381000; www.centrepoint galway.com; MC, V), close to the campus of NUI Galway, have a more stylish, bachelor-pad kind of look, with comfy leather sofas, neutral fabrics, and stripped pine floors. Visitors have a choice of two-sleeper (€190 per week) and three-sleeper apartments (€240 per week), from June through August.

€€   **Gort na Coribe** (Opposite Dunnes Stores on Headford Rd.; ☎ 091/746400; info@gortnacoiribe.ie; MC, V) offers visitors accommodation for up to six people

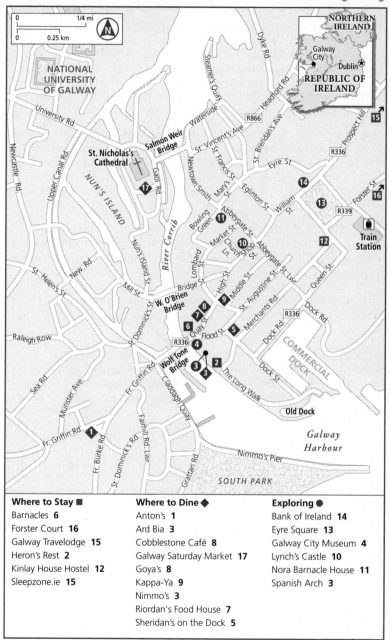

Where to Stay ■

Barnacles **6**
Forster Court **16**
Galway Travelodge **15**
Heron's Rest **2**
Kinlay House Hostel **12**
Sleepzone.ie **15**

Where to Dine ◆

Anton's **1**
Ard Bia **3**
Cobblestone Café **8**
Galway Saturday Market **17**
Goya's **8**
Kappa-Ya **9**
Nimmo's **3**
Riordan's Food House **7**
Sheridan's on the Dock **5**

Exploring ●

Bank of Ireland **14**
Eyre Square **13**
Galway City Museum **4**
Lynch's Castle **10**
Nora Barnacle House **11**
Spanish Arch **3**

A Stay in Salthill

B&Bs tend to be more plentiful as you head out of the city, and the seaside resort of Salthill, located on Ireland's longest beach, and just a couple of kilometers outside the city, is fairly bristling with them. To get here, renting a car is an option, but a taxi from the city center will cost you about €10, and most of the resort is centrally located.

€–€€   Berna Kelly's award-winning **Devondell** ✹✹ (Devon Park; ☎ 091/528306; www.devondell.com; cash only) is a quaint four-bedroom house renowned for its breakfast—homemade bread and preserves, good local produce—and its genial welcome. Beds are funny old brass numbers, something like you might find in the nursery of a Big House. Period furniture adorns the rooms, all named after local flowers. B&B rates start at €80 for a double room.

€–€€   Across the road from the town's promenade, the nine-bedroom **Ocean Crest House** (Oceanwave; ☎ 091/589028; www.oceanbb.com; cash only) has an unremarkable modern exterior, but a relaxed, cozy interior. I'm talking old Chesterfield sofas, quaint period furniture, and rather dainty (but comfy) beds, with views of both Galway Bay and the Burren Mountains. All of this goes for €70 to €110 per double room, including breakfast (of course).

€–€€   If golf is your thing, **Marian Lodge** (Knocknacarra Rd.; ☎ 091/521678; www.marian-lodge.com; cash only), sited just around the corner from the picturesque Galway Golf Club, under the guidance of Donegal-born landlady Celine Molloy, is the place to go. Chatty, knowledgeable Celine has created a haven for golfers, not to mention flower lovers. Everywhere you look are hanging baskets and potted plants, but the effect is cheerful rather than oppressive. Beds are the good, orthopedic sort, essential for recovery after those challenging 18 holes (p. 272), and Celine's home-baked bread is a real winner. Your bed and breakfast will

in a number of apartments and town houses from €450 a week. Okay, they might look as if your oldest maiden aunt got busy with the matching fabrics, but that seems a small price to pay for such in-room niceties as multi-channel TV and a free phone pizza delivery line. That maiden aunt was pretty thoughtful after all. Saturday to Saturday rentals only.

Hotels, Guesthouses & B&Bs

€–€€   Covered in rambling old creeper with lovely mature gardens, the nine-bedroom **Corrib Haven** (107 Upper Newcastle; ☎ 091/524171; corribhaven@eircom.net; cash only), is a pleasant spot, less than 5 minutes' drive from the city center. Yes, the rooms are a bit chintzy, but they all have pretty views and the general feel is tranquil. Also, this is a good place from which to explore Connemara as the region's main road, the N59, starts just outside the door. Rates start at €60 double and include breakfast.

€€   Napoleon said of his soldiers that "an army marches on its stomach" and the same could be said of travelers. If food is important to you, you'll love the **Heron's Rest** ✭ (Longwalk, Spanish Arch; ☎ 086/337-9343; www.theheronsrest. com; AE, MC, V), as it serves possibly the best breakfast in the city. Think French toast with grilled banana, maple syrup, and bacon, and mixed forest fruit pancakes served with raspberry and lime coulis, ready to greet you after a nights' sleep (from €110–€130 a night). Open from May to September, novel in-room extras include a pair of binoculars and a crystal decanter of port—essential kit for taking in a long summer evening by Claddagh Harbor, home to Europe's largest colony of white swans ("Arthur" the heron also makes a daily appearance in the mornings, hence the name). All rooms have direct sea views and straightforward, modern decor, but not all have private bathrooms, so be sure to ask before booking.

€€–€€€   We all know what we get with a Travelodge—good, clean, chipper, family-friendly, fuss free accommodation—and the **Galway Travelodge** 🄺 (Joyce Roundabout, Tuam Rd.; ☎ 091/781400, www.travelodgegalway.com, MC, V) is everything it should be, in a great city center location. Rooms are modern and bright, with cushy duvets and king size beds, and will do for either three adults and a child, or two adults and two children. Though rates here officially start at €169 per room per night, we've seen this rate drop to an enticing €74 per night thanks to last-minute online deals. And families should note that the double rate also works for "family rooms," with a trundle-like couch for the young 'uns to sleep on. No dining room, of course, but a cafe selling drinks and snacks instead.

€€€   A standard hotel, but with a genuinely caring staff and a terrific location (right near Eyre Sq.) the **Forster Court** ✭ (Forster St.; ☎ 091/564111; www.forstercourthotel.com; AE, MC, V) is a solid choice in Galway, perfect for the traveler who just wants a comfortable, clean place to crash (average €130 a night, though online specials can halve that). Rooms are forgettable looking, but loaded with nice extras like free Wi-Fi, 24-hour room service, and powerful showers.

Hostels

€   The pick of the lot is **Barnacles** ✭✭ (Quay St., near Spanish Arch; ☎ 091/568644; www.barnacles.ie; MC, V), situated opposite the Quay's Bar—the place to grab a stool outside and watch the city drift by on a sunny day. Barnacles is high on its own atmosphere too, built in a medieval town house dating back to the 14th century. Rooms are bright and clean and beds comfy, with hypoallergenic duvets. Towels, hot water, and a staff philosophy of going well beyond the basics to ensure your comfort also hit home. Rates start at €56 per night for a double or twin room during the week, and €64 per night on weekends. Beds in 12-bed dorms start at just €13. Swell extras include "pizza and pasta" nights and "chips and dips" movie nights, at no additional cost, plus two bikes guests can borrow for free.

Embrace the Galway Hooker

We're talking spirits, not ladies of the night! Galway Hooker ale is undoubtedly one of the hidden gems of the county, and is available in select county bars, including **Tigh Neachtain** (p. 277) and the **Roisin Dubh** (p. 275). A smooth, pale ale similar to Samuel Adams in the U.S., it goes down almost too easy.

€   That generous feeling of "more for less" is also in operation at the recently upgraded **Kinlay House Hostel** ✸ (Merchants Road, off Eyre Sq.; ☎ 091/565244; www.kinlaygalway.ie; MC, V). It isn't the most aesthetically impressive spot—it looks like the maiden aunt might have had a hand in kitting this place out as well, though on a restricted budget this time—but, with clean, restful double and twin rooms starting at €42 per night, and up to €60 during the summer, it is a more-than-honest option. Dorm beds can be had for just €16. General manager Declan Sharkey is open to a bit of haggling now and again; guests who have pushed for a deal in the past have earned a 10% reduction, or complimentary towel. Free Wi-Fi is also included in the price.

€–€€   Massive **Sleepzone.ie** (Bothar na mBan, off Prospect Hill; ☎ 091/566999; www.sleepzone.ie, cash only)—200 beds!—has a pleasant outdoor terrace for BBQ and free Wi-Fi, though is otherwise unremarkable. Double and twin rooms can be had for as little as €30 per night, from November to January, rising to €76 in high season and €15 for a dorm bed. Annoyances: The push button timed shower is pretty irritating and the breakfast nothing to write home about. However, the company also operates a hostel in Connemara, which means that tour/accommodation deals are negotiable, making this a possible good bet.

DINING FOR ALL TASTES

Galway's seaside location lends itself to a booming seafood industry, so by and large, seafood you find on most of the city's menus is of pretty high standard—especially if it was likely swimming around the day before. The area around Eyre Square is teeming with fast food joints, but as you head down towards the Spanish Arch, dining options become more diverse as the streets begin to narrow. Stumble off the main, pedestrian thoroughfares and you'll find a range of cafes serving cheap eats; stick to the well-trodden paths, and you may be sharing the dining room only with your fellow tourists.

€   A few euro goes a long way at **Anton's** (Father Griffin Rd.; ☎ 091/567801; www.antonscafe.com; Mon–Sat 9am–6pm; cash only), a small, family owned cafe, an excellent value lunch option popular with the aesthetically minded—every month features a showcase by a different artist. A wide range of sandwiches are available for just €5.50—we're big fans of the Cambozola cheese and roasted pepper chutney—and a variety of quirky salads for just €8.50. Smoked chicken with apricots? Trust me, it works.

€   Most people come to **Riordan's Food House** (7 Quay St.; ☎ 091/567810; www.riordans.2ya.com; Mon–Sat 12:30–10:30pm; Sun 11am–10pm; cash only) in the early afternoon, after a heavy day's shopping (it's almost a ritual) to rid themselves of their small change before they head home. It's not impossible to have a three-course meal here for under €20, with starters around €6 and mains all weighing in at €9, although it's the chicken wings (€4.75) or seafood chowder (€4.50) that are the real bargains. It's a simple place, unassuming green frontage, exposed stone walls, basic wooden furniture, but staff are usually charming, the portions only come in one size (large), and most importantly of all, you're in the heart of Galway's cultural quarter, Quay Street.

€–€€   So often the best places to eat are those off the beaten track, and it's quite possible you could spend days trawling the teeming mass that is Quay Street without ever stumbling into the peaceful, pedestrian quarter known as Kirwan's Lane. And if so, that would be a major pity; no visit to Galway could be complete without sampling two of its loveliest little cafes, **Goya's** ✹✹ (Kirwan's Lane, off Lombard St.; ☎ 091/567010; www.goyas.ie; Mon–Sat 9am–6pm; MC, V) and the **Cobblestone Café** ✹✹ (Kirwan's Lane, off Lombard St.; ☎ 091/567227; Mon–Sat 9:30am–6pm; cash only). Goya's proprietor, Emer Murray, is one of the finest baking talents in the country, and should you be visiting friends for dinner during your stay, you'll be looked upon favorably with Goya's 3-Layer Chocolate Gateaux (€25) under your arm. Of course, many also come to Goya's for the lunchtime plat du jour, from 12:30 to 3pm—check the blackboard on the way in. The chicken pie (€9.95), made with mushrooms, leeks, and a white wine sauce is legendary, while plenty of sandwiches and salads start at €7.95. The Cobblestone Café, meanwhile, may be small, but owner Kate Wright's love of cooking and, more important, culinary ability is stoutly evident in a predominantly Mediterranean-themed menu, including paellas, quiches, and even a wonderful curried parsnip soup for €3.20 (also try the Tunisian Orange Cake, which won a recent Amnesty International sponsored dessert competition . . . seriously!). It's a must-stop for vegetarians, or visitors who want a change from the calorie-laden menus in other cafes. Cozy in winter, bright and airy in summer, it's a slice of rural Ireland in the heart of the city.

Eat your Weight in Oysters

From a culinary perspective, September is the best time to visit Galway, with the both the **Clarenbridge Oyster Festival** (mid–Sept, Stradbally, Clarinbridge, 10 min. drive south of Galway City; ☎ 091/796766; www.clarenbridge.com; free admission) and the **Galway Oyster Festival** (late Sept, various venues around Galway City center, ☎ 091/587992; www.galwayoysterfest.com; free admission) offering visitors a chance to indulge their crustacean cravings. Skip lunch before getting there as you'll want to take advantage of the platters of free samples that will be circled through the crowd. Get ready to feel the love.

A Market Meal

The **Galway Saturday Market** (Beside St. Nicholas Church, off Lombard St; Sat 9am–5pm; cash only), is a hot spot for those seeking quirky one-off gifts; for everyone else, it's a chance to savor some of the city's best al fresco grub. **Yummy Crepes** is a decade-old institution that offers a decent selection of sweet and savory crepes, ranging from the basic—a ham, cheese, and onion crepe is €6—to the more gourmet—the "Big Mick," with ham, three cheeses, sun-dried tomatoes, pesto, and Dijon mustard for just €7. Veggie lovers can savor a madras, pea, and potato curry (€3.50) or stuffed chapatti (€2.50) from the **Bean Tree** stall. Follow that up with some sushi from the **Kappa-Ya**—owners Yoshimi and Junichi, incidentally, run the best Japanese restaurant in Galway elsewhere in the city (**Kappa-Ya**, Middle St.; ☎ 086/354-3616; Tues–Sat 12:30–6pm; dinner by reservation only; MC, V)—and you're unlikely to be needing to stop for dinner for some time to come.

€€–€€€　If cheese is your thing, you'll be right at home in Galway. Competition is fierce, but frankly there are few families in the city, or in the rest of the country for that matter, who have done more for Irish food culture than the Sheridans. While the cheese-monger business is certainly worth a visit (16 Church Yard St.; ☎ 091/564829; www.sheridanscheesemongers.com), the family's signature pub/cafe, **Sheridan's on the Dock** ✦✦ (New Docks Rd.; ☎ 091/564905; Mon–Fri 4:30–9:30pm; Sat 12:30–10pm; AE, MC, V), offers the best of both worlds. A blackboard outlines the small range of menu items, such as a smoked seafood board, or lamb and barley stew, while the assorted cheese board for €9 is a great option to share. If you can nab a table outside, enjoy an "up close and personal" opportunity to watch the fish-laden trawlers return home to dock. With one of the best, quirkiest wine lists in the city, a plentiful supply of Galway Hooker ale (they claim to pull the "cheapest pint in Galway"), and trad sessions that last well into the night, this is everything that's best about the city.

€€–€€€　You could try and pin down exactly which nationalities are represented on the menu at **Ard Bia** ✦✦✦ (Spanish Arch; ☎ 091/539897; www.ardbia.com; Tues–Sat 10:30am–3pm and 6–10pm; MC V)—the general consensus is that it falls somewhere between New Zealand and Lebanese—but to be honest, I'd rather spend my time eating here than talking. Together with its more fine-dining sister restaurant, **Nimmo's** ✦✦✦ (Underneath Ard Bia; ☎ 091/561114; Tues–Sat 6:30–9:30pm; MC, V), Aoibheann McNamara's eateries specialize in the element of surprise, with flavors weaving together on dishes such as St. Tolas goat cheese, sage, and roasted pumpkin risotto (€16). However, the lunch menu is where the real deals are, with fish of the day at €14, Galway Bay mussel and smoked haddock chowder (€7.50), and the Ard Bia chickpea and coriander burger for just €10. Eclectic Middle Eastern dishes dot the menu, while the gubbeen or mezze platter is possibly the best value item on the dinner menu at

€9.50. Regular art exhibitions and a private members supper club on weekends round off what is considered one of Galway's finest foodie experiences—no wonder the translation of the Gaelic "Ard Bia" is "High Food."

WHY YOU'RE HERE: TOP SIGHTS & ATTRACTIONS

Galway isn't a city where history is relegated to a few dusty museums. The narrow, cobblestone streets of the city center have been trudged for close to 900 years, and the area around Quay Street, High Street, and Cross Street is a mecca for visitors, and here, history doesn't cost a penny. Expect to be serenaded as you make your way around the city, especially on weekends, as the pedestrian center is filled with every type of busker, from singer-songwriters to jazz quartets, ensuring the hum of the city lasts long into the evening.

If you'd like to explore the streets with an expert at your side, top-notch guided tours are available from **Legend Tours** ✦✦✦ (Forster St.; ☎ 087/778-2887, www.legendtours.ie; €10; tours twice daily). Tour guide Conor Riordan knows Galway inside out, and is able to translate his knowledge and passion into an amusing, memorable flow of information. I'll also recommend a watery tour via the **Corrib Princess** ✦ (Furbo Hill; ☎ 091/592447; www.corribprincess.ie; €14; Apr–Oct), which departs from Woodquay for 90-minute sailings three times a day. With a commentator on board to point out historic castles, and other sights, it's a fun way to immerse yourself in the historic monuments and natural amenities that make the River Corrib one of the most spectacular waterways in Ireland.

Most visitors to the city stumble across **Eyre Square** sooner or later—if traveling by train or bus, it's actually the first thing you see once you disembark—and if you're lucky enough to drop in on a sunny day, this is the perfect location for a lazy afternoon. The square features a green area, named John F. Kennedy Park after the former U.S. president. While in the area, be sure to check out the **silver sword** and **great mace,** housed in the **Bank of Ireland** (19 Eyre Sq.; ☎ 091/563181); dating from the 17th century, they are some of the finest remaining examples of Galway silver. From here, it's just a short stroll to Shop Street, home of **Lynch's Castle.** Now operating as a bank (AIB, Shop St.; ☎ 091/567041), the castle was built in 1320, and was the home of the Lynch family, one of the original tribes of Galway. Coats of arms and stone works adorn the facade, while the interior boasts very fine fireplaces, which date from the reign of Henry VIII. Guests are free to wander in and look around—no transaction necessary.

The **Spanish Arch** stands at the end of Quay Street, a tribute to Galway's merchant past. One of four arches built in 1594 to protect the quays, the Spanish Arch takes its name from the hordes of Spanish merchant ships that used the city to import wine and brandy into the West. In 1755, the arches were partially destroyed by a tsunami generated by an earthquake near Lisbon in Portugal. Right beside it, you'll find the new state-of-the-art **Galway City Museum** (☎ 091/567641; free admission; daily 10am–7pm), which offers guests a walkthrough of the city's colorful history. Housed within are a statue of one of Galway's most famous sons, poet Padraig O'Conaire, a genuine "Galway hooker" fishing vessel, and a focus on Claddagh village, a small fishing community that developed close to where the museum now stands.

Little more than two small rooms and a tiny back yard, the **Nora Barnacle House** (Bowling Green, off Abbeygate St.; ☎ 091/564743; www.norabarnacle. com; €2; summer Mon–Sat 10am–5pm) is a museum dedicated to the sultry wife of Ireland's greatest writer, James Joyce. Packed with Joycean artifacts, the house has been lovingly converted to commemorate the woman who inspired some of the best books in the English language as well as being known for her own pithy sense of humor. This place is catnip for Joyce lovers.

Lastly, the **Galway Irish Crystal Heritage Centre** (Merlin Park, just outside the city; ☎ 091/757311; www.galwaycrystal.ie; free admission; guided tours €4; Mon–Fri 9am–5:30pm; Sat 10am–5:30pm; Sun 11am–5pm) is a chance to immerse oneself in the intricate world of crystal craft. Visitors can watch the craftsmen through each stage of crystal manufacture, from blowing to hand-cutting, with the chance to bring the experience home to sit on your mantle. To get there, follow N6 out of Galway (Dublin Rd.); Merlin Park is just beyond GMIT.

THE OTHER GALWAY

For every tourist trap, there's a side of Galway that only the locals see—as a visitor, you can find that other side, if you don't mind rooting it out. It may be the "other" Galway from a tourist point of view, but take part in one of these activities and you'll soon feel like a local.

Obsessive fans of U2—and there's no shortage of them over here—will undoubtedly remember the "giant heads" that launched most of their shows during the 90s. These bizarre creations were the work of Galway group **Macnas** (☎ 091/561462; www.macnas.com), whose dedication to performance art over the years has earned them distinction at home and abroad. Needless to say, the colorful troupe is always on the lookout for volunteers for their latest ambitious project, and offer a series of free creative workshops (drumming perhaps, or mask making or costuming), generally taking place in May and June.

Galway was the first county in Ireland to host an All Ireland hurling final, way back in 1887, and the county's love of Gaelic games has continued unabated since—with four All Ireland hurling titles and nine All Ireland football crowns under their belt, they're not too bad at it either. Few experiences in the city are as invigorating or passionate as a GAA (Gaelic Athletic Association) championship match—don't be afraid to don maroon and white, the local colors and join in the singing (avoid wearing green and red, the colors of loathed neighbors Mayo—not that you'll be in any danger, but you may find yourself the butt of jokes). The Tribesmen, as the team is known, play their home games at **Pearse Stadium** (Roackbarton Rd., Salthill; ☎ 091/583173; www.pearsestadium.ie), a short distance from Salthill Promenade; keep an eye out for schedules on **www.galwaygaa.ie** while a range of tickets are available through **Ticketmaster** (www.ticketmaster.ie).

ACTIVE GALWAY

Golfers are well accommodated in Galway, and **Galway Golf Club** (Blackrock, Salthill; ☎ 091/522033; www.galwaygolf.com), situated in Salthill, is recognized as one of the country's finest, with a heritage dating back to 1895 and breathtaking views of Galway harbor. A members' club, visitors are not allowed on Tuesdays, Sundays, and certain Saturdays, while green fees are a modest-for-golf €50 Monday to Friday, and €60 weekends, for both men and women. Further out of town, **Barna Golf Club** (beside Paddy's Cross Roads, outside Barna; ☎ 091/592677; www.bearnagolfclub.com; green fees Mon–Fri €35, Sat and Sun €50), designed by RJ Brown, is a parkland course set over 100 hectares (247 acres) and is fast earning a reputation as one of the West's most challenging courses.

Festive Galway

Galway is a county renowned for the *craic,* and the abundance of festivals dotted throughout the year is a testament to locals' willingness to get into the business of fun. The most notable of these is probably the July **Galway Arts Festival** (various venues in Galway City; ☎ 091/566577; www.galway artsfestival.com), with music, dance, literature, and art. The festival celebrated its 30th anniversary in 2008, featuring performances by artists of the caliber of Blondie, Philip Glass, and Joni Mitchell, as well as a host of dramatic performances, readings, comedy shows, and of course the Festival Parade. Keep an eye out for performances by local theatre group **Macnas** (p. 272), which generally form the centerpiece for the festival. Over 100,000 people descend on Galway in July for the festival, so if you're planning on visiting at this time, some serious advance booking of hotels and restaurants is recommended.

In April, Galway's literary heritage is celebrated at the **Cúirt International Festival of Literature** (Various venues; ☎ 091/565886; http://galwayartscentre.ie/cuirt.htm), which in previous years has hosted a big-name writers, from Allen Ginsberg and J.M. Coetzee to Chuck Palahniuk and Irvine Welsh. Readings, workshops, and debates fill the 5-day festival.

Sports in Galway are dominated by the **Galway Races Summer Festival** (Ballybrit racecourse, off the N17; ☎ 091/753870; www.galwayraces.com; €20, €30 Wed and Thurs), one of the country's premier horseracing events, which attract spectators from all walks of life—it's been said that politicians spend more time debating in the races' corporate hospitality tents than in the Irish parliament itself. Taking place over 1 week starting the last Monday in July, the event attracts over 200,000 people from across the country. Expect no shortage of glam on Ladies' Day (Thurs), with the best dressed ladies battling for attention (and an ample-size shopping voucher), while Sunday, the final day, is traditionally "Mad Hatters" day, with the most peculiar hat creation scooping a range of prizes.

If the Galway rain isn't wet enough for you, **Bow Waves Sailing and Powerboat School** (Harbour Enterprise Park; ☎ 091/560560; www.bowwaves.com), situated just outside Galway City center, offers a range of sailing courses for adults and children, as well as a host of family offers. Dinghy, yacht, keelboat, and powerboat sailing courses are available, from beginner to advanced.

ATTENTION SHOPPERS!

The city center of Galway bristles with jolly shops, many of them quirky and crafty. The **Kilkenny Shop** ★★★ (6 High St.; ☎ 091/566110; www.kilkenny shop.com) is a treasure chest of high-concept Irish design, including pottery by

Stephen Pearce, crystal by John Rocha, bags, accessories, and shoes by Orla Kiely, and silver jewelry by Newbridge.

Anyone with a wedding on the way (or just a lonely ring finger)—should make **Dillon's Claddagh Gold** ✸✸ (Quay St.; ☎ 091/566365; www.claddaghring.ie) a must stop; the firm has been making the world famous Claddagh Friendship Ring since 1750, and only relocated from its original premises in William Street to Quay Street in the 1990s. A small museum on site charts the history of the Claddagh ring, which has adorned the fingers of everyone from Winston Churchill to Walt Disney.

One local institution, **Cobwebs** ✸ (7 Quay Lane; ☎ 091/564388), which recently celebrated its 35th birthday, has had a revamp and is looking better than ever. Yes, the store is packed with modern designs and pretty engagement rings, but there is also an excellent selection of antique pieces, collected by the owner who has both considerable knowledge and passion in that area. Clever, delicate lockets, broaches, pendants, and rings are historically perfect and great value, while the charming collection of teddy bears and excellent selection of unusual cufflinks are worth a browse.

Books are big in Galway, particularly appealingly musty old hard-backs, and **Charlie Byrne's Bookshop** ✸ (The Cornstore, Middle St.; ☎ 091/561766; www.charliebyrne.com) has a rock-solid selection of Irish-interest titles, as well as plenty of cheaper, more disposable paperbacks to get you through those wet days.

Although local fashion can incline towards the tie-dyed and overly bright, there is plenty of high style to be had too, as anyone who has ever spent a day at the Galway Races will know. **Les Jumelles** ✸ (11 Upper Abbeygate St.; ☎ 091/564540) is indeed owned by twin sisters and works a chic-boho look very well. Alongside major European labels they also stock Irish fashion darlings Lainey Keogh, Louise Kennedy, and Mary Grant. Although definitely not cheap, the twice-yearly sales are the real deal, with avalanche-style discounts on many fabulous pieces, so if you're around in January or July, be sure to pop in.

Vintage is very much part of the Galway aesthetic, and **Twice as Nice** (5 Quay St.; ☎ 091/566332) have a good selection of clothes, jewelry, and accessories, along with some lovely old linen and lace.

Royal Tara (Tara Hall, Mervue; ☎ 091/705602) fine bone china and **Galway Irish Crystal Heritage Centre** (p. 272) both have "seconds" or factory shops alongside the main outlets outside the city, where you will pick up perfectly good-quality pieces at a decent discount. Galway Irish Crystal, in particular, is a good bet for those who like the genre but don't fancy paying the higher-profile Waterford and Tipperary Crystal prices. **Clarenbridge Crystal** (Clarenbridge, on the N18; ☎ 091/796178) is also locally made, hand-cut, and decorated in a factory about 16km (10 miles) south of the city, and has a shop about a kilometer and a half (about a mile)

Store Hours

Unless otherwise stated, shops in Galway keep the usual opening hours—roughly 9:30am to 6pm, with late opening on Friday, until around 8pm. During high season (July and Aug) most also open on a Sunday.

Druid Theatre

The vibrancy of the Galway arts scene is nowhere more evident than in **Druid Theater Company** ✪✪✪ (Flood St.; ☎ 091/568660; www.druid theatre.com), under the careful stewardship of legendary director Garry Hynes. This was the very first professional theater founded outside of Dublin, back in 1975, and was in no small part responsible for reinvigorating the Dublin theatrical scene by providing a bit of much-needed competition. Garry Hynes, the first woman ever to win a Tony Award for Best Director (for Martin McDonagh's *The Beauty Queen of Leenane,* in 1998) was among the three original founders and is still the creative and driving force behind this remarkable company. Consistently inspired by the works of J.M. Synge, in 2007 Druid staged the ambitious DruidSynge project, a marathon showing of all six of Synge's classic plays in 1 day. As well as reanimating the established cannon of Irish literature, the energetic Hynes also champions a host of younger playwrights, such as Enda Walshe and Marina Carr, and has contributed, in no small measure, to their establishment. Along with playing the Town Hall Theatre (p. 275), the Druid Theatre Company also host a number of performances at the Chapel Lane Theatre. Early booking is essential.

farther down the road selling decanters, glasses, bowls, and table wear at prices rather better than you will find elsewhere.

NIGHTLIFE

Galway's bohemian lifestyle has instilled it with a vibrant arts scene, with numerous theater and performance art groups competing for attention in the city's many venues. The **Town Hall Theatre** (Courthouse Sq.; ☎ 091/569777; www.townhall theatregalway.com, www.ticketlord.com) is where you'll find the major arts events in the city, with everything from musicals to comedy to orchestral performances finding a home in this multi-purpose space. Regular guests include the Druid Theatre Company (see above), the Abbey Theatre Company, and the Royal Shakespeare Company, as well as a host of international musical and acting talent. Best of all, not a week goes by without a series of new performances, especially in the run up to the Galway Arts Festival (p. 273).

The **Galway Youth Theatre Group,** based at the nearby Galway Arts Centre, host regular performances at their own Nun's Island theatre space (Nuns Island; ☎ 091/565886), an affordable alternative to other venues in the city, with admission charges generally around €10.

Dance & Music Clubs

Rock music is the thing at the city's top live venue, the **Roisin Dubh** (Dominick St.; ☎ 091/586540; www.roisindubh.net), and while the many international acts that frequent the venue can command ticket prices in excess of €30, most gigs come in at around the €10 mark, with many midweek nights free of charge. Located on vibrant Dominick Street, the intimate venue got a complete overhaul in 2004, including a new state-of-the-art sound system, but happily, the notorious atmosphere hasn't changed a bit. Many local and international acts also appear at the **Quays Bar** (Quay St.; ☎ 091/568347; €8–€12) and at the **Radisson Hotel** (Lough Atalia Rd.; ☎ 091/538300; www.radissonhotelgalway.com; over €30).

Galway is teeming with nightclubs—homage to the strong student population—and most offer discounted rates during midweek, with admission on Mondays, Tuesdays, and Wednesdays generally gratis. Bear in mind that during the week, most Galway clubs attract a younger crowd, with the older generation generally saving themselves for the weekend.

The Central Park Group operates two of the city's most popular nightclubs, **Central Park** (Upper Abbeygate St.; ☎ 091/565976; www.centralparkclub.com; Fri €8, Sat €12, Sun €6) and **Halo** (Upper Abbeygate St.; ☎ 091/565976; www.halonightclub.com; Fri €10, Sat €14), both of which spin a mix of the latest chart hits and dance-floor tracks from the past few years. The **GPO** (Eglinton St.; ☎ 091/563073; www.gpo.ie; €5–€15), just off Eyre Square, has always attracted an older, dressier crowd, featuring international DJs of the calibre of Roger Sanchez and Fatboy Slim, while **Cuba** (Prospect Hill, Eyre Sq.; ☎ 091/565991; www.cuba.ie; €10–€15), set over two floors, covers a wide spectrum of musical styles during the week—anything from rock classics on Monday and disco on Thursday to dance-floor fillers at the weekend.

Pubs of Note

The smoking ban in Ireland has been received in differing ways by the pub trade and pub going punters. While the lack of foresight in some pubs has forced smokers to huddle under basic tarpaulins outside, others have thrived by creating novel smoking areas that are, in many ways, cozier than the crowded bar inside. The **Dew Drop Inn** ✶ (also known as Myles Lee, Mainguard St.; ☎ 091/561070) is one of those places: While the two rooms that make up the complex are brightly decorated with comfortable seating, it can get a bit cramped at weekends. The smoking area, meanwhile, is heated, well covered, and packed with snug seating—it's the best little back room in the city, as long as there aren't too many puffing away beside you.

Should you be leaving the Dew Drop at a respectable hour, you'll more than likely hear a cacophonous commotion taking place down the road—it's nothing to worry about; it's just another night at **Tig Cóilí** ✶✶ (Mainguard St., junction with Shop St.; ☎ 091/561294). The little pub is renowned for its traditional Irish music sessions, featuring artists from home and abroad, and while bars like the Quays around the corner thrive on the tourist dollar, here you'll mainly find locals soaking up the sounds of the city. If you see a crowd around the door, don't panic; the pub may not be quite full—the music sessions generally take place near the door, and there may well be seating down the back.

One of the first bars you'll encounter when leaving the train station (or the last before you leave) is also one of Galway's best. If you're in need of liquid refreshment, **Garvey's Inn** ✶✶ (Eyre Sq., just beside train station; ☎ 091/562224; www.garveysinn.com) serves one of the best pints in the city, and boasts high ceilings and period features—the bar originally opened in the mid-1800s, so it's a bit

A Raucous Pub Hop

No visit to Galway is complete without doing what's been locally termed the "Quay Street Shuffle"—a pub crawl through the heart of the old city to some of its most renowned venues. Start at the junction of Cross and Quay streets at the notorious **Tigh Neachtain** ✪✪✪ (Naughton's, Cross St.; ☎ 091/568820), a lively spot that has attracted everyone from buskers to businessmen since 1894, and is packed with cozy snugs and alcoves in which to savor your pint of plain.

Across the road, the **Quays Bar** ✪✪ (Quay St.; ☎ 091/568347) is a rustic, old-world spot with an interior salvaged from a French medieval church. Don't be surprised to hear a foreign voice or two—it's something of a tourist magnet—but make sure you take a good look around; the bar is spilt into two parts; as well as the larger, newer half, there's also the "pub within a pub," in the form of former 19th century bar Delia Lydon's.

Stumble further down the street to the **Spanish Arch** ✪✪✪ (Quay St.; ☎ 091/569600; info@spanisharchhotel.ie), one of the best spots in the city for an impromptu trad session (most of the pub is surrounded by a former monastery wall to keep the noise out), and, if you're still up for it, finish the night off by soaking up the atmosphere in the cavernous **Front Door** (High St.; ☎ 091/566186; www.frontdoorpub.com), on High Street, a 500-capacity venue that remains open until 2am.

like drinking in a museum. If you fancy something a little stronger, ask the barman about the pub's collection of fine whiskies, and if it all gets a bit too much for you later in the day, there are a number of bedrooms above the pub (they can be a bit loud, however) for €110 a night.

GALWAY COUNTY

Galway City may be the hub for most of the county, but the excitement shouldn't end once you leave the city limits. Over the next few pages, we focus on the best the rest of the county has to offer, starting with one of the most remote—and beautiful—parts of the Irish landscape.

THE ARAN ISLANDS

Perched at the edge of Galway Bay, the last stop before tackling the mighty Atlantic, the Aran Islands are possibly the most weather-beaten set of rocks in Ireland, which is reflected in the stony landscape and barren terrain. Nonetheless, generations of Irish have called these islands—Inis Mor, Inis Meain, and Inis Oirr—home. The islands are awash with history: The stunning ancient fort of Dun Aenghus still stands proudly on the west coast of Inis Mor, 3,000 years on from when it was constructed, while Robert Flaherty's powerful 1934 documentary, *Man of Aran* (screened daily in the Aran Heritage Centre, p. 279) portrays a side to Irish history that is still remarkably visible on some parts of the island. For the most part, though, the Aran Islands have modernized in the past few years; better roads make it easy to get around (bike is best), and the islanders have finally managed to track down an electricity source that doesn't cut out several times a day (as was the case when I first visited, some 10 years ago). John Millington Synge once described the Aran Islands as a "little corner on the face of the world. [The] people who live in it have a peace and dignity from which we are shut for ever." Time can't change that.

Getting There & Getting Around

Getting to the islands is easy. **Aran Island Ferries** (☎ 091/568903; www.aranisland ferries.com; round-trip €25; 7 daily sailings summer, 2 winter) depart from Rossaveal, about 1 hour from Galway City (coaches depart from Kinlay House hostel three times daily). **Aran Direct** (☎ 091/566535; www.arandirect.com; round-trip €25) also operate from Rossaveal, with three sailings daily to Inis Mor. Travel time around 40 minutes. For those in a hurry—or prone to seasickness—**Aer Arann** (☎ 091/593034; www.aerarannislands.com; €40 per person, based on a group of 4 or more, day trip) operates flights to the island from Aerfort na Minna (p. 263).

　Inis Mor, Inis Meain, and **Inis Oirr** are all easily explored either by minibus, taxi, or preferably by bike—the largest of the three, Inis Mor, is just 12km by 3km (7½ x 2 miles) in size.

Where to Stay & Dine

€   It's difficult to find a guesthouse—or indeed anything else—on the stunningly beautiful Inis Mor, the largest of the Aran Islands, that doesn't have some sort of character. **Mainistir House** ★★★ (☎ 099/61169; www.mainistirhouse aran.com; MC, V), operated by ebullient host Joel d'Anjou, is rightly famous for both its adorably quirky rooms—which have an almost Far Eastern silken tent appeal, so deeply jewel-toned are their wall colors and decor—and its nightly gourmet spectacular, the "vaguely vegetarian buffet" (€12, there are a few meat dishes thrown into the mix). Open for 14 years and upgraded recently, Mainistir House also offers truly excellent value accommodation, with hostel beds available for €18, or one of eight private rooms, starting at €50 each, though only one has a private bathroom, and that for the slightly inflated price of €70. A light continental breakfast is factored in. It's located a 20 minute walk from the harbor.

€€   **Man of Aran Cottages** ★★★ (☎ 099/61301; www.manofarancottage.com; closed Nov–Feb; cash only), also located on Inis Mor around 6km (4 miles) from Kilronan (minibus available), was the setting for the movie *Man of Aran,* and it's not difficult to see why. Located right beside the sea, this tiny three-bedroom B&B (only one with private bathroom but for such character, the slight hardship seems well worth it) operated by Joe and Maura Wolfe is everything you'd expect of a guesthouse in such a remote part of the country: a thatched roof, exposed wooden beams and stone walls, simple furniture, and whitewashed walls—to be honest, I don't know how much of it is put on for the tourists, but I still like it. The guesthouse is also renowned for its devotion to organic produce and quality cuisine, as Maura spent some time working as a chef at Buckingham Palace. Breakfast, lunch, and dinner are lovingly crafted for guests using the best herbs and vegetables the couple's organic garden will provide. Rates start at €80 per night for a standard double (€90 for the en suite room), while dinner at the property will set you back

€35. If you plan on exploring the island on foot or bicycle, make sure you ask the ever-obliging Maura to whip you up one of her legendary packed lunches.

€€   The 9th century church of Dun Aenghus is generally recognized as the Aran Islands' premier tourist attraction, but I would make a case for Treasa Joyce, owner of **Kilmurvey House** ✪✪ (☎ 099/61218; www.kilmurveyhouse.com; cash only), as a close second. A truly charming lady, Treasa's 12-bedroom property stands on the land that leads up to the church itself, meaning all guests get free access. This 150-year-old property has real country elegance: high ceilings, imposing portraits of former landowners, pretty china, and a top quality beach just 2 minutes' walk away. Kilmurvey House boasts a strong level of repeat guests, especially cycling groups. Unfortunately, Treasa was in the process of scaling back her fantastic dinner operation to just "3 or 4 nights a week" when I called on her, although she still cooks a wonderful breakfast—fruit, fresh pastries, homemade bread, and jam. The most striking thing about Kilmurvey House is its peaceful aura—while all the bedrooms are en suite, not one features a TV. As the woman herself says, "The idea is to provide a time away from all that." Who are we to argue? Nightly costs are €90 to €110 per double room including breakfast; dinner €30. The house is 7km (4 miles) from the harbor, but minibus transportation is available.

Why You're Here: Exploring the Islands

Inis Mor is the largest of the three Aran Islands, and it's here that you'll find the most activities, but how you choose to view the island generally depends on how fit you are. Cycling tours are especially popular with groups from continental Europe and the U.S., and **Aran Bike Hire** (Inishmore; ☎ 099/61132; www.aranbikehire.com; €10 per bike per day, with deposit) is a good place to start, located at the end of the pier just as you step off the ferry. **Mullins Bicycle Hire** (☎ 099/61132) and **BNN Bicycle Hire** (☎ 099/61402) offer similar rates, from the tiny village of **Kilronan,** a short stroll from the pier. Inis Mor is arranged in such a manner that the often hilly main road, which features many of the island's historical sites, and the flatter coast road, meet in Kilronan.

  Another popular option is to see the island by bus, generally over the course of 2 to 3 hours. My personal favorite is the **Dún Aonghas Tour** (☎ 099/61329; www.dunaonghastours.com) with local Bertie Flaherty, a knowledgeable, chatty fellow who is endearingly passionate about his work. **Noel Mahon Tours** (Kilronan; ☎ 087/778-2775; www.tourbusaranislands.com) and **Aran Bus Tours** (☎ 087/056-3285; www.aranbustours.com) will also do the job.

  All tours take in several of the island's key attractions: **Dun Aonghasa,** a 2,500-year-old fort perched atop 91m (300 ft.) high cliffs, **Na Seacht d'Teampaill,** the ruins of a religious study center from the 8th century and the setting for Robert Flaherty's powerful 1934 documentary, *Man of Aran.*

  The **Aran Heritage Centre** (Cill Ronain; ☎ 099/61355; www.visitaranislands.com; free admission; daily Apr–May and Sept–Oct 11am–5pm; Jun–Aug 10am–7pm) is also worth a visit; here you can find out about some of the island's more notable natives, such as poet Martin O'Direain and novelist Liam O'Flaherty, and learn about life on the island in the 1930s—*Man of Aran* is screened up to six times daily in the center and if you have never before come across this slow-moving masterpiece of cinéma vérité, now is the best possible time to make up the deficit.

Attention Shoppers!

The humble Aran jumper has come on leaps and bounds since its sheep's wool origins; recent years have seen them modeled by the likes of Sarah Jessica Parker and Sharon Stone, so quit sneering. Head to the **Aran Sweater Market** (☎ 064/39756) on Inis Mor, the largest of the Aran Islands, and if there's any Irish lurking in your family tree, they'll track down your hereditary stitching pattern and create a jumper just for you.

CONNEMARA

Parts of **Connemara**, which runs from Lough Corrib in the east to the mighty Atlantic Ocean in the west, look like a distant planet, with rocky outcrops and acres of barren wasteland. In fact, there's a part of Europa, one of Jupiter's moons, named Conamara Chaos after the Galway region. For all its wilderness, however, Connemara remains one of the most beautiful parts of the country, and a visit is highly rewarding, if only for the sense of perspective it delivers on the frustrations of daily life.

Lay of the Land

The area commonly referred to as Connemara is made up of the civil parishes of Moyrus, Ballynakill, Omey, Ballindoon, and Inishbofin, though most simply think of it as the area west of Galway City (from roughly Oughterard to the raging Atlantic Ocean). Clifden is its largest town and makes a good hopping-off point for exploring the rest of the area. To the north of Clifden is Ireland's only fjord, the splendid Killary Fiord; it's other big draw is Connemara National Park, an eclectic area of mountains, bogs, heaths, and grasslands.

Getting There & Getting Around

You can hop on a bus from Galway to Clifden and the region's other small towns; **Bus Éireann** (☎ 091/562000; www.buseireann.ie) has daily service, leaving every 3 hours or so (services varies by season and day of week), costing €11 one-way and €15 round-trip between Galway and Clifden. But the bus likely won't go everywhere you want and schedules aren't always convenient. You'll do better simply renting a car and hitting the **N59.** The heart of the Connemara region is about 65km (40 miles) west of Galway City.

Where to Stay & Dine

CLIFDEN

€€   Breakfast is big at the **Connemara Country Lodge** (Westport Rd., 500m/1,640 ft. from Clifden town center; ☎ 095/22122; connemara@unison.ie; cash only), not least because the owner, Mary Corbett, a trained ballad singer, violinist, and character, is sometimes moved to break into a traditional ballad over the bacon and eggs (p. 285). The ten basic but pleasant bedrooms are en suite, but shower only. Rates start at €70 double.

€€   Further down the Westport Road, Catriona and Patrick O'Toole, proprietors of **Buttermilk Lodge** (400m/1,312 ft. along Westport Rd. outside Connemara village; ☎ 095/21951; buttermilklodge@eircom.net; cash only), as well as being convivial hosts, breed sheep and picture-postcard Connemara ponies

Dine on the Orient Express

The magnificent **Glenlo Abbey** (along the N59 from Galway to Clifden; ☎ 091/526666; www.glenlo.com; reservations essential) is rightly renowned for its picturesque setting and attention to detail—it's a big hit with weddings—but casual visitors shouldn't leave the county without paying a visit to the hotel's Pullman Restaurant. Set in an actual 1920s railway carriage, the Pullman was used to transport Winston Churchill's remains to their final resting place and in later years played a starring role in the Agatha Christie film *Murder on the Orient Express*. Now grounded, these days it's more famous for its fine cuisine (€12–€30) . . . but keep an eye on that waiter with the shifty eyes.

for a living. It's a real taste of rural Ireland, and Catriona and Patrick, who are sweetly proud of their extended family, will quite happily escort you, Toby the sheepdog, and Harley the golden retriever down to their field to meet the menagerie. The guesthouse itself is inviting and warm, with a peat fire burning away in the corner (although the carpets and curtains are a throwback to the 1980s), and the rooms themselves, while basic, are perfectly comfortable. Rates start at €70, with deals available for stays of 2 nights or more. Breakfast is a real highlight here—the local butcher consistently wins awards for his homemade sausages and black and white puddings.

LETTERFRACK
€€€   Set in a restored cottage, **Pangur Bán Restaurant** ✪✪✪ (Letterfrack village, opposite Connemara National Park; ☎ 095/41243; www.pangurban.com; Mon–Sat 6–9pm, Sun 10am–4:30pm; MC V)—the name is a nod to a 9th-century poem about a white cat—looks unassuming enough from the outside, but few restaurants in the country offer as satisfying and adventurous a menu as John Walsh's stone-fronted eatery. Think prawn tempura with poached pear and black bean sauce (€8), fillet of Irish cod with asparagus risotto (€23), or pork fillet parcels with cranberries, mint, and spinach sauce (€22). This is a sensory adventure, and well worth the 15km (9 miles) trip from Clifden. Two courses will generally set you back around €20, and special deals are available for larger groups. If you'd like to learn how to make what you're eating, consider taking a class at the cooking school here (p. 284). Letterfrack, incidentally, was the location chosen by Marconi for his first transatlantic duplex wireless transmission some 95 years ago. Reservations necessary.

LOUGHREA
€   **Fare Green Food** (Millenium House, Ewstbridge, Loughrea; ☎ 091/870911; Mon–Fri 8am–6:30pm; Sat 9am–6pm; Sun seasonally; cash only) is a quaint delicatessen/cafe that lives up to its name. Owner Maureen Fynes is a staunch advocate of organic produce. The main focus of this operation is to provide healthy meals, as well as top quality loose leaf tea, making it a worthwhile pit-stop or a longer, lingering lunch. The homemade bread and scones are so good you'll

want to take them with you, while the cafe also offers a variety of lunchtime specials, such as a soup and a variety of wraps for €7.95, soup with homemade bread for €4.95, or a range of organic salads for €6.95.

OUGHTERARD/ROSSCAHILL

€   Connemara's limestone base gives it an almost lunar landscape, and while the rocky scarps and sweeping, flat vales in the area are breathtaking, a small change of scenery is always a welcome respite. Brigit's Garden is just such a location: a landscaped set of four gardens themed around the Celtic seasonal festivals, set among 4½ hectares (11 acres) of woodland and wildflower meadows. Within the gardens is **Brigit's Garden Café** ★ (2km/1 mile from N59 between Oughterard and Moycullen; ☎ 091/550905; www.brigitsgarden.ie; May–Sept daily 10am–6pm; MC, V), a little piece of paradise for weary travelers on the road back to the city. Open seasonally, owner Jenny Beale's hallmark is freshly prepared food featuring herbs and vegetables from the garden. Try the homemade vegetable soup with brown bread (€4.50), goat cheese and courgette quiche (€8.50), topped off with Nico's French pear tart (€4.75).

€€   If you're drawn to the area, consider bunking at the **Corrib Wave Guesthouse** kids (Portacarron, Oughterard; ☎ 091/552147; www.corribwave.com; MC, V), which features cheerful rooms, including a number of family rooms, chatty, knowledgeable hosts, and views out across Lough Corrib. Rates start at €80 double.

CLONBUR

€€–€€€   There's a local saying that "you could meet anyone in Clonbur." Well, Edward Lynch's **Fairhill House Hotel** (5km/3miles west of Cong, follow signs for An Fhairce [Clonbur in Irish]; ☎ 094/954-6176; fairhillhouse@ eircom.net; cash only) is a good place to start. Established in 1830, the hotel was brought up to three-star standard 4 years ago, cementing its strong local following—some of Lynch's guests have been coming for over 30 years. Located almost 2km (1 mile) from one of the biggest free fishing lakes in Europe means its popular with angling enthusiasts, while Ashford Castle, 5 minutes down the road, is a convenient option for dinner. Rates start at just €65 (Nov–Mar) and don't go above €80 for the rest of the year, while 2 nights B&B and one evening meal is available for a reasonable €145. The rooms are modern and comfortable; try and nab a room with a balcony for stunning views of the Clonbur landscape. The signature seafood chowder is the thing to go for in the restaurant, but the bar also does good seafood and always seems to be packed with happy locals.

Why You're Here: Exploring Connemara

There's a saying in these parts that "for every star God put in the sky, He cast a million stones upon the ground of Connemara." It's true, to a point; stone plains dominate the landscape, with mosses and lichens the only form of nature in many places. But Connemara is also a landscape of many guises: Limestone plains sit alongside bog and marshland, pockmarked by myriad lakes. If you're making your own way around this beautiful area, definitely take in the **Connemara National Park** ★★★ (13km/8 miles from Clifden, near Letterfrack on the N59; ☎ 095/ 41054; www.connemaranationalpark.ie; free admission; May–Aug daily 9:30am–6pm;

free daily guided walks) for a ramble through this inspiring area. As well as a visitors center, the park offers guests the choice of two short walking trails: the Ellis Wood Nature Trail and the Sruffanboy Trail. Both take about 20 minutes to complete, but bear in mind that the Sruffanboy trail takes in a couple of steep hills.

Beyond its spectacular natural sights, Connemara is awash with heritage, and it's difficult to drive more than 15 minutes in any direction without stumbling across a monument or building with serious historical pedigree. By far the most popular attraction is **Kylemore Abbey** ★★☆ (80km/50 miles from Galway on N59 between Recess and Letterfrack; ☎ 095/41146; www.kylemoreabbey.com; €7.50; visitor center, abbey, and church year-round daily 9am–5pm; Victorian Walled Garden Apr–Sept daily 10am–4:30pm) a quiet hideaway that still operates as a Benedictine monastery. Built by wealthy English politician Mitchell Henry in 1870 in honor of his wife, the Abbey became the home of the Irish Benedictine Nuns following the First World War, after they fled their convent in war-torn Belgium. The abbey is a work of art, embellished with limestone carvings, impressive gothic arches and angelic gargoyles. In the south transept a beautiful stained glass window depicts the five graces: Fortitude, Faith, Charity, Hope, and Chastity (be honest, how many of them do *you* adhere to?). Whether it's the reclusive setting, hidden in its own valley by the shores of Lough Corrib, the serenity of the lovingly kept Victorian Garden, or just the blissful peace that pervades through the abbey itself, visiting is a wonderful way to spend an afternoon. Empty your mind, gaze on the ancient stones, and ponder the many mysteries of life.

Connemara by Bike or Bus

Two-wheeling it is an ideal way to take in the wonders of Connemara. Starting at Maam Cross, about 35km (22 miles) from Galway, an 85km (53 mile) cycle route takes in breathtaking scenery, boundless ruins and monastic sites, and a plethora of villages with more pubs than houses. Everything you might remember from those old picture postcards—including roads packed with sheep or other livestock. Rush hour in Ireland, as the saying goes. Don't forget the puncture repair kit.

For those of us that don't have the luxury of time, a number of tour providers serve the area well. **Healy Coaches** (☎ 091/753335; www.healytours.ie; €22; discounts online) operate daily coach tours of the Connemara landscape, running from Forster Street in Galway City center every day at 10 and 11:30am. Moycullen, Oughterard, Lough Corrib, Inagh Valley, Maam Cross, Clifden, Recess, and Spiddal are among the towns and villages visited, as well as the magnificent **Kylemore Abbey** (p. 283). The average tour lasts around 7 or 8 hours, and is a cheap, compact way to sample the beauty of the Connemara region. Better still is **Aran Islands Direct** (Forster St.; ☎ 091/553188; www.arandirect.com; €25), which also operate a Connemara tour, taking in all of the above locations; with it you get the bonus of a 2½-hour stop at Kylemore Abbey.

A Literary Side Trip

If books are your thing, you will probably already know all about **Coole Park** ✪✪ (near Gort, close to the junctions of the N18 and N66; ☎ 091/631804; www.coolepark.ie; free admission; visitor center Mar–Sept; park year-round), the residence of the late Lady Augusta Gregory, associate and friend to many of Ireland's greatest writers and artists, including George Bernard Shaw and W.B. Yeats, who spent long periods of tranquil, creative time at the estate house. Walking around this 178 hectare (440 acre) estate, you can't but feel invigorated knowing that some of the nation's paramount writing talent trod the same path—make sure to visit the "signature tree," which features carved initials by everyone from Douglas Hyde, Ireland's first president, to Yeats himself. The visitors' center charts the history of Lady Gregory, with an exhibition outlining the great figures of the Irish literary revival. Close by is **Thoor Ballylee**, a 16th century tower where Yeats lived from 1921 to 1929, during which time he wrote the extraordinary *Sailing to Byzantium*.

Also of historical note is **Aughnanure Castle** (3km/2 miles south of Oughterard; ☎ 091/552214; €2.90; Mar–Oct daily 9:30am–6pm). Built by the wealthy deBurgo family in the 15th century, it was the principal residence of the O'Flaherty clan—a warmongering lot who came to symbolize native Irish opposition to the ruling English classes in Galway City (for several generations). These are the same O'Flaherty's who are referenced in a notice over the west gate of the city; stuck up in 1562 by the then mayor, it reads, "From the Ferocious O'Flahertys may God protect us."

For something a bit different than abbeys and bogs, head to **Connemara Smokehouse** (Bunowen Pier, Ballyconeely, around 8km/5 miles from Clifden on the R341; ☎ 095/23739; www.smokehouse.ie), a seafood business operated by the Roberts family for over 30 years. Specialists in wild smoked salmon, honey roast smoked salmon, gravaldax, and smoked tuna, the business is primarily a retail outlet, but smokehouse tours are available during the summer, on Wednesdays at 3pm. Make sure you bring some spending money—after watching expert Graham Roberts hand fillet, smoke, and slice your own cut of salmon, you won't want to leave without some samples.

The Other Connemara

Galway cuisine is largely dictated by the sea—an undulating Western seaboard, facing onto the mighty Atlantic, gives it a 689km (428 mile) coastline—and while sampling local oysters and sea bream is a fine way to spend your holiday, cooking for yourself is an invigorating way to immerse yourself in the "flavour of the West." John Walsh, chef/proprietor of **Pangur Bán** (Letterfrack, opposite the Connemara National Park; ☎ 095/41243; www.pangurban.com; €75) boasts that his in-house cooking school is the "first of its kind in Connemara," and while many imitators have sprung up in the years and months since, I still believe this to be the best. Set in the 300-year-old thatched cottage that also doubles as a fine restaurant, John takes students through the history of Galway cuisine, and talks visitors through the preparation of everything from homemade bread—he's one of the most inventive bakers in the country, by the way—to a range of starters and main courses. With plenty of fish, of course.

Love horses? Don't mind mucking out a few stables? The **Slieve Aughty Riding Centre** (Kylebrack West, Loughrea; ☎ 090/974-5246; www.riding centre.com; 2-week working holidays start at €400, €200 a week, including full-board) is a perfectly respectable B&B and riding center in its own right, but between September and May of each year, equine fanatics descend on the picturesque Loughrea school to help the Zyderlaan family tend to the horses, manage the farm and organic garden, and perform general maintenance for two periods of 2 weeks. The center is popular with students—although the oldest visitor to date was a sprightly 67—and a working day at the farm lasts about 4 hours, after which time you get 2 full hours riding time in the in-house arena, cross-country, or up in the stunning Slieve Aughty mountains.

Many come to the **Connemara Country Lodge Guesthouse** (Westport Rd., 500m/1,640 ft. from Clifden town center; ☎ 095/22122; connemara@unison.ie) for the quaint accommodation (p. 280), cheery staff, and hearty grub; most stay for the chance to put their vocal chords to the test. The owner, Mary Corbett, a trained ballad singer, violinist, and all-round character, has been known to break into a traditional ballad over breakfast, and guests are encouraged to put down the cutlery and join in. As well as outlining the history of each ballad in a range of languages, Mary is a fine teacher, and it's hard not to get wrapped up in the enjoyment of it all. She'll even sit down and teach you a tune or two at no extra charge. If you plan on sticking around, you're bound to be called on to deliver a party piece or two at the regular "Irish Nights," when Mary ropes her daughters in for a full-on trad-session. "Singing for your supper" has just taken on a whole new meaning.

Active Connemara

Galway is a treasure trove of outdoor activities, and given the abundance of coastline, not to mention the dominating presence of Lough Corrib, watersports enthusiasts are well provided for. The **Killary Adventure Company** (☎ 095/43411; www.killaryadventure.com) situated on the Killary Fjord, close to the town of Leenane, offers kayaking, windsurfing, and sailing activities as well as the rock climbing, abseiling, orienteering, archery, and—for those who have the nerve—bungee jumping. Two-day weekend adventure packages are available for groups of four or more, starting at €159, which includes full-board, while individual activities range from €40 to €85.

For those who prefer swinging clubs to conquering the wild, the **Connemara Championship Golf Links** (Ballyconneely, near Clifden; ☎ 095/23502 or 095/23602; www.connemaragolflinks.com), designed by noted course designer Eddie Hackett, are nestled between the Twelve Bens mountains and mighty Atlantic in Ballyconeely, west Galway. It's a 72-par course that measures over 7,000 yards. Green fees start at €25 during the winter and rise to €65 in the summer, although twilight package deals are available—€30 for 9 holes after 3pm, set against a dusky Atlantic backdrop.

A range of walking holidays are available in the Connemara region including a number of short walks that you can do yourself, such as the **Diamond Hill**

Inishbofin: For the Birds

Inishbofin translates literally into English to "the island of the white cow," but actually, cows of any color are rare in this part of the world. Over the years, everyone from monks to pirates have used this small island, located 8km (5 miles) off the coast of Connemara, as a place of exile. These days, Inishbofin is a breeding ground for dozens of species of birds—including the rare corncrake. Which means that plenty of ornithologists flock to the **Dolphin Hotel and Restaurant** ✹✹ 🆆 (Middlequarter, Inishbofin; ☎ 095/45991; www.dolphinhotel.ie; MC, V). Pat and Catherine Coyne opened the Dolphin as a restaurant in 2000, and added 11 plain, almost monastic, but spotless bedrooms in 2006 (rates start at €90). Last year the Dolphin became one of a handful of restaurants in Galway to be members of the Irish Seafood Circle, meaning their seafood is top quality. Try the Inishbofin crab claws or seafood chowder (€6.50) for lunch. In keeping with the overall harmony of its surroundings, the Coynes use their own organic garden to supply all herbs, and have installed solar power for hot water and underfloor heating—no easy feat given the indifferent Connemara weather.

Loop (about 2 hr.) from the **Connemara Visitors Centre** (Letterfrack; ☎ 095/41054). The Irish tourist board website **www.discoverireland.ie** is a good place to find out about routes in the area, as is the Visitors Centre.

Attention Shoppers!

Venture away from the city on the N59 and in Oughterard you will find Leah Begg's lifestyle store, **Eggliving** (Main St., Oughterard; ☎ 091/557914; www.egg living.ie), a charming, eclectic jumble of house and garden items, along with a gallery showcasing constantly changing local and international artists. Bleached ash garden furniture, retro cookie cutters, children's rag dolls, polka dot dog bowls—everything is injected with an infectious spirit of fun.

Still on the N59, past Clifden, and about a 40-minute drive from Galway, Letterfrack is an ideal spot to admire the dramatic Atlantic coastline, as well as factor in a quick stop by **Avoca Handweavers** (Letterfrack; ☎ 095/41058). Known locally as "the possibly shop," because one enthusiastic international reviewer described it as "possibly the most interesting shop in the West," this sister-store to the Dublin and Wicklow outlets is stocked with delightful Irish crafts, gifts, clothes, soft furnishings, mohair rugs, cashmere throws, glassware, ironwork, and jewelry—and not a piece of kitsch in sight.

Alongside Mary Corbit's Connemara Country Lodge (p. 280) in Clifden, is a pretty little thatched cottage housing the **Connemara Woollen Mills,** a must-see for anyone determined to track down knitted sweaters, either of the traditional Aran variety or more contemporary, brightly colored lamb's wool. Prices start at about €50 for a machine knit.

8 Along the Shannon

Peaceful, less-visited counties along Ireland's spine

by Keith Bain

SOME CALL IT HIDDEN IRELAND. SOME CALL IT THE IRISH OUTBACK. SOME might even call it the ass-end of nowhere. However you wish to label the less-visited, largely undiscovered Irish midlands, this is an ideal place for tranquil respite from the multitudes plowing their way through the heavily touted regions along the coast. We're calling it the spine, because it really is made up of a central column of midland counties that hold the country together; it's also a region through which Ireland's biggest river, the Shannon, flows like the country's central artery—its spinal cord, if you like—and innumerable lakes and waterways throughout make this a paradise for water lovers. Many are drawn here for marathon fishing weeks or simply to cruise the waterways by boat.

What to look out for here? Vast, under-populated areas; huge stretches of wide open blanket bog; and a prevailing palette of green. While the main towns don't feel at all like backwaters, you'll find less pressure here to see a long list of attractions, and more time to hone your social skills. And while some guides may ignore this region altogether, they'd be missing some rock-solid sights: The country's most important early Christian site is here at Clonmacnoise; Ireland's largest castle, Tullynally, is just outside Castlepollard, and near another ecclesiastical wonder, Fore; the planned Georgian town of Birr has drop-dead gardens at its castle; the grand manor house at Strokestown houses one of Ireland's most evocative museums, focused on the Great Famine; and the glittering Lakelands of the water-soaked northern midlands are dappled with sleepy villages.

Ireland's spine may not be the most visually exciting place to visit—certainly the mostly landlocked landscape lacks the drama of the coast—but you won't miss the masses of tourists who've chosen to devote themselves to Ireland's better-known regions.

DON'T LEAVE IRELAND'S SPINE WITHOUT . . .

PAYING TRIBUTE TO EARLY CHRISTIAN HERITAGE Clonmacnoise, near Athlone, was once the most important seat of learning in Europe and a beacon of Christianity that burned bright while the continent was sweating out the Dark Ages. See p. 296.

UNDERSTANDING THE AWFUL PARADOX OF THE GREAT IRISH FAMINE Strokestown is the ultimate planned Georgian town; although it's tiny, its main road is the widest in Ireland and leads to one of the most intriguing aristocratic mansions you can visit. Not only is the house filled with fascinating foibles collected by its wealthy landlords, but the stirring Famine Museum sheds light on the most heartbreaking event in Irish history. See p. 304.

GETTING INTO THE BOWELS OF THE EARTH WITH A REAL MINER In Leitrim, coal mining was big business in the 19th century, and the mine at Arigna operated until 1990. Many died either while working or due to limestone and coal dust exposure. Now part of the mine is a museum where former miners guide you along a shaft where thousands of men spent years picking away at the coalface. See p. 299.

DRINKING AT IRELAND'S OLDEST PUB   Athlone isn't really on the mainstream tourist circuit, but its location on the banks on the Shannon means that it has been drawing all sorts of people for hundreds of years. And if archaeological evidence is to be trusted, its visitors have been socializing here since as far back as 900 A.D.—at Seán's Pub—purported to be the oldest watering hole in the country, and perhaps the world. See p. 296.

VISITING   FAIRYTALE   CASTLES   &   MAGICAL   GARDENS Complementing the midlands' numerous waterways and loughs, are many magnificent gardens, planted around monumental castles and mansions, built for wealthy landowners who were themselves "planted" in Ireland. Best of these are the mature demesne around Birr Castle (p. 291); the lakeside grounds of Belvedere House (p. 297); and the ornamental parkland around colossal Tullynally Castle (p. 298).

GETTING AROUND

To get the most out of a visit to this region, **rent a car.** Many of the major attractions are away from the towns, and you'll need your own steam to get to them. Traffic is generally problem free, except when it comes to getting through and around larger towns like Mullingar, Athlone, Longford, and Carrick-on-Shannon; it's generally always wise to park as soon as possible and explore these places on foot. The only other issue you'll have is with being stuck (rather frequently) behind tractors on narrow roads. But, hey, that's Ireland.

Fairly regular (usually daily) **buses** service the major towns outlined in this chapter, while every village sees at least one bus per week; visit www.buseireann.ie to check schedules. **Trains** connect Athlone, Mullingar, Longford Town, Carrick-on-Shannon, and Boyle with each other and with major centers to the east and west. Visit www.irishrail.ie for schedule information.

THE SOUTH MIDLANDS: BIRR & AROUND

Sedate Birr is a tidy, handsome town with a perfect tree-lined Georgian layout. In fact, it is generally considered to be the finest, most complete Georgian town in Ireland, and having never been industrialized, has retained enormous charm. Centered on what is widely acknowledged as the oldest inhabited home in Ireland—Birr Castle—the peaceable town is also strategically situated for day trips to Lough Derg and to the Slieve Bloom Mountains (p. 292). Initially a

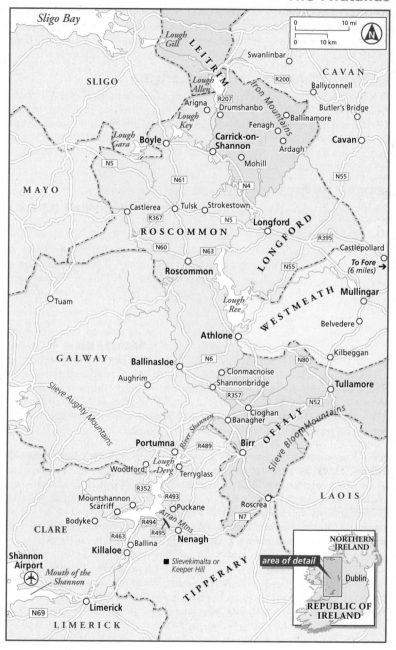

Sligo Bay

Lough Gill

LEITRIM

Swanlinbar

R200

C A V A N

Ballyconnell

Lough Allen

SLIGO

Iron Mountains

Arigna

R207

Drumshanbo

Butler's Bridge

Lough Key

Ballinamore

Fenagh

Lough Gara

Boyle

Carrick-on-Shannon

Ardagh

Cavan

N5

Mohill

N61

N4

N55

Castlerea

Tulsk

Strokestown

R367

Longford

N5

R O S C O M M O N

LONGFORD

R395

Castlepollard

N60

N63

To Fore (6 miles) →

Roscommon

N55

Tuam

Lough Ree

WESTMEATH

Mullingar

Belvedere

Athlone

Kilbeggan

N6

G A L W A Y

Ballinasloe

N80

Aughrim

Clonmacnoise

Shannonbridge

Tullamore

R357

N52

Cloghan

O F F A L Y

Slieve Aughty Mountains

Banagher

Slieve Bloom Mountains

Portumna

River Shannon

R489

Birr

Woodford

Lough Derg

Terryglass

L A O I S

R352

R493

Mountshannon

Scarriff

Puckane

Roscrea

Bodyke

R494

Arran Mtns

N7

C L A R E

R463

R495

Nenagh

Killaloe

Ballina

Shannon Airport

Slievekimalta or Keeper Hill

Mouth of the Shannon

T I P P E R A R Y

N69

Limerick

L I M E R I C K

0   10 mi
0   10 km

NORTHERN IRELAND

area of detail

Dublin

REPUBLIC OF IRELAND

monastic town founded by St. Brendan of Birr, it was taken over by the Normans in the 13th century and during the Plantation was given to the Parson family who still reside in the castle. Its demesne—an enormous, splendid garden—is the town's chief attraction, sheltering some ambitious scientific inventions.

GETTING THERE & GETTING AROUND

While it's an ideal starting point for exploring Ireland's spine, Birr is not exactly a major town; it is, however easily accessible from just about anywhere, including Dublin and Shannon, which is the nearest airport. Birr lies at the junction of the **N52** and the **N62**. Daily **buses** link Birr with Dublin (2½ hr.), Athlone (50 min.), and Limerick (90 min.). Birr is small and easy to negotiate, with a compact center revolving around Emmett Square.

WHERE TO STAY & DINE

On the shores of nearby Lough Derg (see below) **Holiday Village** (Killaloe, Co. Clare; ☎ 061/376777; www.loughderg.net) rents cottages right on the water's edge. They're a bit "mix and match" in their looks but fine for an unpretentious lake stay, with a children's playground, tennis courts, and shop on site. Three varieties are available in various configurations and though bedrooms are a bit wee (the three-bedroom which goes for between €395 and €675 is really best for five people, not six), the open plan living rooms will give your group sufficient space to stretch out.

€€   Right near the town center, amidst a row of terraced Georgian houses, Noreen and Martin Kearns offer modest luxury at **Townsend House** ✸ (Townsend St.; ☎ 057/912-1276; townsendhousebandb@eircom.net; MC, V). The bedrooms (€80 double) are individually decorated with wood antique dressers, carved wardrobes, plush drapes, carpets, and decent-size tiled bathrooms. (Room 1 is especially well proportioned and has a tub, too.) You can enjoy a glass of vino or, this being Ireland, a well pulled pint of Guinness at the end of the day in the lovely and intimate wine bar downstairs.

€€   Diagonally across town, right next to the Castle, **Spinner's Town House** ✸✸ (Castle St.; ☎ 057/912-1673; www.spinnerstownhouse.com; MC, V) offers guests a choice of bright, light-filled "standard" bedrooms (from €80 double) or so-called "gothic" rooms, which are designed for romance—textured with a darker palette and more expensive (from €100). Either way, all are soothing, relaxing spaces in which contemporary minimalist styling—wooden floors, shuttered windows, and framed antique postcards depicting a much earlier Birr—blends seamlessly with the redesign of this historic 300-year-old former wool mill. A few rooms share a bathroom, and of these, no. 108 is a top choice, rendered in dark ocher, with a marvelous wrought iron bed. The public spaces have intriguing historical displays, such as old Guinness cask registers (ancient register books once used in the Guinness warehouse, now part of the hotel) above the stairway, and in one cabinet, a display of keys that once opened every door in town. The owners offer last-minute deals, so you might be able to swing a 10% to 20% walk-in discount if you arrive after 6pm (but not in summer, please). Although pricey, **Spinner's Bistro** ✸✸ (Wed–Mon 6:30–9:30pm; Fri–Sat 6:30–10:30pm) is the best place in town for dinner, with inventive dishes; if you arrive early, you can order from a cheaper menu with less extraordinary-sounding, but no less satisfying items in the €12 to €17 range, and a "value menu" offering two courses for €17.

€–€€€€   You know that a place called the **Thatch** ✦✦✦ (Crinkle, Birr; ☎ 057/912-0682; www.thethatchcrinkill.com; Oct–Apr daily Tues–Sun 6:30–9pm; May–Sept Tues–Sun 6:30–9pm; DC, MC, V) set in a tiny village called—Lord help us!—Crinkle (5km/3 miles from Birr) is going to be just overflowing with charm. And so it is. At almost 200 years, this thatched-roof hostelry is one of Offaly's oldest pubs and a delightful place to dine. It's been in Des Connole's family for five generations and gets my vote not only for the food but for the gracious service. Whether you're in the snug pub ordering from the affordable bar menu (served daily 12:30–4pm; all mains €7–€10), or decide to splash out on a full-blown meal in the quaint country-style restaurant (all exposed brick and wooden floors), you'll be ordering from the same kitchen, which turns out finely rendered fresh fish and an especially wide range of meat dishes (even kangaroo and ostrich). If you pitch up early enough, you can try out the "early bird" menu (Mon–Sat 5–7:30pm). On my last visit, I had tasty fillets of pork, stuffed with apricot, and topped with apple chutney and a wild mushroom sauce (€18), served with mountains of potatoes—mash, au gratin, and garlic—on the side. Yum . . . and the extra carbs make the meal filling enough to share between two.

WHY YOU'RE HERE: TOP SIGHTS & ATTRACTIONS

Birr Castle Demesne ✦✦✦ (☎ 057/912-0336; www.birrcastle.com; €9; daily Mar–Oct 9am–6pm; Nov–Feb 10am–4pm) has been called "a green jewel," and for anyone who can appreciate the majesty of mature, well-tended foliage, this is a must. The demesne (pronounced "domain") consists of 48.5 hectares (120 acres) beautifully laid-out gardens, filled with rare and exotic plants, many of which were collected by the Parson family, who have lived here since 1620. During their tenure, the family has famously produced a rather impressive number of inventors—private home schooling with the best tutors from Trinity College (rather than being sent off to posh English colleges designed for the aristocratic elite) meant that children in this family learned unusually practical skills, and developed a keen interest in science. Among the technological inventions developed by the Parson boys is the so-called Leviathan of Parsonstown, the world's largest telescope completed in 1845 after spending nearly 20 years and at least £20,000 developing it. Restoration of the mammoth instrument cost £1 million in the mid-1990s, and there are sometimes demonstrations of how it works. In 1897, another inventive Parsons lad—Charles Algernon, the 3rd Earl of Rosse—developed the steam turbine; the original is still in place near the castle at Waterfall Point, and supplied electricity to the castle and the town until the 1950s.

Since they were so busy toiling over their inventions—and spending vast sums of money perfecting them—the Parson men never really got round to generating sustainable wealth; they did, however, develop other skills that allowed them to hang onto their family estate. After the Irish Land Act stripped landowning aristocrats of any land over and above their private demesne, most were left without any income and were forced to sell off their properties. However, the Earls of Rosse were well practiced in the art of marrying wealthy English heiresses (Charles

Active Pursuits on "Pleasure Lake"

Formed by a widening of the River Shannon, **Lough Derg** (www.discover loughderg.ie)—popularly known as "Ireland's Pleasure Lake"—stretches for 35km (21¾ miles) between Portumna in the north and the twin towns of Ballina (in County Tipperary) and Killaloe (actually on the County Clare side of the lake, just 23km/14 miles from Limerick City) to the south. The largest of three lakes on the Shannon, Lough Derg is a much-vaunted watersports destination, luring large crowds in the summer months; if you're looking for tranquillity, you may want to give it a skip. With its Yacht Club established as early as 1835, Lough Derg remains a favorite with boating enthusiasts; you can rent boats from **Lough Derg Holiday Village** (Killaloe, Co. Clare; ☎ 061/376777; www.loughderg.net) for €15 per hour (2-hr. minimum; fuel included), or €45 per half-day (4 hr.). If you're new to watersports, the **University of Limerick Activity Centre** (Two-Mile Gate, Killaloe, Co. Clare; ☎ 061/376622; www.ulac.ie) offers training in a broad range of water-based activities. You can take sailing courses; develop kayaking skills for flatwater and whitewater conditions; or learn to windsurf. Most of these activities cost around €200 for a packed 2-day weekend, while you can get your 1-day powerboating certifi-

Algernon apparently wooed his wife in a very butch way: with his amazing needle-work!), and they used the money earned off "their" English estates to fund this one. They also managed to finance the upkeep of the gardens, which include trees from China and Tibet; the world's tallest grey poplar; and spectacular golden willows on the banks of small lakes that harbor swans, ducks, and even otter. In fact, there are at least 50 trees here that are recognized British Isles champions (the tallest of their species)—no mean feat for a family garden. Although the castle itself is not usually open to the public, the view of the garden-facing facade (completed in 1840, although the castle originally faced the town) is impressive, as are the moat walls, built to provide work during the Great Famine.

Nature enthusiasts can use Birr as a base for excursions to Lough Derg, one of the country's favorite water-getaway resorts (p. 290), at the edge of northern Tipperary; or to the Slieve Bloom Mountains, which loom—albeit from a rather gentle 600m (1,968 ft.)—to the southeast, along Offaly's border with Laois. Here, the Slieve Bloom Way is a 50km (31-mile) walking trail that circles back on itself and takes you through some less-explored terrain, including some of the most intriguing bogland in the country; despite the limited altitude, views to the valleys below are spectacular. Roscrea, just across the border in Tipperary, is another heritage town, this time with roots as a 7th-century monastic settlement; the place is studded with early ecclesiastical ruins, and you can pick up information and a "heritage walk" map at the 700-year-old **Roscrea Castle** ★ (Heritage Card or €3.70; daily 10am–6pm), built by the Normans to control the Slighe Dala, one of the five great roads of ancient Ireland.

THE OTHER BIRR: GETTING YOUR FINGERS DIRTY

Looking to make your green thumb substantially more leaf colored? Birr may be your Nirvana. While heritage gardens abound on the Emerald Isle, Birr is among the very finest, and it regularly accepts volunteers. At the **Birr Scientific and Heritage Foundation** (☎ 057/912-0336 or 057/912-0340; mail@birrcastle.com), you'll not only gain experience in good old-fashioned gardening (a skill you'll soon discover to be hugely underrated), but get to learn alongside experts who descend on Birr to work with some of the exotic plants found here. And all the while, your boss is an honest-to-goodness aristocrat—the Earl of Rosse.

Volunteer stints are a minimum of 1 month with the basics all covered. Simple accommodation—a bed, bathroom, and cooking facilities—is provided free of charge, with one or two students per room in a shared cottage. You'll fend for yourself food-wise, but will be provided with any available produce. If you complete the program, you also walk away with a certificate, and the experience has earned some former volunteers jobs at formidable gardens elsewhere.

NIGHTLIFE

If you're staying in Birr, make a point of stopping by at **Chestnut** ✿✿✿ (Green St.; ☎ 087/220-8524; Mon–Fri 8–11pm; Sat 3pm–2am; Sun 3–11:30pm), the ultimate contemporary take on a small town bar, with a, suave atmosphere and an aura of calm gentility. Clodagh Fay, the owner, works behind the bar herself, and brings her pot-bellied grey and black cat—Come Here—to work with her. Yes, it's that kind of place—the type of relaxed spot I'd like to make my local hangout: Goldfrapp on the stereo, and, it being winter, red leather armchairs in front of a warming fire, accompanied by piles of magazines. The place brings real "cool" to Birr, too; there's free Wi-Fi, and in winter there are film club evenings. Art exhibitions happen year-round, and summer features live music (with an emphasis on reggae and rockabilly) and an orchard beer garden. Around the corner, for a more sedate, gentlemanly, old-fashioned kind of vibe, head for **Kelly's Bar** ✿ (Green St.; ☎ 057/912-0175), a crisp, proper pub with display cases filled with quality vintage goods.

CENTRAL MIDLANDS: ATHLONE & COUNTY WESTMEATH

As with many of the towns straddling the Shannon River, Athlone started out as an important crossing point, and in 1210, after the town became an Anglo-Norman stronghold, a castle was built on the river bank to protect the ford—it was around this that the city evolved. The castle remains Athlone's oldest complete building, and the area that sprung up around it—known as "The Left Bank"—is the rejuvenated heart of historic Athlone, an alluring rabbit warren of winding streets, vividly colored buildings and enough eateries, shops, and pubs (including Ireland's oldest) to make your head spin. The town became a key stronghold after the Battle of the Boyne, and after several battles British troops were garrisoned here until 1922. It's only in very recent years that Athlone has begun stirring as a tourist destination.

Now it's pretty much regarded as the capital of the Irish Midlands, and its position on the Shannon and close to a number of fine lakes makes it ideal for water and fishing enthusiasts. Each July athletes here plunge into the Shannon for the swimming leg of the Waterways Ireland triAthlone, and in 2010, Athlone will host the European Triathlon Championships.

Devote a couple of hours to a stroll through the Left Bank, then set out on a day trip to see the nearby ruins at **Clonmacnoise.** You can visit the atmospheric whiskey distillery at **Kilbeggan,** or—if you just want to soak up some fresh air— cruise along the Shannon, or hire a boat to float on **Lough Ree.**

In his youth, James Joyce was a regular visitor to **Mullingar,** once a major center for the midlands beef industry, over in Westmeath's east. Joyce even set several scenes in his novel *Ulysses* at the Greville Arms Hotel, where he stayed when his father was in town on government business. Mullingar is a lively town with few attractions (other than its line-up of pubs, the enormous **Christ the King Cathedral,** and **Belvedere House** just outside the city), but it's a useful pit-stop between Kilbeggan and two interesting detours farther north—**Tullynally Castle** in Castlepollard, and the mysterious ecclesiastical ruins at **Fore.**

GETTING THERE & GETTING AROUND

Athlone lies on the **N6** which links Dublin and Galway. If you're traveling from Birr, take the **N62** north until you hit the N6; turn left for Athlone, or right if you want to go directly to Kilbeggan or Mullingar.

For Clonmacnoise, which is 21km (13 miles) from Athlone, take the N6 towards Dublin and after about 3km (2 miles), take the N62 south; at the village of Ballinahown, take the **R444** and follow signs to the site.

Athlone's castle houses a summer-only **tourist office** (☎ 090/644-2100; www.athlone.ie); there's a year-round **information center** at Clonmacnoise.

WHERE TO STAY & DINE

Athlone

€–€€   If you like being in the heart of the action, then stay at the **Bastion** ✸✸ (2 Bastion St.; ☎ 090/649-4954; www.thebastion.net; MC, V), owned by Vinny and Anthony, who grew up in this lovely, rambling house in the Left Bank. The brothers have filled their cheerful, contemporary-boho B&B with artifacts, artworks, and souvenirs from all over the world—most recently Vietnam and Peru. Perhaps the oddest piece is the angry stuffed otter at the entrance. No matter, bedrooms (seven of them) are upbeat and all individually styled. The attic room (no. 1; €85 double)—with wooden floors and different levels—has space enough for four people, and a small outdoor terrace. The price for a midrange double is €75, and there are two rooms with shared bathroom for €60. Across the road, the brothers have a very spacious bachelor pad–style unit with a mini kitchenette (fridge, kettle, and toaster), little sitting area, and dining table. It's not really self-catering, but you could use it for takeaway meals; it costs €85.

€€   On the outskirts of Athlone, in what almost feels like the edge of the countryside, Mary and Brian Fagg operate a homey, hands-on little B&B at their home, **Cornamagh House** ✸ (Cornamagh, Athlone; ☎ 090/647-4171; www. cornamaghhouse.com; cash only). Mary once operated the cafe at the top of Athlone Castle and she baked scones to lure visitors up from the tourist office; now she welcomes guests into her home with tea and the same freshly baked goodies. She also prepares the fluffiest scrambled eggs in Ireland, does laundry for guests, and provides the inside scoop on the area. Bedrooms are fairly standard, but some have views over the adjacent old farm field where you can watch horses frolicking. The Faggs really make an effort to welcome you into their home, and will drop you at restaurants (with the number for a taxi) rather than risk your getting lost. All rooms have private bathrooms (although one is not en suite), and cost €70 double or €50 single.

€–€€€   Back down in the Left Bank is one of Athlone's best-value eateries, **Pavarotti's** ★ (kids) (Fry Place; ☎ 090/649-3066; daily 6pm–late; MC, V), always packed with locals who come to feast on big portions of fresh, tasty Italian (well, mostly) fare. Pizzas are 12-inch and cost between €7.85 and €10, pastas are traditional and similarly priced (mostly €8–€12), and the catch of the day (€14) is served with seasonal vegetables.

€€–€€€€   Also on the Left Bank in an ancient, lopsided yellow house, is one of the country's top Thai restaurants, **kin khao thai** ★★ (1 Abbey Ln.; ☎ 090/649-8805; www.kinkhaothai.ie; daily 5:30–10:30pm; Wed–Fri 12:30–2:30pm; Sun 1:30–3:30pm; MC, V). Run by Adam Lyons (he's Irish), his Thai wife Janya and an all-Thai crew, the food here has a welcome authenticity and sometimes, heat. While most main courses are pushing the €20 mark, early diners (Mon–Thurs till 7:30pm, or Fri–Sat 7pm) can try a two-course set menu (with tea or coffee) for the same price; lunch, too, is a more affordable affair.

€€–€€€€   Just outside Athlone, the village of Glasson (which Goldsmith called "the village of roses") is where locals go to escape. Perched at the edge of Lough Ree, is a **restaurant** ★ (kids) (☎ 090/648-5155; Mar–Nov Wed–Mon 6:30–10pm; MC, V) attached to a cluster of self-catering units, **Killinure Chalets** (www.killinurechalets.com), owned by a German-Irish couple. They've brought their heritage to bear here, creating an eatery that's more like a forest cabin-turned-beer hall and one that serves tasty, but unapologetically simple food—roast chicken, €14; half crispy duck, €19; organic smoked salmon, €19. The cottages cater mostly to fisherman, and are rudimentary, but a good value at €400 per week (two twin rooms, small kitchen, shower, porch, plenty of space), and just a stone's throw from the water's edge. All in all a friendly, visit-worthy place.

Mullingar

There's no need to overnight in Mullingar, but you may want to make a detour for a pint, a meal, or a listen to some music at **Danny Byrnes** ★★ (Pierce St.; ☎ 044/934-3792; danny.byrnes@hotmail.com; Mon–Thurs 10:30am–11:30pm; Fri–Sat 10:30am–midnight; Sun 12:30–11pm; MC, V). Designers have created a chic-Gothic ambience here: flickering candles, red and burgundy lighting, gathered drapes, leather sofas, dark wooden ceilings, and even an old-fashioned library in one corner. Tables are arranged in all sorts of hidden, round-the-corner spaces and there's excellent lounge music. On Sundays, roast meats, chicken curry, and freshly baked fish is served to hungry diners (€11, with veg and mash); also on offer was pepper steak or roast duck for €12. Diners walk away with bulging plates at this weekly "event" (Sun 12:30–5pm). For the rest of the week, it's a la carte (and pricier) fare, but you'll never leave hungry.

WHY YOU'RE HERE: TOP SIGHTS & ATTRACTIONS

On the Shannon's Left Bank

In Athlone itself, you'll want to restrict your time to the pretty little historic enclave of the **Left Bank** ✪✪✪ which sits in the shadow of **Athlone Castle.** The names of the little winding streets reveal much about the past: **Bastion Street** was the outer edge of medieval Athlone, where an old bastion wall was located; **O'Connell Street** is named after Daniel "The Liberator" O'Connell who stayed here on a visit, and whose son managed the first branch of the Bank of Ireland, also located on this street. And, among the pretty shopfronts on Main Street, you'll find the beguilingly simple entrance to **Seán's Bar** ✪✪✪ (Main St., Athlone; ☎ 090/649-2358; www.seansbar.ie), which has received Guinness Record recognition as the oldest bar in Ireland, with evidence that there's been a hostelry here since as early as 900 A.D.; apparently this was once an inn whose owner, Luain, guided people across the ford in the river. Athlone—or *Atha Luain*—actually means "Ford of Luain," suggesting that Seán's Bar predates the town itself. When the pub was excavated for renovations in 1970, the ancient walls were found to be made of wattle and wicker, and coins dating back to the earliest days of the inn's existence were also found. Even if you don't fancy a drink, step inside to check out the fascinating displays on the walls.

For many, getting out on the Shannon itself is a great joy, and there are plenty of operators willing to take you on fast-paced trips or leisurely outings. **Shannonsafari** (36 Silverquay; ☎ 090/647-9558; www.shannonsafari.ie) goes a step further and also offers powerboat lessons (€100–€200); a 1-hour leisure cruise is €20.

Clonmacnoise

Of all Ireland's early Christian settlements, **Clonmacnoise** ✪✪✪ (Shannonbridge; ☎ 090/967-4195; www.heritageireland.ie; Heritage Card or €5.30; daily mid-May to mid-Sept 9am–7pm; mid-Mar to mid-May and mid-Sept–Oct 10am–6pm; Nov to mid-Mar 10am–5:30pm), a short drive from Athlone across the border in County Offaly, is the unequivocal must-see. While Europe was firmly stuck in the grip of the Dark Ages, this was a thriving scholastic center, a university attended by Europe's privileged sons with as many as 3,000 learned souls living in the medieval equivalent of a city, albeit one relatively cut off from the rest of the world. Founded by St. Ciarán in the mid-6th century, this was where the first Irish book, *The Book of the Dun Cow*, was written; it lasted about 1,000 years until Henry VIII finally shut it down in 1552. St. Ciarán himself is believed to be buried here, as is Rory O'Connor, the last high king of Ireland.

Today, it not only retains the aura of a great history, but enjoys a perfectly isolated setting at the edge of the Shannon—this, combined with a near-total absence of modern development (aside from the mandatory "visitor center," of course) makes Clonmacnoise an enchanting place to visit, particularly if you're not in a hurry. Not that it was always peaceful here. As you pick through the ruins, investigating the 10th-century cathedral (a good example of Hiberno-Romanesque architecture), fantastically carved high crosses, and graveslabs with curious clues to their history, you'll see evidence of threat from invaders. Most notable are the **round towers** which were used for defense. In its medieval heyday, Clonmacnoise's prosperity meant that it was a regular target for attack—by the Vikings (eight times), by warring Irish clans (27 times), and by the Normans (six times), who each came to steal whatever plunder they could lift. Much of the real devastation was by the English, though, particularly after they were garrisoned in Athlone.

A short film details the significance of monastic sites such as Clonmacnoise, and there's a middling exhibition explaining the significance of the carved high crosses (which have been relocated indoors).

The Spirit of Kilbeggan

The drive from Athlone to Kilbeggan can be slower than expected due to snail's pace traffic through smaller towns like Moate along the N6; but it's worth it to get to **Locke's Distillery** ✪✪✪ (Lower Main St. Kilbeggan; ☎ 057/933-2134; www.lockesdistillerymuseum.ie; €6.50; daily Apr–Oct 9am–6pm; Nov–Mar 10am–4pm), especially if you're either a whiskey fan, or are curious to see some Old World technology in action. Locke's claims to be the oldest licensed pot-still in the world, and it's awesome to see how this booze factory was producing the "water of life" as far back as 1757. Although it's now a museum, most of the original machinery has been restored to working order, so you get a live demonstration of the entire production process; there's even a giant waterwheel which once powered the distillery. Often, it's the monumental scale of the equipment that's is visually intriguing—in one room, a gigantic steam engine, built in Glasgow in 1887, looks like it was dreamt up by Tim Burton. The sounds, smells, and—eventually—the tastes are all 100% genuine. There are even coopers who still pound away with hammers preparing whiskey barrels, one of them refusing to wear his earmuffs. At the end of your guided tour (around ½ hr.), you can pick up a traditionally styled jar of Locke's single malt (€44), and visit the attached cafe for an affordable meal. Then explore the little village.

Mullingar Environs

Adultery, family feuds, exotic plants! You'll find all these at **Belvedere House Gardens** ✪ 🧒 (4km/2½ miles south of Mullingar; ☎ 044/934-9060; www.belvedere-house.ie; €8.75; daily Mar–Apr and Sept–Oct 10:30am–7pm; May–Aug 9:30am–9pm; Nov–Feb 10:30am–4:30pm; house closed from 5pm all year), which is as well known for its scandalous history as it is for its sumptuous gardens (and on the tour you'll learn about both). Built on the shores of Lough Ennell by Robert Rochfort, later the Earl of Belvedere, the original hunting and fishing lodge was designed by the esteemed German architect Richard Castle (Cassels) in 1740 (Castle also designed Leinster House, Powerscourt Estate, and Russborough House, among others). Robert was a jealous man, rightly it turned out, because he discovered that his wife had been having an affair with his own younger brother (even bearing him a son). In retaliation, he had her locked away, Rapunzel-like. He then dotted the estate with magnificent follies—facade-like walls designed to look like bits of old architecture—to block views of neighboring family members. His famous "Jealous Wall," for example, looks like an ancient ruin, and obstructed the view of his hated brother's neighboring estate. A warning to the romantics among you: While Belvedere should be a spectacular outing, it can tend to feel like little more than an over-elaborate children's playground. The grounds, however, and especially the nonsensical follies, make for an interesting diversion, and the setting on Lough Ennel's shore is quite lovely.

North of Mullingar lies the one-circle town of **Castlepollard**, famous as the site of **Tullynally Castle** ✸✸ (Granard Rd., 1.5km/1 mile from Castlepollard; ☎ 044/61159; www.tullynallycastle.com), the obscenely massive, fairytale-style home of the Pakenhams, who've been here for 350 years. What was initially a "square tower of stone" was later remodeled as a Georgian manse, and then in the 19th century gained all manner of Gothic Revival additions, transforming it into the monster-building you see today; it is the largest castle in Ireland and was the first castle in Europe to have central heating. The current Earl of Longford is prize-winning author Thomas Pakenham, whose chief interests are history and trees (his book *Meetings with Remarkable Trees* became a radio and TV series). Many people come simply to walk through the castle **gardens** (€6; May–Jun Sat–Sun 4–6pm; Jul to mid-Aug daily 4–6pm), which cover around 12 hectares (30 acres); from the grounds you get a good look at the multi-turreted, bastioned, and steepled castle facade. It's a great shame, however, that the castle interior is only open to large pre-booked groups; the best you'll manage is getting a look at the castle courtyard during a visit to the tea room. *Tip:* Outside the summer season, the entrance to the castle grounds is often open, and I've noticed people park their cars at the entrance and simply walk in. As long as you mind your own business, you may be able to get a look at the castle with a similarly brazen approach.

East of Castlepollard (take the R195) you venture into refreshingly remote countryside. Follow signs to **Fore** (5km/3 miles)—set in a verdant valley between two low hills. Scattered over a small area near the village, are the various ecclesiastical unattended ruins of **Fore Abbey** ✸✸, interesting for their association with the so-called Seven Wonders of Fore. These minor "miracles" are supposedly connected with the 7th-century monk, St. Fechin, who had magical powers and who founded the abbey. On one side of the road is what's left of **St. Fechin's Church** as well as a 15th-century tower—the **Anchorite's Cell,** so-called because a hermit who had sequestered himself inside after vowing to live out his days there, actually killed himself trying to escape; in the process, he became one of the ironic seven wonders. On the other side of the road, a dead tree has become a sort of shrine, gaudily decorated with anything passersby have managed to tie to its branches; this represents "the wood that will not burn," another of the wonders. Some distance behind the tree, are the remains of a 13th-century Benedictine monastery, with some Gothic detailing still intact. Even if you've limited interest in the supernatural (signs at the site explain the other wonders, including a stream that supposedly flows uphill), the setting is wonderful, and this makes for a great place to stop with a self-packed lunch; or you can visit the nearby **coffee shop** (☎ 044/966-1780).

NIGHTLIFE

Situated in the heart of the Left Bank, **Dean Crowe Theatre and Arts Centre** (Chapel St., Athlone; ☎ 090/649-2129; www.deancrowetheatre.com) maintains a year-round program of dramas, comedies, and musicals; most of the work is on tour from around the country. I've already highlighted **Seán's Bar** ✸✸✸ (Main St., Athlone; ☎ 090/649-2358; www.seansbar.ie) as Ireland's oldest pub, but don't think of it merely as an historical attraction—this place pumps, and although it gets ridiculously crowded, it has an atmosphere that's second-to-none. Traditional music sessions happen later in the night, and there's a beer garden out back when overcrowding sets in. If you feel like the floor is moving even before you've touched a pint, don't panic—the whole place is lopsided.

THE NORTHERN MIDLANDS: LONGFORD, LEITRIM & ROSCOMMON

Although it's hardly a blip on the tourist trail, the bustling and colorful town of Longford is conveniently central (it's on the Dublin-Sligo road) and packs a punch with its busy-for-a-backwaters nightlife. Longford is conveniently close to one of the Republic's most interesting stately houses—Strokestown—in the middle of vast, famously flat and dreary Roscommon. Not only is it the ultimate example of a planned town—with the widest main road in Ireland—but the house is home to the emotionally grueling Famine Museum. From Strokestown, you can continue north to see the remarkable 12th-century Cistercian abbey in Boyle, a small town which outdoorsy types use as a base for the beautiful Lough Key Forest Park.

Boyle is a short drive from Carrick-on-Shannon, just over the border in County Leitrim, which borders six other counties and stretches as far as the coast, making it the only Midlands county that isn't completely landlocked—although its coastline is a mere 4km (2½ miles). Largely undiscovered and notoriously underpopulated, Leitrim has been referred to as the Cinderella County—Carrick, its main town, is really blossoming these days, attracting numerous Irish vacationers. In the shadow of the evocatively named Iron Mountains, the village of Ballinamore is a serene and friendly place to stretch out, either with a fishing rod or on a good hike of the region. Based here—or in nearby Fenagh—you'll have access not only to all the regional sights, but also the beautiful Lakeland county of Fermanagh across the nearby border in Northern Ireland.

> " *They don't price Leitrim by the hectare, but by the gallon!* "
> –Popular saying

It's as though the farther north you get in the midlands, the more laid-back things become, so if you favor a mellow getaway, don't discount these peaceable kingdoms at the top of the spine.

GETTING THERE & GETTING AROUND

At the top of Ireland's backbone, counties Longford, Roscommon, and Leitrim are among the least visited by tourists; however, this doesn't mean that they're not well-placed for exploration. The town of **Longford** is on the N4, which connects Dublin with Sligo, and also passes through Carrick-on-Shannon, Leitrim's county town.

Longford's neighbor to the west, County Roscommon, often feels like a vast expanse of nothing; so as you drive the N5 to reach **Strokestown,** and then follow the N61, north to Boyle, don't be alarmed by the surprisingly long stretches

The Midlands' Lettered Men (& Woman)

Although sparsely populated, the Irish midlands have spawned a number of significant literary figures.

County Longford is popularly associated with **Oliver Goldsmith,** the 18th-century playwright and novelist who based one of his greatest works—*She Stoops to Conquer*—on his experiences in Ardagh, one of the prettiest villages in the midlands. Goldsmith apparently turned up at the aristocratic Ardagh House one night in 1744 and mistook it for an inn; the posh Featherston family who owned the mansion decided to play along and entertained Goldstone as though they were indeed servants. The deception intrigued him so much that it inspired his most famous play (initially titled *Mistakes of a Night*), with a plot that has in turn inspired countless romantic comedies.

Few contemporary readers have heard of **Maria Edgeworth,** who was born in England, but settled in Longford with her family at a young age. She is considered to be the first Irish person to write a realistic novel about Ireland; her first was *Castle Rackrent,* published 1800. Her work is said to have influenced Thackeray, Sir Walter Scott, and even Turgeynev.

Leitrim, too, has its bard, **John McGahern,** who died in 2006 and was widely considered the most important Irish writer since Samuel Beckett. Most of his work is set around the small towns of Ballinamore and Mohill. Most evocative is *That They May Face the Rising Sun* (also published as *The Lake*), a gentle, ruminative account of a year in the lives of the lakeshore inhabitants. At the same time, it echoes with commentary on the violence that has stained Irish history. By all accounts, the peaceful Midlands have inspired some formidable texts.

of uneventful roadway. **Boyle,** in northern Roscommon, is right near the border with County Sligo; the N4 north goes to Sligo Town, while the N4 east connects Boyle with nearby **Carrick-on-Shannon,** the only place of any discernible size in County Leitrim.

North of Carrick, the R280 reaches Leitrim's brief stretch of coastline, passing beautiful lakelands and the undiscovered glens of Leitrim along the way. Take the R209 to reach the tranquil villages of **Fenagh** and **Ballinamore,** near the Cavan border.

WHERE TO STAY & DINE
Longford

€–€€€   If you want to see where Longford's in-the-know foodies hang out, then march directly up the stairs to **Aubergine** ★★★ (1st Floor, The White House, 17 Ballymahon St.; ☎ 043/48633; Mon–Sat noon–4pm; Fri–Sat 6–9:30pm; Sun 2–7:30pm; MC, V) on the town's bustling main street. This buzzy, bistro-style cafe is easy on the eye and at night fills up with a young, smart, enviable crowd. Unexpected pairings are the lure here and really deliver (last time I visited, I was wowed by a duo of cod and salmon wrapped in Parma ham); mains at dinner tend to run between €16 to €20. As usual, lunch is a much less pricey affair. Expect to pay less than €10 for such dishes as smoked haddock lasagna (€8.50), beef stew with Guinness (€9.50), or baked beef and pasta ziti (€8.50). Desserts are simple and sinful, so leave room.

€€–€€€   Built for the Earl of Longford in the 1750s **Viewmount House** ✪✪✪ (Dublin Rd.; ☎ 043/41919; www.viewmounthouse.com; AE, MC, V) is, without a doubt, one of my favorite B&Bs in all of Ireland. Though some might consider it a splurge (doubles go for €110), I'd say rates are low for what you get, which is the unique opportunity to stay in a smartly renovated, terrifically historic house with an aristocratic pedigree. Owners Beryl and James Kearney have poured heart and hard-work into this property, both restoring it and adding on a more contemporary wing that flows cleverly out of the Georgian space without ruining the look and feel of the original. Bedrooms in the old house are huge, lavish, and impeccably put together with antiques wrestled from auctions, high-quality textiles, sumptuous mattresses, and wonderful wood-floor bathrooms with a choice of tub or shower; ask for room 3—done out in subtle purple, it has a lovely garden view. In the new wing, things are rather more contemporary and designed as loft-style "suites" with either a lounge area below and bedroom upstairs, or an extra bed in the upstairs section so it can be used by families (these go for €120–€130). Set in tree-filled grounds, Viewmount has its own restaurant, and the Kearneys, who are astute art collectors, lovers of gardening, and involved with Longford community, are excellent hosts.

Boyle

If Abbey House (below) is full, you can check in at **Úna Bhán Tourism** (grounds of King House; ☎ 071/966-3033; www.unabhan.net)—dedicated to "anything that helps the town"—and speak to Roy or Patricia about booking in local B&Bs. They won't charge anything, but will call around to find a place that suits your budget. They're also terrific sources for information on fishing in the area.

€€   The best-situated lodgings in Boyle are at Christina Mitchell's **Abbey House** ✪✪ (☎ 071/966-2385; www.abbeyhouse.net; cash only), where you can enjoy turf fires and traditional B&B hospitality in a splendid Victorian house, or rent out a self-catering unit built right up against the walls of Boyle's 12th-century abbey. On the other side of the house is the Boyle River, creating the illusion that you're out in the countryside, despite being a short walk from the town. For €72 you get biggish, homey bedrooms in a large house with an authentic Old World ambience—it's 180 years old, yes, but doesn't feel too old-fashioned. Of the three cute self-catering "cottages" on the property, two were formerly stables; ask for "Abbey Lodge," which is the largest unit. Each has a double as well as a twin room; plenty of wardrobe space; kitchen; cozy, furnace-warmed lounge; and access to laundry facilities. You'll pay €320 per week (May–Aug), and a little less out of season.

€€–€€€   With the ambience of a country pub, all in wood with a great big blazing fire, the **Moving Stairs** ✪✪ (The Crescent; ☎ 071/966-3586; food served Tues–Sun 5–10pm; Sun 4–9pm; MC, V) hosts dining and upbeat drinking downstairs, and live music (with country and western bands from Cork to Nashville) upstairs. Try the lip-smacking Hungarian goulash (€13) or the tender-roasted lamb shank (€15); but if you fancy a big plate of local beef, order one of the near-overwhelming steaks (the largest costs €18). The kitchen uses only organic, locally sourced ingredients. The soundtrack is great, too—even when the traditional tunes aren't live, they're intoxicating, and tinged with experimental riffs that let you know the owner understands music.

Carrick-on-Shannon

The town of Carrick-on-Shannon itself isn't overly supplied with attractions, so the popular activities, as you might expect, are waterborne. Locals and visitors alike are enamored with boating, and you can choose from plenty of cruises, including a Saturday late-nighter on the **Moonriver** (☎ 071/962-1777; www.moon-river.net) with music, booze, and an over-23 crowd up for a huge party, starting at 11:30pm. Tickets cost €12, but what you do at the bar is extra.

€€–€€€   As for sleeps, you have another historic beauty on offer here. And I'd like to underscore this trend: In this less-touristed area of the country, lavishly restored historic homes are much less expensive to stay in than they would be in, say, County Kerry, so if you're visiting this neck of the woods, do take advantage of this opportunity. Case in point: Rosaleen and Tom Maher's **Hollywell** ✪✪✪ (kids) (Liberty Hill; ☎ 071/962-1124; hollywell@esatbiz.com; AE, MC, V), which has been around since the 1730s. Overlooking the river and the town on the opposite shore, this is a fine creeper-clad Georgian manse, studded with flower boxes and stuffed full of antiques (including three disemboweled, silent grandfather clocks), family portraits, and a wonderful sense of keen-eyed luxury without any pretenses. Upstairs, the four guest rooms all boast big beds, orthopedic mattresses, fine-quality linens, and bedspreads, as well as wardrobes, books, and CD players (TVs would ruin the ambience entirely); bathrooms are a little on the snug side. The two "standard" rooms cost €100 to €110 double, it's an additional €20 for one of the two front-facing rooms, which are massive, with bigger bathrooms (and tubs) and windows affording views over the river. One of these has an extra single bed, and the other has room for another bed in addition to the divan that's already there; these are a good option if you're traveling with children. Hollywell is a true measure of Irish hospitality, and it's a short walk across the bridge into town.

€€–€€€€   Easily one of the finest pub-style eateries in Ireland, the **Oarsman** ✪✪✪ (Bridge St.; ☎ 071/962-1733; www.oarsman.com; Tues–Sat noon–3:30pm and 6:45–9:30pm; MC, V) is wildly popular—arrive even on a weekday afternoon, and there's a near-scrum for tables. So if you have to, skip the tables and dine at the bar; a full menu's offered there and the service is just as good. At lunch, there's always a dish of the day (around €11)—I last had a tastily marinated pork chop, served with stir-fried leek, courgette, and onion with herb mash and a pepper, celery, and orange salsa, and I'm smacking my lips just writing about it. A signature choice is Beef Wellington (€11) made with minced Irish beef and buttered leek in a puff pastry, it's also served on mash, this time with a peppercorn cream sauce. There are good vegetarian options, as well as seafood chowder, sandwiches, wraps, and soup. The evening menu is more expensive, but what you get for the extra euros is special (anything they do with lamb comes highly recommended). And sometimes I like to just sip my espresso and soak up the good vibes; the Oarsman is a little addictive.

In & Around Ballinamore

€–€€ It's not only the seemingly endless line-up of welcoming pubs that makes Ballinamore feel ultra-hospitable, but also the warm reception you'll find at **Hamill's B&B** ✪✪ 🄺 (Town Centre; ☎ 087/227-8195 or 071/964-421; www.hamillsbedandbreakfast.com; MC, V). While Damien and Bernadette Hamill's decade-old guesthouse is slap-bang in the center of the town, it's also located off the main street, so you're away from traffic noise where there's plenty of parking; it also means that kids are that much safer and have a bit of a garden to play in (along with the Hamill's three sociable youngsters). Accommodations (€60–€80 double; €40–€45 single) are spacious, with good pine furniture and decent-size bathrooms (with a tub-and-shower combo) that you can happily get your entire body into without any tricky maneuvers. There's none of the fussy, dated styling that's become typical of some of the older home-turned-guesthouse lodgings you find throughout Ireland, and Damien attends to all the painting, fixing, and refurbishing himself (he also irons the sheets, would you believe, and will make sandwiches if you're spending the day out on the lake), so things tend to be in top nick. Many visitors to Ballinamore come for the fishing, and although he's no fisherman himself, Damien will help you get organized with that; he'll also lend you a few irons if you feel inclined to spend a day on the local 9-hole course (€20 for a day).

€€ A few miles from Ballinamore, on the edge of Fenagh Lake, the **Old Rectory** ✪✪ 🄺 (Fenagh; ☎ 071/964-4089; www.theoldrectoryireland.com; MC, V) is heaven for kids with its playroom-cum-conservatory and trampoline. Bicycles and canoes are available, and there's an easy, direct route down to the lake. That's not to say grownups won't dig the place, too. Hey, there's a hot tub with lovely lake views and six antique-furnished guest rooms (€80 double), and also a self-catering garden cottage for anyone wanting to stay awhile (€350 per week, suitable for two). All in all, a genuinely pleasing place. In case you were wondering, the house was formerly the rectory of the church next door. The B&B's open in the summer months only (Apr–Sept).

WHY YOU'RE HERE: TOP SIGHTS & ATTRACTIONS
County of Saints, Sinners & Wordsmiths

While the most celebrated name associated with Longford is playwright Oliver Goldsmith, it may interest you to know that Mel Gibson's mother also hails from these parts, and her son is apparently named after Saint Mel, who was active in Longford County in the 5th century. He—the saint, not the actor—gave his name to **St. Mel's Cathedral** ✪, which is the town's architectural highlight, built in the Renaissance style (which means it resembles a city hall), with a 60m (200-ft.) domed tower; if you get a chance, go inside to check out its mosaic floors and arched baroque ceilings.

Otherwise, aside from simply wandering the town's streets and sampling its alluring pubs, you'll want to leave it to visit the immaculately maintained heritage town of **Ardagh** ✮✮✮ (10km/6 miles from Longford), a mellow little spot with some 75 residents and the original St. Mel's Cathedral, apparently founded by St. Patrick. At one stage it was served by a nun who went on to become St. Brigid. Ardagh House, built in the early-1700s is the village's most sumptuous piece of architecture where Goldsmith inadvertently became the butt of a joke that was to evolve into the plot of his most famous play (p. 300).

Best Laid Plans of Men & Monsters

While Longford Town is not exactly essentially viewing, if you do make it to this stretch of the midlands, then one unmissable stop is the planned estate town of Strokestown, known for having Ireland's broadest main street, and laid out—as you will instantly notice—on a cross-plan.

But, unless town-planning is your thing, the reason to stop here is to visit **Strokestown Park House & Gardens** ✮✮✮ (Strokestown; ☎ 071/963-3013; www.strokestownpark.ie; house, gardens, and famine museum €14; mid-Mar to Oct daily 9:30am–5:45pm). Once upon a time, this was among the finest plantation estates in Ireland, the preserve of the aristocratic Pakenham Mahon family from 1653 until 1981. Now, peasants like you and me get to roam the corridors and explore the stately chambers formerly inhabited by some really nasty, ignoble types (see below). The house is filled with grand architectural detail and sumptuous furnishings and decoration. A highlight is the Georgian kitchen—one of the finest in Europe. It has a gallery from which the lady of the house could drop recipes, oversee the cooking process, and pass down measured quantities of precious ingredients to the servants below.

Strokestown is appealing not only for the authentic way in which the house has been restored, but also for its evocative **Famine Museum** ✮✮✮, which is chockablock with absorbing details and historical anecdotes around the Great Irish Famine, perhaps the greatest human tragedy of the 19th century. The most startling fact around the famine is that Ireland continued to export food throughout the crisis—it was only the poor who were suffering, forced to pay rent, even when they had nothing to eat, their regular potato food source having been wiped out by the potato blight. It's no accident that this museum is housed here. When Stokestown House was purchased from Olive Packenham Mahon in 1981, alarming revelations came to light. Mildewed letters dating back to the Great Famine were discovered—in these were the pleas of tenant farmers seeking assistance, or work, from Dennis Mahon who had inherited the property in 1845. But the heartless landowner, rather than showing mercy, evicted people en masse, and personally sent many to Quebec. In fact, he evicted some 3,006 people in 1 year—that's more than the total number who were evicted from County Cork. He was so hated, in fact, that he became the first landlord to be assassinated; two men were hanged for his murder. On display here is the gun used to kill him, along with eviction notices and crowbars that would have been used to turn people out of their homes. The museum also opens up the famine crisis to a contemporary perspective, drawing saddening parallels with issues of starvation that afflict third world countries today. After the museum, you can meditate on what you've learned with a walk around the estate gardens, and there's a cafe at the entrance occupying an old granary which predates the mansion.

Boyle's Fine Abbey

In the northernmost corner of Roscommon, Boyle is a polite, pretty village that quickly spreads out into the countryside; Irish families love to come here to explore the Forest Park, at the edge of island-studded Lough Key. Apparently the town grew around a traveler's hostel built on the advice of St. Patrick, who visited in 435 A.D.; that inn is now long gone, but Boyle is home to two important architectural sites. Like something straight out of *The Name of the Rose*, **Boyle Abbey** ★★ (Boyle; ☎ 071/966-2604; www.heritageireland.ie; free admission while restoration continues; Easter–Oct daily 10am–6pm) was built by the Cistercians in the 12th and 13th centuries, and although its roof is long gone, it retains its haunting atmosphere. Built during a transition phase in Irish architecture, the ruins reveal original Romanesque elements complemented by additions (the arches, for example) from the later Gothic movement. Although there are hourly tours of the abbey, you might want to look out especially for the weathered sheela-na-gig carving which is an overtly carnal, or erotic, image of a female; also, look for carvings of cockerels, which hint at the Cistercian's French origins. The round tower is a reminder of the many attacks that the abbey endured, particularly after the Elizabethans turned it into a military barracks; Cromwell's forces besieged it in 1645.

A short stroll from the abbey, at the edge of Boyle's town center, **King House** (Main St.; ☎ 071/966-3242; www.kinghouse.ie; €7; Apr–Sept daily 10am–6pm) is a lavish and expansive Georgian Mansion built in the 1730s as the original home of the self-made King family, who later built and lived at famed and fabled Rockingham (which perished in flames 50 years ago).

In Search of Black Gold

If you've never been down a mine shaft or suffer from any kind of claustrophobia, the **Arigna Mining Experience** ★★★ (Arigna, Co. Roscommon; ☎ 071/964-6466; www.arignaminingexperience.ie; €10; daily 10am–5pm) might be quite frightening. In fact, you might wish to stay above ground and admire the view over the valley below while those of sturdier constitution follow one of the miners-turned-guides into the disused mining tunnels that comprise this fascinating attraction. Arigna's mining history began in the 1600s when iron works were established here; later, coal was discovered here and mined as an alternative to the rapidly diminishing supply of timber that had been used to produce charcoal for the ironworks smelting process. Coal mining kept the local economy afloat even after the ironworks floundered. Visitors to Arigna don mine helmets and are led into the often-narrow, sometimes pitch-black pits and tunnels that were dug out in the search for the "black diamond." Much of this shoveling was done by hand, and often by men lying on their sides, in the damp and muck, for the better part of a day. And as you plunge deeper into the mine shaft, you become increasingly aware that the heavy weight of the rock above you is held up by nothing more than what looks like cheap timber. Along the way, your guide, who would have spent years "working the 'gob'" until the mine finally closed in 1990, explains (in an often unfathomable accent, I must admit) how the men toiled under atrocious conditions. With the frightening, terrifying reality of all that unpredictable weight above them, they were also dealing with the terrible noise of rumbling machinery and the non-stop hammering, banging, and, of course, blasting. At one point, sound effects simulate such a blast, and at another, your guide turns off all the lights and you realize just how dark, lonely, and terrifying this job must have been. And then there are tales of when things went wrong . . .

Tours of Arigna last around 40 minutes and when I went, one small child became very scared, while I myself was a little nervous; it's not a dangerous tour at all, but the bleak tunnels evoke a sense of imminent danger, and it's hard not to be disturbed by the fact that our fellow human beings were subjected to such harrowing and, frankly, inhuman working conditions. You might never complain about your job again.

THE OTHER NORTHERN MIDLANDS

As you might expect in such remote and laid-back parts, just stepping into the local pub can provoke interest in the "stranger"; let folks know that you're from faraway and are keen to know more about local life, and you'll leave with arm-loads of friends.

If you're looking to learn from the locals, or learn with the locals, your first stop should be the **Dock** (St. George's Terrace; ☎ 071/965-0820; www.thedock.ie), Carrick-on-Shannon's all-purpose arts and culture space, which not only has a theater and regular art exhibitions, but also runs regular events, including dance classes, and workshops with different artists and crafters. It's worth popping in—even if there's nothing happening, you can usually pick up a conversation in the little cafe here.

Nearby, poke your head into Ken Cunningham's little studio shop, **Leitrim Crystal** (☎ 086/395-1717 or 071/962-2255). Ken is a master glass-cutter who doesn't mind having visitors watch him etch designs onto the ornamental and practical glassware he prepares. In fact, I think he loves people taking an interest in what he's doing, and he's got so many orders flying in, he won't put pressure on you to buy. It's mesmerizing to lean in over his shoulder and watch the precision with which he rapidly shaves away the glass to produce various patterns (it's a lot more intimate than the experience at Waterford Crystal). When I popped by, a brief chat about the difficulties of glass-cutting turned into a lengthy conversation about South African politics.

If you happen to be in Boyle over the weekend, stop by the weekly **farmers' market** ✿✿, which happens on Saturdays from 10am to 2pm on the grounds of King House. For a short time, this becomes the hub of village life.

ACTIVE LEITRIM

Abundant lakes and waterways make Leitrim a fisherman's paradise. With a season that stretches from late-March until October, and a 40.5-hectare (100-acre) spring-fed lough nearby, one of the most pleasant bases from which to tackle your **fishing** is the peaceful village of Ballinamore. Daily licenses cost €10 (or €40 per year), and can be purchased from the most unusual store you'll venture into anywhere in Ireland: **The Forge (aka Dee's Shop;** ☎ 087/625740), which is on

Ballinamore's main road (if for some reason you can't find it, just ask anyone). Dee, originally from the U.S., not only stocks anything and everything in her chaotic little store (from fish bait to *bodhráns,* and essential oils), she'll also provide insider intelligence on where to hike or cast a line, even telling you where the best wading spots are. Even if you're not into fishing, don't pass up the chance to venture into Dee's phantasmagoric emporium.

ATTENTION, SHOPPERS!

Run by Nick Kaszuk and Joanna Moss, **Trinity Rare Books** ✪✪ (Bridge St., Carrick-on-Shannon; ☎ 071/962-2144; www.trinityrarebooks.com; Mon–Sat 9:30am–6pm; Sun 1–5pm) is a great place to pick up well-priced works of Irish literature; there are classics as well as contemporary novels. Also in Carrick-on-Shannon, at the Dock art center, browse the fine selection of arts and crafts at the **Leitrim Design House** (☎ 071/965-0550; www.intoleitrim.com); the small shop represents over 250 artists, and has some wonderful ceramics, beautiful photography, and interesting jewelry.

9 Counties Mayo, Sligo & Donegal

Big skies & earthy drama in the Northwest

by Keith Bain & Emily Hourican

IRELAND IS FAMOUS FOR ITS GREAT WESTERN SEABOARD, BUT WHEREAS THE other coastal beauty spots, like Kerry, west Cork, and Connemara were discovered by tourists decades—even centuries ago—Mayo, Donegal, and, to a lesser extent, Sligo proved harder to crack. The terrain was more inaccessible, the roads even worse, the winds even stronger, the language less likely to be English. That's all changing now but the northwest remains far less developed touristically. It's particularly suited to those who like bracing walks, long scenic drives, trad music (Sligo, in particular, has a near endless series of music festivals), dining on the freshest fish, and—when duty calls—occasionally roughing it. Here, getting closer to nature is a given—whether you're ascending mountains at the edge of the sea, hiking through splendid woodlands, or perhaps grabbing a surfboard and conquering tubular waves. For those who enjoy ticking off highlights, the northernmost point in the country (at the top of Donegal) is here, and Sligo has more megalithic sites per square meter than any other part of the country.

DON'T LEAVE THE NORTHWEST WITHOUT . . .

PUBBING IN SLIGO OR WESTPORT   Small enough to be intimate, but large enough to get lost in (on your first day anyway), these are two of the handsomest and hippest towns in Ireland, each boasting a splendiferous trad music scene and some of the friendliest pubs on the Emerald Isle. See p. 319.

SINKING INTO A SEAWEED BATH   For over 100 years, travelers have been lounging in the hot seaweed baths at Enniscrone (p. 342) and then climbing into individual cedarwood chests for a steam bath. A true Edwardian experience.

LODGING IN A COUNTRY MANSION ON A VAST ESTATE   And believe it or not, you can do it for under €100 per person a night at Temple House (p. 334) or Markree Castle (p. 333). If those are still to rich for your blood, the northwest has some of the loveliest **hostels** in Europe. Try Gyreum in Sligo (p. 334) or one of the many in Donegal (p. 347).

ISLAND HOPPING   Go out to Donegal's Tory Island (p. 356), to be greeted by the king; or to Sligo's abandoned Innishmurray Island (p. 340) and curse your enemies on the ancient cursing stones.

VISITING A MEGALITHIC SITE   The northwest has megalithic tombs a thousand years older than Stonehenge. Best choices—the Carrowmore or the Carrowkeel passage tombs (p. 337).

WALKING THE SLIEVE LEAGUE CLIFFS   Donegal's cliffs aren't as famous as the cliffs of Moher and don't have that staggering sheer drop of a view, but they're higher, and much less crowded, and best of all don't foist upon tourists a useless visitor centre (or parking fees). See p. 350.

RECITING YEATS   Go on, memorize a few lines, one for every place you visit: "I will arise and go now and go to Innishfree"—"The wind has bundled up the clouds high over Knocknarea"—"Under bare Ben Bulben's head/In Drumcliff churchyard Yeats is laid." See p. 338.

A BRIEF HISTORY OF THE NORTHWEST

Mayo and Sligo are in the ancient province of Connaught and Donegal of Ulster, a boundary still marked by a difference in the accent. Although part of two different provinces, these three counties share a great deal of history, mainly because they share geography. All three suffered terribly in the famine because of poor land. Until very recently emigration was a fact of life for all families. To counteract the poverty of the soil, each has a strong tradition of cottage industries—particularly Donegal, which had (and has) a weaving industry. Mayo and Sligo (whose Irish name *Sligeach* means "shelly place") counted on their salmon and trout-rich rivers to feed their fishing industries.

Going further back, this whole area is known for its megalithic sites, many dating as far back as 5000 B.C., so this must have been a significant region in the Neolithic age. Mayo and Donegal are similar in their remoteness, which is why both have strong *Gaeltacht* (or Irish language) communities. Immune to the political and cultural changes coming out of Dublin, they kept hold of their traditions for longer.

COUNTY MAYO

Mayo is a county of radical oppositions. On the one hand it has some of the poorest soil and the windiest shores in Ireland, so that in the last century whenever people referred to Mayo, they added, like a litany, "Mayo—God help us!" On the other hand it has, in Ashford Castle, not just Ireland's, but one of the world's most luxurious hotels. It was erected here because Mayo boasts some of the country's finest scenery from mountains similar to Connemara's, in south Mayo to the lush riverside scenery around Ballina, by way of the majestic, barren bogs of Achill Island and Belmullet. But it's not all about landscapes—Westport rivals Sligo as the hippest town in the northwest.

GETTING THERE & GETTING AROUND

You can get to Westport and Castlebar by **train** (☎ 071/916-9888; www.irishrail.ie) from Dublin (€15–€24), and by **bus** (☎ 071/916-0066; www.buseireann.ie; €16 one-way from Dublin, €24 round-trip). Westport is also served by buses from Galway, Clifton, Sligo, and Athlone. Within Mayo, as with all rural Irish counties, you're reliant on the rather infrequent bus services.

Coming in to the county with a **rental car,** therefore is likely your least stressful (and most enjoyable) strategy. Mayo does have an airport, built to serve the Marian shrine at Knock, but flying into it is insanely pricey (so not advised).

CONG

Southern Mayo is very much a continuation of Connemara (p. 280)—as you move northwards, the Maamturk Mountains become the Partry Mountains. Just over the border with Galway County is **Cong,** a small, pretty village which always sounds to us like something out of the Far East, although actually the Gaelic *Cung* means "narrow strip of land." It lies just before **Lough Corrib.** If you spend more than 5 minutes here you'll know Cong's claim to fame: This is where John Ford shot *The Quiet Man,* starring John Wayne and the red-haired, Dublin-born Maureen O'Hara. There's a *Quiet Man* museum here, which is a replica of the cottage in the film, and a hostel which screens the film *every* night. It all harkens back to an era when Ireland was thrilled to have a Hollywood presence (it's now completely blasé, what with *Braveheart, Angela's Ashes, Saving Private Ryan,* and just about every blockbuster you can think of, being shot here). Cong also has **Ashford Castle,** where Pierce Brosnan got married and everyone from Princess Grace to John Travolta has stayed.

Accommodations, Both Standard & Not

Cong does not lack for accommodations, yet it gets very busy and if you're visiting in summer, you'd do well to reserve ahead for a room in one of its many B&Bs or small hotels.

€   With rentals in the village and a hostel, campgrounds, and a B&B on their land that abuts Ashford Castle, Margaret and Gerry Collins have hit all the bases in Cong. They also are taking the *Quiet Man* connection as far as it can go, playing it nightly at the **Cong Hostel** (Quay Rd.; ☎ 094/954-6089; www.quietman-cong.com; MC, V). That may well be the most charming feature at this very spare, institutional looking hostel with an awkward layout and creaking floors. I mention it simply for those who want to avail themselves of the €20 a night bunks (in four-bedded rooms), though I'll warn you: linens are an additional cost, and the shower costs €1 for every 5-minutes of water. Twin and double rooms (€56 per night) have private bathrooms but are as frill-free in terms of decor and amenities. If you bring your own tent, the **caravan and camping park** costs €15 to €20 a night.

€€   Across the road from the hostel, things couldn't be more different at the Collins's pristine **Michaleen's Manor** ✰✰ (Lisloughrey, Quay Rd.; ☎ 094/954-6089; www.congbb.com; MC, V), their substantially smarter B&B named after the matchmaker in *The Quiet Man.* And the entire B&B is a tribute to the film—the sizeable, cheerful rooms are named after the movie's characters, and tasteful memorabilia decorates the walls. Good showers, bright color schemes, and spruce linens and fabrics make accommodations feel a whole lot more luxurious than they necessarily are—and you certainly won't find anything for this price (€75 double, €55 single) in the center of Cong. If you can, ask to book room 10 ("The Bishop") where brilliant white bedcovers account for a slightly more

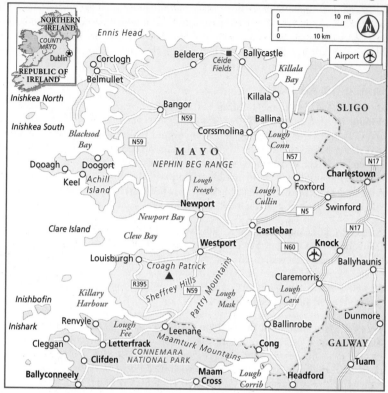

contemporary ambience. There's also a pair of interconnecting rooms (done out in shades of lilac) that are especially useful for families (children pay 10% less). It's actually pretty lavish for a B&B with a sauna and hot tub, and DVD in each room (no points for guessing what movie you can borrow here).

The Collins also have four rental units—you've a choice of cottage or apartment—each with two bedrooms, easily sleeping four. Decorated with care and designed for comfort, they offer full kitchens and functional living areas. Prices are fair at €500 per week in summer, negotiable the rest of the year. "We'll take whatever we can get," says Margaret!

€€   In Cong village, right around the corner from the Abbey, the lime green **Danagher's Hotel** (Abbey St.; ☎ 094/954-6028; MC, V) has an artfully disheveled appearance when you first step inside (even the floorboards, which squeak considerably, seem to slope off the horizontal). But up above the bar and restaurant (there's no formal lobby area) are ten decent, not-too-tiny bedrooms with good, if compact, bathrooms (all with tubs). Rooms have a somewhat mix 'n' match aesthetic (every wall in the house seems to be a different color), but they all have solid beds made up with lovely white quilts. Ideal for sharing, each one has a double and a single bed, except for 5 and 6 which are larger and offer king-size and single beds, and an extra pullout sleeper—great for families. The owners believe that guests have the right to sleep in when on holiday, so breakfast can be served at just about any time you like. You'll usually pay €80 to €90 double, and as little as €70 during the low season; children sharing with parents score a discount, depending on age.

Dining for All Tastes

€–€€   You'll smell the roasting coffee from the street as you approach the **Hungry Monk** (Abbey St; ☎ 094/954-5842; Mar–Oct Tues–Sun 10am–6pm; cash only). Despite the low ceiling and lino-covered tables, the small room is bright and cheerful, and there are handsome paintings on the wall (by the owner, Robert Devereux). He also has an artistic way with sandwiches (€7.95–€8.50) and salads, mixing unlikely ingredients like bacon with hazelnuts, strawberry balsamic salsa, and apple with bacon and brie. If your needs stretch beyond tea and coffee, you can order a half a bottle of house red for €5.

€–€€€   For something more substantial, head to **Mary Kate's Kitchen** at Danagher's Hotel (Abbey St.; daily noon–9pm; MC, V), which offers solid bar food all day—steaks, stews, traditional bacon and cabbage (€13), and good old chicken curry with rice (€13)—and also fine salads (€14–€15), sandwiches (€3.50), and toasties (€4.50). Trad session nightly in summer and frequently during the rest of the year.

€€–€€€€   **Cullen's at the Cottage** (☎ 094/954-5332; daily 11:30am–9:30pm; MC, V), situated on the grounds of the Ashford estate has two big lures: Its spectacular views of the property, and tasty meals at far less than you'd pay at the castle itself. A traditional thatched cottage with tiled floors, white walls, and wooden tables Cullen's is overseen by Castle head chef, Stefan Matz, and offers a bistro-style menu with an emphasis on seafood. You can have soup and sandwiches go for about €12 or go all out for lobster . . . and pay a lot more.

Why You're Here: Top Sights & Attractions

Fans of the movie will probably make a bee-line for **The Quiet Man Heritage Centre** (Quiet Man Cottage Museum, Circular Rd.; ☎ 094/954-6089; €5; Mar 17-Oct 31 10:30am–4:30pm) but we can't imagine why you'd want to pay €5 to go in (you've seen the movie and are now practically on set, why would you want to see an exhibition?) Instead, ask to join one of the more engaging, 90-minute **tours** (€15). Gerry Collins, *Quiet Man* fan extraordinaire, takes visitors to locations from the film sharing anecdotes along the way. Be warned that you'll also be asked to enact key scenes from the movie at the relevant locations. Extroverts are especially welcome.

Hollywood devotion aside, the real reason you've come to Cong is for the sumptuous scenery. The village is actually set on an island, and is surrounded by waterways and lush greenery; it really does seem like a set created for an overly romantic Hollywood love story. There's even a castle: magnificent **Ashford Castle** ★★ (☎ 800/346-7007 toll-free U.S. or 094/954-6003; www.ashford.ie), its massive stone walls a foil for the lake and grounds on which it's set. The castle was built in 1228 by the Anglo-Norman de Burgo family after they defeated the

The Other Cong: Walk the Hawk

It's likely that falconry—the practice of using trained birds of prey to pursue game for their human handlers—is some 4,000 years old. Accounts vary on where it was first developed; some say Mesopotamia (the area known as Iraq today), others China, Japan, or Mongolia. What's clear is this practice, which many consider both a sport and an art, is a mesmerizing spectacle to behold and a fascinating tie to the past.

At **Ireland's School of Falconry** ✪✪✪ (Ashford Castle, Cong; ☎ 087/297-6092 or 094/954-6820; www.falconry.ie; daily 9am–4:30pm), novices have the unique opportunity to not only watch these raptors take wing, but to handle Harris hawks (the only hawks that will fly with strangers). Participants are outfitted with thick, leather gloves (for the birds to perch on) and then learn how to encourage the bird to fly from—and return to—their gloved hand. What most surprised us when we took the course was how intimate the relationship between man and bird quickly becomes. The hawks we held intently watched every move we made, eager to do our bidding. And it's exhilarating to extend your arm and then watch as the hawks effortlessly glide, majestically descending from the branch of a far-off tree, and touching down with perfect precision on your wrist.

A hawk walk isn't cheap at €70 for an hour, with discounts if there are two or more of you, but I think this unique opportunity is worth the splurge. Under certain conditions, it may be possible to walk with an owl, when you can witness a hunting simulation during which a live rabbit is used as a lure (it's not for the squeamish).

O'Connors (Connacht's royal family). Over the centuries, the castle has found itself under various masters, growing all the while in size and splendor—in 1715 a lodge in the style of a 17th-century French chateau was added. Sir Benjamin Guinness purchased the estate in 1852; he expanded the estate to 10,520 hectares (26,000 acres), planted thousands of trees and gave the castle two massive Victorian extensions. Ashford became a hotel after it was sold to Noel Huggard in 1939; in 1951 Ashford Castle and its grounds became part of the backdrop for *The Quiet Man*. Besides John Wayne (the film's star), the castle is known to have hosted such luminaries as Ronald Reagan, Princess Grace of Monaco, King George V, Oscar Wilde, and Senator Edward Kennedy.

To keep the crowds at bay, the proprietors allow non-patrons to enjoy the handsome grounds here for a fee (€5 in the summer, although we just walked into the grounds when we last visited in autumn; if you arrive early, there's usually no-one checking). You'll also have a legitimate reason to visit if you're intending to visit its **School of Falconry** (see above).

Back in the village, explore the ruins of **Cong Abbey** (Abbey St.; ☎ 094/954-6542; free admission), an early Irish Romanesque building right opposite the Tourist Office, dating from the 12th and 13th centuries.

WESTPORT

Westport isn't Mayo's capital, but it's by far the county's liveliest and most hand-some town. It's unusual among Irish country towns in that it was designed to an actual plan (by James Wyatt in 1780) rather than simply evolving willy-nilly, and boy, can you feel the difference. Aim to spend at least a few nights here as Westport truly has everything—great nightlife, good places to eat, and proximity to beautiful beaches and walks. Its only downside? Westport's population of 5,000 is said to rise to about 22,000 during the summer so at peak season you may be more likely to meet fellow travelers than locals here.

Getting There & Getting Around

From Connemara, the **N59** continues up along the rugged coast of Mayo to Westport. The route shares much of Connemara's beauty but is less touristed.

Westport itself has two main, parallel thoroughfares—**James Street** which bounds the striking **Octogonal square,** and **Bridge Street,** which has a clock tower at its southern end. Navigate by this clocktower, which has four streets radi-ating off it. To the north is the tree-lined **Mall,** which runs along the canalized **Carrowbeg River.** The town is situated on **Clew Bay,** with many of the best places to eat along the harbor. A 35-minute drive to the west is the sleepy and charming village of **Louisburgh,** which has nifty beaches where Westporters go to swim. A few buses a day make the 35-minute drive (€6.50).

Accommodations, Both Standard & Not

Westport's recent building boom means a wide variety of lodging, including inter-esting hostels, good B&Bs, and a high number of cheerful hotels. Though the rental market is also strong, negotiating rentals can be confusing. A lot of the same housing pops up on different sites . . . often with different price tags.

We'd recommend looking to a local agency, like **Atlantic Coast Holiday Homes** (Distillery Rd., Westport; ☎ 098/27711; www.achh.ie) to help sort the gold from the dross. In business since the 1990's, its portfolio is diverse—from two-bedroomed apartments in Westport town to country cottages, and almost all properties are three- or four-star rated by Bord Fáilte, which means that certain standards must necessarily be in place and maintained. Additionally, owners Pat Aylward and Bob Kilkelly check out the properties before adopting them into their portfolio, and do occasional inspections; based on the properties we've seen, they have a clear sense of good quality. Weekly off-season prices start from €300 to €450, while in July and August you're looking at between €500 and €800 per week. A big downside: Their rates are sometimes higher than prices on other web-sites (though they're sometimes willing to negotiate; ask).

Before booking with Atlantic Coast, we'd suggest comparing its prices with those offered on the Mayo tourist office site, **www.mayo-ireland.ie,** which acts as a hosting site for both agencies, and individuals with only one or two properties to rent. You'll find property photos and contact information on the website allow-ing you to phone owners directly and haggle. Among the spectacular deals there:

◆ **Brookside Cottage** ✷✷ (in Cushin, 5km/3½ miles from Westport; ☎ 098/ 359118): A gorgeous, 100-year-old farmhouse with old-fashioned decor—cast iron beds, an open fireplace, low stone walls surrounding the lovely garden— with all the modern amenities. The cottage sleeps six people in four bedrooms and costs just €280 per week most of the year, €330 to €380 when things get a bit busy, and €580 when Westport is wall to wall with visitors.

♦ **Garavan's** ✠ (Drummin; ☎ 098/21845; www.garavans.com): Another six-sleeper farmhouse, this one goes for between €230 and €450. The house gets loads of light, has brightly colored walls, and has most of the conveniences of home—only in an altogether more relaxed, totally rural setting.

♦ **Harbour Mill** (Westport Quay, Westport; ☎ 098/28555; www.theharbour mill.com): Professionally managed apartments down at the harbor, with a full-time reception, sauna, Jacuzzi, swimming pool, and children's playroom all set in a reconstructed 18th-century mill. What we like about these apartments are their spaciousness, and the inclusion of all the standard modern amenities in neat, open-plan kitchens. Each has two bathrooms (one en suite), while bedrooms (a double bed in one, and two singles in the other) have a woodsy feel. Rates start at €399 to €499 per week, up to €649 in July and August; add €100 per week for an extra person.

€ Westport's hostels are such unique, interesting, and attractive places to stay—one converted from a mill and the other from a monastery—that they get a lot of folks who generally don't settle for hostels elsewhere. We're talking families and older travelers, who are catered to with double and family rooms (as well as a check-out time of 10am that deters rowdy all-nighter type guests). Both include a rudimentary breakfast in their prices. The **Old Mill Holiday Hostel** ✠ (Barrack Yard, James St; ☎ 098/27045; www.oldmillhostel.com; MC, V) still looks very much like the mill/brewery it once was, thanks to its wooden beams and thick stone walls. These enclose six- and seven-bed dorms with neat bunk beds (€19 per person), double rooms, and a family suite with three bedrooms (€25 per person). None of these rooms has a private bathroom so the price is high compared to other hostels. The converted monastery **Abbeywood Hostel** ✠✠ (Newport Rd.; ☎ 098/25496; www.abbeywoodhouse.com; late-Apr to late-Sept; weekends rest of year; closed Jan–Feb; MC, V), is right in the center of town, though it has a very discreet, private feel. It has retained the original stained glass windows and has some antique furniture but recent renovations have added orthopedic mattresses and power showers. Prices are similar to the Old Mill—€18 per person for the 10-bed dorm, €22 per person for the four-bed, and €25 per person for the private rooms, one double, one triple (although that just has a bunk perched above a double bed, so is only suitable for a strictly nuclear family). Again, no rooms with private bathrooms but breakfast is slightly better than the Old Mill's.

€€ The **Boulevard Guesthouse** ✠✠ (kids) (South Mall; ☎ 098/25138; www. boulevard-guesthouse.com; cash only) also occupies a prime location in the heart of town, in walking distance to everything. It's an extremely cozy place, with individually styled bedrooms that are saturated with color (one room's all different shades of calming blue, another blue and yellow, and so on). Rooms also boast amenities that you don't often find in B&B's like proper bedside lamps and writing tables. If you value your space (or are traveling with children), ask for room 1, which is especially large and super-stylish (dark wooden furnishings against maroon- and cream-colored walls), or—if you don't mind another set of steps—see if the family-size bedroom at the top of the house is available. Out back, there's

A Horse Drawn Home

One charming rental option: a **Mayo Horse-drawn Caravan** ✪ (kids) (☎ 094/903-2054; www.horsedrawncaravan.com). Brightly painted, traditional Romany-style rounded wooden caravans, these old-style "RV's" are drawn by large, peaceful draught horses and amble round the South Mayo roads, stopping at sights on the way. Inside the caravans make the most of space—they sleep four, the folding table turning into one of the beds at night. Lighting is provided by gas or electricity, and you can cook on an inside gas ring.

These carriages are an option even for those who wouldn't consider themselves part of the "horsey set." An instructor accompanies you around the roads at Belcarra (near Castlebar) and before you go out on your own, teaches you how to harness, drive, and care for the horses. Then, you travel about 10km (6 miles) a day and stop at selected farmhouses, where your horse is stabled. Instructors are within reach, should you need help harnessing in the morning.

Perhaps because of the hands-on help, it's not dirt cheap: Prices start at €720 a week from May to mid-July and rise to €930 mid-July through August, plus you have to pay €21 a night for pitching fees, and €2 a night for electric hook-ups. But your kids will adore it, and you'll certainly have some story to tell when you get home. One week may be too long for most families, so we'd advise the 3-day trip for €370 (but usually only available in May, June, and Sept).

a very pretty garden where a few chickens roam and provide eggs for breakfasts, served here with big helpings of French press coffee. Doubles tend to run €70, and a family room (for four people) will be €120 but if you're planning on staying for three or more nights, the owners will give you an even better rate.

€€ **Glenderan Bed & Breakfast** ✪✪ (kids) (Rosbeg; ☎ 098/26585; www. glenderan.com; closed Nov–Feb; cash only) is 600m (1,968 ft.) from Westport's Quayside area—not too far from the town center, yet perfect if you want to escape the noise that many visitors complain about in this hard-partying town. A handsome, slate-roofed house on a .5 hectare (1-acre) property with lovely gardens and outdoor seating areas, Glenderan has been well-conceived for guest use. Bedrooms (€76 double, €55 single, children half price) are particularly good-looking, with sleigh beds, good orthopedic mattresses, and smart, eye-catching linens. On chillier evenings, turf fires are lit in the sitting room, and your hosts, Dermot and Ann O'Flaherty, make an effort to create a homey atmosphere. Breakfasts are taken in a glass-walled conservatory, and include a choice that goes beyond the usual full Irish fry-up.

€€–€€€€ **Clewbay Hotel** ✪ (James St.; ☎ 098/28088; www.clewbayhotel. com; MC, V) is an upgrade of an older hotel that has been considerably smartened up and prettified, and the bedrooms have received more than a mere lick of paint. They now have soft beds with plush linens, and designer wallpaper, modern lamps, and tidy wood furnishing to create a little oasis of calm right in the heart of busy Westport. Rates are a mixed bag, with an assortment of deals and special packages, although you'll always pay far more on weekends. The best offers (we've caught many a "2-nights-plus-dinner" deal for €89 per person) are available online, so surf there first when weighing up your options; otherwise, expect to pay €100 to €130 weeknights, €140 up on weekends.

Dining for All Tastes

Westport fancies itself the Kinsale of the Northwest (that is, a gastronomic mecca) and it does have good places to eat, although perhaps not as good as it thinks. However between cheerful Italians, fish by the harbor, and evangelical organic cafes, we're certainly not complaining. The harbor is the place for good seafood while around Bridge Street are cheap and cheerful pasta places.

€–€€ McCormacks on Bridge Street is one of Westport's most famous butchers, and has been in the same family for six generations. Annette McCormack has now opened a cafe/restaurant with gallery (or vice versa) upstairs. **McCormacks at The Andrew Stone Gallery** ★ (Bridge St; ☎ 098/25619; Mon–Tues and Thurs–Sat 10:15am–4:45pm; MC, V) lets you enjoy art while you eat, and food while you gaze. This is deli fare—chowder (€5), quiches (€8.60)—as well as meat dishes (and you can trust the meat) like stews, casseroles, and the Irish favorite, bacon and cabbage (all €10). Everything is home baked and locally sourced.

€–€€€ Down at the Quay, with a big, grassy waterside beer garden, the **Tower Bar & Restaurant** ★ 🅺🅸🅳🆂 (Westport Harbour; ☎ 098/26534; daily 12:30–9pm; MC, V) caters to anyone and everyone—there a children's playground outside, and the bar puts on live music on weekends (trad on Sun). When it comes to what's on the menu, the emphasis is on Mayo-sourced ingredients, using them in everything from freshly made sandwiches (€4–€4.50) to more substantial bar meals that include Thai curry (€16), burgers (€12–€14), and ultra-fresh Clew Bay mussels done in a creamy, mouthwatering garlic sauce (€15). There's also a kids menu. You'll know the place when you see it, a modern version of a fortified medieval round tower.

€–€€€€ **Sol Rio** ★ (Bridge St.; ☎ 098/28944; www.solriowestport.com; Wed–Mon noon–3pm and 6–10pm; MC, V) serves up good quality pastas and lasagnas, as well as seafood dishes—prawns, mussels, oysters—in a pleasant first floor room (take heed of the smallish chairs, though). At lunch you can order from a very reasonable menu with most mains costing between €7.50 and €11; lunch is also when you can try a selection of choice traditional "Irish meals" (€8.20–€11) including Irish stew and the chef's famed fish pie. At night Sol Rio is pricier, but there are still good, affordable choices, notably pizzas for €11 to €15.

€€–€€€€ Owner Robert Cabot of **Cabot's Source** ★★★ (High St.; ☎ 098/29771; Wed–Sun 6–10pm; cash only) explains his cooking philosophy in four words: "source locally, cook slowly." But in truth, the food here is much more sophisticated than that implies thanks to Cabot's terrific chef, a Jordanian chap named Nafar, who isn't afraid to give a Middle Eastern "zing" to Irish food-stuffs. So you might find yourself dining on a spice-laden spinach soup (€4.50) or tucking into a platter of pitas and spreads (€11 hummus, beetroot paste, baba ganoush) or a succulent steak (€22). Prices are reasonable, with dinner mains starting at just €3.50 (though some veer into the low €20s), and take-out deli food is also available. One warning: The room is small, holding just about 20 diners, so call in advance for dinner reservations.

Why You're Here: Top Sights & Attractions

Westport's major touristic lure is a stately home turned amusement park called **Westport House** ★ (kids) (entrance from Westport Harbour; ☎ 098/25438; www.westporthouse.ie; house and gardens €11.50; house, gardens, and attractions, €21; hour and gardens Apr–Sept 10am–6pm; park June–Sept 10am–6pm). Along with the historic mansion (see below) its grounds hold fairground rides (log rides, toy railroads, and so on), an animal and bird park with petting zoo, pitch and putt, pedalo boats, and in-the-pipeline kayaking, combat games . . . you name it. It's all a bit dizzying and purists may complain that this is all lessening the dignity of an old family seat. But let's face it: There are a lot of dignified estates and ruins round the west of Ireland, whereas there aren't too many places for kids to blow off steam, so we're all for it.

Except . . . it ain't cheap. We can understand having to pay for attractions (although €16.50 for kids is pretty outrageous!), but €11.50 just to see the house and gardens seems steep. And don't go if rain threatens. That would really be a waste of money.

Don't skip the place either just because you don't have rugrats in tow. The house and gardens are truly an eyeful. The graceful house was built in 1730 by James Wyatt, who also designed Westport town for the Brownes. Like so many Georgian houses the rather austere exterior hides a rococo interior, with wonderful corniced ceilings, mahogany doors, a Chinese salon, and heaps of silver plate. Paintings by Sir James Lavery, James Arthur O'Connor, and most notably the great English portraitist, Sir Joshua Reynolds grace the walls.

Hours are bit confusing: House and gardens, 22 March to the end of October daily, 11:30am to 5:30pm; attractions, Easter week 11:30am to 5:30pm, May Sundays only, June to September daily, 11:30am to 5:30pm.

Active Westport

Along with the fairgrounds at Westport House, families will enjoy sampling the nearby beaches including:

- **Bertra Beach** (Murrisk, a 20-min. drive on the R335 towards Louisburgh): Nearest to Westport the waters here are clean and patrolled by lifeguards in the summer months, making it ideal for swimming, Great springy dunes also endear it to walkers.
- **Old Head** (10 min. further along R335): Sheltered by cliffs and woodlands, with a lifeguard on duty in the summer, Old Head gets a bit crowded for our tastes. However, if you're traveling with kids who'd like to pal around with other tikes, this is a decent choice.
- **Silver Strand** (45 min. from Westport at the end of R335 at Killary Harbor): Silver Strand is a long, frequently deserted sandy beach. It sits directly on

Galway Bay so the views are spectacular; young families will also enjoy explor-ing the dunes here. Like the other two we've listed, it's consistently awarded a "blue flag" which means the waters are clean enough for swimming.

Attention Shoppers!

The **Whyte House in Westport** (Market Lane; ☎ 098/50891) is indeed a white-painted shop but it gets its name from proprietor Karen Whyte. A stylish gift shop, it stocks mostly homeware, but also carries clothes and local art. Whyte stocks such rarefied labels that many people travel from Dublin to visit the shop.

For food gifts (or just treats for yourself), head to **Marlene's Chocolate Haven** (The Courtyard, James St; ☎ 098/24564; www.chocolatehaven.net). Belgian chocolate only is used as a base here, though it's spun into many varieties of milk, dark, and white.

Jams, cheeses, hams, spices, breads, and cakes are on sale each Thursday at the country market held at the Town Hall; for another swell Mayo country market go to the **Parish Centre** (Cornmarket, Ballinarobe) on Saturday mornings.

Nightlife

Nobody should come to Westport without checking out the pubs—even if you only drink orange juice in them. Start off in **McGing's** (on High St.; ☎ 098/26870) one of those plain, functional looking Irish pubs, with carpets, low ceil-ings, and nothing particular in the decor (*Tip:* Pubs that look like this are usually the ones with the most loyal local followings, therefore they inevitably provide the most engaging *craic;* by contrast the ones you should be wary of are the wood-paneled tourist traps.) The Guinness here is renowned and you'll also hear good music, not just trad but occasionally jazz and bluegrass as well.

The town's most famous pub is **Matt Molloy's** (Bridge St.; ☎ 098/26655; www.mattmolloy.com), owned by the eponymous flautist of the great Irish band, the **Chieftains.** It's a real session pub—no TV, but music memorabilia on the walls—that by now is so famous it's full of tourists. You should still go in, just don't spend all your time here.

If you prefer your nightlife pumping and heaving, then head for the main nightclub at the **Castle Court Hotel** (Castlebar Rd.; ☎ 098/55088), where things can get pretty sweaty on weekends.

DAY TRIPS FROM WESTPORT
Pilgrim's Trails

Emily first tried climbing **Croagh Patrick** ✿✿✿ (Murrisk, R335 from Westport) at the tender age of seven and being either very pious or very competitive insisted on doing it bare foot . . . so didn't get very far. But hundreds, made of sterner stuff than a 7-year-old's, manage it barefoot every year. This is one of Ireland's foremost places of pilgrimage—in A.D. 441 St. Patrick is said to have fasted the 40 days of Lent on the summit, and then hurled the snakes of Ireland off the precipice. On St. Patrick's Day (Mar 17), the Feast of the Assumption (Aug 15), and, especially, Reek Day (the last Sun in July), tens of thousands march to the summit. On Reek Day mass is celebrated in the small chapel at the top, built in 1905. It's a strenu-ous, but not difficult, climb—the path is *very* well-worn—and from the summit are great views of Clew Bay and Slieve League to the North. This climb isn't about

Amazing Grace

Though the Broadway musical, *The Pirate Queen,* based on the life story of Grace O'Malley, or Granuaile (c. 1530–c. 1603), proved a huge financial disaster, the tale of the woman is a true blockbuster. Grace O'Malley was one of the great Elizabethan figures, a feminist and a nationalist icon. Daughter of a local chieftain, she had her headquarters on Clare Island and policed the waters from Galway Bay to Donegal Bay—she claimed she was imposing taxes on ships in her waters; the Dublin government called her a pirate. She didn't limit her attacks to ships but also ransacked fortresses along the mainland, engaging at once in clan warfare and fighting the English. Her meeting with Elizabeth I at Greenwich Palace was an extraordinary event—bringing together the two most redoubtable women of their age—and the queen took to the pirate, and promised to recall the bloodthirsty governor of Connaught, Sir Richard Bingham, if Grace stopped fomenting rebellion. Bingham was duly recalled, but then sent back, so Grace continued her raids, and became a mythic figure. A film of her life is scheduled for 2009.

To learn more about Grace, there's a **Granuaile Centre** in the library at Louisburgh (☎ 098/66341; €4; June–Sept daily 10am–6pm), which offers the ubiquitous multimedia tour. The fine, intimidating, square **tower house** at the harbor on Clare Island was her headquarters, and there's another in **Achill Island.** The stone plaque in **Clare Abbey** is said to mark her resting place, but that's disputed. The great Irish song, "Óro Sé do Bheatha Bhaile," ("Hail, welcome home") commemorates her.

discovering isolated places of beauty, it's about tapping into the communal spirit and over 2,000 years of Christian pilgrimage. Count on 2 hours up and an hour down.

The starting point is the **Visitor's Centre** (☎ 098/64114; info@croagh-patrick.com for specific closing times; Mar 17–Oct daily 11am–4:30pm) in Murrisk on the R335 from Westport. It's a useful center with packed lunches, showers, guided tours of the mountain (which you probably won't need), and a pretty good cafe. Opposite the Centre, in a small park, is the **National Famine Monument,** by John Behan, unveiled in 1997 for the 150th anniversary of the famine. Also a place of pilgrimage, it's a haunting bronze sculpture of a coffin ship, with skeletons in its hull, depicting the thousands who died on the trip to America. A similar sculpture, outside the U.N. building in New York, represents those immigrants who survived the trip to America.

Two by Sea: Clare Island & Inishturk Island

Cut off from the mainland, Mayo's "island zone"—Clare, Arranmore, and Tory—are inhabited by small communities and nowhere near as popular as the Aran Islands off Galway's coast. Consequently the folks here are delighted to meet, greet, and involve visitors. This is particularly true with **Clare Island** ✹✹ which is inhabited . . . but just barely (there are 130 people now, compared to about 1,600 in Grace O'Malley's time; see p. 320). A day trip (or half-day) will give you just enough time to swim and take some scenic walks around the island and perhaps learn a bit about Clare's culture and history.

Take a boat from Roonagh Quay on Clew Bay. Seven boats a day sail from May to Sept (with an additional two per day in July and Aug). From October through April, expect two boats a day. Contact **O'Malley Ferries** (www.omalley ferries.com; ☎ 086/600-0204 or 098/25045); or **O'Grady Ferries** (www.clare islandferry.com; ☎ 086/851-5003 or 098/28288). Admission on each is €15 round-trip. The journey takes 15 minutes. A leaflet you pick up on the boat will map out the five walks round the island, or you may prefer to rent bikes from the pier (**O'Learys,** ☎ 098/25640). The squat, menacing tower you see at the harbor is Grace O'Malley's (p. 320). The 13th-century **Cistercian Abbey** is worth checking out for the frescoes, which show dragons, griffins, hunts, and—the premier activity in old Ireland—cattle raids. We'd advise bringing a sack lunch, though the **Bay View Hotel** (☎ 098/26307) does serve food if you're starving.

To the south of Clare Island is **Inishturk Island** ✹✹ a smaller, less-developed isle with half the population. The journey there takes three times as long, but we love the walk from the harbor to the north, round a small lake to the watchtower (takes about 40 min.); and to the south is a lovely, sheltered beach (worth traveling for when you're in windy Mayo!). **O'Grady Ferries** (see above) serves this island with departures from Roonagh Quay three times a day (except Thurs when there's only a 9:30am sailing). The price is €20 round-trip.

One by Land: Achill Island

Famed **Achill Island** has two distinct sides: One is the remote, non-materialistic, spectacularly beautiful place of pale northern light and turf-cutting, where fiddles strike up and stories abound. That's the Achill of Irish artist Paul Henry (whose iconic paintings of Achill's peaks and women cutting turf can be seen in the National Gallery, Dublin), and of German Nobel prize winning writer, Heinrich Böll, who wrote a exquisite book, *An Irish Journal,* about his time here in the 1950s. The other is an overly touristic Achill, trading on its past, luring in Germans (in particular) on the trail of Böll. That's the Achill a friend recently gave out about: "It's all bungalow blitz! And it's not even an island!" (This in reference to the bridge connecting Achill to the mainland, although in fact Achill's always been more of a peninsula.)

The truth lies somewhere in between, or as another friend, who grew up on Achill says: "You have to tap the vein." Yes, there are too many bungalows and the recent building boom brought in some questionable housing (one estate is referred to dismissively by locals as "Toblerone houses" for obvious reasons to do with the shape). But there are still acres and acres where there's nothing but magic scenery; and musicians, artists, and film-makers still come here for the light and the unique feeling—like beret-clad Camille Souter, who's lived in Achill for years.

So how to make the most of it? Try and come at festival time—and there is quite a lot of festival time—when the whole island pulls together: Scoil Acla arts and culture festival at end July, Heinrich Böll literary festival in early-May, a walking festival in mid-March, the Yawl sailing festival from end July to

The Other Clare Island: Volunteer Vacation Opportunities

There are few better places in the world to learn about sustainable lifestyles than the tiny isle of Clare, where a big shortage—a shortage of human beings!—means that those who live off the land must do it in remarkably creative ways. It also means that locals are eager to welcome outsiders to volunteer in their community for a spell, not only for the help they can provide, but for the variety of having an outsider living in their midst. For volunteers, the rewards are possibly even greater: You'll get an up-close look at traditional values, gentler routines, and a notable absence of things you may take for granted back home (and you'll certainly learn new skills in the process).

Volunteer workers are welcomed in exchange for accommodation and food. You can help out on two organic farms or flex your muscles at the yoga retreat center, where there is also some small-scale farming activity (but where food is strictly vegetarian and an interest in chakras is a help). Here's the lowdown on what you can expect:

 ❖ **Bernie Winter** (Kill; ☎ 098/28997) runs a 14 hectare (35-acre) lowland farm and uses traditional methods to grow potatoes, oats, hay, vegetables, and herbs. Three cows provide butter (Bernie milks and churns by hand, so you'll learn those skills); a working donkey is used to bring turf from the bog and sea weed for the garden; and about 100 sheep roam (come at the right time and you'll learn shearing the old-fashioned way). Volunteers get their own bedroom in Bernie's cottage.

September—and those are just the perennials. There are one-off events organized throughout the year, see **www.achilltourism.com/events**.

Try the following one day-itinerary: Take the **Atlantic Drive** round the south end of the island from Achill Sound (where you'll cross over from the mainland), past **Carrick Kildavet** ✯ another of Grace O'Malley's 15th-century tower houses, virtually intact, presumably because nothing could dent the formidable thickness of those walls. Follow the road round to **Dooega,** and take the second road to the right as you arrive at Dooega, veering left along a small track up to the view-rich summit of the **Minaun cliffs.**

Double back and rejoin the main road, following signs to the village of **Keel,** one of the island's principal hubs. Keel's beach is particularly popular with surfers; if that describes you, stop off at **Blackfield** (Closhreid, road into town; ☎ 087/ 249-5175 or 098/43590; www.blackfield.com), to rent a surfboard (€24 per day for a board, wetsuit, and roof rack), or sign up for a lesson.

Next, head west to **Keem Bay,** probably the island's most beautiful beach, surrounded by steep grassy hills (ideal for walking) and well-sheltered for swimming. If you're lucky and the weather's good, you'll see basking sharks (not dangerous!).

- Musically inclined? Consider volunteering with **Billy Gallagher** (Lecarrow; ☎ 098/26745) who has 17 hectares (42 acres) on the west of the island. Besides farming with sheep, Billy is a top-notch accordionist and especially welcomes anyone interested in traditional Irish music. Bring your own instrument and you may find yourself part of a two-man band. By day, though, you'll be spending more time with the furry flocks.

- The type of work you'll do at Christophe and Ciara's **Clare Island Retreat Centre** (Ballytoohey; ☎ 098/25412; www.ecofarm.ie) runs the gamut from gardening, farm work, house maintenance, child minding, cooking, building, and the general running of the farm (a 97-hectare/240-acre spread) and retreat center. They prefer to have help from people who share an interest in organic or biodynamic food production and sustainable living. If you're into yoga (or would like to learn), that's a bonus, and you may get to join classes from time to time, although the main focus of being here will be to work. Volunteers are provided with digs (in summer you stay in a *yurt*, a Himalayan tent-style dwelling) and quality meals prepared by your health-conscious hosts. In exchange, you'll work a 6-day week.

For more details on Clare's organic farm volunteering programs, check out www.clareisland.info/wwofing.html. For more opportunities in organic Irish farming, see our full write up of **Willing Workers on Organic Farms** (WWOOF), p. 473.

After your swim, take the road back the way you came, and at Keel, head north, and about 2km (1 mile) to your left you'll see the **Slievemore Deserted Village** ✹✹, a haunting site of nearly a hundred stone cottages, roofless but with walls, doorways, and naves. No-one is sure exactly why or when this village was abandoned—it's currently being excavated by the **Achill Archaeological Field School** (☎ 098/43564; www.achill-fieldschool.com), which organizes rather expensive tours of the island (€20 per person, minimum of 15 people required). Finally continue on the road another 2km (1 mile) and a signpost will take you up a 10-minute walk to a **dolmen** tomb and a great view of **Keel Bay**.

BELMULLET PENINSULA

In few places in Ireland do you feel the presence of the Atlantic as strongly as on this barren windswept peninsula. What trees there are, are bent sideways by the wind, and the landscape is mostly bare and lonely bog, rising in the northwest tip to the magnificent Broadhaven cliffs. It's a magical, unspoiled landscape, the fields dotted with bog cotton, small paths leading over hills and winding down to rolling sandy beaches. Under-developed touristically, you will have to rough it a

The Other, Painterly Achill

For more than 2 decades, Seosamh Ó'Dálaigh has been rendering the Achill landscape in bright, vivid paintings that have made him something of a cultural icon in these parts. In 1985, Ó'Dálaigh set up the Yawl Art Gallery, as well as the **Ó'Dálaigh School of Painting** (Achill-Mulranny Rd., Owenduff, Tonrageel; ☎ 098/36137; www.achillpainting.com), where he continues to draw artists and art enthusiasts from across the globe. Classes are pressure free and held in a wonderfully tranquil environment thanks to Ó'Dálaigh, a supportive mentor. Weekend courses run once a month May through September (2 days for €100), while there are also weeklong courses June to September (5 days for €200). Classes include a demo on the various mediums (oil, watercolor, pastels, acrylics, and drawing techniques). Students then visit scenic areas on the peninsula to put brush to canvas.

bit—there's not the level of shops or accommodations that you'll find in other parts of Ireland. This, of course, is the point—to speak in fashion lingo, Belmullet is "the new black," the new Achill, the new untamed district. But if you can't cope without cozy cafes and Wi-Fi, better keep away.

Getting There & Getting Around

All approaches to Belmullet are beautiful but our favorite is the **N59,** one of the most scenic roads in Ireland. The drive's about an hour and a half from Westport to Belmullet town by car. If walking follow the **Bangor Trail** from Newport.

Belmullet town is at the entrance to the peninsula and is frankly no great shakes, although you'll find comfortable places to stay and a decent restaurant. This town was actually built much later than other places on the peninsula—the first places to be settled were the peripheries which were key locations for lighthouses and coast guard houses. **Ballyglass Lighthouse** in the north and the particularly handsome **Black Sod Lighthouse** in the south are still standing.

Worth noting is that many of the place names on road signs only appear in Irish, because this is a Gaeltacht area and evangelists seem bent on removing the English place-names. (Not the best way of enticing tourists to this isolated area!) So look out for the following signs: *Béal an Mhuirthead* (Belmullet) and *Cois Farraige* (to the Beach).

Where to Stay & Dine

There aren't a huge amount of options on Belmullet because it's only recently opened to tourism. Below are our two top picks for each.

€€€   Máirín (pronounced Maureen) and Gerry Murphy's B&B and rental options, **Drom Caoin** ✪✪ 🧒 (Belmullet; ☎ 097/81195; www.belmullet-accommodation.com; AE, MC, V) would be our first port of call. A short walk from Belmullet town, with views onto Blacksod Bay and Achill Island, theirs is a big, luxurious, light-filled 1970s bungalow, in which they brought up nine children. It's been converted into a modern B&B, plus—for those who want a dash more privacy and want to be able to cook for themselves—two apartment-style units. The Murphys have gone for an uncluttered, easy style, with a muted color scheme and lots of pine. The B&B accommodations are compact (and built under a pitched roof), yes, but they're impeccably clean and well maintained. Doubles go for €70, and are just a fraction more (€76) in July and August. The **apartments** are €70 to €80 per night, €450 to €550 per week; one sleeps three, while the other has a loft bedroom and a pull-out couch that provides space for three children in addition to two grown-ups in the master bedroom. Each has washing machines, dryers, a well-equipped kitchen, a dining area, and TV. A final plug: Máirín is a human dynamo and knows everything about the area. She'll arrange your visit completely, if you like. It's a bit like having an on-site travel agent.

€€ You don't come to Belmullet for its great cuisine. Over the years, we've only found one place we'd recommend. **An Chéibh** (Barrack St.; ☎ 097/81007; summer Mon–Sat 12:30–9pm; winter Mon–Sat 12:30–8pm; Sun 1–7:30pm; AE, MC, V) proudly announces its awards on its door, and you can't miss this large indigo building on the main street. The decor is wood-lined and nautical (*chéibh* means anchor). The food—mostly fish, but also steak and pasta—is hearty and decent, but not spectacular. The seafood platter (€23) is enough to feed two, though it's a little weighted on the salmon side.

Why You're Here: Top Sights & Attractions

You're here to swim, walk, play golf (**www.belmulletgolfclub.ie** or ask at the Broadhaven Hotel), or to take a boat out to the off-shore island. A good target on your walks or drives is **Black Sod Lighthouse** ★ at the southernmost tip of the peninsula. It isn't open to the public but it's a fine Victorian building with a fascinating history: In June 1944, lighthouse keeper Ted Sweeney predicted storms in the English channel and delayed the D-Day landing by 24 hours.

An Outing to Goose Islands

Gé is Irish for goose and **Inishkea Islands** (Inis Gé) ★★ means Goose Islands. They are home to barnacle geese in winter—in summer the geese head up to Greenland—numerous bird species, and grey seals. There was a community of humans on the islands up until 1935, when, following the policy of the day, everyone was cleared to the mainland. Now there's the rather eerie harbor, a string of abandoned houses, and a roofless school—moving evidence of a world left behind by the former inhabitants. It's a stark, haunting place for a visit, but is also popular with birders, and the beach is a fun picnicking spot—you're likely to be ogled by curious seals that'll poke their heads through the water's surface. Contact the **Broadhaven Bay Hotel** (☎ 097/20600; www.broadhavenbay.com), which organizes full or half-day trips on the 40-ft. boat, *An Géaróidín.*

You'll find two blue flag (government approved) beaches on the road from Belmullet to Black Sod. Our favorite is the Mullaghroe (or Mullach Rua) strand, a left turn (signposted) off the main road. An enticing curved and sandy shore with clear water—it looks tropical but feels Nordic.

A Side-Trip to Ballina in North Mayo

On the R314 from Bangor or Belmullet, you hug the coastline, passing stunning scenery and then, to your right, a distinctive pyramid-shaped building looms up. This is the visitor center of **Céide Fields** (see below). Through the small one-street village of **Ballycastle,** you can't miss stunning **Downpatrick Head,** with its arresting stack of rock, and **Doonbristy,** just separated from the main cliff. Legend has it that when St. Patrick was fighting with the devil he landed such a blow that he detached part of the headland. The road will then take you through another small town, past beaches and **ruined abbeys** (p. 327) to bustling **Ballina**—it's in no way handsome but a surprise after all the isolated scenery.

The area's main draw, the **Céide Fields** ✸ (Ballycastle; ☎ 096/43325; €3.70; daily mid-Mar to May and Oct–Nov 10am–5pm; June–Sept 10am–6pm) is intellec-tually astonishing—these remains date from 5,000 years ago!—but visually a bit of a let-down if you're not an archaeologist. It just looks like a pile of auld stones. For once the Visitor's Centre is essential—we're not usually fans of these centers, which can detract from the site—but in this case the audiovisual presentation and the exhibits really are a help to understanding why this rubble is significant. After the audiovisual, there's a guided tour around the fields—you'll see walled farms and animal pens, which have been excavated from the bog over the past 30 years. Remarkably a local farmer, Patrick Caulfield, was the first, in the 1930s, to sus-pect that there was more than met than eye under the turf. His son grew up to be an archaeologist and confirmed his father's hunch.

Though it's not as celebrated, we'd say don't pass up the chance to visit the **Round Tower** ✸✸ as you drive through Killala town. Dating back to a monastic settlement in the 12th century, it was damaged by lightning in the last century

---

North Mayo Sculpture Trail (Tir Sáile)

In 1993 fifteen site-specific sculptures were commissioned along the coastline from Belmullet to Ballina, the largest public arts exhibition ever undertaken in Ireland. The sites vary from a disused quarry to sand dunes to agricultural land to stony fields, and the works reference local history and legend. Sculptures are deliberately placed close to the rugged coast-line so you have to work—walk, climb or scramble—to get to many of them. We wouldn't necessarily advise following the trail from 1 to 15 (or A to O, on maps they're lettered), but while walking round Belmullet (three sculptures) and Ballycastle (four or five in the area) you can use the sculp-tures as focal points. The *North Mayo Sculpture Trail book* is available in tourist offices or check out **www.mayo-ireland.ie**, which provides a map to the Trail.

The Other North Mayo

Marjorie Nolan's cooking has made her one of County Mayo's local heroes. She's written three cookbooks, is a regular on TV cooking programs, does radio broadcasts, has an online cooking show, and writes for a major Irish weekly, getting her marvelous recipes and kitchen know-how out to people all over Ireland. Hundreds of Irish food fans also make a point of coming to her home in Ballina to attend demonstration classes at **Marjorie's Kitchen** (Brigown B&B, Quay Rd., Ballina; ☎ 087/230-4986 or 096/22609; www.mayo-ireland.ie/brigown.htm; marjorieskitchen@hotmail.com). Meet her, and you'll understand why. She's a genuine dynamo, with enough energy to light up a small town. Besides enhancing her students' repertoire of recipes, she pumps them full of fantastically simple, yet profound, tips that go towards making food preparation that much easier (who knew you could freeze eggs! Marjorie let us in on that secret).

Marjorie's classes are fashioned to make learning about cooking enjoyable, fun, and social. She likes to base what she teaches on her students' personal preferences, so she'll first find out what sweet and savory dishes you're fond of and then work those kinds of dishes into her course. Class content is quite diverse—from serving seafood to making homemade jams—and there are classes in traditional Irish cooking, too. In these latter sessions, you'll pick up recipes for good old Irish stew, boxty, white soda bread, Irish tea brack, bacon and cabbage, and Marjorie's famous Mayo coddle. Marjorie's one-off classes happen two or three times per month on Saturdays from 10am till 3 or 3:30pm; these sessions—which

and repaired by Bishop Verschoyle in 1841. Nobody quite knows why it's here but at 25m (82 ft.) high, with a small doorway 3m (10 ft.) off the ground, it's thought to have been used as a place of storage, and, probably, protection for townspeople. A good trick is to stand close to the tower and look up. If the sky is clear with drifting clouds, the tower seems to sway as the clouds pass over.

A few kilometres out of Killala, off the R314 towards Ballina are the ruins of two abbeys, **Moyne Abbey** and **Rosserk Abbey** ✦✦✦, which have a shared history. Both were founded in the mid-15th century; both were sacked by Sir Richard Bingham, Elizabeth I's governor of Connaught, in 1591; but both, if sadly deserted since 1800 (when the last friar died in Moyne Abbey), are remarkably well-preserved and romantically set in splendid isolation—no visitor centers, no tours, no entry fees, just "bare ruined choirs where late the sweet birds sang."

Moyne Abbey was founded by the Burke family in 1460 and built in the late Irish Gothic style. The 15th-century Cloisters are in excellent condition as is the five-storey tower. It's a trek to get to, across fields (one of which worryingly has a sign saying "Beware of the Bull"). Locals assured me that there was no bull, just a farmer, who's fighting with the Heritage Board, and trying to scare off access to the Abbey. We took the locals on faith; and saw no bull, and the intrepid trek rather added to the experience.

Rosserk Abbey, a few kilometres on towards Ballina, is even better preserved. Founded in 1441 by the Joyce family, only the roof is missing. The magnificent arched window is still etched against the sky and you can climb the winding staircase to look across the bay.

COUNTY SLIGO

William Butler Yeats, in his poetry, and his brother Jack Butler Yeats, in his paintings, immortalized Sligo, so that by now, it's almost impossible to see the county except through their eyes. Even if you're totally indifferent to the arts, you won't be able to avoid the Yeatses on your visit—spot a lovely lake, and someone will helpfully inform you in which poem it appears in; take a swim and you'll be told how Jack painted this bay; head into the center of Sligo town and that witty, expressionist statue by the river turns out to be W.B.

Yet despite this being "Yeats Country," and home to one of the country's best traditional music scenes (plus a truly remarkable number of megalithic sites), Sligo remains relatively underdeveloped touristically—like the rest of the northwest, you won't find the crowds you get in Kerry and Galway. The town of Sligo's got a village feel but is (just) big enough to get lost in (for the first day anyway). Its situation, on the River Garavogue and under two legendary peaks— Knocknarea and the flat-topped Ben Bulben—is superb. Home to an art college and an institute of technology, Sligo's atmosphere is studenty, bohemian, friendly, and conducive to pub crawls. And those pubs are the kind that made Ireland famous—dark, snug places you can while away hours in, meeting people and listening to trad sessions.

Altogether, this area of mountains, lakes, rivers, Neolithic tombs and a sassy capital town offers wonderful hikes, swimming, surfing, fishing, pubs, trad music, and hideaway retreats.

LAY OF THE LAND

With the **River Gavarogue** running right though the center, Sligo Town is easily navigable. To the west are the adjacent bus and train stations, a 10-minute walk in a straight line from the center, which is loosely bounded by four streets— Stephen, O'Connell, Grattan, and Bridge streets. Museums, galleries, bars, and restaurants are clustered round here, with **Sligo Abbey** a short walk along the river to the east.

Just outside the town (10–15 min. drive) are **Strandhill** to the west and **Rosses Point** to the north. Once small fishing villages, these are now suburbs of the town—buses run to and from them all day until two in the morning. They're the nearest places to swim, surf, play golf, or hear trad music by the bay. Strandhill is for surfers—the beach is too dangerous for swimming—and is more grungy and laid back. Rosses Point has golf and is correspondingly staider, but its beaches are safer and it has good, affordable restaurants.

Farther afield, **South Sligo** is a large area stretching from **Lough Arrow** (one of Europe's best brown trout lakes and studded with tiny islands) in the east to the lesser known and smaller **Lough Talt** in the west. If you're not here at festival

time—mid-July in the town of **Tubbercurry,** end of August to the beginning September in **Gorteen**—and you're not a fisherman, there's frankly less reason to visit the Southern areas of Sligo.

West Sligo, closer to Mayo's Ballina than Sligo Town, has some of the county's best beaches and surfing spots. The rather run-down village of **Easkey,** in particular, is famous among surfers for its reef breaks—the waves break over rocks, not sand, making them hollower and faster. This area also boasts one of the county's main attractions: the Edwardian seaweed baths at Enniscrone.

GETTING THERE & GETTING AROUND

You can get to Sligo Town by **bus** (☎ 071/916-0066, www.buseireann.ie) from Dublin (€16 one-way, €25 round-trip), Donegal, Derry, Galway, Ballina, Castlebar, and Westport; and from Dublin (€36 one-way) by either **train** (☎ 071/916-9888; www.irishrail.ie), or **air** (Standhill airport; ☎ 071/916-8280; www.sligoairport.com). Occasionally costs for flights drop to as little as €50 round-trip but that's not common. Factoring in price and convenience, the train is probably best from Dublin (much more comfortable than the bus).

Within Sligo County you'll be reliant on buses, which run frequently between the capital and all the main towns, but don't link the towns together—for example you can't go from Tubbercurry to Enniscrone, you have to pass through the capital. There is no public transport within Sligo town (it's too small to need it) but there are frequent buses to Rosses Point and Strandhill, 20 minutes away. You can rent **bikes** from **Flanagan's Cycle Hire** (Market Yard; ☎ 071/914-4477) or may want to rely on a rental car.

ACCOMMODATIONS BOTH STANDARD & NOT

Because of its quality student apartments, available for weekly rental in the summer, Sligo Town has some of the best alternative accommodation in the northwest. We wouldn't recommend any of the hostels in town, unless you're happy to really rough it, but there are spiffier, low budget digs in Strandhill in the form of two well-located campgrounds. **Strandhill Caravan and Camping Park** (☎ 071/916-8111; €19 for tent for two; Apr–Sept) is right on the beach, a pleasant, medium-size (55 spots) well-maintained campground with a game room, on-site laundry, and pay showers. **Greenlands Caravan and Camping Park** ★ (☎ 071/917-7113; tent €18 for two; Easter–Sept) is about twice as big (120 pitches) and boasts lovely views of Sligo Bay (it's set right off the sand traps of a golf course). Like the Strandhill site, it has recreation facilities, laundry, and pay showers, but it also has a camper kitchen and facilities for disabled travelers which may have endeared it to the readers of *Practical Caravan* magazine who voted this campground "Best in Ireland."

Summer-Only Rentals in Sligo Town

€€€   Clean, functional, and extremely well-equipped apartments are the lure at **Gateway Apartments** ★★ (Ballinode; ☎ 071/914-5618; www.gateway apartments.ie; AE, MC, V) managed by a private rental company for students at the Sligo Institute of Technology. Which does mean that these digs are only an option from mid-June to the end of August (apartments are student's stomping grounds

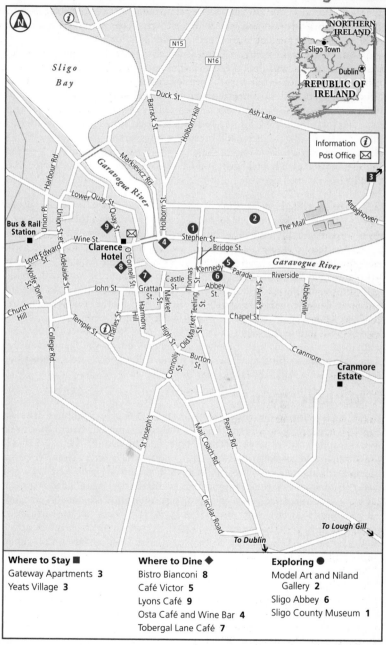

Where to Stay ■
Gateway Apartments **3**
Yeats Village **3**

Where to Dine ◆
Bistro Bianconi **8**
Café Victor **5**
Lyons Café **9**
Osta Café and Wine Bar **4**
Tobergal Lane Café **7**

Exploring ●
Model Art and Niland Gallery **2**
Sligo Abbey **6**
Sligo County Museum **1**

during the school year). The flats occupy nine modern two-storey blocks situated just 10 minutes (by foot) from the center of town. Accommodations are designed to be functional: There are narrow beds (singles only, we're afraid), writing desks, and wash basins in the bedrooms, and armchairs, a sofa, fully equipped kitchens, washing machines, and dining tables in the open-plan living area-cum-kitchen. While they're not five star luxury, neither are they student grot—everything's ultra-clean and tidy, and linens and eating utensils are provided. The rates are pretty unbeatable: You'll pay €65 to €75 for a one-bedroom apartment (sleeps two), but just €80 to €90 for two-bedroom (sleeps four adults, or two adults and three children). They're better still for longer stays, as the price drops to €295 to €345 weekly for a one-bedroom; €345 to €410 two bedroom. The apartments can also be used on a **hostel** basis: You pay €30 for a private single room, or €20 for a bed in a shared twin unit.

€€€ **Yeats Village** ✪ 🅺🅸🅳🆂 (Ballinode; ☎ 071/913-8945; www.yeatsvillage.ie; MC, V) is another development for students happy to spend their college days in bland, architecturally unexciting, but perfectly clean and functional digs. There's a mixture here of houses, sleeping six, and apartments, sleeping three or four. Accommodations have a studenty feel—think wood-frame sofas and the odd potted plant intended to liven the place up a bit. If you're traveling with children, however, the layout might be useful. The houses, for example, have four single bedrooms (sharing two bathrooms) and one en suite twin. Prices are similar to the Gateway Apartments (see above)—€350/week for apartments and €550 for the houses, with midweek 3-night deals for €200 to €300. You get slightly less for your money—no bed linen supplied, and there's an on-site launderette rather than individual washing machines, but this is still a good, second-choice, again just a 10-minute walk from the center of town.

Hotels, B&Bs & Hostels

€–€€   For surfers, the village of Strandhill—just a few minutes drive from Sligo—is something of a mecca. Far and away the most convenient spot to hang your wetsuit is **Knocknarea House** (Shore Rd., Strandhill; ☎ 071/916-8313; www.strandhillaccommodation.com; cash only), which offers clean, good-value bedrooms. Although no longer run as a B&B, the private units here are a generous step up from hostel accommodation, a mix of well-maintained rooms with carpets and textured wallpaper, solid pine furniture, good-size mirrors, and smallish beds neatly covered with duvets and blankets. Rooms (all upstairs) are supplied with tiny TVs, hairdryers, and Wi-Fi access; you've a choice of attached shower (€60–€70 double) or units with shared facilities (€50–€60 double). Although breakfast isn't served, guests have access to the kitchen in the **Strandhill Hostel** (same contact details) next door, which is a second lodging choice if you're counting euros more fastidiously and don't mind bunking up (dorm beds start at €16, and are slightly pricier at weekends). Based here, you'll be within spitting distance of those fearsome, hypnotic waves, and in stumbling distance of several reliable eateries and the town's favorite pub. When the hostel fills up with surfers (storage for surfboards is available), things can get quite lively—although strict rules curb late-night noise.

€€ Farther out of Sligo Town, near the pier in the tiny village of Aughris (off the N59 Sligo-Ballina Road) is the **Beach Bar,** a noted gastro-pub (p. 336). The family owners have long offered bed and breakfast at **Aughris House** (on the Coast Rd. to Aughris Pier, Templeboy; ☎ 071/916-6703; www.thebeachbarsligo.com; cash only), a pink bungalow right beside the pub. It has nine bedrooms with attached showers (€60–€70 double), although they're now cutting down on the number of rooms available to guests. Different colors, mostly bold, have been used throughout the house, so there's a rather eclectic, homegrown look to the place—silk flowers appear alongside real plants, duvet covers don't necessarily match the curtains, and color combinations will have you scratching your head. But, all the beds are back-supporting (if smallish), and the bedrooms stand out for their exceptional cleanliness. We love the fact that you can hear the constant tumble of waves (the beach is just a few steps away), but perhaps the main reason for staying is the helpfulness of the MacDermotts, who will arrange boat trips to the island and tell you exactly where to go on your walks.

€€ Back in Sligo Town, conveniently located right beside the bus and train station, the **Southern** (Strandhill Rd.; ☎ 071/916-2101; www.thesligosouthern hotel.com; MC, V) was once part of the Great Southern hotel chain that's owned by the national rail company. Now part of the Brian McEniff chain, it's still got a comfortable, catering-to-the-business traveler feel. We're fans of all the Great Southern Hotels: We like their spacious foyers, soft furnishings, friendly staff, and rooms that are lifted above the average by the height of the ceilings, and their prices. Here €90 double is usually the rate and it's a fair deal. Don't take breakfast though; at €14 extra it's not worth it.

€€€€ Because castle upkeep costs a pretty penny, castle stays usually do as well. An exception to that rule is **Markree Castle** ✯✯ (Collooney, 10km/6 miles outside Sligo Town, off the N4 road to Dublin; ☎ 071/916-7800, www. markreecastle.ie; AE, MC, V); while not cheap (single rates start at €90 a night, double from €150, though online discounts sometimes drop the nightly rate to €100 double) it is, perhaps, a doable splurge. Set in 202 hectares (500 acres) of park and woodland, Markree Castle has been in the Cooper family for 370 years. Although there's been a castle here since 1400, the present design is 19th century and opulent. An enormous log fire burns in the vast hall and the staircase sweeps up to stained glass windows. Not all the furniture is in keeping with that era and it's not all five-star comfort and *chateleine* luxury. We've heard some of the guests grumbling about uncomfortable beds and lack of modern conveniences. But for our tastes Markree has a lovable eccentricity and (for this type of stay) a welcome affordability—we put being able to horse-ride, practice clay shooting, or just roam acres of woodlands above Wi-Fi. The dining room is also stunning, but frankly, the setting far exceeds the food (set dinner €30).

Elsewhere in County Sligo

Old-school snipe and duck shoots; the chance to fish from the 200km (124 miles) Temple House Lake; or the ability to wander at will on a huge hereditary estate. These are the unique experiences on offer to those who rent one of two atmospheric

Cairn Sweet Cairn

Ireland is gaining a bit of a reputation for innovative budget accommodations, and one of the reasons is **Gyreum Eco-Lodge** ✪✪✪ (Riverstown; ☎ 071/916-5994; www.gyreum.com; MC, V), which puts an ecologically sensitive spin on the hostel concept. As you approach, you'll see a low circular building which looks, in keeping with the megalithic sites in the area, like a cairn (although it's also been likened to a vast Christmas pudding). Inside, classical music will alert you that this is a place of calm retreat. Colum Stapleton, who built this unique structure, will tell you that the big airy, central hall (with its 360° views of Sligo's cairned mountains and Lough Arrow) is aligned to both the winter and the summer solstices. Off this warm, wooden hall are a handful of "dorms," private rooms, washrooms, a kitchen, and conservatories. The fascinating conceptualization has additional eco-friendly features, like geothermal heating, naturally filtered water, and a complicated sewerage works system (much of the waste is composted and then given to the neighboring farmer in exchange for eggs).

Book ahead to secure one of the private rooms; there are two small-but-big-for-a-hostel doubles (with proper wooden beds and decent mattresses, books on bookshelves, a basin, and even bedside lamps for €50–€54 double), although loos and showers are shared with guests in the two "dorms." These cozy six-bed and five-bed rooms (€17–€21 per bed, the price goes up weekends), are also suitable for families (children are half price weekdays), although, frankly, we think your kids would be thrilled to spend the night in one of the capsule-like tents (€17, sleeping one or two people) permanently set up in that main hall. They're supplied with thick mattresses and are a superb alternative to camping outside in the cold, while actually providing more privacy than a traditional dormitory. Linen—which includes great thick duvets on the beds—is provided; there's a guest kitchen (with an eco-friendly dishwasher!); a TV and VCR (with selection of art-house films) are on standby for bad weather days; and there's even a Finnish sauna, and a pool table. The lodge welcomes volunteer workers through WWOOF (p. 473).

homes on the grounds of the renowned **Temple House** ✪✪✪ (Ballinacrow, Ballymote; ☎ 071/918-3329; www.templehouse.ie; AE, MC, V), a stunning Georgian mansion set in 405 hectares (1,000 acres) of woodland. By renting a cottage rather than staying at the lodge itself (which is a guesthouse), you not only get a good dose of privacy but pay just €25 to €55 a night per person (half those amounts if you bed four in the houses rather than two) instead of the €180 double a B&B stay entails (or €160 if your shower isn't en suite). Those better rates are for two darling cottages, with such amenities as open fireplaces, porches, porticos, and satellite TV. Of these, the finest (and largest) is the "Gardener's Cottage," which is a characterful Victorian number with a sharply pitched roof making it look a bit like something out of a fairytale. It sleeps eight people, has every amenity and convenience you could wish for (along with primo views) and goes for €500 to €995 per week. If you're happy with far less space, then "The Front Lodge," right next to the main gate to the estate (and consequently less secluded) is more affordable at €350 off season to €750 in August. Here things are cheerful (decorated with contemporary canvases), but a bit sparse—and all the pine furniture they've used does feel a touch incongruous in a period house. Both cottages have outdoor barbeque facilities and a parking area.

DINING FOR ALL TASTES

Sligo Town has a lot of places to eat, but in many the food is very average—decent, but nothing special. Fortunately there are exceptions, and lunch in particular can be a treat.

€   Our pick for breakfast and lunch in Sligo goes to the recently opened **Café Victor** ✪✪✪ (JFK Parade; ☎ 071/914-0440; Mon–Fri 8am–5pm; Sat 10am–5pm; cash only), a short walk along the river, past Sligo Abbey. A small basement cafe, it seats just 35 in a room bedecked with paintings by local artists. Guests sit at the square pine tables, or at the bar; entertainment is provided by peering into the open kitchen and watching the cooks (it's reassuring, too). Breakfast is varied and great value: €6.50 for the full Irish, €5.50 for bacon and maple syrup pancakes. At lunch four types of soup are generally on offer for €5 and a hearty main like beef chili and rice (€6) or roasted pepper and goat cheese (€6). Owner Nora Healion has created a funky little cafe with great ambience, and even her (excellent) coffee is €.15 cheaper than anywhere else.

€–€€   **Osta Café and Wine Bar** ✪✪ (Garavogue Weir View, near Hyde Bridge, Stephen St.; ☎ 071/914-4639; www.osta.ie; Mon–Wed 8am–7pm; Thurs–Sat 8am–8pm; Sun noon–5pm; cash only) is another nifty lunch spot which stays open until the early evening with a tapas and wine selection. Owner Brid Torrades is a leader in the Euro-Toques and Slow Food campaigns for better food, which means the produce is organic, Fair Trade, locally sourced where possible, and home-cooked. Expect sandwiches (€4.50) with free-range egg and chive mayonnaise, wraps, and paninis (€6.50) with interesting fillings like roasted vegetables and pine nuts. The charcuterie and cheese plates (both €9.95) showcase Ireland's top products. Daily vegetarian and meat specials are chalked up on the black board. The breads and cakes in particular are top-notch (try the Bakewell tart, €3.50) and come from her bakery at Ballinafad. Brid has now opened another outlet, close by, the **Tobergal Lane Café** (Tobergal Lane, off O'Connell St; ☎ 071/914-6599; Thurs–Sat 10am–10pm; Sun–Wed 10am–7pm; MC, V). This serves similar food, but larger portions—more bistro style—and has a full bar license and much more seating.

€   In business since 1878, and still owner-run, the store Henry Lyons and Co., with its original shopfront and mosaic tiles, is a Sligo landmark and runs **Lyons Café** (Quay St; ☎ 071/914-2969; daily 9am–12pm; lunch 12:30–2pm; MC, V). Traditional family-operated shops are sadly disappearing all over Ireland but this one is very popular and should hopefully stay the course. Chef Gary Stafford serves locally sourced, often organic, meals. The menu changes but good soups (€5) are a feature as is a vegetarian plate.

€€–€€€   You're not spoiled for choice in West Sligo, it's true, but most wouldn't find it a hardship to take their daily meals at the **Beach Bar** 🌟🌟 (Aughris Head, Templeboy; ☎ 071/917-6465; www.thebeachbarsligo.com; food served daily 1–8pm in summer; Sat–Sun in winter; MC, V). A lovely thatched and flag-stoned building, it's been here since the 18th century, when it was a *shibín* (small inn) known as Maggie Maye's. Hearty home cooking is *de regeur* including seafood chowder (€5), bangers and mash (€10), with mouth-watering traditional puds (desserts), like apple crumble and cheesecake (€4.50–€5). And if you're lucky a session will start up in the pub while you're dining or drinking.

€€€   With robust and plentiful Italian food at reasonable prices, it's not hard to see why **Bistro Bianconi** (O'Connell St., Sligo Town; ☎ 071/914-1744; MC, V) is popular. Its success has led to its opening outlets in Dublin and Galway. Starters include minestrone soup (€6.35), garlic bread (€4.95), and chicken and bacon salad (€7.85). Mains are mostly pasta dishes—like Bolognese cannelloni (€19) and seafood lasagna (€19). Pizzas are between €12 and €14. This cheerful, bustling place now says "franchise" to us—the food has become a little more standardized, but it's still a good bet for a quick meal.

WHY YOU'RE HERE: TOP SIGHTS & ATTRACTIONS

Sligo Town itself doesn't have too many major sights, except for the flagship **Model Art and Niland Gallery** 🌟🌟 (The Mall, Sligo; ☎ 071/914-1405; www.modelart.ie; hours and prices not set at press time), which is scheduled to reopen after several years of renovation in 2009 (the website lists alternative venues around town for exhibits during their building renovation). Its highlight is a gallery of Jack Yeats paintings which covers all the Sligo locales you've come to know. It also is a regional powerhouse for contemporary art including film, music, and literature. Visit the website for upcoming programs.

Sligo's most impressive older building is **Sligo Abbey** 🌟 (Abbey St; ☎ 071/ 914-6406; €2.10; Mar–Oct daily 10am–6pm; Nov–Jan Sat and Sun 9:30am–4:30pm), founded in 1252 by the Norman leader Sir Maurice Fitzgerald (who also founded the town). It defines the term "survivor": The original was burnt to the ground in 1412, it was torched and ransacked in 1641, and ravaged at least three other times in the intervening centuries (what you see today dates mostly to the 18th century). Despite all this brutality, it's wonderfully well preserved, particularly the cloisters. (Look out for the high altar and the decorated tombs, one with the carvings of a Catherine's wheel, and St. Peter's keys.)

Before heading out into the countryside for sights associated with Yeats' poems, get a flavor of the man himself at the **Sligo County Museum** 🌟 (Stephen St; ☎ 071/914-2212; free admission; summer Tues–Sat 10am–5pm; winter 2–5pm). An impressive former manse, it houses manuscripts, photos, letters, newspaper clippings, and the poet's Nobel Prize, as well as paintings by his brother, Jack, and contemporaries George Russell and Sean Keating. This being Sligo, the museum's other focus goes back several thousand years, with an exhibition of finds from the area's megalithic sights, including one downright weird one: a firkin of so-called "bog butter" (a waxy substance archeologists found buried in the peat, which they assume is preserved butter, though they're not sure).

Just outside Sligo Town

Sligo County is home to some of the oldest megalithic tombs in Europe and some of the oldest stone architecture anywhere in the world (the structures you'll see here are a good 500 years older than the pyramids). The most famous of these tomb complexes, the **Megalithic tombs at Carrowmore** ★★ (☎ 071/916-1534; €2.10; daily 10am–6pm) lie 5km (3 miles) outside Sligo Town (follow R292 from Strandhill). Thirty tombs are visible today with another thirty apparently buried and though they're lower to the ground than they once were—the movement of soil over the centuries has covered the bases of these structures which likely once stood nearly 2m (6 ft.) off the ground—they still impress. Archaeologists are quarrelling (as they do) over dates—most of the tombs date from 4300 B.C. to 3500 B.C., but some have been placed as far back as 5400 B.C. Whatever—they're Neolithic, and unusually early, and have the stern, unknowable mien of Stonehenge (which they pre-date by a thousand years). The majority are small passage tombs (which get their name from the fact that there's a small passage, leading to a chamber topped by a capstone where human remains were interred) and dolmens, frequently surrounded by a stone circle. When you realize that this circle has not been moved for thousands of years you begin to feel the majesty of the place.

The site stretches over almost 4km (2½ miles) in a complex pattern of circles—some of the tombs are in adjacent farms. Make sure to see the central cairn, **Tomb 51,** known as Lisoghil, which has carvings on the side. You can pick up a map for the site as well as a bit of knowledge on the many mysteries surrounding Carrowmore at the visitor's center.

King of the Trad Fests

There's something extra toe-tapping about Sligo trad fiddle playing. Made famous worldwide in the early 20th century by local hero Michael Coleman, it's a style known for its bouncy rhythms, light bowing, and decorative flourishes. Every summer, musicians come from around Ireland and the globe to master it at the **South Sligo Summer School** (Tubbercurry; ☎ 071/918-2151; www.sssschool.org) festival. Established in 1987, this week-long trad dance and musical festival is held in mid-July and it's terrifically inclusive. Along with classes for advanced players in all sorts of instruments, beginners are encouraged to learn the basics of Irish music and dance with morning classes (€95 for the week) in set-dancing, *bodhrán*, tin whistle, *uileann* pipes, and *sean-nós* singing (that's the West of Ireland singing, generally without accompaniment, that sounds almost like speaking). Even if you have two left feet (and a tin ear), it's worth molding your trip to coincide with this festival. You won't be expected to take class to attend; most simply soak up the great sounds at daily recitals, lectures, *ceilís*, concerts, and pub sessions in venues throughout the town.

On Yeats' Trail: Mountains, Water-falls, Lake Isles & Country Estates

Along with this guidebook, consider bringing a book of Yeats' poetry with you to Sligo. It will offer a crisp, compelling and, yes, poetic introduction to the region. Here are some of our favorite verses and the areas that inspired them:

The wind has bundled up the clouds high over Knocknarea / And thrown the thunder on the stones for all that Maeve can say. Yeats' words come back to you when you're climbing up to the **Tomb of Queen Maeve on Knocknarea** ✹✹✹ (first left when you drive south out of Strandhill, then left at the crossroads to begin mountain walk; 45 min. to summit). Clouds will likely be bundled on the mountain-top ahead and when you reach Maeve's tomb—an enormous cairn, made up of half a million stones, which you can see from miles away—you can imagine that doughty queen curs-ing the winds as they whistle round you. She may or may not have actu-ally existed but her mythical character, as related in the ancient saga, *Táin Bó Cúailnge* (Cattle Raid of Cooley), shows her as feisty, imperious, bawdy, and unforgettable.

Where the wandering water rushes / From the hills above Glencar is how to greet the enchanting **Glencar Lake and Waterfall** ✹✹, east of Drumcliff, on the road to Manorhamilton, and the inspiration for the wistful poem learned by every Irish schoolchild. The waters in the lake are too icy for swimming but the shores are great for walks.

I will arise and go now and go to Innisfree, goes Yeats's most famous poem—so famous that 1,000 boy scouts marched to the top of a hill to recite it, apparently causing the poet to faint in horror. Well here's the Lake Isle of Innisfree, an island set in a large, beautiful 8km (5 mile) lake, which has **Parke's Castle** (Sligo Dromahaire Road on the NE shore of Lough Gill; ☎ 071/916-4149; €2.90; Mar–Oct daily 10am–6pm) on its shores. Originally belonging to the Gaelic O'Rourke family, the structure was con-fiscated during the 17th-century plantation and given to Robert Parke, who built much of the present structure. Despite its current name it's

South Sligo

Overlooking Lough Arrow, the **Carrowkeel passage tombs** ✹✹✹ (signposted off the N4) are less numerous and famous than Carrowmore's but also less crowded with visitors and they have an unbeatable location on a hill, so we pre-fer them. You also have to work harder to get to them—the last kilometer has to be walked. Fourteen tombs (also called cairns), dolmens, and stone circles are here and they appeared to be aligned with the setting sun (try to time your visit to considered a fortified manor house rather than castle. Having fallen into disuse it was, until a generation ago, employed by a local farmer to house his cattle but it's now excellently renovated. We're not generally fans of audio-visual shows of photos and narration, but the one here is beautifully shot and excellently narrated.

Light at evening, Lissadell, great windows open to the south. Although a handsome neo-Classical building, **Lissadell House** ✸ (Lissadell, Ballinfull, 7km/4 miles on the N15/Bundoran Rd.; ☎ 071/916-3150, www.lissadell house.com; house €6, house and gardens €12; house tours on the hour; daily 10:30am–6pm) can't match the magnificent story told by this poem. This is where Yeats's friends, Eva Gore-Booth and Constance Marcievicz, grew up. Marcievicz took part in the 1916 rebellion and was the first woman to be elected to the Irish parliament. (There is a statue, and bizarrely, a swimming pool named for her in Dublin.) The house remained in the Gore-Booth family until a few years ago, when it was brought by barristers Edward Walsh and Constance Cassidy as a family home for their seven children. They've spent a lot restoring it, which perhaps explains the rather steep entrance fee. However, even if you're not an Irish history or a Yeats fanatic, this is a fine tour, with the long gallery, handsome chandeliers, zodiac clock, and paintings by Ireland's foremost painters—Jack Yeats, Paul Henry, and A.E. The Gore-Booths, by the way, are related somewhere along the line to Al Gore and Gore Vidal. Closed.

Under bare Ben Bulben's head / In Drumcliff churchyard Yeats is laid. The poet was buried as he wanted to be, at the foot of Ben Bulben, in **Drumcliff cemetery,** though he died in France in 1939 and his body wasn't repatriated till after the Second World War. The grave is easy to find, near the entry of the small churchyard, a simple stone with the inscription: "Cast a cold Eye / On Life, on Death / Horseman, pass by!" (You're probably not on a horse, but this is still a good epitaph.) The small horizontal stone is for his wife, Georgie.

coincide with the sun going down to test this theory). You can even climb inside some of the passage graves. ***Note:*** Come prepared. There's no visitor center, bathroom facilities, or food stands here.

Second most important attraction in this area is Ireland's largest sanctuary for birds of prey. The **Irish Raptor Research Centre** ✸✸ 🧒 (Ballinacrow; ☎ 071/918-9310; www.eaglesflying.com; €9; Apr–Nov 10:30am–12:30pm and 2:30pm–4:30pm) was opened in 2003 to the public (it was established in 1999) and since

Places that Once Were

Deserted villages dot Ireland, a reminder of famine and emigration, which have blighted Ireland, particularly the West, up until the present day. On the road to Aughris Head from Sligo, you'll come to a particularly evocative **Deserted Village.** Take a left at the crossroads and turn right up a small lane. The remnants of the village you see was thriving in 1873 with a population of 400 but poverty and emigration reduced it, and now ruins are all that remain.

For a deserted island and a truly haunting experience, go out to **Innishmurray Island** ✷✷. Innishmurray had a small community up until 1948 when, following the official, but misguided policy of the time, it was cleared and everyone settled on the mainland. Today, the boat leaves you at a natural harbor of huge flagstones—you can then spend a few hours rambling, and taking in the wildlife. You'll see birds, seals, and—if you're there in winter—even barnacle geese. Of note are ruins of an early monastic site, including the monks' beehive cells and the well of St. Molaise (monks sought out isolated, bleak spots believing the deprivation brought them closer to God). Inside the monastic compound, on an altar, are the legendary cursing stones—islanders in the 19th century used them to curse interfering coast guards (who allegedly all perished) and during the second World War a woman from the mainland used them to curse Hitler (also effectively). So if you have any enemies . . .

To get there, you'll need to take a private boat from Aughris Pier, or Mullaghmore. The 70-minute journey is weather dependent. Phone Joe ☎ 087/667-4522, or Francis ☎ 086/067-5833, or ask at the Beach Bar

then it's been astonishing visitors with its demonstrations on the keen intelligence of eagles, hawk, vultures, owls, and other magnificent birds. Flying demonstrations led by the research scientists here, start at 11am and 3pm, last 60 minutes and even include a chance to touch some of the birds—but ask first! The golden eagles released in Glenveagh National Park in Sligo were reared here.

THE OTHER SLIGO

The Northwest is a festival zone. This is good news for you if you want to meet locals because festivals always need extra hands. **Itchyfeet** (www.itchyfeet.ie) is a Sligo-based organization with a hand in festivals and events all round the northwest; besides organizing their own festival, they host two regular club nights, host visiting musicians, put on workshops (mostly in music, but also in diverse activities like kite-making), and in general experiment with their philosophy that entertainment should have an educational component of some kind.

They're always looking for helpers to assist in different activities—from marshalling parades (when you're paired up with someone local) to meeting, greeting, and looking after visiting musicians and artists (so you get to rub shoulders with the talent). Because there's a strong educational component to Itchyfeet's work, you can be assured of either picking up some new knowledge during your time as a volunteer, or at the very least get to hear good-quality music or spend time in the company of interesting artists and performers. They welcome helpers of "all and any ability," and all you need to do is send an email.

ACTIVE SLIGO

Swimming in Strandhill is banned—the waves are too big and dangerous. Those same waves are, however, a huge draw for surfers (experts and newcomers), and world champion Kelly Slater surfs not far from here when he wants to hide from the crowds. An excellent family-run surf school, **Perfect Day Surf School** (☎ 087/202-9399; www.perfectdaysurfing.com) has its base here, and has as one of its teachers the man who helped kick off the surf craze here back in the '70s: Tom Hickey. Tom (who once won a place in the European Championship) is one of the most patient and enthusiastic instructors you'll find, and he enjoys nothing more than seeing his students conquer the challenge of getting up on the board for the first time. A 2-hour surfing lesson costs €30, including the use of the board and a wetsuit. A one-to-one session is €50. Note that with the ban on swimming, you are only allowed to enter the water if you are a legitimate watersportsman or are taking a lesson. You cannot rent boards here.

You can, however, swim at **Rosses Point Beach** which has a blue flag, which means its waters are pristine (or it did when we went to press—these flags are as meticulously earned as Michelin stars—the water is checked *weekly* so beaches do sometimes go through periods when they lose them). Jack B. Yeats painted the beach and bay frequently from here.

Walks around Sligo vary from gentle ambles along pristine stretches of beach, to tackling sweatier hillside and mountain terrain. The Strandhill walk southwest along the headland is wonderful—it's 2km (1 mile) to **Cullenamore Strand,** which has quieter waters for swimming. Follow the coast back around to a broad bay, where you should be able to spot a seal or two (there are over 200).

A more rigorous climbing walk is "doing" **Knocknarea Mountain** (452m/1,480 ft.); you start your 2-hour jaunt up to Maeve's Cairn from the car park near Ransboro, on the Strandhill Road (the R292), not far from Sligo Town. The route which should take 45 to 60 minutes; views from the top take in Sligo Bay and the Ox Mountains, as well as Donegal and Mayo. For a tougher climb, you might consider tackling famous **Benbulben,** which rises to 527m (1,070 ft.).

For an unspoiled lakeside walk, make your way around Lough Arrow or Lough Key, starting at Castlebaldwin; 10 different circular walks range in length from 4km to 12.3km (2–8 miles). For detailed route information, visit www.walkireland.ie, or www.discoverireland.ie/northwest.

In southern Sligo, it's popular to rent a boat to explore **Lough Arrow** and its islands—and, of course, if fishing is your thing, you'll certainly want to cast a line here. Poles and boats can be rented from local fishermen (try **John Hargadon** ☎ 071/966-6666 or **David Grey** ☎ 071/916-5491; €30–€60 depending on type of boat and equipment you require).

Slipping & Sliding in Sligo's Sensual Seaweed

Seaweed bathing has been around for over 300 years. And, seaweed has been an important element in Celtic culture for much longer than that—the colors that have predominated in Celtic clothing through the centuries are a result of seaweed being used as a dye—yup, now we understand what all that green is *really* about.

In the Victorian era, there were well over 150 seaweed bathing venues across Ireland. **Kilcullen's Seaweed Baths** ✪✪✪ (Enniscrone; ☎ 096/36238; www.kilcullensseaweedbaths.com; summer daily 10am–9pm; winter Mon–Fri 12pm–8pm; Sat–Sun 10am–8pm) was the original and some think, the best Irish spa. In fact, there have been baths here since the 19th century and they're now in their 5th generation of ownership by the Kilcullen family, who happily haven't been tempted to turn them into a generic 21st-century spa. The current building opened in 1915 and all fittings are still intact—this is a true Edwardian bathing experience. Take a hot seaweed bath (€24), then be enclosed in your individual cedarwood cabinet for a steam bath, and then splash yourself with a bucket of ice-cold sea water. You'll feel amazing! Massages are also available but pricey at €60 an hour.

A second choice, located in the surfing mecca of Strandhill, is **Voya** ✪✪✪ (Strandhill; ☎ 071/916-8686; www.voya.ie; daily 10am–7:30pm)—which was previously known more prosaically as the "Celtic Seaweed Baths." Voya takes its new identity from clients' suggestions that bathing in seaweed is akin to taking a "personal *voya*ge," which is certainly true of our first experience in a bath full of seaweed. Here the basic treatment is €25 and there's a cheaper rate if you share your treatments with a partner.

Don't think luxury spa (there are no fluffy robes or supermodels at either), but rather an opportunity to rejuvenate, luxuriate, and detoxify. The experience couldn't be more simple—or more satisfying—the hand-harvested *Fucus serratus* seaweed (fresh from the Atlantic) is steamed and then immersed in hot fresh saltwater in a bathtub; the heat causes the plant to release polyphenyls, iodine, and minerals which form a polysaccharide gel (the same gel used to heal burn victims) in which you soak (along with the seaweed) after a short steam bath to open your pores. Around 85% of the seaweed plant comprises vitamins and minerals since the plant filters those from its home water to survive. This impressive concentration of nutrients is of benefit to you when you climb in that warm, weedy water. Besides being an utterly relaxing (and surprisingly sensual) experience, the bath helps to detoxify the body (it's especially good for hangovers), working as a powerful cure-all, soothing tired muscles, nursing stiff joints, healing skin disorder (good for eczema), and even moisturizing the hair. You'll feel the effects soon after climbing into the bath—your heart rate decreases and you're overcome by a sense of calm.

ATTENTION SHOPPERS!

Pottery is a feature of Irish arts and crafts—actually, it's a feature of former peasant cultures everywhere—and a lot of it is mediocre but we like **Linda Gault's** (The Factory, Quay St., down the alley beside Harp Tavern; ☎ 071/911-4155, lindagault@hotmail.com) serene and simple work—she does lamps, bowls, and plates, glazed and with a superb finish, not rough and rustic. Prices are about €110 for a lamp, but she has good sales.

Also in Sligo, **Michael Quirke** (Wine St; ☎ 071/914-2620) has a real following for his wood carvings. He works very quickly and will make you an individual carving for about €80. His specialty is figures from mythology.

Onto food: Obviously you don't want to be buying perishables to take home, but you might like to enjoy Sligo's famed cheese, honey, jams, chocolate, and cakes while you're here (and Irish fruit cake lasts forever—traditionally you used your wedding cake for the christening of your first child, who was *always* born less than a year later). For all these goodies, head to **Cosgrove's** (32 Market St; ☎ 071/914-2809), a delicatessen emporium which has been there for generations and has always specialized in exotic produce.

NIGHTLIFE

Don't confine Sligo's pubs and bars to the night—some of the very best times for drinking a pint and hearing a trad session are the afternoons. In summer it's light until past 10pm so you can go into one of these dark intimate pubs at 4pm, wile away a few hours, and come out blinking to find it's still light outside.

If it's Thursday or Tuesday head up to **Shoot the Crows** ✪✪✪ (Grattan St.; ☎ 071/916-2554), our favorite pub in Sligo. Dark, lively, and intimate, it's as cool as it's name and if you don't make some friends or at least night acquaintances here, you're just not trying. You should continue to chat, but break off every once in a while to concentrate on the music. Try to get a feeling for it—when it's really cooking, the whole pub will stop talking and start listening.

Head up to **McGarrigles** (O'Connell St.; ☎ 071/914-1667) for last orders. Try not to have to go to the toilet as this will frankly put you off McGarrigles.

Trad Music: Where & When

You can hear trad music any day of the week in Sligo (except, usually, Fri). Here's a quick run-down:

Monday: The Harp Tavern (Quay St.; ☎ 071/914-2473)
Tuesday: Shoot the Crows (Castle St.; ☎ 071/916-2554)
Wednesday: McGarrigles (O'Connel St.; ☎ 071/914-1667)
Thursday: Shoot the Crows
Saturday: Fureys Sheela na Gig (Bridge St.; ☎ 071/914-3825)
Sunday: McGarrigles

Most sessions start around 9:30pm, but some of the best ones are impromptu and will start much earlier or later.

Regardless, this is a great music venue. There may even be an open mic in case the feeling takes you.

Finally end up, like everyone else in Sligo in the **Clarence Hotel** (Wine St.; ☎ 071/914-2211; €8 before 11pm, €12 after). Set in stunning Georgian buildings, DJs here can be very very good—if you're lucky you'll hear Underworld's Darren Emerson or Dublin's latest star, Mundy. Stagger out of the Clarence at 3am. Accompany the crowd to the nearest chippie. Keep your ears out for word of a party . . .

If you're not the pubhopping type, head instead to Sligo's fantastic small theater, the **Blue Raincoat Theatre Company** (The Factory, Quay St., down the alley beside Harp Tavern; ☎ 071/917-0431; www.blueraincoat.com) which is located in a former dockland warehouse. Opened by Marcel Marceau in 1993 and recently refurbished, it's a blackbox performance space that seats 85. The company's 12 ensemble players put on Irish and European plays, frequently those neglected by mainstream theater. They're particularly good at adapting novels and stories to the stage. Recent highlights included Flann O'Brien's surreal masterpiece, *The Third Policeman*, and Lewis Carroll's *Alice in Wonderland*.

COUNTY DONEGAL

"The wilds of Donegal" is an old Irish phrase, still in use, for somewhere very remote, very rugged, and very isolated. And northwest Donegal remains at the furthest reach of the country—a place of jagged beauty and few people. It's 7 hours' drive from Dublin but could be a million miles—many of the people won't even be speaking English, because the parish of Gweedore is home to the country's largest Gaeltacht community.

Donegal breaks a lot of records—it has the highest cliffs in Ireland and the most northerly point, plus the country's only golden eagles, and the famous tweed. It's Ireland's second-largest county, after Cork, and arguably it's most spectacular. The serrated coastline and long sandy beaches are almost ridiculously beautiful. The people are correspondingly hard-edged but also warm and genuine. They're tough and attractive and you feel immediately a Northern no-nonsense to them, which is quite different to the easy charm down south.

On the downside, there is still a lack of good places to eat and quality accommodation in the remotest regions. In fact a rule of thumb for Donegal seems to be the more beautiful the landscape, the less likely a hip cafe. But don't let that put you off. You can, after all, find hip cafes all over the world, but golden eagles and hilltop ring forts are harder to come by.

GETTING THERE & GETTING AROUND

Donegal isn't on the train line, which means you're reliant on rental **cars** or the **bus** (☎ 074/912-1309, www.buseireann.ie; €18 one-way from Dublin, €25 round-trip); correspondingly Donegal has a lot of private bus companies, including **Patrick Gallagher** (☎ 074/913-7037); **Gallagher Coaches** (☎ 074/953-1107; www.gallagherscoaches.com), and **John McGinley** (☎ 074/913-5201; www.johnmcginley.com; from Dublin, €20 one-way, €30 round-trip), great for intercity and inter-regional links within the county.

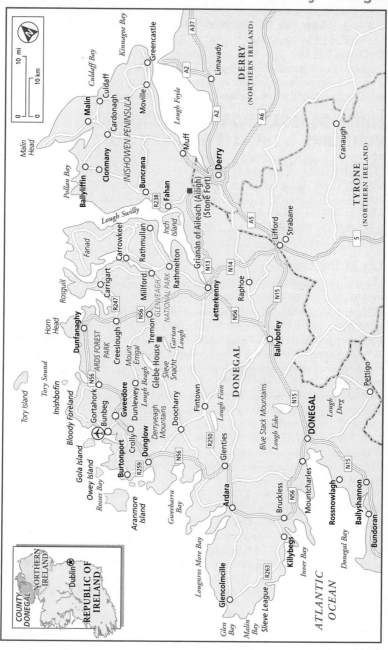

You may also want to approach from the north, if you've started off your trip in Belfast. **Ulster Bus** (☎ 028/9066-6630; www.translink.co.uk) charges £16.50 one-way and £25 round-trip.

Donegal is the only area in the northwest we'd advise flying into from Dublin—this is because the airport is in **Gweedore,** close to the main sights, but a very long drive from Dublin, so it can be worth paying the €60 or so round-trip fare and saving yourself effort (see **www.aerarann.com**).

SOUTH DONEGAL: DONEGAL TOWN, BALLYSHANNON, BUNDORAN & THE SLIEVE LEAGUE CLIFFS

Not all of Donegal is the wilds—the south, around Bundoran, Ballyshannon, and Donegal Town, feels more like Sligo and Leitrim—a leafy landscape of large lakes, winding rivers, impressive trees, and small, cheerful towns. You'll find comfortable places to stay and eat round here, and some people like to base themselves in south Donegal and take day trips to the "wilds"—Bundoran is too far south as a base but from Donegal Town you can easily strike out to Glencolmcille and the cliffs of Slieve League (just half an hour away).

Lay of the Land

Just over the border with Sligo is **Bundoran,** Donegal's southernmost town and its surfing mecca. Just 6km (4 miles) north of Bundoran is **Ballyshannon,** always billed as Ireland's oldest town (apparently the Scythians landed here around 2700 B.C.). More to the point, it's the birthplace of the great blues-rock guitarist Rory Gallagher and site of Ireland's best folk festival (www.ballyshannonfolkfestival.com) in early August. Music-lovers come here on pilgrimage; everyone else will find this a jaunty town, with brightly painted Georgian buildings and a clocktower on the main street to navigate by.

The coast road takes you on to **Rossnowlagh,** where there are good cliff walks and a wide surfing beach. Rejoining the main road, 16km (10 miles) north is **Donegal Town,** not the county capital (that's Lifford) or the largest town (that's Letterkenny), but the main town in the area and the most touristic in all Donegal with plenty of hotels, restaurants, craft shops, and, of course the famous tweed. There aren't any famous sights or beautiful churches in Donegal Town, but it's got a good feel and a lively nightlife.

Most visitors to Donegal Town explore the surrounding territory, **Lough Eske** and the **Bluestack Mountains,** where there are wonderful walks.

Leaving Donegal Town by the coast road, you'll see the castle at **St. John's Point,** with great views over Donegal Bay. Heading north you come to the still very active fishing port of **Killybegs,** and then it's the scenic drive past the awesome **Slieve League** cliffs, or you can go directly from **Carrick** to **Glencolmcille,** named for the 6th century St. Columba, or St. Colm Cille—here you'll see megalithic and monastic remains, a sturdy little village, and great cliff walks.

Accommodations, Both Standard & Not

Those looking for rental opportunities in Donegal town should first consult **Donegal Direct** (www.donegaldirect.ie), the official Donegal Tourism site which only lists Bord Fáilte approved accommodation. An informational, rather than a booking site (it will direct you to another site or contact number for actual book-ings), it has the fullest range of options for this section of Donegal. Some exam-ples of what can be found on it include:

◆ **Ashwood Apartments** (Mill Park Hotel, Killybegs; ☎ 087/281-3209 or 074/974-0729; www.ashwooddonegal.com), adjacent to a hotel, include the free use of that facility's leisure center (full pool, gym, steam room, and Jacuzzi). At €670 a week in July and August and €530 a week in June and September, that's really not bad. So though these clean, well-equipped 2-bed-roomed apartments are in a slightly soulless new complex (10-min. walk from the center of town) and don't have oodles of personality, we consider them a good value.

◆ **Assaroe Falls** ★★ (☎ 087/661-4244; www.assaroefalls.com) is a modern complex with 18 elegant apartments (think glass-topped tables, black leather sofas, wide screen TVs) going for just €550 a week high season for a one-bedroom, €650 a week for a two bedroom, and €750 a week for three bed-rooms (a remarkable bargain). You can also book by the night (higher rates).

The best website we've found for rentals in the Donegal countryside is **www.donegalcottageholidays.com**, an exemplary site with photos, amenities, prices, locations, proximity to beaches/shops/pubs, and a short description of the various areas. The site covers all Donegal, so it's the ideal place to start hunting when planning a week or two in this county. Brian, who owns and runs the site, visits just about all the properties himself to make sure they're up to snuff and photograph them before posting. Most houses and cottages on the site sleep between five and eight people and online prices for July and August average just €600 to €800, a boon if you favor space and are traveling with children.

€ Family-run **Donegal Town Independent Hostel** (Killybegs Rd.; ☎ 074/972-2805; MC, V) which is on the town outskirts—about 1km (about a mile) from the Diamond, is the best option for penny-pinchers. Its most obvious bonus is hostess Linda Cunningham, who will give you tea and tell you all you need to know about the area. Dorms with 4 or 6 bunk beds cost €17 per person, two standard double rooms (sharing a bathroom) are €20 per person and two double en suite represent a good value at €22 per person. The double beds are more com-fortable than the bunks, which can be a bit saggy. One of the double en suites has a bunk bed so can do as a family room—the price for this, Linda says, "she makes up on the spot—maybe €65 or €70 for the room," so do haggle!

€€ Donegal Town is good if you want a night out, otherwise many travelers prefer to stay round scenic and quiet Lough Eske, 8km (5 miles) away. Possibly one of the loveliest spots in this part of the country is a warm, welcoming and exceptionally good-value B&B called the **Arches** ★★★ (Lough Eske; ☎ 074/972-2029; http://homepage.eircom.net/~archescountryhse/index.htm; MC, V) where Noreen McGinty charges €70 to €80 double and each spacious bedroom has a gorgeous view of the lake through a huge picture window. Bedrooms are spa-cious and handsomely laid out, with large beds (thick, plush mattresses, too, with great linens), solid wood furniture, and carefully placed amenities (which include your own satellite decoder for the TV). If you're in a position to pick one (easy, really, since Noreen is so accommodating), opt for one of the two upstairs corner units—one of these has views not only of Lough Eske, but also of the Bluestack Mountains.

€€   Also around Lough Eske, **Rhugorse** ✿✿ (Lough Eske; ☎ 074/972-1685; www.lougheske.com; Apr 1–Oct 30; MC, V) is among our favorite places to stay. It's a big, comfortable '70s house, enjoying amazing views down to Lough Eske. The family room, with en suite bathroom (the other two rooms have showers) is the pick of the crop, being large and airy, with big bay windows. Gráinne (pronounced *Gra*-nee-a) McGettigan has a direct, down-to-earth warmth and you know as soon as you meet her what further investigation confirms—this house is an enemy to dust, germs, uncomfortable mattresses, and shoddiness in any form. Nightly rate here is €90 double.

€€   We'd also like to warmly recommend **Ard na Bréatha** ✿✿ (Droomrooske Middle; ☎ 074/972-2288; www.ardnabreatha.com; mid-Jan to mid-Nov; MC, V) on the outskirts of Donegal town—1.5km (about a mile) from center, on the road to Lough Eske. Albert and Theresa Morrow's guesthouse is pretty and welcoming with such niceties as wrought-iron beds and handsome pine furniture. On site are a fully licensed bar, with a roaring fire, and a small, excellent restaurant. But because guest rooms are in an attached barn, guests aren't disturbed by noise from the eatery. All in all you get the intimacy and good pricing of a B&B with the convenience of a hotel. B&B is €98 double but if you opt to dine here (and you should) you'll get a package deal—3 nights B&B with one five-course meal for €169 per person total.

Dining for All Tastes

€–€€   Donegal Town has a lot of places to eat—most of them mid-range and decent, but not spectacular. An exception is the **Blueberry Tea Room** ✿✿ (Castle St.; ☎ 074/972-2933; Mon–Sat 9am–7pm; cash only) which is right in the center of Donegal Town, both geographically and culturally (it often feels like a club house for locals). As for the food, it's straightforward, but delicious and served in unusually generous portions. The menu is broad, meaning there's something for all tastes from basic sandwiches (from €3.30,) to salads (€4.95–€9.95) and fresh pastas (€9.95) to such daily specials as organic chargrilled salmon with salad and homemade bread (€12). Be careful: You'll have to pass some dangerously enticing cakes on the walk in. If you get one, share: Portions are humongous.

€–€€€   From tea to **Aroma Coffee** ✿ (Craft Village, 1.5 km/1 mile outside town on the old Ballyshannon Rd.; ☎ 074/972-3222; Mon–Sat 9:30am–5:30pm; MC, V): a tiny cafe and veritable mecca for foodies (so try and arrive either before noon or after 2pm to get a seat, though if it's sunny, there's a big outdoor eating space). Owner Tom Dooley and Mexican chef Arturo de Alba Gonzalez source great ingredients to produce food with flair (set lunch is €7.50, most mains €10 a la carte). Coffee is excellent and should be taken with the Tunisian Orange cake €4.50.

The Very Reason You Came to Ireland . . .

It's been extensively touted by all kinds of media as one of the finest B&Bs in Ireland, and we, too, have lost our hearts to the **Green Gate** ✪✪✪ (Ardara; ☎ 074/954-1546; www.thegreengate.eu; cash only), which is quite unlike any other lodging experience. Situated above the delightful village of Ardara, the Green Gate is a rather magical cluster of white-washed cottages restored many years ago by French philosopher and writer, Paul Chatenoud. Now he runs this hilltop getaway as what he likes to call "a free estate," which means that there's a touch of bohemia here—there are no silly strictures (breakfast is whenever you want it, for example) and the only thing Paul doesn't tolerate is snooty, demanding guests in search of luxury (as Paul is quick to point out, "no TV, no computers, no e-mail" . . . which, in our books, spells "freedom").

The setting is gloriously remote and isolated, and yet a very short drive from Ardara's 13 pubs, and within easy reach of a number of fine beaches. Of the four bedrooms, three are in a converted thatched shed (€90 double), a "Hobbit"-like space, each with a handsome little bathroom (with a skylight above the tub), quality antique furnishings, and low doorways. A fourth room (€110 double) occupies a separate slate-roofed cottage and is somewhat more spacious, with mesmeric views from both the bed and the bathtub (there's also a bidet in this bathroom).

Prepare for great continental breakfasts (with 20 different jams and marmalades made by Paul's neighbor), turf-fuelled fires in Paul's cozy, homey kitchen, and riveting conversations. It may seem ironic that a Frenchman has created the ideal, most idyllic Irish getaway, but perhaps it takes a foreigner to recognize the loveliness that others might have too-easily taken for granted.

€–€€€ The sweet village of Ardara has 13 pubs, but those in the know go to **Nancy's** ✪✪✪ (Front St.; ☎ 074/954-1187; food served Easter–Halloween daily noon–9pm; Halloween–Easter Sat and Sun only; bar open till 1am; cash only), now in the McHugh family for seven generations. A thick-walled space filled with a motley collection of tables and chairs (there's hardly a matching pair), artworks hanging all askew, it has a formidable collection of mugs dangling above the small bar. Best of all, the rich aroma of fresh seafood greets you as you step in from the bracing air outside. While you can order an open sandwich (mostly €8.90), the seafood here is especially memorable. Try "Charlie's Supper," a tantalizing combination of prawns and smoked salmon gently warmed in a sweet chili, garlic, and lemon sauce (€13) . . . which makes our mouths water just thinking about it. During the summer months, there's live music (folk and rock) over weekends.

€–€€€€   Your best bet in Bundoran is **Madden's Bridge Bar** (West End Bundoran; ☎ 071/984-2050; www.maddensbridgebar.com; food served 12:30–8:30pm; MC, V) where surfers, swimmers, and musicians gather. A big, wood-paneled bar, leads into a restaurant upstairs serving all-day snacks along with lunches and dinners. Large groups tend to settle into the booths to devour chicken wings (€7.25), or prawns and crab claws (€11), before moving onto burgers (€11). Owner Declan Madden keeps it local where possible, such as Irish beef Guinness stew. He also has a very good deli with home-baked cakes and tarts as well as salami, olives, and sundried tomatoes.

Why You're Here: Top Sights & Attractions

The big castle that looms over Donegal Town, **Donegal or O'Donnell's castle** ★ (☎ 074/973-2405; Heritage card or €3.70; Mar–Oct daily 10am–6pm; Nov to mid-Mar Fri–Sun 9:30am–4:30pm), was home to the county's premier family, the O'Donnells, whose most famous scion was the 16th-century firebrand, Red Hugh O'Donnell, who led a rebellion against the English and had an amazing knack of escaping from jail. The original castle was 15th century and used by the O'Donnells as a defensive fortress; the 17th-century owner, English captain Basil Brooke, made it more of a home—today both influences can be seen. It's worth a visit to see the Persian rugs, French tapestries, the 14 (!) fireplaces, and to get a sense of how the rich lived back then.

Rather pretentiously styled an Aqua Adventure Playground **Waterworld** ★ kids (Bundoran; ☎ 071/984-1172; www.waterworldbundoran.com; €10.50, children 7 and under €8, children 2 and under €4; June-end Aug and Easter week daily 10am–7pm; Apr, May, and Sept Sat and Sun 10am–7pm), is in reality a big slide 'n' splash, beloved of kids, but made bearable for adults by a steam room, sauna, and seaweed baths (assuming you have someone to watch your kids in the pool, and want to pay the €22.50 for the spa). There's a wave pool and three different slides, including the Whizzer Slide (Ireland's fastest). Noisy fun but there's nothing this child-friendly in the rest of Donegal.

SLIEVE LEAGUE CLIFFS

The big draws in the area are the **Slieve League cliffs** ★★★, which we call a must-see. They're allegedly the highest marine cliffs in Europe, though they're only the sixth highest cliffs in Europe—all these stats get confusing, and it really doesn't matter. These are very high and much less crowded than the Cliffs of Moher in Clare (p. 236). They're also better for walking (until you get near the summit, which is tricky). An abiding memory of author Emily's is hiking to the top and then dashing down. The turf beneath is springy as a trampoline.

To get to the cliffs, take the drive from Teelin to Bunglass (the views are mighty dramatic), but be careful round those hairpin bends. From the Bunglass carpark, follow the path up to One Man's Pass, named for obvious reasons—the narrow path to the summit has to be taken in single file. This is vertiginous, and definitely not advisable if it's windy or misty, but the view 600m (2,000 ft.) down to the sea is breath-taking.

Active South Donegal

Just north of Donegal Town, lovely **Lough Eske** is ideal for gentle, well sign-posted walks that won't require too much of your time. More dedicated hikers should consider the **Bluestack Way,** which points you across small hills, through woodland and onto open bogs. Bring a packed lunch and eat it in one of the ruined houses you'll find on the trail. Most exciting is the waterfall, **Ashdoonan Falls**—Author Emily climbed all the way up it and then bounced down on her backside, laughing all the way like a dervish. For trail maps to all these places pick up a copy of the *Ordnance Survey Map, No. 11*, and perhaps *The Bluestack Guide* (€10; usually available from the Tourist Office in Donegal Town). Better still, contact the **Bluestack Centre** (☎ 074/973-5563; www.donegalbluestacks. com) in Letterbarra, which is just 3km (2 miles) from the Bluestack trail. Another source for information on hiking in the region is **www.northwestwalking guides.com**.

Surfers coming to Donegal will undoubtedly have heard about Bundoran, one of the sport's great Ireland locations. The reef and breaks are world class and the town has hosted two European championships. If you're new to **surfing** and fancy picking up a new skill, head either to **Surf World** ✹✹ (Main St., Bundoran; ☎ 071/984-1223; www.surfworldireland.com), which is owned by the family of Richie Fitzgerald, a world champion, or **Bundoran Surf Co.** (Main St., Bundoran; ☎ 071/984-1968; www.bundoransurfco.com), where you can rent boards for €20 and wetsuits for €10 per day. Here, you can also bag a "surf 'n' stay" package, from €55 per person for a night's B&B plus a surfing lesson; there are packages for up to 7 nights (€290 inclusive of five lessons). Accommodation in a shared dorm is only marginally cheaper.

Attention Shoppers!

Magee of Donegal (The Diamond, Donegal Town; ☎ 074/972-2669; www.magee donegal.com) has been famous for its tweed for centuries. The nice surprise is that they've kept up with the times—styles are simple, well-cut, wearable, faintly conservative, and not too expensive. It's better for men's clothes, though it has some women's styles.

You may want to buy an Aran sweater while here—those creamy, patterned fishermen's jumpers that are absolutely gorgeous though a bit tarnished by their popularity. If you do, or want to get other knitwear, head to Ardara, Donegal, where you'll pay half the price anywhere else. Check out **John Molloy's** (☎ 074/ 954-1133), 1km (less than a mile) outside Ardara town, or **Kennedy's** (☎ 074/ 954-1303), up from the Diamond in the center of Donegal Town.

GWEEDORE, GLENVEAGH NATIONAL PARK & THE INISHOWEN PENINSULA

The county's most popular attraction, the Glenveagh National Park, stretches east of Gweedore, around the Derryveagh Mountains and Lough Beagh. A thickly wooded valley, with a castle at its heart, it seems to have emerged straight from a fairytale. In this area you'll also see internationally acclaimed artists—Picasso, Modigliani, Renoir—in practically the only collection outside Ireland's major cities, as well as the primitive painters of Tory Island. Head even farther to the Inishowen Peninsula and you'll have reached Ireland's most northerly point. So you've got landscape, wildlife, art, bragging rights for reaching the great north and some great pubs—not too bad for the wilds of Donegal!

Lay of the Land

The gateway to Gweedore is the tiny village of **Crolly,** after which you can go inland towards **Glenveigh National Park,** or take the coast road round to **Horn Head.** The stunning coast road (R257) takes you through a number of charming villages, picturesque harbors, and even a carefully restored famine workhouse (at Dunfanaghey). If you're thinking of going to **Tory Island,** hop on the ferry either at **Bunbeg** or **Magheroarty** (the journey's a hair quicker from the latter). Inland, you'll hit the bleak, barren landscape of the **Bloody Foreland,** not named after a massacre but for the color the setting sun makes on the heather.

Whether you take the coastal or inland roads is a bit of a toss up. The inland road is quicker and not less scenic because you go past **Mount Errigal,** and onto the **Derryveagh Mountains,** where the National Park is located.

Most heading to the Inishowen Peninsula, meanwhile, go from **Letterkenny** northeast on the N13. Just off this road before **Burnfoot** and the start of the peninsula proper, is the large fort, **Grianán Ailigh,** one of the largest ring forts in Ireland. Keeping northwest, past **Buncrana** along the scenic drive to **Dunree Head,** and further north, to spectacular **Dunaff Head.** A few miles beyond that is **Pollan Strand,** where you'll see the ruins of the 16th-century **Carrickabraghy Castle.** The road winds slightly south to **Carndonagh,** before going north again to **Malin** village, perched prettily on **Trawbreaga Bay.** Now you're heading to the northernmost tip of the country, **Malin Head.** You can take a windy walk along the headland and you'll know you're at the tip when you reach the ruins of a Napoleonic tower, **Bamba's Crown.**

Accommodations, Both Standard & Not

This region offers some of the best budget accommodation in the country. A real effort has been made to take advantage of the stunning locations and to renovate or design buildings in keeping with the landscape.

€   A small hostel, with cozy rooms, **Screag an Iolair** ★★ (Crolly; ☎ 074/954-8593; isai@eircom.net; Apr–Sept; cash only) has two great assets—it's 244m (800 ft.) up in the Cnoc na Farraigh Mountains (hence the hostel's name, which means "Eagle's Nest"), with fine views across to Arranmore Island, and its position as a haunt of musicians from all over the world. When we were last there, Japanese and Bavarian harpists were guests (coincidentally) so the evening turned into a harp festival. It can sleep 30 but owners Eamonn and Mireille keep a few beds spare each evening because this is a traditional walkers' hostel (there's been an inn here for 200 years) and they don't like turning away exhausted hikers arriving late. There are three small dorms (€18 per person), a family room with double bed and a pair of bunks (€20 per person), and a sweet garret, with a double bed, called "Heidi's room" (€20). None of the rooms have a private bathroom, but it's all very clean and mattresses are firm (they're changed every 3 years as policy). A well-equipped kitchen for guests is available to guests but no TV. They're pretty technophobic—you're asked to switch off your mobile phone, and don't even think about going online.

€   At the foot of Mount Errigal, in the perfect position for climbing the peak, is the **Errigal Hostel** ★ (Dunlewey; ☎ 074/953-1180; www.errigalhostel.com; MC, V), which has been located here for 40 years but the current building is brand

---

All Aboard for Dunfanaghy

For a hostel stay with a difference, climb aboard the **Carriage** ✪✪ (Corcreggan Mill, Dunfanaghy; ☎ 074/910-0814; www.the-carriage-hostel-corcreggan.com; cash only), where guests stay in compact dorms or private rooms fashioned from the hull of a disused train carriage. Each dorm has two double bunks carved from railway sleeper-size chunks of wood (so they're pretty darn solid); in addition, they're supplied with a basin and a chair, meaning that they're pretty basic. But, behind the carriage are ultra-homey public areas, including a fire-warmed lounge, dining room, well-equipped kitchen, showers, and laundry facilities. Antique pictures, decorative bits of nostalgia, and a selection of literature help give these peaceable digs a touch of class—a welcome break from the usual institutional hostel atmosphere—greatly enhanced by the personable attitude of Desmond, the owner. Dorm beds cost €18, and there are private doubles, too, which are an encouraging €43. And, before you ask: No! The carriage does not move . . . it's cemented down.

---

new, and no expense has been spared on design. It's now a slick but discreet building of brick, glass, and wood. Since the maximum number of beds per dorm is six (€21 per person), and there are rooms with four beds and also just two beds (which are en suite and cost €25 per person), it hardly feels like a hostel. Best of all, it's wonderfully clean and light-filled, with comfortable, modern furniture and shiny wooden floors. There's even a play area for children. Unless you absolutely insist on being hand-served your full Irish breakfast, we really don't see why you'd pay more for a B&B.

€€   **Bunbeg House** ✪ (The Harbour, Bunbeg; ☎ 074/953-1305; www.bunbeg house.com; closed Oct–Feb; MC, V) is a family-run guesthouse secreted away in an enviable spot overlooking Bunbeg Harbour. It offers 14 fairly large guest rooms (€80–€90), reached via long, wide passageways. Not only that, but they've a huge, airy, wood-floor dining room, and a nifty bar with Guinness on tap to accompany the watery views. Unlike your standard B&B, you can also get home-cooked bar meals and dinners here—ranging from sandwiches to steaks and a great deal in between. Your hosts take good care of their guests, too—if you fancy a spot of fishing, Andrew will even take you out in their dinghy so you can cast a line. While bedrooms aren't luxurious, they're wonderfully large with wood-framed beds, good mattresses, and basic amenities (kettle, TV, decent-enough shower cubicles). Try to secure room 20, which has two double beds and distinctive views of the harbor inlet and the river). Children under 16 pay half price, and under-10s are rarely charged at all.

€€–€€€   If you make it to the Inishowen Peninsula you'll definitely dine at **McGrory's of Culdaff** ✪✪✪ 🧒 (Culdaff; ☎ 074/937-9104; www.mcgrorys.ie; Tues–Thurs 6:30–9pm; Fri–Sat 6:30–9:30pm; AE, MC, V), first to say you've been here (it's a real institution), second to move seamlessly after dinner to the Backroom Bar to hear brilliant live music, and third, because you'll eat well. The polished cherrywood dining room offers steaks, seafood, and vegetarian options, however we'd plump for the **Front Bar** (food from 12:30–8:30pm), which is much jollier and a better value. You'll get chowder (€6), a prime sirloin steak sandwich (€11), Inishowen rock oysters (a dozen for €12), and wild, local mussels, which are certainly worth the €17 (try them in garlic onion cream and white wine sauce). Special children's portions are available, too. If you're here Tuesday or Friday, trad musicians will come in after your meal, and you'll be here all night.

€€–€€€   Finally, if it's an honest-to-goodness hotel you fancy, look no further than Gweedore's stalwart early-20th-century **Seaview Hotel** ✪ (on the R237, Bunbeg, Gweedore; ☎ 074/953-1159 or 074/953-1076; www.seaviewhotel gweedore.com; MC, V), which has 36 spacious rooms (they don't make them like this anymore), a rollicking big pub, bistro, and a disco (yes, even out here in the Gweedore wilderness). Guest rooms, which all have neat, old-school bathrooms with tubs, have been refurbished to a pleasing standard in recent years, so the furniture and fittings are from the 21st century—dark wood and brushed metal prevails. Bizarrely, suites cost the same as the other bedrooms (off season, they're €80 during the week, and €100 on weekends though packages sometimes drop the rates to €120 for 2 nights and dinner; in the summer you're most likely to pay €140 a night.)

Dining for All Tastes

€–€€   Despite its cheeky name, **Muck 'n' Muffins** ✪ (Market Sq., Dunfanaghy; ☎ 074/913-6780; www.mucknmuffins.com; summer Mon–Sat 9:30am–9pm; Sun 10:30am–9pm; winter daily 9am–5pm; closed Sun Dec–St. Patrick's Day; MC, V) is actually an irresistibly quaint cafe above a pottery studio right near the heart of Dunfanaghy. Here, sisters Deborah and Emma Moore operate a low-key coffee shop where they serve delicious stuffed rolls and sandwiches (€3.25–€3.95), as well as salads (€8.50), light meals, and delicious sweets. Since acquiring a wine license a few years back (€4.50 glass; €17 bottle), they've also thrown in lasagnas,

---

Dunfanaghy's Green Man

No, not a leprechaun. The **Green Man** ✪✪✪ (Main St., Dunfanaghy; ☎ 074/910-0800; Mon–Sat 9:30am–6pm; Sun 10am–2pm; MC, V) is a little deli and fine food store that you'd probably never expect to find in such a remote village. But this lovely shop sells a wide range of organic and whole foods, around 15 to 20 Irish cheeses, jams, sundried tomatoes, pickled olives, smoked chicken, duck liver pâté, and even—if you're in the mood for a splurge—steamed lobster (€25/kg). You can pick up a loaf of Guinness bread for €3.25, or snack on homemade muffins (€1.55), and it's useful if you're looking for health products. Be warned, this place gets busy in summer, so consider placing your order a day in advance.

quiches, and baked potatoes (each served with salad; €9.50), and in summer and during special events will stay open into the evening (it's a great place to meet the locals).

€–€€   You come to **Maggie Dan's** (Gortahork; ☎ 074/916-5630; www.maggie dans.ie; daily 6–10pm; bring cash as credit card payments attract a €6 fee) for the atmosphere: There's an open piano for customers to use at will (okay, this can be a negative as well as a positive), and minor theatrical events (including music) happen from time to time. A ragtag, bohemian atmosphere prevails in this 19th-century house with its motley collection of chairs and sofas and assorted tables. Presiding over it all is arguably the cheekiest proprietor in All Ireland—so be prepared for his cheerful banter and pray he decides not to take the mickey out of you. Food-wise, choices are pretty much limited to pizza (choose three standard toppings on a 10-incher and pay just €6, or grab a 14-incher for €10 and share it between two), and we can't say the pizza is consistent (sometimes they're a bit doughy) but at €6, who's really complaining?

€–€€€€   Take the Creeslough Road to Port na Blagh, where you'll find the **Cove Restaurant** (☎ 074/913-6300; Tues–Sun 6–9pm; MC, V) over-looking the harbor. It's small and popular so even if you've booked, you'll probably have to wait for your table at the upstairs bar, before being taken downstairs to the dining room, with its open fire and surprisingly good art on the walls. Start with the trademark chowder (€7.50), or whole boned quail (€9.50), then move onto monkfish (€24) or pork belly (€20). You can pay less if you opt for the set dinner (€20–€25).

Why You're Here: Top Sights & Attractions

Glenveagh National Park ✰✰✰ (☎ 074/913-0790; www.glenveaghnational park.ie; daily Apr–Sept 10am–6pm; Oct–Mar 9am–5pm; castle guided tour €3, free general admission) is a huge swath of 6,475 hectares (16,000 acres) stretching over the Derryveagh mountains and comprising bogs, hills, woodland, and lakes. The park was donated to the state by an Irish-American, Henry McIlhenny, who lived here from 1937 to 1983, and by his generous act cancelled out some of the bad feeling round the estate. The first owner, John Adair ruthlessly evicted 244 tenants in April 1861, an act bitterly recorded as the Derryveagh Convictions. His reason: They were ruining the view. Today's unimpeded views—beyond the flora, look out for hares, deer, plovers, falcons, and most excitingly, since 2001, golden eagles (the best time to see these is in winter, when the young birds are released)—are all the more poignant thanks to this sorrowful history. After the Adairs, the owner was another Irish-American, Arthur Kingsley Porter, who disappeared in mysterious circumstances.

Aim to spend a few hours in the park; follow one of six walks, ranging from the easy 1km (less than a mile) **Garden Trail,** through the cultivated gardens to the 8km (5-mile) Glen Walk, past Lough Veagh. Part of the delight of visiting here is contrasting the formal, 4 hectares (10 acres) of gardens, filled with rare plants from across the globe to the rugged scenery in this "Glen of the Birches" (the meaning for Glenveagh) with its purple moor grasses and densely wooded areas. The **Visitor's Centre** is at the northern end of Lough Veagh, off the R251.

It has a presentation on the area's ecology, which isn't essential, and a pretty good **restaurant.** Buses (€2) leave from the Visitor's Centre to the slightly kitschy but romantic looking neo-Gothic **Glenveagh Castle** within the park (we think you can skip the castle and concentrate on the park).

McIlhenny's good friend, the English artist Derek Hill, was equally generous and donated to the area its next most visited attraction, the **Glebe House** ★★★ (4km/2.5 miles from the Park, towards Letterkenny on the R25; €2.90 includes tour; June to end-Sept Sat–Thurs 11am–6:30pm). Hill, an inspired collector as well as a fine artist, created in this stern, handsome Georgian presbytery a riotous, eclectic interior, where William Morris wallpaper backs Picasso and Modigliani prints, trinkets from the seaside, and the primitive art of the Tory Islanders (see below). In 1981 he abruptly up and left, gifting the house and its priceless contents to the state. The converted stables are used for visiting exhibitions.

Donegal's distinctive **Mount Errigal,** shaped like a pile of sugar, with its summit generally lost in clouds, offers a rugged challenge, good for the reasonably fit (count about 3½ hr. including descent). The trail is marked from the R251, a little way past Errigal youth hostel and the views from three quarters of the way up are primo—we've only ever seen mist from the summit, but we hear from other trekkers that on a clear day, the views are heart stopping.

Bird-watchers in particular will love **Horn Head,** the dramatic rock face north of Dunfanaghy, where puffins, gannets, storm petrels, and the endangered corn-crake nest. The east road (starts at west end of Dunfanaghy village) rises steeply to the heather-clad cliffs. It's an exhilarating climb, almost frightening in places, and takes about 5 hours to do the perimeter. An easier walk is to go from the Horn Head Bridge, just outside Dunfanaghy, and walk west across the dunes to the beautiful Tramore Beach and further north, to Pollaguill Bay and beach. From here you'll see **Marble Arch,** a tremendous naturally occurring arch, over 20m (66 ft.) high, cut by the sea into Trawbreaga Head.

Tory Island

Derek Hill (see above) is even more associated with **Tory Island** ★★★ (☎ 074/ 953-1320, www.toryislandferry.com) than with the Glebe House. A gregarious portrait painter (among his subjects was the Prince of Wales), he also craved solitude and found it on this remote island, where he lived in a tiny hut, and painted majestic views from the cliffs. His presence initiated a remarkable outpouring of primitive art among islanders, many of whom had never picked up a paintbrush before his arrival. Their pieces are of variable quality but some of them, notably those by James Dixon, are excellent. The islanders' work can be seen in the gallery on the island, Dixon's former home.

To get there, take either the ferry from Bunbeg harbour (Apr–Oct at 9am) or from Magheroarty (Apr–Oct at 11:30am and 5pm and July–Aug at 1:30pm). Both are about €20 round-trip, but realize that this isn't a guaranteed day trip: The last sailing back is 6pm and doesn't always go because of weather, so count on staying the night. Not that that's a bad thing. You'll be met at the harbor by the elected king, Patsey Dan Rodgers—he makes it his business to shake the hand of every visitor. From the harbor you walk up to a jaunty terrace of brightly painted houses, gallantly facing the mainland, their backs to the vast Atlantic. Tory has only 150 people and it's small—4km (2½ miles) long, 1.5km (1 mile) wide—so you can walk it easily. Most spectacular are the sheer cliffs, which drop down one side of the island. It's delightful to lie on the springy grass at the edge of the cliff and watch the seabirds far below. A distinctive T-shaped cross, the **Tau cross,** one of only two in Ireland, is set in the west pier, a reminder of St. Colmcille's monastic settlement here in the 6th century.

There are only a few options if you spend the night—hotel, hostel, and a few B&Bs. Expect to pay between €55 and €60 for the night; the **tourist center** (www.oileanthorai.com; ☎ 074/913-5502) will make arrangements for you. Don't fret if you end up stuck here; the evenings in the Social Club can be lively.

Inishowen Peninsula Sights

The massive ring fort **Grianán of Aileach (Ailigh)** ✪✪ perched on a hill off the main road from Letterkenny and before Burnfoot, was the residence of the O'Neills, the great chieftains of this area. An important building, it was included by Ptolemy in his second-century A.D. map of the world and became an important Christian site, too, when, in A.D. 430, St. Patrick baptized King Owen (the same king who gives Inish*owen* its name). However the building you're seeing isn't the one Ptolemy recorded—that was sacked and ransacked in the 12th century and reconstructed by Walter Bernard of Derry in the late 19th century. So who knows how authentic this is? It reminds me somewhat of Knossos in Crete, another major 19th-century reconstruction—you're torn between bemusement at the cavalier way these Victorians re-imagined an unknowable site, and appreciation that what you're seeing is more arresting than the alternative—a pile of old stones, that only archaeologists can understand. In any case, it's the area's most popular attraction, so climb up here, take in the fantastic view, and don't, unless you're hungry, bother with the **Visitor Centre** (☎ 074/936-8080), back on the main road. The food is pretty good at the restaurant here but the exhibition isn't.

The most famous walking destination in the area, **Malin Head** (coastal road along the north of Trawbrega Bay), isn't actually the most beautiful. In fact it's fairly flat landscape, not on a par with Donegal's finest. However we like standing by the ruins of the Napoleonic tower, imagining that it was built to spy on the French if they ever thought of attacking Britain through the far north (unlikely!) and appreciating that there's nothing but Scotland and Iceland between us and the Arctic Circle.

A better walk though is round **Pollan Bay,** near Ballyliffan, where you can climb up the ruins of **Carrickabraghy Castle** and peer through the empty window, or doorway, at the shore. If the tide is in, you'll see water spurting through from the "hissing rock" beside it.

Nightlife

Nightlife in Gweedore and Dunfanaghy revolves almost exclusively around pubs and trad music sessions. Two of the county's most famous pubs are in this area. Just before Crolly, you'll see a sign for **Leo's Tavern** (Meenaleck, Crolly; ☎ 074/ 954-8143), run by one of Ireland's first musical families. Leo and Baba Brennan were members of 1950s–1960s show bands, but it's their kids who've really gone global—three of them, Máire, Pól, and Ciarán, are in the group **Clannad,** and another is the reclusive singer **Enya,** whose voice you will have heard in the film *The Lord of the Rings: The Fellowship of the Ring.* Of course the kids' numerous awards still festoon the walls. Thursdays are the big nights here. Unsurprisingly, it's pretty touristic, with Enya fans making the pilgrimage from all over the world.

Across the road **Tessie's** (Meenaleck, Crolly; ☎ 074/954-8124) has more locals and is now the choice of those who hate going with the crowd. It's also got a primo trad session on Sundays.

To the North, **Teach Húdaí Beag** ("Hughdie's Small House," Bunberg; ☎ 074/953-1016), by the harbor, used to be the kind of small, smoky room you'd spend hours in, losing track of time. Now the smokers are all outside, but it still hosts one of the best trad sessions every Monday evening (sometimes as many as two dozen musicians participate), and a smaller one on Friday.

Farther up the coast, stone-fronted **Teach Billie** (Gortahork; no phone) is a welcoming spot where it's easy to get caught up in the *craic* as little huddles of regulars drift frequently and fluently between English and Irish—this is surely a prime location for the local lads (and lasses) to share the day's gossip. The trad music sessions that erupt here are so rollicking that they often end up on YouTube.

10 New Peace, New Future: Belfast

Once a hotbed of sectarian troubles, now a city on the move

by Keith Bain

BELFAST—SHAKEN, STIRRED, BATTERED, ALMOST BROKEN. YET BELFAST IS unmistakably Ireland's comeback kid. Having sloughed off the worst of a violent hangover, Belfast is a city determined to throw off any lingering shackles of a troubled past. Without the constant threat and fear, life has taken on a consumerist bent, producing a buoyant, bouncing society keen to catch up on all that it missed out on during years of civil conflict. During the socially crippling Troubles, Belfast's center was frequently reduced to a ghost town, but now the inner city is a social hotbed drawing thousands of revelers who come specifically for weekends of fun.

Yet, with so much "new" going on, you really don't have to look far to get a sense of Belfast's past. Betwixt the ultra-chichi nightclubs and extravagant new hotels, Belfast still has what must be the best selection of traditional pubs in the world. The city remains an architectural wonderland, with an exciting mix of elegant Old World structures—myriad churches, public and university buildings, Victorian redbrick townhouses, retired warehouses, and disused linen mills—jostling to become the next candidate for restoration. In West Belfast—ground zero for much of the Troubles—communities are hard at work rebuilding society through innovative projects that make this an exciting place to visit in its own right. And you'll still see ugly reminders of the past. Schools and playgrounds shrouded by ominously high fences—silent witnesses to inter-communal hatred—and fortified police stations.

In the whispered asides and darker corners, one senses the slightest glimmer of anxiety that the balance of peace is a nimble tightrope walk. And somehow that feeds into the sense of Belfast having a more vital personality—a reborn misfit filled with optimism, yet cautious of battle scars from a former life. Whether you're a city lover, culture vulture, or someone who's intrigued by history, don't discount Belfast. If ever there was a time to look beyond reputation, it's when considering a trip to this feisty little city.

DON'T LEAVE BELFAST WITHOUT . . .

PARTAKING OF THE *CRAIC* IN THE MOST ATMOSPHERIC PUBS IN THE WORLD Belfast's pub scene is arguably its finest tradition, kept alive by authentic hostelries where there's always excellent *craic*—good conversation—and, later at night, a live traditional music session.

LEARNING ABOUT THE ART OF PEACE   One of the most astonishing tours you can take is through West Belfast's Falls Road area, generally considered ground zero throughout the appalling years of the Troubles, now known for its many poignant murals. For an intimate encounter with this historic neighborhood, go on a 3-hour walking tour with a former IRA prisoner. See p. 378.

GOING TO MARKET   The liveliest Saturday mornings are at St. George's Market; shop with the locals for the freshest farm goods, and then chill to live music, performed free. See p. 386.

A BRIEF HISTORY OF BELFAST

Belfast is young; it only found its feet about 400 years ago when, during the Plantation of Ulster, a tiny village—inhabited by native Catholics—was given to an Englishman, Arthur Chichester. His son became the Earl of Donegall, and the strengthening status of this now aristocratic family was mirrored in the fortunes of the town. From humble beginnings as a collection of forts gathered around the mouth of the river Farset, Béal Feirste (the "sandy ford") built itself up on merchant trade, later adding manufacturing. During the Victorian-era, Belfast was the world leader in each of its major industries: linen (thanks to skilled French Huguenots settlers), rope-making, and shipbuilding. Queen Victoria granted Belfast city status in 1888, when it was the largest, most industrialized city in Ireland. It was a century when, riding high on a wave of imminent glories, the city fathers started building its great architectural landmarks—the University and City Hall. Then, in 1912, Belfast built the largest passenger liner ever, and just as disaster befell the *Titanic,* so too began the decline of the city.

Even during times of prosperity, conflict always existed between Catholics and Protestants. When six of Ulster's nine counties were left out of the agreement that created an independent Republic of Ireland free of British rule, Belfast found itself the capital of a new Northern Ireland, which politicians had determined to have a Protestant, and therefore pro-British, majority. For the Catholic minority, the fight had only just begun. Belfast, as the North's political and economic heart, was to see the worst of the conflict: an impossible riddle dubbed "the Troubles."

By 1969, the city was gripped by tension and urban conflict. For decades, emotions ran high, and bomb blasts, gunfire attacks, and many deaths painted a nasty, inhospitable image of Belfast and Northern Ireland. The violence committed by both Loyalists (Protestants who identify as British and want Northern Ireland to remain a part of the United Kingdom) and Republicans (Catholics who consider themselves Irish and want Northern Ireland to be absorbed into the Republic) tore society apart and the world's media portrayed a city at war.

Today, following the 1994 cease-fire agreement and many reconciliatory discussions, negotiations and turnabouts, Northern Ireland's government seems to have arrived at a compromise. In 2007, DUP leader Ian Paisley agreed to lead the government with Sinn Féin leader, Martin MacGuinness, as his deputy. The streets of Belfast carry an atmosphere of hope, maintained in no small measure by the vast quantities of cash being pumped into the city's rejuvenation. Ironically, its "Titanic Quarter" is the most visible sign of the city's newfound prosperity, where the largest waterfront development in Europe is under construction. By 2012, a century after the great ship went down, Belfast expects to be celebrating its comeback, not only with a new permanent *Titanic* exhibition at the water's edge, but a prosperous community living the high life in a once-derelict area that for decades was a physical embodiment of the city's decline.

LAY OF THE LAND

Concentrated around the head of a vast natural harbor, Belfast is hemmed in by hills keeping urban sprawl in check. At the height of its industrialization, the port and its docks were the lifeblood of the city, and the main commercial buildings are still clustered close to the channels where ships once docked. Those docklands are now the revitalized **Titanic Quarter.** The main part of the city, with nearly all principal areas of interest and most attractions, lodgings, restaurants, and nightlife, are west of the River Lagan. Immediately north of the city's heart (**City Hall**) is **Cathedral Quarter,** a formerly derelict area once known as Sailors Town. Now it's the city's cultural hub. Just west of the **Central Business District (CBD)** is Great Victoria Road which psychologically divides **West Belfast** from the traditionally more-prosperous center. West Belfast was the scene of much of the community violence that plagued the city during the period known as the Troubles; **the Falls**—centered on Falls Road—is a Republican neighborhood, and remains segregated from its Protestant, Unionist neighbor, **Shankill,** by a massive Peace Wall, designed to prevent inter-community attacks. Great Victoria Road runs south towards traditionally prosperous suburbs as well as feisty **Queen's Quarter,** home to Queen's University—the city's student hub and hotbed of social intercourse.

GETTING THERE

BY AIR

Belfast has two airports and is connected to destinations in Europe, North America, and other parts of the United Kingdom as well as the Republic of Ireland. You cannot fly to Belfast from Dublin, which is less than 2 hours away by car.

Most international flights arrive at **Belfast International Airport** (☎ 028/9448-4848; www.belfastairport.com), located at Aldergrove, 30.5km (19 miles) north of the city; it takes around 30 minutes to drive into town on the M2. Catch the frequent **Ulsterbus Airport Express** from right out in front of the terminal for just £6 (£9 round-trip) and you'll be delivered promptly to the Europa Buscentre in the city center. Tickets are available on the bus, or from the Airport Tourist Information Desk. A **taxi** into the city will cost around £25.

Just 5km (3 miles) north of Belfast's CBD is the newer, smaller **George Best Belfast City Airport** (☎ 028/9093-9093; www.belfastcityairport.com), the main hub for low-cost airlines, such as Ryannair and British Midlands, that service the region. The **Airport Express bus** (£1.30 one-way; £2.20 round-trip) provides regular city transfers. A **taxi** should cost £6.

BY LAND

As the commercial and political hub of Northern Ireland, Belfast has good public transport connections with the rest of country; you'll find that **bus** connections tend to be more extensive and far-reaching, while **trains** are better for travel from bigger hubs. For information about both bus and rail services, you can either call

☎ 028/9066-6630, or visit www.translink.co.uk. The **Enterprise** rail service runs between Dublin and Belfast eight times a day (five times on Sun), and takes around 2 hours (£25 one-way; £36 round-trip). Belfast also enjoys regular bus connections with Dublin; in conjunction with Bus Éireann, **Ulsterbus** operates the high-frequency Goldline Express Service, with around-the-clock hourly trips between Belfast's Europa Buscentre and Dublin's Busaras Bus Station (£11.10 one-way; £16.30 round-trip); the Express Coach service from Dublin Airport to Belfast also takes around 2 hours (£9.65 one-way; £14.10 round-trip).

BY SEA

You can cross the waters between Belfast and Liverpool in 8 hours with **Norfolkline** (Victoria Business Park, West Bank Rd., Belfast; ☎ 028/9077-9090; www.norfolkline-ferries.co.uk). If you book online, you'll pay £99 to £170 per car plus driver and up to two passengers (Easter, July, and Aug are most expensive, and night crossings are almost double the price). Telephone bookings and payments made at the departure terminal are more expensive. The journey between Belfast and Stranraer in Scotland lasts 90 minutes and costs £55 to £100 per car plus driver and £18 per passenger (Sat travel is pricier, as are the months of July and Aug); contact **Stena Line** (☎ 028/9074-7747; www.stenaline.com).

GETTING AROUND

You'll have little difficulty exploring the compact center **on foot.** In fact, traffic (and the struggle to find affordable parking) can be so infuriating that hoofing it will save time as well as money. Belfast has an excellent **bus** network, with all routes commencing at Donegall Square (bang in the center, around City Hall); a kiosk sells tickets and is well posted with timetables. Buses are an affordable and reliable way to get around; a Metro Day Ticket costs £3.50 and can be used anywhere, anytime on any city bus route (Mon–Sat), while a £2.50 version can be used after 10am and all-day Sunday. Along Falls Road, you can hail a special black **taxi** just about anywhere; these only go back and forth along Falls Road and work a bit like a miniature bus service (they're shared); for £1.10 per person you'll get dropped off anywhere along the Falls Road (terminating on the outskirts of the CBD) as long as your cab is headed in the right direction. For general taxi numbers, turn to p. 395.

ACCOMMODATIONS, BOTH STANDARD & NOT

Being so close to just about anywhere in Northern Ireland means that Belfast is a good base from which to explore the rest of the country; all the most popular attractions are easily accessible as day-trips from here, so consider staying here for city life buzz combined with the possibility of more competitive hotel rates (that's hotels only; outside Belfast better value is to be had in B&Bs and guesthouses).

SELF-CATERING HOUSES & APARTMENTS

Most of Belfast's rental options are geared towards business travelers who spend protracted periods in the city; they provide a more affordable option than the smart hotels, and more comfort and space than the budget hotels. Each will have a full-scale kitchen, another wallet pleaser as you won't be forced to eat out each night.

Where to Stay & Dine in Belfast

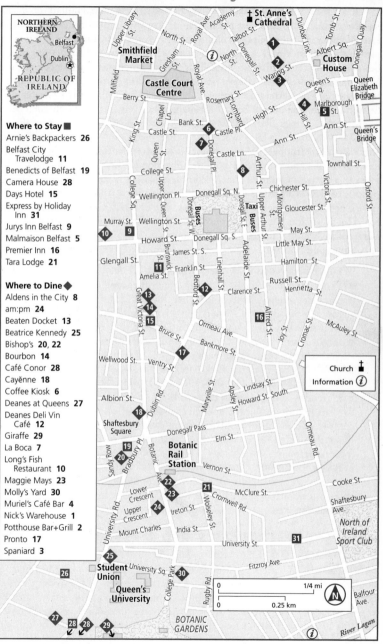

Where to Stay ■
Arnie's Backpackers **26**
Belfast City
  Travelodge **11**
Benedicts of Belfast **19**
Camera House **28**
Days Hotel **15**
Express by Holiday
  Inn **31**
Jurys Inn Belfast **9**
Malmaison Belfast **5**
Premier Inn **16**
Tara Lodge **21**

Where to Dine ◆
Aldens in the City **8**
am:pm **24**
Beaten Docket **13**
Beatrice Kennedy **25**
Bishop's **20, 22**
Bourbon **14**
Café Conor **28**
Cayenne **18**
Coffee Kiosk **6**
Deanes at Queens **27**
Deanes Deli Vin
  Café **12**
Giraffe **29**
La Boca **7**
Long's Fish
  Restaurant **10**
Maggie Mays **23**
Molly's Yard **30**
Muriel's Café Bar **4**
Nick's Warehouse **1**
Potthouse Bar+Grill **2**
Pronto **17**
Spaniard **3**

Of the local agencies, **Urban Holiday Rentals** (www.urbanholidayrentals.com), has the widest reach and best prices. Though only founded in mid-2008, it represents about 30 properties, including penthouses specifically suited to two people. Unlike most rental agencies, properties are priced per night, but you get better deals if you rent by the week. The current range starts with a one-bedroom Victorian apartment that sleeps two people for £80 per night, or £450 per week. Five-bedroom modern houses are available for £225 per night (or £995 per week).

Some good deals are to be had through private lets, sometimes hidden behind high-minded names like **7castles Luxury Self Catering** (☎ 0771/470-0018; www.7castles.co.uk), which is actually a three-bedroom semi-detached house in south Belfast. Although it's a 10-minute drive from the center, public transport is easily accessible, and this residential neighborhood is interesting in its own right. Having a house to yourself means complete privacy, and this pad has off-street parking as well as a garden area where you can throw a BBQ. The house sleeps up to five people, for which you pay a weekly rate of £475; shorter rentals are possible. The downside: There's just one bathroom, although there's a separate downstairs toilet. Still, it's an ideal base for families.

Other good options:

- **BT1Apartments.co.uk** ✯ (Margarita Plaza, 82 Adelaide St.; ☎ 028/4062-9215 or 0774/618-9220): Offering much the same aesthetic sophistication (fresh white linens, silky cushions, beechwood furnishings, and that ultra-in-vogue neo-baroque wall paper) as a luxury hotel suite but with the added convenience of your own kitchen, this apartment is right in the center of the action (a short walk from City Hall) and packed with modern appliances. It's a one-bedroom space designed for a couple, but including a sofa-bed, just in case. Nightly rates start at £79, £450 for a week.
- **Somerset Studios** ✯ (☎ 028/9022-6183; www.staybelfastcity.com): Loft-style trendy—a duplex with exposed brick and contemporary kitchens—this flat isn't luxurious, but includes all that you might need to make your stay as comfortable as possible (dishwashers, washing machines, DVD players). Rates start at £450 per week (but can reach up to £600) for this two-bedroom apartment. Shorter stays: £80 to £100 per night.
- **Staying in Belfast** (www.stayinginbelfast.co.uk): Two centrally located, chic, modern apartments, each with two double bedrooms. The more affordable option starts at just £395 per week (or £65 per night); it even has a small back garden area.

HOTELS, GUESTHOUSES & BED & BREAKFASTS

£ All Seasons ✯✯ (356 Lisburn Rd.; ☎ 028/9068-2814; www.allseasons belfast.com; MC, V), a homey little B&B—with eight bedrooms (£30 single; £50 double; £60 triple)—remains one of the city's finest values. The roomy, carpeted bedrooms are simply done out with pine furnishings, soft white sheets, and '80s-style duvets; any amenities that aren't in the rooms (like hair dryers and irons) are available on request. Brand new bedrooms on the top floor have rooftop views and powerful showers. Breakfast is a full-throttle Ulster fry. If you're traveling with children, the owner offers a self-catering semi-detached house ✯✯ right next door. For £80 to £100 per night (or £500–£600 per week), you get two bedrooms

A Room Is a Room Is a Room . . .

Catering to the almost endless influx of visitors who come to Belfast for special events, music concerts, business, and all kinds of nighttime fun, are several budget hotels right in and around the city center. You'll find extraordinarily good rates and—so typical of Belfast—friendly service, even if your bedroom feels a little boxy, carbon-copied, and very "standard." Here's a selection, starting with the cheapest:

- **Belfast City Travelodge** (15 Brunswick St.; ☎ 0870/191-1687; www. travelodge.co.uk): Room-only rates start at £59 per night. Within spitting distance of City Hall and Great Victoria Street.
- **Premier Inn** (Alfred St.; ☎ 0870/850-6316; www.premierinn.com): Weekend rates start at £65 per room, while Sunday to Thursday it's £70. Plus, family rooms are the same rate as doubles, so if your kids are under 16 you could score big time.
- **Express by Holiday Inn** (106a University St.; ☎ 028/9031-1909; www.exhi-belfast.com): Breakfast is included in the £65 you could pay for a double room, which features "budget-smart" decor. There's free parking, too.
- **Days Hotel** (40 Hope St.; ☎ 028/9024-2494; www.dayshotelbelfast. co.uk): The location looks seedy and rundown, but you step off the street into a lively lobby and leave all that behind. Rooms start at £75.

(one en suite) and a comfy fire-warmed sitting room with fully kitted kitchenette. Situated on Belfast's boutique shopping strip, All Seasons is a 10-minute bus trip to the city center, or just £3 by taxi.

£–££   Closer to the action (near the University Quarter) **Camera House** ✮✮ (44 Wellington Park; ☎ 028/9066-9026; www.cameraguesthouse.com; MC, V) was so-named because it was used by photographers who came to take pictures during the Troubles in the '60s and '70s. Young owners Bronagh and Peter took over and thoroughly refurbished it in early-2007, uncovering original architectural features throughout. The refurb wasn't just cosmetic; new showers were put in, crisp white sheets and duvets were introduced, and Wi-Fi was installed. Guests are treated to a full, all organic breakfast. All this sounds expensive, but en suite doubles cost £61, and if you're willing to share a bathroom, the price drops to £56. Three people in a family-size en suite room (the one on the second floor includes a fine view) pay just £78. Singles start at £34 (with shared bathroom), or £48 en suite.

££   Arriving at Olive and Roger Nicholson's **Ravenhill House** ✮✮✮ (690 Ravenhill Rd.; ☎ 028/9020-7444; www.ravenhillhouse.com; MC, V) you might just walk in on the aroma of baking soda bread. And it's that sensory reminder of being in a country home that always strikes me when I think of Ravenhill, a handsome Victorian house a little way out of the center, near vibrant Ormeau Road, a fun little enclave worth exploring in its own right. Built in 1886 by a wealthy distiller, the Nicholsons have taken care to retain the original character of the spaces. The upstairs bedrooms (£70–£80 double and £45–£55 single) have special, personal touches, like vintage "Roberts" radios; all have a relaxed, cozy, country ambience, though each is individually styled. Downstairs, the sitting room has a piano, an iMac for checking e-mail, and a collection of CDs and books. Incidentally, besides baking delicious breads, Roger also prepares award-winning breakfasts using locally sourced ingredients.

££–££££   Back in town, practically next door to the Grand Opera House, and a block away from City Hall, **Jurys Inn Belfast** ✸ (Fisherwick Place, Great Victoria St.; ☎ 028/9053-3500, 0870/410-0800 for reservations; www.jurysinns. com; MC, V) is part of an Irish budget chain specializing in comfortable-but-standard-looking rooms (bottom line: They're neat and clean, and the mattresses are top quality) sold at an ever-changing "rate of the day." This approach ensures that Jurys is always busy and buzzing. Business yuppies do deals over the breakfast buffet; tourist mobs gear up for bus rides through the city; and city slickers glam it up for evening cocktails in the popular bar—all making this one of the most bustling lodgings in town. As for rates, you might bag a room for as little as £69 (up to three adults sharing) though on other nights £120 might be more likely; it's a crap shoot.

££   A turn-of-the-century rectory in the University quarter has been restored, refurbished, and dutifully converted into a family home and, for 15 years now, also a B&B called, predictably, the **Old Rectory** ✸✸✸ (148 Malone Rd.; ☎ 028/9066-7882; www.anoldrectory.co.uk; cash only). It's one of my favorite lodgings, with a mix of six individual, well appointed bedrooms. If you value space, ask for the Malone room, downstairs—it's accessible for guests with disabilities and is more like a mini-suite, with flatscreen TV, a sofa, fridge, and a selection of magazines. Myrtlefield is another pretty option, with an old-fashioned tub. There's a thoughtfulness here, too; guests are spoiled with yummy welcome trays, and breakfasts are especially healthy—one of the owners is the executive chef at the Europa Hotel. Doubles are an excellent value at £75; singles cost £39 (private bathroom in the hall), or £49 (attached bathroom).

££   As much as **Benedicts of Belfast** ✸✸ (7–21 Bradbury Place, Shaftesbury Sq.; ☎ 028/9059-1999; www.benedictshotel.co.uk; AE, DC, MC, V) looks like a renovated historic property, everything was built from scratch just over a decade ago, mostly using French antique pieces, and—in the bar—even parts of an old Catholic church. It's an impressive forgery; the space feels like it belongs to another, more eccentric era—stone tile floors, chandeliers, a big fat pillar right in the middle of the lobby, and Van Morrison singing the blues in the background. Bedrooms are *très* luxe, with waist-high king-size beds and crisp linens; contemporary color schemes and eye-catching decor. A double or twin room costs £80, or you can lob on an extra £10 and upgrade to executive digs which are slightly bigger, have spa baths, and large flatscreen TVs. Singles are £70. The buzzy downstairs **restaurant** ✸✸ has a "Beat the Clock" special between 5:30 and 7pm;

depending on the dish you choose, you pay either £10 or the equivalent of the time you place your order (so if you order at 5:45pm, you pay £5.45). Yes, it's a crazy town. A warning: The bar is hugely popular and open till 2:30am, with live music Monday to Wednesday and DJs the rest of the week. If you'd rather not be near that kind of energy (and noise), you'd better go elsewhere, 'cause the late-night party sounds do travel.

£££ Rooms at the **Tara Lodge** ✪✪ (36 Cromwell Rd.; ☎ 028/9059-0900; www.taralodge.com; AE, DC, MC, V), a guesthouse-turned-hotel in the University district, have a luxe, contemporary feel (that contrasts mightily with the dull looking lobby and dining room). I'm talking plush, luxurious linens, flatscreen TVs plus DVD, and a completely overhauled modern bathroom with a tub-shower combo and toiletries in each of the £85 guest rooms. Some, however, are more spacious than others (try to snag corner unit 7; or one of the light-filled, view-happy rooms on the higher floors in the annex). Free Wi-Fi.

£££–££££ My favorite hotel in central Belfast is a social hotbed; at night the bar buzzes until the wee hours, while the restaurant pumps with the energy of up-and-coming Belfast. And the dirty little secret is that you can bag a plush, luxurious room at the **Malmaison Belfast** ✪✪✪ (34–38 Victoria St.; ☎ 028/9022-0200; www.malmaison.com; AE, MC, V) for an extraordinarily low rate if you plan properly and book online. While the standard rate for a room is £150 in mid-summer, when you go online, you're often able to score a promotional price of £95 (room only). Similarly, you should sign up for their electronic newsletter; I once received word of a £79 room only Easter deal. Occupying a pair of former seed warehouses, with one of the most distinctive facades in the city, Malmaison (part of a deluxe small hotel chain in the U.K.) is within walking distance to the city center. Decor emphasizes a sense of drama; the designers like to describe the bedrooms as "bordellos," with lots of sensual fabrics and seductive, decadent colors. All this and they're well kitted out with excellent mattresses, CD players, powerful showers, and oversized toiletries that'll last you the rest of your holiday.

HOSTELS & UNIVERSITY ROOMS

£ In the heart of the University district, but far away from the booze-inspired pandemonium that erupts there, **Arnie's Backpackers** ✪ (63 Fitzwilliam St.; ☎ 028/9024-2867; www.arniesbackpackers.co.uk; cash only) is the most inviting of Belfast's five centrally located hostels. You'll not only receive a warm welcome, but a homey, relaxed environment. The budget travelers who stay here are quieter than you find at most hostels (that may be because it's a small place with only 22 beds). Besides the comfortable lounge (with a book collection, board games, and place to stretch out), there's a small kitchen and laundry room. The only drawback tends to be spatial: Because the hostel is really a converted Victorian townhouse, it can be a slightly tight squeeze in the dorms and there's sometimes a bit of a queue for the shower.

£ A useful alternative to hostel digs—but only if you're on your lonesome—is a private room in **Queen's University's Elms Village** (78 Malone Rd.; ☎ 028/9097-4525; www.qub.ac.uk/sacc; MC, V) where, when I visited, en suite singles cost just £38, with breakfast, unlimited Internet, and privacy. The major drawback is that they're only available during the university's summer break which runs from mid-June until the end of July. If you want to book, you need to write to Jane O'Loughlin (accommodation@qub.ac.uk) and provide you name, phone number, e-mail address, and the dates you require.

DINING FOR ALL TASTES

While Belfast's top-notch restaurants have prices that will have you breaking into a sweat, the city has plenty of pubs, cafes, delis, and sandwich bars where you can affordably take care of those hunger pangs. There's also no need to always dine in; plenty of eateries offer cheaper deals on take-out meals, and there's absolutely nothing wrong with popping into one of the many local supermarkets and grabbing a pre-packaged sandwich for a picnic in one of Belfast's lovely parks or lawns. Many pubs across the city also serve affordable, sometimes very tasty meals, so see the "Nightlife," section on p. 386 for a few of the best.

THE CITY CENTER & ALONG GREAT VICTORIA STREET

£–££   Deli by day, popular little wine bar by night, **Deanes Deli Vin Café** ✪✪ (44 Bedford St.; ☎ 028/9024-8830; www.michaeldeane.co.uk; Mon–Tues noon–3pm and 5–9pm; Wed–Fri noon–3pm and 5–10pm; Sat noon–10pm; AE, MC, V) has a yuppy pedigree, but is nevertheless an unpretentious place for light meals—soups, salads, and delicious, health-conscious made-to-order sandwiches (choose from the chalked up options, preferably one doused in their exquisite chili aubergine chutney). On the beverage side are smoothies, special teas, or even a glass (or bottle) of wine. A sandwich here will cost £4.50 to £5.25, and comes with french fries. Place your order at the counter, and it'll be brought to your table by handsome waiters.

£–££   While there's a pretty down-to-earth pub downstairs, upstairs at the **Beaten Docket** (48 Great Victoria St.; ☎ 028/9024-2986; daily 11:30am–8:30pm; MC, V), has the ambience of a 1950s gentlemen's club—all earthy tones and stylish wood flooring. The food is just as testosterone laden: homemade steak stew (£4.75, or under £3 between noon and 2pm); steak and Guinness pie (£7); a big, fat "Bookmakers Sandwich" (sirloin steak on ciabatta, with your choice of

---

Pit Stop

Catering to office workers and anyone between the University area and the city center, **Pronto** ✪ (32–36 Venture Gate, Dublin Rd,; ☎ 028/9027-8969; Mon–Sat 7:30am–sundown; cash only) is a gem of a takeaway joint, with excellent coffee, top-quality hand-cut sandwiches, paninis, wraps, and light, hot meals, like lasagna, vegetable quiche, and Texan beef chili. Nothing costs more than £4, and most sandwiches—filled with interesting ingredients (like pastrami, brie, rocket, and red currant jelly; or sausage and Irish cheddar)—are under £3.

Caffeine Break

Where Donegall Place and Castle Place meet, you can't miss the **Coffee Kiosk** ✪✪, a bright red booth just big enough for two baristas and an espresso machine. For my money, these chaps make the best (and definitely the cheapest) coffee in town; £1.50 for a double espressos, or coffee and a sandwich for £3.75. And while you're sipping from your paper cup, take in some of Belfast's most underrated architecture—in one of the oldest areas in the city.

---

sauce; £9); and that northern Irish specialty, sausage and champ (mash with a thick gravy), for £6.45. Admittedly, it's not nouvelle cuisine, but grab a plush alcove seat at the window, admire the sumptuous architecture, and you probably won't give a damn. A "beaten docket," in case you were wondering, is a losing ticket in horse racing—and probably many of the customers watching the races on the telly here have one of those in their pockets.

£-££££   Baby sibling to long-established Aldens, just outside the city, **Aldens in the City** ✪✪ (12-14 Callender St.; ☎ 028/9024-5385; www.aldensinthecity.com; Mon–Wed 8am–5:30pm; Thurs 8am–6pm; Fri 9:30am–6pm; MC, V) feels flash and modern with its lime green accents gleaming through its large glass frontage. But it's really only part restaurant and part deli; take your pick of gourmet sandwiches (£4–£7), hearty soups (£3–£6), or opt for the more complex (and pricey) fare for which Aldens is renowned. It's very popular with local office workers—always a good sign.

££-££££   **Bourbon** ✪✪ (60 Great Victoria St.; ☎ 028/9033-2121; www.bourbon restaurant.com; Mon–Fri noon–2:30pm; Mon–Thurs 5–10pm, Fri–Sat 5–11pm; MC, V), justifies it's over-the-top design by imagining itself in another time and place, specifically New Orleans. Dramatic decor takes its cue from the nearby Grand Opera House, and while some might find the busy mix of baroque and bohemia—palm trees, statues, chandeliers, and detailed plasterwork—way too much, if you take it all in the spirit in which it comes, you'll probably have a great deal of fun. Menu choices are wide-ranging, many of them traditional Irish dishes with subtle Cajun and Polynesian influences thrown in by head chef, Billy Burns. As always, prices across the board drop considerably at lunch (mains £7.50–£13). Arrive between 5 and 6:45pm, and you can partake of the pre-theater special deal: £13 for a starter plus one of the simpler mains.

££-££££   **Cayènne** ✪✪✪ (Shaftesbury Sq., Great Victoria St.; ☎ 028/9033-1532; Tues–Fri noon–2:30pm; Mon–Thurs 5–10pm; Fri 5–11pm; Sat 6–11pm; Sun 5–9pm; AE, DC, MC, V) is the brainchild of the city's first celebrity chef couple, Paul and Jeanne Rankin. It's not only a haven of cool, with its art-gallery looks, but the menu offers exciting variety, as the chefs cleverly infuse traditional, local ingredients with foreign—mostly Asian and even north African—spices and techniques.

Quirky dishes include wok tea smoked salmon (£16), and white miso broth with scallops, foie gras, and enoki mushrooms (£5.75). I'm a huge fan of the five spice glazed free range pigeon (£17), one of the tastiest dishes in town, served with sweet corn and scallion pancakes. For those on a budget (and who isn't?), there are specially priced menus (like a two-course set lunch for £12). Perhaps it's fair to say that while some of the city's other hot restaurants also offer exquisite dining, Cayënne has fairer pricing. Yes, it's a splurge to dine here, but not necessarily a damaging one.

CATHEDRAL QUARTER

£–££   The **Spaniard** ✯✯ (3 Skipper St.; ☎ 028/9023-2448; www.thespaniard bar.com; food served Sun–Wed noon–6pm; Thurs–Sat noon–8pm; MC, V), a cramped and crammed-with-atmosphere pub, won the "Oscar" for the top pub in Northern Ireland in 2007. It looks and feels a bit like the miniature museum that might have exploded out of Salvador Dali's imagination—were he a fan of retro-pop-disco . . . or something like that. Nevertheless, the grub is hugely satisfying, from big bowls of hearty soup (£4), to ciabattas filled with either chargrilled steak or chicken, bacon, cheese, and red chili jam, and topped off with chips and salad for £7. They're not afraid to spice things up, either, so beware when you order anything with chili. And, after your meal, you can slip into one of the sofas in the room at the back and browse the small library kept here. Bill Murray dined here every day while he was in town shooting *City of Ember.*

£–££   The creative minds behind the Spaniard are also responsible for **Muriel's Café Bar** ✯✯ (12 Church Ln.; ☎ 028/9033-2445; Mon–Fri 8:30am–1am; Sat 10am–1pm; Sun 10am–midnight; MC, V). It occupies the premises of what was previously the smallest pub in Northern Ireland, but now it's been expanded, and the downstairs pub is dressed to look like an old world hat shop. You can grab one of the outdoor tables (prime people-watching terrain), head to the hat-filled bar area, or recline in comfortable sofas in the little neo-baroque lounge above; at night a DJ spins mellow tunes. Breakfast is served until mid-morning, after which you can choose from the selection in the deli cabinet alongside the bar, or dip into the day's small menu for combinations that you wouldn't have dreamed possible: a salad of chorizo, roast cherry tomatoes, and watermelon, served on toasted bread with arugula and salsa verde (£6); or salt and pepper chicken with chimichurri sauce, served on sourdough bread (£5). After 8pm, the assortment of very sexy-looking meat and cheese platters (£8) go perfectly with wine.

££–££££   Belfast's first Argentine-style eatery, **La Boca** ✯✯ (6 Fountain St.; ☎ 028/9032-3087; www.labocabelfast.com; Mon–Wed 9am–7pm; Thurs–Fri 9am–10pm; Sat 10am–10pm; MC, V) is the brainchild of Pedro Nesbitt, born in Argentina while his Belfast parents were there working. By day the high ceilings and massive windows ensure that the venue is bright and airy, while at night it's all sexy, Latin cafe (Fri features live music and tango). It's a fabulous change from pub dining; specialties include the Gaucho steak sandwich with jalapeño mayo and chimichurri (£7.25); *choripan* (a Buenos Aires street vendor meal of chorizo sausage with chimichurri in bread, £6.75); and slow roast pork belly with chorizo and white bean locro (£13); and that Argentinean staple—*bife*—either rib-eye

(£15) or sirloin (£16), with chimichurri, served with frites. A platter of 5 different *tapas* selections is £10—perfect for sharing; or get 3 *tapas* and a bottle of wine for £15.

££–£££   Industrial posh is the look designers were after when thinking up the chunky concrete communal tables at the **Potthouse Bar+Grill** (1 Hill St.; ☎ 028/9024-4044; www.potthouse.co.uk; dining Mon–Sat noon–9pm; Sun 2–9pm; MC, V). I think the clientele's good looks outdo the decor, so this tends to be a place I come to schmooze and watch the social drama unfold. Oh, and also for the dining specials. Sunday to Thursday you pay £25 for two people choosing any starter (or salad) and just about any main dish, plus a bottle of house wine. Fresh ingredients are important here, so the menu changes regularly, but I last enjoyed a Potthouse salad (it has slices of black pudding thrown in for that Belfast twist) and some tasty venison sausages, with creamy mash.

££–££££   What was once a bonded whiskey warehouse in the dodgy part of town (yes, where the sailors hung out) has been **Nick's Warehouse** ✩✩✩ (35 Hill St.; ☎ 028/9043-9690; www.nickswarehouse.co.uk; Mon 10am–5pm; Tues–Fri 10am–10pm; Sat 6–10pm; reservations advisable for restaurant; AE, DC, MC, V) since 1989. This was Belfast's first wine bar, and the venue that breathed life into the derelict and forsaken area now proudly labeled Cathedral Quarter. Nick Price remains esteemed in the Belfast culinary scene, not least because of what he's done to grow the concept of "Modern Irish" cuisine. An open-mindedness about dining possibilities means that at lunchtime you can get hearty casseroles and stews—or meatloaf with melted Reblochon cheese and homemade ketchup—in the downstairs informal Anix, where all lunch mains are under £8, or you can head upstairs to the slightly formal restaurant to enjoy a two-course meal for £17. It's the type of carefully thought-out cuisine that creatively bridges that often too-wide divide between simple and fancy. Sadly, at dinner prices inch up.

QUEEN'S QUARTER

As anyone knows, where there are students in abundance, there's bound to be an endless supply of cheap eating possibilities, not to mention many late-night re-fueling spots. Queen's Quarter is no exception, so if you're fumbling around looking for a quick bite, this is where the action is.

You'll have no problem spotting the many large-size adverts for special deals that sound too good to be true (loud posters everywhere proclaim "two-for-one lunch" and "meal and a pint for £5"). Some of these offers will be posted outside respectable eateries like **Molly's Yard** (1 College Green Mews, Botanic Ave.; ☎ 028/9032-2600; Mon–Sat noon–9:30pm; MC, V), where a two-course meal costs £20. Then there's the contemporary-styled **am:pm** (67–69 Botanic Ave.; ☎ 028/9023-9443; www.ampmbelfast.com; Mon–Thurs noon–11pm; Fri noon–midnight; Sat noon–1am; Sun noon–10pm; MC, V), which has two eclectic menus (at lunchtime there is a wider selection of lighter items)—from sandwiches (£4.25–£8), pizzas (£7.25–£9), and pastas (£6.95–£11) to grills (£10–£20)—but offers a "Beat-the-Clock" menu (where the time you order is the price you pay) on weekdays between 5 and 7pm. For all-day dining, **Giraffe** (54–56 Stranmillis Rd.; ☎ 028/9050-9820; daily 8am–late; MC, V) is a popular cafe-restaurant in the

Classic Fish 'n' Chips

Long's Fish Restaurant ✭ (39 Athol St.; ☎ 028/9032-1848; Mon–Fri 11:45am–6:30pm; Sat noon–6pm; cash only) is the oldest fish shop in town and despite the Formica and paneled wood decor, still draws a loyal clientele that stretches from penny-pinching students to high-end millionaires who know about a great investment. Even after almost a century, there's nothing here over £4.50.

If it's a late-night take-out you're after, Long's modern competitor, **Bishop's,** looks positively up-market by comparison, and has evolved into a chain that caters especially to those who've been on the town (and who might not care too much if the food arrives cold). It, too, serves fish and chips (up to £6), as well as chips with burgers (under £5) and similarly hunger-busting fare. There are three outlets: 30 Bradbury Place (☎ 028/9043-9070; Thurs–Sat 10am–3am; Sun 10am–1am; Mon–Wed 10am–2am; cash only); 48 Botanic Ave. (☎ 028/9023-7787; Sun–Wed noon–11pm; Thurs–Sat noon–2am); and 137 Stranmillis Rd. (☎ 028/9038-1234; daily 11:30am–11pm).

lively Stranmillis area. Breakfasts are particularly popular (triple-stack pancakes, £3; panini filled with bacon, sausage, and cheese, £5), and meals are available to takeaway, too.

£–££   For the ultimate in all-day dining, there's no beating the cheeky, diner-style **Maggie Mays** ✭✭ (50 Botanic Ave.; ☎ 028/9032-2662; Mon–Sat 7:45am–11:15pm; Sun 10am–11:15pm; cash only), where you'll see loads of locals taking the edge off last night's boozing. Order at the counter and then wait at your wood-bench booth; although there's a menu, don't miss the chalked up deals on the wall. Meals are simple, but filling and satisfying: big bowls of hearty beef steak stew for £4; sandwiches from £3; and homemade burgers served on a floury bap (a large, flat bread roll) with various toppings and hand-cut chips on the side (£5.50). Nothing on the menu is more than £7, and there's a cool BYO policy (for beer and wine), with a £1.50 corkage fee; or order tea for a pound!

£–££££   Across the road from the Botanic Gardens, the one-time studio of local painter William Conor has been converted into a pleasant daytime eatery with brightly painted canvases on walls beneath a large overhead skylight. **Café Conor** ✭ (11a Stranmillis Rd.; ☎ 028/9066-3266; www.cafeconor.com; daily 9am–11pm; MC, V) is busy all day thanks to a mixed line-up of dishes, including some traditional Irish favorites. Breakfasts (until noon weekdays and until 3pm weekends) include waffles with bacon and maple syrup (£4) or a traditional Ulster fry (small £4, large £5.75). Later in the day, the menu offers everything from homemade soup of the day (£4.75), to Cajun chicken (£10), to old school fish and chips and mushy peas (£9.75). If you want something typically Irish, done with a dash of flair, try Conor's sausages—made with pork, apple, and cider, and then drizzled

Eating in the West

Few visitors to Belfast—even those who are most keen to discover more about the history of the Troubles along Falls Road—ever bother to eat or drink in West Belfast. It's a shame, really, since eating locally is a great way to hang with a crowd you might never otherwise have gotten to know. And you'll find more affordable meals, too.

While there are a couple of favorite eateries in West Belfast, the one I prefer is family-run **Temple** ✫✫ (kids) (62 Andersonstown Rd.; ☎ 028/9020-2060; Mon–Thurs 5pm–late; Fri–Sun 11am–late; MC, V). A real neighborhood restaurant, you'll often see large Catholic families out together, either in the middle of some celebration, or perhaps having just visited nearby Milltown Cemetery. In many ways, the interior is a bit of a surprise in working class Andersonstown—it's almost stylish with wood floors, exposed brick walls, and cottage-style tables and chairs. A well-priced wine list (with South African whites and reds for £9) complements a menu filled with traditional Irish dishes, where the emphasis is on wholesome, filling, good-value food. While there are some choices for vegetarians, meat is emphasized: grilled pork and leek sausages (£8); honey and thyme pork chops (£8.45); roast rib-eye (£8.45); prime Irish beef (£8). A two-course set menu costs £12, and three courses is £15. It's a good idea to reserve on weekends when there's a separate breakfast and lunch menu, too.

with a sauce of Irish whiskey cream and crushed peppercorns—served with champ (mashed potato) and market-sourced greens (£9.25).

££–££££   The latest fine-looking establishment in celebrity restaurateur Michael Deane's little empire is just across the road from Queen's University and so is named **Deanes at Queens** ✫✫✫ (1 College Gardens; ☎ 028/9038-2111; www.michaeldeane.co.uk; Mon–Sat 11:30am–5pm; Mon–Tues 5:30–9pm; Wed–Sat 5:30–10pm; AE, MC, V). Like all of Deane's outlets it excels at simple food done to within an inch of perfection. Most of what's on his lunchtime menu (including homemade burgers, beef sausages, and pastas) is priced around £7 and includes some more interesting items—like potted smoked eel on crostini and cress (£6.50); or fish pie with flaky pastry (£10). Specials run through the late afternoon (3–5pm), and dinner includes a few slightly pricier items. A service charge of 10% is added to your bill.

££–££££   Candles, starched white napkins, and glistening wine glasses suggest that chic, intimate little **Beatrice Kennedy** ✫✫ (44 University Rd.; ☎ 028/9020-2290; www.beatricekennedy.co.uk; Tues–Sat 5–10:15pm; Sun 12:30–2:30pm and 5–8:15pm; MC, V) might have some heart-stopping prices. Which it does—evening mains range from £16 to £18. But, if you're looking for that one-off romantic dinner, that needn't put you off. Owner and chef Jim McCarthy has developed an express menu for those of us with lighter wallets. Between 5 and

7pm you can get a two-course meal for just £13. Jim is known for his fish and game dishes, and there are usually a number of seafood options among both starters and main courses.

WHY YOU'RE HERE: TOP SIGHTS & ATTRACTIONS

BELFAST CITY CENTER: CITY HALL & ITS NEIGHBORS

A logical starting point for any exploration of Belfast is the Edwardian **City Hall** ✪✪✪, which really does feel as though it's at the heart of the city; an utterly over-the-top nod to imperial whimsy, novelist E.M. Forster called it "a costly Renaissance pile, which shouts 'Dublin can't beat me' from all its pediments and domes." Completed in 1906, it was here, in 1912, that the Solemn League and Covenant, protesting against the Home Rule Bill, was signed; legend recalls that one signatory, Rev. Henry Montgomery, signed in his own blood. It's easy to get lost in the macro-spectacle of the architecture, but try to look out for some of the symbolism buried in the sculptural effects; see, for example, if you can work out what the three figures at Queen Victoria's feet are meant to represent.

At the time of writing, the City Hall is closed to the public for renovation; it should be making its comeback in 2010. In the meanwhile, you'll have to make do with admiring the flashy exterior, perhaps from the **Belfast Wheel** ✪✪ (☎ 028/9031-0607; £6.50; Sun–Thurs 10am–9pm, Fri–Sat 10am–10pm), a long-term temporary attraction similar to the London Eye. This gargantuan 365-ton Ferris wheel allows riders to reach the highest point in the city—even if only for a few brief seconds as your gondola climbs 60m (197 ft.) above the ground at the summit of its revolution. Each ride lasts three rotations, includes recorded commentary and takes around 12 to 14 minutes.

Facing City Hall from the corner on Donegall Square West, is the beautiful turn-of-the-century **Scottish Provident Building** ✪✪ worth admiring for the detailed paneling on the facade; you'll see sphinxes, dolphins, lions' heads, and 17 images of the queen in different guises. At the center of all this, look for representations of the activities that made Belfast great: weaving, printing, ropemaking, and shipbuilding. Across the road, spare a few moments for the **Linen Hall Library** ✪ (17 Donegall Sq. North; ☎ 028/9032-1707; www.linenhall.com; Mon–Fri 9:30am–5:30pm; Sat 9:30am–1pm), Belfast's oldest repository of books, founded in 1788 and now occupying a former linen warehouse. Free weekly tours take place on Wednesdays at 11:30am (book in advance to secure a place), but you'll enjoy it even on your own.

Near City Hall, **Victoria Square** (www.victoriasquare.com) is the newly opened (Mar 2008) shopping center that has had the whole city talking. Covering 14 acres (5⅔ hectares) of ground space, the idiosyncratic building has really opened up the city center, extending Royal Avenue and Donegall Place right down to the edge of the burgeoning Titanic Quarter. Its futuristic design, with 4 levels encapsulated by an iconic glass dome, tries hard to bring the outside indoors, with large glass wing ceilings that work as skylights. Beneath the dome, a convoluted system of escalators, elevators, and a dizzying corkscrew-spiral staircase leads up to an observation deck with **wraparound views** ✪✪✪ over the top of the city; grab a free ticket for entry from the ground floor customer services

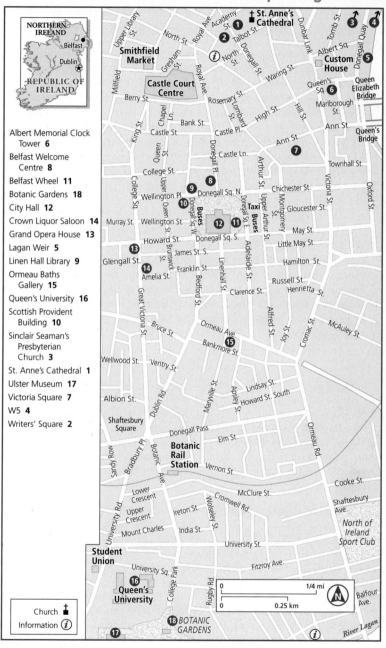

NORTHERN
IRELAND
Belfast
Dublin
REPUBLIC OF
IRELAND

Albert Memorial Clock
Tower **6**

Belfast Welcome
Centre **8**

Belfast Wheel **11**

Botanic Gardens **18**

City Hall **12**

Crown Liquor Saloon **14**

Grand Opera House **13**

Lagan Weir **5**

Linen Hall Library **9**

Ormeau Baths
Gallery **15**

Queen's University **16**

Scottish Provident
Building **10**

Sinclair Seaman's
Presbyterian
Church **3**

St. Anne's Cathedral **1**

Ulster Museum **17**

Victoria Square **7**

W5 **4**

Writers' Square **2**

Church ✝
Information ⓘ

Taking It All in with a Cabbie

A popular way of seeing Belfast (and far more personal than using one of the many bus tours) is to go on a **Black Taxi Tour** ✸✸✸, of which there are now several versions, all covering more or less the same ground. You'll be driven around in one of Belfast's famous cabs by a feisty local lad who'll talk you through his understanding and interpretation of the historical context of what you're seeing along the way. Typically, the tour won't be all serious, since these chaps are known for their stand-out wit. You'll get a fairly broad coverage of the city's most popular sights, from City Hall to the Albert Memorial Clock Tower to the *Titanic* dockside area, and—probably most importantly—a view of the famed political murals in the Falls and Shankill areas, as well as seeing the Peace Wall and the infamous Crumlin Road Jail and Courthouse.

Tours like these don't come cheap; it's around £25 for up to three people, and £8 per additional passenger. Most tours last between 1 and 1½ hours. One of the top tours is offered by Walter of **Experience Black Taxi Tours of Belfast** (☎ 077/2106-7752). The tours are far more useful (if pricier) than the walking tours, which only get to the main attractions in the center (which you can do on your own and with this book). Reserve through **Belfast Welcome Centre** (47 Donegall Place; ☎ 028/9024-6609; www.gotobelfast.com).

desk. Don't panic if you feel the floor move under you when you're up there—it sways 8mm off center.

On the southern fringe of the city center, the **Ormeau Baths Gallery** ✸✸ (18a Ormeau Ave.; ☎ 028/9032-1402; www.ormeaubaths.co.uk; free admission; Tues–Sat 10am–5:30pm) occupies a decidedly unusual-looking building; in the days before private bathrooms, this was the public wash house. Now the space is kept free of water and is used for important exhibitions often showcasing Irish artists and photographers.

CATHEDRAL QUARTER

Not too many years ago, nobody wanted much to do with the inner city area around St. Anne's Cathedral. Then the artists and entrepreneurs moved in, and now there's so much going on here that you can't move two steps without seeing something that's provocative, entertaining, or worth putting into your belly.

A stone from each of Ireland's 32 counties was used in the construction of **St. Anne's Cathedral** ✸ (Donegall St.; ☎ 028/9032-8332; www.belfastcathedral.com; free admission, £2 donation expected; daily 10am–4pm), the area's architectural centerpiece. Although the decision to build a cathedral came when Queen Victoria granted Belfast its city status, it was only completed in 1981. As you enter, you'll find a floor made of Irish marble, cleverly designed as a kind of symbolic maze: Follow the black path (of sin) and you'll come to a dead end, but the white path leads to the sanctuary. The pillars down the nave are crowned with capitals representing different aspects of Belfast life (from womanhood to ship-building). In more recent times the cathedral's gone postmodern with the addition of a gigantic heavenwards-pointing steel spike—the "Spire of Hope"—that looks like it's about to launch out of the church building. A 53-m (175-ft.) sculpture in brush-finished steel, the spike—lit up to good effect at night—is even more impressive when you enter the church and witness how the spike actually plunges down into the building, penetrating the austere space. Across the road from the cathedral is **Writers' Square,** basically an open air tribute to the literary figures who have been associated with the city.

Near Belfast's docklands, and built on land reclaimed from the sea, it's little wonder that **Albert Memorial Clock Tower** ✯✯ now leans 1.25m (4 ft.) off the vertical. Standing 35m (113 ft.) tall, it looks like Belfast's very own Leaning Tower, an imposing landmark at the bottom end of High Street, which connects the quayside areas with the city center. All along High Street, narrow side streets, known as "entries," give on to some of the most atmospheric nooks and crannies of the city, not to mention some of the oldest and best-loved pubs.

GREAT VICTORIA STREET & THE GOLDEN MILE

The **Crown Liquor Saloon** ✯✯✯ (46 Great Victoria St.; ☎ 028/9027-9901; www.nationaltrust.org.uk; Mon–Sat 11:30am–11pm; Sun 12:30–10pm) is perhaps the only drinking hole owned by a national heritage preservation agency (the National Trust mercifully doesn't charge entry here). Built between 1839 and 1840, the ornate tile and glass detailing of the interior is as spellbinding as the glittering mosaic exterior might lead you to believe—it's a striking example (and one of the few in existence) of a High Victorian saloon, and still lit by gas. It is so opulently decorated, with embossed ceilings, engraved glasswork, and beautiful Italian tiles that it's easy for the first-timer to forget about ordering a drink. Take a peek at the private snugs (booths), decorated with lions and gryphons, where patrons once only had to push a button to be served.

Across the street is the **Grand Opera House** ✯✯ (Great Victoria St.; ☎ 028/9024-1919; www.goh.co.uk; tours £5; Wed–Sat 11am–noon) has been a subject of some debate among architectural purists. In recent years, the original 1894 opera building—designed by Frank Matcham, considered the leading theater designer of his generation—has acquired a modernist wing, which parasitically sticks out of the daintier pastel-painted, plasterwork-enriched, twin-domed Victorian original. The addition follows major expansion in the years following two bomb blasts. If you don't get the chance to catch a performance (remember to check out the ceiling's swirling angel fresco), then at least try for one of the tours.

QUEEN'S QUARTER, THE UNIVERSITY & BEYOND

When Samuel Beckett taught in Belfast, he famously referred to his students as "rich and thick." But you've got to take your hats off to them for choosing to study at such a beautiful campus. Designed by the preeminent Charles Lanyon (whose buildings are everywhere in Belfast), the main building of **Queen's University** ✯✯ (University Rd.; www.qub.ac.uk; free admission) was completed in 1849 and built in a loving synthesis of soft red brick and sandstone. Referred to as the Lanyon Building, it borrows from the Gothic and Tudor character of the great medieval universities. Feel free to poke around; the **Queen's Visitor Centre** (on the left, past the main University entrance; ☎ 028/9033-5252; Oct–Apr Mon–Fri 10am–4pm; May–Sept Mon–Sat 10am–4pm) doubles as a tourism point. It's also where you can pick up a map of the University, which you can use to explore its many interesting buildings, like Elmwood Hall ✪✪ across the road, and the Union Theological College ✪ around the corner.

Just south of Queen's University, is the enchanting **Botanic Gardens** ✪✪ (Stranmillis Rd.; ☎ 028/9032-4902; free admission; sunrise–sunset) which is as much a hub of Belfast sociability as it was in the heady days of industrial prosperity when it drew multitudes of Victorian strollers. Nowadays, when the sun makes an appearance, it seems as if every student is out on the grass tossing a Frisbee. The star attraction here is probably the **Palm House** (Apr–Aug Mon–Fri 10am–5pm; Sat–Sun 1–5pm; Sept–Mar Mon–Fri 10am–4pm; Sat–Sun 2–4pm), another Lanyon project, this time a massive sweat lodge for plants, built of glass and iron.

Also on the ground of the Botanic Gardens, is the **Ulster Museum** (Stranmillis Rd.; ☎ 028/9038-3000; www.ulstermuseum.org.uk) which is shut at this writing but due to reopen, after massive renovations, sometime in 2009. As the name implies, the museum houses a studied collection of objects, artworks, and artifacts (some curious, some banal) connected with the history of the northern part of Ireland, or the province known as Ulster.

WEST BELFAST & THE GAELTACHT QUARTER

Falls Road gives its name to the area known the world over as the Falls. The part of the city most strongly associated with the Troubles, it's lodged in popular memory as the headquarters of Republicanism and of the IRA. Here you'll see murals honoring those who died, and those who went on hunger strikes in prolonged prison protests. Today, many of the activities and events that happen in this emerging Gaeltacht Quarter (an area committed to fostering Irish culture and language) are deliberately aimed at encouraging renewal in the face of the years of social disenfranchisement. It's not necessarily a pretty neighborhood, with stark reminders of violent conflict and poverty, but it's an important one for visitors to experience. And those seeking visual beauty should know that it backs right onto urban parkland, the **Bog Meadows** wetland reserve, and the **Belfast Hills** countryside, centered on Divis and the Black Mountain where you can escape for fresh air walks with spectacular views over the city.

> ❝ Are ye a Catholic or a Protestant?" "God knows I'm an atheist." "Sure, but are you a Catholic or a Protestant atheist? ❞
>
> —Long-standing Belfast joke

By far, the most engaging way in which to see the Falls is on a **political walking tour** ✪✪✪ (£8; Mon–Sat 11am; Sun 2pm) organized by the West Belfast community initiative **Coisté** (10 Beechmount Ave.; ☎ 028/9020-0770; www.coiste.ie), and led by ex-IRA prisoners who, having served time for their political struggle, are now pro-actively reaching out to the outside world. Not only do these men—who have such remarkable stories to tell—take visitors on stupendously eye-opening walks through the Falls Road area, but they are also involved in inter-community projects designed to literally cross the Peace Walls and hopefully bring Republicans and Loyalists together. I took one of these walks with Seamus Kelly who trains up the "tour guides"—only, he's not just a training coordinator, but a man who spent ten years in prison for his IRA activities. No matter what your feelings about freedom fighters, terrorist or paramilitaries, I must tell you that this turned out to be one of the most enlightening, entertaining, and heartfelt experiences I've ever had while visiting a city. Some of what I learned cut so close to the emotional bone, went so deep under the skin, and came from a place so personal, that I felt like I'd known Seamus all my life.

A typical tour lasts 3 hours, and covers the history-saturated stretch from **Divis Tower** (an unsightly low-income block where, until 2005, the top 2 floors were used by the British Army for surveillance of the local community), and all the way to **Milltown Cemetery.** Along the way, you gain an insider's perspective on the political murals starting with those that cover the **International Peace Wall.** Your guide will point out bullet holes, and present you with a riveting historical account in a narrative that's as thrilling as it is heartbreaking.

If you want a slightly more balanced tour, Coisté can arrange for one that takes in part of the Falls, and then, in conjunction with Loyalist guides, explores **Shankill Road** in a similar manner. While you can explore West Belfast on your own, you'll get far more out of the experience with the intimate local knowledge and personal understanding that one of these guides brings to the experience.

Beyond Milltown Cemetery, where Falls Road splits in two, you can either take a black cab shared taxi back to the city (make sure it's going in the right direction), or continue on (preferably with a cab, since it's one heck of a long distance through pretty unattractive neighborhoods) to **Colin Glen Forest Park,** for a scenic ramble.

NORTH BELFAST & THE SHANKILL

Belfast's **Shankill Road** area is synonymous with so-called Orange culture. Like the Catholic Falls area, Shankill is a nucleus of Protestant Unionism, and is where you'll see many of the remnants of the Troubles, such as fence-protected buildings, as well as pro-Unionist and strongly paramilitary murals. One of the dominant features is the massive **Peace Wall** that divides Shankill from the Falls, a stark and spine-chilling reminder of the hatred that drove neighbors to persecute and kill one another. As you explore Shankill Road, be sure to dip down some of the side-streets where you'll find residential enclaves and many more murals.

Running parallel to Shankill is Crumlin Road, notorious for the creepy and infamous **Crumlin Road Gaol.** Designed by prolific Charles Lanyon, the gaol opened in 1845 and functioned until as recently as 1996. It housed such luminous inmates as Gerry Adams, Eamon De Valera, and Lenny Murphy, the leader of the Shankill Butchers. Plans are afoot to transform the prison into a museum. Crumlin Road becomes Clifton Street, and near the intersection with the Westlink Motorway, you can cast your eyes over the facade of the **Belfast Orange Hall** (Clifton Street Orange Hall), another spooky reminder of the agitation between Unionists and Republicans; the facade of this building—protected by a large barricade fence—features Belfast's only equestrian statue.

North of the city, along the Antrim Road lie Belfast Castle, Cave Hill, and the zoo. I'm not a fan of the Scottish baronial-style **castle** (free admission; daily

---

Set Sail for Heaven

In the city's north, down by the docks in the old maritime quarter evocatively known as **Sailortown**, there's little left to recall the days when the area would have been crawling with sailors, prostitutes, and assorted cut-throats who would not be out of place in *Pirates of the Caribbean*. One idiosyncratic leftover is **Sinclair Seaman's Presbyterian Church** ★★ (Corporation Sq.; ☎ 028/9071-5997; Wed 2–4:30pm). Built for the many sailors who called in to Belfast with no place to worship, it's themed along nautical lines, with a pulpit designed like a ship's prow and miniature lifeboat collection boxes ("They look small," one of the church elders told me, "but they hold a lot"). Before services, the brass bell from a decommissioned warship, HMS *Hood,* is rung; and during weddings, the bride and groom stand on an image of an anchor to symbolize their union. Today, there's an active congregation and the minister still makes it his business to visit every ship that calls in at the port.

9am–6pm); built in 1865 for the Marquis of Donegall, it's been rather unceremoniously transformed into a dining venue. Instead of visiting it, park your car (the castle parking area is 4km/2½ miles north of Belfast), put on your walking shoes, and head up along one of the marked paths in **Cave Hill Country Park** ★★★, affording hikers panoramic views over the city and Belfast Lough, crossing meadows, moorland, and heath. The most challenging route is the Cave Hill Trail, which passes the caves and then goes up a steeper path to Hightown Fort.

One place where kids will be engaged is **Belfast Zoo** (kids) (Antrim Rd.; ☎ 028/9077-6277; www.belfastzoo.co.uk; £8.10; daily Mar 21–Sept 10am–7pm; Oct–Mar 20 10am–4pm), where animals are held in high esteem and good conditions. Over 140 different types of animals are on display, ranging from tiny pygmy marmosets to massive Asian elephants, and a 45-year-old gorilla named Delilah; many of the animals here are endangered and the zoo has an intensive breeding program. In 2008, a rainforest house was introduced, bringing in two-toed sloth, fruit bats, and some exotic birds. Metro buses go from City Hall (Donegall Square West) to the zoo. By car, take the M2 motorway and exit at junction 2, then follow the signs. *Note:* Last entry is up to 2 hours prior to closing.

THE TITANIC QUARTER

2012 will be the 100th anniversary of the sinking of the *Titanic.* It's odd that the city that built it would want to be remembered for it, yet Belfast's most prestigious regeneration project has been dubbed the **Titanic Quarter** (www.titanicquarter.com), rapidly gaining momentum as the largest waterfront in Europe. Between the time I write this and the time you visit Belfast, there will be massive development throughout the all-but-abandoned dockyards of Belfast.

As a port city, Belfast's quays are intimately associated with the origins of the city. In the 17th century, the banks of the Farset became the first quaysides and

Look Closer . . .

The large salmon sculpture near Lagan Weir is entitled *Bigfish* and is by the artist John Kindness; look closely and you'll see that the tiled ceramic "scales" are actually decorated with pieces of text and images linked with the history of the city.

the Farset was used to transport goods into the city. Today, the Farset runs beneath the city's High Street—a humungous tunnel carries the river underneath the city.

The **Lagan Weir,** which spans the river, was opened in March 1994 and cost £14 million; the start of the city waterfront regeneration program, it sparked the revival that is transforming Belfast into the waking giant that she aspires to be.

A winding ramp provides access to the footbridge above the weir, allowing you to cross the Lagan (on the footbridge you'll get a better view of the two famous yellow Harland and Wolff cranes, Samson and Goliath, the largest in the world). If you cross the bridge to the other side of the river, you'll be in Queen's Quay, and a 5-minute walk takes you to the Odyssey Pavilion (see below), and—beyond this—the slipways and massive construction yards where the *Titanic* was built and from where it set off on its first and final voyage.

The Odyssey is a sprawling neon day-glo entertainment mall—IMAX cinema, arena, bars, video arcades, restaurants—right on the water's edge. It's also the location of the city's top children's attraction, a science learning center called **W5–Whowhatwherewhenwhy** (☎ 028/9046-7700; www.w5online.co.uk; £7; Mon–Sat 10am–6pm; Sun noon–6pm), several floors of interactive exhibits designed to bring the hard facts of physics, chemistry, biology, and the natural sciences to life in imaginative ways. Visitors can film themselves presenting the weather report, take a lie detector test, or play a cool air harp that works with lasers. Overall it's a worthwhile stop for families.

THE OTHER BELFAST

Journalist and novelist Gavin Esler once said: "My Belfast is the world's biggest village. It's not that everybody knows each other in this city—it's just that it often feels that way." You, too, may start feeling that way after several days here, especially if you try the following experiences.

STIMULATING MIND & IMAGINATION

If you scan the University notice boards, you'll find postings for public lectures, and although these are very often serious intellectual discussions on obscure topics ("The Ethnicity of Englishness & the Hit of the Irish Real" is probably not everyone's cup of tea), they're often followed by a lively drinks reception where you can get to know the academics.

Also connected to the university, and founded in honor of the Nobel laureate who studied and taught here, is the **Seamus Heaney Centre of Poetry** (English Department; ☎ 028/9097-1070; www.qub.ac.uk/heaneycentre), which puts on a regular program of talks, readings, and lectures that are well-attended by Belfast's impressively loyal followers of poetry.

Belfast by Boat

It can be enlightening to actually see and experience the city from the water itself, learning, as you go, about the history of what was once the scene of the largest shipbuilding industry on the planet. You can take just such a tour with the **Lagan Boat Company** ★★ (48 St. John's Close, 2 Laganbank Rd.; ☎ 028/9033-0844 or 077/1891-0423; www.laganboat company.com). Running commentary by an honest-to-goodness "Aye-aye, Captain" emcee helps bring everything into perspective and makes for a most evocative journey of discovery. As you cruise through the harbor, ogling the rusting, monstrous machinery, stationary warships, and derelict harbor offices, you'll get unique views of a world where up to 32,000 men once worked to produce great ships, many of them losing their hearing while hammering rivets. You'll learn how the shipbuilding company, Harland and Wolfe, churned out a ship a week, and how anywhere between 5,000 and 14,000 men lost their lives working here. And if you think you got the gist of the *Titanic* story from watching James Cameron's 3-hour movie, you're wrong . . . this tour reveals how fate intervened to secure the conditions that resulted in the *Titanic*'s rapid demise. **Titanic Tour** happens Friday to Monday at 12:30, 2, and 3:30pm (£10). The same company operates an alternative **River Lagan Tour** (at the same times Tues–Thurs only; same price), which follows the Lagan upstream as far as the Stranmillis Weir.

The **Linen Hall Library** (p. 374) sustains an active calendar that draws in the public for lively interactive sessions—readings, discussions, debates—that tend to revolve around literary and intellectual themes. From time to time, the library holds discussions of selected books (you'll need to prepare by actually reading the chosen piece of literature, but there's no cost involved). Other events include readings by award-winning writers, storytelling sessions, and children's workshops. To know exactly what's going on and when, pick up the Library's pocket-size program booklet.

Regular workshops, discussions, lectures, and even high profile master classes are also held at the **Grand Opera House** (p. 377), free and open to interested and curious members of the public—often connected to some aspect of what is currently being performed. So, for example, during the run of the Peter Shaffer drama, *Equus,* in early 2008, there was a special "theatre day" with the assistant director answering questions about the production.

LEARN TO DANCE TO A DIFFERENT BEAT

Though it has dozens of learning opportunities (in everything from tai chi to creative writing), the **Crescent Arts Centre** (165 Ormeau Rd.; ☎ 028/9024-2338; www.crescentarts.org) is best known, and rightly so, for its classes in Irish set dancing. If you've never tried set dancing before, you've nothing to fear—it must be one of the most sociable, fun and easy-to-pick up dance forms around. Typically someone on a microphone will explain each of the moves in the dance (there are many different forms), and then call them out so you can put them into action. They're often simple, easy-to-execute moves, like "advance" (go forward), "retreat" (move backward), "hold hands with your partner," "form an archway," "march," and "duck." In some dances, there are just a handful of steps to remember, so even a klutz can manage them, even after a few pints. Classes are held at **Rosemary Hall All Souls Church** on Elmwood Avenue, Mondays 8 to 10pm, and cost £3; call ☎ 028/9266-3565 for details.

Incidentally, once you're addicted to set-dancing, you can find out about regular events—this time outside the classroom—from **An Droichead** (20 Cooke St., Ormeau Rd.; ☎ 028/9028-8818; www.androichead.com), a local Irish cultural organization.

IN THE BELLY OF THE GAELTACHT

At the heart of West Belfast's Gaeltacht Quarter is **Cultúrlann McAdam Ó Fiaich** (216 Falls Rd.; ☎ 028/9096-4180; www.culturlann.com), a cultural collective. Its main activities range from shows and cultural entertainment, to workshops and Irish language classes—anything to keep Irish culture alive and active in the midst of a city where globalization is clearly the order of the day. A lot of what goes on is in Irish, so while you won't necessarily understand some of the readings or drama productions, you will get to hear Irish being spoken, and there's always someone who'll be keen to chat to you about the meaning behind the foreign words. There's live traditional music in the cafe each Saturday morning (free

---

Careful Conversations

Belfasters always have time to chat. You can walk into any pub (or shop, or restaurant), and strike up conversation without much effort. However, if you want to discuss delicate subjects—politics and religion, which are pretty interchangeable here—don't pounce right in. Ask lots of questions if you're curious, but there's no need to express an opinion, even if you think you have one. It's fine to prefer one brand of stout over another, but in a city where there's been open war on the streets over religious and political dogma, it's best not to get involved or challenge people's beliefs. Ignore this simple social courtesy, and there's every chance that even the most relaxed stranger could be incited to take you on (in fierce debate or even physically). Before treading on tender toes, consider these pithy words from Thomas Lynch's memoir, *Booking Passage:* "In Belfast as in Baghdad there is no choice to opt out of conflict. Everyone is something. Everyone believes or disbelieves in something. Whether lapsed or devoted, militant or indifferent, orthodox or not; whether disbeliever or misbehaver, nonconformist or reformer, everyone is bound by ancient codes of tribe and blood, belief and conflict. And hate, like love, forms its habits and attachments." Meaning: Don't take sides.

admission) and monthly *céili* dance sessions (which you join in for £5) on certain Sunday nights.

HEY, SMARTYPANTS!

For opportunities to mingle in a more free-form fashion, don't discount quiz nights, held in pubs all over the city. The **Bot** and the **Eg** and **Bar Twelve** (Crescent Town House, 13 Lower Crescent; ☎ 028/9032-3349), have brain-teasing events on Tuesdays from 10pm. The aim of the game is always fun (they kick off after a few rounds of drinks have already been poured), and while the quizzes are a test of general knowledge, you'll probably get by a little better if you manage to convince someone local to join your team. There's bound to be a few questions that are nigh-impossible for foreigners to answer—unless you take an interest in football (soccer) or rugby. Nevertheless, for an entry costing as little as £2, you could walk away with an Xbox 360.

LEND A HAND

Belfast also presents many opportunities to volunteer. You might contribute your services to an upcoming festival, or commit yourself to a charitable or community-development enterprise, picking up experience, new skills, and locally based colleagues and friends in the process. **VSB** (www.vsb.org.uk) is an umbrella organization that identifies volunteering opportunities and in 2008, was involved with over 760 volunteer groups in the greater Belfast area. Some activities you might do for a day or two of your vacation:

   ◆ Assisting with renovation work on the Nomadic (the small vessel that transferred passengers from Cherbourg to the ill-fated *Titanic*).
   ◆ Helping in East Belfast's Lagan Valley Regional Park (planting trees, conducting species surveys).
   ◆ Conducting interviews with immigrant poets, musicians, and artists.

Since volunteers are generally drawn from the local community, don't expect to receive accommodation in return for services rendered, but there are no charges for giving up your time, either.

ACTIVE BELFAST

A good 3-hour walk gets you to **McArt's Fort** at the summit (330m/1,100 ft.) of Cave Hill ✭✭ (p. 380); the reward is the finest view over the city and the entire Belfast Lough. Another wonderful walk (although only when the weather is decent) is to the top of **Black Mountain** (1¾ hr. return), or through the **Colin Glen Forest Park** ✭. For information on these trails, contact the **Belfast Hills Partnership** (☎ 028/9060-3466; www.belfasthills.org).

You can also walk or cycle along the 13km (8-mile) **Lagan Towpath,** which runs alongside the Lagan waterway from the Botanic Gardens all the way to the city of Lisburn.

The **Belfast Welcome Centre** (p. 395) has a "Belfast by Bike" cycling map, and bikes can be rented from **McConvey Cycles** (183 Ormeau Rd.; ☎ 028/9033-0322; www.rentabikebelfast.com; £15 touring bike, £20 mountain bike).

ATTENTION, SHOPPERS!

Shopping centers have longer hours during the week (9am–7pm), while Thursday is a late-night shopping day (till 9pm). Small shops tend to open around noon or 1pm on Sundays, and close around 5 or 6pm.

CLOTHING

When **Victoria Square** (www.victoriasquare.com) opened in March 2008, people came from all over Northern Ireland for a peek at the top-quality designer lines that many associate with London's high streets. Not to be outdone, and for many years considered the top retail center in Belfast, **CastleCourt** (Royal Ave; ☎ 028/9023-4591) still has famous names, including La Senza, Paranoid, and Remus Uomo. The boutiques along **Lisburn Road,** south of the city center, are great if you prefer to avoid the lookalike consumerism of malls.

More sensibly minded shoppers should head for **Best Vintage** ✪✪ (11 Wellington Place; ☎ 028/9031-2784; www.bestvintage.com), right near City Hall, which holds tightly packed racks of vintage shirts, jackets, jeans, and trilby hats—straight from the '60s, '70s, and '80s. Some clothing goes for as little as £5.

Retro and vintage clothing with an offbeat edge is what you'll find at **Rusty Zip** (28 Botanic Ave.; ☎ 028/9024-9700) at the edge of the University Quarter. From ra-ra skirts to tuxedos, the shelves and racks are packed with eye-catching, fetching, and downright unusual designs. Also with a good range of vintage wear, **Liberty Blue** (19–21 Lombard St.; ☎ 028/9043-7745) is an affordable, spunky place to shop for pretty, original dresses.

Gentlemen, if you're type for whom only the very best will do, then you must at least browse the shelves at **Smyth and Gibson Shirtmakers** ✪✪✪ (Bedford House, 16–22 Bedford St.; ☎ 028/9023-0388; www.smythandgibson.com) where handmade tailored shirts are sold from a gallery-quality space. For a more casual look, **Yoke** (5 Wellington St.; ☎ 028/9023-6900), just off Donegall Square, does cool lines in men clothing, like Supremebeing, Goi Goi, and Scotch & Soda.

MUSIC

Opposite Castlecourt's rear entrance, near Smithfield Market, is Ireland's oldest record store, McBurney's aka the **Premier** ✪ (3/5 Smithfield Sq. North; ☎ 028/9024-0896; www.premiere.co.uk) which has been trading since 1926 and is still very much a family affair. Head here for traditional Irish music, although you'll find pop, country, and other genres as well. But the music store to visit if you want to rub shoulders with a legend is **Phoenix Records** ✪✪✪ (Haymarket Arcade, Royal Ave.; ☎ 028/9023-9308) run by musician, DJ, and legendary record producer, Terri Hooley. The selection here is far deeper than at McBurney's, with good local releases and plenty of alternative music.

ARTS, CRAFTS & SOUVENIRS

If you're looking for souvenirs with a local flavor, but like me don't go in for fluffy neon leprechauns, then make some time for **Wicker Man** ✪✪ (44–46 High St.; ☎ 028/9024-3550; www.thewickerman.co.uk) where a range of good-quality crafts, artworks, and occasionally works of whimsy have been gathered together under one roof: organic handmade soaps, Celtic linens, pewter goblets, *bodhráns*

Let's Go to Market

Although it only happens twice a week, **St. George's Market** ★★★ (12 East Bridge St.; ☎ 028/9043-5704; www.belfastcity.gov.uk/markets; look out for the free bus going to the market) is one of the most vibrant day-time gathering places in Ireland. On Fridays it's more of a commercial market, thronged by all kinds of people come to buy weird, wonderful, and totally banal goods—you'll come across everything from knock-off Calvin Klein underwear and cheap football shirts to artisanal cheeses and marinated olives. Saturday, it feels more like a social outing attended by a cool, yuppy crowd, with fresher than fresh foods (fruits, vegetables, and excellent fish displays). Live music accompanies the shopping—often it's traditional, and always upbeat. It's a good place to arrive fairly hungry; you can grab a double wild boar hotdog from **El Toro Grill** for just £2, and give a small donation for a cup of **Fairtrade Charity Coffee.** While you're roaming, don't miss the absolutely spectacular display of cheeses under the blue canopy near the center of the market, and consider the range of salads and *tapas* ingredients—artichoke hearts, sundried tomatoes, and pickled olives—available from the **Olive Tree Company.** Also be on the lookout for colorful, slightly exotic jewelry by Lisa Shilliday, known to her clients as **Lish Designs** (☎ 077/4708-4323; www.lishdesigns.com).

(around £43), and other uniquely Irish musical instruments. I particularly fancy the jewelry here (some made by Peter, the Wicker Man himself).

On an altogether more serious note, and if you do happen to be trawling Falls Road, pop in at **Republican Merchandising** (52/53 Falls Rd.; ☎ 028/9024-3371), which is actually owned by Sinn Fein, which has its offices right next door (so you can't miss it if you are in this neck of the woods). It's stocked with heady political literature; for a very intimate, heartfelt account, I recommend Bobby Sands' *One Day in My Life.* Also thrown into the mix are bits of Resistance memorabilia and strong reminders of the struggle for independence from British rule. There's a decent selection of traditional music here, too.

NIGHTLIFE

On weekends, expect to see white stretch limos carrying screaming lasses singing along to twee pop songs, while on the sidewalks, ultra-coiffed lads strut through Queen's Quarter ready to take the night by storm. As the night wears on, it'll be groups of boozy men spilling out of bars and onto the streets in search of fast, greasy food with high-heeled, be-stockinged girls not far behind.

But really any day of the week, you'll be overwhelmed by the volume of nighttime opportunities in Belfast. Step into the **Belfast Welcome Centre** (p. 395) and the staff should be able to bundle you with event guides and program booklets; resources that you'll find helpful include *Belfast in Your Pocket* (www.inyourpocket.com), a small format magazine, and the *big list,* a newspaper-style free publication that details the wide range of entertainment offerings.

You can purchase tickets for many events in the city through **Ticketmaster** (located in the Virgin Megastore in the city center; www.ticketmaster.ie).

CULTURAL PURSUITS

The **Grand Opera House** ★★ (Great Victoria St.; ☎ 028/9024-1919; www.goh.co.uk) is a fine venue for those who take their staged entertainment seriously. The line-up includes ballet, opera, dance, and major dramas. In addition to the main theater, the Baby Grand, a smaller on-site venue, hosts some of the most popular shows in town. Ticket prices range from £5 to around £40; matinees are considerably cheaper.

With an ongoing line-up of performance artists, comedians, musicians, and anyone else on the creative cutting edge, the **Black Box** ★★★ (18 Hill St.; ☎ 028/9024-4400; www.blackboxbelfast.com) is an intimate space flying high on the Cathedral Quarter's artsy credentials. Most shows are one-offs, so ticket prices vary and there are occasional freebies.

Old Museum Arts Centre (7 College Sq. North; ☎ 028/9023-3332; www.oldmuseumartscentre.org) offers a line-up that tends to be more experimental and, some might say, self-consciously serious. Along with live theater it hosts indy film screenings as well.

Live Music & Entertainment

Locals still consider **Ulster Hall** (Great Victoria St.; ☎ 028/9032-3900; www.ulsterhall.co.uk) the city's premiere classical music venue; at the time of writing, it was behind luminous green construction screens, undergoing an upgrade to the tune of £7.5 million. Apparently, it will be reopening sometime in 2009, when it will become the new home of the Ulster Orchestra.

The massive, purpose-built **Waterfront Hall** (Lanyon Place; ☎ 028/9033-4455; www.waterfront.co.uk), is an ultra-modern theater space designed for blockbuster concerts that run the gamut from classical to pop. The main auditorium hosts an eclectic mix that has included top orchestras, the Soweto Gospel Choir, Kris Kristofferson, Lou Reed, and Björk. And that's just the music side; you can also head here for the World Irish Dancing Championships, such odd attractions as the Shaolin Monks and psycho-illusionist Derren Brown, and rotating list of top comedy acts; the most affordable tickets range from £15 up to about £30.

Besides being the city's indoor sports venue—where ice hockey is the major draw—the **Odyssey Arena** (2 Queens Quay; ☎ 028/9076-6000; www.odysseyarena.com) fills up for big name rock and pop concerts, typically catering to the masses. Kylie Minogue and Dolly Parton played here in 2008, giving you a pretty good idea how diverse the menu can be.

Queen's University has a full music program throughout the year, showcasing artists-in-residence, up-and-coming jazz performers, and some of the world's most important contemporary composers. Much of it is free and happens at different venues around the University. Pick up the quarterly program, *Music at Queens* from the **Queen's Visitor Centre** (p. 378), or visit www.qub.ac.uk/music. The student union, **Mandela Hall** (75–87 University Rd.; ☎ 028/9097-1062) hosts pretty mean concerts—U2 did an early gig here.

The **Belfast Empire Music Hall** (Botanic Ave; ☎ 028/9024-9276; www.the belfastempire.com) hosts Irish and U.K. favorites, from reggae to indie rock artists, as well as a plethora of tribute groups, which have a loyal fan base here in Belfast. Belfast-based duo, Oppenheimer (comparable with Daft Punk), are worth catching here. Cover charge varies, but quite a few shows are free. There's legendary stand up comedy Tuesdays at 8pm (£7).

South of the city center, on Ormeau Avenue, **Limelight** (☎ 028/9032-5942; www.the-limelight.co.uk) is the place to get a peek at the big names of tomorrow; bands such as Kaiser Chiefs and Scissor Sisters have cut their teeth here.

DRINKING & RELAXING

Pubs are generally open all day until 11pm. They'll stay open later on Fridays and Saturdays and close earlier on Sundays. Bars can generally go longer, and many have late-licenses. Some clubs only open late at night and then go through the night, often till as late as 6am on weekends and bank holidays.

Belfast's Historic Pubs

Belfast's most famous venue, the **Crown Liquor Saloon** ★★★ (46 Great Victoria St.; ☎ 028/9027-9901) is not just a stand-out sightseeing attraction, but very much a working bar; I can imagine no more memorable a place to enjoy your first pint of Guinness than in the warm glow of this archetypal gas-lit pub (see p. 389 for more history).

One of the highlights of a visit to the Cathedral Quarter is time spent in the **John Hewitt** ★★★ (51 Donegall St.; ☎ 028/9023-3768) which celebrates a decade of existence in 2009, but feels so much older. Named for a local socialist-leaning poet, it's popular with journalists and other arty hacks drawn here by the intellectual vibe and the music sessions that happen every night (from 9 or 10pm) except Wednesday. Film screenings and small theater performances are on the bill, too.

Just around the corner, down a cobbled alleyway, is one of Belfast's liveliest and loveliest, the **Duke of York** ★★★ (7 Commercial Court; ☎ 028/9024-1062). Packed full of eye-catching memorabilia, it sometimes feels more like a busy museum (but one where everyone just happens to be boozing). Sinn Fein stalwart Gerry Adams used to be a bartender here.

In the oldest building in Belfast, **McHugh's Bar** ★★ (29–31 Queen's Sq.; ☎ 028/9050-9990) traces its origins back to 1711, and is a good place to pop into while you're exploring the Laganside area or poking around Custom House; the bar is right beside the Albert Memorial Clock Tower. Look for sculptures of bare bottoms that hang from the walls—they're reminders of the days when ladies of the night plied their trade in this area (and, possibly, in this pub).

Promoting itself as the oldest tavern in town, **White's Tavern** ★★ (2–4 Winecellar Entry, off Lombard St.; ☎ 028/9024-3080) actually started out in 1630 as a booze wholesaler pushing its wares to other pubs; it only opened to the public in 1860. The upstairs DJ venue (indie rock on Fri, jazz and lounge on Sat) looks and feels just like a 1950's sitting room.

Tipple Tour

A fun way to see a good selection of Belfast's finest pubs is with **Historical Pub Tours of Belfast** ★★★ (☎ 028/9268-3665; www.belfast pubtours.com; £6; May–Oct Thurs 7pm; Sat 4pm), a 2-hour walking tour that introduces you to the history and background of each of the venues you visit. These are not just opportunities to do a pub crawl (although there's usually time enough in each bar for you to have a pint), but insightful expeditions during which your guide (who's on friendly terms with all the publicans) also tells you about some of the city's top sights and lets you in on local secrets (myths, too). The tours start at the Crown Liquor Saloon and cover around six pubs; the itinerary changes nightly.

Bittles Bar ★★ (70 Upper Church Lane, Victoria Sq.; ☎ 028/9031-1088) can be a bit of a tight squeeze, but it's worth the effort. Besides being the city's most slender pub, Belfast's only "flat-iron building," it's well known for its anachronistic paintings of Irish literary heroes.

Because it's quite a way out of the center, in a lively part of South Belfast, few outsiders frequent **Errigle Inn** ★★★ (312–320 Ormeau Rd.; ☎ 028/9064-1410), a pub going back to the 1930s; seek out the warming authenticity and traditional atmosphere of the wood-paneled **Oak Bar** ★★★, where the stained glass and solid furniture sets the scene for many intellectualized pint-drinking sessions (when the writers who frequent this place start talking, they do so with a great degree of flair). Meanwhile, the **Real Music Room** is where singer-songwriters show off their talents.

Belfast's "Modern" Watering Holes

I've already sung its praises as a dining venue, but the **Spaniard** ★★★ (3 Skipper St.; ☎ 028/9023-2448) is also a delightful nighttime haunt. Here "there's no rugby—ever," ensuring of vibe that draws barristers, artists, restaurateurs, and photographers to mix spiritedly while anything from Dido to punk to Motown plays in the background. At night, there's dancing (and listening) upstairs, and Thursday nights with legendary DJ Terri Hooley are hot.

Young hipsters rub shoulders with a suave older crowd in the oh-so-cool and up-market **Apartment** ★★ (2 Donegall Sq. West; ☎ 028/9050-9777) right across the road from City Hall. A class-A pick-up joint, it's filled with superbly coiffed locals with two things on their minds: cocktails (all around £5; how about a ginger and lemongrass martini?) and sex.

NIGHTCLUBS FOR AN ALL-NIGHT BOOGIE

Although the glass dancefloor at the **Sugar Room** ★★ (1 Hill St.; ☎ 028/9024-4044; www.potthouse.co.uk) has earned notoriety (and popularity) for allowing folks downstairs to see a little more flesh than more prudish dancers would prefer, if you like your house tunes hard and sexy you'll be among friends here. Most big events cost £10, but you'll find yourself in a queue if you don't pitch early for the "first come, first served" door policy; doors open at 10pm.

Milk ✦✦✦ (12–14 Tomb St.; ☎ 028/9027-8876; www.clubmilk.com; Thurs–Sun 9pm–3am) is considered Northern Ireland's best club, known for its pounding American house and garage. There are two levels of clubbing and plenty of bars. Belfast's most decadent parties are hosted here by **Vibe** ✦✦✦; visit www.ilovevibe.com to pre-book a place on the guest list—these Sunday night events are very popular.

Belfast's most attractive club, **La Lea** ✦✦✦ (43 Franklin St.; ☎ 028/902-30200) has designer-quality interiors, a strict door policy, and an elegant crowd looking to boogie to Old Skool (Fri), funky house (Sat), and anything danceable (Sun). Cover varies (£3–£10); doors open at 9 or 10pm.

GAY BELFAST

Belfast's LGBT scene is friendly and inclusive, and mixes partying and human-rights campaigning with equal vigor. Northern Ireland is officially 1 day ahead in terms of the U.K.'s civil partnership legislation, as the law to allow gays to be legally partnered was passed here a day before they were in England. Belfast's Pride festival has been happening since 1991; it runs from late-July through early-August. For the lowdown on the scene, contact **QueerSpace** (☎ 028/9089-0200; www.queerspace.org.uk) an "activist factory" of socially minded individuals who sponsor all sorts of events. QueerSpace organizes a walking group called "Out 'n' About," which usually sets off on the last Sunday of the month at 10:45am; it's a great way to meet members without the influence of alcohol or throbbing music.

Named for a popular Victorian-era dockside bar that was frequented by gay men and ladies of the night back in the day, **Declan Lavery's Dubarrys** ✦ (10–14 Gresham St.; ☎ 028/9032-3590; www.dubarrysbar.co.uk) is situated among Belfast's sex shops, and is an uproariously "anything goes" kind of place where old and young (mostly, but not exclusively, men) mix, mingle, and exchange prolonged glances. On Fridays, the top floor "Seduction Lounge" is set aside for Lick, ladies-only parties (men can come as guests).

Starting with a fantastic silver statue of Lenin poking out of the wall over the entrance, the mock-Soviet design theme at **Kremlin** ✦✦ (96 Donegall St.; ☎ 028/9080-9700; www.kremlin-belfast.com; £5) continues throughout its warren of dance floors, passages, and stages. You'll meet (or be pinched, squeezed, and hugged by) people everywhere: on the way-too-cheesy pop and disco floor, and at any of the numerous bars where vodka-and-Red Bull far outsells Guinness. Kremlin is hands-down the hottest club in Belfast and consequently popular with many straight clubbers. Apparently, it's the biggest gay club in Ireland.

Adjoining Kremlin, but reached via its own entrance around the corner, **Union Street** ✦✦ (14 Union St.; ☎ 028/9031-6060; www.unionstreetpub.com) occupies a former shoe factory and is widely considered one of the smartest bars in town. It's famous for its open-plan washrooms: Situated right behind one of the bar counters, clubbers can actually see into the toilets, so you can watch people washing their hands or checking their make-up, and behind them, guys taking aim at the latrine.

A SIDE TRIP TO ARMAGH CITY

In the 8th century Armagh was known as the "City of Saints and Scholars," for the extraordinary men of letters who trained and studied at the famous school established by St. Patrick (which at one time was thought to have 7,000 students). A number of these scholars earned renown for spreading Christianity across northern Europe. Its status was such that at one stage the Roman Catholic Holy See considered relocating here to escape the frequent attacks on Rome.

If that had happened, Armagh—and indeed, Ireland—might have been a very different place. Instead, with a population of just 54,000, Armagh is one of the most attractive cities in Ireland, with an assortment of museums and a world-class observatory; you can explore all the major sights in just a few hours.

GETTING THERE

Ulsterbus (☎ 028/9033-3000; www.ulsterbus.co.uk) has regular scheduled coach services between Belfast and Armagh, and also links Armagh with other major towns in Northern Ireland as well as important cities in the Republic. By **road,** Armagh is a relatively short drive from Omagh (around an hour on the **A5/A28**), and the drive from Belfast should take no more than an hour.

WHY YOU'RE HERE: TOP SIGHTS & ATTRACTIONS

The St. Patrick Threesome

It's worth doing a comparative study between Armagh's two cathedrals dedicated to St. Patrick—these are, after all, the seats of power that give Armagh its slightly aristocratic air. Start by standing in the shadow of the twin-spired **Roman Catholic Cathedral** ✪ (☎ 028/3752-2638; www.armagharchdiocese.org; free admission; Mon–Sat 10am–sunset), commissioned only after the repeal of penal laws against Catholic worship. The effect of the design is almost to make potential worshippers

---

Stealing Gulliver

Armagh's **Public Library** ✪✪ (43 Abbey St.; ☎ 028/3752-3142; www.armaghrobinsonlibrary.org; Mon–Fri 10am–1pm and 2–4pm) is the oldest in Northern Ireland. Founded in 1771 by Archbishop Richard Robinson, much of the library was his private stock of rare books from the 17th and 18th centuries. Among them is Sir Walter Raleigh's *History of the World* (1614), and a book by John Gerson printed in 1488. But the most interesting part of the collection is a copy of a first edition of Jonathan Swift's *Gulliver's Travels,* with the author's handwritten scribblings and amendments. In one of the craziest events to hit Armagh in recent memory, the manuscript was actually "kidnapped" in 1999, presumably by paramilitaries. Fortunately, the precious book turned up 9 months later in Dublin after an anonymous telephone tip-off.

Road Bowling in County Armagh

There are some things for which the phrase "seeing is believing" must have been invented, and one of them can be witnessed in County Armagh.

As far as strange and unusual sports go, **road bowling** must rank way up there—the concept is so extraordinarily foreign to anyone raised where roads were made for vehicles! Here, bowling is on a stretch of tarred, public road. And in spite of this apparent madness, road bowling is not only a popular sport in certain parts of Ireland—Cork and Armagh are major centers—but also big business, with players often placing enormous bets on themselves and one another, making this far less the amateur sport you might imagine. Take a gander at the website of the **Irish Road Bowling Association** (www.irishroadbowling.ie) for an idea of how popular it is. There was a time when the activity was banned. I've met people in Armagh who had their bowls confiscated by the police when they were children.

So, how does it work? Simple really. Players take turns throwing their bowl, a heavy cast iron ball (adult bowls are 28 oz., while youths play with 14 oz. bowls), from a starting point and then picking it up and throwing from its final position, until it goes beyond a predetermined end point (usually a mile or two from the start). The player (or team) to reach the

whimper in the face of the immense struggle undergone by this arm of Christianity in Ireland—approach from the front, and the facade, its spires and staring statues of clergymen loom powerfully overhead. The cathedral did not go up without considerable effort—although building began in 1840, the Famine put off construction for a number of years and it was only functional in 1873, and completed in 1904. Still, it makes its presence felt today, with two stone bishops engaged in a permanent stare-down with the Church of Ireland Cathedral just a few hundred yards away. On either side of the entrance, are statues of St. Patrick and St. Malachy, both in anachronistically modern garb. Atmospherically dark, the interior is lit by stained glass windows and flickering votive lights that cause the goldleaf in the wall and floor mosaics to shimmer.

St. Patrick's **Church of Ireland Cathedral** ✪✪✪ (☎ 028/3752-3142; www.stpatricks-cathedral.org; free admission; daily Apr–Oct 10am–5pm; Nov–Mar 10am–4pm; guided tours June–Aug Mon–Sat 11:30am and 2:30pm) is on higher ground, apparently where Patrick founded his first church in 445. The church that now stands here—one of many that have been destroyed at least 17 times by all sorts of calamity, usually fire—is compact and beautiful. Having been renovated, restored, rebuilt, and appended so many times over the centuries, it's impossible to say what parts, if any, of the church are original. The exterior walls are studded with gargoyle-like creatures, some of them like Disney caricatures. Somewhere on the grounds is buried Brian Boru, the first High King of Ireland, finish in the least number of throws is the winner. Although fairly straight stretches of quiet road are the best, good players are able to skillfully cope with bends, undulations, and a variety of road surfaces.

Road bowling attracts fairly large crowds and there's always plenty of excitement, no doubt enhanced by the laying on of bets (when I was last in Armagh during an important match, I heard talk of £20,000 on the line for a single throw of the bowl!). Joining road bowling spectators is a sure fire way to meet people. Remember that you'll be doing plenty of walking along the way (miles and miles of it), as the crowd moves with the bowling action; be prepared to avoid flying bowls, and have a blast.

Occasionally, events will be open to casual participants, so you could even have a go at it yourself, although I suggest you watch a few rounds before trying your luck. Road bowling isn't particularly well advertised, but in Armagh you need only ask a few locals to get an idea of when something is going down. Be sure to get specific directions to the road in question and, for goodness sake, be careful as you drive towards the "sports ground."

although with all the building that's gone on here, I'd imagine his bones have become displaced.

The interior, which Thackeray called "almost too handsome," is filled with tributes and memorials to past archbishops as well as to military men. The most interesting pieces in the church, however, are Iron Age figures, such as the one-armed "Tandragee Man." Legendarily one of Ireland's greatest kings, he lost his arm, and his throne, but true to form, the hero cast himself an arm of silver and won his throne back using that.

Nearby, the St. Patrick's **Trian Centre** 🧒 (English St.; www.visitarmagh.com; £5; Mon–Sat 10am–5pm; Sun 2–5pm), offers three exhibitions connected to Armagh's history, but none of them are nearly as enjoyable as simply wandering through the Mall or visiting either of the cathedrals. Kids may like it though. In the "scriptorium" they get to try their hand at quill-writing and they'll get to dress up at the start of the Land of Lilliput exhibit as they listen to voices enact an abridged version of Gulliver's Travels, celebrated here because Jonathan Swift spent quite a bit of time in Armagh, frequently sponging off wealthy friends who lived at Markethill.

The Mall, Museums, Observatory & Palace Stables

For a glimpse at how the ideals of pure Georgian terracing were meant to transform choked urban centers into salubrious tracts of civilized development, spend some time wandering through the **Mall** ✪✪✪. On its eastern flank is the free-to-visit **County Museum** (☎ 028/3752-3070; www.magni.org; Mon–Fri 10am–5pm; Sat 10am–1pm and 2–5pm), an old-fashioned and outdated collection of ancient and more recent relics spanning the great divide between pre-history and modernity; for the most part, you're left to figure out what it all means by yourself.

Military enthusiasts might want to spend some time roaming the densely curated **Royal Irish Fusilier Museum** (☎ 028/3752-2911; free admission; Mon–Fri 10am–12:30pm and 1–4pm), also on the Mall East, which is definitely only for specialists, but does engage with Armagh's history in some depth.

From the Mall, it's a short uphill walk to another part of Robinson's substantial legacy—**Armagh Observatory** (College Hill; ☎ 028/3752-2928; www.arm.ac.uk; grounds open Mon–Fri 9:30am–4:30pm), where around 25 scientists are diligently scanning the stars in order to expand our knowledge of the universe. Robinson established the observatory in 1790 and it remains one of the premiere astronomical centers in the U.K. In the 1960s, the Observatory's director secured funding to establish the **Armagh Planetarium** (☎ 028/3752-3689; www.armagh planet.com) where a Mars Goto projector allows visitors to get up close and personal to the Red Planet.

Back on earth, the **Palace Stables Heritage Centre** 🧒 (☎ 028/3752-1801; £5; May and Sept Sat 10am–5pm; Sun noon–5pm; June–Aug Mon–Sat 10am–5pm; Sun noon–5pm) is another of those immersive living history experiences where actors dressed up in period costume lead you around the premises while attempting to re-create life as it might have been in the late-18th century. To cut to the chase: It's best for those with children.

The ABCs of Belfast

Area Code The area code for Belfast and for all of Northern Ireland is **028**.

ATMs & Banks ATMs are ubiquitous; some centrally located banks with on-site round-the-clock ATMs include **Bank of Ireland** (54 Donegall Place; ☎ 028/9023-4334), **Ulster Bank** (Donegall Square East; ☎ 028/9027-6000), and **Northern Bank** (14 Donegall Square West; ☎ 028/9024-5277). Banks generally operate Monday to Friday, 9:30am to 4:30pm; some banks do open on Saturday mornings.

Emergencies Dial ☎ **999** for any emergency, including police, ambulance, and fire services.

Hospital Belfast City Hospital is at 91 Lisburn Rd. (☎ 028/9032-9241).

Internet You can surf the Net at the **Belfast Welcome Centre** (p. 395; £1 for 20 min.) and also at several Internet cafes and coffee shops around the city, such as **Revelations, the Internet Café** (Shaftesbury Square; ☎ 028/9032-0337) for around £4 per hour.

Opening Hours In Belfast, larger city center **stores,** particularly those in shopping centers, have longer-than-normal shopping hours during the week (9am–7pm), while Thursday is a late-night shopping day (till 9pm); **shops** tend to open around noon or 1pm on Sundays, and close around 5 or 6pm. For more detailed information, visit www.ulster shopper.co.uk. **Pubs** are open from 11am to 11pm, Monday to Thursday, till around 11:30pm Friday and Saturday, and 12:30 to 10pm on Sundays. Some **bars** and **clubs** have much later opening hours and tend to vary wildly.

Police Call ☎ **999** in case of any emergency.

Postal Services The main **post office** is in the center of the city (12 Bridge St.; ☎ 028/2459-8466). It's open Monday and Wednesday to Saturday 9am to 5:30pm, Tuesday 9:30am to 5:30pm, and Sunday 9am to 5pm. It closes for lunch noon to 1pm. The post office is good for much more than sending postcards; you can also exchange currency and cash travelers checks without commission charges. If you want to ship goods abroad, go to **Mail Boxes Etc.** (Thomas House, 47 Botanic Ave; ☎ 028/9024-7888; www.mbebelfast.co.uk; Mon–Fri 9:30am–5:30pm) who serve as agents for a number of shipping companies; they'll even collect your package free of charge if you're within a 5km (3 mile) radius of their shop.

Restrooms Victoria Square shopping center has the cleanest, slickest loos in town, and they're free. Other shopping centers also have free-to-use toilet facilities. Around the city center you'll see a number of pay-to-use electronic toilet booths that look a bit like futuristic space pods. They're fully automated and cost 20p (15 min.); a computerized voice talks you through the entire process.

Taxis Cabs run around-the-clock and are metered. Try **City Cab** (☎ 028/9024-2000), **Value Cabs** (☎ 028/9080-9080), or **fonaCAB** (☎ 028/9033-3333; www.foacab.com). The minimum fare is £2.70 (for up to .5km/$^7/_{10}$ mile), after which the meter kicks in.

Tourist Offices **The Belfast Welcome Centre** (☎ 028/9024-6609; www.gotobelfast.com) is in the heart of the city, right near the City Hall at 47 Donegall Place; it's open Monday to Sunday, 9am to 5:30pm and stays open until 7pm June to September. It's a one-stop tourist information center, where you can also book accommodations throughout Northern Ireland and even some in the Republic, use Internet, avail of a left luggage facility, and purchase tickets for tours and events.

11 Spectacular Antrim & Down

The Giant's Causeway, peaceful glens & St. Patrick's footsteps

by Keith Bain

ANCIENT IRISH SUPERSTARS, FINN MCCOOL AND ST. PATRICK, SHARE TOP billing as the characters who have—in spirit at least—most colorfully shaped the history of the eastern counties of Antrim and Down, both known for their majestic natural beauty. Along Antrim's rugged coast, Finn McCool—widely billed as Ireland's coolest giant and perhaps the best known and understood of all its mythical characters—is legendarily held responsible for creating one of Ireland's most popular visitor attractions: the Giant's Causeway.

County Down's ambience is shadowed by a giant of another sort, the ecclesiastical hero credited with transforming Ireland into a bastion of Christian practice. When he returned to Ireland as a missionary, it's believed that Patrick arrived at Strangford Lough, a long, narrow body of water that separates the Ards Peninsula from the Lecale—the lolling, drumlin-dotted hinterland of County Down. And as if taking its cue from pious Patrick, bucolic Down is blessed with an abundance of wide-open space, iconic rural vistas, and the ever-present backdrop of the brooding Mountains of Mourne. Although without the dramatic scenic splendor of Antrim's coastline, Down stands out for its heavenly serenity—it remains one of Ireland's least discovered regions.

Okay, so McCool is fictional, and the facts on St. Patrick are dodgy at best, but that's all the more reason to head out in search of their legacies. What you'll see along the way will be half the reward.

DON'T LEAVE ANTRIM & DOWN WITHOUT . . .

WALKING IN THE GIANT'S FOOTSTEPS   Yes, it's one of the most popular attractions in Ireland, but the massive, hexagonal stepping stones at Giant's Causeway are not only spectacular to behold, but within striking distance of many of Antrim's marquee natural sights. See p. 410.

SEEKING OUT THE LITTLE FOLK IN THE ANTRIM GLENS   Antrim's nine glens are places of undeniable beauty—idyllic woodland valleys carved out of the land at the edge of the sea—but they are imbued with a rich folkloric heritage that still includes fairies, giants, and other mythical creatures. It's said that

Counties Antrim & Down

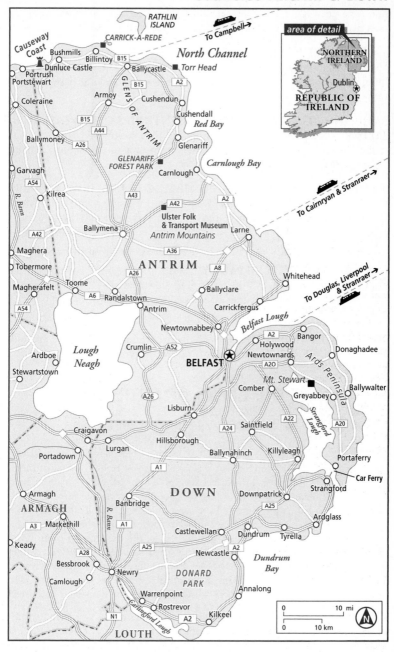

RATHLIN ISLAND

CARRICK-A-REDE

To Campbell →

North Channel

Causeway Coast

Bushmills
Billintoy
Dunluce Castle
B15
Portrush
Portstewart
Ballycastle
Torr Head

area of detail

NORTHERN IRELAND

Dublin

REPUBLIC OF IRELAND

Coleraine
Armoy
B15
Cushendun

Cushendall
Red Bay

Ballymoney
A44
A26
Glenariff

Garvagh
A54
GLENARIFF FOREST PARK
Carnlough
Carnlough Bay

Kilrea
A43
A42
A2

Ulster Folk & Transport Museum
Antrim Mountains
Larne

Ballymena

Maghera
A42
A36

Tobermore
A26
A8

Magherafelt
Toome
A6
Ballyclare
Whitehead

Randalstown
Carrickfergus
To Cairnryan & Stranraer →

Ardboe
Lough Neagh
Antrim
Newtownabbey
Belfast Lough
To Douglas, Liverpool & Stranraer →

Stewartstown
Crumlin
A52
BELFAST
Bangor
Donaghadee

Holywood
Newtownards
A2

Mt. Stewart
Comber
Greyabbey
Ballywalter

A26
Lisburn
A20
Ards Peninsula

Craigavon
A24
Saintfield
A22
Strangford Lough
A20

Portadown
Lurgan
Hillsborough
Killyleagh
Portaferry

A1
Ballynahinch
Car Ferry

Armagh
DOWN
Downpatrick
Strangford

ARMAGH
Banbridge
A25
Ardglass

A3
Markethill
A1
Castlewellan
Dundrum
Tyrella

Keady
A28
A25
Newcastle
A2
Dundrum Bay

Bessbrook
DONARD PARK
Annalong

Camlough
Newry
Warrenpoint
Rostrevor
Kilkeel

N1
A2
0   10 mi
0   10 km

LOUTH

397

non-believers will never see the "gentle folk," but whether you believe or not, you can't deny the fairy-tale allure of the glens themselves. See p. 403.

MOONWALKING TO A ROCKY ISLAND   Just a few short steps on the Carrick-a-Rede rope-bridge is all it takes to walk from the mainland to a tiny, uninhabited rock island; look down, however, and the crashing waves below will make you think you've left this orbit. See p. 412.

SAMPLING THE FIREWATER AT A CENTURIES-OLD WHISKEY DIS-TILLERY   The best whiskey-tour in Ireland is in Bushmills where the distillers might not be turning water into wine, but are creating something just as magical (as you'll discover in the tasting room). See p. 412.

TRAIPSING THROUGH THE CRUMBLING RUINS OF A CLIFF-EDGE CASTLE   It may not be the most magnificent castle in creation, but I do love the way Dunluce—on Antrim's northern coast—is practically hanging off the edge of a cliff. So much so, in fact, that the kitchen once dropped right into the sea below. See p. 413.

CONNECTING WITH ST. PADDY   Ireland's ecclesiastical father may or may not lie buried next to the church on a hill in Downpatrick; this was, however, the place where St. Patrick started his crusade to turn the pagan Irish into Christians. See p. 423.

WALKING IN THE MOURNES   Down's Mountains of Mourne are said to have inspired C.S. Lewis's Kingdom of Narnia; they remain a sublime landscape, perfect for hikers. See p. 426.

THE GLENS OF ANTRIM

Ruggedly beautiful, the Antrim Coast sweeps and curves around post-glacial beaches and weathered headlands—white chalk and dark basalt rock—that stretch into the sea like witches' fingers. Travel the full 100km (62 miles) between Larne and Portrush, and you'll see the best coastal scenery Northern Ireland has to offer. Just north of Larne (an unremarkable port town), you reach the first of the nine famed and fabled Glens of Antrim, a collection of forested valleys giving on to idyllic bays, and sheltered by spellbinding rock formations, rugged hills, and mountains that wrap haphazardly around the coast. Grassy fields roll almost all the way down to the water's edge, and time and again you'll discover that the slowly moving white rocks are actually sheep, grazing amidst the tremendous calm. It's relatively unspoiled, with a sprinkling of villages, mostly tiny and unassuming, drawing what little business there is from outlying farms and summer sightseers. A vague sense of isolation keeps human numbers low, too, so many of the villages retain a quirky, unique atmosphere—perfect for anyone wanting a real sense of "getting away from it all," particularly if you arrive during quieter periods.

A BRIEF HISTORY OF THE GLENS

Millennia ago, Ice Age glaciers worked their magic along Antrim's coast, tearing nine rugged wedges out of the existing mountain; nature and time conspired to nurture a series of micro-environments within these valleys, spawning unusual forest vegetation that makes the region unique in All Ireland. Remote and isolated, this was where communities of monks—no doubt drawn by the quiet and peaceful seclusion—settled around 1,300 years ago. Over the centuries the Antrim Mountains kept what farms did exist in the glens well cut off from the outside world. In fact, Scotland was always considered closer and more accessible than the Irish hinterland, and it was only in 1832 that construction of the road into the glens began. Such isolation meant that Celtic culture and Irish language flourished here, and even today whispers of Celtic mythology penetrate local life—just ask anyone about Cushendall's Fairy Hill, Tiveragh.

LAY OF THE LAND

From south to north, as you're most likely to encounter them if driving or riding along the coast from Belfast along the **A2,** here's the lowdown on the nine Glens of Antrim and their villages:

GLENARM   The most southerly of the glens, this is where the Earls of Antrim have had their castle since Randal MacDonnell left Dunluce Castle to build his hunting estate here; the present castle was built in 1636, but has been burnt, renovated, and adapted so frequently, there's not much left of the original. Lined with colorful buildings, sleepy **Glenarm village** comprises a single road and some unfortunate concrete development round the seafront. The compact road leads to a gateway which now gives access to the glen itself; park here and set off alongside the river. For what it's worth, you'll be able to catch a glimpse of MacDonnell's hideously restored castle.

GLENCLOY   Next up, Glencloy meets the ocean at **Carnlough,** a town once closely linked to its nearby limestone quarries, an industry established here by the Marquis of Londonderry to relieve famine pressure in the 1840s; now it's a seaside village concentrating on tourism, boosted by the existence of its historic sea-facing hotel, once owned by Winston Churchill. Indeed, besides staring at the fishing boats bobbing around in the shabby little harbor, most of what there is to see in Carnlough hangs on the hotel's walls, which are chockablock with memorabilia.

Continuing from Carnlough, the plummeting hills take on a more dramatic outlook, forming natural stone sculptures that line the road. Soaring, monumental cliffs give way to sheer drops. At other points, you look below to find you're just a few feet above the rocky shore. Around the vast headland at Garron Point, is the tiny enclave of **Waterfoot,** where—unless you stick your head into one of the pubs—you might think the place is completely abandoned.

GLENARIFF   Miniature Waterfoot provides access to the most naturally glamorous of all the glens. Pretty indeed, this "Queen of the Glens" is set in a deep U-shaped valley where lush forests, waterfalls, and streams, provide precisely the sort of setting that have inspired fantastic legends. If you only have time to explore one of the glens, you'll want to focus your attentions here, taking full advantage of the marked trails within the **Glenariff Forest Park.**

Acknowledged by locals as the "Capital of the Glens," the little village of **Cushendall,** just around the corner from Waterfoot, is not only a useful base for seeing Glenariff, but nearby Glenballyeamon and Glenaan, too. With a number of B&Bs, Cushendall also has the most infrastructure, including a small hotel, several restaurants and bars, and a supermarket. It does not, however, have a petrol station.

GLENDUN   Nearby, **Cushendun** is a tiny village at the head of Glendun, held to be famous—and unique—because a string of Cornish-style houses were built here in the 1920s. With a broad sweep of gently curving beach, a motley collection of fishing boats, its rugged mountains to the back and these quaint white-washed cottages, Cushendun is certainly worthy of a visit.

GLENCORP, GLENSHESK & GLENTAISIE   The road (A2) from Cushendall towards Cushendun, cuts through short, wide **Glencorp,** marked by stone walls and gorse-studded hills. On the eastern slope, a prominent round hill, **Tieveragh,** is said to be home to multitudes of fairies who come out in a procession on May Eve (Apr 30).

Beyond Cushendun, the coastal drive around Torr Head towards Ballycastle gives access to some of my favorite views and hidden experiences along this entire coast. Virtually a metropolis compared with other villages along the coast, **Ballycastle** sits at the head of the northernmost glens, **Glenshesk** and **Glentaisie.**

GETTING THERE & GETTING AROUND

For the easiest access to the Glens, you'll probably want either your own car, or a bicycle. Although distances between the glens and their villages are small, some of the best parts are away from the main road that cuts through here. Public transport is a good money-saving option, of course. The **Antrim Coaster** (Ulsterbus 252) runs a circular route through the Antrim Glens from Belfast (departing 9:05am from Europa Buscentre), stopping at Glenarm (10:40am), Carnlough (10:46am), Waterfoot (11:05am), Cushendall (11:10am), and Cushendun (11:25am), and then continuing to Ballycastle (11:53am), Giant's Causeway, Bushmills, Portrush, and Coleraine (in County Derry). Buy an "All Day Rambler" ticket for £4.30, allowing you to make as many stops along the route you like.

ACCOMMODATIONS, BOTH STANDARD & NOT

If you're looking to rent a house or cottage in Northern Ireland, first visit **www.nischa.com**, website of the **Northern Ireland Self-Catering Holidays Association (NISCHA).** From the menu, you can either choose "Browse Map," allowing you to browse options by county, or "Full Search" which searches by your criteria for the type of place you're looking for. Once a property is selected, very detailed descriptions appear, along with photographs, prices, and the all contact details for the property. Bookings are done directly with the owners, but you have the assurance that all of the listed properties are regularly inspected by the Northern Ireland Tourism Board. Antrim has many listings, but you should remember to specify "coastal" when entering your criteria, so you really do end up with a pad that potentially has a sea view.

NISCHA may also refer you on to another "direct to owner" site where you can compare rental prices: **Cottages in Ireland** (☎ 0870/236-1630; www.cottages inireland.com) specializes in freestanding, mostly rural cottages (the ones I've seen have a character and charm) in Northern Ireland and Donegal. While some of the cottages were purpose-built for guests, many are traditional homes or converted historic properties; the site grades each of the cottages, but I wouldn't place too much faith in that as the star-rating generally alludes to amenities, which as we all know, aren't the be all and end all. Like NISCHA, this isn't an agency, but a marketing and booking service, which means that you'll be dealing directly with the owners when it comes to arranging check-in details and sorting out any problems that may arise. A few have on-site management (or assistance nearby), but in most cases, you'll want to ask about what access you'll have to a maintenance person if something goes wrong.

So, there's no shortage of rental home opportunities in and around the Glens of Antrim. But the one I prefer for it's near-perfect elevated location overlooking the Bay of Cushendun has got to be the **Coach House** ✦✦ (185 Torr Rd., Cushendun; ☎ 028/2176-1252; maggie.scally@hotmail.com; cash only). With two double bedrooms, a full kitchen, and private garden, it's a fine base from which to explore the glens. And, did I mention the view? On a clear day it stretches all the way to Scotland's Mull of Kintyre. All this can be yours for a full week for just £395 in summer and £280 in winter; shorter period rentals would depend of availability (unlikely in mid-summer) but you could get the house for £120 to £145 for 2 nights, or £145 to £165 for 3 nights. And, while some self-catering options leave you feeling a little isolated and insecure because you don't quite know where everything is or how things work, you always have the security of knowing that the proprietor is in the B&B next door (p. 402).

If camping is your thing, you can set up base opposite the entrance to Glenariff Forest Park (p. 403), where authorities have a **campsite** (98 Glenariff Rd.; ☎ 028/2955-6000; cash only), with modern facilities and electricity points for caravans. It's informally run, and you can't pre-book, but you can call ahead to check on availability. A park ranger does the rounds early in the day or at night and collects £8 to £11 per tent.

£   Considering the spectacular views afforded by its location above Cushendall village, you just won't believe your good fortune when checking in at Jim and Olive McAuley's wonderfully neat, clean, and remarkably priced **Cullentra House** ✦✦ (16 Cloughs Rd., Cushendall; ☎ 028/2177-1762; www.cullentrahouseireland.com; cash only). Jim, a local headmaster, is a fount of information on what to see and do in the area. Olive, a former nurse, takes care to constantly upgrade the bedrooms: Crisp, fresh linens and considered, coordinated color schemes are telling of personal attention to detail. All the rooms (most of which are spacious) are en suite (showers only) and have amenities such as TVs, Wi-Fi, trouser press, and tea and coffee facilities; you'll pay just £46 double, or £30 single. One thing you must know is that when staying here, you really will get a sense that you're staying with a local family, so it's not a place for anyone looking for the anonymity of hotel. By the way, August is particularly busy, so you'd need to book up to 8 months in advance.

£   Another unassuming B&B, this one with smashing views over all Glenariff— the "The Queen of the Glens"—is Donnell and Elizabeth O'Loan's **Sanda** ✦ (29 Kilmore Rd., Glenariff; ☎ 028/2177-1785; www.sandabnb.com; cash only), situated just 1km (⅗ mile) inland from Waterfoot, en route to the Glenariff Forest Park. Lovely, compact, and decent, with just two pastel toned bedrooms (one double and one slightly larger twin, both £50), with homey duvets, TVs, and bedside lamps; there's an attached shower and toilet, while the basin is in the bedroom. There's also an extra room without bathroom, which is suitable for small children. This peaceful home makes a good base for discovering the history of the glens; Donnell used to be a teacher and is a member of the local historical society and he loves to share his knowledge. He can also help with researching local genealogical history if you've come searching for your roots, and there are lots of books on the region to browse through. Best of all, you'll probably never forget the view over the glen as you enjoy a hearty Irish breakfast.

££   If you like the sound of the Coach House (discussed above), but aren't in the market for a week-long stay, then how about owner Maggie Scally's B&B right next door? She calls it the **Villa Farmhouse** ✸✸ (same contact details; cash only) and it is one of the most pleasant and attractive lodging options in the Glens. A 19th-century Tudor farmhouse, whitewashed with traditional dark timber beams, this is another place where you're constantly falling in love with the views. Inside, it's quaint and homey, and very well taken care of. At £60 double, it's a little pricier than other B&Bs in the area, but you'll thank your lucky stars for the rare chance to stay in such an idyllic location.

££   There are two moderately priced hotels in Antrim's glens. One is Cushendall's central, appropriately christened the **Glens Hotel** (6 Cost Rd., Cushendall; ☎ 028/2177-1223; www.theglenshotel.com; MC, V) which is truly laid back, retaining much of the traditional character of a small town lodge, devoid of pretense. Locals hang out in the little bar-cum-lounge, and there's quite a nifty conservatory-style glassed-in sitting area from where you can enjoy views over the seafront, even when the weather doesn't cooperate. Bedrooms are a very mixed bag and mostly not very pretty; nevertheless, when I last looked around, four units affording views had been refurbished with relatively plush decor and pine poster beds. A few rooms have biggish bathrooms (and tubs), but most are really tiny (and are shower only). Lodgings may be modest, but if you'd prefer a hotel this is a fairly decent bet at £70.

DINING FOR ALL TASTES

£   Glenarm's languid charm spills into cheerful little **Sally's Coffee Shoppe** (36 Toberwine St., Glenarm; ☎ 028/2884-1139; Thurs–Mon 9am–5pm; cash only) which you can't miss on the main road through the village. It's perfect for a pick-me-up after exploring the glen. There's a selection of attentively prepared sandwiches (around £3–£4), but I'd opt for the warm wild boar salad (£2.75) any day. Surprisingly for such a small village, the coffee here is excellent.

£–££   Perhaps it's because there's really nowhere else to eat in Cushendun, but **Mary McBride's Bar & Restaurant** ✸ (2 Main St., Cushendun; ☎ 028/2176-1511; Sat–Sun 12:30–8pm; MC, V) is a much-loved spot for laid back weekend dining, drawing locals as well as tourists from throughout the Glens. The fare is standard pub grub, but it's the buzz that accompanies your time here that makes all the difference. The menu is a mix of fish, chicken, steak, and vegetable dishes, but you can also order toasted sandwiches (£3.80), homemade lasagna (£6.75), and burgers (£5.50). But, if I were you, I'd opt for good old reliable steak and Guinness pie, served with peas and chips, for £6.

£–££   In the heart of Cushendall's tiny village, above Joe and Shelia McCollam's massively popular pub, and offering an "upmarket" experience at small village prices, is **Upstairs@Joe's** ✯ (23 Mill St., Cushendall; ☎ 028/2177-2630; Mon-Sat noon–6pm; MC, V). Chef Pol Shields comes up with new menus each month, adjusting to what's in season or how temperatures might impact preferences; what I appreciate most, is how healthy all his dishes are, and how much flavor he manages to pack in. Taking his cue from the location, the menu is always strong on fish. If there's tuna—usually a seared loin cutlet, perhaps with garlic mash and wild mushroom jus (around £12)—that's where I'd put my money. Your dining experience is complemented by a fairly sophisticated, yet affordable wine list (£11–£25 per bottle.).

££   Right across the street from Joes, I've heard groans of excitement when diners are served their sizzling steaks (£13) at **Harrys** ✯✯ (10 Mill St., Cushendall; ☎ 028/2177-2022; www.harryscushendall.com; daily noon–9:30pm; MC, V). Harry and Julia McMahon offer a pub menu (most dishes and sandwiches £6–£7), but, I think it's rather worth ordering a proper meal. Start with the homemade pâté (£3.50), followed by salmon steak given zest and tang with a flavorful lemon and garlic sauce (£9.50) or perhaps one of their sophisticated specials like honey-roasted duck in orange and Cointreau sauce (£11), or vegetable samosas (£7).

WHY YOU'RE HERE: EXPLORING THE GLENS
As I've mentioned, your best bet for a 1-day taster of the Glens is to plunge head-first into the **Glenariff Forest Park** ✯✯✯ (Glenariff Rd., Glenariff; ☎ 028/2175-8232; www.forestserviceni.gov.uk; £4 car, £1.50 per person; daily Apr–Sept 8am–8pm; Oct–Mar 10am–sunset) where you can hike to your hearts content, following well-marked trails that give a good idea of distances and also of what you're going to see along the way. In spring, the forest floor is covered with a dizzying pattern of bluebells, white wood sorrel, and wild garlic; in summer, sweet-smelling woodruff combines with the deep blue of bugle. This is a likely place to see the difficult-to-spot red squirrel, as well as excellent birdlife. Of course, it can get busy and crowded in summer.

The Waterfall Walks Trail is probably the most commonly followed trail, with 5km (3 miles) of stairways, pathways, and boardwalks on stilts. But if you prefer to linger, then take the 9km (5½-mile) Scenic Trail, which takes you to an elevation of 260m (853 ft.), rewarded by unforgettable views over the glen and (weather permitting) as far as Scotland.

Money Saving Tip: An alternative, slightly sneaky, way of getting in to the Park, but without paying to park your car, is to follow earlier signs to **Laragh Lodge** (120 Glen Rd., Glenariff; ☎ 028/2175-8221; www.laraghlodge.com; MC, V), a restaurant (food served daily noon–9pm) and bar (open till midnight), where you can leave your car and then follow one of the paths to the Park entrance. Technically, if you sneak in like this, it's only polite to return to Laragh for a drink or a meal—grab a window seat for views of the nearby waterfall, perhaps over late lunch.

If you follow the road that runs from the tower down towards the sea, you'll eventually come to the ruins of ancient **Layd Church** ✪✪, which has an eerie, beautifully situated graveyard that was the traditional burial place of the McDonnells, the Scottish lords who became the Earls of Antrim. It's an enchanting spot, with a stream, an unusual 14th-century headstone (it's the one with a hole in it, albeit with the wrong date carved into it), and an impressive vista of Red Bay (with Scotland in the distance).

A popular activity—particularly for anyone interested in architectural peculiarities—is simply trolling around the heritage village of **Cushendun** ✪; it's unique enough to be "owned" in its entirety by the National Trust (don't worry—there's no entry fee). In 1912, the village was commissioned as a set of 7 houses on a square, and the architect, Clough William-Ellis, created a series of Cornish-style cottages which would be aesthetically perfect if there weren't some signs of modern development creeping in around town. Still, there's a lovely long beach here, and Mary McBride's (p. 402) is a fine pub.

From Cushendun towards Ballycastle, the Torr Scenic Road leads past the **Torr Head** ✪✪✪ promontory, the site of an ancient fort. It's surely one of my favorite spots along the Antrim Coast, reached by following a steep, windy road that goes past ruined houses; from the car park, you half-climb up to a disused coastguard lookout and then simply drink in the views. Look for the Scottish islands of Jura and Islay (to the north-west), and the Mull of Kintyre should be visible in clear weather. Scan the water, too, for commonly sighted porpoises, and rarely seen minke whales.

THE OTHER GLENS OF ANTRIM

One thing's for sure—Irish folk have the gift of the gab. Whether you meet them in a pub and get the lowdown on some private matter, or engage them in debate on meatier topics, this is a nation of wonderful orators. While some people will spin fantastic yarns about just about anything you care to imagine, a few are so gifted that they've elevated this traditional social practice to an art form and become professional storytellers. One of Ireland's top storytellers is Liz Weir who has penned books of children's stories (including *Boom Chicka Boom*) and done a storytelling series for BBC Radio. She's also been all over the world with her talent and regularly organizes music and storytelling sessions for visitors to her hostel-style digs, **Ballyeamon Camping Barn** (127 Ballyeamon Rd.; ☎ 028/2175-8451 or 028/2175-8699; www.taleteam.demon.co.uk; cash only). Overlooking Glenariff Forest Park, just 8km (5 miles) from Cushendall, the "Barn" has 14 bunk beds in a dorm. Laundry, kitchen, and Internet facilities are provided, and you have the opportunity to solicit your hostess for some tall and magical tales—possibly connected with the many fairies believed to reside in the glens.

NIGHTLIFE

Considered just about the finest venues for traditional music sessions anywhere along the Antrim coast, **McCollam's** ✪✪ (23 Mill St.; ☎ 028/2177-1876) is bang in the center of Cushendall, and usually opens sometime in the afternoon or early evening, definitely by 7pm. There's music on Sunday and Friday nights, and more

---

Drink Up & You Eat for Free

I'm a big fan of Waterfoot's wood-paneled **Saffron Bar** ★★ (4–6 Main St., Waterfoot; ☎ 028/2177-2906) where regulars pile in on weekends to share gossip, throw darts, and half-heartedly keep an eye on the televised sports; it's a great place to rub shoulders with those who live in the glens. The owners not only serve cheaper-than-usual pints (£2.40 for a Guinness), but on Friday and Saturday afternoons, they hand out free sandwiches and bowls of tasty homemade soup. A great treat after exploring Glenariff Forest Park just a few kilometers down the drag. And, if that's not reason enough, there are also live music sessions Friday to Sunday evenings.

---

frequently during peak summer months when you'll find many more visitors cramming into the pub. Last rounds are called at midnight, but you can continue drinking with the regulars till quite a bit later.

BALLYCASTLE, BUSHMILLS & THE CAUSEWAY COAST

It's worth getting under the skin of slightly ramshackle Ballycastle, a vivacious little town that lies on the coast roughly midway between the Giant's Causeway and Cushendun. A central location makes it viable for exploring not only the Causeway Coast, but also the Glens of Antrim; and because it's the only town of any substantial size for kilometers, it's incredibly lively, with a vibrant pub scene, fanatical following of the sport of hurling, and a blue flag beach. Ballycastle is also where you can catch ferries to Rathlin Island. Bushmills is famed for one thing only, and that's whiskey. The small town is where the world's oldest licensed distillery still turns out millions of liters of the triple distilled "water of life" and because it's so near the world-renowned Giant's Causeway, is popular even among teetotalers. But, really, your main focus in this area should be the coast between Ballycastle and Bushmills—this is where you'll discover the fantastic stepping-stone highway built by Finn McCool; the miniature adventure of the Carrick-a-Rede rope bridge; and the cliff-hugging Dunluce Castle. Not to mention Cliffside walks where you can make your own discoveries.

GETTING THERE & GETTING AROUND

The coast-skirting **A2** links Ballycastle with Bushmills. Smaller roads to reach the Giant's Causeway, the Carrick-a-Rede rope bridge (at Ballintoy), and Dunluce Castle, are clearly marked off the A2.

In summer, the **Causeway Rambler** (Ulsterbus 402; ☎ 028/7032-5400; www.translink.co.uk) runs between Bushmills and Carrick-a-Rede (23 min.); the Rambler also stops at the Giant's Causeway and Dunseverick Castle along the way. An "All Day Rambler" ticket costs £4.30, allowing you to stop at as many different spots along the way as you wish; there are seven departures in each direction through the day. The **Antrim Coaster** (Ulsterbus 252) runs a circular route via the Antrim Glens from Belfast at 9:05am (from Europa Buscentre), stopping at the Giant's Causeway, and then continuing to Bushmills, Portrush, and Coleraine (in County Derry). Again, your best ticket option is an "All Day Rambler" for £4.30. The nearest **train** halt for the Giant's Causeway is at Portrush, 13km (8 miles) away; journey time from Belfast is about 2½ hours and costs around £10, depending on which connection you use.

The **Ulster Way** hiking trail follows a coastal path that links Ballycastle with all the sights along this route and continues as far as Portrush and beyond, down to County Derry.

For assistance with local sightseeing, accommodation bookings (£2 service fee), transport queries (including bike rental), and information about getting to Rathlin Island, stop in at Ballycastle's **tourist office** (Sheskburn Hosue, 7 Mary St.; ☎ 028/2076-2024; July–Aug Mon–Fri 9:30am–7pm; Sat 10am–6pm; Sun 2–6pm; Sept–June Mon–Fri 9:30am–5pm).

ACCOMMODATIONS, BOTH STANDARD & NOT
In & Near Ballycastle

Mary McGinn lovingly refers to her hilltop property, just 3.25km (2 miles) from Ballycastle, as "a special piece of heaven," and—after falling in love with the views from up here—I can't fault her judgment. "Stonechat" and "Cuckoo's Nest" are the two self-catering **Crockatinney Cottages** (80A/80B Whitecastle Rd.; ☎ 028/2076-3451; www.crockatinneycottages.com; cash only), which she rents out to anyone seeking to partake of her idea of heaven. Spacious, fully furnished modern homes-away-from-home, each has one en suite master bedroom, and a second bedroom, plus a separate bathroom with bath and shower; bedrooms are done out in cottage-style pine furniture, but the overall look is actually quite slick, with tiled floors, contemporary artworks, and even some modern lounge furniture. A fully kitted kitchen with open-plan dining and living area is complemented by a sun lounge. Centrally heated, the cottages also have traditional open fires (ask for turf to fuel this if you want to feel like a real local). Up here, you're far away from traffic, and noise, and any of the unsightliness of town life; there's even a play area for kids. The weekly rate (Sat–Sat) is £550, while a 3-night weekend costs £300; heating and electricity are included in the price.

£   Facing the marina, and wedged up against the famous Marine Hotel in an old, narrow house, is small, homey **Ballycastle Backpackers** (4 North St.; ☎ 028/2076-3612 or 077/7323-7890; cash only) which I've found comfortable (and neat and clean) enough, and certainly the most economical place in town to crash. Dorm beds are £11, but a small private double or twin room with a wash basin, some hanging space and mattresses that won't kill your back, costs £28 (facilities are shared). There's a kitchen for you to use, a lounge where you can chill out, and you get a key to the front door, so you won't have to deal with lock-out or curfew. If you'd prefer more privacy, but still want a good deal, the owners also rent a renovated self-catering cottage behind the hostel. It's nothing fancy, but has two small en suite bedrooms (one double, one twin) above a lounge with open fireplace and open-plan fully fitted kitchenette. The main drawback is that it's hemmed in by the hostel, which you have to walk through to get to the cottage, but at just £35 per room per night (in quieter periods, you needn't take the whole cottage), you should probably overlook such a minor inconvenience.

£   Ballycastle's loveliest B&B is Valerie Greene's proudly maintained **Fragrens** ✦ (34 Quay Rd.; ☎ 028/2076-2168; MC, V), which I've found to be comfortable, reliable, and actually quite charming, thanks in no small measure to Valerie's welcoming nature. Valerie's personality also spills into the decor, which is quite cottage-like, with lots of pinewood and floral fabrics and linens, and individual color schemes in each of the bedrooms. Rooms are either in the main, original house or in the annex cottage (which feels just a touch more private); all the rooms have private bathrooms, little TVs, and a kettle. There's also plenty of off-street parking. You order breakfast from a menu (rather than being asked if you want a "full fry" as is the practice in so many B&Bs) and dine in a pleasant little conservatory. Most enchanting of all, is the price: £50 for a double room, or £70 the family unit that takes three adults or two adults and two children.

££   About 7 minutes outside Ballycastle, **Glenmore House** ✦ (Whitepark Rd.; ☎ 028/2076-3584; www.glenmore.biz; MC, V) has more in common with a small inn or hotel than a B&B, yet it still retains a hands-on, family-run sensibility. John is a farmer-turned-hotelier; he finds time (between looking after the few sheep) to chat endlessly about anything and everything (he once explained that he could talk the hind legs off a donkey). His daughter (an excellent vocalist and *bodhrán*-player) arranges traditional music sessions in the bar over weekends, and his wife organizes homey meals in the restaurant-cum-breakfast room. Always looking to improve, John seems to add a new feature with every season. Bedrooms are spacious and more than adequate, and at £56 double, something of a bargain; single rooms are £30. John also offers caravan and camping facilities (£13 per camp site) with showers and kitchen facilities. Glenmore is very popular with fishermen and walkers who come here in droves in summer to face off against the golfers.

££   Five minutes from Ballycastle, and just 15 minutes from the Giant's Causeway, **Crockatinney Guest House** ✦✦ (80 Whitepark Rd.; ☎ 028/2076-8801; www.crockatinneyguesthouse.co.uk; cash only) is so fantastically situated, you'll wonder why anyone would choose to stay in town. Thanks to a slight elevation, the property overlooks the Bay of Ballycastle, a dormant volcano, Fair Head Cliff, and—on a good day (always on a good day)—the Mull of Kintyre, in Scotland. Named for the islands off the coast, the bedrooms are modestly proportioned, but done out with a sense of style (even if that style is a bit "quaint")—great linens, pine wardrobes, and attached showers; it's all very no-nonsense and sensible. Thanks to the views, breakfast turns out to be more an event than a feeding session; I could sit in the neat little dining room for hours just watching the sea.

Near the Giant's Causeway

The best self-catering deal along the Causeway Coast are the **Ballylinny Cottages** ✦✦✦ (7 Causeway Rd., Bushmills; ☎ 077/7188-6516; www.giants causeway.co.uk; MC, V), a cluster of fully equipped units within spitting distance

---

Cheap Irish Stew, All Day

All kinds of fun can be had at Ballycastle's big, popular, and ceaselessly busy **Central Bar & Restaurant** ★ 🐾 (Ann St.; ☎ 028/2076-3877; daily noon–1:30am; MC, V), which draws a mixed crowd for its non-stop pints, affordable pub grub, and—later at night—upstairs disco. You can get Irish stew here for just £2.50 (usually until 8pm, for other dishes the kitchen closes at 5pm), so there's no excuse for not supplementing your Guinness with real nourishment. The back dining section is especially popular with families with children, who tend to take over in here until around 8pm; after that a younger crowd starts drifting in and the volume of the *craic* increases dramatically.

---

of the Giant's Causeway. Occupying white farm-style bungalows are 11 different units of different configurations and styles. You can choose from more traditional "cottagey" units—with bedrooms downstairs and living room upstairs, wooden floors, fireplace, complete kitchen, and coastal views—or quite modern, contemporary-style units built as recently as 2007. The latter tend to have chic furniture and state-of-the-art amenities, not to mention big picture windows. In the end, it's all about taste. On top of all the standard amenities you expect, kitchens come with coffeemakers, dishwashers, and washer/dryer facilities so you can sort out your own laundry; there's also Wi-Fi access. Although you should make a point of insisting on a good view when you book, I can tell you that "Portnaboe" (one of the larger units) has an outlook that is quite heart-stopping. As for prices, they vary greatly. By way of example, a two-bedroom unit comfortably sleeps five people and costs £190 for 2 nights (only available Sept–June); in peak season (July–Aug) the same place will cost £490 for a full week. A tennis court is onsite, as well a little shop for basic supplies.

££   If you want to bed down right at the Giant's Causeway—literally—choose the **Causeway Hotel** (40 Causeway Rd., Bushmills; ☎ 028/2073-1210 or 028/2073-1226; www.giants-causeway-hotel.com; MC, V). Despite its flaws (it's old-fashioned and a bit rundown) it exudes loads of character and affords views that many people return for time and again. By staying here (or simply stopping here for a cup of coffee) you'll also avoid paying to park your car at the adjacent Giant's Causeway Visitor Centre. The big toss-up is deciding whether you want a more spacious (and modern) room, or would prefer to soak up the decaying ambience in one of the original (1836) bedrooms, which are definitely smaller and feature lots of flaking paint (run-down but tolerable). Entertainment? The atmosphere in the cozy little pub can be quite spirited; alternatively, designate a driver and head off to nearby Ballycastle or Portrush for some serious social intrigue. The damage? £70 double in low season (Sept–Mar) and £85 in high season (July–Aug).

Ballintoy

££   Clearly, dining comes first at strategically located **Fullerton Arms** (22 Main St.; ☎ 028/2076-9613; www.fullertonrms.co.uk; MC, V), a pleasant-enough little inn where the popular restaurant regularly drowns out all signs that there are a clutch of neat little bedrooms upstairs (£70 double). Insist on one with a sea view. Ballintoy is midway between Ballycastle and the Giant's Causeway and is another one road village, this time with the sea on one side of the road and the town on the other.

DINING FOR ALL TASTES

If you're staying in either of the Bushmills or Giant's Causeway hotels discussed above, your best bet for dining might be to either stick to your hotel, or to make an outing of it—either to Ballycastle, where there's plenty of choice and some unexpected party atmosphere on weekends, or to Portrush, an unattractive seaside resort where the various Ramore (see below) eateries are among my favorite spots for fun dining, followed by fun at the bar.

Wining, Dining & Carousing in Portrush

Portrush is a mad, mad little seaside resort right near the border between Antrim and Londonderry. It's popular with surfers as well as bevies of teens and students who flock to its promenades, sleazy games arcades, and tired shops to do lots of conspiratorial "hanging around." That's why it's so surprising to me that it's home to some of the most exciting eating and drinking venues in Northern Ireland. Make your way to the harbor and you'll find killer atmosphere at massive, modish **Ramore—The Wine Bar** ✿✿✿ (The Harbour; ☎ 028/7082-4313; www.ramorerestaurant.com; Mon–Sat 12:15–2:15pm and 5–10pm; Sun 12:30–3pm and 5–9pm; MC, V), where the market in fun, upbeat dining has been wholeheartedly cornered. People start queuing early on weekends to ensure they get in, but even if you turn up late, don't shrug off the waiting list; you can grab a seat at the ultra-cool bar and investigate the wine list (house blends £10–£13) while you wait. Order and pay at the counter, choosing from a pretty eclectic menu: rump steak burgers (£6); Peking duckling with orange caramel sauce (£11); Thai monkfish red curry served in a clay hotpot (£14); garlic chicken and Dublin Bay prawns (£11); and chalked up specials.

An equally large crowd waits just around the corner, at another of Ramore's throbbing venues, the **Harbour Bistro** (The Harbour; ☎ 028/ 7082-2430; Mon–Fri 5–10pm; Sat 5–10:30pm; Sun 4–9pm; MC, V). Here, it's a similar menu, but a slightly different atmosphere, where you entertain yourself at the groovy, traditional **Harbour Bar** ✿✿✿ downstairs, before being called to your table. All in all, the stuff of a very glam night out.

Ballycastle is your best bet for dining, and actually has a number of reputable eateries, but here are suggestions for places where you won't break the bank, and where you will feel like you're supping with the locals.

£   Donnelly's Bakery & Coffee Shop (28 Ann St.; ☎ 028/2076-3236; www. donnellysbakery.co.uk; Mon–Sat 7am–6pm; cash only) has takeaway meals downstairs in the bakery; and sit down options upstairs at the diner-style eatery. Simple food but good, all-day breakfast costs £3 to £4, and at lunchtime you can grab shepherd's pie and chips for £4.

£–£££   In a cozy, slightly nautically themed space above Conolley's Bar (with its boozy clientele and busy pool tables), is **Anzac Bistro** ★★ kids (5 Market St.; ☎ 028/2076-8469; Mon–Fri 5–9pm; Sat–Sun noon–9pm; MC, V), a fine place for what locals call a *scrans*—a good meal—in an unassuming, family-friendly environment. I'm talking large plates of satisfying, attentively prepared grub a notch above what's being served elsewhere in town. At dinner you can order popular items like steak and chicken kebabs (served with tossed salad, £7.45), steaks for between £10 and £17, or fresh local fish that's chalked up on the board. Lunch is only served on weekends.

WHY YOU'RE HERE: TOP SIGHTS & ATTRACTIONS
With a little effort, you can squeeze all the major sights into a single day, particularly during the summer when access to the main draw, the Giant's Causeway, runs into the early evening.

The Giant's Causeway: Finn McCool's Basalt Stepping Stones
Certainly, they are one of the must-see wonders of the earth, and no matter how many photos you've seen, there's always a slight gasp when you come upon them for the first time. Basically, they're close on 40,000 basalt columns, astonishingly all polygonal in appearance and imaginatively arranged as if to form a gigantic walkway into the sea. The columns are a result, or so say the experts, of molten basalt being blasted out of the bowels of the earth some 60 million years ago; when it cooled, what were formed are the crystallized shapes—mostly hexagonal—that have been attracting fascinated tourists since the end of the 17th century. It's called the **Giant's Causeway** ★★★ because Irish lore tells a far more imaginative and romantic tale. The giant Finn McCool fell in love with a large lass on the Scottish isle of Staffa, and in order to get to her, he laid out these neat stepping stones, the other end of which can also be seen at Staffa. Things turned nasty when the giantess's Scottish lover caught wind of Finn's shenanigans and an earth-shaker of a fight broke out; in the chaos, Finn actually ripped out a big piece of Ulster and threw it at his opponent. As with so many legends, there's a point to all of this: The hole left in Ulster is now Lough Neagh and the uprooted missile is the Isle of Man.

To see Finn's basalt handiwork you're meant to park your car at the **Giant's Causeway Visitor Centre** (44 Causeway Rd.; ☎ 028/2073-1855; www.national trust.org.uk; £5 per car; daily Apr–Sept 10am–7pm; Oct–Mar 10am–5pm; closed Christmas week), where your experience is first held up by a mood-killing souvenir-cum-craft shop, a 12-minute audio-visual presentation (£1), and a scuttle of

Building the Trust: Saving on Northern Ireland's Heritage Sites

Scattered across the United Kingdom are hundreds of heritage sites managed by a government agency called **The National Trust.** Quite a number of these properties are in Northern Ireland. While entrance to a handful of these attractions is free (Belfast's Crown Liquor Saloon is one), most aren't and some attract hefty entrance fees. If you're not a U.K. citizen, always check that you're paying the standard admission, rather than the slightly higher "Gift Aid" price which is really a tax incentive scheme from which you can't benefit. ***Note:*** Discounted rates apply at all these sites for children (about half-price) and families ($2\frac{1}{2}$ times the normal adult admission), and children under 5 go free to all these sites.

If you're planning to visit a large number of National Trust properties, consider investing in annual membership (for purchase at any of their locations) which may just save you a few quid—but only really worthwhile if you're planning to also tour England, Scotland, or Wales, where your membership will be valid for scores more sites. The cost of annual National Trust membership is £46 for one adult, whereas family membership (valid for two adults and their children or grandchildren under 18 years of age) is £82. There's more good news for couples (residing at the same address), who pay a combined, discounted annual membership of £77. To make the decision easier, here's a list of adult ticket charges at Northern Ireland's National Trust sites that we've recommended:

Site	One Adult	Family	Parking
Giant's Causeway (Antrim)	free	free	£5
Carrick-A-Rede (Antrim)	£3.36	£8.54	free
Mount Stewart (Down)	£6.36	£15.90	free
Caste Ward (Down)	£7.06	£18.10	free
The Argory (Armagh)	£5	£12.54	£3.50
Ardress House (Armagh)	£4	£10	free
Castle Coole (Fermanagh)	£5	£12.27	free
Florence Court (Fermanagh)	£5	£12.27	£3.50
TOTAL	£35.78	£89.62	£12

So if you're a keen sightseer with a car that needs to be parked, you could save £1.78 per adult (not a heck of a lot), £6.56 per couple, or £19.62 per family on these eight sites alone . . . even more worthwhile for those of you planning further sightseeing in Great Britain within 1 year.

tourists trying to figure out what to do next. Here's what you do: Head straight through the shop and follow the lower path down to the water's edge. Within about 5 minutes, you'll be eyeballing the hexagonal pillars and walking over them, probably in a state of disbelief. If the 1.5km (1-mile) walk sounds too extreme to you, there's also an eco-friendly minivan that shuttles tourists between the visitor center and the stone patchwork for £2 round-trip.

When you've had your fill, make your way farther along the path you came down on, this time heading upwards to reach the **Organ,** an incredible rock formation which really does resemble its namesake when viewed from a distance; touch the stone to feel how it has been weathered over the centuries and smoothed by pounding water. For more awe-inspiring views and increasing peace and quiet, continue along this path as far as is permitted (erosion sometimes forces closures along the way), before turning back. Then, instead of going back down to the columns, follow the steep steps up to the ridge overlooking the Causeway, where you'll find yourself on the Causeway Coast Cliff Path. If you're feeling energetic, you can walk all the way to **Dunseverick Castle,** 7km (4½ miles) away, and beyond to the Carrick-a-Rede rope bridge (see below), 16km (10 miles) away. Alternatively, you can head back to the visitor center, and perhaps head over to the Causeway Hotel for a sundowner.

Hanging in There: the Carrick-a-Rede Rope Bridge

Not quite the rickety rope bridge adventure you might imagine, but this clever tourist attraction is definitely one of those "gotta do it, gotta say I done it" experiences, and I must confess to finding the seafront terrain here in some ways even more gloriously beautiful than around the Giant's Causeway. The **Carrick-a-Rede** ✪✪ (119a Whitepark Rd., Ballintoy; ☎ 028/2076-9839; www.nationaltrust.org.uk; £3.36; daily Mar–May 25 and Sept–Nov 2 10am–5:15pm; May 26–Aug 10am–6:15pm) is nothing more than a rope bridge some 20m (67 ft.) long, but it's your distance—30m (98 ft.) above the surface of the water, with waves crashing fiercely against the rocks below—that gives this experience its edge. For 350 years, the gap between the mainland and rocky Carrick Island was spanned by fishermen who strung their rope bridge to hang nets in the path of migrating salmon. These days, the bridge is taken down for the winter and then raised into place just before the tourist season starts; so while you'll feel ever so slightly like a moonwalker, commercialization has literally taken most of the play out of the swing-bridge (although vertigo sufferers do tend to cross very slowly). Incidentally, once you've crossed over, there's very little to explore on miniscule Carrick Island, but it sure is a pretty place to be. Also note that there's a 1km (⅔-mile) walk—along cliffs overlooking Larrybane Bay—from the car park to the bridge.

The drawback of Carrick-a-Rede? Even when it's quiet, it can feel a little congested—and on the bridge itself, you pretty much have to move one way or the other if someone else is trying to clamber on. Solution? Arrive before it opens and (carefully) hurry to be the first across.

Bushmills: Straight Up, with a Dash of Water

While imbibing one's favorite poison, usually hygienically distilled and then bottled to exacting standards, it's difficult to imagine how such intricate processes were carried out 100 years ago, never mind back in 1608, which is when the **Old**

Bushmills Distillery ✦✦✦ (Bushmills; ☎ 028/2073-1521; www.bushmills.com; £6; guided tours Mar–Oct Mon–Sat 9:15am–5pm; Sun noon–5pm; Nov–Feb Mon–Fri 10am–4:15pm; Sat–Sun 12:30–4:15pm; last tour about 1 hr. before closing) became what is now the oldest legal whiskey producer in the world. It remains the only grain-to-glass distillery in Ireland. Today, besides just tasting and talking about the ingenious liquor, you can get a behind-the-scenes gander at the production process, starting with the mashing process in which crushed barley (or grist) is stirred up by a furious machine that would not look out of place in one of those James Bond deadly escape sequences. Because you're being led through the very factory where the whiskey is transformed—from a mix of malted barley, yeast, and water, into a fine spirit—you get a full on sensory experience complete with the loud noise of heavy machinery and the sickly sweet odors of fermentation.

Most intriguing is the still house where the intricate process of distillation actually takes place; like something from an alchemist's laboratory straight out of the middle ages, with a gigantic copper still shaped like a wizard's hat, yet hooked up to a super-modern computer system that regulates the process. As you'll know from all the hype around Irish whiskey, it's distilled three times rather than twice (which is the practice in Scotland). After this third distillation, the cask strength spirit has an alcohol volume of 83%. This potent, clear liquid is then reduced with distilled water and left to mature in barrels during which time it loses 2% of its alcohol volume each year. And yes, you see the guys with their white lab coats and testing pipettes, so you know the whole process isn't magic after all.

On a detour to the bottling plant you will have a choice of whiskeys to sample—if the special anniversary brand "1608" is available to taste, jump at the chance; it's exceptional.

Tours are often booked up in advance in the summer, so it's always a good idea to call and reserve a place; from November to March, tours are available daily, but you need to call to find out when. Last tours usually set off at 4pm. *Note:* The bottling plant shuts down for the weekend at midday on Friday, so you ideally want to catch a weekday tour, and no later than 10am Fridays.

Hanging on the Edge: Dunluce Castle

It may not be the biggest castle, nor the best preserved, but the views from the precariously positioned **Dunluce Castle** ✦✦ (Coastal Rd., near Portrush; ☎ 028/2073-1938; www.ehsni.gov.uk; £2; daily Apr–Sept 10am–6pm; Oct–Mar 10am–5pm) are stellar; the dramatic setting affords views of Portrush and, across the water, Donegal's Inishowen Head.

Owned by the MacDonnells of Antrim, it's assumed that a fort has stood here since early-Christian times; certainly, the precarious cliff-hugging position indicates its suitability as a defensive structure, but most of what is now visible and available for you to investigate was built in the 16th and 17th centuries, the oldest parts being the round towers and curtain walls. Although the castle was attacked by Elizabethan cannons back in 1584, the most dramatic event in Dunluce's history happened one evening in 1639 when—much to the horror of the lady of the house, Catherine Manner, wife of Randal MacDonnell, the 1st Earl of Antrim—the sea-facing wall of the kitchen simply dropped into the sea taking several servants to their doom. A real city girl who in any case hated the

A Mini-Adventure that No One Speaks About

A detour to **Kinbane** ★★★ rewards visitors with a ruin, a headland, an adventure, and a divine photo op. Shhh . . . it's a local secret that very few visitors experience, though Kinbane is signposted off the main road between Ballycastle and the Giant's Causeway (keep a lookout). To get there you'll follow a windy narrow road down to a spot near the seafront, where you'll find a parking area and a path. Take the steep steps for your first photo op: a glorious view of Rathlin Island, Scotland, the mainland, and even some waterfalls. Keep going forward and wear decent footware as you're going to have to hop over a low wooden gate or two (ignore signs warning you to consider turning back); do stay away from the edges, where the long grass makes it difficult to see exactly what you're treading on. You also need to be extremely careful if the ground is wet. This area is not managed, so there is no responsible authority keeping the place up or to contact should you need help. Kinbane means "White Headland" and describes chalk-colored sheer drop at the very end of the headland that protects the crescent sweep of the Sea of Moyle. The headland juts out into the sea and features the remains of a castle built by Colla McDonnell in 1544; all that's left is the gate tower, but from up here, you look back toward the mainland, taking in the imposing basalt headland of Gobe Feagh ("Raven's Point") and juniper-clad grassy slopes. Only a flock of nonplussed sheep and the remains of a diminutive salmon fishery that closed in the late-1980s signal any nod to modern civilization. One suggestion: Consider packing a picnic and enjoy it out here in perfect solitude.

sound of the waves, Ms. Manner took this as her opportunity to move out of the castle and so inspired hubby Randal to relocate to Glenarm, where the Antrim Earls have been ever since. Don't be put off by the tale of the disappearing kitchen wall, since what remains of the kitchen court provides unforgettable views. In other parts of the castle, you'll come across quite discernibly different stages of architectural development, with partially visible bartizans (pepper pot turrets) characteristic of Scottish design, medieval, Renaissance, and Jacobean elements each marking different sets of home improvement carried out by a short-lived succession of owners.

THE OTHER CAUSEWAY COAST

Despite its size, Ballycastle is known throughout Ireland as an important center for the ancient Gaelic sport of hurling. You frequently see youngsters walking down the road with a hurley (the hurler's ash wood stick, also called a *camán*) in one hand, bouncing the leather *slíothar* (the ball) off its curved end. It can be a thrill to witness just how skillfully accurate these young players can be—particularly if you manage to catch them in action on the field, or even practicing on one

Oi! What's that You Called Me?

While in Antrim, you may come across a few examples of the Ulster-Scots dialect. *"Wee"* is easy, and we all know it means "small," which is usually used with some affection; but if someone calls you a *"lig,"* they think you're a stupid lout or a clumsy idiot . . . or at best, a clown. A *"borgeegle"* describes a botched job, *"yaffle"* means to eat speedily and noisily, and if someone says you're *"thran,"* it means they think you're awkward. To learn more about the Ulster-Scots dialect and explore an online dictionary, visit **www.ulsterscotsagency.com**.

of several fields around town, when they don't just bounce that ball, but whack it with brutal force and inevitable accuracy.

Ballycastle is also a great place to catch a local amateur game at no cost. The sport is fast, hard, mesmerizing, and at times, confusing . . . which makes it a great springboard for conversations with the other spectators. Ask about the rules and the scoring system, and you'll soon be able to get into the advanced details—like which team is a favorite to win this year's championship, or why hardly any of the senior players wear helmets (under-18s must wear them, fortunately). To find out when there's the likelihood of catching a game, pop in to **O'Neill's Sport House** (6–8 Ann St., Ballycastle; ☎ 028/2076-9940) and ask one of the lads about any weekend fixtures; the guys are usually so keen to help, they'll go out of their way to get the lowdown for you. Incidentally, you can buy your very own hurley here for around £8 to £16.

Explore the Area's Unique Heritage

"Ulster-Scots," is a term you're likely to hear from time to time in Ulster—particularly in northern Antrim, a region strongly associated with the culture and traditions of an Irish ethnic group originally from Scotland (tens of thousands fled to Ireland in the 1690s to escape famine in Scotland). While it's a politicized, complex identity issue, there are those who are keen on preserving some of the more sociable and enjoyable aspects of Ulster-Scots culture, including the unique dialect and music. **Bushmills Ulster Scots Heritage** (19a Main St., Bushmills; ☎ 028/2073-1761; www.bushmillsheritage.com) is one group that's pretty passionate about keeping the flame of Ulster-Scots culture alive. Besides being very active in community life (and Bushmills is a *very* Protestant town), it hosts discussions, workshops, and all kinds of events designed to promote an active interest in all things Ulster-Scots and these are open to folks of all backgrounds, even tourists. So, you can sign up for an introduction to Ulster-Scots language, or test your aptitude for *lambeg* drumming, Scottish dancing, or the tin whistle. From time to time, there are storytelling courses; and fun days with all kinds of entertainments—dance performances, poetry readings, and craft markets—are organized throughout the year, often complemented by the music of celebrated Ulster-Scots bands, informative lectures (on subjects like the significance of tartan), and even specialty Ulster-Scots food.

ATTENTION, SHOPPERS!

After generous helpings of *crathur* at Old Bushmills Distillery, there's only one shop in town that's managed to ignite any desire to shop: **therapy** ★★ (47 Main St., Bushmills; ☎ 028/2073-2727 or 078/0105-3428). Its Pam McAlister's unexpectedly cool little fashion boutique with fine threads on the racks and funky music to put you in a spending mood. Labels include U.K. designer Peter Werth, hot menswear by "Made in LUKE," and Linq. Pam does great sale racks, sometimes lobbing as much as 70% off superior lines; when I was last scrounging around, I found gorgeous T-shirts for a mere £5 and elegant fitted formal shirts for as little as £13.

If you want to leave the region with something special to remember your visit by, consider getting a hand-crafted *bodhrán* made by **Paul McAuley** (21 Leyland Park, Ballycastle; ☎ 028/2076-3126; www.irishbodhrans.com) who is himself a skillful player (catch him at the House of McDonnell; see below). These drum-family instruments—available in various sizes, from 23cm to 46cm (9–18 in.) in diameter—are made by stretching treated goat or deer skin across a circular wooden (ash or birch) frame. Paul can make the handheld drum to your specifications—learning to play it, however, is up to you.

NIGHTLIFE

At the heart of Ballycastle's social scene since April 1766, the **House of McDonnell** ★★★ (71 Castle St.; ☎ 028/2076-2975; www.houseofmcdonnell.com)—known colloquially as "Wee Tom's," in fond recognition of owner Tom O'Neill's diminutive frame—hosts superb trad music sessions on Friday nights (from around 10pm), when it seems as if the entire local population crams into this narrow space. One word of warning: If you're a bloke, be prepared for what one regular called "the filthiest toilets in Ireland, probably!"

RATHLIN ISLAND

Rathlin is Northern Ireland's only inhabited offshore island, located 9.6km (6 miles) from the mainland, across the Sea of Moyle. The L-shaped island is 9.6km (6 miles) long and just 1.6km (1 mile) wide. It was here that the Scottish king, Robert the Bruce, took refuge in a cave in 1306 when he was driven out of Scotland by Edward I of England. Legend has it that Robert was so inspired by the sight of a spider repeatedly making efforts to spin a web that he went on to triumph at the Battle of Bannockburn; a festival is held here each June to commemorate Robert's time here. Rathlin is also where Marconi tested the world's first commercial radio transmission in 1898, broadcasting across the water to Ballycastle; these days the island is pretty well connected, both telephonically, and by ferry from Ballycastle with **Caledonian MacBryne Ferries** (☎ 080/0066-5000; www.calmac.co.uk; £10 round-trip; timetables are seasonal with more frequent departures Apr–Sept).

Rathlin's rugged landscape makes for adventurous hiking (contact **Paul Quinn Walking Tours;** ☎ 028/7032-7960), and there is a cycling route, too (bike rental, ☎ 028/2076-3954). But the island's top draw is its bird-watching. During the summer—the season kicks off in early May—the **RSPB Seabird Centre** (Royal Society for the Protection of Birds; ☎ 028/2076-0062; www.rspb.org.uk), at the

West Lighthouse (6km/3¾ miles from the harbor) is where you need to be to watch razorbills, kittiwakes, guillemots, and those delightful puffins (which head off again in mid-Aug). These birds nest in the island's rocky cliffs and sea stacks, best viewed from the center's viewpoint.

Incidentally, Rathlin is closely associated with the mythological female spirit known as the *banshee;* apparently, her hideous wailing is occasionally heard at night. Although she is seldom seen, if you do happen to glimpse a woman in a grey hooded cloak, you might want to check your ancestry: Legend tells that she comes to forewarn members of certain ancient Irish families—the O'Neills, O'Briens, O'Connors, O'Gradys, and Cavanaghs—of their death.

WHERE TO STAY & DINE ON THE ISLAND

££   Spending the night on Rathlin is the North's ultimate "get away from it all" experience. I'd recommend the **Manor House** (The Harbour, Rathlin Island; ☎ 028/ 2076-3964; www.rathlinmanorhouse.co.uk; cash only) which has not only been renovated to a comfortable standard, but also has a restaurant with acceptable grub. The rooms vary—from snug singles (£35), to more generously sized doubles and twins (£65), and some have attached bathrooms, while others have private facilities down the hall—but they're all neat and clean, and while unspectacular in terms of decor and furniture, the views from those facing the harbor are probably deal-clinchers. So try to make sure you book room 5, so you can lie in bed and watch the tide roll in and out.

DOWNPATRICK & THE LECALE

County Down is deeply associated with Ireland's patron saint Patrick, known for driving the snakes out of Ireland, imbuing the shamrock with spiritual significance, and turning his enemies into animals. These days, St. Patrick turns more commercial tricks, not only as inspiration for some of the biggest parades and booziest parties to mark the anniversary of his death (Mar 17), but also for anyone trying to lure visitors to the busy little town of Downpatrick, supposedly where the saint is buried. While slightly congested Downpatrick, with an attractive Georgian Mall, can be a base for exploring the surrounding countryside, there is little in town beyond its modern St. Patrick interpretative center to really hold your interest; head out into the surrounding Lecale countryside, however, and there are fine, if often subtle, attractions—quaint villages, enchanting coastal roads, Norman round towers, moody ecclesiastical ruins, and the architecturally schizophrenic Castle Ward poised at the edge of pristine Strangford Lough. A challenging sailing destination in its own right, the lough is known for its biodiversity, luring seabirds such as terns, grebes, oyster catchers, plovers, and mallards, and—in spring and summer—snow geese. But, your enduring memory of Down will be of wending your way along country roads through vast tracts of green, punctuated by drumlins—small, iconic hills formed by glacial deposits at the end of the last Ice Age.

A BRIEF HISTORY OF DOWNPATRICK

Strangford Lough—now a popular and important maritime destination—was once the scene of major Viking incursions. Best remembered of these Norsemen

St. Paddy: A Brief Demystification

Ireland's patron saint is so much a part of local mythology, so imbedded in Irish symbols, and so much an excuse for a parade and a party, that perhaps a quick look at the man behind all the hype is in order. Be warned, though, that much of what is known about him is based on speculation—we have only two autobiographical accounts upon which to build his biography.

As a teenager, Patrick was captured by Irish slave traders—he may have come from southwest England, Wales, Scotland, or even Tours in France. He probably came from a wealthy Roman—and therefore Christian—family, and he was convinced that his capture was a punishment for forsaking God, so perhaps he'd been less than well behaved in his youth. He became a slave shepherd boy in Ireland (either on Antrim's Slemish Mountains or in County Mayo). Patrick claims that during his slavery, he prayed up to 100 times per day, and after a particularly lucid vision of the angel Victoricus, he fled, traveling 322km (200 miles) to the south of Ireland. Back home, he entered the priesthood and 10 years later became a bishop. Then: More visions—this time of Irish voices begging him to return to the Emerald Isle.

He was not the first Christian missionary in Ireland; in fact, the pope sent a bishop to Ireland in 431, a year prior to Patrick's arrival. But Patrick seems to have been the more effective of the two, having formidable powers of persuasion. His first conversion happened to be brother of the High King of Ulster and Patrick famously used the shamrock to explain the metaphysics of the Holy Trinity, which is why the little green plant is now a national symbol. Apparently no sissy, he would also employ physical force to get his point across. He's also said to have shown concern for the rights of women—almost unheard of among saints—so might have gotten support from the ladies.

And as for the notion that St. Patrick drove all the snakes from Ireland? Well, we all know that there were never any snakes in Ireland, but at the time when he came to Ireland, pagan worship frequently involved animal cults. One argument is that the snake legend refers to the destruction of such cults and therefore the banishment of Satan, symbolically perceived as a serpent by contemporary Christians. Whatever the case, Patrick must have been incredibly busy during his time in Ireland; although the extent of his travels and the number of converts he is responsible for is unclear, his impact was immense and there are records of him showing up all over the place. He established the city of Armagh at the ecclesiastical capital of Ireland, and is believed to have died sometime between 460 and 490, after which a cult steadily grew around his teachings, and within a few hundred years he had become the stuff of Irish legend. Not bad for a shepherd slave.

is the last Viking warrior king, Magnus Barelegs. Barelegs—who earned his nickname because during battle he wore the legless dress of the Irish—earned a special reputation not only for his endurance as a fighter, but because he married a local tribeswoman, making him yet another conquering hero who apparently succumbed to the powerful charms of the Irish. Today, the likes of Magnus are celebrated hereabouts during annual Viking festivals, attracting Scandinavians who don costumes and reenact those heady days around the Lough.

The Vikings plundered and burned Downpatrick in 989, but the town was much revitalized after 1177, when the Norman knight, John de Courcy, invaded Ulster with a team of just 22 knights and 300 foot soldiers, and defeated local boy Rory MacDunlevy at Downpatrick. Steeled by his victory, de Courcy drew power from what he perceived to be the area's spiritual significance: This was, after all, where St. Patrick first landed when he returned to Ireland as a missionary in the 5th century, and where he had given his first sermon—just outside Downpatrick, in the little village of Saul—soon after he converted the local chieftain to Christianity. In fact, the chieftain had been so enthralled by Patrick's powers of persuasion that he provided him with a barn in which to preach, and it was there that legend tells us St. Patrick built his first church. De Courcy did much to stimulate the cult of Patrick; he built a Benedictine house of worship on the site of a former Celtic monastery on a low hill in Downpatrick, and reburied what he believed to be the remains of the saint in the adjacent graveyard. Although de Courcy was eventually forced out of Ulster in 1204, he had by then attached sufficient importance to the town, which he renamed Downpatrick—"the fort of Patrick"—for it to become the busy county market town it remains today.

GETTING THERE & GETTING AROUND

Downpatrick, the main market town in County Down, lies more or less directly south of Belfast. If you're traveling by car, take the **A24/A7** for the most direct route (37km/23 miles); the road trip shouldn't take more than 1 hour. Buses run from Belfast to Downpatrick **bus station** (83 Market St.; ☎ 048/4461-2384) regularly, with reduced service on Sundays; the trip takes 1 hour and costs around £5. From Downpatrick buses run to various towns throughout the Lecale, including Newcastle, 35 minutes away (£3.20), and Strangford (£2.90), less than half an hour away.

Beyond the elegant houses around **English Street** and along the **Mall** leading up to the cathedral, there's little to see, and its central roads are frequently congested, making getting through the town irritating.

My favorite place to stay in the Lecale is the bucolic village of **Killyleagh,** just north of Downpatrick, at the edge of Strangford Lough. Exploring the Lecale is a cinch—it's a relatively tiny region, and most of the time you'll find yourself on quiet country roads, meandering through verdant farmlands, or along the coastline, occasionally spotting medieval Norman towers and passing through hassle-free fishing villages with disorganized road systems.

WHERE TO STAY & DINE
In & Around Downpatrick

£   Carved out of the same spaces that have served as guest accommodations for 4 centuries, the rooms at **Denvir's** ✸ (14–16 English St.; ☎ 028/4461-2012;

Day-Tripping through the Ards Peninsula

Here's a day's outing that you can do either from your base in Belfast, or as a way of combining the journey from Belfast to the Lecale Region with rewarding sightseeing. Start out no later than mid-morning, heading out of Belfast along the A2, which will take you to:

Ulster Folk & Transport Museum ★★ kids (Cultra, 11.5km/7 miles east of Belfast, County Down; ☎ 028/9042-8428; www.nmni.com; combined ticket £7; Mar–June Mon–Fri 10am–5pm; Sat 10am–6pm; Sun 11am–6pm; July–Sept Mon–Sat 10am–6pm; Sun 11am–6pm; Oct–Feb Mon–Fri 10am–4pm; Sat 10am–5pm; Sun 11am–5pm), which is actually two distinct museums. The **Folk Museum** is an open-air exhibition in which an entire town—Ballycultra—has been assembled alongside a collection of rural farmsteads. Upon arrival, you're given a map, which you'll need to explore each of the 50-odd buildings—schools, farmsteads, forges, mills, pubs, shops, churches, and even an old-style movie house screening a Charlie Chaplin flick. It all feels a bit like a movie lot, despite the sights, smells, and pettable farm animals.

The **Transport Museum** is the Folk Museum's antithesis since most of what's on show is collected inside a massive enclosure. For the mechanically minded, it's a dream-come-true, with entire locomotives, dozens of cars, buses, trams, and all kinds of bizarre, weird, and wonderful devices designed (and many failed) to help mankind move with the least amount of energy. I think the most interesting exhibits are those strange contraptions that didn't quite make it onto the showroom floors, like oddball electrical scooters and the De Lorean, which really did only ever make it big on the silver screen—as the time-jumping vehicle in the *Back to the Future* films. In another gallery are exhibitions of early transport—yes, donkey carts, carriages, and buggies—and air transport (including a flight simulator, £1.50).

From Cultra, take the coastal road that passes through **Bangor** and **Donaghadee.** When you hit **Ballywalter,** take the turn-off for **Greyabbey,** just 5 minutes west. Here, stop to explore:

www.denvirshotel.com; MC, V), just down the way from Down Cathedral, are spacious and generally comfortable. Featuring sleigh-beds (with soft linens, but slightly lumpy mattresses), okay reproduction furniture, and framed Jack Vetriano prints against caramel-colored walls, these six bedrooms offer the best opportunity in town for a decent night's sleep. Which you might just need after an evening in one of the two downstairs bars (one dated 1642), where things can get kinda crazy. Actually, you won't need even a single pint to feel a little woozy here: The off-kilter shapes of the rooms, leaning walls, uneven floors, and bulging brick- and plasterwork will probably do it to you (it's an old, old house). Breakfast is served in a wood-beamed, stone-floored cellar and also serves as a romantic

The evocative 12th-century **Cistercian Abbey** ✪✪✪, Ireland's first completely Gothic construction, founded by Affreca, the wife of the Norman knight, John de Courcey, in 1193. The lawns here are ideal for picnicking on a summer's day.

On the other side of Greyabbey village, when you hit the A20, you'll catch your first sight of **Strangford Lough;** you'll need to double back briefly toward Newtownards, heading north along the A20 to reach one of the more interesting attractions on the Ards:

Mount Stewart House, Garden, and Temple of the Winds ✪✪ (Portaferry Rd.; ☎ 028/4278-8387; www.nationaltrust.org.uk/mountstewart; £6.36 gardens and house tour; lakeside gardens daily 10am–sunset; house and formal gardens highly seasonal opening times, call ahead). An 18th-century neoclassical mansion, Mount Stewart is renowned for its Spanish and Italian gardens plump with rare plants from around the globe; there are also formal fantasy gardens here incorporating bizarre sculptures and artfully laid-out flower beds. The house—although not quite as spectacular, perhaps, as the gardens—is eccentrically furnished with, among other items, a major George Stubbs equestrian painting (considered among Britain's top 100 artworks), and the 22 chairs that were used by delegates at the Congress of Vienna. Be sure to take in the views across Strangford Lough from the **Temple of the Winds** (Apr–Oct Sun 2–5pm).

The remainder of your Ards' sojourn takes you south to Portaferry; for most of the journey, you'll have views of the lough on your right. The little town has a popular pub, the **Fiddler's Green** ✪ (10–12 Church St.; ☎ 028/4272-8393; www.fiddlersgreenportaferry.com) with decent meals, quality B&B accommodation (from £44, or £50 en suite), and live traditional music Friday to Sunday. To get across the lough to Strangford, and the Lecale, follow signs for the **ferry** (car plus driver: £5.30 one-way, £8.50 same-day return; pedestrians and passengers: £1.10 or £1.80 return).

dinner venue. You'll pay £60 for a double room; a special package includes dinner and a bottle of wine for £75.

££ Another oldie but goodie **Ballymote House** ✪✪ (Killough Rd., Downpatrick; ☎ 028/4461-5500; www.ballymotehouse.com; cash only) was built back in 1730, making it the earliest unfortified house in Down. Reminders of upper class living are everywhere: in the fine gardens, the stable of 10 lively horses at the back, the endless antiques, and such telling objects as a stuffed fox head, a portrait of Oliver Cromwell, and Wedgwood china. The main guest room (the one you want; £80) boasts a handmade bed, 150-year-old Parisian curtains, a beautiful antique writing desk, and views (from the bedroom and the bathroom) of the surrounding landscape. Two single bedrooms suitable for children and solo travelers are available for £40. As enthralling as the house, believe it or not, is your hostess Nicola Manningham-Buller, a vibrant, always busy woman. With Nicola, there are no half-measures, and because she's so fussy about food ingredients, she goes to the trouble of preparing her own jams, and has sausages specially made from a personal recipe; these are the sorts of special treats you get at breakfast. One suggestion: Print a map for directions to Ballymote as there often isn't a sign indicating where to turn off.

Killyleagh

£   For light—and dare I say, healthy—eating, pop into **Picnic** ✸ (47 High St., Killyleagh; ☎ 028/4482-8525; Mon–Fri 7am–6pm; Sat and holidays 10am–4pm; cash only), a deli-style eatery serving freshly baked focaccias, paninis, and bagels—which you fill with various fresh, locally sourced ingredients displayed behind the counter. Everything's available to go or eat in, including homemade soups, pâtés, pies, and the like. When you step inside, the aroma of freshly brewed coffee will probably make you want to hang around, but remember that it's more expensive if you take a seat.

££   Once the local Bank of Ulster, **Dufferin Coaching Inn** ✸✸✸ 🄺🄸🄳🄼 (33 High St., Killyleagh; ☎ 028/4482-1134; www.dufferincoachinginn.com; MC, V) is among my favorite places to stay in Northern Ireland, located in the particularly picturesque village of Killyleagh (pronounced Killy-lay), site of Ireland's oldest inhabited castle. Just 10 minutes from comparatively bustling Downpatrick, Killyleagh has the advantage of being right on Strangford Lough—walk up to the church for really absorbing views. Dufferin is now in the most capable hands of Leontine Haines, a former Dublin-based nurse, she came to Killyleagh to relax into small town life and instead has become the very epicenter of the community—she always has the local scoop, and knows everyone. Her spacious inn is immaculate and quite elegant. Bedrooms are all done out with great flair: four-poster beds, crisp linens, thick-pile mattresses, large wardrobes, and attention to little difference-making details, like adding light switches that you can reach from your bed. My choice would be the most recently added room—a massive ground unit with a handsome bathroom. It's one of Ireland's best deals, too: £70 double.

£–££   Right next door the **Dufferin Arms** ✸✸ (High St., Killyleagh; ☎ 028/4482-1182; www.dufferinarms.co.uk; food served Mon–Thurs noon–3pm and 5:30–8:30pm; Fri–Sun noon–8:30pm; MC, V) is both a mightily hospitable pub (packed with locals and the odd stuffed animal) and a reliable provider of victuals, serving good, tasty grub Monday to Thursday, and a more ambitious restaurant selection over weekends. Whichever way you go, you can't help notice the care taken to give old favorites a slightly new dimension. So, duck sausages are used for Dufferin-style bangers and mash (£7.25), and the burgers are made with Finnebrogue venison and served in a granary bap with salsa and salad (£7). Portions are substantial and can be shared.

Strangford, by the Lough

££   Peter and Caroline McErlean are so darn passionate about the **Cuan** ✸✸ (Strangford Village; ☎ 028/4488-1222; www.thecuan.com; dining room daily noon–9pm; MC, V) that it's almost embarrassing. But they have reason to be proud: Their solid little restaurant (plus pub, guest inn, and fish and chips takeaway) is the very epicenter of life in Strangford, an attractive conservation village with the ferry connection to Portaferry on the Ards' side of the Lough. Locals come for the comfortable atmosphere and the excellent cuisine—Peter (originally a baker from Belfast) is often seen wandering around in his tall chef's hat, auditing reactions to his work in the kitchen. Menu choices range from traditional pub-style meals, like steak and Guinness pie (£9) and Peter's legendary seafood chowder (served with smoked salmon and organic wheaten bread; £9), to surprises like pan-fried Portovo pheasant sausage (£10). As for the accommodations they're carpeted, with pine furniture and flat screen TVs—basically neat and functional looking. At £80 double, though, they're nowhere near as sumptuous or character-filled as you'll find at Dufferin Coaching Inn (see above), and certainly not as good value (there's a massive family room, too).

A Mansion by the Sea

£££ There's eccentricity—and sometimes, briefly, no electricity—at David Corbett's rambling family manse, **Tyrella House** ★ (Tyrella, A2 between Ardglass and Clough; ☎ 028/4485-1422; www.hiddenireland.com/tyrella; closed Dec–Feb; AE, V). Built in three major stages, the oldest dating back to 1704, the varying architectural characteristics within different parts of the house means that each of the upstairs bedrooms has entirely individual qualities; the most attractive is the massive Georgian Room (1810) with its many large windows framing stunning views of the gardens, grounds, and Mourne Mountains in the mid-distance. A carved antique woodframe bed and dainty period furnishings are complemented by electric blankets, bowls of fruit, a coffeemaker, and a kettle; the only drawback is that the bath (complete with rickety ancient plumbing) has no shower. The smaller William and Mary Room (1704), does have a shower, however, so think about that when booking. With piles of magazines that date to the 1980s, plumbing from the Ark, and original antiques throughout the house, a stay here offers insight into the obvious difficulties that go with the upkeep of old, rambling buildings. David keeps horses on the sprawling estate—available for polo lessons or galloping along the beach—and feels his job is to make sure his guests enjoy "a bit of fun," whether encouraging them to take a dip at Tyrella Beach, or helping them discover some of Down's hidden gems. He prepares breakfast and on request does dinners (with garden vegetables and homegrown lamb; £25), too. Rooms go for £90 a night.

WHY YOU'RE HERE: TOP SIGHTS & ATTRACTIONS
In & Around Downpatrick

In Downpatrick itself, the main attractions are clustered close together near the Mall and on the road leading up to the hill upon which stands **Down Cathedral** ★ (Hilltop, English St.; ☎ 028/4461-4922; www.downcathedral.org; free admission; Mon–Sat 9:30am–4:30pm; Sun 2–5pm)—visible from any point in town. It's here that the spiritual father of Ireland is believed to be buried. His tombstone is easy to find in a plot alongside the church; it's engraved with a single word—"Patric"— in evocative Celtic lettering. If this is the grave of St. Patrick, who died in 461, it's evidence of well over 1,500 years of Christian heritage on this site. Originally a

12th century Norman church, which replaced an earlier Celtic construction, the cathedral was pretty much destroyed in 1316 and lay in ruins until 1790 when restoration (or rather, rebuilding) to its present state began. Parts of the walls and some of the pillars are original, however, and the enormous organ at the back of the church is one of Ireland's most impressive.

Down the road, just below the Cathedral, is the modernist **Saint Patrick Centre** (The Mall; ☎ 028/4461-9000; www.saintpatrickcentre.com; £4.90; Sept–June Mon–Sat 9:30am–5pm; July–Aug Mon–Sat 9:30am–6pm; Sun 2–6pm), an audio-visual interpretative exhibition which, frankly, takes itself just a little too seriously. The slow-moving audio-visual vignettes, strong-handed proselytizing, and bland voice playing the part of Patrick make the saint sound far duller than he could ever have been. One thing's for sure, even the IMAX movie (that's really a way of getting you to pay for a prolonged marketing film about County Down and its neighbor, Armagh) won't help you understand why there's so much crazy drinking on St. Patrick's Day.

Nearby, in the town's 18th-century former gaol, **Down County Museum** (The Mall; ☎ 028/4461-5218; www.downcountymuseum.com; free admission; Mon–Fri 10am–5pm; Sat–Sun 1–5pm), provides a traditional, old-fashioned museum experience, but if you don't have a serious interest in local history, it'll really just be chewing up time you could be spending out in the country. If you're interested in the moving image, spend some time on the **Digital Film Archives** which turn up some intriguing historic footage. Ignore the horrid exhibition space in the gaol cells at the back entirely.

Finally, my favorite spot in the immediate vicinity of Downpatrick is **Inch Abbey** ✸✸, 1.6km (1 mile) outside town. Although little more than a ruin now—it was built for Cistercian monks imported from Lancashire in the 12th century, and burnt down in 1404—it's a hugely atmospheric site with a sublime lakeside setting. Pack a picnic and dine on the grass while cacophonous ravens dart above your head.

Architectural Confusion at Castle Ward

A short drive from Downpatrick will take you to one of Ireland's most impressive estates, **Castle Ward** ✸✸✸ (near Strangford; ☎ 028/4488-1204; www.ntni. org.uk; grounds only: £4.40; House Tour: £2.70; grounds: daily Oct–Mar 10am–4pm; Apr–Sept 10am–8pm; house: daily July–Aug and Easter week 1–6pm; Apr–June and Sept Sat–Sun 1–6pm), "famed," as its National Trust caretakers put it, "for it's mixture of architectural styles." Which rather undersells the bizarre clash of stylistic elements—neo-Gothic and Classical—that might suggest that a war between two very adamant architects broke out here during the design phase. Apparently, the eclectic appearance results from the much divided tastes of the owners. Lord Bangor, whose predilection was for the studied classicism of Palladian design, brought his preferences to bear on the front entrance. Lady Anne, who favored the contemporary Gothic look so popular during the late-1700s (when designs were drawn up), left her mark on the garden-facing wing. Whatever the real reason for the peculiar mismarriage, the effect suggests that two building projects were joined at the hip, since the segregated design splits the house right down the middle and runs as deep as the choice of mundane everyday items inside. Needless to say, Anne and Bernard's marriage did not last into eternity, but their home does provide insight into the extreme lengths, given enough cash, some of us go to in order to make a point. It also showcases a barrage of unusual timesaving artistic "tricks"—ordinary objects dipped in plaster and displayed as sculptural effects—that may or may not inspire your admiration. On a good day, the grounds make for salubrious exploration, with a lake, tower houses, and children's play center. In June, Castle Ward is the venue for a show-stopping opera festival, one of Lecale's most anticipated events. ***Note:*** Much to my—and your—irritation, you cannot visit the house interior without first paying the much heftier fee just to enter the grounds, so while the House Tour may sound like a bargain, be prepared to fork out £7.10 per adult in total to see the castle from the inside.

THE OTHER LECALE

If you're up for an energetic socializing-and-learning experience, consider signing up for a set dancing class. As scary as that might sound, you should know that even if you have two left feet, set dancing is not only great fun, but relatively easy to get the hang of—and there are no Lord of the Dance expectations whatsoever. It's basically a form of line-dancing, with ordered moves that play out to form a routine—or set. This is a fast and lively way to meet new people, literally rubbing shoulders with them while "advancing" and "retreating" according to the commands of the person on the mike.

Classes in Downpatrick are held at the **Russell Gaelic Union GAA Clubhouse** (Old Course Rd., Flying Horse Rd; no phone); a weekly session on Tuesdays from September through May at 7:30pm. Classes last 2 hours and include tea. You can also look into classes by renowned tutor, Ashley Ray, who gives instruction all over the county, including at Downpatrick's busy **Down Arts Centre** (2–6 Irish St.; ☎ 028/4461-0747), which is at the heart of County Down's cultural scene. She usually teaches basic set dancing steps prior to an evening of more "serious" *ceili,* when you're supposed to know the meaning of the moves. Usually, there's an afternoon "warm-up" beginners session—the ideal platform to lose your inhibitions. Once you've found your rhythm, you just won't want to stop. Three hours of intro training costs about £3, while the advanced evening costs £6. Classes are not held during summer.

Incidentally, the Arts Centre is a community initiative that offers all sorts of workshops from lessons in *bodhrán* (an Irish musical instrument that looks a bit like a tambourine), to a lectures on Irish heritage. The Centre also organizes workshops designed for kids, and hosts events such as Viking banquets, where you're sure to discover the wilder side of Down. For a look at what's lined up when you're in the area, visit **www.downdistrictevents.com**.

NIGHTLIFE

Down Arts Centre (see above) is also the Lecale's main venue for music and theater events—an eclectic mix that spans contemporary quartets, racy stand-up comedy, folk musicians, and old-masters like Voltaire. Pick up the Centre's Ultimate Guide, a comprehensive seasonal listing of arts events throughout Down.

Dufferin Arms (p. 422) is the prime nighttime hang-out in the Lecale. I've met such an eclectic and interesting mix of locals here—artisans, blue-collar workers, and even the sociable chairman of Down County Council. It's presided over by Jarvis, an always-charming barman who pulls consistently good pints of Guinness.

THE MOUNTAINS OF MOURNE

Among the most striking of Ireland's mountain ranges, the evocatively named Mountains of Mourne are perhaps the best-known on the island, having inspired both C.S. Lewis's imaginary Kingdom of Narnia and a much-loved song by Percy French. Formed of igneous granite 65 million years ago, the range stretches 24km (15 miles) from Newcastle to Rostrevor, yet the mountain summits are grouped together in an unusually compact area just 11.25km (7 miles) wide, imbuing them with a special beauty. The highest peak is Slieve Donard, rising to 850m (2,788 ft.)—not exactly mind-blowing stuff, but as the rugged peaks "sweep down to the sea," they provide good hiking terrain, crisscrossed by dry stone walls that divvy up the farmlands and help hikers keep their bearings.

LAY OF THE LAND

The Mountains of Mourne really do "sweep down to sea," and they do so across a short stretch of Down's coast between the Victorian seaside resort of **Newcastle** and the Down-Armagh border town of **Newry,** to the west. You can follow the coastal road between Newcastle and Rostrevor with the Mournes stretching above you on one side, or you can go through narrow country roads that twist and weave around the lower reaches of the mountains themselves.

Newcastle's **Tourist Information Centre** (10–14 Central Promenade; ☎ 028/4372-2222; July–Aug Mon–Sat 9:30am–7pm; Sun 1–7pm; Sept–June Mon–Sat 10am–5pm; Sun 2–5pm) provides general assistance and also sells a variety of maps for walkers; pick up Mourne Mountain Walks (£6), a set of 10 different walks on handy waterproof cards. A most extensive online resource for the entire Mourne region is **www.mournelive.com**.

GETTING THERE & GETTING AROUND

Newcastle is 51km (32 miles) directly south of Belfast; it's about an hour away by car. **Ulsterbus** (☎ 028/9066-6630; www.translink.co.uk) has a regular bus service from Belfast's Europa Buscentre to Newcastle (almost 30 trips daily Mon–Fri, reduced service on weekends); it takes around 80 minutes. If you're **driving** from Downpatrick, Killyleagh, or Strangford, I'd first head to the seaside village of Ardglass, and then follow the coastal-hugging route (the A2) around Dundrum Bay, with Norman towers and quaint harbor villages along the way. Consider breaking the short journey with a stop in peaceful Dundrum; a walk up to its hilltop castle will be rewarded with spectacular views.

The **Ulsterbus Mourne Rambler** does regular circuits of the Mournes. There are six departures per day, with 13 strategic stops before returning to Newcastle (the whole circuit takes 70 min.). Call for updates, schedules, and an idea of where the bus is at any given time. All-day tickets cost £4.70.

WHERE TO STAY & DINE

The most convenient base for excursions into the mountains is the seaside resort of Newcastle, where holiday tack is offset by exquisite mountain views and a popular beach. But, if you prefer a more laidback setting (and aren't relying on public transport), you can flee from the action by settling in for the more tranquil charms of Dundrum, where you can admire the seascape from atop its ruined Anglo-Norman castle.

If you're looking to devote some time to the Mourne mountains, you might want to rent a cottage or house; see p. 400 for two useful rental websites. A wide range of options (with photos, full contact details, and links to private websites) is listed at **www.mournemountains.com**—just click on "Accommodation" and then "Self Catering." The listings include individual as well as clustered properties. Expect to pay between £300 and £450 for a two-bedroom place that sleeps four; usually the more rural the setting, the lower the price, but the less likelihood of having access to assistance when something breaks down—another consideration if you book a privately owned property. One set of rentals featured on this site that is particularly lovely are the stone cottages offered by **Mourne Cottages** (www.mournecottages.com), so look at those first.

In & Around Newcastle

In a freshly restored low-rise Victorian building on the seafront, the most professionally run apartment rental option in Newcastle is **Snooze** ★★ (5 South Promenade; ☎ 028/4372-6002; www.snoozeapartments.co.uk; AE, MC, V). Verging on luxury (although a bit too minimalist to be in that category), these four apartments come with plenty of natural light, unrestricted views of Newcastle Bay and the Mourne Mountains, a lounge where you can really stretch out, and well-equipped kitchens where you can cook up a storm. Bedrooms are fairly snug, and the "children's rooms" use bunk beds but they all have wardrobes and comfy mattresses. And the bunk system also means that a two-bedroom unit sleeps up to six people (though with just one bathroom, I'd say they're best suited to four). Original Victorian fireplaces have been left as features in the living room, where the owners have also packed in plenty of modern "necessities"—TV, DVD, dishwasher, washer-dryer, and ironing equipment. Given that you'll want for very little—linens, towels, and heating are all included—I think they offer quite reasonable value at £450 for a week (two bedrooms), and £350 (one bedroom); rates for 2 or 3 night stays are also available.

£ Catering to the many hikers and outdoorsy types who come to explore the Mountains of Mourne **Newcastle Youth Hostel** (30 Downs Rd.; ☎ 028/4372-2133; MC, V) is right across the road from the beachfront. Equipped with a self-catering kitchen, dining room, and a lounge (with TV, a dated-but-detailed ordinance survey Mourne area map, and loudly ticking clock), it's got most of what a budget traveler might need. While the bunk bedded dorms are decent enough, the design of the place is a bit awkward, though, with doors opening out over stairways, and irritating push button faucets that make it impossible for a two-handed person to mix hot and cold water.

£–££ If you don't mind being a little out of town, a hospitable B&B choice is **Briers Country House** (39 Middle Tollymore Rd.; ☎ 028/4372-4347; www.the briers.co.uk; MC, V), where a family welcomes you into their 18th-century home and then provides homey comforts, including—if you arrange them—evening

---

Camping Under the Stars

Camping is available at **Tollymore Forest Park** (176 Tullybrannigan Rd.; ☎ 028/4372-2428) as well as at **Castlewellan Forest Park** (Main St., Castlewellan; ☎ 028/4377-8664). Both sites are well maintained; rates at each range from £9 (May–June and Sept) to £13 (July–Aug).

---

meals in their reputable restaurant. Accommodations are really nothing fancy, with furniture and decor that you'll probably consider dated (I do), but they're cozy and the mattresses are good. And the price doesn't hurt a bit either: Doubles cost from £45 to £60, season-dependent, and you'll get a better deal if you stay for more than 2 nights.

£–££   For my money, Newcastle's loveliest place to eat is **Seasalt Delicatessen & Bistro** ✪✪ (51 Central Promenade; ☎ 028/4372-5027; www.seasaltnew castle.com; Sun–Thurs 9am–6pm; Fri–Sat 9am–9pm; MC, V), which is small, but light-filled, and—thanks to its water-facing window frontage—affords some sense of being at the seaside. The food here is wholesome and delicious: seafood chowder (£4), freshly made lamb burgers (with a tangy homemade curry dressing and just-out-of-the-oven garlic bread; £6.25), sandwiches stuffed with your choice of ingredients (I always fancy their goat cheese, olives, sundried tomatoes, peppers, and pesto—yum!), and there's an evening "Irish-style" tapas menu. You can bring your own wine (there's a bottle store nearby) and pay only £1.50 corkage fee.

££   Along with a major promenade upgrade, several new eateries opened in Newcastle just prior to the 2008 summer season, and none of them as eagerly anticipated as the **Mourne Café** (107 Central Promenade; ☎ 028/4372-6401; Mon–Fri 11:30am–8:30pm; Sat–Sun 9:30am–late), an offshoot of the famous Mourne Seafood Bar, with branches in Dundrum (see below) and Belfast; prices at this Newcastle establishment are reasonable, too, even if the decor is a little too "upmarket-contemporary" if you're taking a break from hiking.

Dundrum

£   With its bright blue walls, flowering window boxes, and central position right across from the harbor, you can't help but be attracted to—or perhaps seduced by—the **Carriage House** ✪✪ (71 Main St.; ☎ 028/4375-1635; www.carriage housedundrum.com; cash only), a tasteful B&B run with affection by Maureen Griffith. She's not only made the effort to assemble interesting, varied, and attractive furniture, combining old and new with effortless flair, but included enough decorative *objets d'art* to ensure there's real personality here. (I also enjoy her menagerie of pets including an adventurous hedgehog!) To add to the feeling that you're being pampered and spoiled (which Maureen does with her generous welcome and wholesome, carefully conceived breakfast spread), is the genuine care taken to bring comfort to the bedrooms. So when you climb into bed with visions of the brooding Mournes vividly in your head, you're enveloped by luxurious cotton linens. Yet, for all her hostess prowess, Maureen must be shy about her talents; she charges just £60 double per night.

££–£££   For a feast of ultra-fresh Dundrum oysters and a pint of Guinness, head right next door to the Carriage House to the **Buck's Head Inn** ✹✹✹ (77 Main St.; ☎ 028/4375-1868; reservations essential; Tues–Sun noon–2:30pm and 5–6:30pm for tea; Mon–Sat 7–9:30pm and Sun 7–8:30pm; DC, MC, V), where the imaginative cooking features plenty of seafood plucked straight from the waters of Dundrum Bay which is, well, right across the road. A plate of oysters goes for around £5 to £6. Buck's Head is equally famed for its Dundrum mussels (how about Thai style—with coconut milk, chili, and ginger?), as well as various interpretations of famed Finnebrogue venison—try chef Alison Crother's braised Finnebrogue sausages (£9) if you're not in the mood for monkfish, shark steak, or whatever else has been caught today. A two-course set menu costs £24.

££–££££   Also on Main Street is one of Down's major successes, the **Mourne Seafood Bar** ✹✹✹ (10 Main St.; ☎ 028/4375-1377; www.mourneseafood.com; Nov–Mar Wed–Sun noon–9:30pm; Apr–Oct daily noon–9:30pm; MC, V), which has spawned branches in Belfast and, more recently, Newcastle. Chef Neil Auterson (who worked under Belfast celeb chef, Paul Rankin, before cheffing in Europe, Martha's Vineyard, and even Down Under) prepares what's in season and what's available; he focuses on fish straight off the local boats, emphasizing relatively unknown species that aren't under threat from over-exploitation. So it's not unusual to find shark on the menu, or perhaps Gurnard, giving you the chance to somewhat spread your culinary wings. Plenty of shellfish, grown on the restaurant's private beds in Carlingford Lough, is also on the menu.

WHY YOU'RE HERE: EXPLORING THE MOURNES

You can set off on foot straight from Newcastle's **Donard Park** (dawn–dusk; free admission) to reach the summit of **Slieve Donard** ✹✹ which looms right behind the town. The walk is quite convoluted, and you'll need to follow signs carefully; it takes around 2½ hours (one-way), and you should know that there are slippery and difficult patches, so be on your toes and wear footwear with good treads. For a more level climb, you can drive to **Bloody Bridge** (5km/3 miles out of Newcastle), where you park and then follow the river up the other side of Slieve Donard to reach the top; it takes as much time, but is a whole lot easier.

Northern Ireland's oldest designated forest park is **Tollymore** ✹✹ (Tully-brannigan Rd.; ☎ 028/4372-2428; www.forestserviceni.gov.uk; £4 cars, £2 pedestrians; daily 10am–sunset) 3km (2 miles) from Newcastle, at the northern foot of the Mournes. Gothic gateways—reminders that this park once belonged to the Earls of Roden—mark the entrance, and there are a variety of scenic routes within, most notably along, and sometimes over, the river. Further north is 450-hectare (1,111-acre) **Castlewellan Forest Park** ✹✹ (signposted from Main St., Castlewellan; ☎ 028/4377-8664; £4 cars, £2 pedestrians; daily 10am–sunset). In addition to woodland walks culminating in exquisite views, the estate, with its Scottish baronial castle, includes a spectacular arboretum for rare and exotic species, a Peace Maze, and Castlewellan Lake.

Tips for Walking in the Mournes

◆ **Don't be deceived by the height of the hills.** They look low, but they may require far more time and effort than you imagine. If you're intending to reach the higher summits, you're likely to spend between 6 and 8 hours getting there and back. Allow around an hour for every 4km (2½ miles) you intend to cover, and also add 1 hour for every 500m (1,500 ft.) that you ascend. Also, don't think that views are necessarily more impressive from the higher summits; a number of the lower hills are less crowded by walkers and provide striking views.

◆ **Take water and food.** There are no stalls along the way.

◆ **The weather can change dramatically with little warning.** Hilltop conditions are often dangerous (particularly when mist or cloud cover impacts visibility). For up-to-the-minute weather information, contact **Weatherline** (☎ 0891/333-111). In winter, be aware that snow and melting ice can seriously impact the degree of difficulty of your walk; dress appropriately and consider taking an ice awl and a walking pole.

◆ **It's not a good idea to walk in the hills alone.** You should inform someone (like your hotelier or guesthouse host) of your intentions before setting off. Take your mobile phone with you, and if you require assistance, call the **Mourne Mountain Rescue team** (☎ 028/9146-3933).

◆ **Be respectful.** Keep in mind that many of the walking routes will take you across land owned by local farmers, and you will pass farm lanes and tracks as you go to higher altitudes. Remember to close gates behind you and take care to respect the property of the farming community.

Another popular hiking route is the 4.75km (3-mile) Viewpoint Walk at **Silent Valley** ★★ (☎ 028/9074-6581; £3 cars, £2 pedestrians; Sept–May daily 10am–4pm; June–Aug daily 10am–6:30pm) which is about a 1.5km (about a mile) from Annalong and 6.5km (4 miles) from Kilkeel, both seaside towns on the A2 between Newcastle and Rostrevor. Although the reservoir project at Silent Valley seems an unlikely place to set out on a scenic jaunt, there are great views along the 5km (3-mile) route.

THE OTHER MOUNTAINS OF MOURNE

While exploring this region, you shouldn't have much difficulty finding local people to engage with—and you needn't only do it at the local bar. Instead take a hike with a local rambling club. The **Mourne Rambling Group** (www.mourneramblers.btinternet.co.uk) have weekly walks of between 4 and 5½ hours (at three different paces for varying abilities) that set out each Sunday. Although this is technically a members club, guests are permitted, although you'll need to call ahead to speak to one of the **New Membership Officers** (Wilfred Green; ☎ 028/9262-1521; or Terry Magowan, ☎ 028/9756-1534). Besides the normal weekly walking events, the group's program might include evening walks with a star-gazing expert, sunrise walks, slideshows (during which members talk about their personal "adventures"), and even an annual rubbish-collecting event where groups clear trash from a particular region.

NIGHTLIFE

In Newcastle, there's often swell *craic* at **Maginn's Donard Lounge & Bar** (21 Main St.; ☎ 028/4372-2614), managed by the same family that runs Maginn's in Castlewellan (also worth a visit). Expect a truly "colloquial" crowd—characters hunched over the bar nursing long pints as though they're the last they'll ever see. Saturday night is often given over to smalltime-legend DJ Finn McKool, when cocktails go for a tantalizing £2.

However, the pub I like to consider my Mourne Mountains "local" has got to be the **Old Killowen Inn** ✫✫ (☎ 028/4173-8601) in Rostrevor (if you're coming from Newcastle, it's on the right as you drive into the village). Owned by a strapping chap named Dan O'Hara, he claims the pub's been in operation since the early 1800s. It's also been a movie set (for *How About You* with Brenda Fricker), and the likes of Richard Attenborough, Vanessa Redgrave, and film director Jim Sheridan have hung out here. You can come in here for a pint or a cup of coffee, and always feel there's some minor intrigue brewing, whether it's punters counting out their next horseracing bet or a local farmer anticipating his wife's "Come home now!" telephone call, this place has atmosphere in buckets. One unusual feature: Paddy Lannon, father of the president of Ireland, works behind the bar.

12 Derry & the Western Counties

The Troubles-scarred city & its history-rich, bucolic neighboring lands

by Keith Bain

AS "BORDER COUNTIES," FERMANAGH, TYRONE, AND DERRY SAW MUCH OF the conflict that dominated the period of the Troubles. Little wonder then that the appeal of this region is only recently catching on.

But appeal it has, and in spades: Tyrone—the largest county in Northern Ireland—is where, in the shadow of the bog-covered Sperrin Mountains, scores of stone circles, dolmens, and wedge tombs were constructed by an ancient people. In the little county of Fermanagh, ancient saints built their monasteries on the islands of glistening Lough Erne; centuries later, moneyed aristocrats established decadent estates that continue to draw visitors attracted to activities on—or around—the county's superb lakelands. And Derry is a poignant city to explore, deeply marked by the Troubles.

Forward-looking locals look back philosophically at the "recreational rioting" and brutal threats of the bad old days, and try to shrug off the horrific memories. They're pushing ahead to promote their culture, help others understand their past, and encourage the world to come to places steeped in exquisite natural beauty and an ancient history.

DON'T LEAVE DERRY & THE WESTERN COUNTIES WITHOUT . . .

STRIKING A POSE ON THE WORLD'S ORIGINAL CATWALK Derry's surrounding walls symbolize the Catholic-Protestant divide. It's said the term "catwalk" originated here, when Catholics would jeer as wealthy Protestants promenaded along the walls, shouting "Look at all them cats!" Circumnavigate the walls (without the jeers) for fab views of the city. See p. 439.

UNDERSTANDING WHY "YOU ARE NOW ENTERING FREE DERRY" Poignant reminders of the Troubles abound in this once-shattered city, none more significant testament than the gable wall bearing this threatening warning to the British military. Visit the wall, Bogside murals, and the Museum of Free Derry. See p. 441.

GETTING DOWN IN THE BOGS   Much of the Sperrin Mountain range is covered by thick boglands, well worth exploring. See p. 446.

LOSING YOURSELF IN A STONE CIRCLE   Tyrone's rural heartland is studded with prehistoric sites. See p. 446.

TOURING LOUGH ERNE   The mirror surface of Fermanagh's Lower Lough Erne is balm for the soul. See p. 450.

SEEING HOW THE OTHER HALF LIVED   Fermanagh is home to two of the most gracious Georgian houses in Ireland. Both Castle Coole (p. 450) and Florence Court (p. 450) provide a time capsule peek at a world of outrageous privilege and architectural decadence.

GETTING AROUND THE WESTERN COUNTIES

Ulsterbus (☎ 028/9033-3000; www.ulsterbus.co.uk) runs daily scheduled services from Belfast to major cities and towns throughout Northern Ireland, and you'll be able to pick up onward trips to some smaller destinations within this region—provided you're not in a particularly big hurry. From June through August, Ulsterbus also operates coach tours from Belfast's **Europa Buscentre** (Glengall St.; ☎ 028/9066-6630) to areas of tourist interest—the Fermanagh Lakelands, Sperrin Mountains, and Armagh City, for example. Included are tours in the Ulster-American Folk Park in County Tyrone—useful only if you're not planning to explore the region in detail.

However, if you intend getting off the main road and exploring the countryside (highly recommended), the best way to travel is by car.

DERRY (LONDONDERRY)

Although Derry—the only remaining completely walled city in Ireland—occupies one of the oldest inhabited sites in All Ireland, you'd be forgiven for never having considered it as a destination. A small city of around 105,000 people, it was once the scene of some of the fiercest Troubles-era conflict; in the not so distant past, in fact, it used to feature what locals called the "afternoon matinee"—daily riots and street battles between the IRA and the RUC. There are few people in Derry who aren't hugely relieved this long-running, violent "show" has now ended.

But that doesn't mean that the great symbols of division have disappeared, and today, Derry's city walls—which once formed a physical barrier between Catholics and Protestants, rich and poor—are the city's prized architectural feature. Still in excellent condition, they provide an opportunity for a bird's-eye promenade of almost the entire city. Don't expect to see too many ancient monuments, though; during the 1970s, a bombing per day was standard, so much of Derry's older heritage literally disappeared. But many visitors to Derry come to gain a deeper understanding of the more recent struggle years, perhaps hearing a perspective on the Troubles that never quite made it into the mainstream media. Derry has several evocative tributes—murals, museums, even entire neighborhoods—that pay witness to the 20th-century conflict; if you're looking for firsthand insight into modern Irish history, Derry delivers.

A BRIEF HISTORY OF DERRY

Derry. *Doire Cholmcille.* Londonderry. The Walled City. The Maiden City. This city has gone by many names over the years, and all those differing tags hold the history of the city.

The original nomenclature can be traced to the 6th century when a monastery was founded here and out of that grew Daire, meaning "an ancient oak grove." We fast forward to the early 17th century, when, thanks to the logistical convenience of the River Foyle, Derry became a major focus of the "Ulster plantation," during which Protestants from England and Scotland were granted land in Ireland, thereby "planting" them on Irish soil. The London trade guilds commissioned a city wall to protect the Scottish and English settlers (basically an investment in a trade partner), and to keep the native Irish out. The walls so strongly cemented ties between Derry and the English capital, in fact, that Derry officially became Londonderry.

In 1688, when, as part of James II's campaign to reclaim the throne of England, a Catholic garrison attempted to enter the city, a group of "Apprentice Boys"—Protestant orphans from London sent to Derry to learn a trade—seized the keys to the city and locked the gates. It was a moment of anti-Catholic, pro-Williamite defiance that rocked Ireland to its core. Their actions resulted in the longest city siege in British history—over 15 weeks, during which 7,000 residents died. The city acquired the nickname, "The Maiden City," as a seedy reference to this siege, reflecting that its walls have never been breached.

"The Relief of Derry" came on July 29th, 1689, when an English ship, the *Mountjoy,* broke through a boom on the River Foyle. James II went on to be defeated by William of Orange at the Battle of the Boyne, while the siege only intensified the rift between Derry's Catholic and Protestant communities.

Derry became the scene of some of the worst episodes of the Troubles during the late-1960s and '70s. In 1969, the impoverished Catholic Bogside area declared itself "Free Derry," banning the police and British military from entering the neighborhood. "Bloody Sunday" (see box on p. 441) was the most famous battle of that period.

Despite the unpleasant social divide, Derry was something of an economic success story. For a time, the city supported the largest textile industry in the world; Derry is even mentioned in Karl Marx's *Das Kapital.* With peace prevailing, Derry seems poised to settle its score with history and revive its economic fortunes. The physical signs of division are still there, though. Around 15,000 Protestants moved out of Derry's West Bank (Cityside) during the Troubles, many relocating to the east bank of the Foyle (known as Waterside). So, while walls no longer divide the communities, the river has become a natural rift between the people.

Incidentally, the official name is Londonderry—which is also the name of the county—since that's the name bestowed by royal charter centuries ago; in mid-2007 a judge ruled that only the Queen could change the name. Officials are petitioning Her Majesty, and everyone's holding their breath.

LAY OF THE LAND

Derry straddles the **River Foyle;** most of what is of interest is on the **West Bank,** where the compact walled city center is located and where most hotels, restaurants, and attractions are—including the **Catholic Bogside** community where so much of the conflict associated with the Troubles transpired.

GETTING THERE & GETTING AROUND

Although it's an unlikely point of entry, **flights** from Dublin, London Stansted, Glasgow, Liverpool, Nottingham, and Bristol land at **City of Derry Airport** (Airport Rd., Eglinton; ☎ 028/7181-0784; www.cityofderryairport.com), 11km (7 miles) from Derry. Buses connect passengers with the city, and there's an information desk (with local tourist assistance) at the airport. Regular **trains** from Belfast arrive at Derry's **Duke Street station** (☎ 028/7134-2228) on the east bank; service is reduced on Sunday. Journey time is 2 hours and includes a free bus transfer from the train station to the **Foyle Street bus terminal** (☎ 0128/9066-6630) on the west bank. Buses pull in here from across Northern Ireland and the Republic. **AIRporter buses** run between Derry's Quayside Shopping Centre and both of Belfast's airports (☎ 028/71269996; www.airporter.co.uk).

Derry is 118km (73 miles) northwest of Belfast on the **A6.**

Derry is fairly small, but it has a convoluted road system that has become even crazier recently as an extensive waterworks upgrade has turned large areas of road into a one-way mess. Avoid driving. The city requires exploration on foot, with few sites beyond walking distance.

ACCOMMODATIONS, BOTH STANDARD & NOT

Rooms move quicker in Derry than you might expect, so book ahead. With one exception, the choices below are within easy walking distance of the walled city.

£   Billed as "the only B&B in the Bogside," Seamus Kennedy's **Abbey House** ✯✯ (4 Abbey St.; ☎ 028/7127-9000; www.abbeyaccommodation.com; cash only) is steeped in the cordial personality of its host which is good news because, in his other life, Seamus is a decorator. He tends to each of the rooms personally, most recently adding leather headboards and chic color schemes. Rooms are always freshly painted, and come with good hanging and packing space, comfortable beds, a desk, and free Wi-Fi. Good value (£50 double), coupled with laid-back hospitality, makes this a stand-out choice. Along with the B&B, Kennedy also offers two townhouses for rent (**www.derryselfcatering.com**). Spacious, smart, and pretty much brand-spanking new, they're places where you can really feel at one with the local community. Brewster House, which sleeps seven, is particularly nice (open fireplace, fab kitchen, big outdoor patio) and costs just £450 to £550 per week, £170 a night.

£   Vivacious Joan Pyne and historian husband, Peter, are mad about old buildings. They've restored two townhouse gems (a few minutes apart from one another) to within an inch of their former glory, offering accommodations at either the **Saddler's House** ✯ (36 Great James St.; ☎ 028/7126-9691 or 028/7126-4223; lucy@fdn.co.uk; MC, V) or the **Merchant's House** ✯✯ (16 Queen St.; same contact details). I'm particularly partial to the latter, the slightly older of the two, built in 1867 by a local tea trader. Although the bathrooms here are shared, I like the fact that the original space hasn't been interfered with (which would have made way for en suite bathrooms). And it's filled with lovely antiques, from pianos and ancient clocks to chandeliers and lithographs. The five bedrooms are rounded off with fine linens and fabrics. Breakfasts are served at the Saddler's House (it's a 5-min. walk) and are sumptuous affairs, with hearty cooked dishes

Rentals in the Rural West

Should you decide you'd like rural rather than Derry City lodgings, here are some wonderfully affordable rentals to consider:

- **Blessingbourne Courtyard Apartments** ✦✦✦ 🄺🄸🄳🄢 (Fivemiletown; ☎ 028/8952-1188 or 078/7057-8729; www.blessingbourne.com) offers luxe digs in award-winning cottage-style apartments that sleep up to five. Set on a vast, sumptuous estate just outside Fivemiletown, they're near the border with County Fermanagh. The estate has its own nature reserve, tennis courts, and a lake with fishing and boating. You have the benefit of round-the-clock on-site assistance. Weekly rates start at £285.

- In Plumbridge, **Ballinasollus Cottage** ✦✦ 🄺🄸🄳🄢 (7 Ballynasollus Rd., Plumbridge; ☎ 028/8164-7618 or 079/0082-6311; www.tyrone cottages.com) is an attractive red sandstone house built in 1871 and recently restored and updated to include modern facilities—it's suitable for a small family. Set on a large woodland property with its own river, it's a great setting off point for walks into the Sperrins. Renting this cottage for a week will cost between £320 and £400.

- With substantially less historical character, but nevertheless built in the traditional "Clachan" style, **Sperrin View Cottages** ✦✦ (199 Termon Rd., Pomeroy; ☎ 028/8775-9036; www.sperrinviewcottages. com) are a cluster of eight purpose-built holiday homes packed with modern conveniences (DVD-players, digital TV, dishwashers, and laundry facilities). The owner, Sean Mallaghan, looks after his guests and takes care of "little problems," should they arise. He also provides a good deal, with weekly rates from £230 to £340 or 1 night at £50 to £60.

- Tucked into the Sperrin foothills, **An Clachan** ✦✦✦ 🄺🄸🄳🄢 (Creggan, near Omagh; ☎ 028/8076-1112; www.an-creagan.com; MC, V) is a group of eight self-catering cottages, purpose-built and designed to impact as little as possible on the natural setting. There are three-, two-, and one-bedroom cottages, each echoing traditional village architecture, with whitewashed stone walls, working fireplaces, and small windows (you must request a TV if you need one). Solar heating ensures that there's hot water. Rates vary according to season. A three-bedroom unit (which sleeps at least six people) costs £330 for a full week in high season (July–Aug), or £220 in the low season (Oct–Mar). By contrast, a one-bedroom cottage costs £220 per week in high season and just £150 in low season.

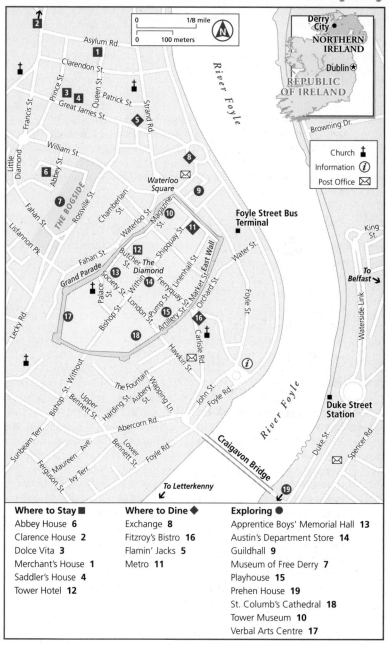

Derry City
NORTHERN IRELAND
Dublin
REPUBLIC OF IRELAND

Church †
Information ⓘ
Post Office ✉

River Foyle

Asylum Rd.
Clarendon St.
Patrick St.
Great James St.
Strand Rd.
William St.
Waterloo Square
Foyle Street Bus Terminal
THE BOGSIDE
Little Diamond
Fahan St.
Lisfannon Pk.
Lecky Rd.
Chamberlain St.
Waterloo St.
Magazine St.
Shipquay St.
Butcher St.
The Diamond
Grand Parade
Fahan St.
Society St.
Palace St.
Bishop St.
London St.
Pump St.
Within
Ferryquay St.
Linenhall St.
East Wall
Market St.
Orchard St.
Water St.
Foyle St.
Artillery St.
Carlisle Rd.
Hawkin St.
The Fountain
Upper Bennett St.
Bishop St. Without
Harding St.
Aubery St.
Wapping Ln.
Abercorn Rd.
Sunbeam Terr.
Maureen Ave.
Ferguson St.
Ivy Terr.
Lower Bennett St.
Foyle Rd.
John St.
Foyle Rd.
Craigavon Bridge
River Foyle
Duke Street Station
Duke St.
Spencer Rd.
Waterside Link
King St.
To Belfast
Browning Dr.
To Letterkenny
Prince St.
Queen St.
Francis St.
Abbey St.
Rossville St.

Where to Stay ■	Where to Dine ◆	Exploring ●
Abbey House **6**	Exchange **8**	Apprentice Boys' Memorial Hall **13**
Clarence House **2**	Fitzroy's Bistro **16**	Austin's Department Store **14**
Dolce Vita **3**	Flamin' Jacks **5**	Guildhall **9**
Merchant's House **1**	Metro **11**	Museum of Free Derry **7**
Saddler's House **4**		Playhouse **15**
Tower Hotel **12**		Prehen House **19**
		St. Columb's Cathedral **18**
		Tower Museum **10**
		Verbal Arts Centre **17**

and home-baked breads. Bedrooms at Saddler's House are rather more compact, and the bathrooms can be a bit of a squeeze (plus showers lack decent pressure). Nevertheless, for such authentic Old World style it's incredible to think that you'll pay just £50 to £55 double (at either house).

££   If you'd prefer to stay somewhere that's more "guesthouse" than B&B (meaning you can get a drink at the bar, and there's a check-in "desk"), another comfortable option, this time rather a far walk from the center, is **Clarence House** ✭ (15 Northland Rd.; ☎ 028/7126-5342; www.guesthouseireland.co.uk; MC, V). Okay, so it's seen better days, but owner Michael Slevin treats guests as though they were staying in a private home. Rates average £70 double, £38 to £45 single with a 10% discount for stays of over 3 days. Plenty of amenities (French press coffee, shoe mitts, a properly working shower), dinners available by arrangement, and an extravagant breakfast spread, all add up to a good stay.

£–£££   If you'd like to be within the walled city, there's only one choice (literally) and that's the **Tower Hotel** ✭✭ 🧒 (Butcher St.; ☎ 028/7137-1000; www. towerhotelderry.com; AE, MC, V), which is architecturally a little out of whack with the historic city. Overtly modern, it features a loungey lobby and bedrooms livened up by intensely red bedspreads and blue carpets (trying to draw your attention away from the dull, modular furniture). The best rooms are spacious (with big bathrooms, too) and have views over the Bogside, so specify such details when you book. Rates without breakfast start at £55 in the low season, up to £99 in high, and this includes rooms that can accommodate a couple plus children (family rooms have fold-out sofa beds). A bar and restaurant, and parking underneath the hotel round out the hotel's amenities.

A Chic Hostel

£   There are other cheap digs in Derry, but nothing as thoughtfully laid out or as style-conscious as **Dolce Vita** ✭✭ (12 Prince's St.; ☎ 028/7128-0542; www. derryhostel.com; MC, V), which—as their tagline suggests—indeed offers "boutique chic" at a "budget price" (you also get about twice the amount of space one usually finds at a hostel). While a bed in a dorm (just four people sharing) costs £11, private rooms are nearly as good a deal at £36 double (or twin). Prices include continental breakfast, Internet, and access to a superb open-plan kitchen where you can cook up a storm before settling down at the designer dining table. Shared showers are tidy; and because some people need to soak after a day on the town, there's also a bathtub. Check-in is at 44 Great James Street, nearby.

DINING FOR ALL TASTES

£–££   For plates piled high with traditional pub grub, served amidst what often feels like a scrum of cheering fans (glued to the set when there's a game on the telly), stride into the vast, wood-paneled interior of the **Metro** ✭ (3–4 Bank Place; ☎ 028/7126-7401; food served Sun–Fri noon–3pm; Sat noon–8pm; MC, V). All the usual suspects are here: Steak and Guinness pie (£6), burgers (£4.50–£4.25), various curries (£6); and they include your choice of side order, ensuring that you won't leave hungry. Remarkably for a common-denominator pub, there's also a special "slimmer's menu."

£–££££ Around the corner from Guildhall, the **Exchange** ★★ (Exchange House, Queens Quay; ☎ 028/7127-3990; www.exchangerestaurant.com; Mon–Sat noon–2:30pm and 5:30–10pm; Sun 4–9pm; AE, MC, V) is one of Derry's slickest venues thanks to such industrial chic touches as exposed white cooling ducts and ultramodish orange lights. A smart crowd chows down on a straightforward "chicken, meat, fish, or veg" menu (£8.50–£16 for most), ordered at the till (it's then brought to your table). International influences like curries or Laska sauces also make an appearance, but have far less spice (stick with the tried and true here). Lunch is cheaper, with good deals on the special of the day (with a side order) for £6.

££–£££ No matter what night of the week it is, **Flamin' Jacks** ★★ (31–35 Strand St.; ☎ 028/7126-6400; Mon–Thurs noon–3pm and 5–10:45pm; Fri–Sat noon–3pm and 4:30–11pm; Sun 12:30–3pm and 4–10pm; MC, V) is perennially packed. As the name suggests, the specialty here is flame-grilled steak (I last had an excellent 8 oz. sirloin smothered in blue cheese sauce, with a Greek side salad for £11), but any of their meat and combo dishes are worthwhile, famous for coming out sizzling hot. The other specialty: "cook your own" dishes where you get to grill your own meat on a hot stone at the table. The intimate space is livened up by leather benches and bizarre, modernist lighting fixtures.

££–£££ **Fitzroy's Bistro** ★★ (2–4 Bridge St., 3 Carlisle Rd.; ☎ 028/7126-6211; www.fitzroysrestaurant.com; Mon–Sat 11am–late, last order 9:45pm; Sun noon–late, last orders 7:45pm; closed 4:30–5:30pm; MC, V) is neo-baroque fantasy (ebony walls, chandeliers, and lots of blinding-white decor) and that goes for the staff, too, who can be a little stagy, trotting around the restaurant floor with their enormous serving trays and long black aprons, but absent when you actually need their attention. You'll appreciate the interesting menu, though, which is more inventive than most with such offerings as Cajun chicken under melted goat cheese served on a bed of stir-fried vegetables (£9) and creamy leek risotto (£9).

WHY YOU'RE HERE: TOP SIGHTS & ATTRACTIONS

To quickly get a feel for how Derry is put together, start by circumnavigating the **city walls** ★★★ (dawn–dusk)—a 1.3km (¾-mile) walk, which is as much an opportunity to learn about the history of the city as it is a chance to quickly grasp its geography. Built at a cost of £11,147, they're among the finest in Europe, with eight uniquely ornamented gates. Original cannons dot the bastions—among them, two Elizabethan cannons inscribed with a Tudor Rose dating from 1590; you'll find them near Shipquay Gate. From atop Bishop's Gate, you get a good view of the Bogside, the Peace Wall, remains of the old gaol, and—within the walled city—the Courthouse, which was the most bombed structure in Derry during the Troubles.

Your wall walk also takes you past the **Apprentice Boys' Memorial Hall** (visits by appointment only), where the fence-protected facade comes from the days when IRA attacks were always a strong possibility. It was created in celebration of the Apprentice Boys, who locked the city gates in the face of King James's Catholic troops, thus igniting the Siege of Londonderry in 1688 (p. 434). The IRA bombed an earlier version of the replica **Walker Monument,** which now stands next to the Hall. The original statue—which is of Derry's Siege-era governor, and therefore a Protestant hero—stood on a column atop the city walls, thus

Getting the Inside Scoop

Touring a new city—particularly when it's stuffed full of tumultuous history and down-on-the-ground intrigue—can be a little frustrating if there's no one to give you the inside scoop. That's why I recommend **Michael Cooper** of **Free Derry Walking Tours** ★★★ (☎ 028/7136-1311 or 077/4317-5709; www.derrybluebadgeguide.com). Michael is a local lad who tells heart-stopping stories, particularly concerning the startling events of the Troubles. While Michael organizes a small squadron of guides who lead various walking as well as driving tours, I'd recommend you insist that he be your expert companion as you set off in search of Derry's hidden history. His walking tours of the Bogside—with a hugely political (that is, intriguing) slant—start at the Free Derry Museum at 10am and 2pm daily and cost £5 per person (a joint ticket that includes admission to the Museum costs £6); walking tours of the walls at noon cover a more general history of Derry (also £5).

These tours are ideal if you're looking for a little more meat on the bone than you might get on a more general walk, such as the fun-but-touristy one offered by City Tours (see below).

always lording it over the Bogside. In 1973, however, the IRA blew up the statue and held its head for ransom.

A fun way to experience the walls is on a walking tour, offered by **City Tours** ★★ (11 Carlisle Rd.; ☎ 028/7127-1996; www.irishtourguides.com; £4); guides are experienced and witty, using various sights along the way to pull together the history of the city (all the while revealing unusual facts, figures, and anecdotes that play like a stand-up comedy routine). Probably the most popular walking tours of the city, they can accommodate fairly large groups; if you're after a tour that's more scholarly, see "Getting the Inside Scoop," above.

One visit-worthy monument in the walled city is **St. Columb's Cathedral** ★★ (London St.; ☎ 028/7126-7313; www.stcolumbscathedral.org; £2; Apr–Oct Mon–Sat 9am–5pm; Nov–Mar 9am–4pm), the oldest building in Derry. Built in 1633, this was the first Protestant cathedral built on the British Isles after the Reformation; paid for by London merchant companies, it wears its Unionist affiliation on its sleeve, with souvenirs from the infamous Siege of Londonderry enshrined within and a memorial to the heroes of the Siege on the grounds. The church's most recognizable celebrity was Cecil Frances Alexander (1818–95), the wife of one of the bishops here; she wrote a surfeit of well-loved hymns, including *Once In Royal David's City, There is a Green Hill Far Away,* and *All Things Bright and Beautiful,* and there is some suggestion that her lyrics were much-inspired by her feelings about Derry City.

In the central square, called the **Diamond,** you'll find **Austin's Department Store,** reputedly the oldest independent department store in the world (15 years older than Macy's). Only a handful of streets are within the walls, and it can be an adventure to simply wander; there's absolutely no chance of getting lost.

The Bogside & Free Derry

The area known as the Bogside is the working class Catholic neighborhood to the immediate northwest of the walled city. Here the **Museum of Free Derry** ✿✿✿ (55 Glenfada Park; ☎ 028/7136-0880; www.museumoffreederry.org; £3; Mon–Fri 9:30am–4:30pm; Apr–Sept Sat 1–4pm; July–Sept Sun 1–4pm) traces the sobering story of the Derry's involvement with the civil rights movement and how this led to the establishment of Free Derry in the 1960s and 1970s, the Battle of the Bogside, and the terrible events of January 30th, 1972—Bloody Sunday.

How Long Must We Sing this Song?

Sadly, the event most closely associated with 20th-century Derry is one of the most tragic single-day events in Irish history: Bloody Sunday, an eruption of violence that left 14 people dead in the wake of a peaceful human rights protest.

On January 30th, 1972, a march to appeal against internment (imprisonment without trial) was held. The march had officially been banned, but 15,000 people showed up anyway. The IRA had assured the organizers that they would stay away from the protest action, and there was reason to believe that it would be a relatively peaceful day. But when the marchers approached the first of the barricades set up by the British Army, a minority of the protesters (a few hundred out of the thousands who turned out that day) continued toward the barricade, angry. Riots broke out, rubber bullets were fired, stones were flung, tear gas exploded, and water cannons opened up.

As the riot seemed to be dying out, five live shots were fired. Two men—one aged 59 and another 15—were hit. And so the bloodshed and carnage got underway. All in all, 13 men fell dead (another died later), and another 15 people were wounded. Six of the dead hadn't seen their 18th birthday. Not one was armed. It had taken less than 30 minutes.

The British army reported that its soldiers had responded to "hundreds of shots" being fired from among the protestors. Just 3 months later, the Widgery tribunal absolved the British battalion from any wrongdoing.

The matter didn't go away, however, and the outcry over this tragedy is considered pivotal in the long, slippery slope that has, finally, led to peace. Bono and his band U2 turned the event into one of the most powerful dancefloor anthems of the 1980s, and the U.K. justice system, having reopened the case, has turned it into one of the longest running investigations in human memory. At a cost of at least £180 million, the Saville Inquiry has been ongoing since the 1990s, and although the published report was expected to be released by the end of 2007, it was still not available in early 2009.

It's not every day that you walk into a museum and are greeted by a polite gentleman who explains how the exhibition works and then—with courageous, trying-to-forget eyes, explains that his own brother was killed in the conflict that the museum works so hard to explain. These moments have a way of haunting us, and hopefully challenging us to be part of the solution; for these moments alone, this museum is worth the time and emotional investment. Don't ignore the computer-stored archive material, with poignant video clips, soundbites, and photographs. *Note:* Parents should be aware that some of the images and video clips are likely to be too harrowing for young children; if you bring the family, you might want to keep an eye on more sensitive kids.

Today, not far from the museum, the most evocative remnant of those awful years is the **white gable wall** painted with the phrase, "You are now entering Free Derry," which first appeared in the Bogside in January 1969, when the first "no go" area was declared. Defiantly, they were first painted as a warning that the people of the Bogside (organized in the large by IRA members and others inspired by the Student Uprisings of the late-sixties) symbolically liberated their own neighborhood, banning the police, the military, and "outsiders." Derry's equivalent of "Amandla" or "We shall overcome," the shiver-inducing slogan today serves as a memorial to the heroes, martyrs, and innocent victims of the Troubles.

The museum is also a good setting off point from which to investigate the **Bogside murals** ✪✪✪, most of which were completed by a trio of artists calling themselves the "Bogside Artists." The murals are easily sighted from the museum and the Walls of Derry. Descriptions of the meaning of each of the murals can be found in front of each painting.

The Guildhall & the Tower Museum

Right outside the city walls, the **Guildhall** ✪✪ (Guildhall Sq.; ☎ 028/7137-7335; www.derrycity.gov.uk; free admission; Mon–Fri 8:30am–5pm) is the city's top architectural draw. Festooned with recessed Gothic arches, turret towers topped by mini onion domes, hooded spires, and a four-sided clock tower, the detailing is so fanciful, you'll be certain you're looking at a church rather than a civic building. First built in 1887, and rebuilt, after a fire in 1912, the Guildhall is open to the public and recommended for its breathtaking stained glass windows (which give a pictorial overview of the city's intrigue-stained history).

For incisive coverage of the history of Derry (and through that the complex story of Ireland itself), devote an hour or two to the **Tower Museum** ✪ (Union Hall Place; ☎ 028/7137-2411; www.derrycity.gov.uk/museums; £4; Oct–Jun Tues–Sat 10am–5pm; July–Aug Mon–Sat 10am–5pm; Sun 11am–3pm; Sept Mon–Sat 10am–5pm). Although not quite as jolly as joining a walking tour of the city itself, there's much to recommend it, especially because the facility uses a number of short films to trace the evolution of the city from ancient times. Whatever you do, don't miss out on the view from the open-air top floor of the museum; take the elevator to the right of the ticket desk.

And, Finally, One Aristocratic Oddity

Derry's most fantastical visit is to quirky **Prehen House** ✪✪✪ (Prehen, Derry; ☎ 028/7134-2829; www.prehen.net; £4; Mar–Oct Tues–Sun 2–5pm), a mansion built in 1740 on an estate alongside Prehen Woods. Packed with curiosities and valuable heirlooms from a wardrobe owned by Empress Josephine, to a library featuring some of the oldest books in Ireland, it's the ancestral home of the Knox family.

Prehen is best known for its association with Derry's legendary Half-Hanged McNaughton. A roguish 18th-century gambler, John McNaughton fell in love with Mary Ann Knox, the 15-year-old daughter of Andrew Knox, and tricked her into a secret marriage. Horrified, the girl's parents prepared to whisk her off to Dublin, but wily McNaughton hijacked the stagecoach and during the ambush accidentally shot and killed his beloved Mary Ann. At the gallows, the rope snapped, so McNaughton survived his execution and was free to go (legally, you can't hang a person twice for the same crime). But, declaring that he didn't want to be remembered as "half-hanged," he returned to the gallows and this time hanged himself. Many say Half-Hanged McNaughton still haunts the bedroom in which Mary Ann's parents once slept and apparently his ghost regularly climbs into bed with guests staying there.

To reach Prehen, head across Craigavon Bridge to Waterside, and turn right into Victoria Road (direction Strabane), following the signs into Prehen after the Everglades Hotel. There is also a bus service to Prehen Park from the city center.

THE OTHER DERRY

For its size, Derry is a hotbed of cultural activity thanks in no small part to the **Playhouse** (St. Columb's Hall, Orchard St.; ☎ 028/7126-8027; www.derryplayhouse. co.uk), one of the largest community arts centers in Ireland. Loads of events, performances, festivals, classes, talks, society get-togethers and workshops pull in people from all walks of life, so this happens to be a great place to spend "untouristy" time with local people. Much of what happens at the Playhouse is suitable for casual, interested visitors, and the manager, Niall McCaughan (niall@derryplay house.co.uk) will let you know what's on if you write to him in advance. Here are some of the activities you might find interesting: traditional Irish dancing classes for adults; lectures on aspects of Derry's heritage; behind-the-scenes tours of the Playhouse premises; and the Magic Lantern Film Club, screening arthouse films followed by a discussion. Every Wednesday from 1:30 to 4pm, the Derry Playhouse Writers meet to share ideas and writing experiences, and anyone is welcome; this is a good opportunity to meet some of the city's creative spirits.

In a modernist space right in the city walls, at the **Verbal Arts Centre** (Stable Lane & Mall Wall, Bishop St. within the walls; ☎ 028/7126-9646; www.verbalarts centre.co.uk), the ancient Irish tradition of storytelling is celebrated in a contemporary context, and considerable focus is given to the sharing of personal histories (particularly important given Derry's ongoing social and political reconciliation). Workshops aren't geared at tourists at all, but visitors are welcome to attend regular events such as the "Foyle Yarnspinners," and bookclub-style readers' circles, which are free and open to anyone; see website for details.

Two Cooking Classes outside the City

Outside Derry in nearby Omagh, you have the chance to learn some new recipes from one of the county's real shining stars. Legendary Norah Brown of **Cook with Norah** (www.learn2cookwithnorah.com; £75), is widely recognized for helping to put Northern Ireland on the culinary map—her involvement in the country's cooking scene earned her an MBE (Member of the Order of the British Empire), which I think means we're supposed to call her Dame Norah. Norah believes that in some ways the isolation experienced during the Troubles may have forced people to hang on to traditional cooking knowledge, much of which she believes may have disappeared in the south.

These are not hands-on cooking classes, but entertaining demonstrations in which Norah reveals some of the finer points of modern Irish cuisine. Each session is 4 hours and Norah goes through a dozen or so recipes in that time. She holds about eight sessions a year, mostly in summer; all include a feast at the end.

Norah has a potent rival in Liz Moore, who leads the cooking classes at the **Belle Isle School of Cookery** ✪✪✪ (Belle Isle Estate, Lisbellaw, Enniskillen; ☎ 028/6638-7231; www.irishcookeryschool.com). Renowned throughout Northern Ireland, Belle Isle is wonderful not only for its setting, with views of the impressive Florence Court Mountains, but for the fun students have while triumphing in the kitchen. "It's not just about picking up skills and learning new recipes," says Liz, "I try to encourage people to love cooking, to love food as much as I do." And, really, when you step into one of Liz's classes, gathered around the counter or the oil-fired Aga stove, in her big, robust kitchen, you really do start, almost instantly, to feel the love. One student showed up not knowing how to boil an egg, and now works in the food industry.

You can choose from a wide range of classes, from 1-day (£120) or weekend courses (£310), right the way up to a 4-week intensive diploma in "Essential Cooking." Most courses are open to anyone over the age of 8; work stations are height-adjustable, and also wheelchair friendly. There are also demonstration classes held on weeknights (these last 2 hr. and start at 7pm; £30); these are sociable evenings where you watch (and learn), drink wine, and taste the samples all the while. The website gives a full rundown of the program for the year—the occasional "Traditional Irish" course does crop up, but otherwise it's a very mixed bag, from "Summer Madness" to "Healthy Eating for Children."

ATTENTION, SHOPPERS!

During the Troubles one piece of graffiti appeared in the Bogside that summed up the spending climate of the time: "Shop now, while shops last!" Shopping in Derry remains a relatively timid experience, without the line-up of elegant boutiques you'll find in Belfast. There are a few stores worth seeking out, though.

Foyle Books ✪✪ (12 Magazine St.; ☎ 028/7137-2530) is the city's largest second-hand store and stocks some intriguing antiquarian tomes. A large section is devoted to Irish language, culture, and history books.

For fashionistas, there's no better place to browse than through the alluring racks at **Chocolate** ✪✪ (Unit 7, Lesley House, Foyle St.; ☎ 028/7136-9023; www.chocolateclothing.co.uk). Challenging the tawdry trend toward cheap and disposable, sharp-eyed Barry Conaghan has cornered the local market for hip and sexy clothing that's good for the dance floor or schmoozing over cocktails.

My other favorite clothing store—and this one is a darn sight more affordable, with plenty of excellent deals on sale items—is **Flip** (3–5 London St.; ☎ 028/7126-5554; www.flipclothing.com), which is one-half of a two-branch chain (the other's in Dublin) that stocks jean, jackets, and urbanwear.

Unique and classical jewelry is sold at the compact antique dealership **Whatnot** (22 Bishop St.; ☎ 028/7128-8333), near the Diamond.

NIGHTLIFE

Derry may be small, but its endless variety of entertainments will blow you away; below are only a few of my favorites.

Cultural Pursuits

One of the most vibrant centers for artistic and cultural activity in Derry is the **Playhouse** (see "The Other Derry," above), and it's one of the few theaters in Ireland that commissions new work. Dave Duggan, the writer of Oscar-nominated *Dance, Lexi, Dance,* cut his teeth here. The Playhouse's newly renovated theater space relaunched in March 2009 with a cutting edge line-up.

For mostly commercial entertainment—theater, comedy, and music—the **Millennium Forum** (Newmarket St.; ☎ 028/7126-4455; www.millenniumforum. co.uk) is the largest purpose-built theater complex in Ireland. In 2008, big scale productions, like *High School Musical,* headed up the year's family program, while superstar comedians Billy Connelly and Lee Evans satisfied less-G-rated tastes (and sold out very early, too). Big name Irish musicians make regular appearances, and there's the odd serious drama with an Irish angle—like Beckett's *Waiting for Godot.*

Drinking Holes, Traditional & Contemporary, with Live Music

You really can't say you've been to Derry until you've spent time at **Peadar O'Donnell's** ★★★ (53 Waterloo St.; ☎ 028/7137-2318), where you'll be hard-pressed not to have a blast. This is particularly true when there's a session involving a brilliant little band called Blacklegminor—usually Wednesdays and Saturdays between 7 and 9pm, occasionally late on a Sunday and on holidays.

On the other side of the walled city, **Sandinos Café-Bar** ★★★ (1 Water St.; ☎ 028/7130-9297; www.sandinos.com) is all about revolution, at least in the decor. Walls are draped with countless bits of radical memorabilia from banners declaring "Free Palestine" to posters of Warhol's tribute to Che Guevera. It's probably not a place you'll appreciate if you were a staunch George W. Bush supporter. Still, the vibe in here is humming and the characters you'll meet willingly share their feelings on politics, free market economies, and more. Aside from the excellent *craic,* spare a moment for the regular line-up of live bands, DJs, jazz, poetry evenings, and even traditional sessions (on Sun afternoons).

You may notice the **Bogside Inn** (32 Westland St.; ☎ 028/7126-9300) while you're investigating the Bogside Murals. Very much a local watering hole, here you'll meet genuine, salt-of-the-earth characters who don't hold their tongues or their opinions for anyone (strictly adults only, I'd say). The walls are hung with striking photographs of some of the poignant moments from the Troubles years, and serve as reminders of how local everyday reality once revolved around military and police intervention. Every Friday, a pint costs just £2.

Pepe's (64 Strand Rd.; ☎ 028/7137-4002) is where you go to dance. Full to the brim with a marvelously mixed and raucous crowd, it's Derry's only gay bar-cum-club, and there's DJ-spun music.

TYRONE COUNTY

Genuinely undiscovered, Northern Ireland's largest county really does offer a chance to get far away from the maddening crowd. The peat-clad slopes and pointed peaks of the Sperrin Mountain range—stretched along the Londonderry and Tyrone border—shelter a lush rural wilderness with some unusual geographic features, rare flora, and some of Ireland's first signs of creative intelligence—left by the country's earliest human inhabitants. You will need a rental car to explore the best of this county.

The townland area of **Creggan** (located midway between Omagh and Cookstown), in particular, is famed in its many prehistoric sites including court tombs, stone circles, and ancient standing stones which archaeologists trace back to the Stone Age. For easy-to-follow insight into the ancient spiritual sites in the Sperrins region, start off at the **An Creagán Visitor Centre** ✶ (on the A505, Creggan, near Omagh; ☎ 028/8076-1112; www.an-creagan.com; Apr–Sept daily 11am–6:30pm; Oct–Mar Mon–Fri 11am–4:30pm). Here, a small exhibition explains some of the local cultural traditions; most importantly, you can pick up a map to the archaeological sites. Forty-four such sites have been discovered within an 8km (5-mile) radius of the town. Of these, I definitely wouldn't miss out on the **Beaghmore Stone Circles** ✶✶✶. Created in the Bronze Age, the site consists of seven stone circles and 10 stone rows. Nobody knows precisely why our ancestors did such strange things with rocks. Some argue that it was an attempt to restore fertility to the soil and prevent the onset of boggy weather conditions that caused peat to envelop the land. There's something profoundly mysterious about them.

Creggan is also known for its **boglands,** and as odd as this might sound, boglands are fascinating places to visit. The blanket bogs you see here are basically big, 2 to 3m (8–10 ft.) thick sponges that cover hills, just like a blanket covers a bed. They're layered with vegetation (which enlivens the hills with vivid colors in spectacular patterns). The so-called **Black Bog** here is said to be one of the largest intact raised bogs in All Ireland.

You can set off on independent walks in the Sperrins, and be engrossed by the landscape—but you'd never know if you'd walked past or over a "bog burst," a "peat beach," without the help of a specialist guide. That's where **Martin Bradley** ✶✶✶ (☎ 0792/678-5706 or 028/7131-8473; martin839@btinternet.com; £90 per group, no minimum or maximum number of participants) comes in, an expert in palaeoecology ("the study of past landscapes and how these environments and their habitats have evolved through time"). Bradley has the unique ability to cut through the hard science with incisive explanations and a slightly offbeat wit, drawing excellent analogies (often with scenes from films) to explain the natural phenomena. His tours are highly recommended.

More recent history is examined at the **Ulster American Folk Park** ✶✶✶ [kids] (2 Mellon Rd., Castletown; ☎ 028/8224-3292; www.folkpark.com; £5 adults; Oct to mid-Mar Mon–Fri 10:30am–5pm; mid-Mar to Sept Mon–Sat 10:30am–6pm; Sun 11am–6:30pm), which examines the topic of why so many people from this region of Ireland (literally millions) immigrated to the Americas. An interactive, outdoor collection of authentic 18th- and 19th-century homesteads and other buildings gathered from different parts of Ulster and the United States, it serves as a sort of

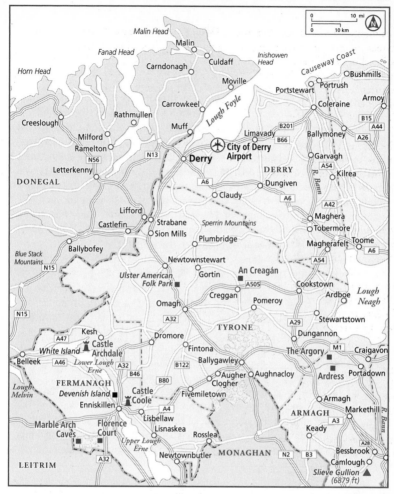

living history museum to show us "moderners" what life might have been like for the people who decided to up and leave Ireland. It's quite well done and particularly appropriate for families.

And there are two shopping opportunities as well. Attracting value-savvy shoppers from as far as Belfast and across the border in the Irish Republic, the **Linen Green** ✪✪ (Moygashel, Dungannon; ☎ 028/8775-3761; www.thelinengreen.com; Mon–Sat 10am–5pm) is the place to score bargains on woven goods and clothing. A conglomeration of outlets that discount big names like Dublin designer Paul Costelloe, Linen Green is just outside the town of Dungannon, about 20km (12½ miles) northwest of Armagh along the A29.

Lake Country Lodgings

Lake Country is so lovely, you may find yourself wishing to extend your day trip to an overnight or perhaps a weeklong visit. If the spirit moves you, here are a few good places to move into:

As hostel accommodations go, the **Bridges** ✺ (The Clinton Centre, Belmore St.; ☎ 028/6634-0110; www.hini.org.uk; MC, V) is a couple of notches above average. Designed as part of the Clinton International Peace Centre (with a totally out-of-place ultra-modern exterior), the hostel prides itself in being Ireland's first public building to use solar panels as well as photo voltaic cells to conserve energy. Spacious digs (£15 for a dorm bed, or £35 double with a bunk bed), extremely clean and well laid-out premises, and a friendly welcome at the desk all make for a decent base from which to explore the lakelands of Fermanagh. There's a laundry room, lounge with TV, and a well-equipped kitchen and dining room if you decide to cook. No curfews or lock-outs (hooray!).

The coach houses, stables, and garden cottages that once were part of the swank **Belle Isle Estate** ✺✺✺ 🌿 (Lisbellaw; ☎ 028/6638-7231; www.belleisle-estate.com) have been transformed into rental apartments, and boy are they swell. Eight in all, they're spacious (with different configurations—some even have two sitting rooms) with smart cane furniture, wood-burning fireplaces, and walls decorated with quality lithographs. Bedrooms have ultra-soft white linens, and kitchens are fully equipped. Rates are surprisingly good, particularly outside summer. By way of example (since the rates vary according to which property you choose), 1 week in a two-bedroom courtyard apartment costs £510 in mid-season (late Mar to late June) and £621 in peak season (late June to end of Aug); in the quiet winter months it's £400. Special rates are also available for 3-night stays; weekends are slightly more expensive. You'll have plenty to do while you're holed up here—besides exploring the enchanting lakeside grounds,

About a kilometer and a half (1 mile) of Dungannon along the A45 toward Coalisland, **Tyrone Crystal** (on the A45, 2.5km/1½ miles from Dungannon en route to Coalisland; ☎ 028/8772-5335; www.tyronecrystal.com; Mon–Sat 9am–5pm) not only sells pricey crystal pieces (a set of six goblets is £129), but offers **factory tours** (£5; Mon–Fri 11am, noon, and 2pm; booking recommended) during which you watch glass being blown and cut by hand.

ENNISKILLEN & THE LAKE DISTRICT

A Tyrone-businessman once told me that "Fermanagh people are so laid-back, they're horizontal." There's clearly some rivalry between the neighboring and, I would say, equally bucolic, counties. You might forgive the people of ultra-mellow Fermanagh for wanting to chill out, though. It's a tiny county steeped in lakeland beauty, and opportunities everywhere to get out on the water or simply you can play tennis, hire a boat, or even join one of the classes that happens at the cooking school here (p. 444).

Rosemary Armstrong runs **Arch House** ★★ 🄺 (Tullyhona, Florencecourt; ☎ 028/6634-8452; www.archhouse.com; MC, V) with a blend of old-fashioned hospitality and well, pizzazz, providing Internet access, laundry service, and preparing restaurant-caliber meals; guests are also invited to watch how she makes those extraordinary-tasting scones she's so brilliant at. All bedrooms have a private bathroom and are quite modestly sized if a trifle twee, with half-canopies and lots of frilly, lacy bits, but the beds and linens are comfortable. While you might imagine yourself spending most of your time dreaming about Rosemary's food, there's plenty to do on this working farm B&B, whether you're more comfortable on or near water, or on horseback. But the big surprise? A double room goes for £52. Children staying in family rooms pay half.

Another recommended farmhouse stay (this time on an organic farm, dating back to the 18th century), is **Dromard House** ★★ (Tamlaght; ☎ 028/6638-7250; www.dromardhouse.com; MC, V). Set within the woodlands of a 73-hectare (180-acre) farm that reaches down to the shore of Lough Erne, it offers homey B&B-style lodgings (£50–£55 double), or a modest-but-cozy self-catering unit for two (£40 per night; £250 per week). Either way, it's a privileged stay in a fetching location; there are walks, views over the lake, and a jetty if you're keen to cast a line. Decor is "quaint country," so don't be surprised to find duck ornaments in the bathrooms, or little kittens sculpted into the headboard. Located over the barn, the self-catering set-up includes a full kitchenette and a lounge-cum-dining area, and the bedroom, while quite compact, is very neat and has views over the farmlands; there is also a sofa bed suitable for a younger child.

saunter idly by. Lough Erne—divided into Lower and Upper sections—stretches across almost the entire county, meaning everywhere you go, you're close to water, and usually bombarded by impressive views.

GETTING THERE
The **A4** links Enniskillen with Belfast and Armagh. Regular **buses** connect Enniskillen with Belfast (2½ hr.), Derry (2 hr.), Dublin (3 hr.), and other major hubs in the Republic as well as the north.

WHY YOU'RE HERE: TOP SIGHTS & ATTRACTIONS
While the lakes are always an obvious focal point, the county is also endowed with two of Northern Ireland's most splendid stately homes.

The spectacularly sumptuous country manor **Castle Coole** ✪✪✪ (Enniskillen; ☎ 028/6632-2690; www.ntni.org.uk; Grounds & House tour: £5; grounds: daily Oct–Mar 10am–4pm; Apr–Sept 10am–8pm; house tours: Apr–May and Sept Sat–Sun 1–6pm; Jun Fri–Wed 1–6pm; July–Aug daily noon–6pm; Easter week daily 1–6pm) is the first and it could very easily be mistaken for a palace. Set on a woodland estate just outside the town of Enniskillen, it's an exceptional example of Neo-classical Georgian architecture, its monumental facade of such delicate coloring—creamy grey stone walls and pillars backed by a hush of pink—that it seems not to be a place for everyday use, but rather to be a thing simply to behold. Particularly intriguing is how so much of the design was concerned with keeping the estate's 90-or-so servants out of sight while they went about the business of keeping its wealthy residents and their guests comfortable. Don't miss the underground tunnel, which was the only entrance to the castle that servants were allowed to use.

Stuck pretty much in the middle of nowhere, **Florence Court** ✪✪✪ (☎ 028/6634-8249; www.ntni.org.uk; House tour: £5, Grounds: £3.50 per car; grounds daily Oct–Mar 10am–4pm; Apr–Sept 10am–8pm; house tours: Apr–May and Sept Sat–Sun 1–6pm; Jun Wed–Mon 1–6pm; July–Aug daily noon–6pm; Easter week daily 1–6pm) is probably the most important 18th-century house in Ulster—a block of grand Georgian endeavor against the backdrop of Cuilcagh Mountains. It's a bit of good luck that the house is here at all, actually, having been severely wracked by fire in 1955. Fortunately, it's been professionally reconstructed, largely thanks to Sir Albert Richardson, an academic so obsessed with the 18th century that he was known to dress up in period costume.

Built by Sir John Cole, the house is large and rambling, its spaces finished with Rococo plasterwork and filled with furniture and objects that—in the right hands—piece together some engaging stories: On the guided tour, often led by a real history buff, you'll learn as much about the house and its inhabitants as you will about how their intrigues relate to the broader history of Fermanagh. **To get here:** Follow the A4 (Sligo Rd.) from Enniskillen; turn left onto the A32 (Swanlinbar Rd.); follow the signs.

Nearby, you can go far deeper than basement level at the **Marble Arch Caves** ✪✪✪ kids (Marlbank Scenic Loop, Florencecourt; ☎ 028/6634-8855; www.marblearchcaves.net; £8; tours mid-Mar to Sept daily 10am–4:30pm; last tour July–Aug 5pm), where a combined walk and short boat trip takes you beneath Fermanagh's surface to discover subterranean rivers, waterfalls, and lakes, and cavernous chambers with walls that look like giant blobs of ice cream. Down here, you'll see all the usual cave features—stalactites, stalagmites, rimstone pools, curtain walls, and unusual mineral deposits. As with all cave tours, it gets cool, so bring a warm top, and have shoes that can deal with occasionally wet rock. The tour, which includes around 1.5km (1 mile) of walking, lasts 75 minutes.

LOWER LOUGH ERNE & ITS ISLANDS

To get a proper feel for the lake district's fabled beauty, you really need to drive right around the Lower lake, and occasionally stop to check out the vistas across the water—particularly impressive at sunrise and sunset—for which you must get close to the shore (there are plenty of roads leading right up close to the edge of the lake, so don't be shy). For a greater sense of adventure, you can also catch a ferry to several Erne islands, some of which feature early Christian ruins. St. Molaise founded a monastery on **Devenish Island** in the 6th century, and the ruins include a 12th-century round tower (well worth seeing if you're into ancient architecture), as well as a 15th-century Augustinian priory, and—in the grave-yard—a carved high cross sure to inspire open-jawed admiration. Devenish is close to Enniskillen; the Kestrel **waterbus** departs from the Round "O" Jetty, a short walk from the town center, while **Devenish Ferries** departs from Trory Point (follow signs to the Trory boat launch off the A32; ☎ 0770/205-2873; operates Easter–Sept only).

Farther north, even more sublime religious artifacts await on **White Island** ✯✯; in the ruins of a 12th-century church are eight Celtic figures, carved in the 6th century. Their otherworldly, mask-like expressions are all the more intriguing for the simple fact that their meaning has yet to be revealed. **Ferries** (☎ 028/6862-1156 or 028/6862-1892; July–Sept daily hourly 11am–6pm; Apr–Jun Sat–Sun) for the island depart from the marina at **Castle Archdale Country Park** (Lisnarick; ☎ 028/6862-1588; free admission; daily 9am–dusk). To get there, head north along the A32, and then take the B82 toward Lisnarick, and look out for the park turnoff. At the marina, you can also hire boats for private use (half-day £55, full-day £80).

13 The Essentials of Planning

by Keith Bain

IRELAND'S SIZE, AND ITS LOCATION ALONGSIDE THE MUCH LARGER ISLAND of Great Britain, often gives visitors a distorted idea of just how much traveling they can cram into their vacation. Don't be deceived. Ireland may be small enough to crisscross several times in 1 day, but if you want to experience its many diverse and often enchanting sights, and—more importantly—if you want to get to know and live the culture, and mingle with the local people, you'll need heaps more time than you imagine. As you'll gather from what you've read throughout this book, some of the best moments in Ireland are ones spent kicking back in pubs, at sporting events, in the living rooms and breakfast rooms of family-run B&Bs. Time, therefore, is not necessarily on your side. Unless, of course, you have plenty of it. If not, you'll want to ensure that you've planned efficiently so that those obvious travel worries are behind you as you set off on what should be an fun adventure, not a chore.

As well, be aware that both Ireland and Northern Ireland can be pricey destinations. Dublin is considered the second most expensive city in Europe, and the power of the euro (the currency used in the Republic of Ireland) and the pound (used in Northern Ireland) outstrip all other currencies.

Don't be disheartened. In researching and writing this book, we've looked for places to stay and eat that can help make Ireland more financially palatable. And in this chapter, I'll be discussing all sorts of ways in which you can plan and budget—both your time and your expenditure—more effectively.

Ireland, being a major destination for travelers from around the world, has gone to great efforts to extensively market itself. If you're looking to supplement the information you'll find in this book, the online resource for both the Republic and for Northern Ireland is **www.discoverireland.com**. It's a very user-friendly site packed with ideas for holidays, an accommodation search engine, information on events and festivals, nitty-gritty pointers, and links to many other sites that serve the Irish tourism machine.

WHEN TO VISIT

Irish **winters** are cold enough that many attractions and guesthouses shut shop between late-October and early-March. Some restaurants might also close or, along with pubs, have shorter operating hours. It gets chilly, yes, and many smaller operators find the cost of heating guest rooms too burdensome when there's only a trickle of visitors anyway.

The converse is true in **summer,** and from June through early-September (peaking in July and Aug) you'll be competing with such a plethora of tourists that your experience may be dampened by more than just Ireland's legendary rain. If you're planning a visit during the busiest tourist season then try to avoid the more hyped destinations (we've provided plenty of clues for getting off the beaten track throughout this book).

If you can time your visit for **spring** or **fall,** you'll be rewarded with lower prices, less-congested streets and less crowded attractions (always a big plus in my mind); you'll also be pleased by the relative absence of tour buses.

Then again, catching a good party might be reason enough to travel, and I wouldn't pass up the chance to be in Ireland for **St. Paddy's Day** (Mar 17).

Visit-Worthy Festivals & Events

Here are just a few of the many events, festivals, and annual happenings that you might like plan your visit around.

March

St Patrick's Day. Prepare to go wild on March 17th: Well and truly the big day for raucous, upbeat celebrations across Ireland. While the festival commemorates the man considered the spiritual father of All Ireland, and who's (misleadingly) billed with having brought Christianity to a once-pagan people, these days, St. Paddy's Day is synonymous with fireworks, all-day drinking, and some of the most imaginative parades you'll encounter (especially in Dublin and Belfast). Can't decide where to catch your float? Visit www.stpatricksday.ie.

Dublin Film Festival. Enjoy 10 days of Irish and international films, including noteworthy premieres, not to mention events attended by celebrities and members of the film fraternity. Which in Ireland, remember, includes the likes of Liam Neeson, Daniel Day-Lewis, Cillian Murphy, and Neil Jordan. Visit www.jdiff.com.

March/April

The World Irish Dancing Championships. For 8 days you can catch the competitive side of what Michael Flatley turned into an international sensation. Over 4,000 leggy contenders pound the floorboards in a different host town every year, either in late March or early April. Check it out at www.worldirishdancing.com.

May

The Cathedral Quarter Arts Festival. For nearly 2 weeks in Belfast's self-proclaimed cultural precinct, you can catch music acts ranging from Sinead O'Connor to the Orb, a poetry slam featuring some of the city's bravest amateur wordsmiths; you can also catch street acts, literary events, and world-class theater. Relatively low-key and wonderfully un-hyped, the festival is a great opportunity to hang out with the locals. For details, see www.cqaf.com.

The Festival of Fools. This lively weekend event draws all kinds of weird, wonderful, and downright silly street theater acts from Ireland and around the world to the sidewalks and pedestrian enclaves of Belfast. From tightrope walkers to postmodern juggling acts and deranged "tour guides," you'll find some kind of wonderful-crazy performance drawing impromptu audiences over the 4 days of the May Bank Holiday Weekend at the start of the month. For information, see www.foolsfestival.com.

Cork International Choral Festival. Yup, people stand in a group and sing. Beautifully. But don't expect your garden-variety harmonizing and hymn-recitation—there's plenty of innovation and rhythmic prowess on display. See www.corkchoral.ie.

Dublin International Gay Theatre Festival. Oscar Wilde, who studied in Dublin, would certainly have approved of this 2 weeks of exclusively gay-themed theater; www.gaytheatre.ie.

Smithwick's Cat Laughs Comedy Festival. Kilkenny is a vibrant little city year-round, but when the stand-ups come to town for a long weekend in the end of May, things go into overdrive, spawning what has been rated one of the top comedy festivals in the world. Check out the program at www.thecatlaughs.com.

Fleadh Nua. Ennis in County Clare hosts one of the country's top traditional music and dance festivals, held towards the end of the month. Enthusiasts scramble from around the county to watch, listen, and learn, and then join the festivities that follow; see the program at www.fleadhnua.com.

June

Music in the Parks. Dublin celebrates summer with concerts in its green spaces all the way through the end of September.

Taste of Dublin. Foodies should come hungry for this kitchen celebration, and discover how New Irish Cuisine is no longer just an aspiration but a full-blown fact. There are cooking demos and tutored wine tastings. You can also catch the **Taste of Cork** festival, a bit later in the month; www.tastefestivals.ie

Dublin LGBTQ Pride Festival. Pink pom-poms are not a requirement, but having had its 25th anniversary in 2008, this 10-day celebration of gay rights serves up more than enough reasons to get your party kit on. Live concerts and DJ-events, rallies and huge costume balls, the ever-popular "Dyke Night," sports days, workshops, poetry readings, and, of course, a big parade, all gets revelers—gay, straight or whatever—out onto the streets, and, er, into the sweatiest clubs. Find out more at www.dublinpride.org.

Bloomsday Festival. On June 16th, fans of James Joyce all over the world celebrate his tome, *Ulysses*. Why? Because events in the novel took place entirely on this day in 1904. And because all the action is set in Dublin, there's an especially huge program of events to look forward to.

Cork Midsummer Festival: Audacious little Cork bills its premiere festival as "Twenty-one days & nights of sensory overload" and you can bet your socks that's exactly what you'll get as theater, music, art, poetry, and entertainments galore turn the city into a cultural wonderland. The festival runs from mid-June through early-July, and kicks off with the totally free Lord Mayor's Festival in the Park, incorporating music, circus acts, street theater, and boat rides to make this the hippest picnic party of the year. During the 2008 festival, thousands of Corkonians went bare for a Spencer Tunick nude photo session. Check out this year's line-up at www.corkfestival.com.

Listowel Writers' Week. In the north of County Kerry, the town of Listowel bursts into action with one of the most anticipated literary festivals in the country. Listen to poets and leading authors, and then meet them face to face, and perhaps share the dance floor with like-minded literature buffs later in the night. www.writersweek.ie.

Kildare Derby Festival. Newbridge, in County Kildare, comes alive with concerts, pageants, exhibitions, a parade, and even a dog show in the build-up to the Irish Derby held at Curragh Racecourse. Check out www.kildare.ie/DerbyFestival.

Killarney Summerfest. Designed for the young and young at heart, Killarney's big, drawn-out June-July summer bonanza kicks off with two big name concerts—in 2008, Westlife (with another superstar, Shayne Ward, as "guest artist") kicked off the festival, and K.T. Tunstall performed on the second night. From then on, anything goes—classical music, parades, horseracing, outdoor theater, and plenty of activities especially for children. Visit www.killarneysummerfest.com for more information.

July

Willie Clancy Summer School. One of Ireland's best music festivals draws scores of traditional musicians and adoring fans (not to mention party die-hards) to the tiny resort town of Miltown Malbay in west County Clare for the first week in July. Besides innumerable music sessions, workshops and lectures keep the intellectual flames alive. Visit www.willieclancy-summerschool.com.

Dublin Circus Festival. Part of the non-stop activity in the Temple Bar cultural precinct, this is a 4-day line-up of local and international circus performances, street theater, and comic mayhem. Study the program at www.templebar.ie.

Kinsale Arts Week. The week that Kinsale spends the whole year preparing for, when the little town puts on a dizzying display of music, theater, art, and spectacular events; some of the entertainment happens on water, and concerts are held at the monumental Charles Fort. Local artists hold workshops, and those in attendance might include international artists, filmmakers, and writers. Book tickets through www.kinsaleartsweek.com.

Galway Film Fleadh. For 6 days, Galway goes film crazy when filmmakers, actors, and writers gather to attend the Irish equivalent of Cannes. Besides a film fare and world cinema screenings, master classes, seminars, public interviews, and debates give the events a steamy intellectual air. And there's a pitching opportunity for Ireland's budding filmmakers. Check out the schedule at www.galway filmfleadh.com.

Galway Arts Festival. For 2 weeks from mid-July, buzzy Galway gets even more hyped-up for this celebration of the arts. Ireland's premiere arts festival has been running for over 30 years now, and attracts 100,000 people each year. Little wonder it's so successful, though—in 2008, the festival featured over 400 artists and performers from around the world, including the Philip Glass Ensemble, Joni Mitchell, Omara Portuondo, Preservation Hall Jazz Band, KT Tunstall, the Dandy Warhols, Ash, and Blondie. Look up this year's schedule at www.galwayartsfestival.ie.

Yeats Festival. County Sligo celebrates the life and work of William Butler Yeats for 2 weeks in late July. Book launches, readings, lectures, and traditional music ensure this is one of the more restrained festivals in Ireland, but the presence of literary heavyweights (like Nobel laureate, Seamus Heaney, in 2008) makes this a unique opportunity for bibliophiles and Yeats fans alike. Find out more about what's on at www.yeats-sligo.com.

Croagh Patrick Pilgrimage. Pilgrims ascend the slopes of Croagh Patrick in County Mayo on the last Sunday of the month as a tribute to St. Patrick.

SprÓg. For children age 5 to 8, this is a 5-day fringe pre-festival to Waterford's annual Spraoi (see below) and starts towards the end of the month. A number of magical performances—theater, music, puppetry, dance—as well as stimulating workshops give visiting children an opportunity to interact with local kids. Visit www.spraoi.com.

August

Feile an Phobail West Belfast Festival. In the working-class suburbs once considered the epicenter of Northern Ireland's political Troubles, this has become one of the biggest community festivals in Europe, with a stunning mix of all kinds of arts, cultural events, and big-name music concerts. Throw in some political discussions, lectures, and seminars and you have a party with a meaningful agenda: to help bring the people of Belfast closer together. Check the weeklong program at www.feilebelfast.com.

Spraoi. Waterford's annual arts festival (www.spraoi.com) is hosted by the Garter Lane Arts Centre and held over the August

Bank Holiday Weekend at the beginning of the month. *The Examiner* has called it "The biggest street party in Ireland" and has an eclectic flavor, usually centered on large-scale street theater productions (some newly commissioned and some international), but also featuring an excellent world music line-up.

Puck Fair. Killorglin's 3-day pagan festival is one of the country's longest-running fairs, held annually on 10th to 12th of August. Each year, there's a horse fair, free family entertainment on the streets, a parade, and a coronation ceremony for King Puck—a mountain goat. One legend attributes the event to an incident during the time of Oliver Cromwell's Roundheads invasion of Ireland—apparently a startled goat alerted the people of Killorglin to the presence of Cromwell's men and so they were ready to protect themselves against the intruders. The festival commemorates the heroic goat, but also bustles with lively entertainment and plenty of elbow-bending. It's a busy time for such a small town, drawing over 100,000 visitors to witness and take part in the revelries. For more information, see www.puckfair.ie.

Kilkenny Arts Festival. Festive Kilkenny shakes its cultural feathers for 10 days each August (for the 36th time in 2009), providing a broad range of art and entertainment events. Catch street theater, multiple-genre music performances, films, parades, and—of course—fireworks. Visit www.kilkennyarts.ie.

Rose of Tralee International Festival. Let's face it—this is a 5-day beauty pageant and an opportunity for everyone and anyone to have a big, rollicking party. It's known the world over and the contestants, too, are from all around the world, provided the young lasses in question come from Irish stock. Although there's a costume ball, parade, fashion show, and other glamorous goings-on, in a turn of irony, the beauty contest coincides with a local horse-racing event—the Tralee Races. If you want to attend the 50th festival in 2009, or have a desire to enter, visit www.roseoftralee.ie. There's even a place for men who fancy themselves serving as "escorts," meaning you get to dress up smart and hang out with the finalists—gentlemen only need apply.

Festival of World Cultures. Celebrating the diversity of human culture, this festival aims to help bridge differences between the various communities that make up Ireland's social fabric. Over a single weekend, a variety of international arts are showcased in a dynamic program of (mostly free) events held in Dún Laoghaire, near Dublin; www.festivalofworldcultures.com.

Fleadh Cheoil na hÉireann. More easily pronounceable as the Festival of Music in Ireland, this annual traditional music competition moves around the country and celebrates its finals in a different town each year. While competitive routines are its raison d'être, the event also showcases concerts, *céilithe*, parades, pageants, and street sessions involving 10,000 musicians who perform with mighty aplomb. In 2008, the 8-day festival happened in Tullamore, County Offaly; to find out about future *Fleadh* venues, visit www.fleadh2009.com.

September

Cape Clear International Storytelling Festival. For one weekend in September, the Gaeltacht island of Cape Clear in County Cork fills up for a celebration of the spoken word, Irish language, and—of course—traditional music. It's very popular, so you may want to set off early, since places on ferries are obviously limited, and plan way ahead if you want to stay on the island overnight. The website (www.capeclearstorytelling.com) provides full information.

Dublin Fringe Festival. For 16 days in September, Dublin dishes up a wild, wide array of theater, music, dance, and comedy events with an emphasis on innovative, experimental, offbeat, avant garde, and highly visual, spectacular entertainment to provide wows as well as stimulate the imagination; www.fringefest.com.

Town of Books Festival. In the tiny village of Graiguenamanagh in County Kilkenny, lovers of books and literature gather for one weekend to celebrate at the country's leading book fair, greatly enhanced with music, dancing, and food; www.booktownireland.com.

Galway International Oyster Festival. For 4 days, oysters take center stage at this spunky little festival, complemented by plenty of Guinness and good traditional music sessions. The World Oyster Opening Competition is held to find the shucking champion, and—surprise, surprise—the Oyster Pearl Competition crowns a "talented and personable young lady"; www.galwayoysterfest.com.

Lisdoonvarna Matchmaking Festival. Traditionally, this event (in west County Clare) aims to hook bachelors up with eligible potential brides, and there's even an official matchmaker who draws couples together. These days the six week-long festival is an expectedly wild opportunity for some liquid-fueled carousing and gallivanting—members of the opposite sex optional; www.matchmakerireland.com

Gaelic Games. The much-anticipated finals of Ireland's traditional sports—hurling and Gaelic football—are held at Dublin's Croke Park stadium this month. Attending at least one game is a sure-fire way to not only fall in love with an adrenaline-heaving sport, but gain first-hand insight into the mighty affection Irish people have for their favorite teams; www.gaa.ie.

Dublin Theatre Festival. Running from late-September and into mid-October, this is the capital's foremost celebration of "serious" theater, with a surfeit of 20 plays on its main program—half are Irish and half are international acts, and they're all top quality, selected to get people talking. There's also a program for children, and the main program dovetails out of the Fringe Festival (see above); www.dublintheatrefestival.com.

October

Cork International Film Festival. Established more than 50 years ago, this festival's line-up includes an impressive selection of Irish and international films, commencing early in the month; www.corkfilmfest.org.

Wexford Opera Festival. Having transformed its existing theater space into a state-of-the art facility for the festival in 2008, Wexford is rolling out the red carpet with more enthusiasm than ever before. Exciting, rare operatic performances give this 2-week festival the edge over similar events elsewhere; www.wexfordopera.com.

Imagine Waterford Arts Festival. All art forms are celebrated in this festival held in late-October and early-November for 11 days; the music line-up runs from traditional Irish to jazz and choral, but there are theater, comedy, dance, and literary events, too; www.waterfordartsfestival.com.

Banks of the Foyle Halloween Carnival. Said to be the best Hallowe'en event in Ireland, if not in Europe, Derry City's celebration of ghouls and goblins starts on October 24th and defies the autumnal gloom with carnivals, fireworks, music, pyrotechnics, traditional games and sports, gala balls, scary storytelling, and loads of food, fun, and an evening of almost mandatory fancy dress.

The Belfast Festival at Queens. Belfast's biggest arts and culture celebration takes over the city for the last 2 weeks of the month (sometimes spilling over into Nov). Masses of comedy, serious drama, traditional and folk music, dance, jazz, and all kinds of events are designed to stimulate the imagination and the intellect (it is hosted primarily by the University, after all). In the past, it's drawn some of the top names, including Dizzy Gillespie,

Laurence Olivier, Ravi Shankar, and Jimi Hendrix, and with Belfast on such a roll, the program seems set to get better and better. Check out www.belfastfestival.com.

Guinness Jazz Festival. One of the largest jazz festivals in Europe hits Cork for 4 days in late-October. For over 30 years, it's been attracting some of the world's top acts, representing a range of styles and influences. Visit www.corkjazzfestival.com.

THE CLIMATE AT A GLANCE

The Irish speak of their "changeable" weather, and it's common to experience four seasons in 1 day. Prepare for mercurial days that might start out snowy and climax in sweat-inducing sunshine (well, maybe just pleasant sunshine). The charts below might give you some idea of how general climate conditions vary through the year, but please don't use them to plan your days. If you're after a really in depth look at local weather, visit **www.accuweather.com,** which provides maps, charts, and forecasts. You can check expected minimum and maximum temperatures, precipitation, wind patterns, and even the UV index. For surfers, there's a section on tides.

Ireland's Average Temperature & Precipitation Stats

Dublin	Jan	Feb	Mar	Apr	May	June	July	Aug	Sept	Oct	Nov	Dec
Ave Temp. (°C)												
High	8	8	10	11	14	17	19	19	17	14	10	8
Low	3	3	3	4	7	10	11	11	10	8	4	3
Ave Temp. (°F)												
High	46	46	49	53	58	63	66	66	62	57	50	47
Low	37	37	38	40	44	49	53	52	49	46	40	38
Rainfall (mm)	69	50	53	51	55	56	50	71	66	70	64	76
Rainfall (inches)	2.7	2	2.1	2	2.2	2.2	2	2.8	2.6	2.8	2.5	3

Belfast	Jan	Feb	Mar	Apr	May	June	July	Aug	Sept	Oct	Nov	Dec
Ave Temp. (°C)												
High	7	7	9	12	14	17	19	18	16	13	9	7
Low	1	1	2	4	6	9	11	11	9	7	3	2
Ave Temp. (°F)												
High	44	44	48	53	58	63	65	65	61	55	48	45
Low	34	34	36	38	43	48	52	51	48	44	38	36
Rainfall (mm)	86	58	67	53	60	63	64	80	85	88	78	78
Rainfall (inches)	3.4	2.3	2.6	2.1	2.4	2.5	2.5	3.1	3.3	3.5	3.1	3.1

Cork City	Jan	Feb	Mar	Apr	May	June	July	Aug	Sept	Oct	Nov	Dec
Ave Temp. (°C)												
High	8	8	9	11	14	17	19	18	16	13	10	8
Low	3	3	3	4	6	9	11	11	9	8	5	4

Ave Temp. (°F)

High	46	46	49	53	57	62	65	65	61	56	50	47
Low	37	37	38	40	44	49	52	52	49	46	40	38
Rainfall (mm)	148	115	97	70	84	68	65	90	97	126	109	136
Rainfall (inches)	5.8	4.5	3.8	2.8	3.3	2.7	2.6	3.5	3.8	5	4.3	5.4

Shannon	Jan	Feb	Mar	Apr	May	June	July	Aug	Sept	Oct	Nov	Dec
Ave Temp. (°C)												
High	8	9	11	13	15	18	19	19	17	14	10	9
Low	3	3	4	5	7	10	12	12	10	8	5	4
Ave Temp. (°F)												
High	47	47	51	55	60	64	67	67	63	58	51	48
Low	37	37	39	41	45	50	54	53	50	46	40	39
Rainfall (mm)	98	71	71	56	60	63	57	82	82	93	95	99
Rainfall (inches)	3.9	2.8	2.8	2.2	2.4	2.5	2.2	3.2	3.2	3.7	3.7	3.9

ENTRY REQUIREMENTS

If you're traveling to Ireland—or anywhere in the world for that matter—you must have a valid passport that expires at least 6 months later than the scheduled end of your visit. Passport applications take a while and require some advance planning. As long as your planned trip to Ireland is 90 days or less, and you're a resident of the U.S., Canada, Australia, New Zealand, or the U.K., you shouldn't require a visa. If you are going to be in Ireland for more than 90 days, or are planning to take up studies or a job while you're in the country, you'll need to plan a little more thoroughly. If you are not an E.U. citizen, stays of over 90 days will require that you register at a local police station, and if you want to work or study, you'll need to get special visas that entitle you to these privileges.

For the latest information on passport and visa requirements for the Republic, contact the **Department of Foreign Affairs** (80 St. Stephen's Green, Dublin 2; ☎ 01/478-0822; www.foreignaffairs.gov.ie).

For Residents of the U.S.   You can download passport applications from the U.S. State Department website at **www.state.gov**; you can then apply either in person or by mail, following the detailed information given on the website. For further queries, call the **National Passport Information Center** (☎ 1-877/487-2778).

For Residents of Australia   You can pick up an application from your local post office or any branch of Passports Australia, but you must schedule an interview at the passport office to present your application materials. Call the **Australian Passport Information Service** (☎ 131-232), or visit the government website at **www.passports.gov.au**.

The Republic of Ireland & Northern Ireland

Remember that we're dealing with two separate countries in this book. The **Republic of Ireland** is a completely independent, autonomous state, often referred to as the "South," particularly by some residents of **Northern Ireland** who are, by contrast, actually citizens of the **United Kingdom of Great Britain and Northern Ireland.** As there is no sign of a border between the two countries, the only real indication that you might get that you've "crossed over" is that speed limit indicators will be in kilometers on the Republic side of the border and in miles in Northern Ireland. This is, of course, one of the important differences to keep in mind when traveling between the two countries as you don't want to find yourself inadvertently breaking the speed limit.

Another major difference is currency, and this issue is discussed in detail under "Money Matters," later in this chapter.

For Residents of Canada   Passport applications are available at travel agencies throughout Canada or from the central **Passport Office** (Department of Foreign Affairs and International Trade, Ottawa, ON K1A 0G3; ☎ 800/567-6868; www.ppt. gc.ca), or any Passport Canada office, which you can locate by using the website. Canada Post offices and Service Canada centers also accept certain types of passport applications, but not all.

For Residents of New Zealand   You can pick up a passport application at any **New Zealand Passport Office** (☎ 0800/225050 in New Zealand or 04/474-8100) or download it from **www.passports.govt.nz**; this website also explains how to complete the application.

For Residents of the U.K.   For a UK passport, you'll need to apply to the **Home Office's Identity & Passport Service;** visit **www.ips.gov.uk** for full details as well as online application forms. There's also a 24/7 **Passport Adviceline** (☎ 0870/521-0410).

CUSTOMS REGULATIONS

If you're an E.U. citizen traveling from an E.U. member state you generally don't need to worry about what goods you're carrying, as long as they're legal. There are limits on certain restricted substances (tobacco products and alcohol), which you would presumably be carrying for own-use only, but the quantities are quite high and way above what anyone going on holiday would be likely to carry.

If, however, you're flying into Ireland from a non-E.U. country, here are the limits on duty-free goods (in other words, if you're carrying more than this, you'll need to declare the fact and pay taxes and duties): 200 cigarettes (or 100 cigarillos or 50 cigars or 250g of tobacco), 1 liter of spirits (or 2 liters of fortified wine or liqueur), 2l of wine, 60ml of perfume, and 250ml of eau de toilette. Adults can also carry goods (including beer) to the value of €175, while children under 15 can carry a value of €90. Children may not bring alcohol or tobacco products in, of course.

If you're arriving in Northern Ireland (or any port of entry in the UK), on a transatlantic flight, the regulations are pretty much identical.

Note that meat, milk, and other animal products are banned along with other obviously undesirable items such as unlicensed drugs and pornography.

WHAT CAN I TAKE HOME?

There are limits on both the quantities and values of goods you can return home with, as well as on the types of things that you're allowed to enter countries with. Returning **American citizens** typically enjoy an $800 duty-free allowance, which means that this is the value of the goods and gifts that you can carry before you need to pay an import duty on what you've purchased. **Canadian citizens** have a C$750 allowance (but only if you've been away for 7 days or more). **Australians** get an allowance of A$900 (A$450 for children under 18); **New Zealanders** NZ$700. In each case, there are additional restrictions on the amount of alcohol and tobacco you can carry with you before being liable for duty.

Generally, customs officials and agricultural authorities don't like you bringing products into their country if they are likely to be a breeding ground for alien pests and diseases. Be aware that organic products, including substances like soil on your hiking boots, wood that hasn't been processed, and any kind of meat, fresh fruit, or vegetable product, will raise suspicion (and possible confiscation) when you pass through customs. Baked goods, chocolate, candy, jams and preserves, teas and coffees—these should all be fine. Cured cheese shouldn't be a problem; if the food you're carrying is in a vacuum-sealed jar it should be okay, unless it contains any meat. In fact, if the foodstuff you're carrying is made from a land or air creature, it's going to be a problem—if it's fresh it'll be prohibited and if it's canned, cured, or dried, it may be restricted depending on current disease scares, so you must declare it. Fish, however, is usually permitted entry to the U.S., so bring on that smoked salmon. Still, you must declare all food items, always, everywhere (in most countries there is a very hefty fine for not declaring food products). Dairy products, including milk, butter, and yogurt are usually allowed, but this all depends on current disease outbreaks and scares. So declare them. One anomaly: hard cured cheeses (like parmesan and cheddar) are fine, but soft cheeses (like brie) or cheeses kept in water (feta, ricotta) are a no-no.

Also restricted at the borders of most territories are counterfeit goods, obscene (pornographic) materials, and drugs of any kind (medications must be declared). Be aware of specialized goods that you have purchased, including heritage items—when entering Australia you need to declare artworks, stamps, and coins, for example.

FINDING A GOOD AIRFARE TO IRELAND

Generally, travelers who need to purchase tickets at the last minute, want the option of changing their itinerary at a moment's notice, or those who choose to fly one-way will be paying premium rates. And sometimes passengers who are simply unlucky also pay more than the fellow in the next seat: Like stock exchange prices, there's little logic to airfares, yet this is what will probably determine your choice of airline.

Playing the Field

Don't only look at the usual suspects when picking a carrier for international travel. Such sites as **www.farecompare.com** will let you know which carriers have the best deals when you're flying and sometimes the results can be surprising. For example, some of the best airfares from Australia to Europe may be offered by Middle Eastern airlines like Emirates (www.emirates.com); compare their rates online.

As well, consider a flight with a stop-over, as this could be a cost saver. **British Airways** (☎ 1-800/AIRWAYS toll-free U.S. and Canada; www.ba.com), **Lufthansa** (☎ 1-800/645-3880 toll-free U.S.; www.lufthansa.com), and **Air France** (☎ 1-800/237-2747 toll-free U.S.; www.airfrance.com) are just a few of the national European carriers that fly between various North American hubs and will get you to Dublin, but only via their own home base airport.

At this writing, trends in international oil prices and an escalating economic crisis are creating fairly volatile, highly speculative airfares, so it's anyone's guess what might lie in store for the immediate future of ticket prices. Whatever the scenario, the tips and advice below will guide you towards getting the best deals on air travel.

High season on most airlines' routes to Dublin is usually from June to the end of August. This is the most expensive and most crowded time to travel. **Low season,** October through February, is when tickets are cheapest. **"Shoulder season,"** when prices are in the middle, is from April to May, and in September.

The next step, once you've settled on a time when you want to travel, is to start shopping around for the most agreeable fares. I always start with such excellent and thorough sites as **www.mobissimo.com**, **www.momondo.com** or **www.kayak.com**, which give an in-depth range of options from both the airline sites directly and such third-party sellers as Orbitz.com and Travelocity.com. Mobissimo actually uses another of my favorite sites, **www.vayama.com**, which is far and away the most aesthetically-pleasing airfare search engine with interactive maps that show you the route you'd be taking as well as a detailed breakdown of the trip and costs involved. UK-based travelers may wish to try **www.justtheflight.co.uk** and **www.wegolo.com**.

Whichever sites you use, a bit of research will quickly give you a fairly good idea of what prices are out there. You may also consider signing up for the Aer Lingus newsletter and the other airlines that service Ireland, as these are often a good way to get wind of special fares (though, of course, this method only works if you have a good amount of time to shop around).

All of this bargain-hunting should be done about four months in advance of your trip as from two to four months out is when most airfare sales start to hit. Book too far in advance, and you could end up paying more than you have to; the same can be said for booking at the very last minute.

From North America   A direct round-trip ticket from New York to Dublin in coach class will cost anywhere between $700 and $1,200; work the system properly, however, and you could get a seat for as little as $550 (most likely in the low season).

Flying time to Dublin from New York, Newark, and Boston is 7¼ hours; from Chicago, 9¼ hours; and from Los Angeles, 11¾ hours. Flying time to Belfast is roughly the same, but there are currently fewer flights to the Northern Irish capital. If you want to head directly to Ireland's west coast, look for flights to Shannon.

From England, Scotland & Wales   Low-cost, no-frills airlines bouncing between Great Britain and other parts of Europe—including Northern Ireland and the Republic of Ireland—have completely transformed travel in the last few years. Top deals are available from increasingly-prominent Irish airlines like **Aer Arann** (www.aerarann.com) and **flyBE** (www.flybe.com), and also from those three budget stalwarts, **RyanAir** (www.ryanair.com), **EasyJet** (www.easyjet.com), and **BMIBaby** (www.bmibaby.com). One big bonus is that these airlines fly to a wider range of Irish destinations (including the "smaller" cities) than you might find with the major airlines, and at rates so low they'll make your head spin. Just be aware of all the rules pertaining to these flights (usually only available online); for example, you can't change your flight dates, and may have to pay a small surcharge for each piece of check-in luggage (on EasyJet, for example, you must pay upfront if you intend on checking any luggage). Also, "no-frills" means no free beverages or food on board, and often quite disagreeable service by check-in staff. The other thing to remember is that prices on these airlines fluctuate considerably, and—like all airlines—vary dramatically according to time of day and day of the week that you fly; shop around between different dates and times for the best bargain and do so as far in advance as possible. Also sign up for electronic newsletters that alert you to specials and sales.

Bear in mind that, occasionally, the big names run cheaper-than-expected fares. Both **British Airways** (☎ 0870/850-9850; www.ba.com) and **Aer Lingus** (☎ 0870/876-5000; www.aerlingus.com) have frequent flights from London's Heathrow to Dublin, and Aer Lingus now also flies to Belfast, occasionally offering the cheapest possible rates (yes, it's called a "price war"). Flying in to Belfast is

One-Way Flights

With the advent of low-cost airlines, and the subsequent burgeoning of internet specials from the so-called legacy carriers (including Aer Lingus in many instances), it's often as cost effective to book flights into one gateway and out of another as it is to book a round-trip. Obviously, this is also a time saving measure as you won't have to double back to return to the airport you flew into. Check prices on both round-trips and one-way fares before booking.

becoming increasingly popular: not only can you generally find cheaper airfares because it's a less-frequented hub, but transport to and from the airport is easier and cheaper. And besides, Dublin is 2 to 3 hours away by car, not too much longer than the time you'll save using a quieter airport.

Flying time from London to Dublin is about an hour, to Belfast is just a little over that.

From Australia & New Zealand   As you well know, there aren't any non-stop flights from this part of the world to the Emerald Isle, but that doesn't mean you can't get there affordably. You'll most likely need to shop around for the best deals to London, and then catch a flight with Aer Lingus or BA, or one of the no-frills airlines (discussed above) to your preferred destination in Ireland. Be aware that London may not necessarily be the cheapest destination, which might mean flying via Paris or Amsterdam—it usually all depends on which national carrier in Europe is offering the best deal. Use the resources discussed earlier in this chapter to get a handle on where the best fare lies, and then see what prices are available through **Flight Centre** (In Australia: ☎ 133-133; www.flightcentre.com.au; in New Zealand: ☎ 0800/243544; www.flightcentre.co.nz), an Australian agency which is usually able to source the best fares to Europe and the UK.

PACKAGES VS. INDEPENDENT BOOKING

Sometimes it's simply cheaper and more convenient to throw in the towel of complete independence and opt for a packaged holiday or tour. Without having to do quite so much planning or preparation—and often for much less than it would cost you to do all the legwork yourself—a package deal can ensure that all the financial details around your transport and accommodation needs are taken care of by experts who can get good deals. Because package organizers negotiate for large numbers at a time, they are often able to get discounted rates that individuals simply can't manage, and those savings should filter through to you. This will take the legwork out of shopping around for the best airfare, hunting down affordable places to stay, and booking the cheapest rental car.

This does not necessarily mean that you'll be in the hub of luxury or that you'll stray too far from the well-trodden tourist path. Though the cheapest of these packages traditionally use mainstream, somewhat dull hotels, booking a travel package can result in big savings, in some cases a $100-a-day or less vacation for airfare and hotel (not including taxes or security fees). And you'll get a clean, convenient place to stay (always with private bathroom), perfect for those simply using their hotel or B&B as a place to crash after a splendid day out; many of the packages also go the other way, ensuring that you stay in rather extraordinary accommodations (if you fork out enough you may end up on an all-castles tour, for example). If you do decide to go for a package, be sure to total all the costs—including additional airport taxes, post-9/11 security fees, fuel surcharges, and car insurance taxes—when you're shopping around; there will be hidden expenses, so look for them. Also remember that best prices are always based on double occupancy, so they're not good for solo travelers.

One package specialist for Ireland is **Sceptre Tours** (☎ 1-800/221-0924 toll-free U.S.; www.sceptretours.com), which—in addition to its escorted motorcoach trips—puts together self-drive and special interest holidays like castle vacations,

Specialized Tours

Some tour companies organize out-of-the-ordinary packages catering to individual tastes or interests. Here are a few worth considering:

- **Cycling Safaris** (☎ 01/260-0749; www.cyclingsafaris.com): Biking adventures, both guided or independent. They also offer walking tours (guided and self-led) through **Irish Ways** (☎ 01/260-0340; www.irishways.com), so you can head out and not worry about getting your luggage from A to B.
- **Go Ireland** (☎ 066/976-2094; www.govisitireland.com): Cycling and walking holidays along Ireland's west coast.
- **Irish Activity Holidays** (☎ 061/366999; www.irishactivityholidays. com): Customized walking and/or golf packages.
- **South West Walks Ireland** (☎ 061/712-8733; www.southwest walksireland.com): Hiking and walking tours of All Ireland.
- **Tailormade Tours** (☎ 066/976-6007; www.tailor-madetours.com): Personalized tours of all sorts anywhere in Ireland.
- **West Cork Calling** (☎ 023/59753; www.westcorkcalling.com): Highly individual holiday packages in West Cork from sports to the arts.

golfing holidays, and even holidays that involve staying only at B&Bs. When you go hunting for what's on offer, scan their "Independent Vacations," which offer really good deals. What's more, their website clearly spells out the different pricings (with or without airfare, and from different American hubs); they're also explicit (as all tour companies should be) about what's included and what's not (airline taxes, airport security fees, and collision waiver insurance for your rental car, are not included, for example). When I last investigated I found a six-night package for just $499 including airfare from New York City, Boston or Washington, DC (other gateways available at an increased price) six nights' accommodations in a villa on the grounds of Adare Manor and a stick-shift car. The deal was for travel from January through March. The catch: four people had to share the villa. For double rate deals, the price rose about $200, though it was still quite a good offer.

In a similar league is **Brian Moore International Tours** (☎ 1-800/982-2299 toll-free U.S.; www.bmit.com), specializing in combining all sorts of options, particularly fly, drive, and stay packages where you determine which guesthouse or B&B you want to stay in. This frees you up to choose your own route, unlike other packages which put you in pre-determined hotels, thus forcing you to see certain parts of the country. For example, you can pick up a package with 5 nights B&B accommodation plus 6 days car rental (with unlimited mileage) for $369 without airfare. A word of advice might be in order, though. Being able to choose your B&B may sound like a good idea, but you do need to realize that B&Bs in certain popular areas can fill up quickly during peak season, so you need to plan ahead to determine which accommodations you want to use and then reserve them as soon as possible. Don't think you can simply knock on the door of any B&B or guesthouse and know for certain that there's room at the inn.

For airfare/car-rental deals from the U.S., **1-800-FLY-EUROPE** (☎ 1-800/ 359-3876 toll-free U.S.; www.1800flyeurope.com) is another good bet, but you need to consider a host of taxes and add-on fees. **Virgin Vacations** (☎ 1-888/ 937-8474 toll-free U.S.; www.virgin-vacations.com) offers fine off-season deals and decent summer packages too; when I last checked, they had 7-day "fly and drive" packages starting at $859 (or $1,299 in peak season) per person; if you think about it, you'd almost be getting the car for free. Another operator is **Celtic Tours** (☎ 1-800/833-4373 toll-free U.S.; www.celtictours.com) which has a number of hotel plus car hire packages (starting at $455 per person for 5 days); flights are extra, however.

Note: With all these packages, when you work out your potential savings, their best quoted rates are always per person sharing (whereas when you rent a car it doesn't matter how many people travel). So if you have more or less than two people in your group, the savings may disappear (not always though; and do check to see if there are discounts for children).

TRAVEL INSURANCE

The simple fact is that things can go wrong, you can make mistakes, lose things, or fall victim to nasty illnesses. But before rushing out and forking over your money for all kinds of policies, check your existing insurance policies and also find out to what extent your credit card company covers you for travel purchased using your card. You may already be covered for lost luggage, canceled tickets, or medical expenses. Also, if you're booking a package, never buy the travel insurance from the company that's selling you travel: if they go belly up, you've lost both your trip and your insurance.

The cost of travel insurance varies widely, depending on the price and length of your trip, your age and health, and the type of trip you're taking. You can get estimates from various providers through **InsureMyTrip.com**.

Trip-Cancellation Insurance   Trip-cancellation insurance will help retrieve your money if you have to back out of a trip or depart early, or if your travel supplier goes bankrupt. Permissible reasons for trip cancellation can range from sickness to natural disasters to the State Department declaring a destination unsafe for travel.

Medical Insurance   Check if your health plan provides overseas coverage; many do not. If yours does, check to see how payment must be done—in most cases, you'll need to pay for services up-front, and will be reimbursed when you return home, after you've filed the necessary paperwork with your insurance company. Besides options at InsureMyTrip.com, medical insurance can be obtained from **MEDEX Assistance** (☎ 1-800/537-2029 toll-free U.S.; www.medexassist.com) or **Travel Assistance International** (☎ 1-800/821-2828 toll-free U.S.; www.travel assistance.com).

Lost-Luggage Insurance   Baggage coverage is limited on international flights; I always recommend that nothing of value ever be packed into check-in luggage. Take any irreplaceable items with you in your carry-on luggage because many

Backpacker Busses

For backpackers, there are some popular packaged tours that can help take the financial load off. Aimed at young budget travelers, **Eirtrail** (☎ 87/612-2501; www.eirtrail.com) does "adventures" through Ireland lasting 1, 2, 3, 6 or 7 days. Travel is by mini-coach (so it's a bit more intimate than being stuck on a tour bus), and digs and breakfast are included. There's a lot of emphasis on fun, so pub tours and opportunities to listen to music are part of the deal. Depending on your budget, you'll have a choice of either hostel accommodation, or more comfortable B&Bs and guesthouses. Eirtrail also allows you (provided you have enough people in your group or family) to create your own tour.

A familiar sight on the Irish tourist landscape are the famous **Paddywagon Tours** (☎ 0800/783-4191; www.paddywagontours.com) which offers a similar deal to Eirtrail, and has an assortment of trips taking in Ireland's highlights. A 6-day trip costs £189, and 3 days is £109; some packages include transfers from London.

valuables (including books, money, jewelry, business papers, and electronics) aren't covered by the airline. Travelers who have had luggage lost or stolen through baggage handler incompetence usually get a bad deal when it comes time to be compensated. If you plan to check items more valuable than what's covered by the standard liability (but rather don't), see if your homeowner's policy covers your valuables—if it doesn't, get baggage insurance as part of your comprehensive travel-insurance package from an insurer. Don't buy insurance at the airport, where it's usually overpriced. Most airlines require that you report delayed, damaged, or lost baggage within 4 hours of arrival. The airlines are required to deliver luggage, once found, directly to your house or destination free of charge.

GETTING AROUND IRELAND

As I mentioned at the very start of this chapter, the biggest mistake visitors to Ireland make is to try and see too many areas in a short amount of time. Ireland looks small, but it's wise to remember that travel in Ireland can be much slower than expected, and routes are often far longer than a scan of the map might suggest. Don't plan to do too much if your time is limited—rather concentrate on a particular area, or pick a few diverse regions and cover them in detail.

BY AIR

Aer Lingus (www.aerlingus.com) flies between Dublin and Shannon (located in the western county of Clare, not far from Limerick City) for about €60 one-way. The major provider of internal flights is **Aer Arann** (www.aerarann.com), which has quite a number of routes, linking Dublin with Cork, Derry, Donegal, Kerry, Knock, Sligo, and Galway; it also connects Cork with Belfast and Galway, and flies between Galway and Waterford. You'll generally have the option of an ultra-cheap

---

Driving in Ireland: The Basics

- ◆ **Drive on the left.**
- ◆ **Remember which country you're in.** Speed limits in Northern Ireland are indicated in miles per hour, while in the Republic, they're in kilometers per hour.
- ◆ **Drive the speed limit.** In Northern Ireland, the speed limits are 30 mph in towns, 60 mph on single carriageways, and 70 mph on dual carriageways and motorways; limits posted on road signs take precedent over these general rules. In the Republic, limits are 50kmph in towns, 80kmph on minor roads, 100kmph on national roads, and 120kmph on motorways.
- ◆ **Buckle up.** Seat belts must be worn by drivers and all passengers by law.
- ◆ **Don't drink and drive.** Driving under the influence of alcohol is a serious offence and authorities are extremely strict in this regard; it is best not to have any alcohol whatsoever if you intend on driving, particularly since you may not be aware of the higher-than-usual alcohol content of Guinness.

"Low Fare" ticket, or a very expensive "Flex Fare." When I recently shopped for a flight between Cork and Belfast (the longest internal flight available), I found a one-way ticket for €35, including taxes.

Think carefully, however, before booking a flight. Often it will take you just as long as driving when you factor in the time spent checking in, going through security and getting to and from the airport.

BY TRAIN & BUS

Train connections are less extensive (not at all useful for small towns or villages) and therefore, to my mind, not quite as useful as **buses.** While they may be more comfortable, they're much pricier than buses, with less frequent departures. In the Republic, trains are operated by **Iarnród Éireann** (Irish Rail; www.irishrail.ie); in Northern Ireland, it's **Northern Ireland Railways** (www.nirailways.co.uk). Try to make all your train travel bookings online, which is considerably cheaper. A variety of rail passes allow unlimited travel for a certain number of days over a specific period of validity.

In the Republic, the national bus network is called **Bus Éireann** (☎ 01/836-6111; www.buseireann.ie). Use the website to find all connections and book your tickets in advance. You'll also see postings about discounted tickets, seasonal specials, and other money-saving options, including cheaper tickets for seniors and students; there are a variety of "unlimited travel" tickets that you can purchase to cover all your bus rides for a certain number of days. Of course, you need to make sure that you really will be moving extensively enough to make these tickets worthwhile. Local tourist information offices should always be able to assist

Irish Rail Routes

North Channel

ATLANTIC OCEAN

Portrush
Ballycastle
Coleraine
Larne Harbour
Derry
Ballymoney
Larne
Whitehead
Carrickfergus
Antrim
Bangor
Belfast York Road
Lurgan
Portadown
BELFAST CENTRAL
Lisburn
Enniskillen
Newry

Irish Sea

Ballina
Sligo
Collooney
Boyle
Carrick-on-Shannon
Foxford
Ballymote
Dromod
Dundalk
Castlebar
MANULLA JUNCTION
Ballyhaunis
Longford
Westport
Claremorris
Castlerea
Mostrim
Drogheda
Mosney
Balbriggan
Skerries
Roscommon
Mullingar
Enfield
Malahide
Tuam
Woodlawn
Athlone
Maynooth
Dublin Connolly
Galway
Athenry
Clara
Ballinasloe
Tullamore
Kildare
DUBLIN
Attymon
PORTARLINGTON
Portlaoise
Dublin Heuston
Dublin Pearse
Dun Laoghaire
Ennistymon
Roscrea
Newbridge
Bray
Greystones
Ennis
Cloughjordan
Athy
Wicklow
Nenagh
Temple-more
BALLYBROPHY
Carlow
Rathdrum
Birdhill
Kilkenny
Muine Bheag
Arklow
Castle-connell
Thurles
Thomastown
Gorey
Limerick
LIMERICK JUNCTION
Clonmel
Enniscorthy
Mouth of the Shannon
Listowel
Charleville
Tipperary
Campile
Wexford
Tralee
Cahir
Rosslare Strand
Farranfore
Rathmore
MALLOW
Carrick-on-Suir
WATERFORD
Rosslare Harbour
Killarney
Banteer
Ballycullane
Bridgetown
Millstreet
Fota
Wellington Bridge
Cork
Cobh

ARAN ISLANDS

St. George's Channel

0   30 mi
0   30 km

with timetable information and can show you where to catch a bus. Bus drivers tend to be friendly and will usually stop to let you alight at a special point of interest if you politely ask them in advance. **Ulsterbus** (☎ 028/9066-6630; www. ulsterbus.co.uk) has very thorough services throughout Northern Ireland, and also runs convenient tours in the summer to accommodate those wishing to get to certain attractions (like the Giant's Causeway) that are not located in or near any major towns.

BY RENTAL CAR

Far and away the best way to explore Ireland is by rental car, but you pay dearly for having your own car here; rental prices are among the highest in Europe, and are pushed up relentlessly by some of the most extreme tax and insurance rates you'd imagine possible. It is always worth your while to shop around online before settling on a car rental company; I go to the hassle of keying in all my details (except credit card information) to determine which company will give me the best rate and the best terms. Remember to check how much mileage and what sort of insurance coverage you're getting before making your assessment.

All the major players are represented in Ireland: **Avis** (www.avis.co.uk), **Budget** (www.budget.ie), **Europcar** (www.europcar.com), **Hertz** (www.hertz.co.uk), and **National** (www.nationalcar.co.uk). In addition, you should check for deals at **Dooley Car Hire** (www.dooleycarrentals.com), an Irish firm represented in the Republic and in Northern Ireland, which has a very user-friendly online quotation and booking system. Because Dan Dooley is familiar with the impact that insurance has on rates, his site clearly shows all costs involved and gives you the totals (for a range of models) in an easy to follow format; and I must say that his prices are very competitive. Another chance to score a decent deal is with **AutoEurope** (☎ 1-888/223-5555; www.autoeurope.com), which significantly undercuts the prices of the major international car-rental agencies, sometimes by as much as 30% (although you'll be shocked to see that insurance practically doubles the cost). Still, I would suggest pricing its vehicles before looking at the other sites.

Travelers should also remember that smaller cars are not only less expensive, but they'll also be cheaper to refuel (gas—or petrol—is ridiculously expensive in Ireland and even pricier in Northern Ireland) and a far better bet when it comes to those narrow rural roads that will take you to some of the more unexpected parts of your journey. Vehicles with manual transmission (stick-shift) are less expensive than automatics.

To Rent or Not to Rent, & When? That Is the Question.

If you're intending to first spend a few days in a major city such as Dublin or Belfast, wait till you head off into the countryside before getting your own car. Negotiating the traffic systems of unfamiliar cities (and even larger towns) can be a nightmare, as can the steep parking rates (and limited free spaces in cities). These cities are best explored on foot and using public transport with a good map.

SAVING MONEY ON ACCOMMODATIONS

Throughout this guide, you'll find information on more affordable lodgings—we've looked for B&Bs, hotels with special deals, self-catering opportunities, and even the occasional hostel and campground. Always bear in mind that many hosts (especially in smaller places) will give discounts for longer stays and cash payments (often, a credit card will attract a small additional fee).

Here are some more tips for saving on your accommodations in Ireland:

Surf the Web   Booking sites are a quick way of getting the lowdown on what sort of rates are out there and also for gauging when prices are up or down. Take a look at **www.irelandhotels.com**, the website of the **Irish Hotels Federation** (☎ 01/808-4419) and **HotelConnect.co.uk** (☎ 0845/230-8888). I also find the search offered by the site **HotelsCombined.com** to be quite comprehensive.

Of course, there are also those sites that basically flog difficult-to-move rooms and hotels that aren't all that visible from a marketing point of view; this is where you may encounter a bargain, although sometimes more useful if you're a last-minute shopper. The British site **LateRooms.com** is a case in point. It's thorough and quick but only of use for last minute deals (the same can be said of **LastMinuteIrelandHotels.com**).

Remember, if you do book through one of these internet booking consortiums, always get a confirmation number and make a printout of any online booking transaction. In my experience, it's also a good idea to save all the fine print detailing the type of room you've paid for (since these systems generally take advance credit card payments); sometimes they bungle the online descriptions and you end up with a windowless room after reading about your penthouse suite.

One thing you should bear in mind is that these sites don't really work for smaller destinations, and they overlook all the interesting, intimate, and "local" establishments. For those use this book.

Take a Temporary Residence   Self-catering apartments, cottages, and houses can represent excellent savings, not least because you don't have the expense of regularly dining out. What's more, you discover a side of life that many tourists never get to see when you go shopping at markets (and even at supermarkets) along with local people. You also usually get a lot more space and privacy when you opt for this kind of deal. Typically, you'll have space for the whole family (and sometimes there are so many bedrooms you don't know what to do with them all).

For perhaps the widest spread of houses and apartments to rent, advertised directly by the owners (although often by local rental agents as well), visit such website as **VRBO** (Vacation Rentals By Owner; www.vrbo.com), **www.rentalo.com**, **www.zonder.com**, and **www.holidayhomesdirect.ie** which may not look or sound very sophisticated, but have such a slew options you're bound to stumble upon something you like. Each property is described in detail by the owners and they tend to list amenities pretty thoroughly; you may flinch at some of the photos, but remember that these are usually not professional advertisements—which, in turn, translates into a lower price, because most of the time you aren't dealing with an agent or firm, but with the owners directly (of course, some agencies do post their stuff here, too). The owners generally ask you to call or email for any extra information and to make a reservation, which can be pretty laborious, so

The Tiffanys of Rental Homes

The **Irish Landmark Trust** ✭✭✭ (25 Eustace St., Temple Bar, Dublin 2; or 50 Bedford St., Belfast; ☎ 01/670-4733; www.irishlandmark.com) is a charity that saves heritage buildings that are at risk of being lost and, after sensitive restoration, gives them a new future by renting them for self-catering holidays. These will be unique properties with a special flavor and genuine charm, often in spectacular locations; restoration of properties is ongoing, so new ones become available from year to year. Each property has also been impeccably furnished, in a manner that fits the look and feel of the architecture. They're generally rented on a weekly basis, but weekend and midweek breaks are also possible. There's just no comparing these properties with those of the mainstream vacation rental agencies. Imagine, for example, the thrill of staying in the Wicklow Head Lighthouse (built in 1781) at Dunbur Head (p. 90); it sleeps four and has stupendous views, and costs in the region of €1,200 per week, depending on season. Meanwhile, on the other side of the island, you can stay in the Lightkeepers' House (p. 237) on the spectacular edge-of-the-earth Loop Head promontory. With room for up to five people, it costs a very affordable €742 to €994 per week, and you'll be assured of one of the most idyllic and exciting settings in all-Ireland. Other properties in the Trust's portfolio include gate lodges, historic cottages, and even (admittedly pricey-but-splurgeworthy) Georgian houses in the heart of Dublin. Stylish, design-conscious and always in excellent nick, these will be rentals that you'll remember for all the right reasons.

filter through the properties that look good to you before embarking on a follow-up mission.

Price is the main reason you book directly through an owner. However, unlike the rental companies we mention below and list throughout the book, there's no third party available to fix a clogged toilet or in the worse case scenario, move you to another house or apartment if you're unhappy. In short, you have no fallback available when you rent directly from an owner. So don't confine your search entirely to direct-to-owner spaces; look at such Irish agencies as **Rent an Irish Cottage** (☎ 61/411109; www.rentacottage.ie) which offers a range of cottages and holiday properties in 23 locations across the west of Ireland—and mostly in towns or villages that you want to visit. The website has an excellent, efficient booking system, and all prices, amenities, and services are clearly spelled out. There are also photos of the cottage you're looking to rent. Rental prices are always better if you take the property for a week (sometimes 2 or 3 nights can cost almost the same as a full 7 days), and prices vary considerably according to season (they tend to double over July and Aug and during important Irish holidays). The "cottages" in question include townhouses and many are purpose-built cluster houses designed for vacationers. In fact, the majority of Irish rental agencies tend to cover mostly holiday developments (where there's a group of look-alike houses on a large plot, typically with extensively-manicured lawns and neat little driveways between them all), so be aware that this is more than likely what you'll encounter when you explore the options they offer.

Another, similar, operation is **West Coast Holidays** (☎ 061/335799; www.west coastholidays.ie), which manages over 700 self-catering units across the length and breadth of Ireland, although many of the different properties tend be concentrated around specific towns, usually favorite Irish holiday destinations. Again, most of what they offer are cluster developments of the "leisure village," "cottage complex," and "holiday apartment" ilk—the vast majority are purpose-built for vacationers. Many of them are rather unwieldy, unattractive modern constructions, at least on the outside—a mix 'n' match of styles and materials that really can be an eyesore. But architectural aesthetics aren't going to make or break your vacation, and the main thing is that they're comfortable on the inside, well-stocked, and suitably maintained. And a good value. Prices for 3-bedroom homes tend to go from €399 in the winter and up to €749 in July and August. One drawback is the cumbersome website where searching for the right price can be a bit of a long-winded process. It might be better just to call or email them directly with all your needs spelled out precisely; one of the advantages of covering developments in only a few specific locations is that their staff know the properties well and can match you with something suited to your requirements. Still, don't agree to anything until you've taken a proper look at photos and fully considered the location.

Stay with the Locals   At one time, Ireland's budget lodging scene was synonymous with makeshift B&Bs where owners would rent out their children's rooms the moment they moved out. In some cases, they wouldn't even wait. If you read Pete McCarthy's hilarious *McCarthy's Bar,* you'll get a good sense of what these homestay-style accommodations are like. These days, there are more and more professional B&Bs, some of them purpose-built, and some of them very snazzy indeed. If you prefer anonymity, stick to the hotels, but if you enjoy meeting people—and often you become privy to all kinds of insider information in this way— then don't turn your nose up at the idea of a B&B. We've recommended scores of them throughout this book, and they range from the ultra-homey to the types that verge on being a boutique hotel.

Here are a few places you can investigate for more such "local" lodgings:

Irish Farmhouse Holidays (www.irishfarmholidays.com) is a booking service for B&Bs, farmhouse stays (which are much like B&Bs, except they're on working farms), and self-catering accommodations. Use the site to instantly book your stay, or find information (including all pricing details and the website address) that will allow you to book directly.

Family Homes of Ireland (www.family-homes.ie) can connect you directly to the proprietors of hundreds of family-run B&Bs and self-catering accommodations throughout the country; you browse by county and select from options listed by locality.

Hidden Ireland (www.hiddenireland.com) offers up-market B&B accommodation in a selection of historic and refined properties; they're mostly pricey, but come with hosts who are especially adept at making you feel welcome—not just in their homes, but to Ireland as well.

Working for Your Daily Bread

As we mentioned in our chapter on the Northwest (p. 308) volunteering on an organic farm is a fascinating way to learn more about rural Ireland...and travel for cheap. Volunteers help out in the fields—whether wrangling animals, milking cows, planting seeds, picking fruit, or whatever—learning specialized skills (such as permaculture) and the intricacies of running an organic farm in the process. At night, they usually bed down for free (food will be free, too).

It goes without saying that you need to have a real interest in acquiring knowledge about organic farming and gardening techniques, that you want to be out in a rural or country location, and that you're committed to positive ecological and environmental practices.

Such farms are scattered all across Ireland, and finding a suitable host simply requires some online research. Check out the website of **WWOOF** (Willing Workers on Organic Farms; www.wwoof.org/wwind), which—for a small subscription fee—will provide you with information about, and contact details for, thousands of organic farms around the world, including 172 in Ireland. In return for your energy—and you need to be prepared to do some honest-to-goodness manual labor (a certain number of hours per day will be pre-determined)—you'll be given meals (which you might help prepare), lodging, and the knowledge you gain during your stay. Some of the farms, like **Hagal Healing Farm** (p. 228), also come with added incentives (yoga sessions, beautiful rivers to swim in, a musician who loves to perform each night), while many farm owners are more reserved and disinterested in workers who've actually come for a cultural experience rather than to work and learn. Bottom line: choose your farm carefully—there's usually more than enough information available to help you make your decision.

Consider a Home Exchange   House-swapping is becoming a more popular and viable means of travel; you stay in their place, they stay in yours, and you both get an authentic and personal experience of the area, the opposite of the escapist retreat that many hotels offer. **HomeLink International** (www.homelink.org) is the largest and oldest home-swapping organization, founded in 1952, with over 13,000 listings worldwide ($110 for a yearly membership) and that's important as the more listings there are, the more options you have. It had 309 in Ireland when I last looked. **HomeExchange.com** ($100 for 17,000 listings) is the same website that enabled Cameron Diaz and Kate Winslet to swap homes and alter the course of their lives in the 2006 film *The Holiday*, and when I recently checked out the site, there were 263 Irish homes listed; again, if you don't find what you're looking for, your second year's membership is free. **InterVac.com** ($95 for over 20,000 listings in 50 countries) is another excellent source for Ireland. Just remember that these exchange companies are only "match-makers" or facilitators, and are not responsible for what happens during the exchange period, although they will monitor complaints.

MONEY MATTERS

As mentioned earlier, different currencies are used in the Republic of Ireland and in Northern Ireland. **Ireland** is fully integrated into the **euro** system, while in **Northern Ireland,** the currency is the **British Pound** (or Sterling, or just simply pound). Although all Sterling notes and coins can be used as legal tender in Northern Ireland, banks here also issue notes that are unique to Northern Ireland (and don't feature images of the Queen)—not that you can get confused, since the name of the currency is clearly indicated on all notes.

Euro notes look the same throughout the European Union's so-called "Euro Zone" countries, although coins can be minted with cultural symbols unique to the place of origin (you'll find a harp on Ireland-minted coins).

The thing to remember is that the currencies are **not interchangeable** and only a few vendors will accept cross-border currency. Try to be prepared by carrying the correct currency.

ATMs are ubiquitous throughout both countries and you'll find them in even the tiniest villages; they typically accept all cards bearing Visa/PLUS, Eurocard/Mastercard, Maestro, and Cirrus symbols. Before leaving home, be sure you're aware of your bank's fee policy for withdrawing money from foreign ATMs. Combined with local fees, you may pay a potentially exorbitant rate per transaction, but sometimes the whole process is free (look for a bank with a "refund all fees" policy; many credit unions also charge low fees for usage abroad). Note, though, that ATM exchange rates are usually as good, if not better than those offered by Bureaus de Change and banks. It's good to have backup in case a machine eats your card, your wallet gets stolen, or the like. Either bring an alternate ATM card, or bring two or three traveler's checks. Traveler's checks can be more hassle than they're worth, but they do offer the security of being replaced if your things are stolen.

Credit cards have relatively good exchange rates, but try to never use them for cash advances, which carry a very high interest rate. Keep in mind that many banks assess a 1% to 3% "transaction fee" on all charges you incur abroad (even if you're using the local currency). If you misplace, lose, or are robbed of your credit card, report the matter by phone: **American Express** (☎ 1-850/882028); **Diner's Club** (☎ 0818/300026); **Mastercard** (☎ 1-800/870866); **Visa** (☎ 1-800/819014). Don't forget to take copies of all banking details and the address and phone number of your home bank with you in case you have any problems with cards not working or going missing.

Credit cards are widely accepted for accommodation and restaurant payments; Visa and Mastercard have far deeper reach than American Express, Discover, or Diner's Club. It's a good idea to carry more than one card, just in case one is not accepted or if there's a problem with the terminal that links one of your cards to the authorizing institution.

Quite a few B&Bs are loathe to accept cards and would—for many obvious reasons—prefer you pay cash; many even have an open and upfront policy of adding an amount on to your bill (usually around 3%) for credit card payments. Wherever you stay or eat, ask beforehand if you intend on paying by credit card;

it's more than once that I've been in an establishment advertising credit card facilities only to have the waiter to turn up at the end of the meal saying that the machine is on the fritz and there's an ATM around the corner.

HEALTH & SAFETY

Crime against tourists is rare. That being said, tourists (or, anyone, really) in large cities are always a target for petty theft, from pickpocketing to car break-ins. I have heard reports of cars being broken into in the parking lots of some major out-of-the-way tourist attractions, so it's a general rule to keep any valuables out of sight (preferably locked in the trunk) if they must be in the car in the first place. It goes without saying that you should never carry large amounts of money on your person, keep your passport in a safe at your hotel, and consider using a money belt to better hide your money. Fanny packs are the worst place to keep money or valuables; they're easily opened and mark you as a tourist. Do not leave bags next to tables or chairs in restaurants and cafes, and—even worse—don't hang them over the backs of chairs. Be vigilant about bags hanging loosely over shoulders, and make sure that bags are zipped or clipped shut after every time you retrieve something. Frankly, these are measures you should adopt all the time, not just when traveling.

There have been infrequent reports of attacks on tourists in cities like Dublin and Cork; circumstances have always been rather sketchy and generally suggest some sort of link to an intoxicating substance—alcohol can be a culprit, so be aware of overdoing it and then getting into a heavy discussion about issues like politics, religion, or the woman standing next to you. You never know who you might be offending.

As for health dangers, your biggest risks may be succumbing to the vagaries of the changeable weather, particularly if you set off on hikes thinking it's going to be a warm summer's day all day. This rarely happens so be prepared for extreme changes in temperature. Mountains can become wet and overcast without warning so always be prepared and always inform someone before heading off.

You also need to be cautious when driving in remote areas where roads are narrow and frequently include heavy farm vehicles and/or animals. It's a good idea to have a mobile phone with you always.

TIPS ON PACKING

That old rule of tossing out half of what you've packed is always a good one to follow; often you only need a quarter of what you've stuffed into that suitcase (which is probably bigger than you require anyway). You might like to stick to a bag that's small enough to pass as hand luggage when you fly; if you're staying in B&Bs and guesthouses during your trip, you'll really want to avoid dragging a large suitcase as you'll likely be dealing with stairs. Also consider how much shopping you intend on doing and what sorts of items you're going to pick up along the way; those things are going to impact the weight of your luggage on the return journey, and I imagine you'd like to avoid paying for excess baggage (which is exorbitant); so, start by packing light.

I need to emphasize that airport authorities in Europe, and particularly in the United Kingdom, have become extremely sticky about luggage weight and the contents of carry-on bags. Most no-frills airlines allow only one piece of carry-on (that *includes* your laptop and handbag) and it must conform to size restrictions. Increasingly, carry-on luggage is weighed at the check-in counter. The rules around liquids, gels, aerosols, and creams taken on board are also strict: You may not carry any of these in quantities greater than 100ml per item, and these must all be in a plastic bag for security inspectors to check. Travel has changed remarkably in the last 5 years, so don't take any chances.

Make sure you have a pair of **sensible walking shoes** that can be used for sightseeing as well as for more energetic hikes and walks in the country; if you're being super-economical, try to get a pair that can double as decent-looking evening shoes. Come **prepared for the cold,** because you will probably experience some of that; in winter, come prepared for the freezing cold. And any time of year, bring an **umbrella,** but get one that folds down into a very compact unit; also bring some sort of **raincoat,** perhaps opting for one that you can crumple down to a very small bundle. I find a small pair of **binoculars** is essential in Ireland—for seeing all sorts of things, including watching birds nesting on distant rocky cliff faces, offshore islands, Scotland from the Antrim coast, attending concerts and operas, and even for admiring ceilings and artworks in churches and other monumental buildings.

While Irish people dress up smartly and tend to look incredibly dashing when they hit the town, they're not overly snooty about what others wear, but that doesn't mean you shouldn't make an effort. **Clubs and bars** in some of the cities may have dress codes, especially on weekends, and in some cases (particularly in Belfast) there may be seemingly strange rules like not wearing branded football (soccer) shirts or chains around your neck if you're a man. The doorman is simply trying to prevent a potential brawl caused by any overt support for a particular team which can actually have a political subtext. It isn't that difficult to look smart and moderately sophisticated in a pair of fitted jeans and tailored shirt. Try out your outfits at home to see what simple, easy-to-pack combinations you can wear while away; you'll want light, durable, and hard-wearing materials so that you don't have to worry about laundry and ironing as much as you might at home. **Laundry services** are expensive and in many places completely non-existent.

SPECIALIZED TRAVEL RESOURCES

FOR FAMILIES

Ireland's best bits are its natural wonders—staggering coastal scenery, splendidly green parks, and lakes, rivers, and beaches—which means this is a splendid destination to keep the Playstation generation engaged in healthier pursuits. And it can be a great reward to see children's imaginations triggered by a walk around a medieval castle or through ancient ruins that remind them of the last fantasy film they watched.

As for all the nitty-gritty details, Ireland is as family-friendly as they come. It's not at all unusual to see children out with their parents even in pubs (during the day at least); every city and small town has playgrounds and parks; and not only are there big discounts for children visiting attractions (which are free to younger children), but there are sports activities, workshops, cooking classes, festivals, and all kinds of fun, engaging events aimed specifically at young people, too. Most public places and visitor attractions also cater for those children, with changing facilities, children's menus, high chairs, and ramps for strollers. It's common for hotels and B&Bs to have rooms with one double bed and one single bed, especially useful if you're traveling with a child who then gets a reduced rate. Children 15 and under pay half price rates on public transport, and under-5s generally travel free on trains.

Recommended family-travel websites include **TravelWithYourKids.com**, with sound advice for long-distance and international travel with children, even telling you how to pack; and **FamilyTravelForum.com** which aids with trip planning and has some great articles on visiting Ireland.

The availability of reliable babysitters will differ dramatically as you travel around the island; in small towns and villages it's quite unlikely that you'll find any assistance, unless you're in a place that draws a large number of domestic tourists or you're staying in a hotel. Still, not all hotels provide the service (due to insurance risks) and even if you're staying at a premium place, you should be aware of a media scare a few years back when it was discovered that certain five-star hotels were not vetting their babysitters. You're highly unlikely to find a B&B or small guesthouse that offers child-minding, although there's no harm in asking—but ask before you make a reservation. Fortunately, there's an online service that you can approach: **Babysitters.ie** can connect you, the parent, to any of almost 20,000 babysitters registered with them (in locations across the Republic and the North). The downside is that you need to register with the service (online); there's a €25 initial cost and the first month costs an additional €8. Remember, though, that you still need to screen the babysitters yourself, since the website only functions as a virtual agency.

FOR TRAVELERS WITH DISABILITIES

Both Ireland and Northern Ireland have laws fostering enhanced facilities for people with disabilities; hotels, restaurants, attractions, public buildings, and public spaces are meant to conform to certain standards that enable all people to have access to and use of the same facilities. Particularly since Ireland hosted the 2003 Special Olympics, access to public facilities and attractions has been much-improved. In reality, however, we're dealing with a country with narrow sidewalks (even the roads are narrow), cobbled streets, difficult-to-adapt historic sites, and many smaller B&Bs with upstairs-only guestrooms. In short, many areas are not wheelchair-friendly, but wherever improvements are possible, they're being implemented.

Discounts for Just about Everyone

Just about every attraction in Ireland offers discounts for seniors, students, children, and families. Throughout this book, we've listed the prices for adults, which is the most expensive entrance fee for each site, but you'll find that seniors and students typically pay just over half the standard price, while children pay half or less. Families (usually 2 adults plus 2 or 3 children) generally pay just more than the equivalent of the ticket price for 2 adults. So there are great savings for many of you.

The Heritage Card

A vast number of important heritage sites—castles, monuments, museums, abbeys, parks, and even natural vistas—throughout the Republic of Ireland are managed by the **Office of Public Works (OPW).** Entrance to many of these is free, but there are also many for which an entrance free is levied; prices range from as little as €1.60 for a gorgeous ruined friary in Ennis, County Clare, to €5.30 for the Rock of Cashel in County Tipperary, Ross Castle in Killarney, Clonmacnoise in County Offaly, and a number of others. If you're a serious sightseer and simply can't miss romping about ruins or seeing the inside of medieval castles, then you might consider investing in a **Heritage Card** (€21 adults, €16 seniors age 60 and over, €8 children age 17 and under and students with valid ID, €55 families) which gets you into all OPW sites free of charge. You also get a booklet with details of all the sites, including quite a number that we haven't covered in this book. You can buy the card at any of the OPW sites, or visit **www.heritageireland.ie.**

A similar scheme operates in Northern Ireland for properties managed by the UK's **National Trust,** a heritage-preservation charity organization; to find out about their annual membership and how it might help you save on sightseeing, see p. 411.

However, disabilities shouldn't stop anyone from traveling. There are more options and resources out there than ever before. Many travel agencies offer customized tours and itineraries for travelers with disabilities. The Irish website **Ableize** (www.ableize.com) provides a directory of resources for people with disabilities who live in Ireland or are visiting; a specific section deals with travel and access. To check up on disabled access in venues (including accommodation, restaurants, entertainment, and shopping), visit **www.accessireland.info**; their listings are far from thorough, but can give you a heads up, at least.

FOR STUDENTS & YOUNGER TRAVELERS

If you're a full-time student, arm yourself with an **International Student Identity Card** (ISIC), which offers substantial savings on rail passes and entrance fees. It also provides you with basic health and life insurance and a 24-hour help line. The card is available for US$22 from **STA Travel** (www.sta.com or www.statravel.com), the biggest student travel agency in the world. If you're no longer a student but are still under 26, you can get an **International Youth Travel Card** (IYTC) for the same price from the same people, entitling you to many discounts. **Travel CUTS** (☎ 1-800/592-2887 toll-free U.S. or 1-866/246-9762 toll-free Canada; www.travelcuts.com) offers similar services for both Canadians and U.S. residents. Australian, New Zealand, and U.K. students should consider deals and offers presented by **Student Flights** (www.studentflights.com), a division of Flight Centre; they organize good deals on air travel, working holidays, and student cards.

Just about all museums and cultural attractions throughout Ireland offer substantial discounts to students—as long as you are simply carrying your valid student identity card. In some instances, you'll get the discount simply for being under a certain age (which may vary from place to place). Always ask if there is a youth or student discount.

FOR GAY & LESBIAN TRAVELERS

While Ireland is a traditional Catholic country in many respects, it is also a part of the E.U. and therefore subscribes to European human rights protocols ensuring freedom of sexual orientation and practice. Gay people are generally accepted and, despite a small margin of homophobia, accorded the same rights as straight people. While you will find people with skewed ideological opinions on this issue—largely based in religious fundamentalism—it's unlikely that you'll encounter too many bigots. That being said, the population size tends to determine the depth of any local gay "scene"; there are only a certain number of cities (and now even a few—very few—towns) where the critical mass of queer numbers has been reached to make it viable for clubs or bars catering specifically to the LGBT community. Obviously, the major cities—Dublin, Belfast, and Cork—have the best nightlife and support groups for gay people (and we've mentioned our top choices—where appropriate—throughout this book). Where communities are insular, aging, and set in their ways, you might want to keep your orientation to yourself and avoid provoking, or bewildering, the locals.

A top site for the gay scene, predominantly in Dublin, but with some coverage of the rest of Ireland, is **www.queerid.com**. Besides extensive listings, the site covers such diverse events as Dublin's Gay Theatre Festival and Mr. Gay Ireland. If you want to read up more extensively on the gay travel scene, check out **www.gay.com**, which has coverage of everything under the rainbow travel umbrella—just click on "Travel." There are articles on the best pink destinations, with info on gay-friendly accommodations, restaurants, and businesses.

For a tour that's aimed specifically at gay travelers (so you'll be in a group), check out the offer at **Hermes Tours** (☎ 1-877/486-4335 toll-free in the U.S. or ☎ 1-315/299-8793; www.hermestours.com). When I last checked, it had an Irish trip scheduled for August/September 2009. **Gay Vacation Travel** (☎ 1-877/515-5100; www.gayvacationtravel.com) is another tour group company specializing in packages exclusively for gay people and arranges Irish vacations from time to time.

The **International Gay and Lesbian Travel Association** (IGLTA; www.iglta.org) offers an online directory of gay-friendly travel businesses; go to their website and click on "Members."

FOR SENIOR TRAVELERS

Although seniors can expect discounted entry to just about all sights and attractions throughout Ireland, one thing that you won't find is a lack of opportunity to socialize. The Irish tend not to put up quite so many barriers between different generations; it's quite appropriate for older people to hang out in pubs and bars and join in the *craic* with revelers many years their junior. The Irish are phenomenally good minglers, so if you're open to mixing with new people—no matter what their age—you should find your attitude reciprocated. Be aware when selecting to stay in B&Bs and historical properties, that many do not have elevators, and often only have upstairs bedrooms; if going up 1 or 2 flights of stairs is likely to be impractical, always ask for a ground floor room and if there isn't one, book elsewhere.

A number of reliable agencies and organizations target the 50-plus market. Boston-based **Elderhostel** (☎ 1-800/4545768 toll-free U.S.; www.elderhostel.org) arranges "learning adventures" for seniors 55 and over (and a spouse or companion of any age, excluding children) in more than 90 countries, including Ireland. Most courses last 2 to 4 weeks. Many include airfare, accommodations in university dormitories or modest inns, meals, and tuition.

STAYING WIRED WHILE WAY

These days just about everywhere you go or stay will have some sort of internet connection. Even some of the smallest B&Bs and guesthouses may offer either a PC or Wi-Fi for checking emails. Internet cafes, and coffee shops or restaurants that offer Wi-Fi as an additional service are generally found in the cities and larger towns, but in villages it's unlikely that you'll get connected unless your host offers Internet. In smaller towns you can usually use the internet in public libraries, although you may need to book a time; the service may be free, or there may be a small fee.

RECOMMENDED READING & VIEWING

BOOKS

Ireland has produced some of the world's most important literary figures, and heaps of titles will have you gasping for want of getting to the land that inspired such resonant, heartfelt prose and poetry. Even if beautiful words aren't really your thing, you'll surely be seduced by the enormous wit and often sharp observations made by shelf-loads of Irish wordsmiths.

Among the geniuses are names like George Bernard Shaw; W. B. Yeats; James Joyce (you should recall *A Portrait of the Artist as a Young Man* from English lit classes, and his more difficult *Ulysses* is set in Dublin over a 1-day period); Oscar Wilde (although more famous for doing you-know-what, he did write *The Picture of Dorian Gray*); Oliver Goldsmith (*The Vicar of Wakefield*); playwrights J. M. Synge and Brian Friel; vampirist Bram Stoker; satirist Jonathan Swift; heavy-drinking Brendan Behan; poet and playwright Samuel Beckett (who basically invented absurdist theater with *Waiting for Godot*); Flann O'Brien (*At Swim-Two-Birds*); Edna O'Brien; Seamus Heaney *(Sweeney Astray);* John McGahern; John Banville (*The Sea* won the Booker Prize in 2005); and—my favorite living Irish author—Colm Tóibín (*The Master, The South, The Story of the Night,* and *Mothers and Sons*). And there are others, too, like William Trevor, and even Sinead O'Connor's brother, Joseph O'Connor (author of *Star of the Sea*). Of these greats, four have won Nobel Prizes for their writing (Shaw, Yeats, Beckett, and Heaney), so it's difficult to choose a short-list of quintessential Irish texts.

Books you will surely enjoy reading include Frank McCourt's *Angela's Ashes.* Although it'll give you the wrong impression of contemporary Limerick, it'll plant you firmly in the fabric of early-20th-century Ireland, and endear the city to you all the more once you visit it; McCourt's style will also prepare you for dry, intelligent Irish wit that goes hand-in-hand with its gripping melancholy. Patrick McCabe's black, black humor infuses his Booker-nominated *The Butcher Boy; Breakfast on Pluto, Emerald Germs of Ireland,* and *Call Me the Breeze* are a few of his other offbeat novels.

There are many enjoyable travelogues, immersive experiential accounts written by visitors to Ireland—often people of Irish descent searching for their "roots." The mainstay of this particular genre has got to be the late Pete McCarthy's laugh-out-loud *McCarthy's Bar,* which is biting and affectionate in equal parts, and does some justice to the very experience of exploring Ireland. More ultra-light reading in this genre includes Evan McHugh's *Pint-sized Ireland*—in search of the perfect Guinness (the name really says it all), and *No News at Throat Lake,* by Lawrence Donegan. A more serious, and deeply moving, "roots memoir" is Thomas Lynch's *Booking Passage.*

Turn to Tim Pat Coogan's *Ireland in the Twentieth Century* if you want historical fact and critique written in engaging prose; if you want to go further back in time, start with R. F. Foster's *Modern Ireland 1600–1972.* Colm Tóibín and Diarmaid Ferriter look at the Great Famine in *The Irish Famine: A Documentary.*

MOVIES

Among the cinematic classics (deservingly, or otherwise) that are set in Ireland, *The Quiet Man* is the one most folks love to talk about; John Ford shot this with John Wayne and Maureen O'Hara (who now still lives in Glengarriff, County Cork) back in 1952, using locations in and around Cong, a village in County Mayo, although it's set on the Isle of Innisfree on Sligo's Lough Gill; the film is about an Irish-American returning to Ireland to find his roots.

In 1970, David Lean almost ended his career when he set *Ryan's Daughter* in beautiful locations around Dingle Peninsula in County Kerry and, according to some critics, buried the characters in the overpowering scenery.

With very little to do with Ireland, except that the mother of the star and director, Mel Gibson, was born there, *Braveheart* was almost entirely shot on the Emerald Isle, and captures some of the atmosphere that one might imagine prevailed at a time when Celtic warriors went into battle carrying axes and swords, and wearing skirts.

Although not set entirely in Ireland, Stanley Kubrick's *Barry Lyndon,* based on a William Thackeray novel about an 18th-century Irish mis-adventurer, includes scenes filmed in Dublin Castle as well as since-destroyed Powerscourt House in County Wicklow. Kubrick captures much of the mood of the period and there's a great deal to be learned about how the social hierarchies of the time functioned.

As commercial as it is, Ron Howard's *Far and Away* provides a glimpse of social conditions in Ireland at the end of the 19th century, and through the eyes of a young Tom Cruise gives an idea of the aspirations of the millions of Irish people who immigrated to America.

Putting a different spin on socio-economic disenfranchised is Alan Parker's *The Commitments,* an uplifting music-powered film about a group of unemployed Dubliners who form a soul band; in 2005 it was voted "Best Irish Film Ever" in a Jameson-sponsored popular poll. If for nothing else, the film will gear you up for the best of Irish word-slinging.

There have been several powerful films dealing with the great political struggle. Although set mostly in London, Jim Sheridan's *In the Name of the Father* looks at the real life story of the Guilford Four, in which four people are falsely convicted of an IRA bombing. The most memorable Irish film ever made is probably Neil Jordan's *The Crying Game*, which tells an intimate IRA story best remembered for having the most shocking—and many would say, transgressive—plot twist in movie history. Liam Neeson played the title role in another Neil Jordan film, *Michael Collins*, an account (albeit with historical inaccuracies) of the eponymous controversial Irish patriot and revolutionary. More recently, *The Wind that Shakes the Barley* is a Ken Loach film about two brothers from County Cork who join the IRA during the time of the Irish War of Independence (1919–21) and the Irish Civil War (1922–23).

In 2003 came Joel Schumacher's scorching mystery thriller, *Veronica Guerin,* starring Cate Blanchett as a reporter who crosses the line with Dublin criminals. But, probably the most important filmmaker to have emerged in Ireland in the last few years is Lenny Abrahamson; his films deal with contemporary issues and bring humanity to often-marginalized "types"—*Adam and Paul,* for example, deals with two Dublin junkies searching for money for their next hit. And to really understand the modern Irish sensibility, try to get hold of John Carney's *Once.* It's a contemporary romantic tale about a Dublin busker and an Eastern European immigrant.

The ABCs of All Ireland

Banks Banks generally operate Monday to Friday 9:30am to 4:30pm; some banks do open on Saturday mornings. ATMs are ubiquitous and you'll find them in all but the smallest of villages.

Dining Concerns If you keep kosher, contact **Kosher Ireland** (www.kosherireland. com) to learn about access to kosher meals throughout your stay. Vegetarians may wish to consult the **Vegetarian Society of Ireland** (www.vegetarian.ie).

Drinking Laws The legal age for the purchase and consumption of alcohol is 18.

Electricity Electrical plugs have three pins, one rectangular and two flat, arranged in a triangle; you'll need an adaptor for 2-pin appliances. Standard voltage throughout Ireland is 220V and frequency 50Hz.

Embassies & Consulates Embassies to the Republic of Ireland are in Dublin (see "ABCs of Dublin," p. 81). For Northern Ireland, most foreign embassies are in London, but the U.S. has a Belfast mission (Queen's House, 14 Queen St.; ☎ 028/903-28239).

Emergencies Dial ☎ **999** or **112** for any emergency, including police (called *gardaí* in the Republic), ambulance, fire services, and rescues services. If your car breaks down, you can contact the **Automobile Association of Ireland** (☎ 01/617-9999 in the Republic; ☎ 0800/887766 or 08457/887766 in Northern Ireland).

Holidays National holidays celebrated in both the Republic and in Northern Ireland are as follows: New Year's Day, St. Patrick's Day (Mar 17th), Good Friday and Easter Monday (which vary from year to year), May Day (May 1st) and Christmas Day. Additionally, in the Republic, there are three bank holidays in June, August and October, and St. Stephen's Day is on December 26th. In Northern Ireland there are 2 bank holidays in May and 1 in August, the Battle of the Boyne is celebrated on July 12th, and Boxing Day is on December 26th.

Hospital Private medical insurance is strongly advised for visitors from non-E.U. countries. E.U. citizens are entitled to free hospital treatment in a public ward and should obtain a European Health Insurance Card before traveling; see www.ehic.ie for details.

Opening Hours **Shops** are generally open from 9am to 6pm Monday to Saturday. In larger towns and cities some shops may open for a few hours on a Sunday.

Police Call ☎ **999** in case of emergency. In the Republic, the police are generally called *gardaí* ("guardians") and are helpful. In Northern Ireland, the police are doing battle with the negative image attracted during the Troubles and consequently tend to be extremely helpful.

Post Office In the Republic, the national postal service is called **An Post;** their post offices are open 9am to 5:30pm Monday to Friday and 9am to 1pm Saturday. Hours may be extended on Saturday in bigger towns. In Northern Ireland, the Royal Mail operates within different hours depending on which city, town or village you're in—as a general guide, post offices are open Monday to Friday 9am to 5:30pm and Saturday 9am to 1pm, but these vary slightly from branch to branch.

Telephones The international dialing code for the Republic of Ireland is **353.** To call Northern Ireland from abroad, use the U.K. country code (**44**), although if you are calling from the Republic of Ireland, you must dial **048** instead. The dialing code (area code) for anywhere within Northern Ireland is **028,** while within the Republic dialing codes vary from one locality to the next.

From the Republic of Ireland: To place an overseas call, dial ☎ **114** for assistance from an operator; for general assistance,

dial ☎ **10.** For local (including Northern Ireland) directory enquiries, dial ☎ **11811** or **11850;** for international enquiries, dial ☎ **11818.**

From Northern Ireland: To place an overseas call, dial ☎ **155** for assistance from an operator; for general assistance, dial ☎ **100.** For local directory enquiries, dial ☎ **192;** for international enquiries, dial ☎ **153.**

To make international calls from within Ireland, first dial 00 (the international access code), followed by the country code for the place you're trying to reach (U.S. and Canada are 1, the U.K. is 44, Australia is 61, New Zealand is 64), then the destination area code and finally the specific number you are trying to reach.

Time Zone Northern Ireland and the Republic of Ireland are in the Western European Time Zone, also known as Greenwich Mean Time. Daylight saving time pushes clocks forward an hour at the start of spring.

Tipping A customary gratuity of 12 to 15% should be added to the restaurant bill if a service charge has not already been added. Do not tip in pubs, unless you are being served at a table. In snazzier bars, staff may expect a tip, but this is at your discretion.

Tourist Offices All cities and most major towns have a tourist information office. The Republic's **Tourism Ireland** (www.discoverireland.com) provides information on travel to and within both the Republic and Northern Ireland. **Fáilte Ireland** is the Republic's tourism authority, while the **Northern Ireland Tourism Board** (www.discovernorthernireland.com) operates in the north.

Weather Detailed information is available on the **National Met Eireann Office** website (www.met.ie).

Index

See also Accommodations and Restaurant indexes, below.

RESTAURANTS

auline frommer's

pauline frommer's
HAWAII
pend less see more

pauline frommer's
ITALY
spend less see more

pauline frommer's
NEW YORK CITY
spend less see more

spend less see more

Budget travel redefined

Discover a fresh take on budget travel with the award-winning guidebook series from travel expert Pauline Frommer. From industry secrets on finding the best hotel rooms to great little neighborhood restaurants and cool, offbeat finds only locals know about, you'll learn how to see more for less — and see it in a more authentic way, without sacrificing comfort for savings.

Also available:

Pauline Frommer's Alaska
Pauline Frommer's Costa Rica
Pauline Frommer's Las Vegas
Pauline Frommer's London

Pauline Frommer's Paris
Pauline Frommer's Washington, D.C.
Pauline Frommer's Walt Disney World
& Orlando

Coming in early 2009

Pauline Frommer's Ireland   Pauline Frommer's Spain

The best trips start here.
Available wherever books are sold.

Frommer's
A Branded Imprint of ⊗WILEY
Now you know.

The new way to
get AROUND town.

Make the most of your stay. Go Day by Day

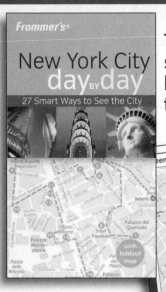

The all-new Day by Day series shows you the best places to visit and the best way to see them.

- Full-color throughout, with hundreds of photos and maps
- Packed with 1–to–3–day itineraries, neighborhood walks, and thematic tours
- Museums, literary haunts, offbeat places, and more
- Star-rated hotel and restaurant listings
- Sturdy foldout map in reclosable plastic wallet
- Foldout front covers with at-a-glance maps and info

The best trips start here.

Frommer's®
A Branded Imprint of ⓦWILEY
Now you know.

BIBLIO RPL Ltée

6 - SEP. 2009